INTRODUCTION TO SOCIOLOGY
A CANADIAN FOCUS

SIXTH EDITION

Edited by

James J. Teevan

University of Western Ontario

and

W. E. Hewitt

University of Western Ontario

Prentice Hall Allyn and Bacon Canada
Scarborough, Ontario

Canadian Cataloguing in Publication Data

Introduction to sociology
6th ed.
Includes 2 indexes.

ISBN 0-13-858598-9

1. Sociology. 2. Canada - Social conditions.
I. Teevan, James J., 1942– . II. Hewitt,
W.E. (Warren Edward), 1954– .

HM51.I57 1998 301 C97-930838-0

Prentice-Hall, Inc., Upper Saddle River, New Jersey
Prentice-Hall International (UK) Limited, London
Prentice-Hall of Australia, Pty. Limited, Sydney
Prentice-Hall Hispanoamericana, S.A., Mexico City
Prentice-Hall of India Private Limited, New Delhi
Prentice-Hall of Japan, Inc., Tokyo
Simon & Schuster Southeast Asia Private Limited, Singapore
Editora Prentice-Hall do Brasil, Ltda., Rio de Janeiro

ISBN 0-13-858598-9

Vice-President, Editorial Director: Laura Pearson
Acquisitions Editor: Rebecca Bersagel
Developmental Editor: Lisa Berland
Copy Editor: John Sweet
Production Editor: Mary Ann McCutcheon
Production Coordinator: Jane Schell
Permissions/Photo Research: Marijke Leupen
Cover Design: Sarah Battersby
Cover Image: National Geographic Image Collection
Page Layout: Debbie Fleming

2 3 4 5 CC 02 01 00 99 98

Printed and bound in the United States

Statistics Canada data used in Tables 5.1, 7.1, 7.2, 7.3, 7.4, 9.3, 10.1, 11.1, 11.2, 11.3, 11.4, 15.2, 15.3, 15.4 and 15.5 and Figures 8.1, 8.2, 8.3, 8.4, 9.1, 15.1 and 15.2 are reproduced by the authority of the Minister of Industry, 1997.

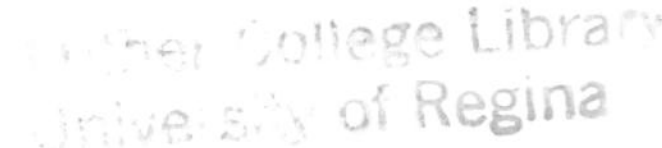

For Christopher,
Class of 2010

TABLE OF CONTENTS

Preface xiv
Acknowledgments xiv
Contributors xiv
For the Instructor xv

Part I Introduction 1

1 **What Is Sociology?** *James J. Teevan & Marion Blute* 3

Introduction 3
Sociology: Its Modern Origins and Varieties 5
Functionalism 7
Conflict theory 8
Symbolic interactionism: an individual perspective 9
Feminist theories 11
Sociology in Canada 12
Future Challenges 17
Questions for Review and Critical Thinking 17
Glossary 18
Suggested Readings 18
Web Sites 19

2 **Research Methods** *James J. Teevan* 21

Introduction 21
Quantitative and Qualitative Methods 21
One quantitative option: survey research 23
A qualitative strategy: participant observation 30
The Methods Compared 33
A common omission: historical and comparative issues 36
Summary 38
Writing a Sociology Library Research Paper 38

Questions for Review and Critical Thinking 40
Glossary 40
Suggested Readings 42
Web Sites 42

Part II Society and the Individual 43

3 Culture *Michael P. Carroll* 45

Introduction 45
Some Basic Concepts 45
Values and norms 45
Social roles 47
Some additional terms 48
Aspects of Culture 52
CBC *Cultural variation 52*
Cultural universals 55
Cultural integration 57
Conceptual Dangers in the Study of Culture 58
Theoretical Perspectives on Culture 62
Functionalism 62
Conflict theory 63
Cultural materialism 65
Feminism(s) 67
Summary 69
Questions for Review and Critical Thinking 70
Glossary 70
Suggested Readings 71
Web Sites 71

4 Socialization *William R. Avison & John H. Kunkel* 73

Introduction 73
The Socialization Process 74
The social context 74
Functions of socialization 75
Biological foundations and limits of socialization 76
Socialization and the life cycle 77
Major Components of Socialization 79
Language 79
Learning 83
Theoretical Approaches to Socialization 87
The psychodynamic perspective 87
The cognitive perspective 87
The symbolic interactionist perspective 90

Socialization and Society 92
Agents and problems 93
Television and socialization 94
Single-parent families 97
Major implications 99
Summary 99
Questions for Review and Critical Thinking 100
Glossary 100
Suggested Readings 101
Web Sites 101

5 Deviance *James J. Teevan* 103

Introduction 103
Definitions of Deviance 103
A functionalist position 104
Conflict positions 105
Other positions 106
Applying a Deviant Label 107
Theories of Deviance 112
Introduction 112
Biological and psychological theories 112
Introduction to sociological theories of deviance 115
CBC *Social structural explanations* 116
Social processes and deviance 126
Putting it all together 131
Summary 132
Questions for Review and Critical Thinking 132
Glossary 132
Suggested Readings 133
Web Sites 134

Part III Social Differentiation 135

6 Gender Relations *Lesley D. Harman* 137

Introduction 137
Gendered order and gendered identity 137
Defining gender 138
Theoretical Perspectives on Gender 139
A functionalist perspective 139
CBC *The symbolic interactionist perspective* 140
A Marxist conflict perspective 141
Feminist perspectives 142
Nature versus Nurture: Myths of Biological Determinism 144

Language and the Gendered Order 148
Getting Gendered: The Development of the Self 150
Trapped in Our Bodies: The Body and Sexuality 152
The Effects of Gender 154
Work and reproduction: the gendered division of labour 154
Health and aging 156
The feminization of poverty 157
Gender and deviance 158
Working Towards Change 159
Summary 161
Questions for Review and Critical Thinking 162
Glossary 163
Suggested Readings 164
Web Sites 164

7 Social Stratification *Edward G. Grabb* **167**

Introduction 167
Concepts and Definitions 167
Power 167
Status and stratum 168
Status hierarchies and power dimensions 168
Ascribed and achieved status 168
Social mobility 169
Class and social class 169
Major Theories of Social Stratification 170
Marx: class, conflict, and the power of property 170
Weber's critique of Marx 174
Structural functionalism: consensus, individualism, and pluralism 176
Combining the major theories to explain modern stratification systems 177
Canada's Stratification Structure 179
Socio-economic hierarchies I: wealth, income, and property 179
CBC *Socio-economic hierarchies II: occupation* 182
Socio-economic hierarchies III: education 186
Racial and ethnic stratification 187
Regional and rural–urban inequalities 190
Gender stratification in Canada 192
Age and social stratification 193
Political power and social stratification 194
Summary 197
Questions for Review and Critical Thinking 197
Glossary 198
Suggested Readings 199
Web Sites 199

8 Race and Ethnic Relations *Carol Agócs* 201

Introduction 201
The Local Ethnic Community: Formation and Development 202
Ethnic Group, Race, and Minority Group: Some Definitions 205
The ethnic group 205
Race and minority group 209
Race and Ethnic Relations in Canada in the Twentieth Century: An Overview 215
CBC *Colonialism and the First Nations* 215
French and British Canadians: two majorities, two solitudes 220
The "other ethnic groups": the shaping of the Canadian mosaic 224
Perspectives on Canadian Race and Ethnic Relations 226
Assimilationism 226
Two-category perspectives 229
Pluralism 230
Summary 232
Questions for Review and Critical Thinking 233
Glossary 233
Suggested Readings 235
Web Sites 235

Part IV Social Institutions 237

9 Families *Roderic Beaujot* 239

Introduction 239
Definitions of Marriage and Family 240
Variability in Family Patterns 240
Number of partners in the marriage 240
Sex codes 242
Consanguine versus nuclear bonds 242
Uniformity of Family Patterns 244
Importance of marriage 244
Incest taboo 244
Importance of inheritance 245
Theoretical Perspectives on Family Change: A Functionalist View 245
The macro-level 245
The micro-level 246
Understanding Gender Roles and the Family: A Conflict View 247
Spousal roles and relations of production 247
Spousal roles and culture 248

Socialization for Marriage and Mate Selection 250
Socialization 250
Dating and premarital intercourse 251
Cohabitation 253
Love in mate selection 254
Homogamy in mate selection 254
Age at marriage 255
Marital and Family Interactions 255
The marital life cycle 255
The structure of marriage 259
Single-parent families 260
Childbearing 261
Childrearing 263
Family change and children 264
Marital Breakdown 264
Decrease in instrumental functions 264
Importance of the expressive dimension 266
Redefinition of the marital commitment 266
Change and Continuity in Family Patterns 267
Summary 269
Questions for Review and Critical Thinking 270
Glossary 270
Suggested Readings 271
Web Sites 271

10 Religion *F.R. Westley & Fred Bird* **273**

Introduction 273
What is Religion? 273
Perspectives on Religion: The Work of Durkheim, Weber, and Marx 275
Emile Durkheim: the causes and consequences of religion 275
Max Weber: religion and social change 279
Marx: religion as ideology 286
Secularization and the Decline of Religion? 288
The secularization process 288
Secularization: a two-way street 288
Bibby and secularization in Canada 289
Redefining the Religious Landscape 291
New religious movements 291
New definitions of religion 293
Summary 297
Questions for Review and Critical Thinking 297
Glossary 298
Suggested Readings 299
Web Sites 299

11 Education *Alan Pomfret* 301

Introduction 301
The Expansion of Education in Canada 301
Educational expansion: a description 302
Explanations of Educational Expansion 304
Functional explanations 304
Capital accumulation explanations 306
The cultural markets explanation 307
The process model of educational expansion 309
Defining, Describing, and Explaining Inequality 311
Expansion, reform, and equality 311
Equality of educational opportunity 312
Persisting patterns of inequality 312
CBC *Explaining inequality 317*
Schooling, Mobility, and Success 323
The Future of Schooling 324
Summary 326
Questions for Review and Critical Thinking 327
Glossary 327
Suggested Readings 328
Web Sites 328

12 Political Sociology *David MacGregor* 331

Introduction 331
Authority and the State 331
Theories of State Control 334
Pluralist theory 334
Élite theory 334
The Marxist view 336
Postmodernism 337
Dependency models 339
Hegel's political theory 340
The Welfare State 342
Neoconservative threats to the Canadian welfare state 343
Canadian Federalism and Political Crisis 345
Who speaks for Canada? 346
Class, Gender, and Politics in Canada 348
Class and political participation 348
Women and politics 349
Summary 351
Questions for Review and Critical Thinking 352
Glossary 352
Suggested Readings 353
Web Sites 353

Part V Social Organization 355

13 Formal Organizations and Work *Bernard Hammond* 357

Introduction 357
What is an organization? 357
Formal organizations, bureaucracies, and informal organizations 358
Historical Development of Formal Organizations 358
Theoretical Perspectives on Formal Organizations 359
The bases of formal organizations 359
Weber on bureaucracy 361
Marx on the state and worker alienation 362
Scientific management 365
The human relations school 366
The structuralist approach 367
Symbolic interactionist perspectives 368
CBC Work and the New Industrial Sociology 370
The impact of Japanese management styles and worker control 371
Summary 376
Questions for Review and Critical Thinking 377
Glossary 378
Suggested Readings 379
Web Sites 379

14 Social Movements *Samuel Clark* 381

Introduction 381
Five Theoretical Approaches 381
Collective behaviour 381
Social breakdown 385
Relative deprivation 386
Collective action 387
Postmodernism and the new social movements 393
A final word in defence of each approach 395
Canadian Social Structure and Collective Action 396
Regional cleavage 397
Ethnic cleavage 402
Summary 407
Questions for Review and Critical Thinking 408
Glossary 408
Suggested Readings 410
Web Sites 410

15 Demography and Population Study *Carl F. Grindstaff* 413

Introduction 413
History of World Population Growth 413
Theories of Population Change 415
The demographic transition 415
Malthusian theory 419
The Growth of Canada's Population: An Overview 420
Variables of Population Growth 421
Mortality 421
Fertility 426
Migration 433
Sex and Age Composition of the Population 437
Summary 439
Questions for Review and Critical Thinking 440
Glossary 440
Suggested Readings 441
Web Sites 441

16 Urbanization *Leslie W. Kennedy* 443

Introduction 443
The Origin and Development of Cities 444
Canadian urban settlement 445
The Urban Transformation 447
The rural–urban shift 447
Suburbanization and rural renaissance 447
Theories of Urban Development 449
Human ecology and competition 449
Social choice theories 452
Social power and the allocation of resources 454
Urban Social Issues: Housing and Crime 459
Urban shelter 459
Community reactions to crime 460
Summary 463
Questions for Review and Critical Thinking 463
Glossary 464
Suggested Readings 464
Web Sites 464

Glossary 465
Bibliography 476
Subject Index 505
Name Index 517
Photo Credits 524

Preface

In this sixth edition of *Introduction to Sociology: A Canadian Focus*, we have made some structural alterations to render the book somewhat more user friendly. Specifically, we have moved Chapter 6, Research Methods, to follow Chapter 1, What is Sociology? Chapter 4, Gender Relations, has been moved to Chapter 6, and is now part of the Social Differentiation section.

Other than these changes, the book retains its original format. Specialists in touch with the most recent research in their individual areas have each contributed a part of the text. As editors, our job has been to integrate this material into a useful and accessible resource that will inform and interest beginning students in the sociological enterprise.

This edition is divided into five parts. The first introduces the field of sociology and its major variants, and includes a brief history of the discipline in Canada. It then discusses the *research methods* or strategies sociologists use to collect the data for their analyses. The next part focuses on society and the individual—the core of sociological thought—and includes discussions about *culture*, the shared way of life that is passed from generation to generation; the learning of culture through a process called *socialization*; and *deviant behaviour* (such as crime or mental illness), which some sociologists believe is due to failed attempts at socialization. Part III considers social differentiation and inequality in Canada. Here, the text examines *gender roles*, a major form of social differentiation and a source of considerable current interest in sociology; *social stratification*, briefly defined as the relatively enduring differences in resources existing between social groups; and Canada's *racial and ethnic groups*. The fourth part looks at social institutions, and contains chapters on the major structures of society: *families, religion, education*, and *politics*. Social organization is examined in the last part, with discussions of *formal organizations and work, social movements, population*, and *urbanization*.

As you will soon see, there is more than one sociological perspective on these various topics. The variety of sociologies is demonstrated throughout this volume, as the authors analyze their subjects and apply these various perspectives to the study of past and present Canadian society.

Acknowledgments

We would again like to take this opportunity to express our appreciation to the various authors included in this text for their cooperation, hard work, and patience. We also gratefully acknowledge the many friends and colleagues who assisted all of us in putting the volume together, as well as the University of Western Ontario's Department of Sociology for its support, financial and otherwise. Many thanks as well to Jody Sadinsky for her assistance in editing the manuscript.

We would like to thank the reviewers, who offered many helpful suggestions: Georgine Hancock, Algonquin College; Rick Holmes, Mohawk College; Eugen Lupri, University of Calgary; and John Peters, Wilfrid Laurier University. Finally, we would like to acknowledge the professional help from the staff of Prentice Hall Canada Inc. Our thanks to Rebecca Bersagel, Lisa Berland, Mary Ann McCutcheon, and John Sweet for their support and encouragement.

James J. Teevan
W.E. Hewitt
1998

Contributors

Carol Agócs
William R. Avison
Roderic Beaujot
Fred Bird
Marion Blute
Michael P. Carroll
Samuel Clark
Edward G. Grabb
Carl F. Grindstaff
Bernard Hammond
Lesley D. Harman
Leslie W. Kennedy
John H. Kunkel
David MacGregor
Alan Pomfret
James J. Teevan—Editor
F.R. Westley

For the Instructor

The contributions of our constituent authors, combined with an editorial emphasis on clear language and uncluttered phraseology, have to date resulted in an instructive text, consistently praised for its uniformity in level and even writing style. In this sixth edition, significant updating and rewriting now make this book tighter, smoother, and more current than ever.

Features of this Edition

1. *Balanced approach to theoretical perspectives:* In this edition we have redoubled our efforts to inject a sound knowledge of sociological theory throughout the text. Chapter 1 provides an even more balanced introduction to the major theoretical paradigms of the discipline, dealing with structural-functionalism, conflict theory, symbolic interactionism, and feminism. These theoretical approaches are also applied more consistently to the specific areas addressed in subsequent chapters.
2. *Research methods given more prominence:* The Research Methods chapter has been moved up to Chapter 2 in the text. This move helps impress upon the student the importance of methodology within the discipline. Also, early presentation helps to facilitate enhanced student understanding of the various strategies employed by researchers in the field, as discussed in subsequent chapters.
3. *Feminist theory:* In response to suggestions from readers and students, the Gender Relations chapter has been relocated to Chapter 6, reflecting its importance as a subject for study within the realm of social inequality generally. In addition, wherever possible, coverage of gender issues in general has been enhanced and integrated throughout the text.
4. *Up-to-date research:* The multi-author approach offers a degree of accuracy and a wealth of information attainable only through specialization. This edition cites the most recent studies possible from Statistics Canada and other sources.
5. *Improved readability:* Throughout the book, passages previously identified as difficult by students and expert reviewers have been rethought and rewritten to produce a clear, concise, and comprehensive text.
6. *More thought-provoking boxed inserts:* Many of the boxed inserts have been replaced with contemporary and topical material of interest to students. Many boxed inserts are now presented in such a way as to promote discussion, through the inclusion of questions related to the material presented.

Established Features

1. *Multi-author perspective:* This text combines the expertise and research base of thirteen subfield specialists with a strong editorial focus to bring you the best of both worlds: the most up-to-date and accurate information—in a dynamic world and ever-developing discipline—explained by experts in each area, presented on a uniform learning level.
2. *Accessible writing style:* The editorial team has always exercised strong control to produce an attractive and complete text with a focus on clear language and uncluttered phraseology. This edition has undergone further change, based on student and reviewer input, in an effort to eliminate difficult passages. The result is a text that engages and motivates students to read on.
3. *Canadian perspective:* Through distinctly Canadian examples and applications, this volume brings students a look at their own sociological environment and areas of particular interest. The text absorbs students through real-world illustrations and discussions of personally and culturally relevant issues. The objective is to centre on the Canadian context; within course time constraints, instructors can best do justice to that material most immediate and familiar to students.
4. *Content coverage:* The volume covers the full spectrum of sociological theory, providing an excellent, balanced view of the major paradigms of the discipline. Core subject areas covered include: research methods, culture, socialization, deviant behavior, gender relations, social stratification, race and ethnic relations, families, religion, education, political sociology, social organizations and work, social movements, demography and population studies, and urbanization.

5. *Part introductions:* The editors have included an introduction at the beginning of each part, designed to help students tie individual chapter topics together by providing context and perspective, and suggesting a focus to guide student learning and emphasize particular concepts. Students develop an understanding of the general picture and of the relationships between separate subfields in an overall sociological context.

6. *Pedagogical aids:* This text is designed to provide a firm informational base while capturing the excitement of sociology. Photos, tables, figures, charts, and extensive use of boxed articles make the book visually stimulating while supplementing written information. The boxed articles present a number of special-interest items and commentary, allowing real-world applications of theoretical perspectives through in-depth discussion of topical cases and viewpoints. Each chapter ends with a summary, a list of key terms, a series of critical thinking exercises composed to spark student interest and debate, a list of suggested readings, and Internet web sites for further exploration. Key terms appear in bold print in the text for easy identification and reference. A full glossary appears at the end of the volume, with page numbers to guide readers to the place in the text where the term is first discussed.

Supplements

This edition is accompanied by a range of invaluable instructional aids, designed to meet student and instructor needs.

1. *Instructor's Manual and Test Item File:* This resource has been developed by co-editor Ted Hewitt. The instructor's manual has been significantly redesigned to ensure maximum utility to the intro-level teacher. The Introduction includes general tips on teaching introductory level sociology, especially in large class format—now a fact of life on most university and college campuses. Chapter sections comprise: (1) a list of chapter headings; (2) a summary of *Introduction to Sociology* chapter contents; (3) a list of learning objectives; (4) a summary of key terms and concepts; (5) issues for class discussion; (6) a summary of chapter-related videos contained on the Prentice Hall Allyn and Bacon Canada/CBC Video Library clips available as a supplement to the text; and (7) a list of NFB videos relevant to the topic. The test bank includes four basic types of question, most new to this edition: (1) fill-in-the-blank; (2) multiple choice; (3) short essay; and (4) true-false. Answers are provided and page numbers appended to each question for easy reference to the text.

2. *Computerized Test Item File:* This computerized file is available in both Windows and Mac format. The test bank contains four basic types of question, and most questions are either new or re-edited for this edition. Questions include: (1) fill-in-the-blank; (2) multiple choice; (3) short essay; and (4) true-false. Answers, page numbers, and difficulty level are appended to each question for easy reference to the text.

CBC

3. *Prentice Hall Allyn and Bacon Canada/CBC Video Library:* A collection of hand-picked CBC video clips prepared for this edition of *Introduction to Sociology* is perhaps the most dynamic of all the supplements you can use to enhance your classes. Prentice Hall and the CBC have worked together to bring you the best Canadian video package available in the College market. Containing segments from various CBC series, these tapes have extremely high production quality, substantial content, and are hosted by well-versed, well-known anchors. Summaries of the topics introduced by the video clips along with discussion questions appear in the Instructor's Manual and the Study Guide.

4. *Study Guide:* This guide provides students with a study aid designed to complement the text. Chapter sections comprise: (1) a summary of objectives; (2) a summary of the chapter-related video clip plus discussion questions, when applicable; (3) a summary of key terms and definitions; (4) self-quiz multiple choice questions; (5) fill-in-the-blank questions; and (6) answers. Students can pinpoint areas of weakness and return to the text for review, as necessary.

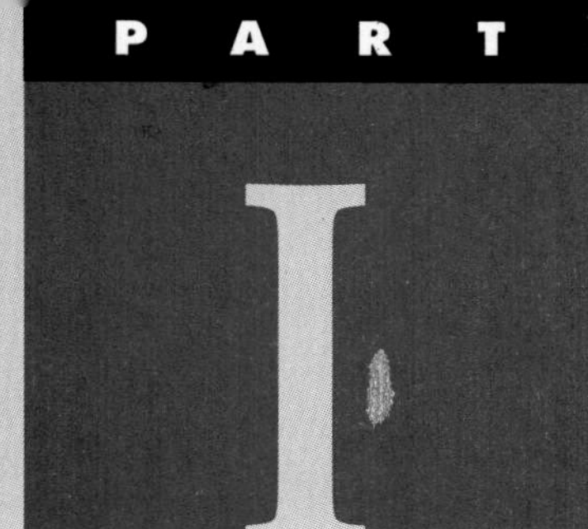

Introduction

In the first part of this book we provide an overview of sociology as a discipline. In Chapter 1 we examine its origins and varieties, and also present a brief history of sociology in Canada. How sociologists conduct their research is the subject of Chapter 2. Although the process generally involves the collection of data to describe or explain social phenomena, there are many specific research strategies from which to choose. Each is explained in a general way, followed by a discussion of its actual practice. An assessment of the relative strengths and weaknesses of the various research methods is also presented. Give each option a careful reading, and then, as the various research problems in need of research are suggested throughout the text, think about the option you might choose.

CHAPTER 1

What Is Sociology?

James J. Teevan & Marion Blute

INTRODUCTION

One of the major concerns of sociology is to explain why members of some groups behave differently from members of other groups. The groups that affect human behaviour include whole societies, collectivities that share a common territory and way of life, such as Canada and the U.S.; smaller groups that share the same status, such as trade unionists, doctors, or right-to-life advocates; even social categories, individuals who may not see themselves as forming social groups at all, but who possess some social characteristic in common, such as having no children, being over six feet tall, or living in the same province. Thus, sociology attempts to answer such questions as why the U.S. has more crime than Canada (see Chapter 3, Culture), whether first-born children are brighter on average than later-born children (see Chapter 4, Socialization), why the crime rate in B.C. is higher than Newfoundland's (see Chapter 5, Deviance), why fewer women than men are in certain professions (see Chapter 6, Gender Relations), or how cohabiting couples differ from those who are married (see Chapter 9, Families).

In seeking to explain such differences, many sociologists adopt a viewpoint developed over a century ago by the French sociologist Emile Durkheim (1858–1917) in his investigation of suicide. Many of Durkheim's contemporaries thought that mental illness, inherited tendencies, or unhappiness might be causes of suicide. Although each of these explanations had merit, Durkheim believed that they focused too much on the person as an isolated individual. Durkheim argued that social factors—factors pertaining either to group structure or to the relationships between individuals in groups—also affect suicide.

Durkheim called these social sources of behaviour **social facts**. Social facts point to social or group-level explanations of behaviour, such as ethnicity, birth order, gender, province, and marital status. They are thus unlike psychological facts, which emphasize individual internal processes such as drives and motives (for a comparison of sociology, psychology, and other social sciences, see Chart 1.1).

In his classic study of nineteenth-century suicide, Durkheim uncovered several differences which pointed to a social cause of suicide: men had higher suicide rates than women, Protestants higher rates than Catholics and Jews, older people higher rates than the young, and single people higher rates than the married (Durkheim, 1897). Durkheim saw the greater frequency of suicide among men, Protestants (cf. van Poppel and Day, 1996), the older, and the unmarried as due in part to the relative social isolation they experienced. As a group, men were more independent than women; Protestants on average were less integrated into religious communities than Catholics and Jews; the older and the unmarried generally had fewer ties to friends and family than the young and the married. Durkheim argued that these social links, found more frequently in some

CHART 1.1 Sociology and the social sciences: A comparison

Sociology	The study of social behavior and relationships, it examines the effects of society and group membership on human behaviour, as well as people's perceptions of their social environment, and the effects of these perceptions on social interaction. There is much overlap between sociology and the other social sciences described below.
Psychology	Primarily the study of individual sources of behaviour, its emphasis is on processes internal to the individual, such as motivation, cognition, learning, perception, and personality.
Social and cultural anthropology	Traditionally the study of small, nonindustrial societies, it has been extended to communities in industrial societies. This discipline tends to study these groups in totality, from their organization and culture, to specific institutions, including their political, economic, familial, religious, and legal systems. Sociologists are more likely to study only some of these topics at any one time in an attempt to achieve a more detailed view of a more limited subject area.
Political science	This discipline looks at government and political life, including the exercise of power and voting. Political sociologists study these issues as well, but usually examine them as they affect and are affected by selected aspects of the broader social context.
Economics	This discipline studies the production, distribution, and consumption of goods and services. As with political sociology, sociologists interested in the economy study these issues in a wider social context.
History	Generally focusing on past human behaviour, history includes both careful description and examination of causal processes, usually in narrative form. Although many historians seek generalizations that hold across several specific historical instances, much historical analysis is confined to the study of individual events or sequences. Historical data, although less accessible than current data, can be used by sociologists for their analyses, but often are not.

groups than in others, act as buffers against suicide. He called the suicides that occur because of the lack of such social ties **egoistic suicides**.

Excessively strong social ties, claimed Durkheim, can also lead to higher suicide rates. This kind of suicide, called **altruistic suicide**, is exemplified by the World War II kamikaze pilots, who chose death for the glory of Japan, or by the members of the Branch Davidian religious sect, who committed suicide in Waco, Texas, in 1993.

Durkheim identified other types of suicide, also with social origins. **Anomic suicides** are found in those societies marked by insufficient rules and regulations, a condition which might arise in times of extensive and rapid social change. In anomic societies individuals experience feelings of unpredictability and of being without limits, and thus may be prone to suicide. **Fatalistic suicides** occur in societies having too many rules and too few options. Individuals in such societies may feel that they are trapped and see suicide as the only way out.

The degree of regulation in society, like the strength of the ties in social groups, is a social and not an individual variable. (Indeed, individuals may be unaware of these conditions.) Thus, in his explanation of suicide, Durkheim demonstrated how social conditions affect human behaviour. Note how sociologists are concerned with *rates* of behaviour—for example, suicide rates among men, and not the suicide of any one man—and with *group differences*, comparing, for example, the suicide rates of married versus single adults (e.g., Trovato, 1991). These data cannot be used to predict any one specific case.

At the same time, neither Durkheim nor sociologists today argue that behaviour is fully determined by the common experiences that may arise from group membership. Sociologists do not deny individual free will; people can and do make choices. But the social environment does affect behaviour, and if the conditions found in some groups are unlike the conditions in other groups, different behaviour may result. Thus, rates of behaviour (e.g., of suicide, divorce, or alcoholism) in various groups (e.g., men and women, Canadians and Americans) may differ according to these differing circumstances.

Suicide is obviously only one of the topics examined by sociologists. In later chapters, additional social facts will be examined in depth. But first let us present a brief discussion of the historical forces that led to the development of sociology and then take a look at its major theoretical approaches.

SOCIOLOGY: ITS MODERN ORIGINS AND VARIETIES

Although sociology existed in various forms prior to the eighteenth century and probably in other parts of the world as well, the French and Industrial revolutions served as important factors in its modern Western development. Each caused upheavals in traditional European life: the French Revolution expanded the potential for democracy; the Industrial Revolution led to a new economy, the further growth of trade and cities, and a radically new organization of work. One result of these two upheavals was that relatively small, simple, rural societies—based on family and tradition, an accepted hierarchy of authority, and at least an outward appearance of consensus—gave way to more urbanized, heterogeneous, dynamic societies, marked by increasing conflict and growing social problems.

At about the same time these social changes were occurring, science and scientific explanations, products of the Enlightenment, were increasingly supplanting religion and theological explanations of natural phenomena. Where earlier explanations

Sociology—A Very Broad Field

Sociologists can and do study just about all aspects of human behaviour. The topics of their research range from the difference between birthday cards intended for women and those intended for men (Brabant and Mooney, 1989) to such crucial issues as the relationship between race and ethnicity and disease (cf. Clarke, 1990). This text will offer you many sociological insights, including how watching television affects people, the myths and reality of gender differences, how wealth is distributed in our country, the changing face of immigration, the effects of divorce on children, supermarket religion, First Nations' protest movements, and the forms of work organization. Below is a selection of other discoveries taken from papers presented at recent professional conferences of sociologists. As you will see, they all reflect Durkheim's belief that social structure and group membership affect behaviour.

- Infants born to women with higher education, economic status, and autonomy are more likely than others to survive their first year of life.
- While parents in Korea prefer the birth of a son, those in Jamaica prefer the birth of a daughter.
- Protestant fundamentalists are becoming more accepting of equality for women.
- Self-identified lesbians are no more likely than others in the population to have suffered childhood or sexual abuse, suggesting that such mistreatment is not a cause.
- People who feel that they are worse off than others have a greater tendency to exhibit negative attitudes toward new immigrants.
- Negative experiences with a condom discourage many men from subsequent use, even those men with multiple sexual partners.
- Regardless of academic ability, children born closely spaced together in time are less likely to pursue higher education than those children born at longer intervals.
- Gossip is a weapon likely to emerge where the principals to the conflict are equals, intimate, and socially homogeneous and where there is no formalized authority structure.

Source: *Adapted from various recent* Sociological Abstracts, *San Diego, CA: Sociological Abstracts Inc.*

The Industrial Revolution heralded a new economy and a radically new organization of work.

were rooted in religious dogma based on authority and faith, scientific explanations were based on *observation* and on *reason*. (For one view of science, see Chart 1.2.) Many people optimistically felt that, just as science had revolutionized industrial production, a science of society, applied to the ills and growing pains of the emerging societies, could bring them to new heights of cooperation, good will, and orderly growth. Credited by some as its founder, Auguste Comte (1798–1857) saw sociology as both a secular religion and a science. Sociologists would be its "priests" who would guide societies through turbulent times and suggest solutions to their social problems. The decline of traditional religion, which tended to see society as divinely fixed and unchangeable and social ills as part of God's will, made possible this new discipline. The excesses of the French Revolution—exemplified by the reign of terror and mass executions—and of the Industrial Revolution—as seen in the conditions of early factories—made it seem mandatory. Thus was born the modern science of sociology (cf. Curtis, 1992).

Almost immediately after its birth, disagreements arose concerning the approach to research which the new science of sociology should take. (This topic will be discussed more fully in Chapter 2, Research Methods.) There were also disputes over the extent to which group membership determines behaviour and how societies are structured. We shall discuss this last topic first.

Some early sociologists, among them Durkheim, argued that society is structured like a human body: a collection of organs, each performing a necessary function. Implicit in this view was the idea that the various segments of society (organs) are cooperative units working for the benefit of society as a whole (the body), and hence, that social ills are temporary phenomena curable by appropriate "medicines" and "repairs."

Others, such as Karl Marx (1818–1883), rejected this analogy and saw society as made up of individuals and groups held together by society's strongest members, who use their power to coerce the weaker elements of society. In this account, social ills are chronic and serious, built into the very structure of society. Cures can only come from radical social change in which the powerful are forcibly overthrown and a more cooperative society established.

Put more simply, some believe societies to be founded upon agreement and consensus, while others assert that power, coercion, and conflict mark their existence. Proponents of these two alternatives, known respectively as *functionalism* (originally structural-functionalism) and *conflict theory*, became major protagonists, each fighting to make its perspective dominant in the new science of society. Later, a third approach—*symbolic interactionism*—emerged, followed by a range of feminist approaches. In the sections that follow, we shall examine each in turn.

CHART 1.2 Characteristics of science[1]

Empirical	Science is empirical, that is, based on observation and experience. Faith, intuition, and common sense may be sources of ideas, but science demands that such insights be subjected to empirical testing.
Explanatory	Science not only describes empirical reality but also uses laws and theories to explain why events occur, and in so doing, follows the rules of logic. For example, if groups with few social ties have higher suicide rates than other groups, and if Protestants are such a group, then it is predicted that Protestants will experience higher suicide rates. This is sometimes called the "covering law" model of scientific explanation.
Simple, parsimonious, and elegant	Science prefers simple to complex explanations and seeks to explain the largest number of diverse kinds of observations with the fewest possible laws and theories. Hence Durkheim, for example, explained higher suicide rates among very diverse groups—men, Protestants, the elderly, and singles—with a single theory. Simple, parsimonious explanations are often said to be elegant and are admired by scientists in the same way that a work of art is admired.
Predictive	Science generally involves stating with a certain degree of probability that if certain events occur, others will follow. In sociology these predictions are not predictions of any one individual's behaviour but focus on group rates of behaviour, for example, on suicide rates among Protestants.
Pure versus applied	Science can be pure, concerned with only the acquisition of knowledge, or it can be applied, concerned with putting that knowledge to use. Sociologists do not fully agree on this issue, some seeking only descriptions and explanations, others to use sociological insights in their attempts to solve social problems.

[1] The above description is best seen as only one view rather than as a universal description of scientific practice. In recent years historians and sociologists have compared this ideal with studies of how science actually is, and has been, conducted in practice, revealing significant discrepancies (cf. Dupré, 1993).

Functionalism

Functionalism generally accepts the consensus viewpoint and originally borrowed three major concepts from biology and medicine: function, equilibrium, and development. The term *function,* first of all, means that social arrangements exist because they somehow benefit society, and points to the importance of each part of society for the functioning and health of the whole. (Note the biological analogy with the parts of the body working together for the benefit of the whole organism.) Following this logic, functionalists could even argue, for example, that female prostitution (male prostitution was generally ignored) is beneficial and functional for society (cf. Davis, 1937). The general functionalist position is that if something persists in society, especially, as in the case of prostitution, in spite of widespread disapproval, then it must serve a function. If it served no function it would disappear.

Specifically, the argument that prostitution is functional begins with the assumption that men possess more sexual energy than can be accommodated in marital structures. Prostitution is seen as an outlet for some of this excess sexual energy. It is a business arrangement, quickly concluded and demanding little or no emotional involvement. Affairs with single women or women married to other men, on the other hand, while satisfying such sexual needs, also generally require greater emotional attachment and they last longer. As such they pose a greater threat to family stability. Therefore, prostitution is beneficial or functional for a society in that it decreases the potential for family disruption and divorce. We shall return in a few paragraphs to a viewpoint that soundly rejects these arguments. A functionalist explanation of sexual jealousy among males will also be examined in Chapter 3, Culture.

Peace and consensus are seen as the natural states of society. Its ability to adapt to occasional, temporary, and minor problems, called **dysfunctions**, and return to a balanced arrangement is called **equilibrium.** Furthermore, because society is in equilibrium, the effects of a change in any one part of society will be felt in other parts of society. For example, eliminating prostitution might lead not only to more family disruption, but also, according to functionalist logic, to greater premarital sexual activity and even to increased rates of sexual assault.

Finally, the concept of *development* is often, although not always, implied in functionalist thought. Social change is seen as gradual, almost evolutionary, and usually in the direction of both greater differentiation (the development of new social forms) and functional integration. Through time, society adapts to its problems and is improved in the process. Thus, to return to our prostitution example, excess sexual energy is a dysfunction; society differentiates (creates) the occupation of prostitute to provide for a return to equilibrium; the family remains intact and society is even improved, since unbroken families are presumed to raise happier, healthier, more productive children than do disrupted families. Once created, prostitution survives only so long as it is functional; should it cease to be so, it would disappear.

Conflict theory

In contrast to functionalism, **conflict theory** suggests that power, not functional interdependence, holds a society together; that conflict, not harmony, is society's natural state; and that revolutions and radical upheavals, not evolution or development, fuel social change and improvement. According to this view, moreover, inequality is the major source of social conflict and is something to be eradicated, not applauded as in the functionalist argument, which sees inequality as necessary to ensure that society's difficult jobs will be filled (see Chapter 7, Social Stratification). Society is viewed as composed of groups acting competitively rather than cooperatively, exploiting and being exploited rather than each fulfilling a function for the whole society.

Reacting to functionalists, a common question raised by conflict sociologists is, "Functional for *whom*?" Conflict sociologists believe existing social arrangements benefit the powerful—such as capitalists and religious or political leaders, usually men, struggling among themselves for dominance—certainly not all of society. Whatever the split, whether it be environmentalists and loggers, anglophone and francophone Canadians, First Nations people

Conflict theory suggests that conflict is society's natural state, and that radical upheavals fuel social improvement.

and later Canadian settlers, students and teachers, there is division and conflict. (Conflict theorists generally do admit to some degree of consensus and cooperation—otherwise society would fall apart—but then suggest that this agreement results from coercion and domination.)

In perhaps the best-known example of conflict theory—and it should be emphasized that Marxism represents only one of several conflict perspectives—Marx argued that contemporary society is held together by capitalist domination, which pits the proletariat (workers) against the bourgeoisie (owners of capital) in a constant struggle for the profit from labour. He saw the relative calm of such societies as based not on consensus or functional interdependence, as functionalists might argue, but on the capitalists' coercion of the proletariat and the workers' lack of awareness of their own exploitation. Only through revolution, Marx argued, could the workers ever hope to change the capitalist-dominated structure of society. (These themes will be explored in Chapter 7, Social Stratification.)

Going back to the female prostitution example, a conflict view would see prostitution not as serving a social need but as marked by power and coercion. Prostitutes are victims forced to work under degrading and dangerous conditions, competing for clients. They are paid as little as possible by their male customers, and much of that is taken by male pimps. Male police officers arrest female prostitutes more often than their male clients. Thus, from a conflict perspective, prostitutes are best viewed as another example of females exploited by males (Lowman, 1992). A radical overhaul of sex roles in society is required to modify the traditionally male-dominated arrangement of prostitution. Such an overhaul might lead, if not to an end to sexual exploitation, then at least to the decriminalization of prostitution or to equal police and judicial treatment of prostitutes and their customers.

Symbolic interactionism: an individual perspective

Despite their different views of society, one emphasizing cooperation, the other exploitation, both functionalists and conflict theorists share a tendency to downplay individual actors in their analyses. Theirs is a *macro*-focus, examining the structure of groups or of societies and their interrelationships, rather than individuals. Moreover, both functionalists and conflict theorists generally see individuals as constrained by the society and social groups to which they belong. While they would agree that behaviour is never fully determined by these conditions and that individual feelings do play a role, choices are limited by the options available, and by the conditions under which they are made.

Symbolic interactionism provides another perspective on social behaviour. It is a *micro*-perspective,

Sociology—A Liberal Discipline?

Informal reports suggest that the social sciences, and sociology in particular, encourage liberal thought. Is this true?

Baer and Lambert (1990) concluded, based on responses from a national sample of Canadian adults, that people who have studied social sciences at university are indeed less likely than people who studied business and the professions to endorse a conservative ideology with respect to the profit motive, the military, big business, and rights of labor. They are also more likely to support government expenditures for social welfare programs.

Baer and Lambert pointed out, however, that business and professional schools may encourage conservative views, pulling their students to the right, rather than social science courses pulling theirs to the left. They also caution that francophone sociology may be more critical and more activist than that in other parts of Canada, and thus more radical. For those interested in reading more on this topic, see Baer and Lambert in Vol. 27: 487–504, of the *Canadian Review of Sociology and Anthropology*, and a rejoinder in that same journal, Vol. 31, pp. 184–195.

one that looks to how individuals *subjectively* interpret their social worlds and then act upon these interpretations. While symbolic interactionists admit that individual perceptions are to some extent affected by social structure and by the experiences group membership entails, they choose to emphasize how individuals actively construct their worlds. For humans, the meaning of things is not intrinsic to the things themselves, but arises through the way people interact with reference to them. For example, the same falling snow can be seen happily by a group of skiers, fearfully by others who have to drive in it, romantically by still others who watch it coating the trees, and resentfully by those who must shovel it. Such reactions determine behaviour. Moreover, if something is perceived or defined as real (Thomas, 1923), it is real in its consequences (see Chapter 4, Socialization). For example, if people perceive, however incorrectly, that immigrants are taking their jobs, they may act in racist ways, regardless of actual employment conditions. People can change their perceptions of reality as they interact with others, can reinterpret the past to fit in with current needs, and can hold several, what may appear to outsiders to be contradictory, perceptions. It is these subjective perceptions, however, that determine their behaviour.

Since humans can react so differently to the same stimuli, symbolic interactionists emphasize free will and the autonomy of individual behaviour. They argue that humans are unlike the elements of the chemist's periodic table—subject to fixed patterns of action—and instead possess autonomy and the ability to make choices. Unlike billiard balls reacting passively to external forces, people act from internal *reasons* rather than external causes. People have options both in their goals and in the means they use to achieve them. Thus, in symbolic interactionism the constraining effects of group membership are downplayed, while individual freedom of choice and autonomy are highlighted.

Returning to the example of prostitution, symbolic interactionists would be more interested in discovering the social patterns among individuals which perpetuate the practice. Thus they might talk to prostitutes and their clients in an attempt to see how each perceives the relationship, how each defines it, and then perhaps how each negotiates the cooperation needed for its conclusion (cf. Visano, 1987, for a study of male prostitution).

Symbolic interactionism focuses on individuals and the autonomy of their behaviour.

Some symbolic interactionist ideas were anticipated in the nineteenth century by the German sociologist Max Weber (1864–1920). Weber succeeded in simultaneously utilizing both a macro- and a micro-perspective. As a macro-sociologist, he saw much conflict in society but believed, in contrast to Marx, that cultural and political forces, in addition to economic powers, play an important role in shaping society. He was especially conscious of the force of bureaucracy in affecting social organization. As a micro-sociologist, Weber believed that sociologists must be able to empathize, to put themselves in the place of the individuals they study, and must attempt to understand, given the actors' goals and interpretations of their situation, the reasons for their actions. Thus, in contrast to Durkheim, he was at least as interested in understanding (***verstehen***) human behaviour as in predicting varying group rates.

For example, in his classic study of the origins of capitalism, *The Protestant Ethic and Spirit of Capitalism* (1904–1905), Weber argued not only from a societal or macro-perspective, that the doctrine of Protestantism was associated with capitalism (in the same sense that Durkheim argued that Protestantism was associated with suicide), but also from a micro-perspective, that the link between the two was subjectively understandable and traceable to the Protestants' interpretation of their worldly role. Weber's assumptions will be explained more fully in Chapter 10, Religion.

Symbolic interactionism was later more fully developed by the twentieth-century American sociologist George Herbert Mead (1863–1931), whose work is discussed in Chapter 4, Socialization. He argued that social interaction is possible because of the ability of individuals to engage in **role taking**, symbolically placing themselves in the role of others with whom they interact, and imagining how those others see them and what they expect of them. Individuals act and respond to one another according to these mental perceptions, not according to any "objective" social reality, Mead argued. Symbolic interactionists since his time have accepted the idea that interaction requires that individuals subjectively define their social environments, interpret the actions of others, and then act on the basis of these interpretations.

Feminist theories

As you will read in Chapter 6, Gender Relations, there is no one "feminism." While all feminists would agree that gender inequality exists, they may disagree on its causes and thus on any "solutions." Some seek radical measures, others more minor adjustments to current arrangements. Correspondingly, there is also no one feminist sociology. Still, it is the most important of the recent perspectives in sociology. Feminist sociology may be broadly defined as one *of* women from their standpoint and *for* women in the political sense of change (cf. Madoo-Lengermann and Niebrugge, 1996). Its first question is always, "And what about the women?" Its most general answer is that women are different, unequal, and oppressed, and that their differentness, inequality, and oppression may vary by women's other characteristics such as race, social class, age, and sexual orientation, among others. It also does not treat gender as one variable among many, as for example Durkheim did in his study of suicide. Instead, its main focus is directly on gender, because gender cross-cuts all aspects of social life.

Along with its focus on women, there is within feminist sociology a general consensus in at least four other areas. First, it tends to be more politically activist than other types of sociology. It has been successful in raising public consciousness: everyone is more aware of spousal violence, date rape, and stalking; growing numbers are aware of the genital mutilation of women practised in some societies.

Second, feminist sociology is more interdisciplinary than other types of sociology. Gender is important in all fields: in economics, history, anthropology, literature, science, and art. As a consequence, feminist sociologists are linked to scholars in these and other fields, more so than is the case for other sociologists. (According to Eichler and Tite [1990], they also tend to be the leaders in these interdisciplinary approaches.)

Third, feminist sociology is more accepting of a broader range of approaches to research. (For a discussion of female-friendly science see Chapter 2, Research Methods.) It sees knowledge as partial and interested, affected by power relations and discovered from a point of view, not total and objective.

Thus it would be related as "I learned" rather than "the data revealed."

Finally, it is less constrained by traditional divisions in sociology and often uses aspects from different sociological perspectives. While very few feminist sociologists claim to be functionalists—it would be very difficult to find one who would defend a division of labour based upon gender as representing a consensual and mutually beneficial arrangement—many feminist sociologists are comfortable with some aspects of both symbolic interactionism and the various conflict approaches. Using the former, they might be concerned with how women and men learn to be feminine and masculine. But there are important disagreements too. Symbolic interactionism is not political enough for many and, worse, it distorts the experience of women in several ways. For example, in taking the role of the other, that other is generally masculine and it is his definition of the situation that prevails. The generalized other is also male, one that encourages women to see themselves as unequal to men.

From conflict theory, some focus on political economy and capitalism, as did Marx, and others on the system of male dominance or patriarchy; still others look to both as sources. (These topics are further discussed in Chapter 6, Gender Relations.) But compared with other conflict theorists, feminist sociologists examine the oppression of women more than the oppression of class, and expand "production" to include non-economic forms ignored by traditional Marxists, including housework, mothering, and "invisible" work—those informal, hidden, and often devalued aspects of social life more often assigned to women.

All four models—functionalism, conflict theory, symbolic interactionism, and feminism—are popular in sociology today. A sociologist's specific choice of model depends in part on the phenomenon being examined. A conflict approach may best explain far-reaching and rapid social change, while functionalism may be used to understand long-lasting, stable, and widespread phenomena. The area of study is important too. Symbolic interactionism is frequently applied to the topic of learning (see Chapter 4, Socialization) while conflict theory is generally not stressed, although it could be. In the case of inequality (see Chapter 6, Gender Relations; Chapter 7, Social Stratification; and Chapter 8, Race and Ethnic Relations) the position is generally reversed. Feminist perspectives are appearing more frequently in all areas of sociology. Generally speaking, however, more than one approach is usually necessary for a full understanding of human behaviour.

SOCIOLOGY IN CANADA

Sociology in Canada has gone through several historical stages (Hiller, 1982). In its earliest phase, sociology in both English and French Canada scarcely existed as a discipline. While in American universities, under the influence of the Protestant-based "social gospel" movement for social reform, sociology was widely established by the turn of the century, the same movement in English Canada initially produced only a few courses in some Baptist colleges, along with some Methodist- and Presbyterian-sponsored social research (Campbell, 1983). Similarly, in French Canada, although the French Catholic sociologist and social reformer Frédéric LePlay gained an audience among some French Canadian intellectuals interested in Catholic social doctrines, the church-controlled educational institutions in Quebec were hostile to Durkheimian-style sociology (Rocher, 1977).

Eventually, however, sociology took hold in both English and French Canada. Both communities were influenced by the "human ecology" approach of Robert Park at the University of Chicago and his student Roderick McKenzie, eventually at the University of Michigan (Shore, 1987). The human ecology approach, discussed in Chapter 16, Urbanization, studies the geographical distribution (often in concentric circles or zones) and natural history (succession and change) of the components of communities. With reference to our earlier discussion, this school's approach to sociology is a mixture of conflict and functional approaches. Change begins with an "invasion" from one zone to another, for example, a shopping mall is built in a residential neighbourhood. Competition ensues between developers and residents (both conflict phenomena), but eventually an "accommodation" is reached. This accommodation could involve a buffer zone, for example—the planting of trees and the construction of small hills to separate the two areas. A symbiotic (mutually beneficial) relationship and equilibrium are then restored, both functional phenomena (cf. Shore, 1987: 109–112).

The first sociology department in Canada was established at McGill University in 1925 under Charles A. Dawson, trained at the University of Chicago and co-author of the first Canadian Sociology textbook, although the extent of the department's independence continued to fluctuate for some years thereafter (Helmes-Hayes, 1994; Palantzas, 1991). It was not until some years later that a group of francophone social scientists assembled at Laval, where a department encompassing ethics and sociology was founded in 1943 (becoming a Sociology department in 1951). In the 1940s the Laval group came under the leadership of Jean-Charles Falardeau, the first professionally trained sociologist in francophone Canada. Falardeau declared "we ought to start looking at French Canada as no longer an entity to save, but as a reality to know" (quoted in Dumas, 1987: 122).

From these two Quebec departments the first classics of Canadian sociology emerged. In subject matter they examined a range of national issues including, for example, Dawson's studies of the settlement process in western Canadian communities, and the work of Everett Hughes (first affiliated with McGill and later with Laval as well) on modernization and ethnic relations in "Cantonville" (Drummondville), a textile town in Quebec. Hughes came to be known as one of the great sociologists of his time and his *French Canada in Transition* (1943) remains an international classic in the discipline.

Not surprisingly, like other aspects of Canadian history, society, and culture, the early American influence on sociology was supplemented with a British one. In addition to Dawson and Hughes, the McGill department in its early years included Leonard Marsh. Marsh had been educated at the London School of Economics, founded to conduct empirical social research and education in the service of socialism. Marsh's teacher there, William (later Lord) Beveridge, became the architect of the British social security system. Similarly, Marsh's early research at McGill, on Canadians "in and out of work" during the Depression, had a lasting impact on Canadian society (Helmes-Hayes and Wilcox-Magill, 1993). In 1932 he helped found The League for Social Reconstruction, a forerunner of the CCF and hence, the New Democratic Party. The recommendations of his *Report on Social Security for Canada* (1943) for the federal government laid the foundation for the Canadian social security system, including family allowances and unemployment insurance.

In 1949, John Porter returned from the London School of Economics to Carleton College in Ottawa (now Carleton University). Sixteen years later he produced another international classic of Canadian sociology, *The Vertical Mosaic: An Analysis of Social Class and Power in Canada* (1965). In it Porter argued that although Canada may be an ethnic and cultural mosaic (a picture made up of small pieces), it is an unequal or vertically stratified one—hence the "vertical mosaic" of the title, a phrase that Marsh had used many years before. We shall have more to say on these topics in Chapter 7, Social Stratification, and Chapter 8, Race and Ethnic Relations.

A second legacy of the British influence on Canadian sociology was to slow its spread beyond Quebec. In Britain sociology was commonly viewed as an ahistorical and "shallow American discipline" (Hiller, 1982: 3; see also Clark, 1975). Thus, although from the 1930s through the 1950s research which can be viewed as sociological was performed in anglophone Canada, it was usually conducted in history, political economy, and even humanities departments; sociology departments just did not exist. The most important stream of this research, and one usually considered native to Canada, was performed at the University of Toronto by Harold Innis and later by S.D. Clark and Marshall McLuhan. Even there, however, the Chicago connection was stronger than has sometimes been supposed (Shore, 1987).

Harold Innis, a historical and institutional economist whom you will encounter in Chapter 12, Political Sociology, was trained at the University of Chicago economics department and influenced by Chicago-style sociological theory. In a trilogy of monographs on mining, the fur trade, and the cod fishery published after 1930, Innis argued that changes in demand for staple products (such as fur, fish, timber, iron ore, and wheat), the physical properties of the staples themselves, the technological means by which they are processed, and their geographical locations relative to transportation and markets shape not only economic but also political and social organization. For example, Innis maintained that the political boundaries of Canada were created by the demand for furs in Europe, the ease with which they were over-exploited in any particular area, the geography of the pre-Cambrian shield and river systems, and the canoe as a means of transportation. He also argued that the perishability of cod, the coastal location of the resource, and the technology for curing it created the characteristic geographical distribution and social organization of Canada's east coast, with its numerous, small, scattered fishing villages.

Late in his life Innis turned from the study of the transportation of goods to the communication of information. He concluded that the physical properties of media, like those of staple goods, had enormous consequences. He contrasted, for example, the relative permanence but unportability of stone and clay tablets with the relative portability but impermanence of papyrus and paper. Innis's work on communications media then influenced a fellow University of Toronto professor, an English professor, who became (along with Northrop Frye, the literary critic) Canada's most internationally celebrated scholar—Marshall McLuhan.

In *The Gutenberg Galaxy: The Making of Typographic Man* (1962) and *Understanding Media: The Extensions of Man* (1964), McLuhan argued that the dominant force in political, social, and cultural change in human history had been changes in the dominant medium of communication—from oral to written to electronic. Various media are extensions of specific human senses; whatever medium predominates distorts perceptions in favour of a

Innis argued that Canada's economic, political, and social organization were shaped by a dependence on staple products.

specific sense. Consequently, media shape not only the economic, political, social, and cultural environment but also the very nature of human consciousness. McLuhan's thesis was almost instantly recognized as the most original idea since Marx's attempt to explain all of human history with the concept of class conflict. "The medium is the message" briefly and clearly stated its central thesis, while phrases such as "the Gutenberg galaxy" and "the global village" succinctly communicated McLuhan's view that those steeped in a print rather than an electronic culture to all intents and purposes inhabit a different universe (see Marchand, 1989). Although McLuhan himself always maintained a rich network of multidisciplinary contacts, friends, and associates, the fairly rapid creation of separate communications departments within universities caused the study of communications to have less influence on sociology and the other social sciences than it might otherwise have had.

Meanwhile, a student of Innis's, Samuel D. Clark, led a small group of sociologists out of the department of political economy at the University of Toronto to establish the first department of sociology in Canada outside of Quebec. For many years Clark was Canada's best-known sociologist. Educated first at the University of Saskatchewan and then at the London School of Economics, McGill's sociology department, and finally under Innis in political economy at Toronto, Clark owed something to all of these influences. *Church and Sect in Canada* (1948) and *Movements of Political Protest in Canada* (1959), for example, include an Innis-style setting of new areas of economic exploitation (in the Canadian west), social disorganization (religious sects and political protest), and a Chicago-style focus on restoration of equilibrium in social organization.

By the early 1960s sociology was tenuously established in Canada. Institutionally it was still limited to Quebec and Toronto. Intellectually it had inherited an interest in the structure of entire communities from the Chicago-style sociology of the twenties. Yet it often combined this focus with political economy and with a historical approach, to take into account change on much longer time-scales than was common in Chicago-style sociology.

In the 1960s the baby-boom generation came of age and simultaneously governments decided that continued economic prosperity depended on a higher proportion of university-educated people. As a consequence new universities, including new sociology departments, sprang up around the country, creating an unprecedented demand in Canada for university teachers of sociology. Large numbers of foreign sociologists, primarily American, immigrated to Canada to take up the newly created positions. By 1970–71, 60 percent of sociology and anthropology professors in Canada were not Canadian citizens (Hiller, 1982: 25). Such mass immigration could not fail to be disruptive, as any community- and ecology-minded sociologist would predict. Conflicts were initiated, some of which have never been resolved entirely.

In English-speaking Canada, the new faculty came into conflict with those already there, and not infrequently with each other. The imported American sociologists were not a homogeneous group. They reflected the many sociologies being practised in the United States. At Harvard, for example, Talcott Parsons had been producing his grand theoretical synthesis integrating a free will/voluntaristic (as opposed to deterministic) view of human action with the kinds of social forces emphasized in the European classics (1937, 1951). At the opposite pole from such "grand theory," a whole technology of polling and survey research had been developed and had spread outward from Columbia University to many other American universities. If some Canadian sociologists thought Chicago-style studies of communities were too ahistorical, one can imagine what they thought of sociologists whose idea of research was almost exclusively to administer surveys of attitudes and beliefs! (This and other research options will be discussed in Chapter 2, Research Methods.) Political conflicts, too, were not uncommon. For some of the newcomers the move to Canada was a straightforward professional one. For others it was an abandonment of a society they viewed as hopelessly racist and war-mongering (this was the period of America's involvement in Vietnam). For still others it was an escape from the protesting students on American campuses. One can imagine the sparks that flew when protesters and the protested-against sometimes found themselves colleagues in the same department. And last but not least, both the old and the newly arrived professors often came into conflict with their students—the old because the sociology of communities did not seem to address the conflict-ridden times adequately, and the new because their knowledge of and sometimes even interest in Canadian society was often elementary at best, at least initially (Hiller, 1979).

As a result of some of these problems, the Association of Universities and Colleges of Canada established a commission on Canadian Studies in 1975. Their report, *To Know Ourselves*, stated that "a curriculum in this country that does not help Canadians in some way to understand the physical and social environment that they live and work in...cannot be justified" (Symons, 1976: 13). This in turn led to federal attempts to place limits on the hiring of foreign academics by Canadian universities. To this day the movement of the 1970s to "Canadianize" university curricula and personnel remains contentious—viewed as hurtful by some and too cautious and incomplete by others (Hofley, 1992).

In Quebec the changes and conflicts were somewhat different, but equally dramatic. The same demographic and economic forces were at work as in English-speaking Canada, but during the "Quiet Revolution" (see Chapter 14, Social Movements) the state took over responsibility for education from the church. As a result the number of sociologists increased and departments were added—first at the University of Montreal and later elsewhere, for example at the University of Quebec at Montreal (cf. Dumas, 1987). Because of the language difference, however, Quebec imported fewer Americans and relied more on people without doctorates and on French Canadians trained in France or the United States. Conflict in Quebec was often associated with the addition of new departments which tended to put forth, in their early days, different interpretations of Quebec society (Renaud et al., 1989). The earlier "modernizing" view which had predominated at Laval was displaced by various Marxist interpretations and by an analysis of Quebec as at once a distinct ("global") society and an ethnic minority—even an "ethnic class" within Canada (Dumas, 1987).

Rocher described how, until about the mid 1960s, "among most of my Quebec francophone colleagues, there was the sense of belonging to a Canadian Sociology and the desire to establish ties and active relationships with anglophone colleagues in other provinces. We felt the need to share with them the fruits of our research and our endeavours" (Rocher, 1992: 66). Perhaps the height of cooperation among English- and French-speaking sociologists was reached during research undertaken for the Royal Commission on Bilingualism and Biculturalism. "One found here French- and English-speaking sociologists and social scientists belonging to different generations conducting studies on various aspects of French-English relations in Canada" (Juteau and Maheu, 1989: 374). Gradually, however, English-language and Quebec sociology in Canada went their own ways, with different journals, professional associations, and intellectual concerns. Rocher (1992) documented this decline in interaction, which he viewed as mirroring the crisis of the "two solitudes" in the larger Canadian society. He related it to a growing preoccupation by Quebec sociologists with changes within Quebec society, their increasing interaction with francophones beyond Canada, and the increasing anglophone unilingualism of Canadian professional meetings (although Canadian Sociology and Anthropology Association (CSAA) publications remain bilingual). Today there exist major differences between the two sociologies. For example, sociology proper in Quebec has remained concerned almost exclusively with macro-sociological questions (Breton, 1989: 563). Associated with this emphasis, according to Béland and Blais (1989), is the infrequent use of quantitative methods in sociology in Quebec. Morris (1991) also found in Quebec sociology a greater emphasis on social policy and on applied rather than pure sociology. For a final example, perhaps because of the greater availability of funding for social research at the provincial level in Quebec, sub-specialties of sociology (such as criminology, demography, and urban and regional studies) have tended to become independently institutionalized there (Juteau and Maheu, 1989: 371).

Careers in Sociology

Later in this book you will read about post-secondary education. You will read how education may be sought as an end in itself or as a means to an end. Whether education is really necessary for the occupation to which you aspire is also briefly discussed. For now, let us assume that you are attending school not only for the love of learning and to gain the credentials necessary to validate your claim to be an educated person, but also as an avenue to an interesting, well-paying job, one that will give you freedom to express your creative talents.

Sociology graduates work in a wide variety of occupations, especially in education, social service agencies, and other government departments. They apply the critical and creative thinking skills they developed in sociology to teaching and research, helping to explain social phenomena; to social welfare programs, seeking to improve people's lives; to the criminal justice system; and to social movements and private organizations working for a better society. Whether as personnel or communications managers or designers and analysts of opinion polls, they generally share an appreciation for the social factors that affect individual behaviour and an optimism for the possibility of social change.

Source: *Adapted from Scott Davies, Clayton Mosher, and Bill O'Grady, 1992. "Canadian sociology and anthropology graduates in the 1980s labor market."* Society, *16 (pp. 39–46).*

FUTURE CHALLENGES

French Canada in Transition, *The Vertical Mosaic*, and *Understanding Media*, among others, are classics of social scientific and sociological scholarship, each contributing in its time to our understanding of ourselves. It remains to be seen whether sociologists of this generation in Canada, many of whom began their careers in the 1960s, will be able to leave a comparable legacy. Clearly, the time for judgment is fast approaching: the wave of retirements that is beginning among university sociologists is coinciding with astonishing changes both internationally and nationally. Can this generation of sociologists, Canadian or otherwise, provide insights into such issues as:

- the consequences of accelerating economic globalization and the continuing gap between rich and poor countries;
- the weakening of existing nation-states, combined with a resurgence of conflict among ethnic/linguistic groups in Europe, the former Soviet Union, and Canada;
- the future of Canadian federalism;
- the continued existence of gender and age discrimination; and
- last but not least, the consequences of the potential incompatibility between the current and projected size of the human population (and its way of life) and the continued existence of a variety of other species on this planet (cf. Marchak, 1990).

As you read in the subsequent chapters of this book about the facts that generations of sociologists have already uncovered, and the theories they have offered to explain them, perhaps you will make your own tentative judgments.

QUESTIONS FOR REVIEW AND CRITICAL THINKING

1. Should each society develop its own kind of sociology, or should sociology be a universal science? How would a Canadian sociology differ from a Chinese variety? Or a Quebec sociology from Maritime, Prairie, Ontario, and B.C. sociologies?

2. How would a conflict explanation of divorce differ from a functional one?

3. Ask your instructors how they became sociologists. Where were they educated? In what kinds of sociology were they trained? What kinds of sociology do they prefer now? How have they experienced the conflicts and changes in Canadian sociology over the last thirty years?

GLOSSARY

altruistic suicide according to Durkheim, the suicide caused by the excessively strong integration found in some groups

anomic suicide according to Durkheim, the suicide caused by feelings of being without limits or of boundlessness, a result of the relative lack of regulation found in some groups

conflict theory the sociological model that portrays society as marked by competition and/or exploitation. Its three major concepts are power, disharmony, and revolution.

dysfunctions the occasional minor, temporary disruptions in social life, as defined by functionalists

egoistic suicide according to Durkheim, the suicide caused by weak interpersonal ties, a result of the lack of integration found in some groups

equilibrium envisioned by functionalist sociologists as the normal state of society, marked by interdependence of parts and by harmony and consensus

fatalistic suicide according to Durkheim, the suicide caused by a decrease in options and feelings of being trapped, a result of the overregulation found in some groups

functionalism the sociological model which portrays society as harmonious and as based on consensus. Its three major concepts are function, equilibrium, and development.

role taking Mead's term for individuals' attempts to put themselves in others' places and to imagine what these others are thinking, so as to make interaction with them easier

social facts social sources or causes of behaviour; used by sociologists to explain rates of behaviour in groups as opposed to individual behaviour

symbolic interactionism the sociological model that argues that individuals subjectively define and interpret their environments, are not fully constrained, and act from reasons, not causes

verstehen the *understanding* of behaviour as opposed to the *predicting* of behaviour

SUGGESTED READINGS

Carroll, William K., Linda Christiansen-Ruffman, Raymond Currie, and Deborah Harrison (eds.)

1992 *Fragile Truths: 25 Years of Sociology and Anthropology in Canada*. Ottawa: Carleton University Press.

This work contains articles on a variety of topics about sociology in Canada, including its relationship to social change, how sociological knowledge is made (including a look at feminist alternatives and the differences between English and French Canadian sociologies), its academic milieu, and finally its professional association.

Hoecker-Drysdale, Susan

1990 "Women sociologists in Canada: the careers of Helen MacGill Hughes, Aileen Dansken Ross, and Jean Robertson Burnett." Pp. 152–176 in Marianne G. Ainley (ed.), *Despite the Odds: Essays on Canadian Women and Science*. Montreal: Véhicule Press.

This article about the lives and careers of three early Canadian women sociologists tells an all-too-familiar story of obstacles, potential contributions frustrated, and accomplishments made but then often poorly (or only belatedly) rewarded and recognized.

Ritzer, George

1996 *Contemporary Sociological Theory*. (4th ed.) New York: McGraw-Hill, Inc.

This theory text, although a bit advanced, describes the major early sociologists as well as perspectives in contemporary sociology including functionalist, conflict, symbolic interactionist, and feminist views.

WEB SITES

http://www.sosig.ac.uk/Subjects/sociol.html

Worldwide Sociology Resources

This page provides links to dozens of sites of interest and potential use to students of sociology, from sociology associations worldwide, to electronic journals, to information on famous sociologists such as Durkheim.

http://www.mcmaster.ca/socscidocs/othdepta.htm

Sociology and Anthropology Organizations and Departments

At this site, you will find a complete listing of and links to sociology departments at post-secondary institutions in Canada, Canadian sociology journals online, and the Canadian Sociology and Anthropology Association.

CHARGEX
VISA

CHAPTER

2

Research Methods

James J. Teevan

INTRODUCTION

Suppose you wanted to know if Canada's divorce rate is changing, if people are more or less happy after they divorce, what types of people tend to remarry more quickly than others, or what happens to children after their parents get a divorce. One way to find answers to these questions would be to look to your personal experiences (or to those of your friends) or to ask authorities such as your parents, teachers, or religious leaders. Another would be to use common sense.

Sociologists are reluctant to use such strategies because of their potential for distortion. For example, though there may have been fewer divorces recently among your family and friends, that does not mean the national rate is going down. Just because it was better for your cousins to be away from the constant fighting of your uncle and aunt does not mean that most children feel better after divorce. The fact that Aunt Liz remarried quickly does not mean that women remarry more quickly than men (the opposite is true). Personal experience is usually not general enough and, worse, is too often based on selective perception—seeing what you want to see—for it to produce accurate statements about the larger society. Authorities too can be wrong or biased in the answers they provide. Common sense may be little better. In most marriages, for example, do opposites attract or do birds of a feather flock together? Which expression of common sense is correct? And finally, what happens when one person's personal experience, or authorities, or common sense, contradict those of another? How is that resolved?

Sociologists thus argue that questions about divorce and other aspects of social life require a research project of some sort. They want to collect and analyze data from a wide variety of settings before drawing any conclusions. The different ways that sociologists conduct their research is the topic of this chapter. It begins with an overview of two basic approaches and then presents in more depth an example of each, examining its relationship to theory, its model, forms of measurement, sampling, and data analysis—terms that will be defined below. An evaluation of the advantages and disadvantages of each approach ends the chapter.

QUANTITATIVE AND QUALITATIVE METHODS

As you read in Chapter 1, Durkheim and Weber had quite different ideas on how to conduct research. Durkheim adopted a position called **positivism**, meaning that he wanted to use the research methods of the natural sciences, appropriately adapted, for the social sciences. Durkheim's successors favour what we today call *quantitative* methods. Counting and precise measurement (see the box on measures of central tendency) of observable behaviour, concentration on a limited number of variables, and prediction are all hallmarks of a quantitative approach. In an example of quantitative research, Cook and Beaujot (1996) found that while marriage and the presence of young children tend to reduce the probability of leaving the workforce for men, the presence of children increases the chances of work interruptions for women, especially if they are not married.

Most quantitative sociologists never actually observe real behaviour. Survey researchers, for example, take only verbal reports of that behaviour from their respondents. Experimenters observe laboratory behaviour, not that found in the real world (see the box on social science experiments). Thus others advocate an alternate approach, one often now called *qualitative*. An early exponent of qualitative methods, Weber argued that the social sciences should not copy the research methods and experimental designs of the natural sciences but should have their own research methods. Human behaviour is unique, he argued, because of the subjective meanings and motivations attached to it. Human beings not only make choices based on these meanings but are also very complex, making any discussion of marriage, children, and work much more involved than was described above. Moreover, sociologists need also to *understand* human behaviour, not just to be able to predict it. Because humans give meanings to their behaviour, because they are complex, because they engage in what Weber called *social action*, or meaningful goal-directed behaviour, the predictions would be incomplete without some understanding and some explanations of the behaviour from the actors' point of view.

To get at these meanings qualitative sociologists can attempt to understand behaviour using a variety of strategies. For example, they may talk at length and in depth with informants (field interviews), simply observe behaviour, or observe while participating themselves and then perhaps asking the actors about the meaning of their behaviour. This last method is called *participant observation*.

Having introduced quantitative and qualitative approaches generally, let us now turn to a specific quantitative approach.

Three Measures of Central Tendency

In everyday speech it is acceptable to talk of an "average," but in summarizing social data we have to be a bit more precise and distinguish among three "averages": the mode, the median, and the mean. Each is illustrated using the following data on the number of years of formal schooling completed by 35 people:

4, 7, 9, 10, 10, 11, 11, 11, 12, 12, 12, 12, 12, 12, 12, 13, 13, 13, 13, 13, 13, 14, 14, 14, 15, 16, 16, 16, 16, 17, 17, 18, 18, 19, 20

The *mode* is the most common value in any series. In the above case it is 12 years. There are 7 people with that number, more than with any other number of years of education. The *median* is the middle score of a set of values, such that half the cases fall above and half below it. In this case, it is the 18th score (17 values below and 17 above), or 13 years of education. Examine the data to verify this answer. Note that arranging the scores from low to high or from high to low makes it easier to find the median. If there are two middle scores, which is the case with an even number of values, the median is found by adding these two scores and dividing by two. The *mean* is found by adding up all of the scores and dividing by the number of scores. The number of scores above is 35, and the total of the scores is 4 plus 7 plus 9, etc., which adds up to 465. Thus, the mean is 465 divided by 35, which equals 13.29 years of education.

Because the other measures provide more information, we rarely use the mode. If the data are skewed (many at one end, few at the other), if a few very extreme values are included, or if the top values are open (e.g., incomes of one million dollars or more) we use the median as it is less sensitive to these distortions than is the mean. In all other instances we generally use the mean.

Does this insert help you to understand why baseball owners used the mean salary and players the median salary in the 1994 strike talks?

One quantitative option: survey research

Survey research is the most common type of research undertaken today and is familiar to most of you in the form of interviews or questionnaires. (See the boxed insert on content analysis for another quantitative option.) It involves asking people questions, either in written or oral form, and recording their answers. Let us now examine its relationship to theory, its model, and strategies for measurement, sampling, and analysis.

Theories and hypotheses

At its most general level, theory refers to the basic approach taken to a subject matter, such as a conflict or feminist approach, mentioned in the first chapter. But these are often very abstract. At a middle level, **theory** gets more specific and is composed of a set of interrelated statements that organizes and summarizes knowledge about some part of the social world. There could, for example, be a theory of crime, or a theory of prejudice. The statements found in these theories are often taken from the conclusions of prior research in which variables are linked to one another or shown to be related. A **variable** for sociologists is something (like income or religion) that takes on different values (varies) in different groups. A relationship between two variables means that they go together in some way, that changes in one accompany changes in the other. For example, level of integration and suicide rates are related, as pointed out in Chapter 1, with the over- and under-integrated more prone to self-destruction. Integration and suicide are the variables, and the fact that extremes in integration may encourage suicide constitutes the relationship between them.

Testable hypotheses can then be derived from such theories. A **hypothesis** is a statement of a *presumed* relationship between two or more variables, usually stated in the form, "Other things being equal, if A, then B." If the A variable occurs, then the B variable also occurs. The B variable is the one being explained, the A variable the explanation. In causal statements A is the cause or **independent variable**, B the effect or **dependent variable**. We might hypothesize that, other things being equal, gender (A) is related to a choice of research methods (B), with men more often favouring a quantitative approach and women more often a qualitative one (cf. Mackie, 1991 and see the box on female-friendly science).

Axiomatic and deductive logic are combined to derive such hypotheses from any theory. **Axiomatic logic** involves making connecting links between related statements, as in, "If A → B and B → C, then A → C." For example, examine the following:

Theoretical statements:

1. Birth order (A) is related to closeness to parents (B) (first-born children are more closely tied to their parents than are later-born).
2. Closeness to parents (B) leads to conservative values (C).

Axiomatic logic:

3. Therefore, birth order (A) is related to conservative values (C) (first-born children more conservative than later-born).

Deductive logic involves deriving a specific statement from a more general statement. Thus, given the general statement that birth order (A) is related to conservative values (C), we can hypothesize that it is related to sexual permissiveness (C_1), with first-borns less sexually permissive. The process could continue with marijuana use being another dependent variable (C_2), with the hypothesis that birth order (A) is related to marijuana use (C_2), and specifically, that proportionally fewer first-born children would use marijuana than would later-born.

But remember that hypotheses include the phrase *other things being equal*. That means that, *at least collectively*, the groups studied should be similar in other social characteristics too. In the current example, first- and later-born children should be the same in terms of age, sex, and religiosity, etc. To compare 15-year-old, religious, first-born girls with 20-year-old, atheist, later-born boys would be an unfair test of the effect of birth order on sexual permissiveness. The ideal of "other things being equal" may be difficult to achieve, but must be attempted because some of these variables are also related to sexual permissiveness.

Model

Models show how variables are related to each other, and are built by combining two or more "if A, then B" statements. Thus, one could develop the following model to explain the relationship between social class and violent crime: Social class is related to age of parents at birth of first child (poorer parents have children at a younger age); age of parents is related to marital breakup (the earlier the onset of family responsibilities, the higher the separation rate); broken families are related to children's school difficulties, especially to failing grade one; early school failure is related to delinquency; and finally, delinquency is related to violent adult criminality. For any two variables in this chain, the variable that occurs first is generally assumed to be an *independent* variable, the later one a *dependent* variable, and the others the *control* variables. We shall explain control variables more fully later.

Measurement

Measurement of their variables is probably the most difficult task survey researchers have to perform. Generally it involves transforming the *theoretical* language of the hypothesis into the operational language of measurement. **Operational definitions** describe the actual procedures or operations used to measure theoretical concepts. For example, an I.Q. score is an operational definition of the theoretical concept of intelligence; counting the number of times per month people attend religious services can be an operational definition of religiosity.

The general strategy in operationalizing variables is to devise simple, directly observable or *empirical* measures of things which may be complex, difficult to measure directly, and hard to observe. Operational definitions, therefore, are what researchers look for or listen to in order to measure their variables.

How would you measure prejudice? Can you operationalize that variable? Suppose some of you said that you would measure prejudice by seeing if people did not like certain groups. Would that be an operational definition? No, because you still would not know what to look for. How do you see "not liking"? Would laughing at jokes that make fun of certain groups be an operational definition of that prejudice? Yes it would, because it is observable and relatively clear—both major requirements of an operational definition. It is an empirical measure which can be heard. Alternatively, you could ask: "Are you prejudiced against (insert name of group), yes or no?" That question is also an operational definition, providing an empirical indicator: the "yes" or "no" response.

Some of you probably do not like either of these operational definitions, the first because unprejudiced people may laugh at these jokes, and the second because people may be evasive in their answers or even lie. These objections raise the issue of the **validity** of operational definitions—the degree to which they actually measure what they claim to measure. Validity is always an issue in constructing and using operational definitions.

Besides being valid, operational definitions must also be reliable. **Reliability** means that measures of a variable should be consistent and not vary either over time or with the person using them. Thermometers, for example, are generally reliable. Operational definitions, however, may lack reliability, as when respondents (1) admit to certain attitudes early in a questionnaire but later on, perhaps because they are growing tired, deny the same attitudes; or (2) tailor their responses to the person asking the questions, for example when female interviewers get different answers than male interviewers. If a measure is unreliable, yielding inconsistent results, it cannot be valid. One of the differing results might represent a valid measure, but researchers would be unable to specify which one it was. Would it be the first? The last? The one given to a male or the one given to a female interviewer? On the other hand, although reliability is necessary for validity, it cannot guarantee it. Even fairly reliable measures such as income may not be valid measures of lifestyle or social class.

Besides reliability and validity, a further potential problem in operationalization is that the same variable can have more than one operational definition. This in turn can have important consequences in the testing of hypotheses. As we will see in Chapter 5, some sociologists, operationally defining criminality as having ever been arrested, argue that poverty is related to criminality. Others, using self-report confessions of crime as their operational measure, find that most people are criminal at one

Female-Friendly Science

Rosser studied some of the ways in which women scientists conduct science differently from men. As part of her research, she attended conferences, talked with and read biographies and autobiographies of practising women scientists, and consulted the emerging literature on "women's ways of knowing." A more "female-friendly science," she concluded, would change current practices. Rosser made a number of suggestions in her book which "attempt to convert the connection of women scientists to their work into methods that will connect students to science" (Rosser, 1990: 55).

Observation

1. Expansion of the kinds of observations beyond those traditionally carried out in scientific research to include various interactions, relationships, or events not seen or considered worthy of observation by traditional scientists operating from an androcentric perspective.
2. Increasing the numbers of observations and remaining longer in the observational stage of the scientific method.
3. Acceptance of the personal experience of women as a valid component of experimental observations.
4. Unwillingness to undertake research likely to have applications of direct benefit to the military, and more likely to propose hypotheses to explore problems of social concern.
5. Consideration of problems that have not been deemed worthy of scientific investigation because of the field with which the problem has been traditionally associated (e.g., midwifery, home economics).
6. Formulation of hypotheses focusing on gender as a crucial part of the question being asked.
7. Investigation of problems of more holistic, global scope (e.g., environmental problems) than the more reduced and limited scale problems traditionally considered.

Methods of Data Gathering

1. Use of a combination of qualitative and quantitative methods.
2. Use of methods from a variety of fields or interdisciplinary approaches to problem solving.
3. Inclusion of females as experimental subjects in research designs.
4. Use of more interactive methods, thereby shortening the distance between observer and the object being studied.

Conclusion and Theories Drawn from Data Gathered

1. Use of precise, gender neutral language in describing their data and presenting their theories.
2. Critique of observations, conclusions drawn, and theories generated, differing from those drawn by the traditional scientist from the same observations.
3. Awareness of other biases such as those of race, class, sexual preference, and religious affiliation which may permeate theories and conclusions drawn from experimental observations.
4. Development of theories that are relational, interdependent, and multicausal rather than hierarchical, reductionistic, and dualistic.

Use of Scientific Information and Practice of Science

1. Use of less competitive models in practising science.
2. Perception of the role of scientist as only one facet which must be smoothly integrated with other aspects of their lives.
3. Placing increased emphasis on strategies such as teaching and communicating with non-scientists to break down the barriers between science and the layperson.
4. Exertion, wherever possible, of positive control over the practical uses of scientific discoveries to place science in its social context.

For more on this and related topics see work by Canadians such as Eichler (1988), Mackie (1991: 16–18), and a volume edited by Tancred-Sherrif (1988) in which it is argued that empowering women scientists is not the answer, for there would still be inequality between the scientist and her subjects. The key is a sharing of power, less hierarchy, and a participatory construction of knowledge with those being studied.

Source: *Sue V. Rosser, 1990.* Female-Friendly Science: Applying Women's Studies Methods and Theories to Attract Students. *New York: Pergamon Press (Chapter 4).*

time or another, regardless of wealth and living conditions. Different operational definitions thus can lead to quite different conclusions (and then quite different "solutions" to the crime problem).

Sampling

Rarely do survey researchers have the time or resources to study everyone they want to. For this reason they usually draw a *sample*, selecting a subset of individuals from the population they wish to study. There are really only two rules of sampling. First, a sample should be *representative* of the population from which it is drawn. Second, conclusions should not be generalized beyond the group from which the sample is drawn.

The second rule is simpler, so we shall discuss it first. It means that if researchers fail to sample from some groups, they cannot say their findings hold for such groups. For example, if researchers draw a sample from sociology students at the University of Alberta and ask them to fill out a questionnaire about Quebec separatism, they cannot then discuss the attitudes of *all* students at the University of Alberta on this topic. They would not know the views of non-sociology students because they omitted them from their sample. Non-sociology students may be unlike sociology students in many ways, including their attitudes toward Quebec separatism. Similarly, the researchers cannot generalize from Alberta sociology students to all sociology students. York and Dalhousie sociology students, among others, were not sampled, and may be quite different from Alberta sociology students in their feelings about Quebec.

The goal of representativeness involves drawing a sample that "looks like" and thus can be used to represent the total population. To accomplish this, researchers could take, for example, a **random sample**. In simple random sampling, all individuals are listed

Researchers usually draw a sample of individuals from the group they wish to examine.

(the result is called a *sampling frame*) and then some are selected for study purely by chance, just like names from a hat or numbered balls from the cages on television lottery shows. For an alternative to this listing see the insert on random digit dialing.

Although preferred in theory because every individual has an equal chance of being selected, random samples in practice are often difficult to achieve. Listing all the individuals from which the sample will be drawn, for example all Canadians, is time consuming, often difficult, and sometimes impossible. Therefore, researchers may opt for a process called cluster sampling or multi-stage random sampling, to simplify the task.

In **cluster sampling**, researchers first randomly sample large units. Then they randomly sample medium units within the large units. Finally, they randomly sample even smaller units within the medium units. For example, they could list all the geographical areas (tracts) used by the census to facilitate enumeration in Canada, and select 100 at random. Then they could list all streets in these census tracts and randomly select 500 of them; and finally, list all residents who live on those streets and randomly select 1000 for interviewing.

Both simple random sampling and cluster sampling permit generalizations to the population—their major goal. Anyone can be chosen and thus the samples should be representative, reflecting the population from which they are drawn. But in reality, researchers using random sampling techniques often cannot generalize to the total population because many of the randomly chosen individuals refuse to be interviewed. For this and other reasons, some researchers turn to also imperfect, but easier to execute, quota samples.

Quota sampling is a less expensive alternative to random sampling and involves a conscious, as opposed to chance, matching of the sample to certain proportions in the population. For example, if researchers know that 35 percent of a population are women in the labour force, 19 percent women at home, 40 percent men in the workforce, 6 percent men at home, they can interview people in exactly those same proportions, thus insuring that the sample is "representative" of the population. The actual respondents are generally chosen by availability—that is, from those who are close and willing to be interviewed, until the final list of respondents conforms to the 35, 19, 40, 6 percent figures. The major drawback to quota sampling is that those who are nearby and cooperative may be quite different from the further away and/or uncooperative segments of the population.

Quota sampling is really a sophisticated version of *accidental sampling*, in which researchers talk to anyone at a selected location, regardless of their social characteristics. Shoppers in a mall and students in introductory sociology classes often form accidental samples. Their strength is their low cost, and this makes them a popular choice; their drawback is the inability to generalize to the larger unsampled population.

In conclusion, limited resources mean that not everyone can be studied. If researchers have much money, they will draw simple random or cluster samples; if less money, quota samples; and with little money, accidental samples. The ability to generalize the findings to the population decreases in the same order, due to increasing doubts concerning representativeness.

University students often form accidental samples. Their drawback is the inability to generalize to the larger population.

"Hello, I Am Calling to Ask Your Opinion...." Sound Familiar?

Telephone interviews are an increasingly popular survey research technique because of their unique advantages, including: lower cost, a better response rate than mailed questionnaires, easier access (many people will not admit interviewers into their homes and many interviewers do not feel safe entering the homes of strangers), and a greater feeling of anonymity. On the down side, people can easily hang up and the overall response rate is lower than for personal interviews. Nevertheless, these are seen as small costs in this increasingly popular alternative to personal interviews (for a discussion see Neuman, 1997).

Random Digit Dialing (RDD) is a sampling technique whereby the telephone numbers to be called are randomly generated by a computer. Since most Canadians have phones, RDD is, in effect, a much cheaper alternative to a listing of all Canadians. It is also better than using a phone directory because it gets around the problem of unlisted and newly-listed numbers. On the other hand, it misses some of the very poorest people, who cannot afford a phone.

Does Drinking Lead to Date Rape? Social Science Experiments

Experiments are better than survey research in demonstrating cause. In the simplest social science experiment (Neuman, 1997 describes more complex designs), subjects are divided by chance into two groups—for example by the flipping of a coin with heads to one group and tails to the other. Once the subjects are in separate groups, a cause (independent variable) is introduced into one of them, called the **experimental group**. Since the cause is introduced to the experimental group only, any effect (dependent variable) should be found in that group only and not in the second or **control group**, which does not experience the cause.

Suppose researchers were interested in the relationship between alcohol and date rape. After random assignment of dating males to either group, alcoholic beverages would be served to the experimental group and soft drinks to the control group. Then both groups could be given a series of hypothetical situations to examine their dating behaviour. They could be asked, "Your date has just said no to sexual intercourse. Would you: (a) respect her wishes, (b) ask again, (c) pressure her to change her mind, (d) continue a bit further to see how serious she is, (e) ignore her and go ahead?" If alcohol reduces inhibitions, the males in the experimental group should more often choose the latter options (c, d, or e) than the males in the control group. If alcohol is not a factor, there would be no difference in answers between the two groups.

A crucial difference between survey research and experiments occurs in their models. The effects of all potential control variables are supposed to be eliminated through the random assignment of subjects to the experimental or control conditions. Such randomization attempts to make true the statement "other things being equal" and means that the experimental and the control groups should be quite similar except for one thing: the independent variable. For example, there should be approximately similar numbers of the very religious, the going-steady, and children of professional parents in each group. Even variables in which the experimenters are not interested—for example, dancing ability—should be approximately the same as a result of this chance assignment. With these "other things being equal," their influence on the dependent variable is then ignored and the model made quite simple, involving only the independent variable, here alcohol, and the dependent variable, response to a date's "no." You will recall that in survey research, control variables must be included in the model because they may affect any relationship between the independent and dependent variables.

Analysis in experiments is then done by comparing the experimental and control groups on the dependent variable. But what if by chance the random assignment did not make the two groups equal in all ways? To examine this possibility, most experimenters take two measures of their dependent variable, here dating behaviour, although perhaps with slightly different but equivalent questions. The first is called a *pre-test*, and comes before the introduction of the independent variable, here alcohol. The second is a *post-test*, since it comes after. Analysis involves looking for changes in predicted dating behaviour between the pre- and post-test in both groups. Any difference in the control group could have been caused by many factors, such as boredom or greater familiarity with the questions on dating, but should not have been caused by alcohol, which its members did not drink. The difference between the experimental group's pre- and post-test, minus any difference in the control group, thus represents the net effects of the independent variable. As in survey research, however, the relationship will not be perfect, and additional causes of date rape can be examined in additional experiments to explain why this is so.

While experiments are good in demonstrating cause and effect, they have their down sides. First, ethical considerations make many experiments impossible. Researchers cannot, for example, force people to attend religious services to examine the effects of such attendance on racial prejudice. They have no control over whether a person is born male or female, to a large or small, rich or poor family—all key variables in social research. Turning to measurement, in the current example a battery of *hypothetical* questions is used to measure actual dating behaviour. Merely being in an experiment can alter people's behaviour as they try to please the experimenters, doing things they think the experimenters want. This is sometimes called the *Hawthorne effect* (see Chapter 13, Formal Organizations and Work). So experimental measures are sometimes even more removed from real behaviour than the measures used in survey research, and thus they have the potential for even greater invalidity. In fact **external validity** refers to whether experimenters can generalize from their experiments to the real world.

Finally, with respect to sampling, experimenters generally need more cooperation than do survey researchers, because subjects in experiments have something done to them. Moreover, many subjects have to return for several sessions of such manipulation. Because of these greater costs in time and effort, subjects for experiments tend to be drawn from accidental samples, with paid volunteers and university students frequent choices. Generalizing experimental results to non-volunteers and to non-university populations should therefore be done only with caution.

Analysis

After collecting their data, researchers must begin analysis, the process of examining the data to look for relationships among the variables. The exact type of analysis depends on the complexity of the hypotheses being studied, but the basic process in survey research involves an examination of relationships between independent and dependent variables. For example, suppose a researcher collected data (see Table 2.1) on threats of punishment and shoplifting. The independent variable (here placed at the top of the table) might be the expected severity of punishment, the dependent variable frequency of shoplifting, and the hypothesized relationship

TABLE 2.1 Relationship between perception of punishment and shoplifting

	Categories of the independent variable			
Categories of the dependent variable	*Expect severe punishment*		*Expect light punishment*	
Shoplift	36%	(21)	78%	(38)
Do not shoplift	64%	(37)	22%	(11)
N	100%	(58)	100%	(49)

that those who expect severe punishment are less likely to shoplift than those who expect only light punishment. *N* refers to the number of individuals in each category of the independent variable: 58 who expect severe punishment and 49 who expect light punishment. These numbers are called *marginals*. Of the 58 who expect severe punishment, 21 shoplift and 37 do not. Of the 49 who expect light punishment, 38 shoplift and 11 do not. These numbers appear in the *cells* where the independent and dependent variables meet. As a general practice researchers do not examine these numbers, called the *raw* data, in their analysis. Percentages allow for better comparisons. The only rule to remember about these percentages is that *each category of the independent variable must add up to 100 percent.* To calculate a percentage, divide the number in any cell by its corresponding marginal *N* and multiply the result by 100, e.g., $37 \div 58 \times 100 = 64$ percent. Here it can be seen that those who expect a more severe punishment are less likely to shoplift (36 percent) than those who expect only a light punishment (78 percent). Again, notice that *each* of the categories of the independent variable adds up to 100 percent.

On the basis of these data it can be concluded that there is a relationship between perception of severity of punishment and shoplifting, but the relationship is not perfect. Some who expect light punishment do not shoplift, while some who expect severe punishment do. Most sociological relationships are like this, incomplete and imperfect. Sociological research usually finds that two variables *tend* to be related under *certain* conditions for *some* people. Collectively human beings are too complex, have too many pressures acting upon them, and possess too many options to exhibit the simpler relationships more characteristic of the natural sciences.

The conditions and kinds of people are the "other things being equal" of the hypothesis. As mentioned, sociologists call these "other things" **control variables**. Survey researchers take into account *statistically* such third or control variables. To do so, they take the original data and divide them into additional tables, one table for each category of the control variable. Suppose we think that threats of punishment work more for girls than for boys, who more often allow peer pressure to make them ignore such consequences. When researchers "control" for sex, they make two identical tables, one for males and one for females. The new tables look exactly like the original, with the same headings and the same categories, and all categories of the independent variable still add up to 100 percent, but in each table the control variable is constant or controlled, meaning that it is the same for everyone in the table, all males or all females, allowing examination of boys and girls separately. These tables could show that the predicted relationship between severity of punishment and shoplifting holds better among girls and less well among boys.

The examination of control variables still does not complete the analysis stage. Sociologists must inspect the cases in the control tables that still do not support their hypotheses, and look for factors that make them exceptions. They must attempt to find out why, for example, boys who expect light punishment still do not shoplift. Perhaps it is because they are very religious. The researchers also must attempt to explain why some girls who expect severe punishment nevertheless do shoplift. Perhaps extreme poverty is a factor in these instances. This finding too must be added to any conclusions drawn.

The list of control variables which serve to qualify the generalizations suggested by the original analysis can be lengthy. Researchers, however, ordinarily collect and analyze data on only those variables logically and closely connected with their independent and dependent variables, and use their knowledge of the field to decide which variables are relevant. The purpose of these controls is to approximate the conditions of the natural science controlled experiment, a basic goal of positivism, to make all other things equal except for variations in the independent and dependent variables. A quite different approach marks the qualitative alternative of participant observation, to which we now turn.

A qualitative strategy: participant observation

Real-life behaviour is directly seen only rarely in most quantitative research. Qualitative researchers, in contrast, generally make such observation a central requirement in their research strategies. There

Content Analysis

Content analysis involves the examination (analysis) of themes (content) from communications such as conversations, letters, newspapers, books, or movies. It is often like survey research in its assumptions and practices. It tends to use deductive logic to derive hypotheses, and to focus on a limited number of variables. Content analysis could involve the use of grounded theory and more complex models, but it usually does not.

In that it generally uses operational definitions, content analysis also resembles a survey research approach to measurement. This practice leads to quantifiability, reliability, and replicability. But the method is less strong on validity. Researchers cannot know whether the values and meanings they assume to lie behind the communications are the actual values and meanings of the original communicators, or whether the audiences understood these values and meanings. Subtle, hidden, or between-the-lines meanings, known perhaps only to the communicators and their audiences, are also problematic for content analysts. Finally, researchers cannot tell if the people acted as their communications would suggest.

As for sampling, content analysis generally involves some form of random sampling procedure, allowing generalizability at least to the sampling frame. Authors, their books, and then certain pages may be cluster-sampled, for just one example. The analysis tends to be quantitative and statistical, much like survey research analysis.

The great strengths of content analysis are (1) because the data are inanimate, researchers do not affect them, a potential error in most quantitative methods; (2) it is inexpensive; and (3) it lends itself to historical and cross-cultural analyses. The main drawbacks concern validity, a potentially serious flaw, and selective survival of documents and other communications. For example, while formal works may survive, day-to-day writings, especially those of the less privileged, are less likely to do so.

are three basic options available to accomplish this task. One occurs when a researcher takes the role of outsider and secretly watches the behaviour of others. A second occurs when an observer secretly joins a group and studies it. Finally, in **participant observation** a researcher asks permission to join and observe a group and to question its members about the meanings of their behaviour. It is this strategy we shall describe in the next section, as it is the most frequently used form of observational research. It overcomes the limitations of the other two forms: unlike the first, it affords access to private behaviour and allows researchers to question the actors; and it is more ethical than the second. In this next section we shall examine theory, models, measurement, sampling, and analysis as they are relevant to participant observation.

Theories and hypotheses

Many qualitative sociologists feel that because most theories about social life are incomplete, with many exceptions (and some of their concepts are not well measured), *perspective* is a better word than *theory*. The use of that term allows a greater flexibility. In addition, the ideal of much participant observational research is to begin a study with minimal preconceptions and to allow the data whenever possible to speak for themselves. These perspectives, then, are sensitizing devices, showing researchers where to look but not limiting their investigations.

Many participant observers thus refuse to derive hypotheses as do survey researchers, but instead use inductive logic, allowing the facts they observe eventually to lead to theoretical generalizations. As deductive logic goes from the general to the specific, **inductive logic** goes from specific facts to general statements. Thus, participant observers tend to collect their data first and conclude with what they call **grounded theory**, theory rooted in and arising from their data. For example, researchers might note that some women tend to ask more questions and to try to extend rather than limit conversations compared to men and then end up with a generalization about how gender affects conversation. The theories come after they examine their

Public behaviour is most amenable to secret observation by a researcher who takes the role of outsider.

data, not before as in most quantitative approaches. (In practice in both qualitative and quantitative methods the relationship between data and theory is more like a circle, with data forcing revisions of theory and theory affecting the type of data collected in a continuous loop.)

Model

Participant observation rarely deals in simple one-independent-and-one-dependent-variable models. Instead, models involve many variables acting at once, as happens in the real world. One common strategy in participant observation is to look initially at many variables and over time to focus in on fewer and fewer variables, thereby simplifying the model as the research progresses. Even with such simplification, however, participant observation ordinarily involves more complicated models than either experiments or survey research. Variables are not isolated, either artificially, as in laboratory experiments, or statistically, as in the control tables of survey research, and thus the models are correspondingly more complex. In addition, the models of participant observers are often more general than specific, in the form of themes and motifs, and arise as the researchers become immersed in the data. A second difference between participant observation and more quantitative methods concerns cause. Qualitative researchers are satisfied in many instances with associations—that is, relationships between variables, without any idea of cause or labels of *independent* and *dependent* variables. When they do look at cause, multiple causes and longer causal chains are stressed.

Measurement

The most important difference in measurement between quantitative methods and participant observation is that participant observers view real behaviour, going beyond both survey research's verbal reports of that behaviour and the artificial behaviour of laboratory experiments. They can also see behaviour the actors are unaware of, behaviour the actors are unable to describe adequately, and even behaviour the actors might not admit to in an interview. If clarification is needed to interpret these observations, explanations from the actors themselves can supplement the researchers' interpretations. Indeed, in their reports, participant observers often allow the actors to explain their behaviour as it makes sense to them. The researcher-controlled "objective" and standardized measures more typical of quantitative researchers become less important while the subjective definitions of the actors become more important. Thus, participant observers more often begin with actor-defined definitions, in contrast to the researcher-defined operational definitions of quantitative methods.

Sampling

Obviously, if researchers live for a time with a group of people to observe them, they cannot study a large number of such groups. The time, money, and effort required would be too costly. Thus, participant observation usually involves only a small number or even just one case, generally chosen because of availability. Sampling considerations extend beyond the choice of group to be studied, however. Inside the group there is much sampling involved; observers cannot be everywhere at all times, or watch all things even in one place. Thus, they sample times, places, people, and behaviours. These samples can be taken randomly or on a quota basis. Often they are not, however, and instead are determined by chance, by the unpredictable flow of the interaction. Still, deliberate bias, including choosing data to support the researchers' preconceived notions, must be avoided whatever the sampling procedure.

Analysis

As previously stated, participant observers often let the actors explain their own behaviour. Some of the actors' explanations may be rationalizations, and in fact their subjective perceptions may be objectively inaccurate, but the explanations still are recorded as motivations behind the actors' behaviours. The participant observers can then add their explanations to those of their informants.

Analysis in participant observation research is often descriptive, attempting to make a coherent portrait of a complex social reality. Numbers are less apparent and words more so. Causal relationships may or may not be specified, but they must be fitted into a larger overall description of the subject matter. In fact, one problem that arises with participant observation is the researchers' inability to describe all that is going on, to complete the picture fully. This occurs because there are just too many facts and too much data to include. Thus, inevitably, participant observers must be selective and edit the information with which they attempt to describe their subject matter. Such decisions are based on their familiarity with the topic, logic, guidance from both colleagues and the actors themselves, and the feelings and intuitions of the researchers. Such a process is hard to plan fully in advance, and must be partly determined in the field.

One common analytical strategy is to examine the data while still in the field, while the research is still going on, with the early analysis rather unfocused and the later increasingly limited. In this way, models and hypotheses that become apparent in those earlier stages can be tested in later ones. This sequential practice is a good way to test grounded theory. *Negative case analysis*, examining those cases that fail to support the generalizations drawn, can then force their revision. Thus, like most social scientists, participant observers use both inductive and deductive logic in examining social reality.

This concludes our brief description of participant observation. More unstructured and flexible than survey research, its exact operations are harder to specify. Still, after reading this section, you should at least be familiar with its logic and rationale. The next section compares participant observation with the previously discussed survey research approach.

THE METHODS COMPARED

Survey research and participant observation can be compared in many ways. Each is strong in some ways and weak in others. Because those in favour of any research strategy emphasize its strengths and downplay its weaknesses, we shall compare them on the same criteria: validity—whether their measures are accurate reflections of social reality; generalizability—whether the conclusions hold beyond the actual group studied; and ability to reveal causes of behaviour (see also the box on causation).

The issues of validity and generalizability are related and are at the heart of the debate between quantitative and qualitative researchers. Participant observers argue that much survey research is invalid, because survey researchers never observe behaviour directly but get only verbal reports of that behaviour. In their desire to please, respondents may slant their answers to what they think the interviewers want to hear. They may even lie, giving socially approved answers that reflect well on them and avoiding responses that place them in an unfavourable light. A related criticism is that survey researchers often examine *attitudes* instead of *behaviour*, although people often act not as their attitudes

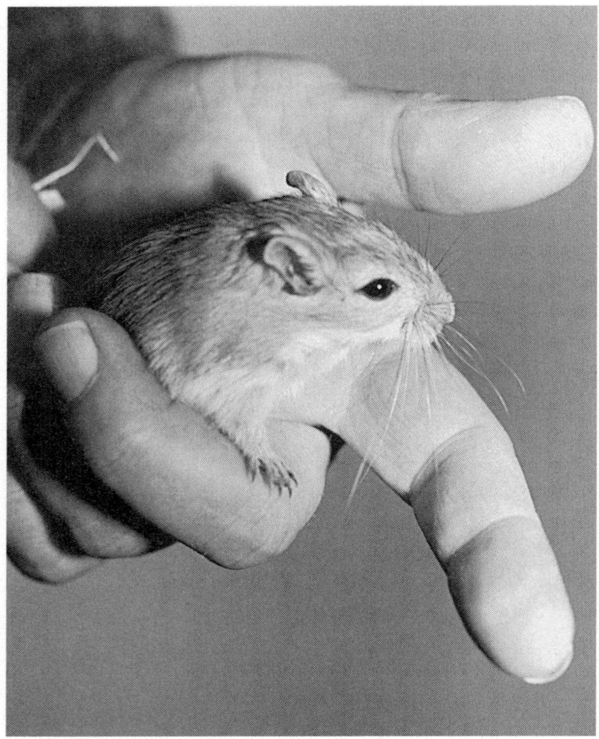

Many social scientists would prefer to apply the methods of natural scientists to their data.

would predict (explaining why more husbands think they *should* share household tasks than actually *do*). Finally, operationalization lets the researcher rather than the actor define and measure behaviour, again raising validity issues.

Survey researchers counter these claims by arguing that careful research design can minimize some validity problems. Self-administered (and cheaper) anonymous questionnaires, as opposed to interviews, for example, can decrease lying and the effects of respondent–researcher interactions. To increase validity, interviewers can be trained to detect misunderstandings and resistance and to encourage candour and honesty. Survey researchers suggest, moreover, that participant observation also yields invalid data, first, because the observers, just by being there, change people's behaviour. People will not act naturally while being observed. Even if they learn to trust their researchers, knowing that they are being watched will still affect their behaviour. Second, quantitative researchers believe that participant observation data are too vulnerable to potential biases, needs, and unconscious distortions of the observers themselves and that different observers will "see" different things and so are unreliable. And while a need for validity checks is all the more important in such instances, the flexibility of the method (seen as a strength by its practitioners) makes **replication**, or the repeating of a study, difficult in participant observation. Thus any invalidity would be harder to uncover than would be the case for quantitative researchers.

A difficulty in making generalizations is another significant criticism survey researchers make of participant observation. With few groups (or sometimes only one group) studied, the chance that the observations may not be representative of other groups is increased. Thus generalizations from participant observation data to the wider but unstudied population should be made only with caution.

Needless to say, this participant observation–survey research debate continues. Qualitative participant observers, while admitting that their small nonrepresentative samples may permit only limited generalization, still lay claim to greater validity, because they observe actual behaviour, over time, and in a natural setting. Moreover, given a choice between validity and generalizability, participant observers feel that validity is the more important criterion to satisfy. A valid picture of even a nonrepresentative sample is preferable to an invalid description of a perfectly random sample. Survey researchers point to their improvements in validity and reject this argument.

Turning to cause, to demonstrate that A causes B, researchers must show not only a logical connection between them, but that A is prior to B and that A and B are not connected only through C, a variable causing both A and B. The random assignment in experiments attempts to rule out all such C variables by making all of them equal, thus insuring that A is the only cause operating. Survey research and participant observation cannot demonstrate this as easily, if at all.

In most survey research, data on independent and dependent variables are collected at the same time, a procedure called **cross-sectional research**. This is quite efficient in terms of cost but a negative side-effect is that researchers often cannot

In participant observation, although people initially may act differently because they know they are being watched, with time most of them begin to trust the observer. Here, Dr. Margaret Mead observes a group of Manus children in the Admiralty Islands in 1928.

demonstrate which variables come first, which are causes and which are effects. For example, as will be discussed more fully in Chapter 4, to what extent does exposure to television violence cause violent behaviour and how often is it the case that violent people choose to watch violent television?

In addition, survey research often deals in **correlations**, demonstrations that changes in one variable are concurrent with changes in another. But variables may "go together" without the correlation between them being causal. Survey researchers must be especially careful about **spurious relationships** in these correlations—assuming that a relationship is causal when it is really only through a third variable, (C), that (A) and (B) are linked. For example, there is a correlation between the amount of money spent in dating relationships (A) and sexual activity (B). Survey research data would reveal that other things being equal, the more money spent, the greater the sexual activity. Is money, an independent variable, causing sexual activity, a dependent variable? No—the real relationships are between involvement (C) and money spent (A), and between involvement (C) and sexual activity (B). The greater the involvement, the more money is spent and the more sexual activity occurs. Interpreting the correlation to mean that money leads to sexual activity is spurious. Survey researchers generally do manage to see through such spurious relationships. Exactly how they accomplish this is a question best left to a more advanced text, but it generally involves examining control variables and their effects on the original relationship. Thus, spuriousness is not an insurmountable problem, but an issue with which survey researchers must deal.

Participant observers, because their research is done over time (called **longitudinal research**), may be better able to see which variable comes first, but they have a problem in that many variables happen at once, making it hard to determine which one(s) is

Does Peeling Onions Make You Cry? Issues of Causation

Philosophers of science have identified at least three distinct types of cause. First is necessary cause, a condition that must be present for a specified effect to occur. In our language, "If no A, then no B." Plants cannot grow without light; thus light is a necessary cause of such growth. A sufficient cause is one that by itself will bring about an effect every time it is introduced, or "If A, then B." But since there are other causes that could also bring about B, it is not a necessary cause. If onions make you cry every time you peel them, peeling onions is a sufficient cause of crying, but since other things could also make you cry, it is not a necessary cause. Finally, a necessary and sufficient cause is one that is both required and adequate to bring on an effect. Such causes are very rare. Even in the plant example, more than light is required for growth in most cases. So although light is a necessary cause, it is not a necessary and sufficient one. Water is also required, as are minerals and nutrients.

Because human beings are so complex and because sociologists rarely can conduct experiments, usually relying on data from which it is difficult to isolate any one cause, sociology generally deals with multiple causes, many acting at once. Thus, sociologists rarely find either sufficient or necessary causes, much less those that are necessary and sufficient. They look for variations in one variable that go along with variations in another, as in the statement "as education increases, so does longevity"—what we just called *correlation*—and then try to demonstrate logically and statistically that there could be a causal relationship.

(are) the cause(s). Their full, rich picture may make it difficult to isolate the specific cause(s) of behaviour. This is one reason some participant observers choose not to focus on cause and instead deal mainly with descriptions.

In sum, validity is potentially stronger in participant observation than in survey research. For generalizability, survey research may be better. Each has difficulty in demonstrating cause and effect. Because no method is without flaws, some researchers engage in **triangulation**, the application of several research methods to the same topic, in the hope that the weaknesses of any one method can be compensated for by the strengths of the others. For example, the findings of a participant observation study may be confirmed by survey research or vice versa.

Quite often the subject of inquiry will point to a choice. Studies of national voting behaviour generally require survey research, and much of the research in education, stratification, and religion reported in this book used survey research. On the other hand, culture, social movements, formal organizations, and areas about which little is known are often examined with participant observation, because of its flexibility.

A common omission: historical and comparative issues

The qualitative and quantitative research techniques described so far collect data over a short period of time, making it difficult to examine long-term changes and trends. *Historical analysis* attempts to fill this gap. Most researchers also confine their work to their own society. *Comparative analysis* requires researchers to study several societies, thus permitting movement beyond societally specific generalizations. Both historical and comparative research also allow a special type of replication, a retesting of hypotheses in new settings, leading researchers either to greater confidence if similar results appear, or to reformulations if conflicting data are uncovered. Because of these strengths, let us examine these methods more closely.

Since it is undertaken after the fact and must rely on whatever data were collected at the time, historical analysis actually entails a variety of research methods. Thus, researchers can perform a qualitative study of diaries or letters written a hundred years ago or can do a statistical quantitative analysis of census data originally collected through survey research. In comparative research too, any method can be used, but it is used repeatedly across cultures.

As a by-product of the versatility of their methods, historical and comparative analysts can use deductive and/or grounded theory. Their models can be simple or complex. Still, it would probably be fair to say that historical analysis is especially attractive to conflict theorists because it best allows a focus on change. We know also that positivists, especially survey researchers, tend to avoid historical sociology. The issues more problematic for historical and comparative analysis relate to measurement and sampling. We shall discuss each in turn.

In collecting their data historians distinguish between primary and secondary sources. **Primary sources** are records produced at the time described by a contemporary of the event, including eyewitness accounts, diaries, and official records. **Secondary sources** are created when individuals report what a primary source said. The potential problems surrounding the validity of secondary sources are readily apparent. The greater the distance in time, in space, and in perspective between the primary and secondary sources, the greater the chance for misinterpretation. But the primary source may be invalid as well. Who wrote it down and why? Did the person deliberately or unwittingly distort the data to tell a certain story? And worse, while the validity of current data can be checked against other current or new data, historical data often cannot be. Thus, validity is always an issue in historical analysis.

Following Their Own Path: Marxist Research Methods

There are several research strategies that appeal to conflict sociologists, reflecting the diversity of conflict approaches outlined in Chapter 1. As a group they may have little in common except for a rejection of Durkheim's positivist stance—that natural sciences methods should be used to study social reality. Here we shall focus on a Marxist conflict model.

Generally those who adopt a Marxist approach are critical of subjective perspectives on social life, such as that of symbolic interactionism. Marxists argue that people are constrained by and not the makers of social reality. But they could be free if someone, perhaps social scientists, would reveal to them their oppression. People have potential but they are deceived and exploited, and have lost control over their own destiny.

Theory is useful to Marxists to the extent that it reveals the causes of the problems faced by the oppressed and helps people see the path to an improved life. The model used in Marxist research concentrates on the potential for change and generally sees the amount of power and resources held, especially economic power and resources, as the major independent variable affecting all other aspects of life. Attention to history, something missing in much functionalist research, is especially important because change, which results from the conflict that arises over ownership of resources, rather than stability is the focus. A *dialectical* approach, which sees history as a series of conflicts over existing material arrangements, is attractive to Marxists. This approach maintains that the seeds for its transformation exist in every society, with the new society that results, in turn, containing the seeds for its own transformation.

Measurement and sampling are not key methodological elements to Marxists, who tend to prefer a critical approach. They like to ask embarrassing questions, to uncover exploitation, and to expose hypocrisy. Marxists look for the conflicts surrounding the unequal distribution of resources, in the hope of encouraging large-scale changes to the status quo. And they prefer to do this in the real world, as opposed to the laboratory.

Nor is analysis, at least in the form of hypothesis testing, so important. Marxists generally "know" what is going on. Instead their role is to act upon their research, a strategy they call **praxis**. They reject Weber's recommendation, that it is not the role of the scientist to suggest social policy, as too passive. Instead they see the role of social scientific analysis specifically as one of unmasking the unjust conditions in the world in order to help the downtrodden see the sources of their ills. Thus research should be action-oriented, a step taken to empower the weak and then to improve the world. Smashing myths and uncovering contradictions are just the first part of that process (cf. Neuman, 1997).

Cross-cultural researchers can collect new data or use available data. One excellent source of existing, generally participant observation, data is the anthropological reports found in the *Encyclopedia of World Cultures*, ten volumes summarizing over 1500 ethnographies of societies around the world. One of the problems with using someone else's data, a procedure called **secondary analysis**, however, is that they may be incomplete, since the original collectors were not aware of the information later researchers would need.

Sampling remains the final stumbling block in historical and comparative research. In the latter, how many and which countries or societies are to be included? Costs multiply quickly. Inside the countries chosen, a representative national sample might be impossible, leading to questionable generalizability. These problems and others result in rather infrequent comparative research. The preference in historical analysis for a complex picture generally results in a small number of cases (as it did in participant observation) and a limited time frame. (Historical studies using census or other official data—see for example Chapter 15, Demography and Population Study—are an obvious exception to this generalization.) The problems of missing or incomplete data may then further reduce the sample size. The end result of these factors is a difficulty in generalizability. Thus, as in contemporary research, researchers tend to choose either simpler measures applied to a large number of cases, or complex pictures of only a few cases. It is always difficult to achieve both full pictures and large samples.

SUMMARY

The earlier discussions of Durkheim and Weber were continued, this time with respect to their different research strategies. Each was illustrated: quantitative (Durkheim) with survey research, qualitative (Weber) with participant observation. The place of theory and hypotheses, types of models, measurement issues, sampling, and simple analysis were presented for both, and their strengths and weaknesses compared. Included in boxes in the chapter were alternative strategies such as content analysis and experiments, along with Marxist and feminist comments on methods.

If you decide to become a sociologist and to conduct research, you thus have many options open to you. Whatever method you choose, the most anyone can reasonably ask of you is honesty, competence, and a healthy scepticism. You should never deliberately choose one method over others because its data will most likely support your preconceived biases; you should be willing to undergo the training that will allow you to be expert at whatever method you choose; and you should be aware of the weaknesses, especially concerning validity and generalizability, of your method. This is a big order, one best saved for an advanced course in research methods.

But before going on to the next general topic of the book, culture, finish this chapter by reading the following short section. If a research paper is required in an introductory sociology course, it will probably involve library research rather than the collection of new data. Consequently, this section deals with writing library research papers.

WRITING A SOCIOLOGY LIBRARY RESEARCH PAPER

The first task in writing any research paper is to define a topic broadly. Students should choose one in which they are interested, as it will make the work easier. The second requirement involves a review of the literature, that is, an examination of existing studies on the chosen topic, for example, homosexuality. Bring a set of 5 × 7 and 3 × 5 inch cards for taking notes. Recent books can be found by looking up "homosexuality" in the library's subject catalogue. The locations of shorter articles on homosexuality can be found in *Sociological Abstracts* (for scholarly journals) and *The Reader's Guide to Periodical Literature* (for popular magazines). A computerized search with a tool called *Sociofile* is even better, saving you much time; unfortunately, some libraries cannot afford *Sociofile.*

The amount of information available will probably be overwhelming. (In rare instances when little is written on a topic, introductory students should probably choose a new topic.) How can the review be made more manageable? Restricting the search to the last five years or so could help, and will make the paper more timely as well. But still there probably will be too much to read. The task is to narrow the subject down sufficiently to make it more manageable. Here the options are many: the focus could be the lifestyles or culture of homosexuals, how the role is learned, the difference between gays and lesbians, or why homosexuality is considered deviant and the extent of hidden homosexuality, whether social class affects homosexual lifestyles, with the rich living one and the poor another, or the discrimination and prejudice homosexuals face. Each of these topics might come out of the next few chapters of this book. What about homosexual families? How does religion treat homosexuality? The possibilities are endless and the earlier stages of even this narrowed review will probably reveal the need for an even more restricted focus.

The next step is to decide the type of research review to be written. Choices here include an integrative review which summarizes what is known on a topic, showing points of agreement and disagreement and issues needing further research; a historical review tracing a topic over time; a cross-cultural review comparing the subject in different societies; even a theoretical review showing how different theoretical positions treat the issue (Neuman, 1997).

The next step involves the cards. For all relevant articles, the author, title, date, name of journal, volume number, and pages should be entered on the top of one of the smaller cards. These cards can be alphabetized later to become the bibliography. On the larger cards, relevant notes on the chosen topic are entered, with the author and enough of the title to identify definitively the source recorded in its own section at the very top. Specific page numbers for all quotes and for any specific ideas borrowed should also be clearly written there for later documentation. For long quotes or whole sections, making a photocopy of the relevant pieces and then taping them to cards may be appropriate, along with the *page number prominently recorded.*

As the cards accumulate, patterns begin to emerge. There seems to be agreement on some matters, disagreement on others. Links between certain aspects of the general topic become clearer and an order becomes apparent. Sorting the cards into categories is the final step before the actual writing. The categories become the basis for an outline of the paper. Avoid the error of poor organization. Many students have well-defined aims, but fail to organize their materials properly. To avoid this they should outline carefully, re-outline, and use subtitles freely according to the information they have found. Proper organization allows movement from point to point in a systematic and non-repetitive way. It also helps to avoid the error of lack of focus. Students who do not have a specific objective in mind may end up merely citing scattered findings, or they may include irrelevant facts, perhaps in the hope that including every fact possible will impress their instructors. The opposite is more often true; students should include only the material directly relevant to the focus of the paper.

The following suggestions about paper form are not rigid rules, but general guidelines.

1. *Introduction.* The introduction to a paper should indicate why the paper is being written. Why is the topic important—is there a need to solve a problem in society, to test a theoretical position, to reveal or discuss a contradiction? The introduction should begin with the most general rationale for the paper and logically proceed to a more specific problem. The last paragraph of this section should indicate what the paper will accomplish, giving a brief outline of the paper.

2. *Results of literature review organized according to purpose of review.* Students should decide which sections of the works they are going to use, and enter them into a computer file (or tape them to larger sheets of paper) along with any necessary bibliographical information, adding their own analysis and summaries as appropriate. Failure to reveal sources and omitting quotation marks are called *plagiarism.* Findings should be clearly presented, supported when necessary with tables, charts, and graphs. (Again, if these are taken from the work of others, proper credit must be given.) Each finding should be explored within the framework of the arguments originally developed in the introduction.

3. *Discussion.* In this section students must discuss the meaning and importance of the points made

in the previous section and show how they relate to the purpose of the investigation as stated in the introduction. In many ways, the discussion is the most important part of the paper as it represents the students' original thoughts, not an organization of the thoughts of others as above. Thus, a great deal of thought and care is required for this section. It makes sense out of the sometimes disparate information included in the previous section. To make linkages between ideas, transitional phrases such as "thus," "moreover," "however," "nevertheless," and "on the other hand" make the writing smoother, although they will not suffice if the connections are also not apparent in the text itself (Bart and Frankel, 1984).

4. *Summary and Conclusion*. Students should briefly summarize the paper here, in so doing showing the progress in knowledge made since the introduction. Suggestions for research that would provide answers to unanswered questions raised in the paper may be included here.

Finally, about the writing itself, consistency is important. Choose a tense and stick to it, for example, "Mundy *says* that homosexuals *are*..." Also choose a person. In general, it is best to write in an impersonal style (avoiding "I," "me," "my," etc.), keeping some distance between author and topic. Plurals ("they," "their") help to avoid the awkward "he/she" construction and the sexism of relying on the singular pronouns of "he" or "she." On the other hand, particularly in discussion sections, students should not be afraid of an occasional "I think" or "I believe." Writing should also be somewhat formal; some students become so informal that rigour and organization suffer. A thesaurus and dictionary are useful to help avoid repetition. Finally, the pages must be numbered and proper footnoting and referencing used. Scholarly journals, for example, the *Canadian Journal of Sociology* or *The Canadian Review of Sociology and Anthropology*, provide good examples of proper reference format. The purpose of references is not to impress readers with the writer's scope of knowledge, but to enable them to find the sources used.

Several revisions are usually necessary. Showing a draft to someone who has experience with this type of assignment can help. If using a word processor, the spell check function will catch obvious errors but it misses such things as confusing *their* for *there*, and *too* for *to*. A friend can help with such proofreading. Finally, papers must be typed and a copy should be kept.

Writing papers is always hard. We hope these suggestions will make the process a bit easier.

QUESTIONS FOR REVIEW AND CRITICAL THINKING

1. Design an experiment to test the advantages and disadvantages of assigning qualified minority teachers to teach children of their own ethnic group, as opposed to having any qualified teacher instruct the children.

2. Which research strategy would be most useful in studying why some of your friends continued their education after high school while others did not? Defend your choice.

3. Design a questionnaire to examine the extent of and reasons for drug use among students.

4. What topics would you like to study in sociology? Do personal values affect your choice? Should you be value-neutral or an activist using research as a tool to improve the world?

GLOSSARY

axiomatic logic the making of connecting links between related statements for deriving hypotheses

cluster sampling a series of random samples taken in units of decreasing size, such as census tracts, then streets, then houses, then residents

content analysis a method of analysis that extracts themes from communications, including letters, books, and newspapers

control variables variables included in a model of behaviour that are neither independent nor dependent variables. They are controlled or held constant to check on apparent relationships between independent and dependent variables.

correlation not to be confused with cause, it is changes in one variable that coincide with changes in another variable

cross-sectional research the type of research that takes place at one point in time as opposed to **longitudinal research**, which can detect change and demonstrate cause because it takes place over a period of time

deductive logic the derivation of a specific statement from a set of more general statements

experimental group the group of subjects in an experiment that is exposed to the independent variable, as opposed to the **control group**, which is not exposed

external validity the ability to generalize research results beyond the artificial laboratory experimental situation to the real world

grounded theory explanations that arise from the data collected and which are thus grounded in reality rather than in deductive logic

hypothesis a statement of a presumed relationship between two or more variables

inductive logic the construction of a generalization from a set of specific statements

operational definition description of the actual procedures used to measure a theoretical concept, as in I.Q. scores being an operational definition of intelligence

participant observation a research strategy whereby a researcher becomes a member of a group in order to study it, and group members are aware that they are being observed

positivism the application of natural science research methods to social science

praxis Marx's concept that research should not be *pure*, conducted just for knowledge's sake, but *applied*, undertaken to improve society

primary versus secondary sources the former are records produced by contemporaries of an event, the latter interpretations of primary sources made by others not immediately present at the event

quota sample a selection of people that matches the sample to the population on the basis of certain selected characteristics

random sample a sample in which every member of the population is eligible for inclusion and individuals are selected by chance

reliability the degree to which repeated measurements of the same variable, using the same or equivalent instruments, are equal

replication repeating a research project in an attempt to verify earlier findings

secondary analysis the examination by a researcher of someone else's data

spurious relationship the appearance that two variables are in a causal relationship, when in fact each is an effect of a common third variable

theory a set of interrelated statements or propositions about a particular subject matter

triangulation the application of several research methods to the same topic in the hope that the weaknesses of any one method may be compensated for by the strengths of the others

validity the degree to which a measure actually measures what it claims to.

variable a characteristic, such as income or religion, that takes on different values among different individuals or groups. Causes are generally called **independent variables**, and effects are usually called **dependent variables**.

SUGGESTED READINGS

Lofland, John and Lyn Lofland

1995 *Analyzing Social Settings*. (3rd ed.) Belmont, CA: Wadsworth.

This volume is an excellent presentation of field research methods. It is readable and contains many illustrations of actual field research.

Neuman, W. Lawrence

1997 *Social Research Methods*. (3rd ed.) Boston, MA: Allyn & Bacon.

This text provides a thorough overview of the research methods discussed in this chapter.

Nock, David

1993 *Star Wars in Canadian Sociology*. Halifax: Fernwood.

This book examines how the personal lives of Canadian sociologists affect their scientific "knowledge." It stands as an attack on positivism and points to the need to examine region as it affects sociological research.

Thompson, Linda

1992 "Feminist methodology for family studies." *Journal of Marriage and the Family* 54: 3-18.

Short and easy to read, this article examines feminist methods in the area of family research. Values and both quantitative and qualitative methods are discussed.

WEB SITES

http://129.97.58.10/discipline/sociology/research.html

Doing Research in Sociology

This site contains useful information on doing research in sociology. Learn how to search for research material in periodicals, newspapers, and social science databases, as well as how to prepare your research report.

http://www.statcan.ca

Statistics Canada

Interested in doing quantitative research on Canadian subjects? At the Statscan web page, you can find the most recent census data on various aspects of life in Canada.

PART II

Society and the Individual

In this section of the book, our central concern is to expand and illustrate Durkheim's claim that social structure and membership in social groups are important determinants of human behaviour. In Chapter 3, culture is defined as the general way of life that is shared by a group of people, is passed on to later generations, and affects their behaviour and perceptions in some way. Culture includes the values and norms that shape social conduct, the rules and conventions of everyday social life. Culture also includes the social roles that people play, and the variety of social conditions under which people live. Values, norms, and roles vary from one society to another. Even within a society, cultural features vary. For instance, the social unit called Canada is composed today of various subgroups whose different racial and ethnic origins and regional locations have given rise to correspondingly different subcultures.

Cultures may be analyzed from various viewpoints. To a functionalist, cultural elements help to make society stable and viable. On the other hand, conflict sociologists analyze culture with reference to power differences in society. They are concerned with questions such as which groups benefit from the way of life that is adopted and who determines the norms and values. As you read the chapter, try to think of alternative explanations that could be substituted for some of the arguments offered.

For culture to affect behaviour, it must be internalized or learned by individual group members. Such internalization may occur when members learn to play roles, for example, the roles of teacher or farmer or daughter. The acquisition of culture is the focus of Chapter 4, Socialization, which argues that there are biological, social, and environmental influences that affect human learning. Social factors are especially important in shaping identity, or a sense of self, and feelings of self-worth. These feelings, in turn, are important determinants of behaviour. Without such social input, humans would be little different from animals. The Socialization chapter also focuses on how individuals adapt to their social environment. While symbolic interactionism is discussed, for example, with reference to the acquisition of a sense of self, the chapter does make a number of assumptions about human adaptation drawn from the functionalist perspective. As an exercise, try to apply a conflict model to the discussion as you read it. Who benefits and gains from the socialization experience should be a constant question in this exercise.

The failure of certain individuals to internalize the norms, values, and "appropriate" social roles contained in their culture is discussed in Chapter 5, Deviance. Crime, considered by many to be the ultimate deviant act, is a major concern here. The chapter examines the social origins of definitions of deviance, including functional and conflict explanations, and shows how these definitions vary across cultures. The role of power and societal reaction are also discussed as factors in the labelling of acts as deviant. The general sociological perspective again is applied: social structure and group membership affect rates of behaviour, this time deviant behaviour.

YAMAHA

CHAPTER

3

Culture

Michael P. Carroll

INTRODUCTION

In observing individuals in a social group—whether a nation, a family, a classroom, or whatever—it soon becomes clear that their behaviour is not random and haphazard. Not all possible behaviours actually occur, and if you were to observe the group long enough, you would notice that certain behaviours tend to occur with a great deal of regularity, almost routinely. Obviously, there is something that produces such order in social life.

Much of that "something" is what sociologists call *culture*. The use of this particular word may confuse some of you because culture also has a perfectly legitimate everyday meaning that has nothing to do with the orderliness of social life. In everyday language, people are "cultured" if they have sophisticated or refined tastes. What this usually means in actual practice is that they enjoy those activities favoured by the educated élite but not by the general public. Hence, drinking French wines is a mark of culture, drinking domestic beer is not; watching a ballet is cultured, watching stock-car racing is not; reading complicated Russian novels is cultured, reading comic books is not.

Social scientists, however, use the word culture in quite a different sense. The most common definition found in sociology texts is one constructed by a nineteenth-century anthropologist named Edward Tylor. For Tylor, culture included "knowledge, belief, art, morals, law, custom, and any other capabilities and habits acquired by man as a member of society" (1871: 1). Notice that this definition gives no clue as to what all the things listed (knowledge, belief, art, etc.) have in common. Upon reflection, though, it turns out that each of the items listed by Tylor is something that (1) is shared by all or almost all the members of some social group; (2) the older members of the group try to pass on to the younger members; and (3) shapes behaviour (as in the case of morals, laws, and custom), or at least structures perceptions of the world (as in the case of the other items listed in Tylor's definition). If we call anything that meets these three criteria a **cultural element** then we can define the **culture** of a given group very simply as the sum total of all the cultural elements associated with that group.

Sociologists consider certain elements of culture to be particularly important. They are values, norms, and roles.

SOME BASIC CONCEPTS

Values and norms

Values are shared, relatively general beliefs that define what is desirable and what is undesirable; they specify general preferences. A belief that divorce is only a last resort for troubled marriages and a preference for abstract paintings are both values. **Norms,**

"Society": Defining an Important Term

Society is probably one of the most commonly used words in all of sociology. Despite that (or more likely because of that), there is no single definition found in all sociology textbooks. Generally, however, sociologists apply the term to any fairly large group of people who (1) share a common culture, (2) think of themselves as having inherited a common set of historical traditions, (3) interact with other group members frequently, and (4) see themselves as being associated with a particular geographic area. The term society is often applied to nations (Canadian society, U.S. society). It can, however, be applied to subgroups within nations (French-Canadian society), or to groups that cut across national boundaries (Western society).

on the other hand, are relatively precise rules specifying which behaviours are permitted and which prohibited for group members. Note that in everyday usage, norm has quite a different meaning—it means average. Here again sociology has constructed its own vocabulary by attaching a new meaning to a familiar word. When a member of a group breaks a group norm by engaging in a prohibited behaviour, other group members will typically *sanction* the deviant member. To sanction is to communicate, in some way, disapproval to the deviant member (a topic to which we shall return in Chapter 5, Deviance).

When asked to give examples of a norm in our society, most students tend to think of laws, such as those against murder and physical assault. Most laws in a society are indeed social norms. The more important point, however, is that your life is governed by many norms that are not laws.

Consider the following case. You feel very close to people who have given you every reason to believe that they are close friends. You then find out that they have systematically lied to you in order to gain some advantage. How would you feel? Quite hurt, probably, and most of you would also feel that their behaviour was wrong. Why? Because most people in this society believe that close friends should neither deceive nor exploit, and a behavioural norm that flows from this belief is that people claiming to be your friends should not lie to you to gain some advantage. Note that your friends have probably not done anything illegal (that is, no laws have been violated), but a norm—in this case an important one—has clearly not been respected.

You are usually not aware, in any explicit way, of many of the norms that structure your behaviour. For instance, there is one particular norm that regulates your daily behaviour, and that is so strongly held that for me to even suggest that you might violate it will make most readers of this chapter somewhat ill. Although students can rarely guess what norm I am talking about, it is easy to express: in this culture, there is a strong prohibition against coming into contact with the bodily discharges (a polite term for such things as urine, feces, pus, vomit, and mucus) of other individuals. Consider how many times in a given day you go to great lengths to make it unlikely that others will come into contact with your bodily discharges. Think too of how sick and repulsed you would be if this norm were broken, if you actually did come into contact with the bodily discharges of others.

Most readers would likely justify their strong reaction to contact with the bodily discharges of other people in terms of hygiene; that is, they would see it as a reaction that helps to avoid disease and for that reason would be very sensible. This is actually a fairly typical sort of rationalization, since people in most societies like to believe that their particular norms make "good sense," and that if the norms were violated something bad would happen. It is fairly easy to demonstrate, however, that our norms relating to bodily discharges involve more than just hygiene.

First of all, the aversion to bodily discharges was present in our society long before we became aware that diseases could be transmitted by germs. Second, many nonindustrial societies had the same strong aversion to bodily discharges and yet never developed a germ theory of disease. Third, even now, in our own society, there are patterns which are hard to explain on the basis of hygiene alone.

Clark and Davis (1989), for instance, found that among Canadian university students certain bodily emissions (like vomit, feces, urine) are more repellent than others (like mother's milk and perspiration). Moreover, some patterns are directly the reverse of what a hygiene hypothesis would lead one to expect. Asked what would be more upsetting to find in the bathtub of a newly rented hotel room, hair near the drain or a dirty footprint, most people choose the hair, although washed hair is less likely to contain germs than dirt.

As another example of the implicit norms governing your behaviour, consider the norms regulating sexual behaviour. What exactly are those norms? Don't respond with the norms that you attribute to supposedly unenlightened people (like your parents). What norms govern your sexual behaviour? Some students might hold to the norm that says that sexual intercourse is acceptable only in a marital context, or at least only when marriage is expected to occur in the near future. Most students do not (Hobart, 1993). Certainly one of the minimal conditions you would impose is that to be acceptable, sexual intercourse must occur with the consent of both partners. The vast majority also believe that there must be "informed consent," which in effect means that both parties must be of a certain age and aware of what they are doing. But in this liberal age, are there any other conditions? Yes. One survey, reported in Chapter 9, Families, indicates that many Canadian university students do add another provision: sexual intercourse is most acceptable when there is evidence of strong affection. This is not to say that sexual intercourse without affection does not occur, but that the preferred behaviour for these students is sexual intercourse between consenting individuals who have a strong affection for one another.

These few examples, of course, do not begin to exhaust the list of norms that regulate daily behaviour; undoubtedly readers can think of many norms not mentioned here. But as soon as you begin to list the norms that regulate your behaviour, it becomes clear that some seem more important than others. For sociologists, the crucial difference between important and less-than-important norms lies in the nature of the reaction of group members when the norm is violated by an individual member. Sumner (1940) long ago introduced two terms, *folkways* and *mores*, to capture this distinction. **Folkways** are those norms that do not evoke severe moral condemnation when violated. The injunction to wear clothes is probably a folkway for most people. If you saw someone running around campus naked, you might feel embarrassed, amused, or titillated, but not morally outraged. **Mores** are those norms whose violation does provoke strong moral condemnation. Our strong moral condemnation of sexual assault, arson, and murder, for instance, suggests that the norms prohibiting these behaviours are mores.

It must be emphasized that the difference between mores and folkways lies in the nature of the reaction produced by the violation of the norm, and not in the *content* of the rule. For instance, one of the norms in our society is that dogs should not be eaten, while one of the norms in contemporary Hindu society is that cow beef should not be eaten. These two norms are similar in content but one is a folkway, the other a *mos* (singular of mores). You may be very upset if you hear that someone has eaten a dog, but you are unlikely to be morally outraged. Yet that sense of moral outrage is exactly what would be evoked among Hindus were someone to openly slaughter, cook, and eat a cow. We shall have much more to say about the importance of audience reactions to norm violations in Chapter 5, Deviance.

Social roles

A **role** is a cluster of behavioural expectations associated with some particular social position within a group or society. For instance, the two social positions of importance in most classroom situations are "teacher" and "student." Most of us expect that a teacher will come to class prepared, will not assign grades arbitrarily, will not show up to class drunk, etc., and so these expectations, taken as a sum, define the teacher role. (As an exercise, you might try to think of the expectations that define the student role.)

A moment's reflection will indicate that one person can occupy several different roles at once. What roles have you occupied during the past week? Brother? Sister? Student? Friend? Enemy? Female? Male? Son? Daughter? This occupation of

A social role is a cluster of expectations about the behaviour that is appropriate for a given individual in a given situation.

multiple roles opens the door to **role conflicts**, that is, situations in which the behavioural expectations associated with one role are inconsistent with those associated with another concurrent role. Some of the clearest contemporary examples of role conflict involve the parent role. The need to care for children—physically, emotionally, and otherwise, or even to arrange for others to care for them on a regular basis—quite often interferes with the demands of a full-time occupation, especially one in a competitive environment. Thus, there is the potential for conflict between the parent role and the full-time worker role, a role conflict that perhaps falls more frequently upon women. (We shall have more to say on this topic in Chapters 6 and 9, Gender Relations and Families.)

In studying roles we must always keep in mind that, without exception, they are social definitions, and thus, to a certain extent, they are arbitrary. This means that roles we take for granted in our own culture may not exist in the same form in other cultures. Here the "mother" role is a particularly good example for making the general point.

In our culture, the traditional definition of the mother role suggests that mothers are supposed to provide their children with emotional support, especially when the children are hurt and frightened, to nurse them when they are first born (with either breast or bottle), and to provide them with guidance as they grow. Some members of our society might even regard these behaviours as natural, as resulting from an innate tendency in most women towards mothering. But let us look at some evidence.

In many European societies prior to the nineteenth century, it was common for biological mothers to send their newborns for care and feeding to a "wet nurse" and her family for a period of one to two years. When these children were returned by the wet nurse, they were often cared for by older siblings or by other relatives, and not by the biological mother. In the case of peasant families, in which the mother had to work alongside the father in the fields, a pattern like this might reflect only economic necessity. It happens, however, that this same pattern was especially strong among the middle and upper classes in traditional Europe. But obviously, if the behaviours that for us are all associated with the single role we think of as "mother" were split up and allocated to a range of different people, then in these societies there was no role that can be said to correspond precisely to the mother role in our own society.

The general point to be made here is that every role is a cluster of expectations about behaviour, but this clustering varies from culture to culture. That our own culture groups together certain behavioural expectations in order to form a particular role does not guarantee that other cultures will group those same expectations together in the same way to form the same role.

Some additional terms

At this point, it will be useful to introduce a few additional terms. The first of these is **subculture**, a group of people within a single society who possess,

On Defining the "Mother" Role

Ask yourself the following question: "Is the increase in the number of married women with families, working outside the home, having a harmful effect on family life?" The odds are that you have a definite opinion on this subject. When a recent Gallup poll asked a similar question of a national sample of Canadians, 53% said that a woman working outside the home did have a harmful effect on family life, 43% said it did not, and only 4% expressed no opinion at all (Bozinoff and Turcotte, 1993).

Now suppose I asked you a second question: "Does the large number of married men with families in the working world have a harmful effect on family life?" Likely you would be taken aback and most of you likely will not have thought about that question in any precise way. But do not feel bad. It is a question that is rarely asked, even by sociologists. While there have been hundreds, possibly thousands of studies on the effects of maternal employment outside the home on children, there have been few on the effects of paternal employment outside the home.

But why does changing "married women, with families" to "married men, with families" convert the question from one on which you have a firm opinion (one way or another) and which has been well-studied by sociologists into one that is puzzling and about which you do not have a firm opinion, and which has *not* been particularly well studied? The answer, presumably, is that you, along with most sociologists, still see the raising of children as being primarily a mother's responsibility, that is, as an expectation that is part of the definition of the "mother" role. Consequently it "makes sense" to you to think about the possible "harmful effects" of something (like working outside the home) that might diminish the amount of time that a mother devotes to her children. Because "primary responsibility for raising children" is *not* an expectation that you have for the role "father," it does not occur to you to think about the "harmful effects" of a father working outside the home.

in addition to the cultural elements they share with the other members of their society, certain distinctive cultural elements that set them apart. Thus, Ukrainians, Jews, Italians, or Iranians residing in Canada are often called subcultures because they share among themselves certain religious or ethnic beliefs and customs that are not characteristic of the Canadian population as a whole. Canadian subcultures will be discussed more fully in Chapter 8, Race and Ethnic Relations.

When the members of a society or a subculture agree that a specific set of norms and values should regulate some broad area of social life, such as the economy, family life, religion, or politics, then that set of norms and values is called an **institution**. Institutions are the subject of later chapters in this text.

The term **material culture** refers to all the physical objects used and produced by the members of a society or a subculture. Thus, for instance, the material culture of a nonindustrial society would include its pottery, the tools it uses to gather and process food, and its sacred objects, while the material culture of our own society would include our televisions, books, automobiles, and houses.

The term **popular culture** refers to those cultural objects and beliefs that are widely distributed across all the social classes in a society, such as comic books and horror films. Since popular culture is by definition widely distributed, larger societies do not usually develop a popular culture until they develop mass media, including print, radio, and television. Also, since relatively expensive things are not likely to achieve a wide distribution, the elements of popular culture are generally inexpensive. For instance, the fact that comic books are relatively inexpensive compared with other sorts of books undoubtedly accounts in part for their popularity, just as the low cost of the dime novel accounted for its popularity during the nineteenth century.

Although sociologists acknowledge the importance of the mass media in creating popular culture, they increasingly recognize that some elements in popular culture are still brought into being by direct, person-to-person exchanges. Consider the case of **urban legends** (see Brunvand, 1989). These

Popular culture refers to those preferences and objects that are widely spread across all the social classes in a society.

are stories that have the following characteristics: (1) they are passed along mainly by word of mouth; (2) the people who repeat these stories believe them to be literally true; (3) the stories are nearly always situated in the very recent past, and are associated with some nearby geographical location; and, most importantly, (4) the stories are almost always completely false. Some of the best-known urban legends include stories about alligators in the sewers of New York, about snakes found in blankets imported from the Orient, about five-year-old boys who are found castrated in shopping centres, about pets put into microwave ovens, about corpses that are mislaid, about Mexican dogs that turn out to be rats, etc.

The importance of these stories lies in the fact that they can tell us something about the unconscious fears that characterize urban societies. For instance, the story about the young boy found castrated in a shopping centre (which has been recorded at hundreds of locations all over North America, and which has really never occurred at any of them) usually includes racial overtones, with the alleged perpetrator often being black. Attributing such an act to a minority group is by no means something new. During the Middle Ages, for instance, Jews were regularly accused of the ritualistic castration and killing of Christian boys, just as, during the early days of the Roman Empire, Christians were regularly accused of the same thing. It seems obvious that the popularity of this modern version of the castrated boy story (and it is a story that is certainly well known to my students) says something about the fears of the dominant white population in North America.

Often urban legends reflect more than one cultural attitude simultaneously. For instance, in the past few years there have been a number of urban legends about AIDS. In one of the oldest and more widespread stories, a man meets an attractive woman in a bar, they go to his hotel room, and they have sexual intercourse. The next morning, when he awakes, the man finds the woman gone and a message scrawled in lipstick on the mirror in the bathroom: "Welcome to the wonderful world of AIDS." At one level, the story can be seen as reflecting our very real worries about this currently incurable disease. But notice that in the story the disease is knowingly spread by a woman to a man. While this pattern of transmission is possible, it is far more common—in the real world—for a man to spread the disease to a woman or another man. Furthermore, while there have been people with AIDS who knowingly spread the disease, most have been males, not females. The fact that the urban legend reverses the observed pattern in order to make a woman the source of danger says something, it has been argued, about prevailing cultural attitudes toward women in our society.

Urban legends are not the only elements of popular culture that can be analyzed in order to investigate prevailing cultural attitudes. Best-selling novels, popular TV shows, jokes, even toys (see the boxed insert on Barbie) can all provide insight into our culture.

More Than Just a Toy: Barbie as Cultural Icon

In Greek mythology Athena sprang fully grown from the head of Zeus and went on to acquire a reputation for cleverness. In 1959, Barbie emerged as a fully formed teenager from somewhere within the Mattel Corporation to become the best-selling toy in the world. Athena was born wearing a suit of armour; Barbie came equipped with a hard plastic body. Athena was virginal but worked with males on a number of difficult tasks; Barbie is virginal (at least semi-virginal) and paired with Ken. But Barbie and Athena differ dramatically in at least two ways: Barbie has lots more stuff and a whole lot more fun!

Barbie's success is phenomenal. In the United States and Canada, the vast majority of girls under the age of twelve have at least one Barbie and it's common for a girl to have several Barbies. What accounts for Barbie's popularity? Partly, it's due to the fact that Barbie and the merchandising package that surrounds her mesh so well with the dominant culture in most capitalistic societies. Barbie, after all, is the quintessential consumer and in the never-ending task of acquiring for Barbie her own special cars, horses, furniture, jewelry, clothing, etc., young girls learn to become the sort of consumer upon whom capitalistic societies depend. Barbie also embodies qualities that have long been favoured in middle-class families: she's pretty, neat, always anxious to have the proper outfit for the proper occasion, and (it goes without saying) intensely heterosexual. Finally, Barbie works to reinforce the traditional gender roles that so many members of the middle class now see as under attack by feminists. She is, after all, concerned with her appearance (her hair in particular), likes nice clothes, and gravitates towards occupations (stewardess, teacher, candy striper, fashion designer, perfume designer, etc.) traditionally associated with women. True, she does occasionally break away from the traditional gender stereotype. In the early 1970s, for instance, Barbie became a medical doctor. The fact is, however, Dr. Barbie never did sell very well (Urla and Swedlund, 1996: 283).

As a cultural icon, however, Barbie is most distinctive on account of her impossible body. Although she has undergone many transformations over the last few decades, and although there are now a variety of Barbies that differ from one another in regard to skin colour and facial features, two things have remained constant: her elongated body and her large breasts. Urla and Swedlund (1996) compared the measurements taken from a sample of different Barbies with the measurements of the statistically "average" female in the United States. Needless to say, they discovered that if Barbie were scaled to the height of the average female, and her bodily proportions remained constant, then she would be clinically anorexic to an extreme degree—albeit unusually buxom. These same authors did a similar study with Barbie's friend Ken. They found that Ken's proportions were also unrealistic when compared with the statistically average male, but (and this, they argue, is the important point here) far less so than Barbie's. To the extent that Barbie's body sets a standard that is impossible for real-life girls to meet, she reinforces a cultural climate in which women must inevitably be considered inferior. Moreover, Urla and Swedlund point out, in the midst of the excesses characteristic of capitalistic societies, a slender body is something that can be achieved only through self-discipline and control; Barbie's hyper-slender body therefore suggests that females are in special need of control and discipline and this too may reinforce male domination or patriarchy (see Chapter 6, Gender Relations).

But nothing is ever simple, and Urla and Swedlund go on to suggest further that we should also pay attention to what Barbie is *not*. For instance, although Barbie has many accessories, a husband and (her own) children are not among them. Barbie is not, in other words, a wife and mother. Nor is she, like so many other dolls, a child to be cared for as a child. On the contrary, Barbie is a strongly sexualized female who conveys an aura of independence. There is, in short, little about Barbie or Barbie's merchandising that can be seen as socializing young girls for a traditional role as mother and wife. To paraphrase the authors: Barbie owns an expensive car and isn't married; she can't be doing everything wrong!

Finally, we must not fall into the trap of regarding young girls as purely passive consumers of what confronts them. Whatever Mattel may intend Barbie to be, young girls are capable of associating their Barbie dolls with a range of roles and personalities. What is needed, these authors suggest, is more research into just what these different roles and personalities are.

In the end, then, Barbie turns out to be surrounded by a fairly complex set of cultural values. These values may not all be consistent with one another but they *are* all very much reflective of the cultural milieu from which Barbie sprang and in which she flourishes.

ASPECTS OF CULTURE

Ever since the nineteenth century, three observations have consistently forced themselves upon virtually every investigator concerned with the study of culture. They are that (1) cultures exhibit enormous variation with regard to their values, norms, and roles; (2) few cultural elements are common to all known societies; and (3) the elements of culture in a given society are often interrelated.

Cultural variation

If we take an overview of the hundreds of societies in the world, past or present, the first thing that strikes us is that there is tremendous variation with regard to the cultural elements found in them. In fact, many societies have values and norms that are directly opposite to those that we might take for granted here.

Some of this cultural variation was apparent in our earlier discussion of the mother role, and other examples of such variation are not difficult to discover. In our society many individuals believe that there exists one god, responsible for all of creation, and they typically describe this god using imagery that is male. Swanson (1960) found that about half the nonindustrial societies in the world also believe in a single god, responsible for creation, although that god is not always seen as a male, or even as having a human likeness. Among the Iroquois, for instance, god was female, while among the South American Lengua, god is a beetle. But the remaining societies in the world either believe in many gods, no one of which is responsible for all creation, or do not believe in personalized gods of any sort. (Related issues will be considered further in Chapter 10, Religion.)

Documenting cultural variation has always been a special concern of anthropologists, and one of the most famous of all the anthropological studies concerned with cultural variation is still Margaret Mead's *Sex and Temperament in Three Primitive Societies* (1935). In this book Mead describes three societies in New Guinea (a large island just to the north of Australia) that she studied in the early 1930s. Mead was concerned most of all with gender roles, and in the first of her societies, the Arapesh, she found that both males and females were cooperative, mild-mannered and gentle, and very much concerned with helping their young. Among the Arapesh, in other words, both males and females seemed to embody the traits that Western societies associate with females. Mead's second society, the Mundugumor, was quite different. Here both males and females were aggressive (and that included being sexually aggressive), uncooperative, jealous, hostile, and relatively unconcerned with parental tasks. To Mead it seemed as if both males and females among the Mundugumor conformed to the gender stereotype associated with males in Western societies. But for Margaret Mead it was her third society, the Tchambuli, that was the most important. Among the Tchambuli, women were confident and efficient, very much involved in economic activities, cooperative (as least with other women), and central to the organization of the household. Tchambuli men, by contrast, seemed relatively passive and peripheral. They concerned themselves mainly with artistic activities of one sort or another, argued among themselves, and—to Mead—seemed maladjusted. Among the Tchambuli, Mead claimed, the gender roles associated with males and females in our own society had been reversed.

For several generations now, Mead's work has been held up as evidence that there are no "fixed" cultural elements, that in the end all cultural arrangements are arbitrary and so, in principle, subject to change. This does not mean, however, that Mead's work has not been criticized. In reviewing the responses to Mead's work, Ward (1996: 47-51) notes two criticisms in particular. First, Mead ignored history in studying the Tchambuli (which was, remember, her most important case). It turns out that at the time of Mead's visit, the Tchambuli had only recently been transferred from one location to another. While Tchambuli women quickly rebuilt the trading networks that had always been their special domain, Tchambuli men were still in the process—while Mead was there—of reestablishing the web of ritual activities that traditionally had been their domain and the source of their prestige. The result was a society in which women seemed more "dominant" than they usually were. Quite apart from her inattention to recent history, Mead has also been criticized for using global terms like "aggressive" and "passive" to describe an entire class of people. More recent feminist thinking suggests that how both males and females behave, even within a single culture, can vary from context to context (see the summary of Thorne's work later in this chapter). On the other hand, despite the criticisms that have been levelled at Mead's work, no one denies that the three societies she studied—despite being in close geographical proximity to one another—were strikingly different from one other and so her work continues to provide clear evidence of just how different cultures can be.

One advantage of becoming aware of cultural variation is that it often gives us a new perspective on things that are happening in our own society. A great many students, for example, seem to think that the high divorce rates associated with contemporary industrial societies are evidence of a declining commitment to traditional "family" values that are characteristic of life in a more traditional society. But the fact is that high divorce rates occur not only in industrial societies. In their study of nearly 200 nonindustrial societies, Broude and Greene (1983) found that divorce was almost universal in about 8 percent of these societies and that it was a relatively common event in another 37 percent. In other words, many traditional societies are more similar to our own society than we think.

Something else that we can "learn" about ourselves in studying other cultures is that many of the behaviours we consider to be deviant (deviance will be considered at length in Chapter 5) are normative elsewhere. For instance, in the late 1800s an anthropologist studying the Zuni (a Native society in New Mexico) brought a Zuni woman to Washington, D.C. The woman, whose name was We'wha, was quickly dubbed a "princess" and soon became the toast of Washington society. There was just one thing: her physical appearance seemed a bit unusual. One newspaper account of the time suggested that We'wha had a relatively broad face, a massive body, and parted her hair strangely (Ward, 1996: 176). In point of fact, We'wha was a biological male who had adopted the behaviours and dress more usually associated with females in Zuni society. The Zuni, like many indigenous societies in North America, recognized that some biological males had an affinity for the female role and encouraged such individuals to take on traits normally associated with females; sometimes as well, biological females took on male roles. Early anthropologists used the term *berdache* to describe these individuals and the role they occupied; more recently, Native scholars have suggested that such people be called "two-spirited." Whatever the term used, these individuals were regarded as engaging in behaviours that were perfectly in accord with Zuni norms. In our own society, by contrast, "two-spirited" individuals would almost certainly be labelled either transvestites or transsexuals, and their behaviour would be seen as deviant, that is, inconsistent with prevailing cultural norms.

Canadian/American value differences

So far we have been talking about cultural variation that exists among relatively distant societies. What happens if we move closer to home, and simply consider Canada and its closest neighbour? There is a fairly extensive descriptive literature on Canadian/American value differences, but the theoretical argument that is most discussed and cited (by sociologists at least) is one put forward by Lipset, an American sociologist, who has presented his argument in a number of publications over a quarter of a century (e.g., Lipset, 1990).

Reduced to its simplest form, Lipset's argument includes two basic hypotheses. The first is that the differing historical experiences of Canada and the United States in the late eighteenth century had a profound and lasting influence on the culture of each region. One part of British North America, the United States, underwent a revolution. That experience, Lipset argued, produced a basic distrust of government and a great emphasis upon individualism. The other part of British North America, Canada, underwent no such revolution and—just as important—became the haven for many who left the United States, having rejected the American Revolution. The result was that in Canada there was a greater trust in government and a greater emphasis upon the group and maintaining harmony within it.

These initial cultural differences were reinforced by other institutional differences between the two countries. Lipset noted, for example, that throughout most of the nineteenth century the two dominant religious organizations in Canada were the Anglican Church in English Canada and the Roman Catholic Church in Quebec. Both of these organizations were hierarchically arranged and had a long history (especially in Europe) of close cooperation with the state. These historical ties made it even more likely that Canadians would have a greater trust in their government and would be less individualistic. In the United States, by contrast, the dominant religious organizations were those Protestant sects that stressed the separation of church and state, and that promoted a religious individuality.

Lipset's second hypothesis is that, once established, these cultural differences between Canada and the United States contributed to a range of other differences. Rates of violent crime, for example, are three to four times higher in the United States. This is true, Lipset noted, even though the number of police officers per 100 000 population is substantially lower in Canada. Lipset argued that Canada has lower rates of violent crime with fewer police because Canadians are less individualistic and have a greater respect for the state. He used the same basic argument to explain why Canada has fewer riots and fewer deaths from political violence; why Canadians are more willing to endorse laws restricting various behaviours (Canadians, for instance, are more likely to endorse laws prohibiting the ownership of handguns, driving cars into downtown areas, door-to-door salespeople, etc.); and why Canada has more government-run welfare programs.

Lipset consistently maintained that his argument is supported less by any one piece of data than by the way everything seems to fit together. The problem is that everything does not fit together. For example, Lipset found Americans more likely to join voluntary organizations. He argued that this reflected their greater distrust of government. That is, since they distrust their government, they are more willing to get things done through voluntary organizations. But Curtis, Lambert, Brown, and Kay (1989) reanalyzed the data Lipset used and found that the greater American commitment to voluntary organizations is due mainly to the fact that Americans are more likely to join church-related organizations. With regard to other sorts of voluntary organizations, such as conservation groups, human rights organizations, charities, etc., there are no systematic differences between the two nationalities.

In other places, Lipset clearly identified very real differences but offered interpretations that do not stand up to direct testing. He was quite correct, for example, in saying that there are more government-run social services in Canada. For Lipset this reflected the greater degree to which Canadians trust their government. But in an article evaluating Lipset's theory, Baer, Grabb, and Johnston (1990) pointed to survey data that indicate that Canadians (both in Quebec and in the rest of the country) are less trustful of government than are Americans.

Often Lipset seems determined to hold on to his theory even when aware of data that do not support his views. Thus, Lipset argued that the greater emphasis upon individualism in the United States hinders the development of class consciousness, which is why a strong socialist movement never developed in that country. In Canada, by contrast, the emphasis upon the group promotes class consciousness, and Canada did develop a strong socialist party in the form of the NDP. The problem is that support for the NDP has been lowest in precisely those regions of Canada, like Quebec and the Maritimes, where even Lipset admitted that a cultural emphasis upon the group has been especially strong. Lipset's response was to equate the Parti Québécois with the NDP in Quebec and to suggest that extensive patronage in the Maritimes has created a web of personal loyalties that encourages the population to support the traditional parties.

Baer, Grabb and Johnston (1993) have suggested that part of the difficulty in testing Lipset's theory is that regional differences *within* Canada and the United States are more important than national differences *between* the two countries. Using a variety of attitudinal measures, for instance, they argued that Quebeckers have become relatively liberal on most issues and that people from the U.S. South are especially conservative. When these two groups (Quebec and the U.S. South) are excluded from the analysis, these authors failed to find any significant attitudinal differences between Canadians and Americans.

In summary, there do appear to be differences between the United States and Canada, and several of these differences seem to make sense under the interpretation that Lipset offered. But there are a significant number of patterns that Lipset's theory cannot account for, and so it seems unlikely that the search for alternative explanations will soon be abandoned.

As we shall see in a few pages, most of the important theoretical perspectives on culture have been developed by anthropologists, not by sociologists. In all cases, anthropological assessments of cultural values in a society have been based on an analysis of things like mythology, religion, literature, folklore, etc., and not upon surveys, or at least surveys of the sort conducted by sociologists. It has seemed obvious to anthropological investigators that a myth or a folktale which has been passed along from generation to generation, for example, is far more likely to say something about cultural values than are the standardized responses (strongly agree, agree, disagree, strongly disagree) to a fixed set of questions created by an investigator. This has seemed especially true when the concern has been to detect those cultural values that people hold strongly but do not consciously think about—those of which they may not be fully aware.

If we wanted to assess Canadian culture using the more traditional anthropological methods, what would we look at instead of survey data? One obvious possibility is Canadian literature. Indeed, a number of commentators (mainly writers and literary critics, not sociologists) have called attention to certain themes that do distinguish Canadian literature from American literature. Lipset (1990) himself reviewed much of the research here, since some of the differences lend support to his theory. Several commentators have suggested, for example, that there is more emphasis upon generational conflict (especially between fathers and their rebellious sons) in American literature and a greater emphasis upon the maintenance of harmonious relationships in Canadian literature. In other cases, the systematic differences identified by previous commentators seem less relevant to Lipset's theory, but are nonetheless interesting in themselves. A higher proportion of the important writers in Canada are women, for instance, and strong female characters are more likely, it has been argued, to appear in Canadian fiction.

The moral? Scholars in other fields assess cultural values with research methods quite different from those used by most sociologists. Anyone seriously interested in the study of Canadian culture would do well to supplement sociology courses with courses in anthropology, Canadian literature, and Canadian art.

Cultural universals

So far we have been concerned only with cultural diversity. But among all the diversity, are there any

Anthropologists often attempt to detect cultural values that are strongly held but not consciously conceptualized.

cultural universals? That is, are there any elements of culture found in every single known society? There do seem to be a few. Every society, for instance, has rules limiting sexual behaviour, though the content and number of these rules vary greatly from society to society. In every known society there is a division of labour by sex, with certain tasks allocated to females and others to males, although the task assignments to either men or women vary among societies.

Some students might think that an *incest taboo*, a norm prohibiting sexual intercourse between parents and children and between siblings, is universal, and they would be right—almost. It turns out that there are about a half-dozen or so societies in which incestuous relationships were permitted for members of the royal family as a way to maintain the purity of the royal lineage. Indeed, in some it was actively encouraged. For instance, between 325 B.C. and 50 B.C., Egypt was ruled by the Ptolemies, a royal dynasty founded by Ptolemy I, one of Alexander the Great's generals, and eleven of the thirteen Ptolemaic kings married either a half- or full sister. There is also evidence that brother/sister marriage was widely practised among commoners in ancient Egypt. One estimate (Roscoe, 1996) suggests that in certain Egyptian communities at least one-sixth of all marriages were between full siblings. The incest taboo, then, is only a near universal.

One of the most important of all cultural universals concerns the relative status of men and women. There are many societies in which men, on average, have more political power and more social prestige than women; these are usually called *patriarchies*. Then there are a fair number of known societies in which men and women are roughly equal in social status, either because one group does not, on the average, have more power and prestige

On Defining the "Father" Role: An Example from Nuer Society

The patriarchal Nuer, an African society, accept two types of marriage that we usually do not. In each the person who plays the role of father for a child is not the biological father. In the first case, a Nuer widow remains bound until her death to transfer rights to her children to her husband's group. This contract becomes effective when her father accepts cattle from her husband's group at the time of her marriage. Ideally, she will remarry her deceased husband's brother or some other member of his group. But even if she simply takes lovers, any children born of those unions will be defined as offspring of her dead husband (hence the term "ghost marriage"). In a rarer form of Nuer marriage, an older wealthy woman may give cattle to a father to "marry" his daughter. The young woman then takes lovers and any children born are defined as the children of the female "father" and belong to the older woman's father's group, even though membership in it is transmitted along the male line. Here we have an exception to the near cultural universal that "fathers" must be males.

Source: *Adapted from Roger M. Keesing, 1981.* Cultural Anthropology: A Contemporary Perspective.(2nd ed.) *New York: Holt, Rinehart and Winston (pp. 216–17).*

than the other, or because greater male power and prestige in certain areas of social life are balanced by greater female power and prestige in other areas of social life. Yet, amid the diversity known to exist among all the societies of the world, there has never existed a true *matriarchy*, that is, a society in which women have more political power and more social prestige than men. The Amazons of myth and legend are just that: myth and legend. What we are dealing with here, then, is a negative universal; that is, with something—matriarchy—that is universally absent from all known societies.

The most important point to make in connection with cultural universals, however, is that the number of such universals is relatively small, at least as compared with the number of ways in which cultures vary.

Cultural integration

Before closing this section it is necessary to point out that many of the elements that comprise a given culture are interrelated, so that a change in one element can produce changes—often quite unintended changes—in other elements. This interrelationship is known as **cultural integration**. The best way to illustrate this process is to consider the extreme case, in which a single cultural change, made with the best of intentions, had ramifications that were massive and utterly disastrous.

An instance of this sort is provided by considering an aboriginal society in Australia called the Yir Yoront. Traditionally, the Yir Yoront travelled throughout various regions of Australia in small bands, each band a cooperative unit that gathered plants for food and hunted animals. In the early decades of the twentieth century, the Anglican Church set up a mission with the goal of converting the Yir Yoront to Christianity. To reward those individuals who came to the mission and took instruction, these missionaries passed out something that they thought would be useful: axes with steel heads. Before this time, the Yir Yoront had used stone-headed axes they had made themselves. A few years after the advent of the Anglican mission, many Yir Yoront bands had ceased to function as cohesive social units and their members had become completely dependent upon handouts from the mission. What happened? For Sharp (1952), the key lay in the impact of those steel axes upon Yir Yoront culture; but to understand this impact you need to know more about that culture.

Most of us probably formed our initial impression of what life in a nonliterate culture is like from the movies, and most movies portray tribal societies as having a chief of some sort. The notion that a small band of individuals should have a single leader strikes us as being perfectly natural and obvious. But in fact, small bands do not always have a single leader. The Yir Yoront did not have chiefs. In this society, any two individuals would determine who had authority over the other by using a complicated system of rules. Basically, these rules specified that older people had authority over younger people, that men had authority over women, and that blood relatives had some authority over other blood relatives. Though these rules tended to concentrate authority in the hands of the older males within a given kinship group, the system was complicated enough that the lines of authority were not always clear. To solve this problem, the Yir Yoront had devised a very concrete procedure for constantly reinforcing these lines of authority; this procedure involved their traditional stone-headed axes.

These axes were used for a variety of tasks that confronted the average Yir Yoront. But, while everybody might need an axe, the axes were the property of the older males within each kinship group. This meant that anyone needing an axe would have to go to one of these individuals. In effect, asking one of these older males for permission to use his axe became a way of acknowledging that male's authority.

Now enter the European missionaries, filled with the typically Western attitude that superior technology (steel axe-heads rather than stone, for instance) is always a good thing. They distributed axes with steel heads to the Yir Yoront who came to the mission, but it turned out that it was mainly women or young men who did so; therefore, these were the people who got the new axes. Having their own axes meant, of course, that they no longer had to go to the older males for the use of an axe. While this might seem very fair and egalitarian to us, the fact remains that, lacking the concrete procedure to reinforce the lines of authority in the society (asking for permission to use an axe), the authority system fell apart, and nothing arose to take its place. Without an authority system, it became difficult to maintain the cooperation among band members necessary for successful hunting and gathering activities. Consequently, the bands ceased to function as independent social groups because some missionaries gave axes to a category of individuals (young men and women) who, under their culture's prevailing social norms, should not have owned them.

Within more differentiated societies, the interrelationship of cultural elements often ensures that the same change will have quite different consequences for different groups. Di Leonardo (1991) presented a good example of this in a discussion of a social movement, calling itself the "Great Way of Former Heaven," which arose in Kwangtung, China, around the turn of the twentieth century, and which defined heterosexuality and childbirth as polluting. A great many women saw this movement as a way of liberating themselves from the restraints of a patriarchal society. The movement's ideology allowed single women to resist the traditional arranged marriages and to take jobs in the local silk industry. Women already in arranged marriages who joined the movement were able to avoid sex (with their husbands and other males) and childbirth, and were able to live with other women. In this case, however, avoiding sex and childbirth meant purchasing other women, concubines, who were obliged to be available for sex with the husbands. The women who became concubines hardly benefited as a result of this social movement. Here then is a case in which a change that raised the status of one group of women had the opposite effect for another group of women in the same society.

The point concerning cultural integration should not be over-emphasized. Cultures are never so tightly integrated that any change will have widespread effects. Whether a particular cultural change introduced within a group will have further cultural ramifications depends upon the particular pattern of interrelationships among the cultural traits found in that group. Tracing out the relationships linking the cultural traits in various groups is one of the primary tasks of the sociologist and the social anthropologist.

CONCEPTUAL DANGERS IN THE STUDY OF CULTURE

The "scientific ideal" suggests that decisions to reject or accept arguments have to do with the fit (or lack of fit) between arguments and the relevant empirical data. But those of you who read the fine print at the bottom of Chart 1.2 in Chapter 1 were told that this ideal is not always met. What we accept as sociological knowledge is sometimes determined as much by our pre-existing biases as by the data that we gather. This bias is an example of what we call **ethnocentrism**. In its most general sense, ethnocentrism refers to the tendency to see things from the point of view of the observer's culture rather than from that of the observed. It occurs frequently, not only among students, but even among social scientists. But this general definition masks degrees of ethnocentrism.

At its worst, ethnocentrism can refer to the tendency to view other cultures as inferior rather than just different. This type of ethnocentrism was especially prevalent during the nineteenth century. For instance, most social anthropologists of the time accepted a view of social evolution which held that societies passed through three stages: savagery, barbarism, and civilization. They also believed that most nonindustrial cultures were stuck at the levels of savagery or barbarism, indicating the low esteem in which they held these cultures.

Though far less common today, ethnocentrism of this sort still crops up now and again. For instance, someone who uses the term "primitive society" to refer to what is really a nonindustrial society might be accused of ethnocentrism, since "primitive" now carries negative connotations that go far beyond a simple consideration of the type of economy found in a society.

A more subtle type of ethnocentrism, harder to spot and probably more common among the readers of this book than the one just described, is the tendency to believe that what is true of your culture is also true of other cultures. Given the nature of our society, two specific biases that flow from this type of ethnocentrism are Eurocentrism and androcentrism.

Eurocentrism is a bit of a misnomer, since it refers to a bias that goes beyond the borders of modern Europe. Basically, a theory or theoretical perspective is said to be Eurocentric when it has been shaped by the values and experiences of the white middle class in Western industrialized societies. In the simplest case, Eurocentrism means assuming that these values and experiences are universally shared. This happens more often (and more easily) than you might expect.

In the early part of this century, archeologists investigating the Ice Age in Europe began discovering female figurines carved out of stone. They were found over a wide area that stretched from France to the Ural mountains, with most being found in Central Europe. In the majority of cases, the breasts, hips, and buttocks of the woman depicted seemed especially large, something which suggested to the (mainly male) archeologists involved that the figurines were associated with fertility. The figurines were promptly dubbed "prehistoric Venuses" (after the Roman goddess of beauty) and accepted as evidence that a fertility goddess had been worshipped in prehistoric Europe.

Over the past few decades professional archeologists, including most feminist archeologists, have challenged the fertility-goddess interpretation of these figurines. First, it seems unlikely that the figurines represent a single goddess or a single anything. Rice (1981), for instance, demonstrated that the figurines display the same diversity with regard to physical traits (some are pregnant, some are not; some are young, some are old; etc.) that you would expect to find among a living population of prehistoric women. This would suggest that the figurines are more likely representations of individual women. But more importantly, nothing in the archeological record itself suggests that the figurines were used for a religious purpose. Indeed, other possible explanations exist.

Townsend (1990) pointed out, for example, that human figurines have been used for a variety of purposes in non-Western societies. In certain First Nations societies in Alaska, shamans had dolls which were thought to travel to another world to retrieve lost souls. Women in Tanzania were often healed by driving their illness into a figurine. In other societies human figures are used in magical procedures designed to harm somebody. In short, there is a range of meanings that the Venus figurines could have had for prehistoric peoples in Europe.

So why has the interpretation of the Venus figurines as prehistoric goddesses become so popular with Western audiences? Most likely because this interpretation conforms to two pre-existing biases that are both Eurocentric. First, in a number of European societies—from the Classical civilizations of Greece and Rome, to the Christian societies of the Middle Ages, to contemporary Roman Catholic societies—people have routinely made statues of the supernatural beings in whom they believe. The practice is familiar to us, it "makes sense." But there's more. Part of the traditional gender stereotype associated with women in the Western tradition is that women are most of all supposed to be mothers, whose primary goal is to bear and nurture children. The idea of a nurturing "mother goddess" responsible for fertility is consistent with this Western stereotype, and so once again the idea of a prehistoric mother goddess seems to "make sense" to us and for that reason seems plausible. In both cases, then, we are assuming that what makes sense to us would have made sense as well to prehistoric peoples. That is Eurocentric thinking.

The idea of a "fertility goddess" conforms to a Eurocentric gender stereotype of women as nurturing beings.

Another common Eurocentric bias has to do with power. When parties of unequal power meet, those with less power often find it necessary to adapt their behaviour to the dictates of those with more power. Since this is something that the more powerful parties rarely have to do, it is something that they can easily miss or overlook. Given the power differences that exist between Western and non-Western societies, this means that contact with the West can (and has) produced changes in non-Western societies that have been overlooked by Western commentators.

For instance, when Europeans made contact with First Nations communities in eastern Canada they reported that these communities were dominated by males, and these early reports were taken at face value by later commentators. By contrast, Leacock (1983) suggested that in the period just before European contact, First Nations communities in eastern Canada were most likely egalitarian, with the political and economic importance of males and females being roughly equal. But the European males who contacted these communities were used to dealing with other males. Because Europe was the more powerful culture, First Nations communities had to adapt to this fact. The result was that as these communities fell under European influence, the economic and political importance of their males increased relative to females. In short, if Leacock is right, the social inequality of males and females in these particular First Nations societies came into existence only after European contact, and this process went entirely unnoticed by European observers.

An unwillingness to acknowledge the ways in which power shapes our interaction with other cultures and the accounts that we construct of other cultures is by no means limited to the distant past. Patai (1994) pointed out that the sociological and anthropological investigators who pour out of North America to study the societies of the developing world are usually white and middle-class and almost always perceived (correctly) by the people they study as having access to all sorts of resources (including simply being on good terms with the local authorities). This may raise expectations on the part of the people being studied (expectations for instance that the investigator may "help" them in some way) and this in turn can shape their response to the investigator's queries.

Androcentrism means "male-centredness." It is a bias that involves (1) seeing things from a male point of view or (2) seeing things in a way that reinforces male privilege in society. One form of androcentric bias, for example, is to systematically develop interpretations of culture which see men as active and women as passive even when the available data are consistent with other interpretations.

For instance, it is routine (and has been for more than a century) for anthropologists to see the manufacture of stone tools by our prehistoric ancestors as one of the first and most important technological innovations in the history of our species. Gero (1991) noted that almost all discussions of stone tool production have assumed that these tools were made by males. But why? Modern experiments have demonstrated that making stone tools does not require great upper body strength, which if it did might give males an advantage. Furthermore, the very sites where archeologists found most stone tools—house floors, base camps, village sites—are quite plausibly areas in which women congregated to carry out their work. This suggested to Gero that at least some stone tools are likely to have been used by women. But if women used stone tools, she argued, there is no particular reason not to suppose that women also made stone tools.

In short, there is no evidence which rules out the possibility that women were as active as (or even more active than) men in the manufacture of stone tools. Why then have anthropology textbooks consistently seen "man the tool-maker" standing so prominently at the dawn of human prehistory and why have the students who have read these texts been so willing to accept this image? Gero's answer is that we have projected a current androcentric image—*men* as the active inventors of important technologies—back on to the past.

Androcentrism also can mean a tendency to prefer theories that believe in innate differences between males and females and which therefore provide a rationale for gender inequalities in society. Implicit in much sociological thinking in the nineteenth and early twentieth centuries, for instance, was the notion that individuals had a limited amount of "vital force" that could be used for thinking and biological reproduction. Since women devoted so much of their vital force towards reproduction, there was less of it available for thinking. This explained (so the argument went) why women were less intelligent than men. The androcentric bias here seems evident. But before you laugh aloud and conclude that modern audiences would never be so gullible as to accept a theory like this, keep in mind that it is still widely believed—both by a number of social scientists and by many university students—that males are more likely to use the right side of their brain than females and that this is why males are better at mathematics than females, even though there is little evidence for this view (see Bleier, 1987; also Chapter 6, Gender Relations). Is talking about unsubstantiated differences in "brain lateralization" really all that different from talking about unsubstantiated differences in the allocation of "vital force"?

Androcentric bias also leads us to choose the male experience over the female experience for study. Traditional anthropological accounts of hunting and gathering societies, for example, devoted far more space to describing hunting activities (usually done by males) than to gathering activities (usually done by females) even when gathering provided most of the food consumed in a society. The simple fact that we call these societies "hunting and gathering societies" rather than "gathering and hunting societies" is for some feminist anthropologists an indication of androcentric bias.

A similar androcentric bias has been seen in the tendency of sociologists to be concerned most of all with what happens in the public arena. There seems to be a sense among sociologists that what happens in public is more important than what happens in private. By contrast, many feminists have suggested that we consider what is public to be important precisely because men are the primary and most visible actors in the public arena.

Finally, androcentrism seems evident in those cases where theories which purport to be about society in general are really about the male experience in society. Gilligan (1982: 18) pointed out, for instance, that the index to Piaget's influential *Moral Development of the Child* (see Chapter 4, Socialization) has four entries under "girls." By contrast, there is no entry at all called "boys." This is because, she argued, "the child" that Piaget discussed at length throughout the book is implicitly assumed to be male. Similarly, Kohlberg (also in the Socialization chapter) used a sample of male college students to develop a theory of moral development and subsequently declared that theory to be universal. Gilligan's (1982) own research demonstrated how starting with a sample of females produces a quite different model of moral development.

THEORETICAL PERSPECTIVES ON CULTURE

Sociologists who study culture have used a range of theoretical perspectives. The most important and best-known analyses of culture, however, have each drawn upon one of four quite different perspectives. These are: (1) functionalism, (2) conflict theory, (3) cultural materialism, and (4) feminism.

Functionalism

Functionalism is a perspective you encountered in Chapter 1, What Is Sociology?, and one that you will see again many times throughout this book. The essence of functionalist explanation, when applied to culture, is that a given norm or value is explained by showing how it contributes to the overall stability or survival of the society in which it is found.

One of the first investigators to use this functional explanation in an explicit way was a social anthropologist named Bronislaw Malinowski. His work, even today, provides some of the clearest examples of functionalist explanation. Malinowski (1954 [1925]) was at one point studying a society located among the Trobriand Islands in the South Pacific. The Trobrianders derived much of their food from fishing in the ocean waters surrounding their islands. What Malinowski found was that every aspect of such ocean fishing was surrounded by an elaborate system of magic. But why did they use magic? At first glance the answer might seem obvious: the Trobrianders used magic because they believed it would help them catch more fish. But, Malinowski argued, if magic is used simply to ensure success, then every society should use magic extensively to ensure success at whatever activity is important to its members. Such widespread use of magic, however, is simply not the case. Some societies, like the Trobrianders, make extensive use of magic; others do not. What accounts for this cultural difference?

In beginning his explanation, Malinowski noted that ocean fishing is an extremely uncertain activity. The Trobrianders had no control over the weather or over the locations at which fish might be caught. Added to this, of course, was the fact that taking a canoe on to the ocean was a relatively dangerous activity. How would you feel if you had to engage in a dangerous and uncertain activity day after day? You would probably feel quite anxious, and Malinowski assumed that the Trobrianders felt the same way. This anxiety would be reduced if you felt, however incorrectly, that you could control your environment. This is precisely the feeling that the use of magic provides. The use of magic allowed the Trobrianders to believe that they could control both the weather and the locations at which fish were to be found. Malinowski's conclusion, then, is that magic is likely to be used whenever people face dangerous and uncertain environments. The Trobrianders faced such an environment, and therefore used magic. Other societies face relatively safe, certain environments, and therefore they do not use magic.

Malinowski had one final bit of data that provided an especially convincing conclusion to his argument. Besides fishing on the open ocean, the Trobrianders also fished in a sheltered lagoon. Unlike ocean fishing, fishing in the lagoon was relatively safe, and since the lagoon was a relatively small place, finding the right place to fish was less of a problem. Given Malinowski's argument, one would expect that magic would not be associated with lagoon fishing. That is exactly what he found. Although the Trobrianders surrounded ocean fishing with much magic, none was associated with lagoon fishing.

Notice how Malinowski's explanation fits the basic functionalist pattern. He explained a given cultural element, in this case the use of magic, by showing how it contributes to the overall stability of the society: magic reduces the anxiety produced by the dangers and uncertainties associated with open-ocean fishing.

The functionalist perspective used by Malinowski influenced not only social anthropologists, but sociologists as well. Perhaps the best examples of functionalist explanation in sociology are contained in a book entitled *Human Society*, written by Kingsley Davis. Published originally in 1949, the book has been reprinted many times. *Human Society* was intended to be an introductory text, though one that explicitly adopted a functionalist perspective. As a result, most of Davis's discussion is devoted to those fairly standard topics, such as socialization, religious institutions, and marriage and the family, that tend to be covered in every introductory textbook. But Davis also devoted an entire chapter to something that would strike many as an unlikely candidate for functionalist explanation: sexual jealousy among males.

Most people probably regard such jealousy as somehow pathological, as resulting from, say, the basic insecurity of males concerning sexual matters. Nevertheless, sexual jealousy among males is found in every known society, and for the functionalist like Davis, that means that it probably contributes to social stability. But how?

Davis started off by making a very crucial assumption—crucial in the sense that if it were false, his entire argument would fall apart. He assumed that, unless a society placed some restrictions upon sexual intercourse, most males would be constantly competing with other males for sexual access, producing much conflict. The conflict, in turn, would prevent the cooperation that must be maintained if society is to survive. This assumption led Davis to conclude that every society must have norms of some sort regulating sexual intercourse. But how are these norms enforced? That is, what ensures that most members of society obey most of the norms most of the time? There has to be some type of deterrent. That is where sexual jealousy comes in.

Jealousy is an emotional response that fosters aggression. Specifically, it fosters aggression against people who have given others a reason to be jealous. Given this fact, Davis argued, a community will encourage its members to be jealous whenever their sexual rights have been violated, sexual rights being those rights guaranteed under the prevailing sexual norms. The fact that the community encourages people to be jealous whenever their sexual rights have been violated will deter individuals who might think of violating those rights. For instance, suppose that one of the sexual norms in a society is that the only person who has a right to sexual intercourse with a married woman is her husband. The foreknowledge that a husband will become jealous (and aggressive) if some other male has intercourse with his wife and the foreknowledge that this jealousy will be encouraged by the community at large would, according to Davis, deter to some degree both the wife and any potential lover from violating that norm. To convince yourself of the reasonableness of the Davis argument, you might think about things the other way around. If it were absolutely certain that people in this society would not get jealous if someone had intercourse with their spouse, would this make adultery more likely? If you answered yes to this question, then you basically agree with Davis's analysis.

A consequence of this formulation is that the only way to eliminate sexual jealousy is to eliminate sexual norms—and if Davis's initial assumption is correct, this cannot be done without producing much social instability. Functionalist explanations of this sort are still popular in sociology, but much less so than they once were. Thus, let us turn to other perspectives, beginning with conflict theory.

Conflict theory

Some conflict theorists, following Marx, lump cultural beliefs under the more general heading of "ideology," the system of thought that serves the interests of the dominant groups in society. This usually means that ideology is seen as something that legitimates existing inequalities of wealth and power, or as something that prevents the less powerful from seeing the true cause of this inequality. Conflict theorists also apply this same perspective to religion (also usually considered to be ideology). You will be considering the Marxist perspective on religion in some detail later in the text.

A conflict approach to culture has been especially influential in connection with the *sociology of knowledge*. This is a subfield of sociology concerned with studying the influence of social factors on what passes for knowledge in a society. Sociologists of knowledge adopt the view that knowledge is a cultural element, and that we acquire knowledge in much the same way that we acquire other cultural elements. This runs counter to the common sense view that what we accept as knowledge is determined mainly by rational criteria, such as the degree to which a piece of knowledge is supported by the available evidence. In any event, the conflict variant of the sociology of knowledge is that forms of knowledge—for example, scientific theories—often become popular in a society as much because they serve the interests of the dominant classes in that society as because they have a basis in fact or anything else.

Do you really think it is a coincidence, a conflict theorist might argue, that Darwin's theory of evolution first became popular in nineteenth-century England? Or are you willing to grant that Darwin's emphasis upon competition and survival of the fittest as the keys to evolution just *might* have been especially appealing in a society in which the rich favoured free economic competition and believed their high status to be mainly the result of their innate abilities?

Or take something closer to home: the theories presented in this book. You have been told—and will be told again and again in this textbook—that functionalism is a major theoretical perspective in sociology. By itself that statement is true. But why? Why, in other words, has functionalism proven so popular with sociologists in North America? A conflict theorist might answer by pointing to the essentially conservative nature of functionalism. It is, after all, a theoretical perspective that emphasizes how cultural elements, such as values and norms, contribute to the stability and smooth functioning of society. Such a perspective, so the argument goes, would naturally be favoured by the dominant groups in society who have a stake in maintaining the status quo.

Re-reading Mother Teresa: A Conflict Approach?

If I asked most of you reading this book to list ten public figures you admire and respect, Mother Teresa would probably appear on a great many lists. Born in 1910 in the former Yugoslavia to Albanian parents, Mother Teresa founded an order of Roman Catholic sisters who today minister to the poor in over eighty countries. From the early 1950s until her retirement for reasons of health in 1990, she personally gathered the dying from the streets of Calcutta, India, and brought them to her hospital where they could die with dignity. As a result, Mother Teresa has often been called a "living saint" and in 1979 was awarded the Nobel Prize for Peace.

Although it rarely makes the news, Mother Teresa has been criticized by a number of Roman Catholic activists, in India and elsewhere. In an interview published in an Italian magazine (*L'Expresso*, September 9, 1990), a Catholic theologian who teaches near Calcutta suggested that it was the Western media that "created" Mother Teresa. He meant that it was the Western media—not the media in India or the rest of the Third World—that first raised her to mythic status. Certainly, it was a Western agency that granted her the Nobel Peace Prize.

Why the criticism? It relates to Mother Teresa's approach to poverty. For her, poverty is something to be alleviated by good works. In her many speeches, she never attacks the root causes of poverty, those social conditions which ensure that the mass of people in the Third World remain poor while relatively few remain rich. Her approach to poverty, in other words, does not threaten entrenched privilege. The conflict approach to religion, to be discussed in Chapter 10, Religion, makes the same point, that religion is a conservative force, one that can be used as a means to calm the masses, a flower on the chain of oppression.

So, how much of the West's regard for Mother Teresa is due to a sincere appreciation of her selflessness (and certainly no one doubts that as an individual she is selfless) and how much to the fact that the West controls and consumes most of the world's resources and finds in Mother Teresa someone whose approach to poverty does not threaten that pattern of control and consumption? Sounds to me like a good discussion question. It shows that in applying a conflict perspective, surprising issues can be raised, even about Mother Teresa.

In Chapter 7, Social Stratification, you will be introduced to a particular functionalist theory dealing with stratification. (You might want to jump ahead to page 176 and read that theory before proceeding here.) This theory suggests that certain occupations both are "more functionally important" to the smooth running of society and require "more talent"—are "harder to fill"—than others, and therefore that the smooth functioning of society depends upon insuring that qualified people move into these more important and harder-to-fill occupations. And how is that done? Why, by insuring that these occupations are given more social rewards (read: money, prestige, and power) than other occupations. *Voilà*: an argument that suggests that stratification is valuable because it contributes to social stability. A conflict theorist would suggest that this theory has proven so durable in sociology (it first appeared in the 1940s) because it suggests that inequality is, well, *good* for society. It would thus be a theory favoured by some middle- and upper-class professors who teach it (and the middle- and upper-class students who learn about it).

The great value of the conflict perspective on culture is that it forces us to challenge a great many attitudes and beliefs that would otherwise be unexamined. Even if in the end we reject a particular conflict account, the exercise of considering it is very much in keeping with the purpose of education. With this in mind, you might try developing a conflict perspective on some of the many campaigns that are important in our society at the moment. Is there any basis for believing, for example, that the current cultural emphasis upon global ecology or upon household recycling works to divert our attention from prevailing injustices and from the groups that are responsible for those injustices? Or what about those campaigns against cancer that adopt a purely medical model, seeing cancer mainly as a disease for which a medical cure must be found, rather than, say, mainly as a condition brought on by things put into our environment by industry? You might surprise yourself.

Cultural materialism

Cultural materialism is a third perspective used to study and explain culture. Cultural materialists de-emphasize ideas and ideology as determinants of cultures, and instead see cultures as adaptations to the needs forced upon social groups by the specific physical environments in which they live.

Cultural materialism sees culture as an adaptation to the needs forced upon us by the nature of the physical environment in which we live.

The essence of cultural materialism is best conveyed by examples, and the best examples of this approach are to be found in the applications developed by Harris (1985). One of his concerns was to explain the Hindu ban on the slaughter of cows. To many Western observers, this ban may seem utterly senseless, a classic example of how religion and the inertia of tradition can stand in the way of rational behaviour (religion and rationality will be discussed in Chapter 10, Religion). Nothing seems more tragic than for Hindu farmers in India to see their families starve rather than kill the sacred cows that wander the countryside. Nevertheless, Harris argued, if you think that the Hindu farmers are in a tragic situation right now, that is nothing compared with the misery and human devastation that would result if those farmers started to slaughter their cows.

How did Harris come to this very counter-intuitive position? He started by noting that there are two basic types of agricultural system in the world today. One, the type used in Canada and most Western nations, is a highly mechanized system that relies on tractors for motive power. Such a system also relies heavily upon petrochemicals, both to fuel the tractors and to provide synthetic fertilizers. The second type is a nonmechanized system that relies on draft animals like oxen for motive power and uses dung for fertilizer. This is the system that characterizes modern India.

There are three reasons why India cannot convert to the more mechanized system of agriculture. First, India currently has insufficient capital either to purchase the required machinery or to establish a system for the distribution of petrochemical products. Second, the experiences in Western nations make it quite clear that one effect of agricultural mechanization is the displacement of people from the country to the city. India's urban areas are already overcrowded and simply cannot absorb a massive influx from the country. Third, although Westerners think that tractors are more efficient than oxen, Harris argued that this is not always true. In India, a tractor can plough a field about ten times faster than can a pair of oxen, but the initial cost of that tractor is something like *twenty* times the cost of the oxen. Given this fact, tractors are more cost-effective than oxen only in the case of large farms that require a lot of ploughing. In the case of small farms—and the vast majority of farms in India are small—oxen are more cost-effective than tractors. India, then, will probably continue to use the nonmechanical type of agriculture for some time to come.

At this point Harris came up with an interesting statistic from Indian government reports: in an average year, the number of oxen available for use by Indian farmers is only about 66 percent of the number of oxen needed by those same farmers. This chronic shortage of oxen is one of the major reasons why thousands of Indian farms fail each year. If Western farmers want new tractors, they go to a dealer, but if Indian farmers want a new ox, they go to—a cow.

We begin to catch a glimmer of the reasoning behind Harris's position. Only by insuring that most of its farms are productive can India feed itself. Only by maintaining a large population of cows can India's farmers be assured that sufficient oxen will be available to make the farms productive. Even with the current ban on the slaughter of cows, there are not enough oxen to go around. Think of how much greater the problem would be if a significant percentage of those cows were slaughtered.

But wait. Isn't there a flaw in the argument? If maintaining a large population of cows is so much in the farmers' self-interest, why do things have to be formalized under the guise of a religious ban? Wouldn't farmers just naturally not slaughter their cows? Harris's response to this criticism is simple. Rains in India are irregular and thus famine is recurrent and unavoidable. Indian farmers are like you or me; if they see their families starving they will be strongly tempted to kill their cows to feed their families. Yet if they do kill those cows during a time of famine, there will be an even greater shortage of oxen than normally occurs, and it will be difficult for agriculture to recover when the famine ends. In fact, killing the cows might easily mean that the famine will never end. The only solution is a total, absolute, and religiously inspired ban on the slaughter of cows. Only a ban of this sort has the remotest chance of overcoming the farmers' temptations to feed themselves and their families during times of famine.

Another well-known example of Harris's cultural materialist approach concerns the ancient Israelites.

The Old Testament *Book of Leviticus* records the religious prohibitions against the Israelites' eating of pork. We also know from other sources that the pig was regarded by the Israelites as a particularly unclean animal. Why pigs? Here again the modern mind tends to prefer hygienic explanations. Pigs, after all, transmit trichinosis, a type of parasitic disease. But, Harris pointed out, from a purely hygienic point of view, cattle are far more unhealthy than pigs. Cattle, for instance, serve as carriers of a disease called anthrax. While trichinosis is rarely fatal, anthrax is deadly. Anthrax epidemics devastated whole populations, including populations in the Middle East, until the disease was brought under control in the nineteenth century. Yet cattle, far from being prohibited in the Old Testament, were held up as a preferred food in *Leviticus*. If the concern were to prohibit the eating of unhealthy animals, then the Old Testament did things backwards by prohibiting the eating of pork and encouraging the eating of beef.

Harris began his own explanation by noting that although "sweat like a pig" is a cliché, the physiological fact is that pigs do not sweat, at least not very much. Remember that the function of sweating is to cool off the body, and all warm-blooded animals must cool off their bodies in a hot climate. Because pigs do not sweat, they must cool themselves off by covering their skin with liquid of some sort, including, for instance, their own urine and feces if nothing else is available.

What all of this means is that the ancient Israelites, since they were living in a very hot climate, would have required enormous amounts of water to raise pigs. But water was scarce in the arid regions of the ancient Middle East, and diverting large amounts of water to the raising of pigs would have left insufficient supplies for the human population. Over the long run, Harris argued, this would have proven economically disastrous. The only solution was a ban on the eating of pigs.

Harris's argument has drawn a lot of criticism, but he has usually been able to turn this criticism to his advantage. Some critics, for instance, pointed out that large numbers of pig bones have been found at archeological sites throughout the Middle East, indicating that the eating of pigs was well established in the region as early as 5000 B.C. Quite correct, responded Harris (1985), but then, as we approach the first millennium before the Christian era, such bones become increasingly rare at Middle Eastern archeological sites. The reason: in 5000 B.C. the Middle East was well forested and pigs can thrive in a shaded forest environment without requiring large amounts of water. What happened between 5000 B.C. and 1000 B.C. is that the Middle East suffered a fairly dramatic deforestation (owing to massive population increases). Many areas in the region became desert, and the raising of pigs became unfeasible. The result was that sometime during the first millennium B.C. the Israelites responded to these changed conditions by developing a ban on pigs.

But wait. If all this is true, then why should the Israelites have been the only Middle Eastern society to develop a ban on pigs? Shouldn't other societies facing the same material conditions have developed the same ban? The fact is, Harris (1985: 83) pointed out, many did. At least three other Middle Eastern civilizations—the Phoenician, the Egyptian, and the Babylonian—came to abhor the pig around the same time as the Israelites.

Students who have found these two examples of cultural materialism interesting should consult Harris (1985), in which he also provides explanations as to why North Americans won't eat horsemeat (though most of Europe does) but love milk (regarded as something like cow spit in traditional China), why Europeans don't eat insects but people living in the Amazon basin do, and why the Aztecs ate other human beings on a scale unheard of anywhere else in the world. Lunch anyone?

Feminism(s)

Let me begin by relating four anecdotes. Anecdote 1: I recently saw a teenaged girl being interviewed on TV. Asked if she were a feminist, she looked startled and then said, "No, I have a boyfriend." Judging from what followed, it appears that she had established a strict equivalence between "feminism" and "lesbian sexuality." Anecdote 2: A colleague teaching a course on methods asked if I could give a short guest lecture on feminist methodology. Anecdote 3: Eichler (1984: 28) reported that in the early 1980s, attempts to include material on women in sociology textbooks were dismissed by many male colleagues as a "sop to women's liberation." Anecdote 4: I was recently told by a friend that her attempts to bring feminist theory into the curriculum at her university were put down as mere "political correctness."

What the first two anecdotes have in common is a failure to understand that *feminism* is a term that encompasses a wide variety of very different things. We made that point briefly in Chapter 1. For some feminists lesbian sexuality is an important issue; for most it is not. Similarly, there is no single "feminist methodology," and in fact there are heated debates among feminist theorists as to how social and cultural phenomena should be investigated. The last two anecdotes demonstrate something else: feminist theory has not yet become a part of mainstream sociology and it quite often provokes a strong and dismissive attitude from established sociologists.

Feminism *is a term that encompasses a wide variety of very different things.*

The fact that much feminist writing is dense, often difficult reading, and little concerned with developing specific analysis of particular situations does not help.

Nevertheless, feminist theory represents one of the most serious challenges to mainstream sociology that has emerged in the past half century. The challenge may eventually fail for any number of reasons or it may succeed and change the nature of sociological investigation. But at this point in time, there is simply no excuse for not discussing that challenge. Sociology classrooms, where this book will be read, seem a good place to start.

Two separate feminist traditions have shaped the study of culture over the past two or three decades, and they are quite different. The first is what many feminist commentators have labelled the "adding women" approach. This tradition rose to prominence during the late 1960s and 1970s and its central concern was to demonstrate the importance of women and women's roles in shaping culture, an importance that had been neglected in earlier studies. It was argued, for instance, that the gathering of food by females, not the hunting of animals by males, was critical in our social evolutionary past. Not only did gathering provide most of the food in earliest human societies, but there are solid reasons for believing that gathering gave rise to complex patterns of group cooperation and communication.

Feminist investigators working in this tradition also forced a reevaluation of those many studies which used observations on modern primates (a group that includes all the various species of apes and monkeys) to make inferences about early human societies (Sperling, 1991). Different types of primates have different types of social organization, and it just happened that traditional (male) investigators have devoted most of their attention to the study of those particular primates, like baboons, whose social organization centres around males defending territorial space. Intensive study of other primate species, like chimpanzees (who are in fact much closer to us in an evolutionary sense), reveals that in these groups the mother–child bond is the most important social relationship.

Although this first tradition of feminist scholarship sought to redirect the study of culture on to new subjects, it did not challenge prevailing research methods or conceptual frameworks. In the late 1970s and 1980s a second tradition of feminist scholarship emerged which did just that. Most of the attempts to identify androcentric and Eurocentric biases in the study of culture, discussed earlier, were made by feminist scholars working in this second tradition.

Some of the scholars working in this second feminist tradition wanted to demonstrate that the ways of conceptualizing the world that have been traditional in sociology often prevented us from seeing important social patterns. An example of this sort of work is Thorne's (1990) study of the culture of children in an elementary school. When Thorne began her study she viewed "male" and "female" as socially constructed gender categories (a topic more fully discussed in Chapter 6, Gender Relations) that were seen to be separate, distinct, and opposed to one another. Male traits were seen to be the opposite of female traits and vice versa. She assumed that the fourth- and fifth-grade children she was studying thought of "gender" in the same way and would use this notion of gender to organize their activities. As a result, Thorne found herself scribbling notes furiously whenever the children seemed to behave in a way that was consistent with this view of gender, as when boys and girls on the playground divided into two separate antagonistic groups.

But as her investigation proceeded, Thorne began to notice that there were lots of other situations in which these very same children behaved quite differently. In some situations, for instance, the children very freely and very easily formed themselves into small, cohesive groups involving both males and females in which gender seemed genuinely irrelevant to them. These are the situations, Thorne argued, that have generally been ignored by sociologists, but they are just as real and just as meaningful as the situations in which girls and boys form themselves into distinct and antagonistic groups. Only by studying both types of situation, she argues, can we come to an understanding of when and why gender becomes important, and indeed what gender "means" to the individuals involved.

Other feminist scholars in this second tradition have been increasingly concerned with demonstrating that many supposedly "scientific" concepts have been shaped by prevailing cultural attitudes and beliefs. Groneman's (1995) study of nymphomania is a good example of the sort of work done here. "Nymphomania" did not exist as a medical category until the late nineteenth century. At that time it was introduced as a medical term designating women characterized by "excessive" sexual desire. In principle, there was a corresponding term for males, satyriasis. But if you look at what medical doctors of the period took as indicators of nymphomania and satyriasis then it quickly becomes clear that the two terms were not symmetrical. Thus, in the case of women, things like adultery, wanting more sex than their spouse, excessive flirtation, and masturbation were often enough to merit a diagnosis of nymphomania. These same things were never enough to justify a diagnosis of satyriasis in men. Groneman suggests that nymphomania was invented so that women who stepped outside the rigidly defined gender roles of the period (such as women who actively pursued sex, something that the society viewed as legitimate for men but not for women) could be defined as "sick" and so treated (and brought into line) by a medical establishment dominated by males. The preferred method of treating nymphomania, incidentally, was surgical removal of the ovaries. To fully appreciate the significance of this, imagine a society in which men who committed adultery, masturbated, or flirted excessively were routinely subjected to castration.

SUMMARY

Social life is patterned, not random, and much of this patterning can be attributed to the fact that every social group possesses a culture. A cultural element is something that is held in common by the members of a group, that affects their behaviour or the way they view the world, and that is passed on to new members. A group's culture is simply the sum total of all the cultural elements associated with that group. There are many types of cultural elements, but the three most important ones for sociologists are values, norms, and roles.

A value is either a very general belief about what is desirable or undesirable, or a general statement of preference. In contrast, norms are those relatively specific expectations we hold about which behaviours are acceptable and which are not. In some cases, the violation of a norm will provoke only a mild response from the members of a group; such norms are called folkways. In other cases, the violation of a norm will provoke a much more severe response; norms of this sort are called mores. Roles are clusters of expectations about behaviour that specify how a given individual is to behave in a particular situation.

Most students of culture are concerned with three observations: (1) that the content of culture varies greatly across the totality of the world's societies; (2) that very few cultural elements are found in all the world's societies; and (3) that the elements of a given culture are often interrelated. However, much of what we see when studying cultures, whether our own or some other, is vulnerable to distortions produced by pre-existing biases. Ethnocentrism is always a danger and Eurocentrism and androcentrism are especially common.

Finally, the most important theoretical perspectives used in the study of culture are: (1) functionalism, (2) conflict theory, (3) cultural materialism, and (4) feminism.

QUESTIONS FOR REVIEW AND CRITICAL THINKING

1. Make a list of at least twenty norms and beliefs you hold and/or activities in which you engage. How would you defend them to an ethnocentric person from another culture? Could you explain smoking cigarettes, drinking alcohol, shaving, dieting, and watching summer reruns or baseball on television to such a person?

2. Choose a set of popular toys and for each toy identify the cultural beliefs and attitudes that it seems to reflect.

3. Read again the argument about Mother Teresa presented in one of the boxes of this chapter. Then identify other individuals who are widely admired in this society, and develop and discuss conflict interpretations of why these individuals are so widely admired.

4. It has been argued that cultural materialism is in the end simply a version of functionalism. How true is this assertion?

GLOSSARY

cultural element anything that (1) is shared in common by the members of some social group; (2) is passed on to new members; and (3) in some way affects their behaviour or their perceptions of the world. Three of the most important elements are values, norms, and roles.

cultural integration the interrelationship of elements in a given culture such that a change in one element can lead to changes, sometimes unexpected, in other elements

cultural materialism a theoretical perspective in which cultural elements are explained by showing how they are pragmatic and rational adaptations to the material environment

cultural universals elements of culture found in all known societies

culture the sum total of all the cultural elements associated with a given social group

ethnocentrism seeing things from the perspective of one's own culture. It includes the belief that one's own culture is superior to others and the belief that what is true of one's culture is true of others. Two of its major variants as they affect the study of culture are *androcentrism* and *Eurocentrism.*

folkways those norms that when violated do not provoke a strong reaction on the part of group members

functionalism applied to culture, the theoretical perspective that explains cultural elements by showing how they contribute to societal stability

institution a specific set of norms and values that the members of a society use to regulate some broad area of social life

material culture the physical objects manufactured or used by the members of a society or subculture

mores those norms that when violated provoke a relatively strong reaction on the part of group members

norms relatively precise rules specifying the behaviours permitted and prohibited for group members

popular culture those preferences and objects that are widely distributed across all social classes in a society

role a cluster of behavioural expectations associated with some particular social position within a group or society

role conflict a situation in which the behavioural expectations of one role are inconsistent with those of a concurrent role

society a group of people who reside in the same geographical area, who communicate extensively among themselves, and who share a common culture

subculture a subset of individuals within a society who are characterized by certain cultural elements that set them apart from others in the society

urban legends oral stories of the recent past, which, although believed to be true, are actually false and reflect unconscious fears

values relatively general beliefs that define right and wrong, or indicate general preferences

SUGGESTED READINGS

Harris, Marvin

1985 *Good to Eat*. New York: Simon and Schuster.

Harris applies cultural materialism to a wide range of food taboos and food preferences, and in the process responds to criticisms made of earlier versions of his arguments. Some of his analyses seem stronger than others, but all are informative and thought provoking.

Lipset, Seymour Martin

1990 *Continental Divide: The Values and Institutions of the United States and Canada*. New York: Routledge.

Lipset systemically compares Canada with the U.S. along a number of different cultural dimensions and relates the differences he finds to the history of each country. His analysis should be read in conjunction with the critiques mentioned in the text.

Mead, Margaret

1935 *Sex and Temperament in Three Primitive Societies*. New York: Morrow.

This is one of the all-time classics in social science. By considering in depth three cultures radically different from our own, at least with regard to sex roles, Mead very forcibly establishes just how much the content of cultures can vary.

Ward, Martha C.

1996 *A World Full of Women*. Boston: Allyn & Bacon.

This book mixes anthropology and sociology in order to focus on activities involving women in a variety of societies, including our own, while simultaneously developing various critiques of the ways that these activities have been viewed by traditional anthropologists and sociologists. It is written for the beginning student.

WEB SITES

http://pubweb.web.co.za/arthur/leglist.html

Legendary Site of the Week

Legends are an integral aspect of society's culture and one of the most intriguing. At this site, read about the latest in mythology, folklore, and urban legends from around the world.

http://www.yahoo.com/text/Regional/Countries/

Yahoo! Country Index

Ever been to Benin, Djibouti, or Mongolia? Make a virtual visit and learn all about cultures from around the world courtesy of this Yahoo! site.

STEAK
ON A KAISER
with
FRENCH FRIES
&
SMALL DRINK
only $4.90
CHICKEN WINGS
FRENCH FRIES
WE SELL
CIGARETTES
FISH & CHIPS
AND SMALL DRINK
only $3.50
SPECIAL
SPECIAL

CHAPTER

4

Socialization

William R. Avison & John H. Kunkel

INTRODUCTION

Every day Canada is invaded by hordes of illiterate barbarians—otherwise known as babies. Yet as they grow older, these babies gradually learn the different roles and skills, the language and norms, and the ideas and beliefs that make it possible for them to develop unique personalities, to get along in and contribute to Canadian society.

The complex lifelong process through which infants become distinct individuals and functioning members of the social group is called **socialization**. This term refers to the acquisition and acceptance of a society's ideas, beliefs, behaviours, roles, motives, thought patterns, and other aspects of day-to-day living. Socialization also implies that society is the source of what is learned. Society's influence may be direct, as when teachers tell students about grammar and mathematics, when parents show their children what to do and believe, or when peers indicate what thoughts are proper and acceptable in a group. Many influences, however, are indirect, as when literature and music convey the meaning and context of culture, or when the mass media interpret current events.

It is also important to note that while sociologists speak of people being socialized into a singular culture, they recognize that individuals may be similarly socialized into various subcultures, such as those represented by ethnic or religious groups.

We can see the significance and dramatic effects of socialization more clearly by examining children raised in nonhuman environments. While there are no well-documented cases of *feral children* (children raised by animals), there have been several instances of children raised together with animals or raised in isolation. Davis (1947), for example, reported the case of Isabelle. This child had contact only with her deaf mother, and for six years lived alone in a dark room apart from the rest of her family. When discovered, she could only croak, was terrified of other people, and in many ways behaved like a frightened animal. But with extensive human contact and professional care, she quickly took on human social characteristics. Within a year, she could speak, write, and add, and at the age of eight and a half, she had caught up with her peers (see the box entitled "Girl in Coop Acts Like Chicken").

Yet, while socialization indicates *how* newborn biological organisms become functioning adult members of society (i.e. through contact with other humans), the process itself does not dictate *what* is learned or how individuals *should* function. Thus, for example, children growing up in any one of Canada's subcultures may be as well socialized as those who grow up within mainstream society. They differ only in the content of the socialization process they have experienced. Indeed, some criminologists have pointed out that it is incorrect to think even of juvenile delinquents as not having been socialized.

Girl in Coop Acts Like Chicken

In the summer of 1980, newspapers carried the story of Isabel Queresma, a nine-year-old girl who had spent most of her days in a chicken coop. She lived with her developmentally disabled mother in a village near Coimbra, in central Portugal. For more than eight years, the mother locked Isabel in a chicken coop in the mornings, gave her the same feed as the chickens (corn and cabbage), and went off to work in the fields. As the mother explained: "Where else could I leave her? I couldn't take her with me, though I feel sorry for her. But she tears and breaks everything up."

Having spent most of her waking hours in the company of chickens, Isabel acted like one. She could not talk and made only squealing sounds, took very small and quick steps, and flapped her arms like wings. Isabel was brought to an institution for the low-functioning developmentally disabled in Lisbon, but she showed no real progress there.

Is such an institution the right place for her? Would your family be a better place for her?

Source: *Adapted from the* London Free Press, *1 July 1980.*

(We shall have more to say on that topic in Chapter 5, Deviance.) Individuals who grow up in subcultures in which "bad" language and lying are accepted, for instance, or where aggression and stealing are respected, are likely to believe that conventional middle-class actions and values are strange and "deviant." Such youngsters are usually quite well socialized, but into a subculture somewhat distinct from the culture of the larger society.

Culture, subcultures, and cultural differences, then, are perpetuated through socialization. But changes, too, can be produced and passed on. Parents typically raise children according to conventional norms; but parents also remember how they were raised, what they missed and enjoyed, and the problems they had. In many ways, parents take into account their own childhood experiences, current circumstances, and the future they expect for their children. These factors often lead to changes in the practices and content of socialization for their children.

THE SOCIALIZATION PROCESS

The social context

Over the years, every person is subjected to many different socialization experiences and lives through a great variety of external events, many of which leave an imprint and affect memories of the past, interpretations of the present, and hopes for the future. Thus, socialization is not a simple cloning process.

For example, in our society, as in most others, boys are raised differently from girls. Parents enforce different rules, have different expectations, give different kinds of presents, and often treat boys and girls very differently. Even when parents make deliberate efforts to treat a daughter and son in the same way, the chances are that relatives, schools, and the larger community will socialize one to meet the cultural definitions of "woman" and the other to fulfil the roles of "man." (We shall discuss this topic more fully in Chapter 6, Gender Relations.) Moreover, even two physiologically normal and intellectually equal children of the same sex who grow up within the same family will have quite different experiences. One is always the younger child; the other has no older sibling. One may be the first born, treated as "mommy's darling," the other an unwanted "accident."

Such variations in a child's early years often (but not always) have significant effects, which last throughout life. Rare indeed are siblings who have the same histories of childhood illnesses, accidents, bruises, or broken bones. Birth order, especially, appears to have several interesting implications (Sulloway, 1996). For example, when first-born children become adults, they tend to be defenders of the status quo in a wide variety of activities, ranging from politics (voting for conservatives) to science (supporting current theories). Presumably this tendency is due to the fact that first-borns usually benefit from existing arrangements; within the family they are likely to have numerous advantages over their younger siblings. When later-born children become adults, they tend to question existing arrangements in numerous areas, for example by being liberals in politics and by defending new scientific theories. A major reason for this willingness to consider and accept new ideas is that these individuals have little to gain from the existing family arrangements and thus have long been open to try new things. The Copernican revolution in astronomy in the sixteenth century, for example, and Darwin's theory of evolution in the nineteenth century were supported largely by scientists who had been later-born children.

Furthermore, in our society, first-born children are likely to be raised by parents who are early in their careers and must count their pennies, and who may have long and frequent interactions with their offspring. But a third or fourth child is likely to grow up when parents are better established in their occupations, and can afford less time but many toys. Most of these children's interactions will probably be with only slightly older siblings, who may provide little stimulation.

Socialization begins at birth and continues throughout life.

The adults who emerge from any family, then, will have some common characteristics, such as language, but they will probably have significant differences in many of their memories, beliefs, and even in their world view and philosophy of life. In a famous study of one Mexican family, for example, an anthropologist (Lewis, 1961) published the autobiographies of four grown children of Jesus Sanchez, along with their father's description of his family's life. These five accounts are so diverse, even conflicting, that it is hard to believe they describe one family and one series of events.

Functions of socialization

The importance of socialization is perhaps best understood by considering the three major purposes it fulfils. First, socialization plays a major role in the *development of the individual personality*. One problem in discussing this function is a lack of agreement, even among psychologists, on the definition of personality. It will be sufficient for our needs here to consider personality as the sum of all individual characteristics that make a person unique and distinctive.

The role of socialization in personality development can be stated concisely. Socialization molds individual tastes and preferences, attitudes and values, and tendencies to act in particular ways in specific situations. There are, of course, limits to the extent to which socialization shapes personality. Most of us are aware that there are biological and genetic restrictions to the scope of socializing influences. The extent of these limitations is a thorny question that we shall deal with later in this chapter.

A second function of socialization is *cultural transmission*. Without socialization people would be unable to communicate with others because they would not have learned a common language. They would have no knowledge of the customs, traditions, norms, or laws of their society, and no sense of their role or place in the social fabric of their culture.

Socialization serves a third important function: *social integration*. Because they have been socialized by other members of their society, people come to share common conceptions of the world—including values, beliefs, norms, and laws—with others in their culture. These similarities may lead them to identify with one another, to recognize that they have similar interests, and, often, to see the advantages of cooperating with one another. As a result, they may be attracted to members of their own culture and interact with them more often than with others. As the members of a society become more integrated, cultural similarities will be further reinforced.

However, as we mentioned earlier, the beliefs, values, norms, and laws that are passed on through socialization are not uniform; they vary. Within our own culture, most people have somewhat different socialization histories, depending on their social and cultural backgrounds. Think of the number of times that you have been in a situation in which you were unsure of the behaviour expected of you. This occurs, for instance, when you attend a service of a religion other than your own, or when you do not know which piece of cutlery to use during a formal dinner.

Biological foundations and limits of socialization

For many years, one of the major debates in the social sciences has focused on the extent to which human behaviour is affected by biological factors as opposed to social or environmental influences. This debate about the effects of **nature versus nurture** is central to the area of socialization. The nature position (or biological determinism) attributes personality characteristics and behaviours to inborn dispositions that have been variously called instincts, inherent traits, or biological propensities. The nurture perspective, on the other hand, argues that human behaviour is independent of biological or genetic influences. Individual personality and actions are conceived to be functions of social or environmental factors. Because of their cognitive abilities, it is argued, human beings have the potential to "overcome" biological and genetic influences. For many years, this debate was waged by social scientists who often took extreme positions. Today, the debate is more sophisticated, and few researchers deny that both social and biological factors play a role in shaping personalities and influencing behaviour. Social scientists now concentrate on discovering which aspects of personality and behaviour are genetically influenced and to what extent. In addition, they are becoming increasingly interested in determining the effect that socializing forces have on identifiable genetic factors.

In fact, it is now accepted that biological characteristics influence personality and behaviour in at least three ways. First, human physiologies are such that humans have certain abilities as a species. The structure of their jaws, mouth, and tongue makes vocalization, and thus language, possible. Their opposable thumbs can touch the tips of their other four fingers and so manipulate tools. Such basic characteristics clearly create the opportunities for certain kinds of behaviour. Second, human physical traits, such as sex and age, also structure personality and social behaviour. Across most cultures, these characteristics are bases for social differentiation. (We mentioned this in the last chapter and shall cover this topic more fully in Chapters 6, Gender Relations, and 7, Social Stratification.) The results—socially assigned identities and roles—lead to different socialization and life experiences for individuals. In these two ways, then, we see how basic biological differences, such as human physiology and individual physical attributes, contribute to variations in human personality and behaviour.

The third way biology influences personality and behaviour is subject to intense debate, but there is good reason to believe that genetic make-up has

Both genetic and environmental factors affect human personality and behaviour.

some direct effect. Researchers use a number of different methods to estimate the effects of genetic make-up on behaviour and personality. One approach involves the comparison of monozygotic and dizygotic twins. Monozygotic twins develop from the splitting of the same egg and have identical genes; people refer to them as identical twins because they are physically so similar to each other. Dizygotic or fraternal twins are like any pair of siblings except that they are born at the same time. They develop from two separately fertilized eggs and, like ordinary brothers or sisters, they do not have exactly the same genes. If monozygotic twins are more similar to each other in their behaviour than are dizygotic twins, this provides evidence, the nature argument goes, that the behaviour or personality trait being measured is more likely due to genetic factors than to environment.

Another technique sometimes used to estimate the effects of genetic make-up on behaviour is the study of adopted children. If these children are more similar to the biological parents from whom they have been separated than to their adoptive parents, this provides evidence for genetic contributions to personality development. On the other hand, if they are more like their adoptive parents, this strengthens the nurture argument.

Using such various research methods, social scientists have uncovered evidence that suggests genetic factors do influence certain personality factors and behaviour, including some types of mental illness and behavioural problems. Plomin (1989) presented a very informative summary of the research on these issues. He concluded that two important personality factors, extroversion and neuroticism, appear to be substantially determined by genetic heritability. He also found considerable evidence indicating that the chances of experiencing mental illness, such as schizophrenia or a depressive disorder, are importantly affected by genetic factors. In addition, recent research on crime, delinquency, and alcoholism suggests that biological influences may also affect these behaviours. At the same time, however, most researchers agree that social factors also play an important role in affecting these behaviours.

The most controversial research in the area of genetics versus nurture concerns intelligence. Recent studies of I.Q. (intelligence quotient) scores have revealed a genetic factor to be operative (for an example see Snyderman and Rothman, 1987) and the evidence is impressive in both quantity and quality, but there are still disagreements regarding the degree to which intelligence is inherited. A major focus of this debate concerns the way in which intelligence is measured. A number of social scientists have asserted that I.Q. tests are imperfect measures of intelligence because they are subject to cultural and class-linked biases (see Brody, 1992). It is argued that certain individuals score poorly on I.Q. tests because their family or subculture does not teach them the specific skills that I.Q. tests measure. Another criticism focuses on the stability of I.Q. scores. If intelligence measures vary over time and can be affected by subtle social pressures, then their usefulness is questionable.

Overall, then, there is some evidence for believing that intelligence is affected by genetic factors. At the same time, social or environmental factors such as education and nurturing in the home definitely have an impact (see the boxed insert on "Family Size, Birth Order and Performance.") An "either-or," nature-versus-nurture approach is simplistic. Intelligence, personality, and behaviour are subject to both genetic and environmental factors in concert with each other. Moreover, the discovery of genetic determinants does not mean that human intelligence, personality, and behaviour are unchangeable. Rather, it is more reasonable to state that social factors can override genetic bases in a variety of circumstances. Much work remains to be done in these areas, however, and many questions remain to be answered.

Socialization and the life cycle

Socialization begins at birth and is most evident during infancy and childhood, but it continues throughout life. In childhood, individuals acquire concrete knowledge, such as the beliefs, customs, and activities of their culture. In later years they learn adult roles, such as that of wife and husband; they may become parents. They learn to perform new roles in the community, and eventually they hope to learn how to age gracefully. Indeed, when people cease to participate in the socialization

Family Size, Birth Order, and Performance

Psychologists in several countries have discovered that children's intellectual performance is greatly influenced by the number of children in the family and their sequential position.

First-born children often do better than the second-born. The third-born generally perform more poorly than the first two, the fourth and fifth tend to do worse, and the sixth even more poorly. Furthermore, children from smaller families consistently outperform those from larger families. (Position in the class structure affects children's intellectual achievements primarily through this size variable: wealthier and better-educated families tend to have fewer children.)

Why are family size and birth order so important for intellectual performance? Zajonc's "confluence model" provides a good answer. He proposed that children's mental development depends on the intellectual environment within their family, and that this environment is a function of the absolute intellectual levels of all family members. Here "level" refers to mental maturity and includes factors such as vocabulary, abstract thinking, and I.Q.

Over time, the intellectual environment changes. For example, an adult may leave the family after a divorce, weakening the intellectual environment. More to the point, as more children are born, the average intellectual level of the family declines, if only because of the greater number of immature minds, and the decline is especially rapid if children are born at short intervals. Fourth children live in a more diluted intellectual climate that is very different from that of first-born. In addition, fourth children are likely to interact more with their (intellectually immature) siblings and less with parents than earlier-born children. Language skills are especially likely to suffer when, for years, these siblings reinforce the youngest child's baby-talk.

An additional factor in the superior performance of earlier-born children is the teaching role that they perform for their younger siblings. This role is intellectually stimulating. Thus, one would expect that last children in large families would be especially handicapped, having no one to teach, and oldest children especially advantaged. Only children, on the other hand, grow up in a rather mature intellectual environment that just about compensates for the absence of younger siblings to teach.

Another element is the time between births. Assuming that children must be older than two before they can tutor, and that infants do not make good students, it follows that closely spaced births provide little opportunity for the intellectual stimulation of tutoring younger siblings.

Source: *Adapted from Robert B. Zajonc, 1983. "Validating the confluence model."* Psychological Bulletin *93 (pp. 457–480).*

process, they may no longer fit into groups or be able to play appropriate roles. Others disapprove of individuals who retain selfish ways after marriage, who do not become effective parents, or who cannot accept new responsibilities; and they feel sorry for adults who deny being over fifty, or who show increasing fear of death.

In this lifelong socialization, individuals frequently learn new beliefs and behaviours long before they are required by new roles, and in various ways they rehearse what it is like to be a spouse, a parent, or a president of a company. Such **anticipatory socialization** enables them to slip smoothly into new positions and perform new roles—assuming their models have been adequate.

Over the years, not only do people acquire new beliefs, actions, and motivations, but they also learn that some old ones are no longer adequate or appropriate. This may occur when individuals realize that their beliefs, customs, and activities differ from those of others, and are indeed only a few of life's many possibilities. Or, it may happen when the habits of childhood are finally discarded, or when people are pressured by others to change, perhaps to act their age. Thus **resocialization**, the replacing of old roles and patterns of thinking with new ones, is also an integral part of life. It is frequently difficult, however, for the old ways interfere with the learning of new ones, and it is not always easy to recognize when the old habits are no longer effective. Studies of prisons, for example, show that new inmates often are subjected to a rather painful resocialization process during which they unlearn bad habits and learn to become "good prisoners."

MAJOR COMPONENTS OF SOCIALIZATION

Perhaps the best way to analyze socialization is to break it down into two major components and to study each in some detail. The most important process is *language acquisition*—including its nature, use, and implications—for it is through language and symbols that people acquire culture. The second process is *learning*, through which individuals acquire beliefs, motives, and ideas, as well as the activities that characterize daily life. These two topics will be discussed in the next two sections.

Language

The nature of language

Some of the happiest occasions within families occur when babies utter their first words. Initially vocabulary is limited, but it expands rapidly until the children have developed a relatively sophisticated means of communicating with others. This process by which language development occurs is central to socialization. Indeed, one of the major functions of families is to assist children in learning a language.

Language is not only a product of socialization but also one of the major processes by which further socialization occurs. Once children have learned a language, the normative expectations, beliefs, and values of a culture can be communicated efficiently to them. Thus, language occupies a unique position in socialization: it is at once a product of socialization and a tool for further cultural learning.

Because people have learned the language of their culture and use it constantly, they seldom pause to think about it. What is language? How is it acquired? What is the relationship between language and culture? These key questions must be answered to understand its important role.

Language is a system of communication that involves the written or verbal communication of shared symbols. All human societies have developed some form of verbal communication and many have a written system as well. While languages differ widely from one another, they also share a number of important characteristics and functions. Let us examine some of these common characteristics.

Most importantly, language is *symbolic*. A symbol is simply a sound or action that stands for something else. In English, the sound uttered for the word *dog* stands for a four-legged, hairy mammal that many Canadians keep as a pet. In French, that same animal is designated *le chien*. The fact that different languages use different symbols to refer to the same thing demonstrates that symbols are shared within, but seldom across, cultures. Indeed, the problems individuals have in learning another language are largely due to difficulties in learning new symbols for objects that already have symbols in their own language.

Second, language is *ideational*. It provides a tool for communicating abstract ideas and concepts. In addition to symbols that are shorthand references to hairy mammals and other concrete objects, language also has symbols such as "love," "patriotism," and "democracy" that refer to very complex feelings, attitudes, values, and ideas.

Another important characteristic of language is its *transmissive* nature. By putting together strings of words in culturally shared ways, people can transmit messages to and exchange ideas with one another. Language is also transmissive in the sense that it continues from one generation to the next. This does not mean, however, that language is constant and unchanging. Indeed, one of the most interesting characteristics of language is its openness. The symbolic content of language is always changing to some degree as new words and definitions (meanings) surface over time. For example, symbols such as "downsizing" and "gigabyte" are relatively new words, while "methinks" and "perchance" are seldom used today. Changes in the meanings of symbols also arise when a particular generation gives a peculiar meaning to a symbol rather than its other, perhaps more usual, meaning. The most obvious examples are slang words, such

The process by which language development occurs is central to socialization.

as "high," referring to the feelings that result from drug and alcohol use rather than to distance above the ground, or "jerk," describing an individual's personality rather than a sharp pull or twist.

The functions of language

Now that we have described the most important characteristics of language, its functions should be more apparent. Language occupies a key role in the development, maintenance, and evolution of a culture. While it is possible to list a large number of purposes that language serves, these can be summarized in three major overlapping functions: *identification*, *integration*, and *socialization*.

Language is often the most easily recognized sign of cultural background. Simply, language enables people to identify other individuals immediately as English, French, Polish, etc. Given this initial information, people often make inferences about other aspects of the speaker's background or personality. The inferences may or may not be correct; nevertheless, people use language to categorize others. Further, language not only identifies cultural origins, it can also assist in identifying social background within a particular culture. For example, many Canadians recognize a distinctive style of speaking that is common among Newfoundlanders, and Newfoundlanders can recognize various mainland accents.

Language may assist in identifying more than just regionality. People's speech patterns often give clues about their social standing. For example, if asked whether they have tickets to the Grey Cup, one person might answer, "I ain't got none," while another might respond, "I don't have any." Most observers would assume that the first person is not as well educated as the second; many would assume that the second person probably occupies a higher social standing.

At the same time that people identify and categorize others on the basis of their language, they also judge them to be more or less like themselves. Sharing the same language can provide a sense of identity with others. This sharing can form the basis for interaction and for a search for other similarities. A shared language can make easier the exchange of ideas, beliefs, and values among members of a culture, which, in turn, can generate a sense of social solidarity.

This integrating function of language can best be appreciated by looking at societies where the bond of a common language is absent. Canada is, of course, a prime example. At various points in the history of this country, considerable bitterness and division have occurred as a result of the linguistic differences that exist. It has been difficult for many Canadians to think of their society as one unified people or culture. The existence of two major language groups has contributed in part to numerous political, legal, and cultural disputes that have restricted the extent of social integration in this country. We shall discuss these topics more fully in other chapters, and mention them now only to illustrate the integrating function of language.

The third major function of language is its contribution to the socialization process. One of the most significant aspects of early childhood is the learning of a language; but even in later years, language remains one of the most important tools for further learning.

Language functions as a socializing mechanism in three ways. First, it is the means by which people learn the content of their culture. Parents, teachers, and peers tell them about their cultural heritage by means of the written and spoken word. Without language, it would be almost impossible for them to have any sense of history, any notion of the norms or laws of their society, or any idea of their own identity. Language is the most efficient means for communicating this information; without it people would learn only those things about their culture that they could immediately experience. Canadians would be incapable of knowing much about the Group of Seven, Louis Riel, Jean Chrétien, or Wayne Gretzky if they could not communicate with other members of their culture. Their ability to read, write, and speak a language opens up a whole world of second-hand or indirect experience to them; it allows them to learn about their culture in the most efficient manner possible.

Second, language operates as a powerful agent of social control. At some point parents and teachers begin to rely upon language as the major means for rewarding and punishing children. In early years, children are encouraged with words of praise, and discouraged from misbehaving with verbal scoldings. As they grow older, language becomes even more important as a socializing influence. As students, their performance in the classroom is evaluated and the results are communicated with grades. Later, they are rewarded or punished, depending upon their performance, with good or bad letters of recommendation. In their jobs, they receive not only monetary rewards, but also, often more importantly, verbal recognition that encourages good work.

Third, language has some influence on the ways in which individuals conceptualize the world; but there is considerable disagreement over the extent of this influence. The debate, to which we shall return later, concerns the interrelationships among language, thought, and culture.

The acquisition of language

Now that we have some sense of the nature and functions of language, a perplexing question comes to mind. How do individuals learn a language? Most of us cannot explain how we acquired our first language. Social scientists who have studied this problem have no simple answer either. In fact, there is a major debate over the processes by which human beings acquire the language of their culture.

Briefly stated, one side of this debate is represented by those who advocate **linguistic empiricism** and the other by those who support **linguistic nativism**. Linguistic empiricists argue that children learn the language of their culture through a process of reinforcement that comes from others who already speak that language. Linguistic nativists, on the other hand, insist that all children have innate, genetically determined capabilities for acquiring language, and that they learn language naturally, as a function of normal maturation. Again we see the nature–nurture debate.

Linguistic empiricists explain language acquisition by referring to principles of learning, to be discussed later in this chapter. They assume that infants naturally engage in babbling the sounds of all languages. Parents and older siblings encourage this babbling, but reinforce, by attention and verbal praise, only the few particular sounds that the children emit which are part of their language. Through this process of selective reinforcement, children's range of vocalization is thought to be shaped. Eventually, children are able to utter the many different sounds that comprise the various words that are recognizable in that culture. Through imitation and further reinforcement, children are able to say certain words. Then, as they mature, they learn to put words together in combinations: "Mommy go," for example. The continuing processes of imitation and reinforcement allow children to construct increasingly more complicated strings of words and to learn that some words fit together better than others.

The linguistic nativists argue that such a learning process is quite unlikely. Because language is infinitely variable (there are innumerable ways of stringing together words), it is impossible for children to learn the complexities of a language in the inefficient manner described by the linguistic empiricists. Nativists believe, instead, that human beings are born with some sort of *generative mechanism* that makes possible the acquisition of a language: rather than learning words or utterances, they say, individuals unconsciously learn the *productive rules* that govern the structures of their language and enable them to use creatively the symbolic content of their culture.

One convincing resolution of this debate is the idea that the acquisition of language is a function of the *interaction* of genetic and cultural factors. This position has been presented effectively in Lenneberg's (1967) classic work. In it he showed that there is a critical period in early childhood during which individuals are most capable of learning a language. Beyond this time period, the acquisition of a language becomes more difficult. Lenneberg estimated that most children complete the major stages of language acquisition by their third birthday, and that from three to ten years of age they refine their grammar and expand their vocabularies.

Cultural learning modifies linguistic use during and after this critical period. The speed with which children acquire language and the sophistication of their vocabularies are undoubtedly due to imitation and reinforcement. In addition, the learning of specific names or symbols for objects in a specific culture is obviously culturally determined. In London, England, people may learn of nappies, spanners, and lifts, while in London, Ontario, the same objects would be diapers, wrenches, and elevators.

In sum, while the basic propensity for learning a language appears to be determined biologically, the learning process is certainly affected by social factors. Thus, we can resolve the linguistic nativism–linguistic empiricism debate with a conclusion analogous to the one resolving the more general nature–nurture debate: language is acquired in the context of an interaction of biological and cultural factors.

Language, thought, and culture

Earlier we noted that language functions as a socialization tool because it influences how we think about or conceptualize the world around us. This point of view stems from anthropological observations of various cultures. In one of the many studies on this subject, researchers noted that the Inuit have several different words for snow: *nutagak* denotes fresh, powder snow, *aniu* means packed snow, *sillik* refers to hard, crusty snow, and so on. For another example, while English has a great capacity for distinguishing among various flying objects—airplanes, helicopters, birds, flies, etc.—the Hopi Indians have a single word that refers to everything that flies, other than birds.

Several different conclusions have been drawn from these observations. **Linguistic relativism** suggests that the nature of language determines and limits the thought patterns of the people who speak it. Another position, **linguistic universalism**, holds that linguistic differences reflect only variations in cultural experiences but do not directly affect patterns of thought in any permanent, unalterable manner.

Whorf (1956) is most closely identified with linguistic relativism. He spent much of his time studying the linguistic patterns of American Indian tribes and observed that differences among the tribes in naming things corresponded to differences in the content of their cultures. For example, Whorf reported that the Navaho language had no means for distinguishing between time and motion, making it impossible for them to comprehend the laws of physics: their system of language cannot accommodate these principles. Whorf therefore concluded that language is a major influence on thought, that a culture's language describes and perpetuates that group's view of the world, and, by implication, that individuals cannot think without having a language.

The opposite viewpoint, linguistic universalism, stresses that differences in language are simply a function of different cultural experiences and do not reflect different thought patterns. Lenneberg (1967) summarized evidence to demonstrate that individuals seem to perceive first (and their culture may direct their attention to what they should perceive), and then attach words to what they observe. Thus, for the linguistic universalist, the various names that Inuit attach to snow are the result of their greater contact with it and their greater need to understand this element of their environment. Furthermore, other Canadians also can distinguish among different types of snow if required. While they do not have one simple word for each kind, they simply add adjectives to describe what they perceive.

As with the debate over the acquisition of language, a middle ground in this conflict makes considerable sense. Most students of language use now accept a weaker version of the Whorfian hypothesis of linguistic relativism. It seems reasonable to believe that cultural experiences exert some influence on the nature of language. In learning a language, people learn names or symbols for objects that are important in their culture. The fact that one culture has a limited number of names for certain things likely blinds it to subtle differences among such things. But the fact that a culture has a wide variety of names for other things makes it just as likely that its awareness of subtle differences among these things is heightened. Most Canadians tend to ignore differences in snow but are aware of variations in different models of automobiles, and the Inuit people's perceptions are similarly influenced: they see many different kinds of snow but are less sensitive to variations in automobiles. But this is not irreversible. Other Canadians can make subtle distinctions about snow if they must; skiers do so regularly. The Inuit could distinguish between an Oldsmobile sedan and a Chrysler station wagon in their own language, given time, enough examples, and necessity.

Learning

In psychology, while there is still some debate concerning the exact nature of learning, there is considerable agreement about learning procedures, the conditions under which learning occurs, and the factors that influence the learning rate. Furthermore, psychologists know quite well how behaviour is maintained, changed, and eliminated. Sociologists have all the knowledge they need, then, concerning the internal processes that underlie learning and the reasons an activity remains or disappears. Nevertheless, much remains to be said about the social factors involved in learning.

By now there are literally thousands of studies in experimental and natural settings, involving people of all ages, capacities, and backgrounds, and concerned with a wide range of simple and complex behaviours. The results of these studies are summarized in the general principle that human behaviour is largely determined by the consequences individuals expect to follow their behaviour. These expected consequences are generally based on individuals' past experiences in similar situations or on their observations of what happens to other people in similar situations (Bandura, 1986).

The consequences of an action can be positive or negative, slight or significant. They may occur soon after the behaviour or much later; they may happen rarely, often, or always; and finally, they may be real or imaginary. People assess the magnitudes and probabilities of the several consequences they foresee and combine them into one overall consequence, which then influences their choice of action. Individuals may not be aware of all the factors they take into account in these considerations, and much of the assessment may be subconscious.

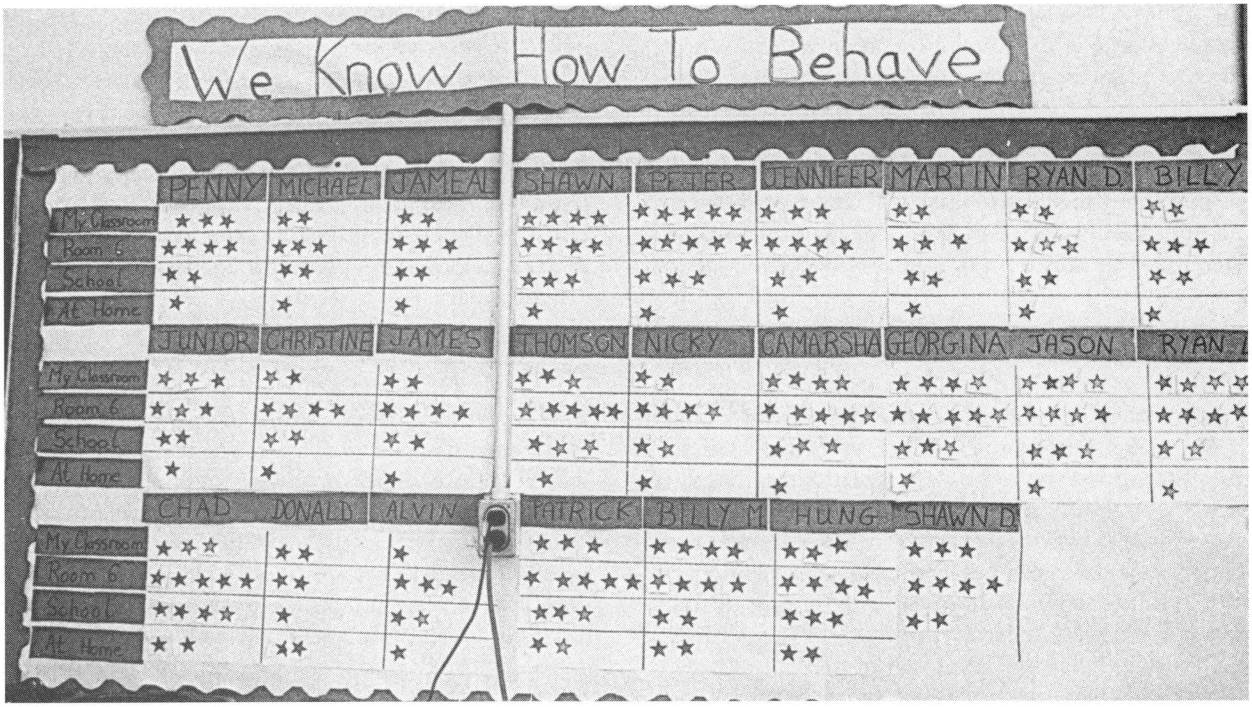

A positive consequence and the context of an action are both significant determinants of behaviour.

Indeed, many activities of daily life are repeated so often that people may not even be aware of the information they are processing. When people develop a habit of taking a certain road to school or work each day, for example, they may not realize that they do this because of the positive consequence, usually called a *reinforcer* or *reward*, which in this case may simply be the quickest and easiest journey possible.

When the overall consequence of an action is positive, the probability of repeating that behaviour increases (or we may say that the activity is strengthened). For example, people who are good (and therefore receive a positive consequence) at math are more likely to continue taking math courses. Conversely, when the overall consequence of an action is negative, the probability of repeating the action declines (or we may say that the behaviour is weakened). People who do poorly (a negative consequence) in sports may avoid them. Behaviour is maintained, sometimes for decades, as in the case of speaking a society's language, when the positive consequences people expect on the basis of past experience actually occur (as when others respond).

A somewhat less significant determinant of behaviour is the *context* in which the action occurs. When people recognize their friends and neighbours at a funeral, they quietly exchange greetings. Part of the context (funeral) serves as a signal that tells them the likely consequences (stares) were they to talk and joke loudly as they do normally.

Thus, any behaviour or complex chain of activities, such as writing a term paper, is the central element of a triad:

context ➔ behaviour ➔ (expected) consequence

The activities permitted or acceptable in any situation, the definitions of "significant" elements of the context, and the content of the "positive" consequences expected vary from one culture to another and over time. Old Order Mennonites define driving a car differently from the way other Canadians do; Christians and non-Christians define

Good Friday differently; and drinkers and non-drinkers would define a beer differently. Sociologists also recognize that there may be subcultural differences in all these elements, not to mention individual variations based on prior socialization experiences. For example, early experiences in reading and abstract thinking, or parental encouragement in mathematics or music, or even the need to deal with numbers in youth (e.g., having a paper route) all vary greatly, and thus some variations in the performance of adults even within the same culture should be expected.

While the basic behavioural principles are relatively simple and the number of relevant variables quite small, daily life usually involves several of them simultaneously, thus leading to considerable complexity. Often these principles and relevant variables are summarized into rules, and social scientists have recently begun to analyze the processes underlying "rule-governed behaviour." (Not all people, of course, understand rules in quite the same way. See Chapter 5, Deviance, for more on this topic.) Most people learn to recognize a yellow traffic light, for example, as a sign to slow down and stop, but for some people it may well be a sign to speed up and beat the red. Similarly, some people learn that a speed limit sign means that they should slow down, while others drive within the speed limit only when they see a police car parked nearby, or when the area has the reputation of being a speed trap. In short, individuals not only learn different activities, but also different meanings in the same context. They learn different expectations of consequences and they have different views of what is "rewarding."

What we must remember is that *perceptions* of context and consequence matter (a central tenet of symbolic interactionism), more so than the actual events. People who view earthly life as a "vale of tears" and who focus on the afterlife will probably behave differently from individuals who believe that life on earth is the only form of existence. The former are likely to value material goods less than the latter; hence the same material consequence (e.g., a high income and what it can buy) will be less significant and powerful in determining their behaviour. Evidently, the analysis of real people and events is much more difficult and complex than the behavioural principles themselves might lead us to suspect.

Moreover, most consequences of activities in daily life are symbolic rather than material—other people's praise or expressions of esteem, for example. While most consequences involve humans (people praise, sell food to, or frown at others), some consequences, especially rewards, are intrinsic parts of the activities themselves—for example, the satisfaction gained from playing a good game of chess, even a losing one, or reading an interesting book, even when not required. Finally, consequences frequently are self-administered. For example, individuals may reward themselves with particular consequences after accomplishing particular behaviour: watch TV only after finishing a math assignment, or say to themselves, "Hey, I've written a pretty good paper." Indeed, Bandura's (1986) work indicates that most daily activities, certainly the efforts of artists and composers, are largely maintained by self-reinforcement. Of course, people also punish themselves for other behaviour: "Boy, I really goofed on that assignment." Most individuals learn early, with the help of parents, to reinforce or curb activities, so that they eventually perform them or avoid them without recognizing what is happening. Eventually they simply feel good or guilty after various activities, even when there are no apparent external consequences. No wonder that people, seeing no evident rewards, ponder why others act as they do.

Many new activities are learned through *modelling* (see the box entitled "Learning Through Immitation"). In this process, individuals observe how a model (usually another person similar to them or someone they want to be like) behaves in a specific context, and then observe whether the model's behaviour is rewarded. Later, when they find themselves in a situation similar to the model's, they may try out the new behaviour previously observed, expecting that any positive consequences the model received will recur in their own case (**vicarious reinforcement**). Verbal instructions, or reading about other people's actions and consequences, will affect them similarly. If they try the new behaviour themselves and positive consequences follow, the behaviour will be maintained and the person observed, actually or verbally, will remain a significant model. But if their initial efforts are not rewarded, the new behaviour is not likely to be repeated and the person observed will become a less significant model. Moreover, just as people learn from a model what to do, they can also learn, when the model's actions are followed by negative consequences, what not to do (**vicarious punishment**).

An understanding of these learning principles can help in determining which activities have a largely genetic base. The term *aggression*, for example, covers a great variety of activities. Not only is the label applied to many different behaviours, but the same activities are sometimes viewed as aggressive and at other times not so. A careful study by Bandura (1973) showed that the decision to attach the label "aggression" to an action depends on the victim's reactions, the circumstances in which the aggressive act occurs, an understanding of the situation and the individuals involved, and, indeed, any identification by the observer with the aggressor or the victim. When one child hits another, for example, others label the action an "aggression" if the recipient cries or expresses pain, if they judge the hitter's facial expression to be mean, if they can see no reason for the act (perhaps because they do not know the history of the relationship), or if they do not know that the children frequently rough-house and belong to a subculture that encourages such behaviour. The most important factors determining the

Learning Through Imitation: A Hockey Analogy

Much of human behaviour is learned through modelling others. In The Game, *Ken Dryden (1983) recalls some examples of modelling.*

In the late 1950s, the CBS network televised NHL games on Saturday afternoon. Before each game, there was a preview show in which a player from each of the teams involved that day would compete in two contests, one of which was a penalty-shot contest. The goalie they used each week was an assistant trainer for the Detroit Red Wings named Julian Klymquiw. Short and left-handed, Klymquiw wore a clear plexiglass mask that arched in front of his face like a shield. None of us had ever heard of him, and his unlikely name made us a little doubtful at first. But it turned out that he was quite good, and most weeks he stopped the great majority of shots taken at him. So, during backyard games of "penalty shots," we pretended to be Julian Klymquiw, not Terry Sawchuk or Glenn Hall. And before each of our contests began, we would perform the ritual that Klymquiw and announcer Bud Palmer performed each week:

"Are you ready, Julian?"

"Yes, Bud."

But the backyard also meant time alone. It was usually after dinner when the "big guys" had homework to do and I would turn on the floodlights at either end of the house and on the porch, and play. It was a private game. I would stand alone in the middle of the yard, a stick in my hands, a tennis ball in front of me, silent, still, then suddenly dash ahead, stickhandling furiously, dodging invisible obstacles for a shot on net. It was Maple Leaf Gardens filled to wildly cheering capacity, a tie game, seconds remaining. I was Frank Mahovlich, or Gordie Howe, I was anyone I wanted to be, and the voice in my head was that of Leafs broadcaster Foster Hewitt: "... there's ten seconds left, Mahovlich, winding up at his own line, at centre, eight seconds, seven, over the blueline, six—he winds up, he shoots, he scores!" The mesh that had been tied to the bottoms of our red metal goalposts until frozen in the ice had been ripped away to hang loose from the crossbars, whipped back like a flag in a stiff breeze. My arms and stick flew into the air, I screamed a scream inside my head, and collected my ball to do it again—many times, for many minutes, the hero of all my own games.

It was a glorious fantasy, and I always heard that voice. It was what made my fantasy seem almost real. For to us, who attended hockey games mostly on TV or radio, an NHL game, a Leafs game, was played with a voice. If I wanted to be Mahovlich or Howe, if I moved my body the way I had seen them move theirs and did nothing else, it would never quite work. But if I heard the voice that said their names while I was playing out that fantasy, I could believe it. Foster Hewitt could make me them.

Source: *K. Dryden, 1983.* The Game. *Toronto: Macmillan (pp. 55–56). Reprinted by permission of Macmillan of Canada, A Division of Canada Publishing Corporation, Toronto.*

use of the aggression label are the recipient's painful reaction and the seemingly insufficient reason for the so-called aggressive action. Furthermore, as Bandura pointed out, aggressive acts are frequently encouraged and indeed rewarded. For example, many societies value both physical strength and the ability to take care of oneself. Thus, people learn to be aggressive, and many kinds of aggression are followed by positive consequences. Hence, genetic factors are not nearly as significant as many people believe.

In summary, psychologists generally are interested in the nature of learning and in studying the factors that influence the shaping, maintenance, modification, and extinction of behaviour. Sociologists, however, tend to take the principles of social learning—the *how* of learning—for granted and focus attention on what is learned by individuals in a society, subculture, neighbourhood, and family. In later chapters we shall see some of the problems that arise when individuals learn different, possibly conflicting things in different social contexts, and we shall see some of the difficulties people experience when they apply what they learned in their youth to their old age, after many changes have occurred.

THEORETICAL APPROACHES TO SOCIALIZATION

Socialization has been studied for several decades, yet our understanding of the process is by no means complete. Indeed, much of what is known about socialization takes the form of theories that reflect one or another view of human nature, behaviour, and society. Some of these theories are based on the results of observation and experiments. Others are derived from more global theories designed to explain all human and social behaviour. Moreover, because socialization can be approached from two distinct starting points, the individual and the society, work done in both psychology and sociology must be considered.

Most psychologists interested in socialization emphasize only a particular aspect of learning or the process of learning itself. A few, such as the followers of Freud (1935) and Maslow (1954), concentrate on the development of the whole human being. Sociologists, on the other hand, tend to emphasize the role of cultural influences and the development of the social individual. They take learning itself for granted and instead focus on the social context of learning and on its implications for the development of individuals who are functioning members of a society and its subcultures.

The theories of socialization that are popular today reflect one or another of three major perspectives regarding personality development. From psychology come the *psychodynamic perspective* and the *cognitive perspective*; from sociology, the *symbolic interactionist perspective*.

The psychodynamic perspective

Writers who adopt this view emphasize a great variety of internal characteristics and processes. We shall consider two examples: Freud's *theory of personality* and Erikson's *theory of life stages*.

Freud: personality development

Today's best-known and most controversial personality theory was developed around the turn of the century by the Viennese physician Sigmund Freud (1935). His theory is based largely on the insights which he derived from his own difficulties and those of his patients.

Freud postulated that the personality of the normal adult consists of three major components. The unconscious forces and instincts with which humans are born are collectively called the **id**. With its physiological basis, the id is the major source of psychic energies (aggressive and libidinal, or sexual) that can be stored, repressed, guided, and expended. The id is that aspect of personality which is impulsive, selfish, and pleasure-seeking, and it operates quite independently of society or culture. As individuals grow up, culture—initially through parents and later through various institutions—represses some aspects of the id. Gradually there emerges the **ego**, consisting of the intellectual and cognitive processes that make individuals unique with certain ideas, beliefs, memories, hopes, and fears. Most of the ego is conscious, and its interactions with the world are guided by the reality principle: ideas and actions are modified to fit the real world, dependent on actual experiences. The third component of personality—the **superego**—consists largely of what is generally called "conscience." Mainly through interactions with their families, individuals acquire the many values and rules of their culture, or, as some would put it, they internalize their society's norms. These values or norms can then guide the ego in reconciling the forces of the id with the limitations and requirements of culture.

The id and its physiological bases, according to Freudians, are largely the same for all human beings. But each culture, operating through such agents as families, schools, and religious institutions (and their equivalents in nonindustrial societies), produces its own type of superego and ego. Indeed, with these two personality components, there are often variations even within a culture. During the socialization process, various elements of the id are repressed to some degree; in fact, the repression of id forces, such as aggression, makes civilization possible. Unfortunately, there is no way to determine which aspects of the id must be repressed, or how much, or in what manner; hence, civilization always produces some degree of discontent.

Normal individuals pass through several stages (first *oral*, then *anal*, *phallic*, *latency*, and finally, *general*), which end in a healthy, mature personality consisting of a strong ego and a well-developed superego (which channels libidinal forces in appropriate directions). The path to adulthood is long and difficult, however, and filled with many conflicts.

Freud's theories have been criticized on many grounds; we will mention only two. First, much of the internal state, such as the components and development of personality, is difficult to investigate empirically. Freud himself considered id, ego, and superego as *hypothetical constructs*, and not real or measurable. The only basis for saying that someone has a strong or weak ego, for example, is the individual's behaviour, from which an observer must infer an internal condition. But another observer who holds a different view of human nature may well reach an entirely different conclusion about the same individual's behaviour. Although the theory prescribes the internal element to look for, inferring the element's existence does not mean it is actually there.

A second major problem is the presumed universality of Freud's concepts and propositions. There is considerable evidence that his concepts are time- and culture-bound, more applicable to upper-middle-class patients of the 1890s and 1900s (the major source of his data) than to other groups. The anthropologist Malinowski (1927), for example, did not find evidence of Freud's *Oedipal conflict* (the tendency for children to direct some sexual attention to the parent of the opposite sex) among the Trobriand Islanders, the group described in the discussion of magic in Chapter 3, Culture. Among the people of those Pacific islands, there is frequent conflict between a boy and his maternal uncle, not his father, largely because the uncle, not the father, is in charge of his discipline. Malinowski concluded that the root of the Oedipal conflict is the family's authority structure rather than the sexual competition of father and son. Feminists are also critical of Freud's assumptions about women (Chodorow, 1978). We shall return to that topic in Chapter 5, Deviance.

Erikson: life stages

Probably the best-known "neo-Freudian" is Erik H. Erikson (1963). One of his major contributions is his description of the eight stages through which most persons pass in the course of a lifetime. He called his theory *psychosocial* because each stage of ego development involves the interaction of the individual's gradually maturing psychological characteristics and the social context of any one time. The stages are not of any particular length, and some people pass through them faster than others. Generally, however, the tasks associated with each stage (such as solving problems and overcoming difficulties) must be successfully completed before going on to the next stage. Incomplete tasks may well mean that the individual will have to return to that stage later, or at least will have considerable trouble when presented with situations requiring skills that should have been mastered previously.

The years of infancy and childhood include four stages. Ideally, during the first stage children develop basic trust (versus distrust); in the second, autonomy (versus shame and doubt); in the third, initiative (versus guilt); and in the fourth, industry (versus inferiority).

During adolescence, the fifth stage, individuals develop a sense of identity. This is frequently a period of identity confusion and identity crises. During the sixth stage, young adults develop intimacy (rather than isolation), while during the seventh stage of full maturity, individuals face the problem of choosing between creativity and stagnation. In the last stage, which is usually entered in old age, individuals must come to terms with the overall quality and evaluation of their lives. Here the major alternatives are integrity or despair.

In each of these eight stages, individuals face difficulties that must be overcome and choices that must be made. Both require interaction with people, and the social context may help or hinder the passage through the stages. Parents and friends are significant throughout life, particularly in the early stages. Co-workers, the people met in the course of daily life, and even strangers may also serve as significant partners in a lifelong series of interactions. These interactions help individuals to pass successfully through the several stages; they help provide a firm sense of identity and the conviction of a useful life.

The cognitive perspective

Not everyone is convinced that the present knowledge of human characteristics is sufficient to construct viable global theories of personality development. Hence, there are also more modest efforts to describe and explain specific aspects of human beings—especially their ways of thinking, and of seeing the social world. For example, cognitive theories explain behaviour in terms of the development of perceptions and thought processes. In this section we will consider a cognitive explanation of "ethical" or "moral" behaviour—Piaget's theory of moral development.

Piaget: moral development

The Swiss psychologist Piaget (1965) was initially interested in children's cognitive development, and especially in progressive changes in reasoning. Through systematic observations of both his own and other children, he discovered that as children mature they use increasingly complex cognitive processes, evaluate more information, and employ more extensive time frames. All individuals pass through the same stages of cognitive development, he maintained, although the speed at which they do so may vary greatly.

Moral development proceeds at the same time as cognitive development and, according to Piaget, it also occurs in stages. During the first stage (from the age of about four to seven) children believe that ethical rules are absolute and come from some higher external authority such as parents. Thus Piaget called this stage the **morality of constraints**, sometimes called *moral realism*. External restrictions (e.g., from parents) on behaviour and the consequences of actions are of prime importance, while intentions do not matter much. Children believe that wrong acts are always punished, and that punishment plays a major part in defining wrong acts.

Between the ages of about seven and nine, most children change their frame of reference, so to speak, to one that Piaget called the **morality of cooperation**, sometimes called *moral autonomy*. Rules (and later on, laws) come to be seen as products of deliberation and agreement, such as the give-and-take on playgrounds, discussions within families, and debates in legislative assemblies. Now motives become increasingly important, and actions are judged not so much in terms of absolute principles as on the basis of particular situations. Children learn that actions are neither always wrong nor always right, but must be judged according to the circumstances involved.

Piaget is no doubt correct that older children reason differently than younger children do and view rules differently. But other researchers have questioned the existence of a small number of definite stages, and it may be more accurate to think of the development of intellectual and moral reasoning as occurring gradually rather than in distinct stages. For example, Kohlberg (1984), who has written extensively on moral development, has expanded on Piaget's work, and proposed his own system of three levels and seven stages. As yet, however, there is no general agreement on its usefulness.

The symbolic interactionist perspective

This approach to socialization focuses on the ways in which the social environment molds and shapes human behaviour; it tends to ignore biological influences in describing how individuals become social beings. In broad terms, it takes the position that interaction among individuals, in the form of language and gestures, shapes a person's *self-concept*. Symbolic interactionists argue that individuals constantly have a view or sense of themselves that is defined and affected by the actions and reactions of other people towards them. For example, if individuals perceive that other people regard them as creative, they will come to define themselves as such. The importance of communication among individuals is thus a key assumption in symbolic interactionism.

As mentioned in the introductory chapter, this theory has been one of the popular perspectives in sociology for some time. Its basic ideas were developed by several philosophers and social scientists during the early years of this century, especially by Cooley (1902), Mead (1934), and Thomas (1923). To understand the basic thrust of symbolic interactionism, it is useful to examine their contributions.

Cooley argued that we come to see ourselves as others see us, much like the view in a mirror.

Cooley: the looking-glass self

Symbolic interactionists emphasize the importance of individuals' perceptions of how other people see them. This idea was developed by Cooley in his early discussions of the **looking-glass self.** He argued that people come to see themselves as others view them, that perceptions of self are much like views in a mirror, or looking glass. Intuitively, this makes sense; most people are affected to some extent by the ways in which their family, peers, and teachers appear to react towards them.

Cooley also maintained that the response to this looking-glass self is a unique set of emotions. If the sense of self satisfies social norms or expectations, individuals feel pride. On the other hand, if the looking-glass self conflicts with such norms, people feel shame. For Cooley, these emotional reactions are of central importance because they have the potential to shape behaviour. Children, for example, may be told frequently by their parents and siblings that they are stupid. If their families are the sole source of information that they have about themselves, eventually they are likely to perceive themselves as stupid. They also know that the people around them value intelligence; thus they come to feel ashamed of themselves. This sense of shame, together with the self-image of "stupid kid," is likely to affect many of their actions. They may become shy and withdrawn, with little confidence in themselves and their abilities (see the box entitled "Parent–Child Relationships and Self–Esteem in Adolescence").

Two important points of Cooley's formulation are still widely accepted today. First, a person's view of self develops out of interaction with others. The looking-glass self is a social concept. It emerges from social experiences in groups, especially primary groups such as family and friendship networks. Second, individuals acquire a sense of self through the process of interpretation. That is, people infer or imagine how they appear to other people. To the extent that individuals belong to social

Parent–Child Relationships and Self-Esteem in

Numerous studies have shown that parent–child relationships influence adolescent self-concept and ego development: families who encourage sensitivity and individuality promote positive self-concepts in their children. Not surprisingly, the higher the quality of the parent–child relationship, the greater the adolescent's self-esteem. In contrast, high levels of control by parents over adolescent children produce lower levels of competence. Excessive control by parents diminishes adolescents' sense of independence and personal control, presumably because excessive parental control inhibits children's development of competence. Furthermore, positive parent–child relationships, those characterized by close attachments and the absence of parent–child conflict, lead to good social adjustment. Avison and McAlpine (1992) studied some of these issues in a survey of over 300 high–school students in southwestern Ontario. They examined the effects of parent–child relationships on young persons' self-esteem, sense of control, and perceptions of social support. They found that adolescents who perceived their mothers and fathers to be caring parents developed stronger self-concepts and were less likely to suffer from feelings of depression.

Differences in the relationships that adolescent girls and boys have with their parents are likely to result in gender differences in psychosocial development. Researchers have observed that mother–daughter, mother–son, father–son, and father–daughter pairs typically involve different levels of emotional intensity. The most intense involvements usually occur in mother–daughter dyads, while father–daughter relationships tend to be the least emotionally intense. Mother–son and father–son dyads fall between these extremes. The greater intensity of mother–child relationships in adolescence may explain why maternal responsiveness has a greater effect on self-concept development than paternal responsiveness. Similarly, adolescents' perceptions of maternal support have a stronger impact on self-esteem than paternal support.

Source: *Adapted from William R. Avison and Donna D. McAlpine, 1992. "Gender differences in symptoms of depression among adolescents."* Journal of Health and Social Behaviour, *33 (pp. 77–96).*

groups and experience a sense of identification or "we-ness" with members of these social groups, they are able to interpret accurately these members' attitudes towards themselves. For Cooley, then, the self-concept is the result of social interaction and social interpretation.

Mead: mind, self, and society

For many, George Herbert Mead's work constitutes the major intellectual foundation of symbolic interactionism. Most of the key concepts developed by Mead can be found in the edited version of his classroom lectures, *Mind, Self, and Society* (1934). For our purposes, the most important aspects of Mead's work are his discussions of the development of the self, the social nature of the self, and the relationship between the self and others in society.

At the heart of Mead's theory is the concept of **role taking**. Mead asserted that social communication between individuals requires that one "take the role of the other." The fundamental principle here is *imagined possibility*. That is, Mead assumed that people constantly strive to put themselves in others' shoes, to imagine what they are thinking. As a result, they are able to see themselves as others see them. For Mead, this is only possible if individuals have the capacity to use a language and interact symbolically. With the development of language and the ability to take the role of the other, the self emerges.

Mead contended that the development of the self takes place in three stages. In the *preparatory stage*, infants simply imitate without understanding what they are doing. Thus, very young children wave when Daddy waves, or "read" with Mommy, or play patty-cake with their older brothers and sisters, without really knowing what they are doing. While this behaviour is largely meaningless, it does indicate that infants are on the verge of role taking.

In the *play stage*, children play actual roles. They pretend to be mother, father, firefighter, teacher; they play house, cops and robbers, doctor. Here, they actually take the roles of others that they have observed. For the first time, children are in a position to reflect upon themselves behaving in a variety of roles. According to Mead, these roles are unstable and transitory because children move from one to another in an unorganized manner. Thus, children as yet have no unified concepts of themselves.

In the *game stage*, a more complete or unified concept of self emerges because children learn to take the role of a number of others. For example, in a game of hide-and-seek, children who are "it" put themselves in the other children's places and attempt to imagine where they will hide. They also know that the others expect to be searched for. By taking on a set of roles rather than one in particular, individuals develop a generalized picture of what is expected of them and how others will act towards them. By playing games and by interacting in a variety of settings, they begin to take the role of the **generalized other** rather than the role of a single, particular other. Their perception of the generalized other embodies their notions of what is expected generally (of normative behaviour), and provides them with a unified concept of how others see them. Evidently, then, the self is social in nature.

Mead further argued that the self involves two distinct aspects, the *I* and the *Me*. The **I** refers to impulsive acts, the spontaneous aspect of human behaviour that is creative and unpredictable. The **Me** represents a social process, individuals' reflections on their own behaviour. Mead viewed this reflection as the embodiment of the generalized other, that is, as an evaluation of how others would respond to the actions of the I. Imagine a situation in which you are listening to a boring lecture from your teacher. At the conclusion of the class, the instructor says, "As you can see, this material was very interesting." Your first, spontaneous reaction would be to disagree loudly, but for some reason you keep silent. Here is a situation in which the impulsive I has been regulated by the Me. You know that such behaviour contradicts the expectations of the generalized other (society, the school, the class) and of at least one particular other (the teacher). The social aspect of the self—the reflective Me—thereby provides the basis for socialization and conformity.

According to Mead, individuals generally differentiate two kinds of "others" whom they take into account. First, there are particular persons whose attitudes and opinions count for a great deal. These individuals may be intimate personal acquaintances (parents, siblings, or peers) or specific prestigious persons (a teacher, boss, or leader). Such individuals are referred to as **significant others**. Second, people also recognize a generalized other, a concept that we have already discussed.

Thomas: the definition of the situation

One last concept completes our discussion of the symbolic interactionist perspective: *the definition of the situation*. Thomas (1923) used this phrase to refer to the thought processes people use to interpret situations. The resulting understandings then help to define what behaviour is appropriate and, in turn, to determine actual behaviour.

Human beings usually share the same definitions of a situation and generally agree on what constitutes appropriate, normative behaviour in various circumstances. To the extent that they do, conformity and social order are possible. However, when such definitions differ, conflict may arise. For example, people who define a party as an opportunity to discuss work issues, when everyone else defines it as a chance to celebrate the end of the school term, are likely to create a certain amount of conflict. Their definition of the situation is contrary to the definitions of others, and their behaviour may create resentment and antagonism. Clearly, shared definitions of the situation arise when individuals are able to take the role of others accurately—in this instance, when they are able to infer correctly the purpose of the gathering that the others have in mind.

SOCIALIZATION AND SOCIETY

As mentioned earlier, learning occurs throughout life, but with increasing age, people learn less rapidly and it becomes more difficult to acquire new behaviours or accept new ideas. In large part this is due to the fact that the new activities are more likely to be inconsistent with the previously learned habits of a lifetime. The best time to learn a second language, for example, is before the age of eight. In addition, the opportunities to learn and practise, so readily available in childhood and youth, are found less frequently in adult situations. Thus, primary socialization is a much easier and usually more successful process than adult socialization. Both, however, can and must occur in a viable social system.

Agents and problems

The family is the most significant agent of primary socialization, but as children grow older, peer groups, schools, and the mass media become increasingly important. People always learn from the close-knit groups of which they are a part, be they family, high-school friends, or the gang at work. But they also learn from contacts with various institutions, such as schools or religious institutions, and from the many organizations to which they belong throughout life. Indeed, Canadians live in a complex, dynamic, and heterogeneous urban-industrial society. In such a context, conflicting demands for appropriate behaviour make the process of socialization more problematic. These conflicting demands often make childhood and youth more difficult periods than they are in societies with the opposite characteristics, where socialization attempts may be more consistent and uniform.

If all members of a culture had caring, competent parents, insightful friends, and knowledgeable teachers, primary socialization could be relatively simple and effective, and childhood and youth could be tranquil. But another of the major problems of socialization is that many agents do not work properly, at least as defined by the larger culture. Some parents do not teach their children the values and norms of the dominant culture (for example, "honesty is the best policy"), and some teachers, not to mention schools, are ineffective in passing on society's basic skills or cultural heritage. Such shortcomings are especially serious in technologically sophisticated societies in which success in life frequently depends on a firm foundation of basic intellectual skills (see the box entitled "Home Versus Day Care").

There are many examples of people who behave awkwardly in a restaurant, or do not act properly at a party, high-school graduates who are functionally illiterate, or have not the vaguest notions about career choices, adults who cannot stand the discipline of a regular job, and old people who are despondent about aging. Some individual and structural factors might well be at work, but to some extent these are examples of inadequate socialization.

Another problem of socialization arises from the fact that much of what people learn in childhood turns out to be inappropriate in later years. The social changes of the last thirty years and those that will occur during the next three decades, for example, require individuals to do things as adults that they did not learn in youth. It is difficult to prepare for a career when there is much uncertainty about the occupational structure in the year 2030. Many of the traditional values learned in childhood, such as having a lifelong occupation or falling in love only once, are no longer self-evidently true. The tasks of parenting are much more complex in a dynamic society than in more traditional cultures, and many families do not keep up with the times well enough to impart effective behaviours and attitudes to their children.

A further problem of socialization concerns the modelling process. There are many people whose behaviour individuals might be tempted to copy, and the mass media describe a host of exotic lifestyles and strange activities. Although most adults in Canadian society are married and have children, dating couples need not look very hard or far to be aware of singles, divorced people, communes, common-law relationships, gay couples, and childless marriages, all of which present alternatives that might seem reasonable. Self-indulgent adults on the society pages, politicians on the election trail, and members of Parliament on late-night television are all potential models. Socialization, therefore, involves not only the actual learning of behaviours, ideas, and values, but also the selection of appropriate models. The very definition of "appropriate," however, is problematic, for it reflects the values of family, peer group, religious organization, and school, among others, none of which may agree on a definition.

Finally, socialization problems may arise from the existence of various subcultures. Each subculture teaches its new members what it considers to be right, proper, and necessary. Ethnic subcultures do

Home Versus Day Care: Which Is Better for Children?

For many years, even very small children have been left at times with relatives or friends while their parents were away or worked. But until the 1950s, the numbers were quite small, because the dominant culture prescribed that mothers should stay at home and raise their children at least until the lower grades of school. Since the 1960s, however, day-care centres have become increasingly significant socialization agents. Today, the majority of mothers work outside of the home, and a large proportion of children spend many hours each day in the company of unrelated children, supervised by others.

The popularity of day-care centres has raised a number of questions, especially about parent–child bonding, children's psychological well-being, and the long-term effects of daily separation. In recent years, the nature and effects of day care have been analyzed by sociologists and other investigators. Most researchers have analyzed the effects of well-run centres staffed by competent professionals catering to stable middle-class families. (The effects of poorly run centres operated by unqualified persons would be quite different, of course.) Most of this research indicates that the bond between mother and child remains strong, even when young children spend considerable time in day-care centres. Indeed, neither the age at which children begin to attend nor the length of time they spend there seems to matter much. There appear to be few significant consequences for children older than two years, although the effects on infants have not yet been firmly established.

Studies typically show, for example, that when day-care and home-care children are separated from their mothers, both groups exhibit about the same amount of distress, such as crying (which varies mainly with age). The social and intellectual development of day-care children older than two years is usually similar to that of children cared for by their mothers. Children from low socio-economic backgrounds, however, seem to develop better, both socially and intellectually, in day-care situations. Indeed, for children who come from broken homes, have incompetent parents, or live in otherwise troubled families, day care tends to provide substantial benefits compared with home care.

Careful investigations of day care reveal what one would expect: the important variables that affect children's mental, social, and physical well-being are the nature and operation of the day-care centre, the competence of the staff, and the children's family background. Finally, the support and stimulation parents provide play a role as well, since children spend at least part of their time at home.

Day-care centres, then, are much like families, schools, and religious institutions. They can be effective socialization agents that help growing children become contributing members of the adult world, or they can have detrimental effects. What matters most is the children's relationship to the care-giver, be it parent, other relative, or stranger. In this instance, more than anything else, it is the quality of the centre and staff, and the way they operate and relate to children, that produce benefits or lead to problems.

Source: *Adapted from Sandra Scarr, 1984.* Mother Care/Other Care. *New York: Basic Books; and Jay Belsky, 1990. "Parental and nonparental child care and children's socioemotional development: A decade in review."* Journal of Marriage and the Family, *52 (pp. 885–903).*

this so routinely that it is hardly noticeable, and few worry much about it. Individuals born into the subculture of Italian immigrants in Toronto have little difficulty acquiring the appropriate behaviours, including language, that enable them to participate fully in the larger Canadian society; or, if they wish, they can spend their lives within the Italian community. Subcultures that are somewhat more segregated, such as Native people or Hutterites, may even provide all the skills, knowledge, and beliefs necessary for a satisfying life outside the dominant culture. Problems arise only when and if the individuals decide to leave their neighbourhoods or groups, and to enter the larger society. We shall discuss this problem of *marginality* more fully in Chapter 8, Race and Ethnic Relations.

Television and socialization

The role of television in the socialization process has been a matter of great interest—and controversy—for many years (Wiegman et al., 1992;

Strasburger, 1995). While television is a potent socializing agent that can have great impact, particularly on children and adolescents, its powers are limited by two factors. First, visual media are most effective in passing on simple subject matter and general ideas. Complex material and specific issues are most effectively transmitted through print. Second, television operates within the context of the viewer's age, gender, and class—as well as intelligence. Indeed, the first three factors (age, gender, and class, usually summarized as a viewer's "family background") have been shown to be at least as significant in their impact on the viewer as the characteristics of television itself.

Unfortunately, conclusions from the research conducted over the last forty years on the role of television in the socialization process have often been inconsistent and even conflicting. The "fuzzy picture" that has emerged arises from the heterogeneity of the populations studied, and from the great variety of methods, time periods, measures, and source materials that have been employed by hundreds of investigators in various countries. To illustrate: most studies of television used to be cross-sectional (done at one point in time), and many still are; that is, the viewing amounts and various behaviours of children are measured simultaneously. Such studies usually find a high correlation between children's TV-watching and aggressiveness, but cannot demonstrate a causal link. Should we conclude that TV makes children aggressive (as many people believe), or do aggressive children watch more TV, or are both phenomena the results of a third factor such as gender? Only longitudinal studies, which follow children over several years and control for all extraneous factors, can give us definite answers. For now, let us say that such investigations show that family, class, culture, gender, and individual differences (especially intelligence and interests) affect television's influence.

The one uncontroversial fact of television's role in socialization is that children and adults spend many hours a week in rooms with TV sets on. A major study during the 1980s, for example, revealed that the average Canadian watched about 3.4 hours of TV per day, up from about 3.2 hours during the 1970s. Amounts varied from about 4 hours in Newfoundland to 3 hours in Alberta. Women over 18 watched more than men (3.8 hours versus 3.2 hours), while older people (60+) watched the most (women 5.1 hours, men 4.5 hours). Contrary to popular complaint, adolescents seem to watch TV least: children from 2 to 11 watched 3.1 hours a day, while youngsters from 12 to 17 watched only 2.7 hours a day (Statistics Canada, *Cultural Statistics. Television Viewing,* Catalogue No. 87-208). Recent research suggests that the amount of actual television viewing may be declining, and that the VCR is gaining significance.

The role of television in the socialization process is the subject of ongoing debate.

Such numbers, however, do not tell the whole story. In order to assess the role of television in the socialization process, sociologists need to know the proportion of children and adults who watch the tube, for how long, what programs they watch, how much attention they pay, and what and how much they assimilate. Unfortunately, the answers are not clear-cut: they may vary by age, gender, and class, and they apparently change over time. For example, studies done in the 1950s and early 1960s suggested

TV has a greater impact than more recent research suggests. Early studies indicated that children who watch more TV engage less in other activities; studies today show the opposite: those who watch more TV are also more activity oriented. Presumably this shift reflects the fact that TV used to be a novelty, but now is so common that it has lost much of its earlier glamour. Similar shifts in attention and subsequent effects were discovered when radio was first introduced. The moral panic ("How can we save our children?") created by TV during the 1950s—and to a lesser degree today, perhaps now shifting to concerns about videos—also existed during the 1920s when radio became part of the socialization process. Indeed, similar moral panic arose when books began to replace verbal recitations of cultural elements during the late fifteenth century.

Most television programs reflect the values and norms of the majority of society, with few programs lagging or in the avant-garde. This is especially apparent in the content, characters, and language of programs. Hence, those who watch become at least acquainted with the dominant cultural values, leading to some homogenizing within a society. But not all viewers are equally influenced: in general, television is particularly effective among those children who initially are outside a culture's mainstream.

One longitudinal study of gender stereotypes, for example, showed that television affected mainly those children, especially girls, who initially had few stereotypes. The more television such girls watched, the more likely they were to accept gender stereotypes; but the effect was greatest for girls with low intelligence and minor for highly intelligent girls. Boys were little affected by TV because they shared cultural stereotypes from the beginning (Morgan, 1982). Parents who raise their children not to have gender or other stereotypes regarding behaviour and occupations may well see their efforts undermined by TV.

The processes by which television influences a person are complex and far from automatic. In the early days, it was widely assumed that viewers were passive objects who blindly accepted what TV offered (and perhaps they were)—proverbial "couch potatoes." Recent studies, however, indicate that most viewers are active subjects who choose times, select programs, and accept material selectively (if at all).

We shall illustrate the complex interplay of television and viewer by considering aggression. Over the years, most studies have shown that children who watch violent acts on TV are more likely in the near future to engage in violent acts themselves (e.g., Wood et al., 1991). But this effect declines over time and depends on gender: boys are much more likely to imitate aggressive acts than are girls. Yet boys are generally more aggressive than girls in the first place.

Bandura's (1973) classic studies of children who watched a film of a punching-bag doll being hit, and a few minutes later hit a doll themselves (or engaged in other aggressive acts), also require careful interpretation. The children may have been imitating novel or interesting behaviour, not necessarily aggression. After all, it is fascinating to a child that, despite being repeatedly knocked down, the doll always stands up again. Indeed, other studies indicate that children use television (and other) models selectively. For example, children tend to imitate those behaviours which they consider novel, interesting, or useful, and this depends on their present situation, upbringing, intelligence, and even personality (Slife and Rychlak, 1982). Aggressive children remember and presumably "learn" more from violent programs (and are more aggressive immediately afterward) than nonaggressive youngsters, just as science-oriented viewers are more likely to select programs with scientific themes and learn from them. To a considerable extent, then, television simply encourages whatever interests the viewers bring with them to the set.

In summary, children watch television selectively, for example, choosing one channel over another, and also learning one action rather than another from the same show. Adults employ the same selection processes. The most important aspect of television in socialization, however, is this: the TV set presents a great variety of models. The models selected, and whether or not viewers imitate them, depend on the intrinsic interest of the modelled action and the expected consequences of copying the modelled behaviour in the real world. Those interests and consequences, in turn, are affected by the age, gender, class, and subculture of the viewers.

Single-parent families

Most children grow up in intact families with mothers and fathers as the major socializing agents. During the last few decades, however, the number of single-parent families in Canada has increased substantially, due largely to higher rates of marital separation and divorce, but also to increases in the number of never-married parents. We shall return to this topic in Chapter 9, Families. For now let us say that several demographic characteristics of single-parent families have important implications for socialization:

1. Approximately 80 percent of these families are headed by females.
2. Both male and female single parents are generally less educated than are parents in intact marriages.
3. There are substantial income disparities between these families and two-parent families.

The increasing number of single-parent families, and the apparent economic disadvantages experienced by many of these families, have prompted considerable research on the impact of parental absence upon children, on juvenile delinquency and

Youth, Social Control, and the Mass Media: A Conflict View

Young people are enthusiastic consumers of the mass media, and over the years such enthusiasm has frequently given cause for concern. Indeed, worries about the content of messages directed at youth accompanied the introduction of comic books and movies.

At that time, many feared that moral degeneration would take place when young people were exposed to "adult" themes. Today, for the most part, we do not advocate shielding young people completely from adult-oriented material. At the same time, some observers worry about how consumption of this material socializes the young into an ethos of consumerism, conformity, and immediate gratification.

For example, magazines directed at young women—"teen-zines"—often send the message that they should intensify their feminine characteristics with cosmetics and fashionable clothing. On the one hand, one could argue that these magazines are simply meeting a market need, insofar as young women want these things. Another, more critical perspective, however, is that such magazines are specifically engineered to *create* a consciousness among young women that only then is defined as a need.

From an analysis of the content of the various mass media aimed at adolescents, it appears that all such organizations share this vested interest. Some of these media do so as agents for other economic interests (e.g., television programs, teen-zines, and fashion magazines). Others, however, do it directly for themselves (e.g., the music industry, with television channels devoted entirely to this task). At the heart of much of this activity is the attempt to sell young people some element of an identity that they have been taught to crave. With this accomplished, identities are sold back to them as products whose purpose is to provide a means of demonstrating their "individuality," however illusive or fleeting.

As a result of decades of influence (and practice), the "leisure industries" that sell music, fashion, and cosmetics now have a largely uncritical army of consumers awaiting the next fads, which often seem more and more outlandish. In spite of their seemingly anti-establishment guise, these activities are tolerated by larger economic interests because the army of willing consumers is the same group that serves as a massive reserve of cheap labour, willing to work under poor conditions, for little pay and few benefits. In addition, distracting young people with these trivial identity-pursuits constitutes a form of social control because it helps prevent them from actively protesting their own disenfranchisement and the loss of a meaningful identity, denied them through a series of laws, customs, and institutional practices. Instead of attempting to condition young people to spend money they do not have, the media might have focused on helping them to develop their intellects and their sense of social responsibility.

Source: *Adapted from James Coté and Anton Allahar, 1994.* Generation on Hold: Coming of Age in the Late Twentieth Century. *Toronto: Stoddart.*

crime (Wells and Rankin, 1991), for example, and on their mental health (Gotlib and Avison, 1993).

While many children living in single-parent families have similar experiences regardless of the reason for the parent's absence, there are some important differences among the families of the separated or divorced, the never-married, and the widowed parent. For just one example of such a difference, the children of widowed single parents are likely to be older than those of separated, divorced, or never-married parents because the death of a parent is more likely to occur when the parent (and thus the child) is older.

Separation or divorce

Amato and Keith (1991) reviewed several studies that compare children from divorced single-parent families with children living in two-parent families on a number of dimensions such as psychological adjustment, social adjustment, self-concept, and misconduct. They found that more recent studies report considerably less impact of divorce on children's behaviours than do older, less well-designed studies. It appears, therefore, that the effects of parental separation or divorce on children may not be as substantial as was previously thought, or that they have declined over time.

How do we interpret these findings? One possibility is that the factors that contribute to separation or divorce are less severe today than they were several years ago. In the past, divorce may have occurred only in the face of extreme conflict, spouse abuse, or spousal pathology. Thus, children from single-parent families in the past may have been exposed to much greater stresses than they are today.

Another possibility is that the stigma of coming from a single-parent home was greater in previous decades than it is today. In the past, children from single-parent families may have encountered more difficulty in getting along with their schoolmates, or they may have experienced some significant labelling by their teachers. Today, children from separated or divorced families are no longer rare, and there are fewer expectations that they will differ significantly from other children.

It also appears that child–parent relationships, parental conflict, and child-rearing styles are important predictors of adjustment among children in divorced families. The maintenance of good parent–child relationships, even in the face of marital discord and disruption, for example, contributes dramatically towards better adjustment among children. Research in the United Kingdom has reported similar patterns: rates of conduct disorder among children of divorced parents are higher, but a strong relationship between children and at least one parent moderates these problems considerably. It appears that parental separation or divorce *per se* may not be as critical for childhood as the existence of parental discord, family conflict, or poor parent–child relationships (Rutter, 1985). Thus, despite the fact that children of divorce may run higher risks of emotional problems, there is good reason to believe that those who maintain a close attachment to at least one parent are less seriously affected by the breakup of the family.

Unmarried parents

The children of unwed parents tend to encounter many difficulties. Most are raised by mothers who are young, poorly educated, and from economically disadvantaged backgrounds. Such women experience considerable deprivation and report numerous difficulties in finding employment, meeting financial needs, and arranging for suitable living accommodations. As a result, unmarried mothers frequently reside in poor neighbourhoods and have few support networks, either formal or informal. These pervasive problems, in turn, are associated with a variety of negative effects on children, such as poor school performance, emotional disturbance, poor physical health, and elevated rates of juvenile delinquency.

Parental death

While some studies of childhood bereavement indicate widespread emotional problems among children, for example depression and anxiety, others have found that children adjust reasonably well to such losses after a relatively short period. Such differences in emotional problems are probably related to conditions that follow a parent's death, especially the redefinition of familial roles. Since the death of a parent usually marks the loss of a set of roles within the family, the redistribution of these roles, along with the responsibilities attached to them, may place additional stress upon children, with varying consequences for their well-being. The surviving parent is likely to experience role burdens which may affect parenting and have negative effects upon the children.

In summary, there are wide variations in the extent to which children in single-parent families experience social, behavioural, and health problems. Whether or not children suffer negative consequences from the loss or absence of a parent seems to be related to the strains that such losses place on families, any resulting problems in parenting, and the absence of social support and other psychosocial resources to buffer the negative consequences.

Major implications

Socialization provides the roots and sets the limits for personality development. Much of adulthood is determined by childhood experiences, and individual potential becomes apparent only to the extent that people have learned the skills, actions, concepts, and words necessary for their expression. Inadequate socialization, such as functional illiteracy, would be a great stumbling block to becoming a poet, and if people have not learned the basics of social graces, they are likely to remain awkward and insecure in their relations with others.

From a societal perspective, socialization contributes to cultural integration and homogeneity. Regardless of individual talents and family background, socialization processes result in a general acceptance of basic values, norms, and skills. At the same time, heterogeneity is perpetuated because the members of various subcultures acquire different beliefs and actions.

Socialization produces members of Canadian society, citizens of a province, and unique individuals. They learn one or both of the official languages and they acquire the values, norms, and beliefs that make them Canadian. They learn to view themselves as Albertans or Newfoundlanders, with certain views of the nation and a certain perspective of history; and they are individuals with unique capacities regardless of geographic area. Without socialization they would know very little, if anything, about themselves, and indeed they would not be human.

SUMMARY

The process of socialization is one of the major links between individuals and groups. This process refers to the several ways in which people acquire the norms and values, beliefs and thoughts, activities and customs of a culture. It is through socialization that people become civilized human beings, unique individuals who can develop their potential, and citizens of a nation.

Socialization occurs throughout life. It begins even before infants learn to respond to certain words of the language of their care-givers and it does not end until after they have learned to adjust to the requirements of a graceful old age. During the intervening years they learn the customs of society, the behaviours demanded by the groups to which they belong, and the skills necessary to develop their capacities. Indeed, individuals frequently anticipate future requirements and prepare themselves for them, and when they enter a new group, they may learn quite different customs.

General human physiology and individual genetic endowment set the limits within which socialization occurs, but its actual content—be it language or behaviour—is defined by the particular culture. Today, there are still disputes regarding the relative importance of society versus biological characteristics. We have suggested both may be very important and have sketched only an outline of this debate.

The major component of socialization is learning, which may occur directly or through modelling. As we saw in the theory section, psychologists know much about the ways in which people learn, but what is learned and why are the province of sociologists.

The unique characteristics and even the self-image of individuals are the results of socialization, since they are developed as people are exposed to a great variety of socialization agents. These agents range from individuals, such as parents and peers, to institutions, such as religion and education, each of which may influence the process well or poorly; if the latter, individuals will be inadequately prepared to perform the roles defined by their society. Disagreement and inconsistency among the agents as to goals may present similar problems.

QUESTIONS FOR REVIEW AND CRITICAL THINKING

1. Observe the behaviour of children between the ages of three and seven for a few hours. Can you list examples of their behaviour that appear to have been shaped by direct reinforcement, by vicarious reinforcement, or by television?

2. Think about your own life history for a few moments. Can you list instances from your own experiences that would be examples of anticipatory socialization? Can you think of any examples in which you were resocialized?

3. Contemplate growing old. What kinds of new socialization experiences would you expect to encounter as you approach the age of sixty?

4. List the names of individuals whom you might consider to be your significant others. Why are their opinions and evaluations so important to you? Can you think of situations in which your anticipation of their reactions changed your behaviour in some way?

GLOSSARY

anticipatory socialization the learning of attitudes, beliefs, and behaviours that will be required for those new roles individuals expect to play in the future

generalized other the conception of what is expected, of normative behaviour; individuals' unified conception of how the world views them

I and Me the two aspects of Mead's conception of the self. The **I** is the impulsive, creative aspect; the **Me** is the reflective aspect that evaluates actions of the I.

id, ego, superego the major components of Freud's model of personality. The **id** is that aspect of personality which is impulsive, selfish, and pleasure-seeking. The **ego** includes the intellectual and cognitive processes that make individuals unique. Most of the ego is conscious, and it is guided by the reality principle: ideas and actions are modified to fit the real world, dependent on actual experiences. The **superego** consists largely of what is generally called "conscience."

linguistic empiricism the view that language is learned by reinforcement from others who already speak that language

linguistic nativism the view that children have an innate capability to learn a language and do so as a function of natural maturation

linguistic relativism the perspective that language determines and limits thinking and perception

linguistic universalism the view that language is a reflection of cultural experiences and that language does not affect thought patterns in any unalterable way

looking-glass self Cooley's expression for people's perceptions of how others see them

morality of constraints the stage of moral development in which children believe that ethical rules are absolute, coming from some higher external authority; sometimes called *moral realism*

morality of cooperation the stage of moral development in which children see rules as products of deliberation and agreement rather than as absolute; sometimes called *moral autonomy*

nature versus nurture the debate over the extent to which human behaviour is affected by biological and genetic factors as opposed to social or environmental ones. Currently, both factors are seen as contributing to the development of personality and the shaping of behaviour.

resocialization the replacing of old attitudes, beliefs, and behaviours with new ones

role taking Mead's term for individuals' attempts to put themselves in others' places and to imagine what the others are thinking so as to make interaction with them easier

significant other any intimate personal acquaintance or specific prestigious person whose attitudes and opinions count for a great deal. Individuals take significant others into account when evaluating their own actions.

socialization the complex set of processes by which infants become distinct and unique individuals as well as members of a society

vicarious punishment the negative consequences individuals observe happening to others (especially a model) and that they expect will follow their own similar actions

vicarious reinforcement the positive consequences individuals observe happening to others (especially a model) and that they expect will follow their own similar actions

SUGGESTED READINGS

Bandura, Albert

1986 *Social Foundations of Thought and Action.* Englewood Cliffs, NJ: Prentice Hall.

Bandura, one of the leaders in this field, provides a comprehensive statement of social learning theory and its empirical foundations.

Berns, Roberta M.

1993 *Child, Family, Community: Socialization and Support.* (3rd ed.) New York: Harcourt Brace Jovanovich.

An excellent summary of theories and research on the problems that individuals face in urban-industrial societies.

Erikson, Erik H.

1963 *Childhood and Society.* (2nd ed.) New York: W.W. Norton and Co.

The classic description of his well-known theory of the stages of personality development, each involving significant social interactions.

Strasburger, Victor C.

1995 *Adolescents and the Media: Medical and Psychological Impact.* Thousand Oaks, CA: Sage.

This up-to-date study examines the effect of various forms of media upon the mental and physical well-being of young people.

WEB SITES

http://paradigm.soci.brocku.ca/~ward/default.html

George's Page

Produced by the Mead Project at Brock University, this page contains useful information on the work of social psychologist George Herbert Mead.

http://www.ucla.edu/current/hotline/violence/toc.htm

UCLA Center for Communication Policy's TV Violence Monitoring Project

Learn about the effects of TV violence as reported in recent research on this important topic. See how your favourite TV show stacks up against others in terms of violent content.

EXCHAN

CHAPTER 5

Deviance

James J. Teevan

INTRODUCTION

When Canadians read in the newspaper about a robber or hear about the depression of a friend, most of them picture the individuals involved. Fewer think about how the behaviour of these individuals is affected by the social environment—such as the province in which they live, the unemployment levels they face, their families and peer groups. Such social factors are of primary concern to sociologists who attempt to discover the role of society in *deviant behaviour*, the general term given to crime, mental illness, alcoholism, and certain other behaviours. What they have discovered concerning society's part in the origin and development of deviant behaviour is the subject of this chapter. It begins with a topic essential for any understanding of deviance: how do societies decide what is deviant and what is not?

DEFINITIONS OF DEVIANCE

The behaviours and conditions that people may consider deviant are quite diverse, ranging from murder, arson, and anarchy to sickness, obesity, and extreme thinness, to breaches of etiquette or over-politeness, to genius. One thing these examples of **deviance** have in common is that each is perceived as somehow not normal. *Normal* can refer to following the rules of society, called *norms*, as described in Chapter 3, Culture, or it can mean "usual" or "average." A second characteristic they share is that each is generally at least somewhat disvalued (Sacco, 1992), surrounded by negative feelings, and thus seen by some people as an acceptable target for social control. This control can range from simple staring and mild ostracism, to more serious reactions such as medical treatment and punishment. Deviance, then, is the "conflict between those who behave in particular ways and those who seek to control their behaviour...and the problems each group creates for the other" (Sacco, 1992: 3).

Not only does deviance include a broad range of behaviour, but there is also great variation across societies in what each considers to be deviant. An example of this was presented in Chapter 3, Culture, in the discussion of how some societies ban the eating of cows, others pigs, and still others, neither. Indeed, anthropologists have shown that most behaviours have been designated as deviant somewhere, at some time, or under certain circumstances, and yet have been accepted elsewhere, at other times, or under other circumstances. For example, in traditional Inuit culture, infanticide and the killing of old people were seen as acceptable means to protect a limited food supply (see Edgerton, 1985).

Most other Canadians would have severely condemned such behaviour. Although the different outlooks are understandable given the unique conditions facing the Inuit, they illustrate the relative definition of deviance, that what is deviant is specific to time, place, and circumstances.

Additional evidence for this variability can be found by looking at homosexual behaviour and suicide. Although considered deviant by many if not most Canadians, both homosexuality and suicide have been tolerated and even encouraged elsewhere. Male homosexual behaviour was accepted and practised in quite a number of societies and was so much the norm in parts of ancient Greece that they did not even have a special word for homosexual (Downing, 1989). Suicide was preferred to dishonour by Japanese Samurai and also practised by Brahmin widows, who threw themselves upon their husbands' burning funeral pyres—an Indian practice called *suttee* (see Edgerton, 1985). Suicide by modern "freedom fighters" who attach bombs to their bodies is also seen as honourable: their gift to the cause. Closer to home, people dying of various painful or degenerative diseases have fought for the right to assisted death. The list could go on. The point is that even suicide is not always considered deviant. Indeed, in twenty-first-century Canada it may become common for the terminally ill to examine the option of suicide, even assisted suicide, with the blessing of family, friends, and medical care-givers, to escape lives sustainable with modern technology but defined as "without quality."

Who then makes the decisions as to what is or is not deviant? For example, who made marijuana illegal, but neither alcohol nor nicotine? Who decided that government lotteries, sometimes described as voluntary taxes on the ever-hopeful poor, should be legal, while bookmaking should not? Further, why were these decisions made? There are several answers to these questions, depending upon how society is viewed, whether in a more functionalist manner, seeing relative harmony, or more in terms of conflict theory.

A functionalist position

Durkheim (1949) took a functionalist position, arguing that definitions of deviance arise out of the **collective conscience**, the values held in common by the vast majority of a society's members. For example, most Canadians would agree that arson, sexual assault, and robbery are deviant acts, and that to weigh 300 kilograms is not normal. According to Durkheim, then, the source of definitions of deviance is society itself.

Moreover, deviance can serve positive functions for society (recall the discussion of prostitution in Chapter 1, What is Sociology?). Deviance, so long as it is not so widespread and/or serious enough to undermine the basic fabric of society, can be beneficial in several ways (Coser, 1964). First, deviants can be used as scapegoats, and serve to unify the rest of society. They can be targets for pent-up tension and aggression. Serving as common enemies, deviants can unite conformists, especially when no external enemies exist, increasing the conformists' cohesion, productivity, and well-being.

Second, deviants can be used to mark the bottom layer of society and to illustrate clearly the meaning of abstract rules. Viewing them enables non-deviants to see exactly what is not allowed (proscribed) or demanded (prescribed), and by comparison allows non-deviants to feel like saints, comfortable and secure in their conformity. In fact, Erikson (1966) argued that if there were no deviants to rally against and to serve as "inferior" comparisons, society would redefine new behaviours as deviant in order to satisfy these needs. He explained accusations of witchcraft in the Puritan settlements of colonial New England in this way.

Third, deviance can call attention to flaws in the social system, serving as an early warning that something is wrong. Thus, like smoke detectors, deviance can help society to avoid other potentially larger problems that could prove more damaging.

Fourth, deviance can begin a process of social adaptation and progress to new and better norms and values. Many advocates of values now commonly accepted were once defined as deviant when, ahead of their time, they pressed for social change. Jesus and Gandhi were deviant in this sense. Nineteenth-century feminists who demanded equality for women were similarly labelled deviant.

Finally, minor forms of deviant behaviour can take the pressure off and serve as safety valves. They permit individuals to let off steam, almost as if in a "time out," and in the process perhaps prevent more serious disruptions. For example, the minor deviance associated with Hallowe'en (or even the major destruction after a home-team world championship) may actually prevent the greater deviance that could erupt without such an outlet.

Conflict positions

Conflict theorists believe that society is held together by coercion rather than cooperation, and argue that definitions of deviance arise out of special interests. Those with power get to have their definitions of deviance prevail while those without power, under constant threat of disapproval from those in control, must get along as best they can.

This general position has two main variants. According to the first, a more Weberian position sometimes called **pluralism**, various segments of society, such as the wealthy, the religious, or even bureaucrats in the criminal justice system, compete to have their definitions of deviance accepted. Becker (1963) called these individuals **moral entrepreneurs**, people and groups who seek to influence the passing of rules and the setting of standards. Although benefit to society is often cited as the rationale behind the definitions of deviance proposed—and these people often see themselves as social reformers—there are sometimes self-serving reasons of equal or greater importance. For example, early twentieth-century Canadian narcotics legislation had among its supporters labour groups. They saw in the anti-opium laws the potential for deporting Chinese immigrants whom they viewed as a threat to their own employment because they would accept lower wages (Solomon and Madison, 1986). Giffen, Endicott, and Lambert (1991) added that once on the books, anti-narcotics legislation is often amended to include additional drugs, not necessarily because the drugs newly proscribed are dangerous but because the drug enforcement bureaucracy needs a broader mandate to justify its continued budget and existence. In Chapter 13, Formal Organizations and Work, we shall explore Weber's view of the growing power of bureaucracy in modern life.

The minor deviance associated with Halloween may actually prevent the greater deviance that could erupt without such an outlet.

In the area of psychiatry, Rohde-Dascher and Price (1992) wrote about the patriarchal origins of psychoanalysis and its sexist view of women's roles. Kaplan (1983) noted that many traditional definitions of mental health are biased against women, with "normal" being equated with male behaviour. To illustrate her point she devised, only somewhat tongue-in-cheek, a female-defined form of mental illness: "restricted personality disorder." It is marked by limited emotionality, even denial of emotional needs, a refusal to admit to being hurt much less to cry, a need always to appear self-assured, the choice of physical or intellectual activities over emotional experiences, and finally a preoccupation with work. How many men suffer some degree of this "illness"?

The second variant of the conflict position accepts Marxist principles and originates from what is sometimes called the *radical* or **critical school**. It sees an economic élite as the major force behind definitions of what is and what is not deviant (cf. Comack and Brickey, 1991). For example, Pirie (1988: 34–5) argued that drug companies had a role in transforming the biologically natural process of menopause into something that would require women to buy the medication they sell in order to remain "feminine."

Difficulties in Moral Entrepreneurship

Sociologists have a long history of opposing censorship. For decades they have been most vocal when conservative moral entrepreneurs have tried to limit freedom of expression. For example, they have fought against those who would limit birth control information and those who would ban communist writings, having little sympathy for claims that such expressions might be offensive to religious views, or serve as the basis for subversive attacks on existing political economy. But today sociologists increasingly face difficult dilemmas in their defence of freedom of expression. When moral entrepreneurs include feminists who seek to suppress pornography and minority groups who do not want certain literary works to be taught in schools because of the unflattering way they are depicted, many sociologists are caught in a bind. Will they lend their support to such groups, the oppressed they traditionally champion, or will they continue to fight censorship? Are liberal (or radical) expressions of censorship different from their conservative counterparts? Can this apparent dilemma for sociologists be resolved? See Brannigan and Goldenberg (1986) for a relevant discussion of pornography and the law of obscenity in Canada.

With either variant of the conflict position, whether it is a single economic élite or several competing groups that define deviance, the general conflict argument is that definitions of deviance often represent special interests. Conflict theorists do not deny that consensus can exist, but they treat it as an issue rather than taking it for granted. Their investigations are directed less towards individual deviants, as might be done by functionalists, than towards the rules and standards themselves and the groups that profit, economically or otherwise, by providing definitions of deviance. Finally, they do not see deviance as functional. It divides rather than unites (cf. Sacco, 1988), as it encourages people to be judgmental, sometimes distrustful of one another, even afraid of whole groups of people. It also deflects attention from the larger issues of inequality, racism, sexism, and the consequences of capitalist greed.

Other positions

Very few sociologists take either an extreme functionalist or an extreme conflict view concerning definitions of deviance. Most would reject as naïve the view that capitalists make all of the laws—if so, how did laws against price-fixing and unfair competition get passed? Most also could not accept a view of a collective conscience without conflict. Witness the amendments to sexual assault legislation made a few years ago. Feminists had to battle long and hard to change earlier versions of the law and the legal system, to reduce police reluctance to lay charges, to lessen the need for corroborative evidence, to increase sentences for offenders, and to allow husbands to be charged. Even in the case of murder, about which many think there is consensus, there are disputes: is abortion murder? euthanasia? execution of criminals? killing in time of war?

In between functionalism and a critical perspective are several compromise views on definitions of deviance. One argues that although conflict explains the origins of some definitions of deviance, consensus explains their continued support. Briefly put, over time the originally less-than-impartial definitions of deviance become widely accepted. A second position softens the idea of conflict between a powerful and a powerless group and points to *negotiation* between and among groups with varying degrees of power (cf. Kent, 1990). For example, people with physical exceptionalities fought for and won the right not to be called "the disabled," and homosexuals have made gains in recent court decisions concerning equal rights, including same-sex spousal benefits.

In the end, each type of deviance should be examined separately to see which explanation best fits. For example, rules about which society is not in full agreement, such as rules against gambling, adult pornography, drug abuse, and other activities which involve willing participants and no specific victim, are often explained by a Weberian conflict perspective (cf. Stebbins, 1988). Gusfield (1986), for example, argued that 1920s prohibition legislation in the U.S. was promoted by rural Protestants who disliked and distrusted a growing urban Catholic population. Fearful that their way of life was threatened by these Catholic immigrants, the Protestants lobbied successfully to make the alcohol the Catholics drank illegal (see Maxim, 1993, for a similar investigation of Ontario dry versus wet counties). In the area of psychiatry, male psychiatrists were historically more influential in creating categories of mental illness than others. *Penis envy* was not a term defined by women; indeed, a wish for women's creative capacities might have led to the condition of "womb envy" had psychoanalysis been female-dominated (cf. Rohde-Dascher and Price, 1992). The fact that the word *hysteria* is derived from the Greek word for uterus reveals some underlying masculine bias in psychiatry. Finally, a lack of power may explain why some things fail to get defined as deviant. Was, for example, the federal government guilty of kidnapping when it "relocated" Japanese-Canadians during World War II? Leroux and Petrunik (1990) also made this argument with respect to elder abuse, which, compared with spousal and child abuse, receives much less reaction from society.

Forms of deviance such as assault and driving while intoxicated, which most people would think of as harmful, may be better explained by Durkheim's consensus position. Crimes against property, especially theft, may need the two-stage explanation: conflict for origin, consensus for current support. The laws were originally made by wealthy property owners who made them after their paying of low wages, creation of unemployment, and a general refusal to share may have encouraged theft. Today, however, most Canadians have some property they would like protected and so most would support the law. Finally, the relative non-enforcement of laws against "capitalist crimes" such as environmental pollution, lack of worker safety, and price-fixing may need a critical analysis.

Whichever theory best fits any specific example of deviance, the general point to remember is that society, either the whole or its more powerful segments, is a crucial variable to consider in examining definitions of deviance. Societies choose to worry about homosexual behaviour or to focus attention on the destruction of endangered species and rainforests, to open new prisons or to emphasize the creation of more jobs. Such decisions determine their deviance. Definitions are not absolute and thus it would be wrong (and ethnocentric) to assume that what is now considered deviant in Canadian society has everywhere always been so, or will everywhere always be so.

APPLYING A DEVIANT LABEL

Whatever acts or conditions a society decides to define as deviant, common sense says that not everyone who fits the definition is discovered. This brings up a second aspect of definitions of deviance: once the definitions exist, audience reactions are crucial in deciding who is and who is not a deviant. Hence, not only are the definitions of deviance social, their application to specific individuals is social too. Official counts of deviance, such as crime (see Table 5.1) and mental illness rates, are then also social products. These ideas are illustrated in Figure 5.1 and the discussion that follows.

In box (1) are *deviants*, so called because they perform deviant acts or are unusual in some way, and because their audiences respond to their deviance. (For convenience, from here on the words "or are unusual in some way" will be omitted.) In box (4) are *innocents*, who perform no deviant acts and receive no audience reactions. So far, there are no major problems, except perhaps for the previously mentioned issue of who gets to define deviance in the first place. The picture is more complicated in boxes (2) and (3), rule breakers and the falsely accused, respectively. **Rule breakers** commit deviant acts, but no one responds to them for some reason. If you ever shoplifted, lied at customs, or sucked your thumb in bed after childhood and either were not caught or if caught were excused for some reason, then you are a rule breaker (see Gabor's [1994] book *Everyone Does It: Crime by the Public* from the University of Toronto Press). If you are secretly homosexual, you are a rule breaker,

TABLE 5.1 Police-reported Incidents, by Most Serious Offence, Canada and the Provinces/Territories, 1994

CANADA Population: 29,248,100	Actual Number	Adults Charged		Youths Charged	
		Male	*Female*	*Male*	*Female*
First degree murder	301	172	18	22	1
Second degree murder	240	168	29	23	2
Manslaughter	49	38	11	3	—
Infanticide	6	—	3	—	1
Homicide — Total	**596**	**378**	**61**	**48**	**4**
Attempted Murder	**918**	**553**	**79**	**103**	**9**
Sexual assault	30,560	9,929	185	1,748	63
Sexual assault with weapon	768	333	11	58	3
Aggravated sexual assault	362	169	7	26	1
Sexual Assault — Total	31,690	10,431	203	1,832	67
Assault	181,400	64,367	9,631	7,577	3,317
Assault with weapon/causing bodily harm	37,706	17,976	3,070	3,391	777
Aggravated assault	2,993	1,761	302	275	45
Unlawfully causing bodily harm	2,599	1,501	179	212	65
Discharge firearm with intent	255	93	5	16	—
Police	5,989	3,634	799	295	111
Other peace-public officers	666	356	63	48	23
Other assaults	4,756	1,496	211	144	51
Non-Sexual Assault — Total	**236,364**	**91,184**	**14,260**	**11,958**	**4,389**
Other sexual offences	**3,812**	**1,181**	**26**	**204**	**21**
Abduction of person <14	339	52	18	3	7
Abduction of person <16	133	13	—	1	—
Abduct contravening custody order	427	50	57	—	—
Abduction no custody order	231	41	19	4	—
Abduction — Total	**1,130**	**156**	**94**	**8**	**7**
Robbery with Firearms	7,371	1,695	74	453	26
With other offensive weapons	9,336	2,240	264	990	131
Other robbery	12,181	2,261	223	1,157	249
Robbery — Total	28,888	6,196	561	2,600	406
Crimes of Violence — Total	**303,398**	**110,079**	**15,284**	**16,653**	**4,903**
Business Premises	110,037	10,487	377	5,111	308
Residence	226,964	15,437	1,128	10,842	1,088
Other	50,876	2,619	131	2,536	154
Breaking and entering — Total	**387,877**	**28,543**	**1,636**	**18,489**	**1,550**
Automobiles	101,779	5,247	405	4,483	630
Trucks	41,361	2,191	128	1,356	140
Motorcycles	6,061	324	5	320	10
Other	10,462	744	14	558	14
Motor Vehicle Theft — Total	**159,663**	**8,506**	**552**	**6,717**	**794**
Bicycles	6,285	117	—	78	2
From motor vehicles	55,928	966	43	546	16
Shoplifting	2,290	367	176	51	37
Other	51,792	3,758	1,020	748	126
Theft over $1,000 — Total	**116,295**	**5,208**	**1,239**	**1,423**	**181**
Bicycles	90,518	775	53	1,063	57
From motor vehicles	295,893	4,689	233	3,429	136
Shoplifting	94,971	29,412	19,539	11,073	8,470
Other	245,982	11,492	2,931	5,095	1,243
Theft $1,000 and under — Total	**727,364**	**46,368**	**22,756**	**20,660**	**9,906**
Have Stolen Goods — Total	**30,522**	**14,375**	**2,132**	**5,922**	**1,077**
Cheques	46,847	8,378	4,255	394	225
Credit Cards	13,287	2,791	946	432	189
Other	43,076	10,232	3,974	747	339
Fraud — Total	**103,210**	**214,401**	**9,175**	**1,573**	**753**
Property Crimes — Total	**1,524,931**	**124,401**	**37,490**	**54,784**	**14,261**

TABLE 5.1 *continued*

CANADA Population: 29,248,100	Actual Number	Adults Charged Male	 Female	Youths Charged Male	 Female
Bawdy house	165	128	269	—	3
Procuring	328	186	118	6	15
Other	5,095	2,289	2,613	1	142
Prostitution — Total	**5,588**	**2,603**	**3,000**	**622**	**160**
Betting house	56	207	51	—	2
Gaming house	116	121	22	1	—
Other	250	218	32	2	—
Gaming and Betting — Total	**422**	**546**	**105**	**3**	**2**
Explosives	448	61	5	72	2
Prohibited weapons	3,567	1,238	89	359	29
Restricted weapons	2,290	856	74	105	6
Other	12,614	4,090	320	1,275	115
Offensive Weapons — Total	**18,919**	**6,245**	**488**	**1,811**	**152**
Arson	13,565	899	148	575	95
Bail violations	65,740	33,689	6,773	5,299	1,738
Counterfeiting currency	20,804	669	102	133	8
Disturbing the peace	51,205	4,403	695	591	124
Escape custody	3,429	1,295	85	1,121	156
Indecent acts	5,656	1,679	215	88	8
Kidnapping	1,820	975	86	110	8
Public morals	439	65	14	5	2
Obstruct peace officer	9,131	5,075	908	451	146
Prisoner unlawfully at large	5,572	3,248	372	655	122
Trespass at night	6,017	623	18	245	7
Mischief	396,596	15,842	1,992	6,875	792
Other Criminal Code Offences	197,598	36,775	5,487	6,012	1,542
Other Crimes — Total	**804,501**	**114,631**	**20,488**	**23,996**	**5,062**
Total Criminal Code (excluding traffic)	**2,632,830**	**349,111**	**73,262**	**95,533**	**24,226**
Criminal Code Traffic — Total	**185,641**	**94,601**	**10,085**	**—**	**—**
Total Criminal Code (including traffic)	**2,818,471**	**443,712**	**83,347**	**95,533**	**24,226**

Source: *Statistics Canada, 1995.* Canadian Crime Statistics 1994, *Catalogue No. 85-205E, Table 3.3.*

FIGURE 5.1 Audience reactions and deviant actors

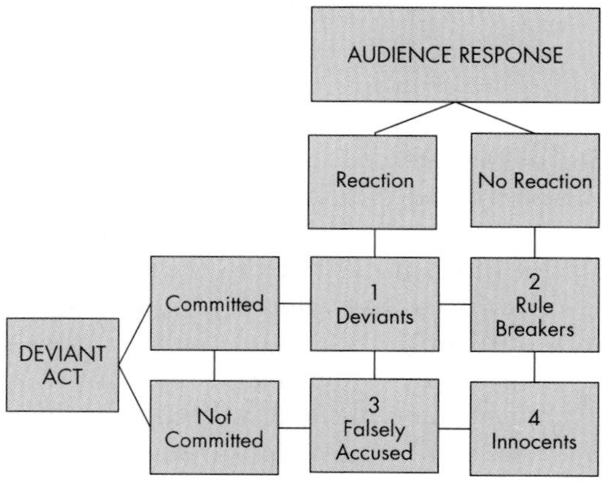

Source*: Howard S. Becker, 1963.* Outsiders. Studies in the Sociology of Deviance. *New York: Free Press (p. 20).*

at least in contemporary Canada. Compare these rule breakers to the *falsely accused* in box (3) who, although they commit no deviant acts, are reacted to as if they have, perhaps even suffering punishment and segregation from innocents and rule breakers alike. Mistakes like this do happen. Looking at actions and reactions, then, it becomes clear that society's reactions and application of the label *deviant* are important aspects of a person's deviance, in some ways even more important than the person's actions themselves.

Conflict sociologists argue that there may be as many or even more rule breakers than deviants, with actual amounts (rule-breaking rates) of alcoholism, drug abuse, crime, and mental illness in Canada all much greater than official data (deviance rates) indicate. For mental illness, Hagan (1991) estimated that as many as 25 percent of Canadians suffer

Society's reactions are important aspects of a person's deviance, in some ways even more important than the person's actions themselves.

psychological impairment. Only about 13 percent of the population sees a doctor for such problems in any one year, however, and an even smaller percentage is hospitalized (Bland, Newman, and Orn, 1990). In the area of crime, most crime is not officially recognized, especially less serious forms, for example marijuana use, petty theft, and minor assaults (cf. Silverman, Teevan, and Sacco, 1995).

These omissions are revealed when researchers ask respondents to report their rule breaking, regardless of whether reactions by others have turned it into deviance. For example, in the past year how often have you driven while even slightly intoxicated? Did you ever shoplift, drink under age, or use illegal drugs? The answers, called self-report data, along with victimization data—responses from victims about their crime experiences—can then be compared with official data. Both reveal a great undercounting of crime. For example, self-report data reveal that 24 percent of Canadians have cheated on their income tax at least once, a percentage quite at variance with official data (Brooks and Doob, 1990).

Sources of this discrepancy between official and unofficial counts of deviance include the number of labellers, from police to psychiatrists, and their resources, for example the number of prison and hospital beds. Any change in the number of either labellers or resources can create corresponding increases or decreases in deviance without changes in the actual rule-breaking rates of behaviour. Such was the case when the addition of more police to a force led to a higher official crime rate (cf. Koenig, 1991). In another sphere, provincial governments are quite aware that the greater the number of doctors licensed, the more illness that is treated, and researchers have argued that the greater availability of psychiatric facilities in urban areas is part of the cause of higher mental illness rates in cities compared with rural areas (Kates and Krett, 1988).

Finally, even with a constant number of labellers, any change in their focus can affect deviance rates. For example, the recent decline in arrests for marijuana use is only partly due to fewer users; another factor is the turning of police attention from marijuana to harder drugs and from users to pushers (Wolff, 1991). The general point to be taken from these examples is that counting deviance is a social activity involving more than the individual deviants themselves. Reactors are a crucial part of the process.

The next issue is whether labellers are biased. Do reactions to the same deviance fall equally upon all people, especially on all groups of people? Most of us can think of examples of rule breakers who were caught and were excused for various reasons. Indeed, there are some fairly widely accepted criteria and rules for excusing deviance (Edgerton, 1985). To illustrate, children under the age of twelve cannot be tried in criminal court. In fact, children, along with the very old, are often excused from obligations that are applied to the rest of society. Drunkenness (though less frequently accepted today), transient physical or mental illness, and being temporarily under the influence of an overwhelming emotion may excuse people from being labelled deviant. Finally, Halloween, funerals, and stag parties are settings that may allow behaviours not normally tolerated.

Despite some grumbling, this lack of uniformity in the application of labels is not generally perceived as a major problem. Sometimes it is even given a positive connotation and called *discretion*, giving officials the *choice* to react or not to react, for example when young offenders are spared and given a second chance (Hackler and Don, 1990). On the other hand, when "discretion" gives rise to accusations of prejudice and discrimination on the basis of gender, race and ethnicity, or social class, then there is a big problem. For example, in a classic study Hagan, Gillis, and Chan (1980) examined police and self-report juvenile delinquency data for an Ontario city, and found some bias. The police expect more delinquency in poorer areas, look for it there, and then find it in what is partially a self-fulfilling prophecy. Had the police been equally observant in wealthier areas, they would have found higher rates of delinquency there as well (see also Wordes and Bynum, 1995).

In the area of mental illness, some conflict theorists argue that all people do things definable as insane, but only some are labelled that way. Do you ever talk to yourself, feel claustrophobic in elevators or crowds, or believe in fantasies because they make you happy? All could be signs of mental illness. Conflict theorists argue that a lack of power is often an important factor (although not the only one) in the labelling of such behaviour as mental illness. Thus, part of the higher official mental illness rates found among single or lower-class individuals, compared with those who are married or middle-class, may be due to their relative lack of resources and their greater vulnerability to being labelled (Scheff, 1984).

Similar arguments are made about the higher rates of mental illness among women. In this case, however, demonstrating bias is a bit more complicated. First, women are more open about their problems and may seek treatment more than men, thus inflating their rates of mental illness (Rhodes and Goering, 1994). Just think who is more likely to ask directions when lost, your mother or your father, and you will see the logic of that statement. (See also Mirowsky and Ross [1995] for a discussion of whether women are more mentally ill, perhaps owing to the heavier burdens they bear, or more often labelled, another manifestation of male control, or both.) Second, the distinction between institutionalized and non-institutionalized care is quite important in this debate. In out-patient treatment there are more mentally ill women than men, but men outnumber women in psychiatric hospitals, partly because men suffer more often from substance abuse, organic psychoses, and those personality disorders which require (often lengthy) hospitalization (Statistics Canada, 1996, *Health Reports, Mental Health Statistics, 1982–83 to 1993–94*). Thus, although women more frequently suffer mental illness than men—approximately a 5:4 ratio (cf. Bland, Newman, and Orn, 1990)—in counts of serious mental illness men exceed women (Mowbray, Herman, and Hazel, 1992), an argument against the general conflict position regarding bias. Finally, in a particularly interesting study, Rosenfield (1982) found that women who suffer substance abuse or personality disorder (illnesses more frequently

Poverty may lead to mental illness. On the other hand, mental illness may lead to poverty via unemployment and a history of unskilled jobs.

found among men) and men who suffer depression or neuroses (more frequently found among women) are hospitalized more often than if they suffer forms of mental illness more "appropriate" to their gender.

Critics of the conflict perspective argue that the bias in the system that reduces the official rates of deviance among the more advantaged, given the same behaviour, is smaller than first appears. Much of the deviance committed by the better-off that gets ignored is both minor and infrequent. Various studies support this conclusion, and suggest that for serious crime or delinquency there is little bias. It is mainly for less serious infractions that unequal treatment inflates the rates of deviance among the disadvantaged. In fact, Henshel (1990: 179) made the point that this potential for bias is greatest in minor crimes, where the language of the law is deliberately vague (e.g., disturbing the peace, loitering, and being a common nuisance), or where enforcement is haphazard (such as possession of minor drugs and minor traffic infractions). Thus, these crimes, rather than homicide, arson, and robbery, may be most vulnerable to biased handling. Indeed, in the area of crime, a general conclusion is that the poor generally do commit the more serious (predatory) crimes, more often (cf. Hartnagel, 1996).

Similarly, in the area of mental illness, most research concludes that level of impairment is more important than power in treatment decisions (cf. Link and Cullen, 1990). As generally is the case for crime and delinquency, the less powerful may be more often labelled for minor forms of mental illness than the more powerful, but for serious psychiatric impairment such bias is less apparent.

In conclusion, when official data are used, be aware that differences in the secrecy and processing of deviance can affect the rates for some groups compared with others. Pay special attention when the less powerful are listed as having higher deviance rates. They may in fact be more frequently deviant, a result perhaps of their poorer living conditions and lack of legitimate opportunities, points to which we shall return. On the other hand it may be that they are being singled out for special treatment (see Stebbins, 1988). But also be critical of those champions of the disadvantaged who say that it is only official bias and attempts at social control that inflate the deviance rates of the poor (also see the box "Race and Ethnicity as Factors in Crime and Delinquency"). In effect they are arguing that poverty and disadvantage have no effect on deviance. But examination of illness, suicide, and mortality rates, especially infant mortality rates, reveals that there are real differences among social groups that probably have little to do with biased audience reactions. In short, there are costs to being disadvantaged, including higher rates of some forms of deviance. Then the debate turns to what causes these real differences, the topic of the next section of this chapter.

THEORIES OF DEVIANCE

Introduction

Before presenting theories of deviance, a few general points are in order. First, the behaviours included within the general area of deviance are too diverse for any one theory to be able to account for why people engage in them. It would be surprising if crime, mental illness, and drug abuse, along with the various other things called deviant, shared exactly the same set of causes. Even within the same area of deviance, different theories would be required to explain, for example, embezzlement versus arson, schizophrenia versus depression, and dependence on tranquillizers versus alcoholism. Second, any one form of deviance may be best explained by a combination of factors taken from several theories, rather than by a single theory. For example, Ratner and McKie (1990) found that violent crime was best explained by ethnicity (it was especially high among Native peoples), but also by unemployment, especially that experienced by males over age twenty-five. This first section will look briefly at several examples of biological and psychological theories, and then we shall move on to their sociological competitors.

Biological and psychological theories

Almost by definition, biological theories of deviance look to individuals. For example, Sheldon (1949)

Race and Ethnicity as Factors in Crime and Delinquency

Any search for relationships between racial or ethnic status and crime raises some thorny issues. Historically, Canadian crime statistics routinely included information on occupation, education, and religion, along with place of birth, a crude measure of ethnicity. Criminologists used this information to discuss group differences in crime just as Durkheim did in his study of suicide. In fact, ethnic differences in crime and delinquency were expected, a natural product of the inequalities symbolized by the vertical ethnic mosaic that is called Canada. Sociologists wrote volumes on the culture conflict arising from the widespread immigration that took place earlier this century and thought it an important explanation of some crime (Sellin, 1938).

Today, however, there are many, and not only minority group members, who think that crime statistics based on race or ethnicity will be used to promote hatred and discrimination (Yi, 1991) and thus should neither be collected nor reported. Too often, they argue, people forget that most members of any racial or ethnic group are not criminal. Below are some of their arguments against collection.

1. Deviance, as pointed out earlier, requires a reaction as well as an action. Since victims, the police, and the courts may react more to criminals from some groups than to others, some of any racial or ethnic differences found in official crime rates may be due to these differential responses or bias and not to actual crime differences.
2. Some of any differences found will be due to the crimes chosen for attention. For example, some crimes, especially white-collar crimes, often get no official reaction. Thus, if ethnic or racial variations are reported, then the specific crimes to which the generalization applies and does not apply should be mentioned.
3. Not only is measuring crime an issue, but rigorous definitions of race and ethnicity are also hard to achieve (cf. Roberts and Gabor, 1990). For example, a lack of agreement on the traits which distinguish the races and the effects of changing political boundaries, in the case of ethnicity, lead to difficulties in unambiguously classifying many individuals into distinct ethnic and racial groups. In addition, increasing intermarriage rates have meant that there are fewer and fewer people in Canada and elsewhere who can claim that all of their ancestors came from only one group.
4. Finally, even if the crime rates of only those individuals who can demonstrate only one racial or ethnic background were collected, which would leave out many Canadians, it would be important to examine the rates of these groups in their homelands, as immigrants to other lands besides Canada, and over time, to see if similar rates occurred. If they did not, then something besides ethnicity and race must be operating.

Taken together, these measurement issues should have warned you that great care should be used in examining variations in crime among racial and ethnic groups. If you decided that such data should not be collected, think now about the criminal justice system's practice of reporting crime statistics by gender and age. Is this practice defensible or is it sexist and ageist? Should crime statistics even be reported by province or city?

hypothesized that body type is related to crime. He argued that muscular individuals or **mesomorphs** are more likely to be assertive, dynamic, and aggressive and that these personality traits are related to greater criminality. Thinner **ectomorphs** and fatter **endomorphs** are less criminal, the former being complainers who withdraw from society, the latter luxury-loving extroverts. A more recent variant of biological explanation examined the effects of levels of testosterone on deviance. Dabbs (1990) concluded that testosterone level is related to: violence and crime at a young age, trouble with parents and school, drug use, a greater number of sex partners, being absent without leave from the army, and being a fraternity "party animal." He also checked for the effects of social class and found that subjects from lower socio-economic backgrounds have on average higher levels of testosterone and are more vulnerable to its effects than their better-off counterparts.

Turning to mental illness, researchers conclude that biology is more important in some forms of mental illness than in others. For example, schizophrenia is more genetic than social in origin, and biological factors are certainly important in the senile psychoses of the elderly. But other forms of mental illness, such as borderline personality disorder, are more likely caused by social factors such as physical abuse, quality of parental care, criminal parents, etc. (Byrne et al., 1990).

In most cases, however, *both* social and biological factors are seen as important. Beisner and Iacono (1990), for example, noted that a predisposition to schizophrenia is biological (and more common among males) but that environmental factors such as poverty and adverse working conditions do play a role in bringing it on. And part of higher mental illness rates among the elderly has to do with their loss of social status and their loneliness, not just biological aging (Stebbins, 1988).

By now you should have a taste for how biological theories look at individual factors in deviance. Several selected psychological theories of deviance may also be noted, even more briefly. They too focus on individuals. For example, criminal behaviour may be traced to individual personality, with the view that criminals are more impulsive and crave excitement more than do non-criminals (cf. Polakowski, 1994). Similarly, Freudians might see some mental illness as the result of an inability of the ego as mediator to handle conflicts between the id, the superego, and the external world.

This presentation of psychological theories is deliberately incomplete. It is intended merely to provide points of comparison for the sociological theories to come, which examine society's role in deviance.

Sociological criticisms of biological and psychological theories

Biological explanations of deviance (cf. Walsh and Gordon, 1995) are generally rejected by sociologists because they too often pay insufficient attention to the social factors that interact with their explanations. Thus, high-testosterone males (biological variable) may be more rewarded and encouraged by others (social variable) for their aggression and may therefore learn (social variable) to be more criminal. Also, because of their extroversion, society may watch them more closely (social variable) and thus be more aware of their deviance. This scrutiny will inflate their deviance rates.

More importantly, on their own ground biological theories have problems. For example, what about the many mesomorphs who become athletes or RCMP officers rather than criminals? Moreover, why don't individuals with the same genes, like monozygotic twins, exhibit the same deviance? Although there is great overlap, there is not a 100 percent concordance in the area of mental illness (Cockerham, 1996). Even though adopted children are more like their biological fathers than their adoptive fathers (with whom they live) in criminality, suggesting a biological link, it cannot be the only factor as many do not follow the path of their criminal biological fathers. And what about their mothers, whose genes they share? They are very infrequently studied.

Another serious deficiency concerns the sometimes wide fluctuations over time in the amounts of deviance. Most official data show, for example, that crime—especially violent crime (Silverman, 1992)—increased dramatically from 1962 to the 1990s. Hartnagel (1992) pointed out that conviction rates for indictable crimes were especially high from 1910 to 1920, a time of immigration and mobility, and much lower in the 1950s compared with earlier and later decades. To take another example, alcoholism, measured indirectly through liver cirrhosis rates, has generally increased throughout the century, at least until the mid-1970s (Newman and Bland, 1987). Since then, even though alcohol consumption has continued to rise, alcoholism appears to have decreased (cf. Eliany, 1991). Did biology change in the same way during these times? No, biological factors, whether they be genes, hormones, or body type, just cannot show the parallel fluctuations which would be expected if they were the causes. So something more than biology is responsible.

Although psychological theories of deviance are generally more appealing to sociologists than biological ones, they are also criticized for the difficulty of measuring some of their concepts and for underestimating the influence of the social factors which precede their psychological factors in deviance. Thus, there is a difference in focus. Psychologists hold social variables such as race, sex, age, and social class constant and then look for differences in psychological variables, while sociologists focus directly on those social variables. Sociologists thus take a step further back in the causal chain; they want to know what social factors are related to inadequate egos or to extroversion and impulsiveness. They want to study the social conditions that would damage even the healthiest mind.

Before leaving this topic, it should be noted that interdisciplinary explanations of deviance are becoming more frequent and the fight for scientific turf among the various disciplines is becoming more sophisticated. These days it is less of an either/or situation. Researchers instead look at the roles that social, psychological, *and* biological factors play and how they can be combined to give the fullest picture of deviance.

Introduction to sociological theories of deviance

Before examining the sociological theories of deviance and seeing how deviance varies across groups and with differing social conditions—tasks that Durkheim's analysis of suicide inspires—a methodological note is in order. In several places the data supporting the theory are taken from official rates of deviance, not rule-breaking rates. This is because official data are both more readily available and more comprehensive than other sources. Self-reported data can lead to different conclusions. It is important to keep this rule breaker-versus-deviant distinction in mind when evaluating explanations of deviance because the causes, correlates, and explanations can be quite different, depending upon whether the smaller number of deviant individuals or the larger number of rule breakers is studied. Thus, always pay attention to the type of data being presented before drawing conclusions. Second, the classification of the theoretical approaches presented is somewhat arbitrary. Different researchers make different distinctions, and some of the theories to be presented have aspects that would allow them to fit into more than one category in the scheme (Silverman, Teevan, and Sacco, 1995).

In the early 1920s, Shaw and McKay (1942) were among the first modern researchers to use a sociological approach to explain deviance. They called it *human ecology*, a study of how different areas or zones in cities exhibit different rates of various types of deviant behaviour. They found that official delinquency rates, along with crime, infant mortality, tuberculosis, mental illness, and truancy rates, were highest in the centre of cities and steadily decreased in concentric circles drawn further away from the centre, reaching their lowest point in the suburbs (see Figure 16.2 in Chapter 16, Urbanization). This pattern occurred regardless of the individuals and racial or ethnic groups that lived in these zones; that is, as new people moved in and others moved out, they took on the rates of the area into which they moved. Thus, Shaw and McKay concluded that something to do with the area affected deviance rates, that social rather than individual explanations were needed, and specifically that *the level of disorganization* of the area caused the differences. Signs of this disorganization include the amount of poverty and unemployment, the presence of condemned buildings, crowding, transiency, and a low rate of home ownership. Combined these factors lead to low levels of cohesion and social control among whomever lives there.

Today the original ecological approach is criticized for paying insufficient attention to the reactions needed to create deviance (are the police more active in the core?), for the ethnocentrism implicit in the term *disorganization* (perhaps it is just a different type of organization), and for difficulties in deciding the causal direction, involving the issue of *social selection* versus *social causation*. Perhaps in some instances these areas attract deviants to them (selection) rather than produce them (causation).

We still see applications of an ecological approach today (although current researchers are more aware of its faults) in studies that reveal that crime rates are generally higher in urban than in rural areas (Sacco, Johnson, and Arnold, 1993). The excess is due mainly to property and vice crimes, which are more common in our cities, and not to crimes against the person, which are found everywhere.

According to a recent U.S. study (Dawson, Grant, Chou, and Pickering, 1995), alcoholism too is found more often in urban than in rural areas, partially as a result of availability. Further, there is generally more mental illness in urban settings than in rural areas (cf. Kates and Krett, 1988). Perhaps the more traditional life and greater community spirit combined with the slower pace (see Chapter 16, Urbanization) and lesser crowding of rural areas work against crime, alcoholism, and mental illness, while the problems found more often in cities increase them. Certainly Kennedy, Silverman, and Forde (1991) found that greater unemployment, higher divorce rates, and inequality are associated with higher rates of homicide in cities, although somewhat inconsistently. But on the other hand, sometimes the data do not fully support, or even contradict, urbanization theories. Canada's territories are not urban, yet their deviance rates are generally higher than the rest of a highly urban Canada. This may reflect the special problems faced by the Inuit (we will discuss this in later chapters). Whatever the explanation, however, difficulties in relying on urbanization as an explanation of deviance are clearly revealed.

Along with urbanization, mobility is also important in deviance (Gabor and Gottheil, 1984). Deviance rates tend to be higher where there is migration and a consequent decrease in the stability of neighbourhoods and social ties. Thus, the highest rates of crime in Canada are found in the territories, British Columbia, and Alberta, where migration is greatest, with the lowest rates in relatively stable Newfoundland, New Brunswick, and Prince Edward Island (Statistics Canada, 1996, *Canadian Crime Statistics, 1994*). This general east-to-west pattern (cf. Hackler and Don, 1990; Kennedy, Silverman, and Forde, 1991) was also discovered by researchers looking at alcoholism and use of alcohol (Eliany, 1991), suicide (Hasselback et al., 1991), homicide, divorce, and sexual assault (Dyck and Newman, 1988). All of these are findings Durkheim would have predicted.

In the next section we shall look at several of the most prominent sociological successors to this basic ecological explanation. Please keep in mind that each theory to be presented may be able to supply some insight into some aspect of some of the many forms of deviance; so the question is not which theory to choose, but how much each can add to the whole picture.

The theories are divided into two types, those that emphasize social structure (a macro-focus) and those that emphasize social process (a micro-focus). The former range from functionalist theories, which see deviance as a temporary, correctable issue, to conflict and radical theories, which see deviance as built into the very structure of society and thus less easily corrected. The specific focus of these structural explanations, moreover, can be on all of society or on certain parts, such as families or the school system. Social process explanations, in contrast, are generally symbolic interactionist and concentrate on how structure is translated by individuals into behaviour. They examine the learning and meanings of behaviour and its unfolding in stages over time. What these structural and process theories have in common is a perception that society is important in creating deviance.

Social structural explanations

Anomie theory

In Canadian society the achievement of wealth and material success is a widely shared goal. The education system, the mass media, parents, and peers all may encourage this pursuit, but these objects of material success are in limited supply and there are not enough legitimate means available for everyone to own an expensive car, nice clothes, and a large house. The discrepancy between the goals a society instils and the legitimate means it provides to achieve those goals can lead to a state of normlessness, a large-scale breakdown of rules, called **anomie**. According to Merton's (1957) functionalist model, the greater the discrepancy, the greater the anomie, and the greater the amount of deviance that can be expected.

Most readers of this book are using an acceptable means, higher education, in their attempt to achieve material success, a legitimate goal. Merton called such behaviour conformity. Conformists accept the goals of society and possess the means to achieve them. Individuals without such access to legitimate means have four options, each considered

The discrepancy between the goals a society instils and the acceptable means the society provides to achieve those goals leads to anomie.

deviant in some way. First, they can lower their goals to the level of their means, and engage in **ritualism**. Ritualists are the honest, hard-working people, often of the lower-middle and working classes, who live in modest, rented homes, own older cars, make some of their own clothes, and take few holidays. Their deviance is that they have given up on the fancy success goals, not that they have broken society's rules.

The second option for those who lack legitimate means is to keep the goals but to engage in what Merton called **innovation**. Innovators range from criminals to plagiarists and cheaters on exams, individuals who use deviant means to achieve non-deviant ends. Rather than becoming bankers and lawyers, innovators become thieves and con artists, in a parallel race to material well-being.

Retreatism, a third category in Merton's anomie model, involves rejecting both the means and the goals of society and instead withdrawing from society. Drug addicts, for example, are considered retreatists and are often scorned by conformists, innovators, and ritualists alike. (Yes, even criminals do not like drug users, finding them too unreliable for the cooperation needed for criminal activity!) On the other hand, retreatists also include members of religious groups who substitute equally valued goals, e.g., salvation or contemplation, for the more common goal of worldly success. Such retreatists generally are more positively viewed than others, but if they become too public or controversial in their activities, as in the case of some religious sects (see Chapter 10, Religion), their behaviour may then be seen as **rebellion**, the final type of deviance in the model. Rebels are in essence active retreatists, individuals who are vocal in their rejection of society's means and goals and who advocate a new social system.

The four types of deviance vary, but they share a common cause according to Merton: not flaws in the individual, but flaws in the structure of society.

Social deprivation and deviance

In support of Merton's ideas, most research shows that official crime rates are higher among the disadvantaged, those with less access to legitimate means such as higher education and full employment (cf. Hartnagel, 1992). For example, Schissel (1992) found unemployment related to homicide. A lack of means and crime often then reinforce one another in a vicious cycle (Huang and Anderson, 1991). For example, for the disadvantaged, a record of delinquency leads to difficulties in finding adult employment, which in turn leads to more crime (Hagan, 1992) and even fewer legitimate opportunities, etc.

Looking specifically at violent crime, we see that the disadvantaged tend not only to be more frequently criminal, but to be more serious and violent in their crimes as well (Ratner and McKie, 1990). As before, there may be some bias behind the actions of some agents in the criminal justice system that inflates the rates, but the assaults and murders you read of in the paper are found more often among the underprivileged. Although Native peoples are only a small percentage of the population, for instance, they are 23 percent of both suspects and victims in homicide cases—a cost of the poverty, crowding, substance abuse, and discrimination they experience (Johnson and Chisholm, 1989).

If hospitalization (official) records are used, social class is related to mental illness, as it is to crime. The data generally suggest that for serious forms of mental illness, the higher the social class, the lower the incidence of mental illness (Kates and Krett, 1988; Lundberg, 1991). Divorce, single parenthood, low education, and multiple disadvantages are also associated with a greater likelihood of mental illness. Less serious forms of mental illness, on the other hand, tend to be relatively more prevalent in the advantaged classes.

The interpretation of this association between mental illness and social class, however, is not straightforward. There is dispute over whether poverty leads to serious mental illness (social causation), or mental illness leads to poverty, via unemployment and unskilled job histories (social selection), with Ortega and Corzine (1990) favouring the latter. We mentioned these ideas in the discussion of the ecological approach. There is some truth in each explanation, but right now the evidence is leaning towards causation. The overriding effects of poverty that lead to stress and mental illness cannot be dismissed (Dohrenwend et al., 1992). Consistent with this finding is the fact that mental illness rates, as measured by hospitalization discharges, are generally higher in the poorer east than the west (Statistics Canada, 1992, *Health Reports, Mental Health Statistics, 1989–90*).

For just one more example of the relationship between deprivation and deviance, although education and income are positively related to the use of alcohol, with the poor and less educated more often abstaining (Eliany, 1991), unemployment is generally related to higher levels of consumption (Gliksman and Rush, 1986). This is especially true for young males (Temple et al., 1991), assuming they can afford the alcohol. Also, when the poor do drink, they often drink in greater quantities (Eliany, 1991).

Merton's focus on the discrepancy between widely accepted goals and the supply of adequate legitimate means for their achievement set the stage for still other theories. For example, Cohen's (1955) theory of gang delinquency argues that many adolescents, especially lower-class boys, do not have the values and skills (means) necessary to succeed on the criteria (goals) demanded by the middle-class school system. Sensing failure and feeling disapproval from teachers and peers alike, the boys band together to seek a group solution to their problem. Rejecting the schools' middle-class standards, which they find so hard to achieve, they establish a **contraculture**, a way of life exactly opposite to the middle-class ideal, but one in which they can succeed. If middle-class values include politeness, promptness, care of property, and reluctance to fight, these boys will be rude, late, destructive, and belligerent. They will measure their self-worth in how malicious, how negative, how useless—in short, how delinquent—they can be. Thus, in a way they are similar to Merton's rebels. (For a more recent discussion of adolescent subcultures and delinquency, see Tanner [1992], who argued that such subcultures are less likely to occur in Canada than in the U.S. because of opposition here to rigid educational streaming, and the presence of varied ethnic groups, which retards the creation of a unified working-class culture.)

Merton's model can also be extended to other applications. He wrote about material success, but his idea of anomie can be applied to all scarce or restricted commodities, from sexual satisfaction, to beauty, to honour and prestige. Often the means to achieve these socially encouraged goals are not sufficiently available. Even when they are, structured inequality or inaccessibility to opportunity prevents many from using them. Agnew (1992) added the idea that escape from pain may be the goal. Failure, abuse at home, and control by parents may lead to a search for new means to avoid or soften the pain such problems cause. So it is not just a lack of means to achieve material success that encourages innovation. Let us look further at the variables of age and gender in this broadened context of anomie.

Virtually all studies reveal that younger people commit more crimes than older people. In 1991, children aged 12 to 17 were 8 percent of the population but 23 percent of those charged with crimes (Statistics Canada, 1992, *Canadian Crime Statistics, 1991*). And the gap between young and old, especially in property and drug offences, may be increasing (Steffensmeier and Streifel, 1991). How is this relevant to anomie? Simply stated, youth more frequently lack means than do older people. They are marginal and segregated in adolescence, awaiting adult status, which is increasingly postponed since they are the frequent victims of the current high unemployment. Many become dependent, even hopeless, and as a consequence turn to drugs and steal what they need. Eliany found young males the most frequent users of marijuana (1991). On top of this, as a group youth are more rebellious than their seniors and always vulnerable to being labelled deviant, sometimes even "asking for" such a reaction after having found it difficult to fit in.

But when the relative powerlessness of youth coincides with a need in young males to assert what they perceive as adult masculinity, an explosive situation too often arises. One report suggested that youths are becoming more violent in their crimes (Statistics Canada, *Canadian Crime Statistics, 1994*, Catalogue 85-205E). Alder (1992) claimed that young men, especially those unemployed and without hope, use fighting both among themselves and against women to demonstrate their masculinity, to show that they are in control (and thus in possession of means).

Nor is this theme new. Lack of means to achieve adult status was used to explain male delinquency by Bloch and Niederhoffer (1958), who argued that boys will try to act strong, cool, independent, and smart, all traits they think adult males possess. Denied or lacking the means to those ends, however, boys' versions of those behaviours often end up as delinquent. Strength is translated into fighting; coolness into alcohol and drug use and dangerous driving; independence into disrespect for authority; and smartness into being a con artist.

Problems with anomie theory

Merton's anomie theory generated much criticism. Some objected to his assumption that everyone shares common success goals. Tepperman (1977), for example, argued that most working-class and poor Canadians never possess lofty goals and aspirations. Another criticism is that anomie theory was developed in the U.S. Lipset's (1990) comparison of Canada and the U.S. described in Chapter 3, Culture, would suggest that Canadians' greater respect for authority should result in less anomie here. Others focused on whether anomie is the effect of absolute poverty or of the contrasts of inequality. As already mentioned, the poorer east has lower crime rates than the wealthier west. Long-standing and widespread poverty, as in the Maritimes, may lead the poor to ritualism, the lowering of goals, and not to crime. The inequality of poverty amidst relative affluence, however, coupled with transiency, as in Alberta and British Columbia, may encourage innovation and crime as a response to the contrast (Kennedy, Silverman, and Forde, 1991). Finally, Ratner and McKie (1990) did not find unemployment a predictor of property crime as anomie theory would predict, and Schissel (1992) found only inflation, but not unemployment, related to robbery and theft.

A larger criticism concerns Merton's apparent acceptance of official crime rates, data which may reflect lower-class crime better than middle- and upper-class crime. These critics argue that anomie theory holds up less well when self-report studies are conducted. This type of data reveals that many of the rich, although law-and-order advocates, are innovators rather than conformists, such as the officials who accept bribes or kickbacks for work contracts or the corporate executives who fix prices or falsely advertise. Their deviance cannot be explained by a lack of means in any usual sense of the word. Only by arguing that these people lack legitimate means to allow them to achieve *extraordinary* goals would anomie theory work (cf. Snider, 1992). In their personal lives, more expensive cars and clothes, larger, more luxurious homes, and longer, more exotic holidays could be the lofty achievements that motivate the innovation of the rich. A similar explanation could be used for doctors who overbill (see the box entitled "Medifraud").

Other, conflict-oriented theorists have noted Merton's failure to examine the forces that cause the inadequacy of means. Anomie theory views crime in functionalist terms, as a dysfunction that greater opportunities can correct. But to many conflict critics, the inherent greed of the capitalist system is the cause of inadequate means. To them, only an extensive reconstruction of society, one that could remove inequality, will suffice. Welfare and unemployment insurance—state interventions to create means—are just insufficient (Schissel, 1992).

Medifraud

Physician fraud, like other white-collar crimes—those illegal activities committed by people in the course of their routine business or professional lives—is infrequently studied. Media attention, public fear, demands for police action, and even criminological research are much more likely to be focused on robbers and burglars. But is this emphasis misplaced? Certainly, if the monetary losses are compared, medifraud is probably one of today's more expensive crimes. Wilson, Lincoln, and Chappell (1986) estimated that Canadians were losing between $300 and $400 million annually to physician dishonesty. The figures would be higher today. Worse, such fraud is hard to detect, with the result that these criminals are infrequently prosecuted and punished.

The forms of medifraud are varied but easy to describe. Physicians can charge for extended (counselling) visits when they actually give regular service, provide extra and unnecessary treatments, make medically unnecessary referrals in return for commissions, or make claims for treatments not given. What is a bit harder to understand is the motivation. After all, physicians' incomes are not at poverty levels. Wilson, Lincoln, and Chappell (1986) argued that some physicians engage in medifraud simply because they want more money, just like other thieves. The rationalizations are different, however. Because their tax bills are high, some of these doctors feel that they deserve the extra compensation. Others, tired of bureaucratic rules and what they regard as government interference in their profession, engage in such dishonesty to gain what they feel is a fair wage. The high probability that they will get away with the fraud simply reinforces such perceptions.

Before you ask your doctor about such practices, remember that most doctors do not abuse the system, and that those who do are not the only white-collar professionals who criminally abuse their positions. University and college teachers, lawyers, accountants, and others all contain within their ranks some white-collar criminals.

Finally, generalize a bit and ask yourself whether there is a parallel situation for white-collar violent crime. Is there a similar inattention to the deaths caused by corporations that pollute the environment and provide unsafe working conditions, while the media, public, police, and criminologists focus on gun-toting or knife-wielding killers?

See Snider's 1993 volume from Nelson, *Bad Business: Corporate Crime in Canada* for more on this topic.

***Source**: Adapted in part from Paul Wilson, Robyn Lincoln, and Duncan Chappell, 1986. "Physician fraud and abuse in Canada: a preliminary examination."* Canadian Journal of Criminology, *28 (pp. 129–46).*

The theory is also sexist, although it would not have appeared so in 1938 when it was first published. Where do women fit in anomie theory? More often denied means than men, they should be highly criminal. Yet perhaps with the exception of Native women, whose crime rate is especially high (La Prairie, 1990), women generally have low crime rates. Indeed, in all societies young males are more criminal by far than any other group (Wilson and Herrnstein, 1985). For example, Ratner and McKie (1990) found that young males aged 16 to 17, followed by males aged 18 to 24, were the groups most implicated in property crime in Ontario. Merton never really dealt with this apparent contradiction. Part of the answer, however, lies in the next criticism. (We shall return to women and crime in other sections as well.)

Cloward and Ohlin (1960) questioned Merton's apparent assumption that deviant means are available to all. They argued that individuals need access to illegitimate means if they are to become innovators and, if denied that access, are forced into ritualism or retreatism. They first need role models or some other means to learn the required skills and then access to opportunities to innovate (1960: 168). Not everyone has the ability, or the chance, to become an embezzler, prostitute, or con artist, they point out. In another context, Gliksman and Rush (1986) used the greater availability of alcohol in cities (where there are more stores, which are usually open longer hours, than in rural areas) to explain the higher urban alcoholism rates. Similarly, the decline in alcoholism experienced during World War II, when supplies declined because the army needed alcohol for the war effort, also can be explained using Cloward and Ohlin's argument concerning the need for opportunities to innovate.

The most important application of this idea of access to illegitimate means, however, may be to explain some of the relationship between gender and crime. Part of the great underrepresentation of women among criminals may be due to women being given fewer opportunities. They may not be accepted by men criminals; they do not spend as much time in places where crimes occur, such as areas around bars; and they are less often in the positions of responsibility needed before one can engage in white-collar crime. Such a view might explain why in eighteenth-century Britain women were 45 percent of the felons (serious criminals), but only 15 percent by the early twentieth century (Feeley and Little, 1991). The growth of industrialism that occurred during the period and the arrival of the Victorian age coincided to restrict women more to the home and thus away from criminal opportunities. We shall return to this subject in Chapter 9, Families.

As you will read several times in this book, however, today women increasingly work outside the home for pay. On the one hand, the increase in the use of such legitimate means should decrease their crime. On the other hand, being in the work environment should increase their opportunities for learning crime. What is the truth? The reality is that women are appearing more frequently in criminal statistics. Whether, as a result of feminism and its effects, women will eventually equal men in their criminality (the convergence hypothesis) is doubtful (cf. Hartnagel, 1992). It has not happened in the area of alcoholism; female alcoholism rates are still less than those of males (Lo, 1995). Moreover, it is generally not the women who support the women's movement who become criminals. The fact is that when women become criminals, they are different from men criminals: their crime tends to be less violent, with more shoplifting and petty thefts, and fewer assaults, robberies, break and enters, and murders (cf. Alder, 1992). Silverman (1992) calculated a 9:1 ratio for men to women among those charged with violent crimes. Girls' delinquency seems to be less serious as well, more theft-oriented but not violent (Reitsma-Street, 1993), although there is some sign of convergence with that of boys (Statistics Canada, 1991, *Juristat Service Bulletin*, vol. 11.6).

Social control theory

Social control theory is a structural theory too, but one quite distinct from the anomie position. The biggest difference is that it sees all people as potential deviants, and then argues that social bonds constrain most individuals into conformity. Its focus is narrower than anomie theory as well, looking not so much on society in general as on families, schools, and other groups which serve as socialization agents, provide the bonds that discourage deviance, and include role models for conformist behaviour.

Hirschi (1969) popularized this position. He maintained that meaningful *attachment* to family and friends pulls people away from deviance. This occurs as they consider the opinions of those others before acting. Besides attachment, other ties include *involvement*, or investment of time and energy in conventional activities, and *beliefs* in pro-social values. Like attachment, they lead to a *commitment* to and respect for the value of conformity, and thus less deviance. Correspondingly, such things as alienation from family, empty time and leisure, and pro-deviant sentiments weaken social control and permit deviance (cf. Brownfield and Thompson, 1991; Gottfredson and Hirschi, 1990). Here we shall examine the effect of a few specific ties only—family, school, social support, and the changes associated with old age.

Let us begin with families, a potentially important resource for both children and spouses. Regarding children, a *meta-analysis*, one which examines all previous research on a topic to reach a general conclusion, found that broken homes are related to delinquency, for both boys and girls. They are more of a factor in minor than in major forms of delinquency and, parallelling this, they are more strongly related to self-report than official data (Wells and Rankin, 1991; LeBlanc et al., 1991). Indirect support for this conclusion comes from McCarthy and Hagan's (1987: 155) historical study of delinquency rates. They found that rates declined during the Depression, even though it was a time of widespread poverty, and attributed the reduction to

A weak attachment to high school, found more frequently among boys in lower-ability groups, is related to delinquency regardless of social class.

the presence at home of more unemployed parents, especially fathers. As they stayed home, fathers exercised greater control, especially over their sons, and as a result the juvenile delinquency rate among boys dropped. Mothers, the traditional controllers of daughters and not as affected by Depression unemployment, continued that control and thus female rates did not decline to the same extent. Delinquency rates then rose during World War II, when parents were away, and eased after the war when parents returned. These shifts are consistent with a social control approach and hard to explain for those who argue for biological causes of delinquency.

For adults the major familial social tie is marriage. Becoming unmarried has effects on drinking (Temple et al., 1991) as does single status generally, especially among males. At the same time, marriage and job stability inhibit criminal behaviour (Sampson and Laub, 1990). Being married also reduces the risk of suicide, as does religious affiliation, another social tie (Hasselback et al., 1991). In addition, marriage reduces chances for mental illness, but its effects vary by type of illness (Williams, Takeuchi, and Adair, 1992) and perhaps gender. Married women have higher rates of mental illness than single women (cf. Gove, 1990), a difference Stebbins (1988) attributed to loneliness among those wives not employed outside the home and to feelings of being overburdened among those trying to juggle the heavy, often conflicting demands of home and work.

Turning to the school as a source of social ties, Hartnagel and Tanner (1986) found that school experience is even more important than social class in predicting delinquency. A weak attachment to high school, found more frequently among boys in lower-ability groups, is related to delinquency regardless of social class. LeBlanc, Vallieres, and McDuff (1993) also found the school experience, including weak performance by the student and discipline by school authorities, to be an important factor in both delinquency and adult crime. Working part-time while in school may also be a factor. Tanner and Krahn (1991) argued that low attachment to school leads to the part-time work, which in turn leads to drinking and also to association with deviant peers who have sought a similar escape from school activities in their part-time work.

With respect to age, older people generally have fewer social ties and thus a greater potential for deviance, according to social control theory. Their crime rates, however, are very low. This may partly reflect a lack of means, but the other social ties mentioned by Hirschi are also a factor. For example, conventional activities and pro-social values, both generally associated with increasing age, inhibit crime. The data for suicide are more in tune with control theory, however, as rates do increase with age (Hasselback et al., 1991). The relationship between alcoholism and age is more difficult to interpret. Data on alcohol use (not alcoholism) reveal that as age increases alcohol use decreases (Eliany, 1991). Still, alcoholism is a problem in the older population, with older people, especially retired men, more likely to drink alone (Eliany, 1991).

With respect to mental illness, rates peak at ages 35 to 44 (Bland, Newman, and Orn, 1990) and then jump again in old age (Statistics Canada, 1992, *Health Reports, Mental Health Statistics, 1989–90*), although patterns vary with specific forms of illness. For example, schizophrenia begins earlier in life and depression generally occurs later (Bland, Newman, and Orn, 1988). Old age may be an especially vulnerable time as senile psychoses increase in prevalence. Part of this is biology, but the loss of status, jobs, friends, and vitality, along with increased poverty, also take their toll (Stebbins, 1988).

Finally, we should add that social support in general may be an important variable in reducing deviance. This theme parallels Durkheim's discussion of suicide discussed in Chapter 1. For example, the availability of confidants and friends can buffer the effects of stress for individuals and can help them avoid mental illness (Noh, Zheng, and Avison, 1994). A similar tendency occurs in the case of alcoholism: loneliness is an important cause, one that hinders attempts to give up drinking (Akerlind and Hornquist, 1992). The higher proportion of male suicides compared with female suicides, a 3:1 ratio (see Dyck and Newman, 1988), is attributed to social support as well.

There are several main criticisms of the social control position. Some critics reject its assumption that all would be deviant if they could. They do not believe that a release from social ties is all that stands between most people and robbing banks, or sexually assaulting or killing others. Rather than focusing on the absence of restraining factors as a cause of crime, these critics still want to look at push factors, at differences in individual motivation to commit crimes. They argue, for example, that anomie theory's concept of strain and the frustration of being encouraged to achieve what turn out to be unachievable goals must have some effect on individual decisions to commit crimes. A related criticism is that social control arguments may be better suited to minor forms of deviance, while other explanations may be needed for serious forms.

From another point of view, however, conflict theorists want to know what weakens the social bonds. Perhaps poverty and other societal flaws weaken the bonds that might otherwise constrain deviance, with any resulting deviance further straining the social bonds. They also ask how control theory can account for the crimes and other deviance of the powerful, those who are closely attached to others, are deeply involved in conventional activities, and appear to be committed to conformity. Are these people tied perhaps to their corporations and not to society at large? For answers to these questions we turn to structural theories that are more conflict-oriented.

Wife Abuse

Smith (1990a) examined some of the social factors associated with wife abuse in Toronto. His results parallel a number of other recent studies on the topic and some of what you have already read in this chapter about deviance. Briefly, he found that low family income, husband unemployment, and low educational and occupational attainment of either spouse are related to physical abuse. Younger women are also more vulnerable. On the other hand, ethnicity and religious affiliation are not significantly related to such abuse.

But there is much dispute surrounding such studies. A primary issue is measurement; many abused women just will not admit, due to shame, fear, or other reasons, their experiences. Thus such abuse always will be undercounted. A second problem concerns the types of abuse to be counted—its physical forms, mental abuse, verbal attacks, economic blackmail and tyranny, other aspects? Restricting the concept of abuse to physical abuse, as is often done, makes it easier to study but ignores its other forms and underestimates its magnitude. Broader definitions and better reporting might have revealed that wife abuse occurs everywhere, under all circumstances, and in all groups, and that the search for correlates is misleading. Indeed most husbands have engaged in some form of it at some time (cf. DeKeseredy, 1992; Lupri, Grandin, and Brinkerhoff, 1994). Abuse is not limited to a few rotten apples; it may instead be built into the very fabric of society, in patriarchy or in capitalism, for example.

Smith and others are aware of such criticisms. Indeed, in another article he pointed out that an ideology of patriarchy is related to abuse and that lower socio-economically situated men are more likely to accept that ideology (1990b). Men's need to be in control, perhaps especially prominent among those denied control at work, often leads to assault, he argued.

Finally comes the issue of how to eradicate wife abuse. Widespread restructuring of society will not come easily or quickly, and time is a luxury women suffering today and tonight cannot afford. While capitalism and patriarchy continue to exist, more specific programs, like arresting abusers, may offer some relief. Why do police daily ignore some domestic violence but virtually no bank robbery (cf. Dobasch and Dobasch, 1992)?

But the police cannot protect everyone and many women do not want their spouse jailed. Some abused women bring charges and later drop them, not because they are weak, but to use as leverage to improve their situation (Mendel-Meadow and Diamond, 1991). They use the threat of the police only as a bargaining tool, to pressure for better treatment—an alternative they prefer to the imprisonment and loss of income offered by the criminal justice system. No strategy pleases everyone in this widespread and difficult problem.

Conflict structural explanations

In their explanation of deviance, radical conflict theorists see much bias in the criminal justice system, focus almost exclusively on capitalism, and often proclaim the necessity for revolution. Less radical conflict theorists are aware of things like capitalist pollution and price-fixing, but also include underclass crimes, like the daily physical assaults to which the oppressed are so frequently vulnerable, in their analyses. They also place somewhat less blame on the police and courts, and accept the possibility of reform. The two views do agree, however, that power is a crucial factor in any explanation of deviance. For radicals it is economic power; for the less radical, other sources of power are important too. Let us start with the less radical position.

Hagan's (1988) approach to deviance uses Marx's measure of class—control over one's labour—in explaining the relationship between social class and deviance, whether it be delinquency, computer crime, homicide, or even fear of crime. It also includes non-economic variables, such as gender of child and family patriarchy. The crucial assumptions in his *power-control* model are that mothers have a greater role in socializing children than do fathers, and daughters are more controlled than sons. The result, claimed Hagan, is higher deviance rates among boys. This gender difference is least pronounced in homes where both mother and father have jobs where they are in control. In these generally wealthier and more egalitarian families mothers have more power and they treat their daughters and sons more similarly. The daughters in turn are more like the sons in their deviance.

Gender differences in deviance are greatest in patriarchal households, which are common when the father is controlled at work and the wife is either not employed outside the home or if so is also controlled. Note how the structure at work affects family structure. In patriarchal families mothers control their daughters more than their sons, leading the girls to be less inclined to take risks and less frequently deviant. Risk-taking is the key intervening variable (cf. Tanner and Krahn, 1991). The data for less serious forms of delinquency support this interpretation and may help to explain why wealthy adolescents engage in some forms of delinquency more than those less well off. They are less coerced, take more risks, and see themselves as above the rules and with freedom to deviate (Hagan and Kay, 1990). On the other hand, for more serious forms of delinquency and crime, it may be that patriarchy leads to male aggression and violent sons (Simpson, 1991), not among the rich, but among the underclasses.

Turning to more radical theorists, we see that they focus more on problems created by capitalism. Unemployment is growing and wages are decreasing, especially in the developed world. Capitalists use the law to remove the underclasses from a glutted labour market and to render them tame (Schissel, 1992). The purpose of the law, according to Spitzer (1975), is to transform "social dynamite," like unemployed youth, into what he calls "social junk," a category in which he included the elderly and mentally ill, also potentially costly but less of a threat to the capitalist order. From the last century's arrests for drunkenness (Brown and Warner, 1992) to current drug laws, some see the legal system as a tool to control the poor. Rather than legalize drugs, capitalists use the government to keep them illegal in order to reduce the potential of the "dangerous" classes for massive and organized civil disturbance (Christie, 1993).

The other distinguishing mark of the radical position is its demand for a total restructuring of society, one that would eradicate inequality and replace current band-aid solutions to the problem of deviance by making more legitimate means available. Critical theorists think that researchers should be part of this transformation, to put their theories into action in what they call *praxis*. (This term was introduced in Chapter 2, Research Methods.)

Before leaving this brief discussion of structural theories, a note is in order. Intellectual opponents as they are, functionalists and radicals often assess each other's position too harshly. Radicals see functionalists as right-wingers, law-and-order advocates, even bigots who blame the true victims of inequality and oppression (the criminals) and seek only minor adjustments to what are major structural faults. Functionalists see radicals as hopeless idealists who blame the rich for everything; as philosophers more than sociologists, holding theories that the data contradict; even as hypocrites whose revolutionary zeal is cushioned by the frequent affluence of their university lives.

The truth is less extreme. The two groups do emphasize different aspects of deviance, but generally each is aware of its complexity. For example, radical theorists admit that Marx wrote little about crime and, as mentioned earlier, they know that not all laws favour capitalists. Some are modifying their views in what is called *left realism* (cf. Young and Matthews, 1992). Functionalists, for their part, are aware of the costs of inequality and of the relativity of law. They also know about the extent of white-collar crime and are fully aware that sanctions for the crimes more frequently committed by the affluent are weak—sentences for auto theft, for example, are often more severe than those for tax evasion—and that the regulatory agencies that police the powerful are overworked, underfinanced, and vulnerable to funding cutbacks (cf. Snider, 1992). What is harder to reconcile are the means each group would use to remedy the situation. One looks more to major restructuring, the other more to individual rehabilitation. Whereas functionalists might increase prison sentences to deter crime, and more conflict-oriented criminologists push for decent wages and day care (Snider, 1991a), radicals still see the need for a revolution.

The major contribution of structural theories in general is to point out that factors beyond individuals are important in explaining deviance. They focus attention on society, on its expectations and the means it provides to individuals to achieve those expectations, and on social ties as constraints on deviance. They have greater difficulty in answering why, given the same social structure, some individuals become innovators while others become ritualists, or why some with few social ties conform while others deviate. Additional answers to these questions come from the social process theories which follow. In general they argue that the choices depend upon individual definitions of the situation, a symbolic interactionist concept.

Social processes and deviance

Differential association

The basic symbolic interactionist position explains deviance by examining how it is experienced and interpreted by individual deviants. Each act of deviance is seen as unique, and a subjective interpretation by the person who performs it will explain even its seemingly irrational aspects (Katz, 1988). One of the earliest symbolic interactionist theories of crime was advanced by Sutherland (1939), who argued that individuals learn crime the same way that they learn conformity—in an interactional setting with others. He maintained that if behaviour—criminal, deviant, or otherwise—is rewarded, it will be repeated. You read about this in Chapter 4, Socialization. The key to the learning of conformity as opposed to deviance is the groups with which individuals interact. If individuals interact more with others who socialize them to value deviance, either directly by rewarding it or indirectly by providing role models and perhaps vicarious reinforcement, they may develop an excess of pro-deviance definitions of the world and become deviant (cf. Heimer and Matsueda, 1994). If, on the other hand, they interact more with others who socialize them to value conformity, they should learn pro-social definitions of the world and become conformist. Thus the name of his theory is **differential association**: learning through association with groups having differing values, such that in the end pro-deviant definitions of the situation exceed conformist definitions. Clinard and Yeager (1980) found differential association theory applicable even to white-collar crime, with executives indoctrinated into a corporate culture that includes definitions and rationalizations favourable to the commission of corporate crime.

Expanding on Sutherland's ideas, Sykes and Matza (1957) argued that most delinquents feel guilty about violating the law and can engage in such illegal behaviour only after rationalizing their guilt through **techniques of neutralization**. These techniques, which are learned and shared among delinquents, permit them to define their behaviour as somehow acceptable and in turn allow them to stay basically committed to conventional society. (Such a view is quite at odds with Cohen's view of delinquents.) Sykes and Matza outlined five such techniques:

1. Denial of injury; for example, "No one gets hurt by shoplifting."
2. Denial of the victim; for example, "The victims deserved what they got."
3. Denial of personal responsibility; for example, "I was drunk when it happened."
4. Condemning the condemners; for example, "Everyone is doing it"; or, "Other people do worse things and get away with it."
5. Appeal to higher loyalties; for example, "I couldn't let my friends down; I had to help them."

Doctors who overbill, it is argued, use a variant of the second technique, claiming that government bureaucracy and artificially low fees force them into this fraud (Wilson, Lincoln, and Chappell, 1986), while some male hustlers may use a variant of the third, arguing that when they engage in homosexual behaviour it is just for the money, not for sexual pleasure. The point is that individuals *drift* in and out of deviant activities, back and forth between conformity and deviance, in contrast to the views of functionalist and conflict theorists alike, who tend to see determinism and a deviant–conformist dichotomy (Matza, 1990).

Evidence against this drift position includes Sampson and Laub's (1990) findings that childhood delinquency is linked to adult crime, alcohol abuse, school failure, unemployment, divorce, economic dependency, and other deviance. No drift is apparent in that overall deviant pattern, and instead social deprivation may be involved. Perhaps drift theory is less applicable to the socially disadvantaged. It is middle-class juvenile delinquency that is more often transient and disappears in adult conformity. Bias may be a factor here. If caught (Hagan, 1992), middle-class delinquents are given a second chance, thus allowing them to return to respectable society. Poorer delinquents live under more adverse conditions and are less frequently given those second chances. As a consequence, they cannot drift out as easily.

A more serious criticism of the whole differential association perspective is that it is circular. What causes the culture that is passed on in intimate groups that then encourages or allows crime and deviance? Answers to this question may require a return to structural theories such as anomie. Also, why do some learn to define deviance as acceptable while others who live in similar circumstances do not? There are no definitive answers to this issue, but the next symbolic interactionist position attempts to provide at least a partial social-process answer to this question.

Labelling theory maintains that society creates deviance through its reactions to people who break its rules.

Labelling

Another quite popular symbolic interactionist perspective on deviance, developed after Sutherland's efforts, is called **labelling theory** (see Schur, 1971, 1984). It poses a challenge to the idea of *deterrence* (using punishment to stop deviance) and maintains that society creates deviance through its reactions to people who break its rules. For example, if adolescents have taken some beer from neighbourhood garages, the victims can react in a number of different ways. First, they can just forget about it. Evans and Himmelfarb (1987) noted that many crime victims choose not to report their crimes (including some serious ones), especially if they define them as trivial or as something about which the police can do nothing. On the other hand, they can treat the theft as a crime and call the police. If they do so, they may have begun what labelling theorists call the **dramatization of evil** (Tannenbaum, 1938) or the **deviance amplifying process** (Wilkins, 1964). Both terms refer to the belief that reacting to deviants, whether this be called treating, rehabilitating, or punishing, may actually increase rather than stop the deviance and may even lead to more serious forms of it. The reactions backfire because of the way in which they are subjectively experienced (recall Thomas's "definition of the situation" in Chapter 4, Socialization) and are dysfunctional rather than functional. Exactly how this happens is outlined in a series of propositions, most of which can be traced back to the work of Lemert.

Lemert (1951) examined stuttering behaviour (cf. Petrunik and Shearing, 1988). He said that many children pause in their speech and have irregular or deviant (as defined by adults) speech patterns.

The stuttering that occurs prior to any reaction to it is an example of what Lemert called **primary deviance**. He believed that if adults ignore these speech problems, many children will outgrow them. On the other hand, calling their attention to the problem may make the children self-conscious. They may become anxious about their speech, may pause, and may speak even more irregularly, perhaps even stuttering. This may lead to more reactions from others, and then more stuttering, in a vicious circle. The children may eventually define themselves as stutterers and the stuttering become permanent. This later stuttering, the effect of being labelled a stutterer, Lemert called **secondary deviance**.

These same ideas were then applied to other forms of deviance: delinquency, mental illness, and even physical incapacity. The general model is one of a *self-fulfilling prophecy*:

1. Primary deviance occurs. It is widespread and caused by many diverse factors.

2. The audience reacts to some of this primary deviance, thus beginning the transformation of the actors involved from rule breakers into deviants.

3. Additional primary deviance occurs and again it has many sources—anomie, differential association, etc.

4. This deviance is followed by a stronger reaction from others, who begin to take steps to segregate the deviants from conformist others. On their part, the deviants seek out others, similarly or previously labelled, who in turn welcome the new recruits as allies and provide them with additional opportunities for deviance.

5. Still more primary deviance may occur, and more reactions follow. Those labelled complain about being singled out and direct some hostility at those who label them, even stereotyping them in return, as when police are called "pigs."

6. These acts generally bring on even stronger audience reactions. In a process called **role engulfment**, "deviant" becomes the master status of those so labelled. Their conformity is ignored or misinterpreted and their deviance magnified out of proportion. Thus, for example, when many people see homosexuals, that is all they see. Their occupation, education, charity, ability at sports—all other aspects—take a second place to the homosexuality. In another context, those never labelled as mentally ill can be nervous and tense some days, even lose their tempers, while recovered mental patients would be "suffering a relapse" were they to behave in a like manner. Basically, the audiences expect deviant behaviour, look for it, and are not disappointed. Even past behaviour may be redefined as deviant in a process called **retrospective interpretation**.

   One result of these activities by reactors is a deviant-versus-conformist dichotomy. People are frequently perceived as one or the other when the reality is they all fall somewhere along a continuum, in at least two senses. First, most deviants conform most of the time: most criminals dress the same way, eat the same foods, and watch the same television shows that conformists do. Second, and more importantly, most people are neither purely deviants nor purely saints. In the area of theft, for example, between professional thieves and absolute law-abiders are those who lie at customs, neglect to return money when too much change is given, do not report all income on their tax forms, etc. Between homosexuals and heterosexuals are not only bisexuals but also those who have engaged as adults at least once, although perhaps under special circumstances, in homosexual behaviour. In the area of mental illness too there is no mentally ill-versus-mentally well dichotomy; the distribution of individuals is a continuum from the most to the least mentally healthy.

7. The process continues as the labellers further isolate the deviants, who in turn spend more and more time with others similarly labelled. The deviants, starting perhaps with the weakest and most vulnerable among them, begin to define themselves as deviant. The stronger are more successful in this battle, and hold out longer before defining themselves as deviant.

8. Finally, deviant behaviour arises from those deviant self-concepts. The acts of the last stage constitute secondary deviance—deviance that arises not from the original various causes of primary deviance, but out of the deviant self-

concepts that result from the isolation, segregation, alienation, and even self-hatred of those labelled deviant. Isolated acts of deviance, to which perhaps the individuals initially are not fully committed, can thus become regular and stabilized, changed into *deviant careers* because of the reactions of others.

Lemert's original ideas on the potential negative effects of audience reactions to deviance were oversimplified by many, some even arguing that reactions cause deviance and that society should therefore never punish or label anyone as deviant. But these are distortions of labelling theory. Its originators wanted to caution official reactors to deviance, to warn them that those who commit deviant acts that are minor and common may turn to rarer, more serious acts if they are cut off from conventional society. For example, if children are segregated for being disruptive in class, a common and minor form of deviance, they may become hostile and angry; they may become truants, incurring greater penalties; eventually they may turn to theft and other less common but major forms of deviance. In the area of mental illness, Scheff (1984) argued that some mental illness is transitory, but it can become longer-lasting if others react to it. For example, those labelled mentally ill may be rewarded for playing sick roles, as when psychiatrists encourage them to accept their illness. On the other hand, their attempts at non-sick roles, to return to previous occupational and family roles for example, may be rebuffed. Confused, ashamed, and anxious, they may eventually accept the role of insanity as the only alternative open to them, and the initially transient mental illness may become chronic (cf. Link, 1991).

In short, labelling theorists seek to investigate the effects of audience reactions. Being symbolic interactionists, they argue that the deviants' definitions of self and of the situation are crucial, and that treatment or punishment, subjectively experienced, may move the individuals in an unintended direction. Moreover, they argue, a deviant does not emerge full-blown but must be developed over time in a process of exchange with the larger society.

In research of this proposition, the effect of imprisonment, perhaps the most extreme form of reaction, has been examined to see whether it deters further crime or whether it increases secondary deviance and criminal careers. Handleby et al. (1990) found, in a sample of 180 boys released from Ontario training schools, that 80 percent were incarcerated again, provincially and/or federally, some as many as five times. These data could be used to support the labelling theorists' position. Additional support comes from Letkemann's (1973) classic study of federal prisons, which found that some inmates learn criminal technical skills in informal relationships with more skilled prisoners, and make the contacts and alliances that will serve to advance their criminal careers after release. If, in addition, employers are reluctant to hire ex-criminals, the resulting unemployment may in turn encourage further criminality. Finally, Kaplan and Fukurai (1992) studied drug use among adolescents and found that negative sanctions lead to self-rejection, then to reduced motivation to conform, to greater interaction with deviant peers, to reevaluation of deviant identities, and finally to an increased predisposition to use drugs. Taken together, these and other studies lend some support to labelling theory's concept of secondary deviance (see also LeBlanc, McDuff, et al., 1991; LeBlanc et al., 1993).

Critics of the proposition that labelling increases deviance argue first that it is too broad. Types of reactions, types of deviants, and types of deviance should be examined to see specifically in which cases the proposition holds true and in which cases deterrence takes place. Perhaps informal reactions from friendly peers can deter rather than lead to secondary deviance. Perhaps those individuals with the most ties to society and more to lose can be deterred by treatment and punishment, rather than pushed to secondary deviance by them. For example, first-time, younger offenders, especially those who value the opinions of their labellers, may be deterred; similarly, Berk et al. (1992) found arrest worked better on spouse abusers who were employed and legally married than on those who were unemployed and not married. Finally, perhaps punishment can deter certain types of deviance; it does deter much shoplifting, and imprisonment appears to deter many robbers and thieves (Schissel, 1992) from repeating their crimes.

With respect to other forms of deviance, there is still debate about the validity of labelling theory. In the area of mental illness, Warren et al. (1989) argued both against and for it. If those labelled mentally ill feel in control of their lives, acceptance of the label may lead to improvement; if not, the label may lead to deterioration and greater illness (secondary deviance). On the other hand, labelling is less relevant to alcoholism (Combes-Orme et al., 1988); gender and other issues are more important. Together these arguments point to the need to qualify the theory, to make it less general. As before, it should not be a choice between either deterrence or labelling; both may be applicable in different circumstances to different forms of deviance.

A final major criticism of labelling questions the existence of secondary deviance. Cannot the causes of primary deviance continue to cause what only appears to be secondary deviance? Critics thus question the transiency of the primary deviance, often arguing that it has deep-seated origins and would have continued with or without labelling. Most of the previous structural theories would support this argument.

Victims and Crime

Criminologists have long been aware that crime victimization is not random, that some individuals are more likely to be victimized than others, and that a few people even suffer repeated victimization (Sacco and Johnson, 1990). This knowledge has led some researchers to focus on the interaction between criminal and victim, and to examine victims and their role in crime. An implicit assumption in their work is that everyone is a potential criminal and what needs to be explained are the factors that turn that potential into reality.

Early studies found that many victims know their criminals, and the term *victim precipitation*, (victims being part of the cause of crime), was even used. Although victims were not seen as a general cause of crime—anomie and other sociological theories were better explanations for that—victims in some circumstances were seen as having a role in their specific victimization. Think about those who leave keys in a running car while they run into a store, leave their houses unlocked, get drunk and then pick a fight, or walk in certain neighbourhoods after dark. Although this conclusion provided hope to some citizens that they could protect themselves from crime, by locking their doors, for example, it was also quickly criticized for coming too close to blaming the victims. Think of date rape—few today accept the view that whatever happened before the assault, from drinking to displays of affection, caused the lack of consent to be ignored.

A more recent focus of such research is the *routine activities approach*, which says that the coming together in time and space of suitable victims, motivated criminals, and the absence of effective social control (a lack of police, for example) are needed for crimes to occur (Kennedy and Baron, 1993). Again, focus is not exclusively on criminals and includes victims. Thus, researchers might examine the effects of the growing number of unattended houses (related perhaps to dual-wage-earner families or increased affluence allowing more holidays) on burglaries, or the number of bars in which young people congregate (combining alcohol and the gathering of crime-prone groups) on assaults. They would look to "hot spots," those specific addresses and intersections which have more than their share of criminal incidents (cf. Gabor, 1990).

While the addition of victims to the equation perhaps adds to an understanding of crime, many, especially conflict theorists, are critical of this type of research. They point out that it would omit much of corporate crime, in which victimization is so diffuse that a focus on specific victims is rare. Worse, it takes attention away from the larger and more general causes of crime: inequality and patriarchy, perhaps. Rather than preventing crime by attacking these overriding issues, looking at the role of the victim can lead only to a band-aid solution; for when some people learn how to reduce their chances of victimization, the chances of others are increased. Crime is merely displaced onto different, more available victims (Gabor, 1990).

Putting it all together

In general, the types of deviance discussed in this chapter are more frequently found among males, the single, the very young or very old, the poor, in cities, and in those provinces with high levels of population mobility. All of these factors share the common condition Durkheim uncovered in his study of suicide: a relative lack of integration. You can see that this social variable is as relevant today as it was one hundred years ago.

In concluding this section on theories of deviance, it must be repeated that the specific causes of deviance are complex, including both individual factors and social factors. To focus on individuals and ignore the role of society gives an incomplete and inaccurate picture. Remember that sociological insights must be added to those of other disciplines that seek to explain the same behaviour. They were never meant to stand alone. Thus, given social conditions such as anomie, poverty, illegal opportunities, and contact with groups that value deviance, the fact that not all individuals who experience these conditions experiment with deviance may call for an examination of individual factors and perhaps social ties. The fact that, after experimenting, only some individuals continue their deviance may also suggest an examination of individual factors. Social variables, like reinforcement, social ties, and labelling, may also be relevant here, however (cf. Tittle, 1995).

Given this qualification, in the general sociological model shown in Figure 5.2, most of the arrows leading to deviance still come from the social factors highlighted in our previous discussions of the effects of social structure and process on deviance. But, as pointed out in Chapter 1, What Is Sociology?, that is what sociology is all about: it seeks social explanations of social rates of behaviour.

Three final cautions are in order. First, the factors discussed in this chapter are sometimes only related to deviance and not necessarily its causes. Sociologists cannot conduct the experiments necessary to establish causation absolutely. This issue was discussed in Chapter 2, Research Methods. Second, there is often more variation within groups than between groups, meaning that the range and variation of behaviour are generally greater inside a group than between groups. For example, the difference between the number of crimes committed by the most and least criminal men is greater than the gap in average crime rates between men and women. This brings us to a third warning: the application of any of the generalizations made in the chapter to any specific individuals would be inappropriate. Being a young male in trouble at school may not have caused your brother's theft spree. Being a married female may not have caused your aunt's depression. Sociology deals with groups, not individuals. These cautions should be added to the previously discussed issues concerning the (often wide) discrepancy between official and self-report deviance rates.

FIGURE 5.2 Model of factors encouraging deviant behaviour

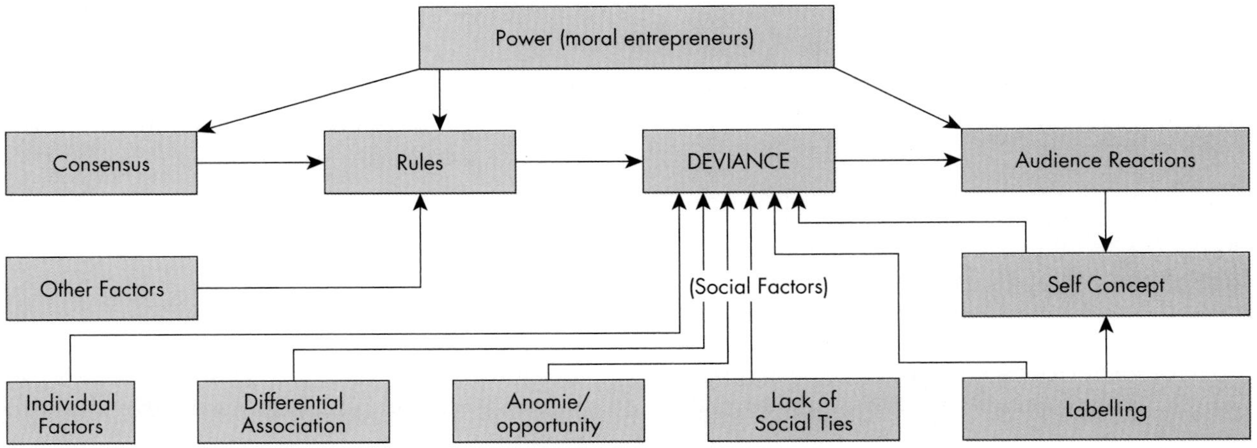

SUMMARY

Deviant behaviour is a designation given by a society to the things it considers somehow not normal and which it sees as worthy of some form of social control. These designations are culturally relative; almost every behaviour has been defined as deviant in some place or at some time, and as non-deviant at other times or in other places. Thus, deviance is a status conferred by society, not a quality intrinsic to the acts themselves.

Sociologists have long debated the sources of these definitions of deviance. Some emphasize a shared, society-wide consensus as the main source. Others focus more on the various social groups that compete to make such decisions. Still others feel that economics is the major force behind definitions of deviance. All three viewpoints and some compromise positions have merit, depending on the type of deviance being considered.

Counting deviance is also an issue. Deviance requires a reaction as well as an action. This rule breaker-versus-deviant controversy goes beyond the obvious idea that not everyone who is deviant gets caught, and looks at bias in the application of the label *deviant*.

Explanations of deviance include biological, psychological, and sociological theories. Sociological explanations examine social structure, including the idea that society does not provide enough means for everyone to achieve the lofty goals it instils, thus opening the door to deviance. Social process theories view deviance as learned in group interactions with others. Either way, social factors "cause" deviance.

Most sociologists prefer their societal explanations of deviance to those that emphasize the individual deviants, including most of those derived from biology and psychology. In questioning the structure of society, the making of social rules, the application of the rules, and specific social conditions including the effects of punishment, they seek social explanations. Still, deviance is to be understood as a complex interaction between the individual and society. Theories that claim to explain deviance must incorporate this fundamental principle.

QUESTIONS FOR REVIEW AND CRITICAL THINKING

1. If the poor had power to write the laws, what changes would you expect to see in the legal system of Canada? What might be the changes if only women made the laws?

2. As an exercise, think about why spousal abuse, long a reality to many women, emerged as a social problem when it did. The modern feminist movement is one part of the answer, but be specific and try to determine what else had changed. Alternatively, think of examples of how success can turn some of yesterday's terrorists and villains into today's revolutionary heroes, and even into elected leaders?

3. Apply labelling theory to growing old in our society, using the attainment of age 65 and retirement as the primary deviance.

4. Consider one or two examples of your own behaviour that others consider deviant. Which theory or theories of deviance best explain them? Which theory or theories are least applicable?

GLOSSARY

anomie theory the explanation that views the widespread discrepancy between a society's goals and the legitimate means it provides to achieve those goals as leading to normlessness and eventually to deviance

collective conscience Durkheim's term for the set of agreed-upon standards of society assumed to have arisen out of consensus

contraculture a way of life in opposition to, not merely distinct from, the larger culture; also called *counterculture*

critical school (also **radical school**) the view that the economic élite is the single major force behind definitions of what is and what is not deviant

deviance a condition or behaviour perceived by society as not normal and at least somewhat disvalued, and thus an acceptable target for social control

deviance amplifying process an argument stating that punishing individuals for minor forms of deviance may backfire and encourage them to take up more major forms of deviance, even deviant careers; related to **dramatization of evil**, the calling of attention to minor acts of deviance

differential association a theory that sees deviance as learned in small-group interaction, wherein an individual internalizes pro-deviant perspectives

ectomorphs, endomorphs, mesomorphs body types (thin, fat, and muscular, respectively) tested for their relationship to personality and then to crime and delinquency

innovation, ritualism, retreatism, rebellion Merton's four deviant adaptations to the problems created when society provides insufficient means to achieve its goals. Innovators find illegitimate means, ritualists water down goals, retreatists give up goals and means, and rebels seek both new goals and new means.

labelling theory the explanation of deviance that argues that societal reactions to minor deviance may alienate those labelled deviant and may cut off their options for conformity, thus leading to greater deviance as an adaptation to the label

moral entrepreneurs people who seek to influence the making of rules and definitions of deviance

pluralism the view that power in modern society is shared among competing interest groups. With respect to deviance, it means that definitions of deviance arise not from consensus, nor from any one group, but from a diversity of sources.

primary versus **secondary deviance** the former includes deviant acts committed prior to any social reaction. These acts arise from a variety of sources. Secondary deviance is that which arises out of the anger, alienation, limited options, and change of self-concept that may occur after a negative social reaction or labelling for primary deviance.

retrospective interpretation applied by society to those actors it considers deviant, it is the redefinition of their past behaviours as deviant as well

role engulfment a process whereby an individual's deviance becomes a master status. Good traits are ignored or misinterpreted, while bad ones are magnified out of proportion.

rule breakers those who commit deviant acts but to whom no one responds as if they have done so, either because they are not caught, or if caught, because they are excused for some reason

techniques of neutralization rationalizations that allow deviants to define their behaviour as acceptable

SUGGESTED READINGS

Corrado, Raymond, Nicholas Bala, Rick Linden, and Marc LeBlanc (eds.)

1992 *Juvenile Justice in Canada*. Toronto: Butterworths.

A discussion of the controversial 1984 Young Offenders Act, this edited volume discusses both the evolution of the law and its effects on Canadian youth.

Gottfredson, Michael, and Travis Hirschi

1990 *A General Theory of Crime*. Stanford, CA: Stanford University Press.

A controversial book from one of the pioneers in control theory, it attacks narrow disciplinary approaches in criminology, even showing how each discipline ignores the data it produces. Why men, adolescents, and minorities commit more crime is explained using concepts of family socialization and self-control.

Linden, Rick (ed.)

1996 *Criminology: A Canadian Perspective.* (3rd ed.) Toronto: Holt, Rinehart and Winston.

A multi-authored, comprehensive venture, this excellent volume includes discussions of law, criminal statistics, theories of crime, and patterns of criminal behaviour.

MacLean, Brian (ed.)

1996 *Crime and Society: Readings in Critical Criminology.* Don Mills: Addison-Wesley.

The readings look at things like white-collar crime, dating violence, and gangs using a critical perspective.

Sacco, Vincent (ed.)

1992 *Deviance: Conformity and Control in Canadian Society.* (2nd ed.) Scarborough, Ont.: Prentice Hall.

Dealing with topics as varied as prostitution, drug use, commercial crime, and political deviance, Sacco's authors examine the distribution, explanations (including the applicability of various theories), and control of such deviance.

Silverman, Robert, James Teevan, and Vincent Sacco (eds.)

1995 *Crime in Canadian Society.* (5th ed.) Toronto: Harcourt Brace.

Collected here are some of the best examples of Canadian research on crime. Included as well are a section on the sociology of law, a discussion of criminal statistics, and summaries of crime theories.

WEB SITES

http://www.sscf.ucsb.edu/soc/honors/deviance

Social Deviance

At this site, you will find definitions of social deviance, and examples of types of deviants. The site also contains links to other sites concerned with various forms of deviant behaviour, from youth gangs to organized crime.

http://www.copnet.org

The Copnet Homepage

The Copnet site provides links to information on crime and law enforcement agencies in Canada and around the world.

PART III
Social Differentiation

The previous chapters looked at culture and its acquisition, or lack of acquisition, by society's members. Research strategies to investigate these and other social phenomena were also examined. In this next section of the book, we focus on social differentiation. The learning of male or female roles is a major focus of Chapter 6, Gender Relations. Various feminist perspectives are offered as the chapter discusses the differences between gender and sex, examines cultural definitions of "masculine" and "feminine," and describes the costs of being a female or male in contemporary Canada. Sexuality, health and aging, poverty, and deviance are examined in turn as they relate to gender. The sources of inequality and the fact that various groups are unequal in their power and privileges are the central concerns of Chapter 7, Social Stratification. Another major topic in this area, especially for Canadians, is the study of the various racial and ethnic groups in society. This topic is examined in Chapter 8, Race and Ethnic Relations.

The analysis of social differentiation is central to all of sociology. First, as a dependent variable (recall Chapter 2, Research Methods), differentiation arises in part from, and then reinforces, various subcultures that are passed on to different groups and individuals in the socialization process. Individuals learn different roles, values, norms, and aspirations by virtue of their being born male or female, into different families, going to different schools, living in different geographical areas, and becoming members of different groups. When this differentiation becomes the basis of a ranking system and of inequality among the groups, it is relevant to the study of social stratification.

Second, social differentiation clearly can act also as an independent variable, with important consequences for the lives of individuals in society. Membership in a gender group, a minority or majority subculture and the occupation of different social ranks can affect aspects of family life, for example one's age at marriage, family size, and chance of divorce. Differentiation can also influence educational aspirations and achievements, church attendance and religious beliefs, and political behaviour; it can affect participation in social movements, health, longevity, and choice of residence. These topics will receive greater attention in the next two sections of the book. For now, remember that social differentiation is a key factor explaining much of the behaviour sociologists study. Keep this in mind as you read the rest of the book.

CHAPTER

6

Gender Relations

Lesley D. Harman

INTRODUCTION

Try to imagine yourself without your body. If you find this difficult, it is because so much of your sense of self comes from your physical presence. Next, try to imagine yourself having been born a member of the other sex. What would you look like? How would you dress? How would you act? How would your opportunities and life chances be different? The difficulty you experience in undertaking these exercises speaks to the social significance of gender.

People experience gender as a condition which partially determines their opportunities and life chances, happiness and sadness, definitions of success and failure. It influences many actions, decisions, and choices made on any given day: what to wear, what to eat, how to interact with others. In fact, most behaviour is greatly affected by what is "gender appropriate." Moreover, because gender norms are so pervasive, they are often invisible. Men rarely question why they do not wear dresses; women are often unaware of why it is that they avoid walking alone at night. Most people rarely think about the way they see themselves during the countless times they look in the mirror. If opportunities are offered or held back because of their maleness or femaleness, individuals may accept this state of affairs as "the way it is" rather than consider it unjust.

Yet it is the very pervasiveness of gender norms that makes them of interest to the sociologist. Why is it so important whether people are female or male? How are life experiences influenced? What are some ways in which these arrangements could be changed? These are just a few of the questions that will be addressed in this chapter.

We shall begin with a discussion of the gendered order and the gendered identity, two levels of analysis that can be applied to the study of gender. Then, we shall define the term gender, and examine the dominant theoretical perspectives applied to its study. That is followed by a consideration of the nature and implications of several prevalent myths of biological determinism, and a discussion of their implications. We shall then look at the ways in which language serves to support an ideology of gender inequality. The process of gender socialization will also be discussed, along with substantive areas concerning the body and sexuality, work and reproduction, health and aging, the feminization of poverty, and gender and deviance.

Gendered order and gendered identity

As with other social phenomena, gender can be analyzed at different levels. At the macro-level we speak of the gendered order; at the micro-level we speak of the gendered identity.

The gendered order refers to the differential treatment individuals are accorded on the basis of gender. This usually takes the form of opportunities offered or opportunities blocked.

The **gendered order** is supported by a fairly rigid set of **gender norms**, an integral part of most cultures, specifying appropriate behaviours for males and females, including a heterosexual assumption that sex between males and females is the only kind acceptable. The gendered order is also supported by an **ideology of gender inequality**. In this belief system, it is generally understood that males are superior to females. Men are more entitled to make decisions, to control resources, and to occupy positions of authority. Although this ideology has been challenged in recent years, particularly through the consciousness-raising of the women's movement, it continues to exert great influence in Canada and elsewhere.

At the micro-level of analysis, sociologists are concerned with how the gendered order is transmitted to and internalized by individual members of society. The **gendered identity** refers to the self as it develops in accordance with an individual's gender and the social definitions of that gender. **Gender socialization** is the process of acquiring a gendered identity, and begins at birth. Infants are born male or female, but through the process of socialization they become masculine or feminine. Through taking on the socially appropriate gender roles, children become integral parts of the larger gendered order. This often occurs in so unconscious a fashion that people may be blinded to its existence. It can be said, then, that the gendered order is socially reproduced through the process of gender socialization.

The two levels of analysis, order and identity, are intimately linked. Structures are reproduced through identities; identities tend to accept structures more or less uncritically. Yet it is clear that neither the gendered order nor the gendered identity are "natural" phenomena in the sense of being universal and immutable. Rather, they are cultural, and hence socially constructed. And the relevance for sociology is that anything that is socially constructed may be reconstructed. In other words, the existing set of relations can be changed.

Defining gender

Gender and *sex* are terms that are often confused, but for sociologists they have distinct meanings and are used to distinguish between biological and social categories. **Sex** is a biological category. With very few exceptions, humans are born decidedly male or female. Sex refers to physiological differences, the most pronounced of which involve hormones, the reproductive organs, and body size. Males are born with reproductive organs (penis, testes) that enable them to impregnate females. Males also have the capacity to develop greater muscle mass and strength than females. Females are born with reproductive organs (ovaries, uterus, vagina, and latent mammary glands) that enable them to bear and nourish babies. They live longer than males and have the capacity to withstand greater pain and stress.

Gender is a social category, referring to the social expectations that are developed and placed upon individuals on the basis of their biological sex. Different gender roles exist for males and females. They are socially created and then learned; people are not born with them. In taking on these roles individuals are expected to become "masculine" or "feminine" and to act in a "masculine" or "feminine" way. Masculinity entails a set of expectations that in Canada often includes dominance, aggressiveness, rationality, physicality, and strength. Femininity entails a set of expectations that often includes submissiveness, passivity, intuition, emotionality, and weakness. While these definitions are slowly changing, they remain fairly strong and distinct.

Acquiring a gendered identity means finding a place somewhere along the continuum between masculinity and femininity.

It can be argued that sex is an *ascribed* characteristic while gender is an *achieved* characteristic, terms you will see in Chapter 7, Social Stratification. Such an argument suggests that people are *born* either male or female, but they *become* masculine or feminine. The process of becoming gendered is one that may be more or less successful, depending on a number of factors including role models, sanctions, and opportunities to deviate from gender norms. Yet the notion that gender is achieved also suggests that there is some degree of freedom of choice about one's gender. From a sociological perspective, it should

Gender roles are socially created and then learned; people are not born with them.

become clear in the pages that follow that the power of the gendered order to influence and shape identity is so great as to suggest, however, that gender may also be seen as ascribed or assigned by society.

THEORETICAL PERSPECTIVES ON GENDER

A functionalist perspective

Functionalists generally take the biological differences between the sexes as evidence that males and females are suited for different types of work. Indeed some, fewer today than previously, see role differentiation between males and females as necessary and positive, and use biological differences to justify what is called the *gendered division of labour*. Such functionalist thought often looks to "the family" as the basic functioning unit of society (Parsons and Bales, 1955). The Parsonian family follows the "head-complement" nuclear family arrangement (see the discussion in Chapter 9, Families) in which the father (the patriarch) is the dominant figure and the decision-maker. The mother in this arrangement is submissive and the conflict mediator.

For Parsons and Bales, this nuclear family arrangement reflected an essential division of labour conforming to broader dimensions of social life. The **instrumental dimension** includes tasks of the **public realm**—the realm of paid labour and commerce, which they argued is the preserve of men. Instrumentality includes rationality, aggressiveness, strength, and domination. Males are socialized within the family into instrumental roles, making them most suited for the dog-eat-dog world of the workplace when they become adults. The instrumental "superior" in the family (the father) serves as the breadwinner and protector of the family in the public realm. The **expressive dimension** consists of the traits necessary for the demands of the **private realm**—the realm of unpaid domestic labour and biological reproduction—and is the preserve of women. Females are socialized within the family into expressive roles, making them most suited for the nurturing demands of the domestic sphere when they become adults. Expressivity includes emotionality, passivity, even weakness. The expressive "superior" of the family (the mother) serves as the unpaid homemaker, nurturer, and care-giver in the private realm. She is expected to give birth and then to care for the needs of the offspring, as well as those of the instrumental superior.

The gendered division of labour as portrayed by Parsons and Bales further assumes that males and females are naturally suited for their respective spheres, and that the distinctiveness of these spheres is both natural and necessary. Instrumental and expressive roles are seen to be complementary, that is, necessary to each other, as well as being necessary to the continued functioning and survival of society.

This functionalist view of the gendered division of labour has been criticized on many grounds. First, in today's society it is simply not representative of the way that most people live. Whether out of choice or necessity, most Canadians find other living arrangements more suitable. These alternatives challenge the assumptions that households must include both a father and mother and their biological offspring, and that the division of labour should be such that women work in the home while men work outside of the home. Census data from 1991 revealed that 13 percent of Canadian households were lone-parent households, 82 percent of these headed by females, and over half of married women worked outside of the home for pay. Increasingly, same-sex couples are raising children. Clearly, contemporary trends do not bear out the picture painted by Parsons and Bales in the 1950s.

Nevertheless, the ideology represented by the functionalist perspective continues to have an impact. In the mass media, education, religion, law, and policy, there is a tendency for men to be portrayed in instrumental roles, and for women to be portrayed in expressive roles. The view that these roles are somehow natural dies hard, although, as we shall see, there is no evidence for such a claim. Arguments concerning complementary roles also tend to overlook the fact that these roles are unequal. Within the typical Parsonian family, the male has financial autonomy and decision-making power. He has a position in the public realm that gives him access to status and resources unavailable to a woman. The female, on the other hand, is isolated in the home, frequently devalued in her role as homemaker, and dependent both emotionally and financially on the male breadwinner. This state of affairs may indeed be complementary, but it certainly gives an advantage to males, to the systematic disadvantage of females. Indeed, a major criticism of the functionalist view is that it justifies an ideology of gender inequality.

The symbolic interactionist perspective

The fundamental premise of symbolic interactionism is that reality is socially constructed, and that the social world is in a constant state of negotiation and renegotiation. Unlike functionalists, symbolic interactionists thus see nothing natural or deterministic about the relationship between sex and gender. Rather, they focus on the ways in which masculinity and femininity are socially constructed (Mackie, 1987). For symbolic interactionists, the process of becoming gendered is a social one that involves the development of a gendered identity. The impact of gender socialization, then, is seen as great indeed.

As evidence for the view that sex and gender need not necessarily be related in a deterministic and immutable way, symbolic interactionists often cite cases in which the acquisition of a gendered identity is not as straightforward as is usually the case. For example, in certain rare instances, male infants are born without a penis and testes. Assumed to be girls, they are raised as such. When a penis later appears and they discover that their genitalia are in fact those of males, *gender confusion* often results (Renzetti and Curran, 1992). Transsexuals provide another example. Here individuals find themselves physically male or female, but socially define themselves as the other sex. Thus their sense of self as a gendered identity is different from their biological sex. People who think of themselves as of one gender, but feel biologically trapped in bodies of the other, may even seek the radical measure of sex-change operations. (See the boxed insert on "Gender Confusion").

"Gender blenders" (Devor, 1989) are individuals who are born anatomically female but who are routinely mistaken for men. Devor reported that for the women she studied, rather than causing a sense of confusion, being mistaken for men led to certain revelations about gender relations. These women realized that being mistaken for a male could have its advantages. It exempted them from the subordinate treatment given to the "feminine" women they saw all around them. "They learned that, as men, they were free to do the things they enjoyed most, where they wanted to, and when they wanted to. As women, they felt humiliated, constrained, and vulnerable to

"Gender Confusion": The Case of Transsexuals

In the 1950s the world was shocked by Christine Jorgensen's sex-change operation in Denmark. The reaction was not much lessened a generation later when Richard Raskind, once captain of the Yale tennis team, army officer, and father, underwent similar surgery and became Renée Richards, professional tennis player and coach of Martina Navratilova.

For men—and many more men undergo this operation than women—the process involves electrolysis, estrogen therapy, the removal of male sexual parts, and sometimes the construction of a vagina; for women it involves a hysterectomy, breast removal, and additional hormones, and, less frequently, the creation of a penis is attempted.

The numbers are not large, but they do relate to what we have been discussing—that gender is a socially constructed phenomenon. Transsexuals are people whose biological sex is inconsistent with their gendered identity. Anatomically they are one sex, but they feel like and want to be defined as a member of the other sex. Needless to say, transsexuals can never create children, but in virtually all other ways they seek to adopt a new sexual identity. It is much more than transvestism, the wearing of clothes of members of the other biological sex. Transsexuals identify with members of the opposite sex so much that they are willing to endure physically and socially painful operations to become members of the other sex.

Why do more men than women undergo this process? Mackie (1985) speculated that sexism is one answer. Men acting in a feminine manner in our society—in their dress, for example—are less tolerated than women who act in a masculine manner. Men beyond a certain age cannot live together without questions being asked. Thus some of the men undergo surgery to avoid the stigma of homosexuality.

Source: *Adapted from Marlene Mackie, 1985.* Constructing Women and Men: Gender Socialization. *Toronto: Holt, Rinehart and Winston (pp. 12ff.).*

sexual attack and violation" (Devor, 1989: 145). (See the boxed insert on "Gender Blending").

An either/or duality between masculinity and femininity is widely accepted in Canadian society as normal and natural. However, it is becoming increasingly clear that socialization into rigid roles is often neither consistent nor enduring and that a blending of the two roles is common. Nowhere is this issue more evident than in the case of homosexual behaviour . It is now estimated that up to 10 percent of the population may reject exclusive heterosexuality, instead engaging in same-sex relationships (homosexuality) or in both homosexual and heterosexual relationships (bisexuality). For these individuals, the social sanctions meted out may be more than outweighed by the new-found freedom of sexual expression. Indeed, the challenge posed by gays and lesbians to the gendered order and its **heterosexual assumption**, that the only natural and appropriate sexual activity is heterosexual, is a profound example of the social construction of gender.

The greatest contribution of the symbolic interactionist perspective to the study of gender is that it recognizes that the process of becoming gendered is a social one, not a natural one. For symbolic interactionists, what can be negotiated can also be renegotiated. This view provides the possibility that the existing gendered order can change, just as gendered identities can be shaped in altogether different ways.

A Marxist conflict perspective

Not surprisingly, most Marxist theorists see gender as a source of social inequality, but they have been unwilling, for the most part, to relinquish the view that social class is the dominant cause of oppression in capitalist society. Patriarchy, or the system of male dominance, is seen to be a product of capitalism, and hence to play a secondary role. The oppression of women, then, is only one manifestation of the injustice of a class-based society.

In his writings, Marx tended to take a position very similar to that of the functionalists on the question of the gendered division of labour. Like functionalists, Marx saw biology as destiny and wrote of

Gender Blending

Sociologist Holly Devor studied fifteen women whom she called "gender blenders": women whose physical appearance caused them to routinely be mistaken for men. The life of a gender blender reveals surprising pleasure and liberation from the constraints of traditional "femininity."

The gender blending females in this study learned well the tenets of the patriarchal gender schema which dominates North American society. They learned that their female sex was supposed to be the irrefutable fact which made them into women and that, as women, they were supposed to behave in a feminine fashion. They also learned, early in their lives, that femininity was patriarchy's way of marking a portion of the population for a secondary status in the service of men.

At the same time as they were learning that femaleness was a stigmatized condition in their society, they were also learning to be proficient at, and take pleasure in, the ways of masculinity. By accident, they discovered that if, as adults, they practised the degree of masculinity to which they had become accustomed as youngsters, they could neutralize some of the stigma of their femaleness as well as enjoy some of the privileges usually reserved for men.

This realization served to reinforce their tendency to masculinity in three ways. Firstly, their masculinity was an accustomed stance which had been with them since their childhoods. They had little desire to change their habits and were thus pleased to find reasons to support their continuance of that behaviour. Secondly, the contrast between their status as women, on the one hand, and the freedom and respectableness they acquired when mistaken for men, on the other, only confirmed and solidified their awareness of the stigmatized condition of womanhood. Their sense of femininity as a contaminant to be avoided was thus enhanced. Thirdly, they simply found joy in the sense of power that walking the streets with the freedom of men imparted to them. That sense of freedom of movement and security of person, on an everyday individual basis, gave them a feeling of exhilaration unmatched in their experience of femininity. They learned that, as men, they were free to do the things they enjoyed most, where they wanted to, and when they wanted to. As women, they felt humiliated, constrained, and vulnerable to sexual attack and violation. Their choice was to buy their public dignity and freedom at the price of their womanhood.

Source: *Holly Devor, 1989.* Gender Blending: Confronting the Limits of Duality. *Bloomington, IN: Indiana University Press (p. 145).*

women "primarily as mothers, housekeepers, and members of the weaker sex" (MacKinnon, 1989: 13). MacKinnon (1989: 256) went so far as to claim that "no distinction exists between these views of Marx and those of contemporary 'pro-family' conservatives." For the most part, Marx's writings on work in capitalist society were exclusively about men.

Engels' much discussed *The Origin of the Family, Private Property, and the State* (1972 [1884]) did give an account of the subjugation of women, arguing that it had its origins with the introduction of private property. With private property came the nuclear family, with men as breadwinners and property owners and women as propertyless reproducers. Engels likened women in the family to the working class, in their economic oppression, and men in the family to the capitalist class.

The historical accuracy of Engels' theory has been questioned (MacKinnon, 1989). His work has also been criticized for its functionalist presupposition that the original gendered division of labour had its roots in the division of labour in heterosexual sexual intercourse (men and women performing different roles), implying a universality and permanence to these relations—in other words, that they cannot be changed. Thus, for the most part, it is left up to more recent feminist theories to provide a systematic critique of the nature of patriarchy in capitalist society.

Feminist perspectives

Feminist perspectives are widely misunderstood. There are in fact many feminisms, and sociologists calling themselves feminists do not always agree.

Most feminist perspectives do agree, however, that Canada is a *patriarchal* society and that gender relations are the dominant tool for the oppression of women. **Patriarchy** is the system of male dominance through which males are systematically accorded greater access to resources and women are systematically oppressed.

Maternal feminism was a movement that took hold in Canada toward the end of the last century. Maternal feminists, such as Nellie McClung and Emily Murphy, held that women's real strength lay in their reproductive capacities. Women's roles as wives and mothers were seen, as in the functionalist perspective, as their true calling and source of status. Efforts to dilute women's maternal role, through the limitation of biological reproduction and work outside of the home, were regarded as threats to their power. Such a view is not widely shared by feminists today, since it is precisely the rigid equation between femaleness and reproduction that is seen to be oppressive.

Liberal feminism takes the view that structural inequality between women and men is the consequence of a lack of equality of opportunities, rights, and education. Liberal feminists tend not to question inequality in society generally, only women's place in existing unequal social structures. They hold that this inequality can be eradicated through the creation of laws and social policies that will alter power relationships. For example, liberal feminists argue that governmental provision of universal day care would free women from the demands of child care and allow them to enter the paid workforce. Liberal feminists also argue that legislation calling for "equal pay for work of equal value" would be effective in eliminating structural inequality in the workforce, so that women and men would be equitably paid for their work outside the home. A major criticism levelled against liberal feminism, however, is that it does not recognize that structural inequalities are rooted in deeper material (capitalist) and ideological (patriarchal) relations which must be challenged and overcome before true equality between the sexes can be achieved. Governments cannot change these relations so easily.

Socialist feminism seeks to meld Marxism and feminism. Those taking this perspective see the roots of gender inequality in the combined oppressiveness of capitalism and patriarchy. Socialist feminists argue that capitalism produces isolating and alienating domestic roles for women in which they occupy a low status and are systematically devalued. It is only through a direct challenge to capitalism that the roots of patriarchy can be destroyed. Some authors (MacKinnon, 1989) have pointed out that this perspective is in fact an "unhappy marriage" between two incompatible views. As we have seen in the discussion of the Marxist perspective, there is a fundamental antagonism surrounding issues of class and gender between Marxists and feminists. This antagonism is not resolved but rather held in tenuous balance by those who call themselves socialist feminists.

Radical feminism is a perspective that sees women's oppression as fundamentally rooted in the system of patriarchy. The approach calls for equality between the sexes through the abolition of male supremacy. Radical feminism has been responsible for raising consciousness and inspiring changes in a variety of areas aimed at reducing the oppression of women. For example, its recognition that violence against women is fundamentally unacceptable has moved Canadian society from one in which the problem of wife battering was laughed out of the House of Commons in the early 1980s to a quite different climate, in which significant government funding is being directed towards education and change in the area of family violence. Awareness that women's voices have been systematically silenced in culture, education, and politics has led to efforts to open up new avenues for expression including women's culture, women's language, women's literature, women's music, and women's "ways of knowing." Some radical feminists argue for the end of women's reproductive role, for it is seen to be the most widespread source of oppression. The search for alternative reproductive technologies, such as *in vitro* fertilization, may also be seen as an avenue for the permanent liberation of women from the masculine domination of their bodies. Others in this category advocate "separatism"—that is, the establishment of separate spheres for women and men.

Generally speaking, the different feminist perspectives address to varying degrees the main sources of female oppression in society, and come to

Masculinity and the "Men's Movements"

As with the diversities in "feminisms," it is important to recognize that there are many "masculinities" present in Canadian society today. The "macho" image has given way to a broader range of choices. Among these, at least three "men's movements" have come onto the 1990s gender politics picture: the profeminist movement, the gay rights movement, and the men's rights movement.

The profeminist movement

Men supporting the profeminist movement are concerned with eradicating the system of patriarchy which has systematically privileged all men. Some adherents of this perspective feel that feminism is the political movement that will liberate men and women alike from the oppression of patriarchy (Salutin, 1993) and permit men to embrace less traditional models of masculinity. One recent, highly visible expression of this movement in Canada has been the "White Ribbon" campaign, in which men across the country have organized against violence against women. This is a significant part of the general societal response to the 1989 Montreal massacre, in which fourteen women were murdered at École Polytechnique, and its aniversary has become recognized across Canada as a time for men to express their support of women's right to be free from violence and to show that not all men are violent.

The gay rights movement

Male homosexuals pose a particular challenge to definitions of masculinity. The choice to engage in same-sex relationships violates the heterosexual assumption of patriarchal society, and continues to be regarded as unnatural and immoral by many citizens. Yet, gay activists have fought against the discrimination and the "gay bashing" which have often resulted from a climate of homophobia, or the fear of homosexuality. Although the Canadian Supreme Court refused, in a close vote, to recognize homosexual marriages, Canada took a leadership role in the liberalization of regulations concerning homosexuals when, in the late 1980s and early 1990s, it lifted its ban on homosexuals in the military, some of its provinces and municipalities extended benefits to same-sex couples, and most provinces extended human rights protection to gays and lesbians.

The men's rights movement

In contrast to the profeminist and gay rights movements, the men's rights movement has emerged to oppose feminist efforts. For some men, strides towards equality for women and gays have been experienced as a form of "reverse discrimination" in which they have begun to feel victimized for being heterosexual males. Various groups have organized to express dissatisfaction with women's rights, and have demanded theirs back.

very different conclusions about how gender inequality can be resolved. They all share, however, a recognition that it is in the areas of biological reproduction and paid labour that the main problems, and their solutions, seem to lie.

NATURE VERSUS NURTURE: MYTHS OF BIOLOGICAL DETERMINISM

The nature-versus-nurture debate, which you saw in Chapter 4, Socialization, is at the root of much of the current confusion and debate over the question of sex and gender. Biological determinism suggests that individual potential is patterned before birth by ascribed hereditary factors, as found in genetic make-up. When applied to the question of gender relations, this appears as the "sex is destiny" argument: social roles and gender are predetermined by biological sex. (See the boxed insert on "Making Sense of *la différence*").

But to arrive at such views, people must take a cultural product and treat it as if it were "natural"—from nature. Some myths reflecting this tendency include "it is natural for boys to be strong and girls to be weak," "it is not natural for boys to cry," "it is not natural for women to have body hair," "it is not

Making Sense of la différence

Few areas of science are as littered with intellectual rubbish as the study of innate mental differences between the sexes. In the nineteenth century, biologists held that a woman's brain was too small for intellect but large enough for household chores. When the tiny-brain theory bit the dust (elephants, after all, have bigger brains than men), scientists began a long, fruitless attempt to locate the biological basis of male superiority in various brain lobes and chromosomes. By the 1960s, sociobiologists were asserting that natural selection, operating throughout the long human prehistory of hunting and gathering, had predisposed males to leadership and exploration and females to crouching around the campfire with the kids.

Recent studies suggest there may be some real differences after all. And why not? We have different hormones and body parts; it would be odd if our brains were 100 percent unisex. The question, as ever: What do these differences mean for our social roles, in particular the division of power and opportunity between the sexes?

Don't look to prehistoric life for an answer. However human beings whiled away their first 100 000 years or so, few of us today make a living tracking down mammoths or digging up tasty roots. Much of our genetic legacy of sex differences has already been rendered moot by that uniquely human invention: technology. Military prowess no longer depends on superior musculature or those bursts of hormones that prime the body for combat at axe range. As for exploration, women—with their lower body weight and oxygen consumption—may be the more "natural" astronauts.

But suppose the feminists' worst-case scenario turns out to be true, and males really are better, on average, at certain mathematical tasks. If this tempts you to shunt all girls back to home economics, you probably need remedial work in the statistics of "averages" yourself. Just as some women are taller and stronger than some men, some are swifter at abstract algebra. Many of the pioneers in the field of X-ray crystallography—which involves three-dimensional visualization and heavy doses of math—were female, including biophysicist Rosalind Franklin, whose work was indispensable to the discovery of the double-helical structure of DNA.

Then there is the problem that haunts all studies of "innate" sex differences: the possibility that the observed differences are really the result of lingering cultural factors. Girls' academic achievement, for example, as well as apparent aptitude and self-esteem, usually takes a nosedive at puberty. Unless nature has selected for smart girls and dumb women, something often goes very wrong at about the middle-school level. Part of the problem may be that males, having been the dominant sex for a few millenniums, still tend to prefer females who make them feel stronger and smarter. Any girl who is bright enough to solve a quadratic equation is smart enough to bat her eyelashes and pretend that she can't.

Teachers too may play a larger role than nature in differentiating between the sexes. Studies show they tend to favour boys by calling on them more often and pushing them harder. Myra and David Sadker, professors of education at American University, have found that girls do better when teachers are sensitized to gender bias and refrain from sexist language, such as the use of "man" to mean all of us. Single-sex classes in math and science can also boost female performance by eliminating favouritism and male disapproval of female achievement.

The success of such simple educational reforms only underscores the basic social issue: Given that there may be real innate mental differences between the sexes, what are we going to do about them? A female advantage in reading emotions could be interpreted to mean that males should be barred from psychiatry—or that they need more coaching. A male advantage in math could be used to confine girls to essays and sonnets—or the decision could be made to compensate by putting more effort into girls' math education. Americans, in effect, already compensate for boys' apparent handicap in verbal skills by making reading the centrepiece of primary-school education.

We are cultural animals, and these are ultimately cultural decisions. In fact, the whole discussion of innate sexual differences is itself heavily shaped by cultural factors. Why, for example, in the U.S. is the study of innate differences such a sexy, well-funded topic right now, which happens to be a time of organized feminist challenge to the ancient sexual division of power? Why do the media tend to get excited when scientists find an area of difference and ignore the many reputable studies that come up with no differences at all?

However science eventually defines it, *la différence* can be amplified or minimized by human cultural arrangements: the choice is up to us, and not our genes.

Source: *Barbara Ehrenreich, 1992. "Making sense of la différence."* Time *139, 3 (p. 43). Reprinted by permission.*

natural for men to stay home with children while women work outside of the home," etc.

A frequent implication of biological determinism is that most highly valued social roles in the public domain are seen to be natural for men because they require "masculine" traits, such as rationality, for their successful performance. Women, on the other hand, are encouraged to be more emotional than men, which in turn may lead to expectations that they are less capable of rational thought and decision-making. Systematically devalued roles, such as care-giving and unpaid domestic labour, are then seen to be natural for women because they require "feminine" traits, such as nurturing, for their successful performance.

The biological determinist argument is fundamental to the functionalist perspective and to most conservative arguments against changes aimed at greater gender equality. It can serve as the basis for discrimination and can inhibit social changes, as can the "nature" (as opposed to nurture) position in general. As one might imagine, researchers have devoted a great deal of effort to determining the validity of this view. The basic issue is the extent to which social traits can be traced to biological sex, if at all. In seeking answers to such questions, most researchers study very young children because they are not very far along in the socialization process, and thus any sexual differences uncovered should be due more to biology than to culture. The conclusions of this research thus far indicate that while there are certainly physical and physiological differences between girls and boys, there is no evidence to suggest either the "natural" complementarity of females and males or the "natural" superiority of males over females. Instead, what is revealed is that much of this way of thinking is based on myths with little basis in fact. In fact it is precisely the social construction of gender and the patterning of the gendered order that produce a self-fulfilling prophecy of male dominance, female submissiveness, and a heterosexual assumption. This is not natural; it is cultural. Five prevalent myths are discussed below (Renzetti and Curran, 1992).

Biological determinism applied to gender relations is seen increasingly as myth.

Myth 1: Boys are born more independent than girls.

The amount of "separation anxiety" experienced by infants upon removal of a parent, and the extent to which infants cling to parents when they are present, are frequently used by researchers as indications of independence versus dependence. Maccoby and Jacklin (1974) examined twenty such studies of children younger than two years of age. Twelve revealed that there are no sex differences, while the rest showed that in some cases boys are more dependent and in others girls are. Thus, the independence of adult males as compared with the dependence of adult females cannot be justified by the claim that these are natural relations.

Myth 2: Boys have superior visual-spatial ability; girls have superior verbal ability.

The predominance of adult males in occupations requiring training in math and the natural sciences, and the tendency to give responsibility for exacting tasks to males, are often attributed to the "natural" superior visual-spatial ability of males. Similarly, the relegation of adult women to more "affective," care-giving, expressive roles is seen as a suitable outcome of their "natural" superior ability to verbalize. Yet, again, we find that efforts of researchers to substantiate such claims have been unsuccessful.

Maccoby and Jacklin (1974) found that in nine studies of newborn children and thirty-three studies of infants a year old or less, there is no evidence of sex difference in spatial perception for newborns and inconsistent findings in spatial perception for infants. Other researchers have upheld this conclusion, finding no sex differences until children have reached adolescence, at which time any results are seriously confounded by environmental factors (Fausto-Sterling, 1985). Cross-cultural studies, moreover, reveal that there is no evidence for a universal superiority of males in the area of visual-spatial ability. Harmatz and Novak (1983) found no sex differences pertaining to that ability among the Inuit.

With regard to verbalization, there has been some support for the view that girls become talkative earlier and to a greater degree than boys, but this is countered by a large number of studies finding no sex differences. Cross-cultural research offers no support for the view that female verbal superiority is universal (Harmatz and Novak, 1983).

The research suggests, then, that visual-spatial and verbal traits often attributed to adult men and women must be understood as heavily influenced by the socialization process rather than as naturally occurring events. In particular, the role of formal education in streaming boys and girls into "typical" male and female areas of study has been criticized for reinforcing these differences (see the discussion in Chapter 11, Education).

Myth 3: Boys are more aggressive; girls are more passive.

Probably the most compelling myth of innate sex differences concerns the belief that males are more aggressive than females. This has variously been attributed to the amount of testosterone in the male body, the greater capacity of males to develop strength, and the erroneous belief that males have a greater sex drive than females.

This highly controversial issue is made more complex by difficulties in defining and measuring aggression, particularly among infants. The interpretation of what is an aggressive act is clearly influenced by cultural definitions of passivity and aggression, which may interact with gender. Condry and Condry (1976), for example, showed a videotape of a baby responding to a jack-in-the-box to female and male college students. The sequence of the baby's response involved being startled, then agitated, and finally starting to cry. The observers who were told that the baby was a boy described it as angry, while those who were told that it was a girl described it as frightened. The authors suggested that such attributions of sex differences tend to be "in the eye of the beholder."

Other researchers have tended to focus on the "activity level" of infants in order to establish innate tendencies towards aggression, and have repeatedly found no sex differences. As children learn and are exposed to role models, their behaviour comes to conform more and more with societal expectations. That is, under the influence of socialization practices, boys become more aggressive and girls less so.

Myth 4: Male and female brains are organized differently.

There has been much debate over the question of brain lateralization, or the belief that the two hemispheres of the brain are responsible for different functions. The left hemisphere is generally thought to be responsible for speech, while the right hemisphere is thought to be responsible for visual perception. Believing that males and females perform these functions at different levels of ability because of biological causes, some scientists have attempted to demonstrate that male and female brains are actually differently organized, and more specifically that females are left-brain dominant, males right-brain dominant.

The research findings have been inconsistent, and demonstrate little more than that the current understanding of the human brain by science is still incomplete. However, it is interesting to note that, in addition to the aspects of brain lateralization mentioned above, "the left hemisphere, as well as being verbal, has also been characterized as intellectual, analytic, and businesslike, while the right hemisphere has been characterized as spontaneous, intuitive, and experiential, as well as spatially skilled" (Frieze, Parsons, Johnson, Rubble, and Zellman, 1978: 93). To find that females are left-brain dominant and males are right-brain dominant, then, would not be in the interest of those who seek to maintain current gender stereotypes that support male superiority in all traits that are considered highly valued. Indeed, it would suggest precisely the opposite: that females would be biologically superior in terms of "masculine" traits, while males would be biologically superior in terms of "feminine" traits (Renzetti and Curran, 1992).

Recent research indicates that there may indeed be differences in the ways in which male and female brains work. For example, the corpus callosum, the tissue connecting the two hemispheres, is up to 23 percent thicker in women than in men (Gorman, 1992). While such differences may exist, it is also a matter of cultural interpretation to assign meaning to them.

Myth 5: Premenstrual syndrome causes women to act in irrational, violent, and even criminal ways.

Women's exclusion from social roles requiring responsibility, sound judgment, and rational decision-making has historically been justified by the claim that women's menstrual cycles interfere with their ability to function rationally. Premenstrual syndrome (PMS) refers to the physiological changes that may occur just before a woman's menstrual period. These include becoming "unreliable, irresponsible, accident-prone, and even violent and suicidal" (Renzetti and Curran, 1992: 34), and the symptoms may range from physical discomfort to mood swings. Researchers have suggested that the majority of North American women suffer from PMS, but exact numbers vary with one's definition of the condition.

The "discovery" of PMS has brought mixed reactions from feminists. On the one hand, many women are pleased that there has been recognition by the medical community of the role played by hormones in the monthly rhythms of the female body. Women who feel they suffer from PMS now may get help more easily from various clinics. Yet others criticize what they call the "social construction" of PMS. They suggest that the "discovery" of the disorder has inadvertently put more power in the hands of the medical community, by giving physicians yet another condition they can diagnose and use to label women as deviant, and by providing the pharmaceutical industry with yet another market for the selling of drugs. The main danger, critics suggest, is that using biological explanations for behaviour can and does result in the legitimation of unequal treatment of women (Laws, Hey, and Eagan, 1985). Indeed, others have argued that there is a social psychological basis to PMS, suggesting that women's attitudes to their menstrual cycles are culturally produced. In North American culture, where menstruation is devalued and even called "the curse," women may develop negative feelings about their monthly periods. (See the boxed insert on "My Hormones Made Me Do It").

What all of these discussions of the "myths" of biological determinism point out is how readily scientists, physicians, lawyers, and judges will accept biologically based explanations of behaviour that tend to support gender stereotypes. Because of this tendency, it is likely that the search for answers in this nature-and-nurture discussion will continue.

LANGUAGE AND THE GENDERED ORDER

One way to understand the cultural valuation of masculinity and femininity is to examine the way that language is gendered. The English language is not gender neutral, nor are the common usages of that language. Language, through persistent patterns, communicates more than just meaning; it also communicates cultural values.

Language use reproduces the gendered order primarily by suggesting that male experience is either universal or more important than female experience. There are several ways in which this occurs. First, the use of "he" or "man" to refer to anyone and everyone suggests that "he" or "man" includes everyone, perhaps even that anyone worth talking

"My Hormones Made Me Do It": PMS and the Law

In December 1980, in a town fifty-two miles northeast of London [England], thirty-seven-year-old Christine English drove her car at full speed directly at her boyfriend, pinning him to a telephone pole and killing him. She was subsequently convicted of manslaughter instead of murder, and she was released on probation because of a mitigating factor in her case: at the time of the crime, her defence attorney argued, English was suffering from a condition known as premenstrual syndrome (PMS), which may cause those afflicted to behave violently. That same year, twenty-nine-year-old Sandie Smith was convicted of killing a co-worker at the London pub where she tended bar, but she too was sentenced to probation on the basis of the premenstrual syndrome defence. As a condition of probation, both English and Smith were required to receive monthly hormone injections to control their PMS symptoms (Glass, 1982; Parlee, 1982).

Understandably, these cases generated considerable controversy, not only in Great Britain, but also in the United States. Legal scholars worried that the courts would be flooded with cases in which female defendants would try to escape punishment for serious crimes by claiming their behaviour was a product of the stress caused by the onset of their monthly periods. Others used the cases to bolster their argument that women are naturally unfit for positions of responsibility and leadership. Dr. Edgar Berman, once the personal physician of Senator Hubert Humphrey, was often quoted on this matter. Said Berman:

If you had an investment in a bank, you wouldn't want the president of your bank making a loan under those raging hormonal influences at that particular period.... There just are physical and psychological inhibitants that limit a female's potential (quoted in Parlee, 1982: 126).

This, of course, generated alarm among feminists. As one physician pointed out:

I don't think anything is going to set back women's causes more than [PMS].... To let women think they become criminal once a month as a result of their physiology is to really debase the status of women. This is to say women are criminal by nature (quoted in Glass, 1982: 8C).

Source: *Claire M. Renzetti and Daniel J. Curran, 1989.* Women, Men and Society: The Sociology of Gender. *Boston: Allyn & Bacon (p. 34).*

about is male. Yet this excludes the experiences of over half of the population. Second, the use of suffixes like "man," although less common today, similarly defines important roles as male roles. For example, "chairman," "workman," and "fireman" could seem to exclude the possibility that females could occupy such roles. The tendency to communicate sexist messages, such as male superiority or the assumption that certain roles must be occupied by either males or females, through language is known as **linguistic sexism**.

Even linguistic usages which do not explicitly exclude may have the same effect in terms of the cultural messages conveyed. When referring to occupations, there are some which are clearly assumed to be held by males, others by females. For example, how many times have you mentioned to friends that you have been to see your doctor and they have responded, "What did he say?" This question implies that the role is occupied by a male. Similarly, if you were to say that the nurse had given you an injection, your friend might ask, "Did she hurt you?," wrongly assuming that all nurses are female.

When asked to change their usage to include women, many argue, "It's only language; what's the fuss?" From a sociological perspective, however, there is really no such thing as "*only* language." Language conveys a whole set of structural relations which are passed on to the young through the process of socialization. We covered this topic in the last chapter. One way in which our perceptions of gender might change is through the gradual move towards what is known as *gender-inclusive language*: language that recognizes and attempts to overcome the sexism contained in the tendencies mentioned above. "What did the doctor say?" and "Did the nurse hurt you?" are examples.

In addition to the structure and use of language, linguistic sexism is also found in the actual dynamics of conversation. Derber (1979) studied male–female dynamics in conversations and found that male–female interactions reflect gender socialization. Males tend to be dominant, to interrupt more frequently, to use the volume of their voices to ensure that they are heard, and to devalue or ignore the conversational contributions of females. Females, on the other hand, tend to be submissive, to tolerate interruptions, and to become "invisible" when overshadowed by dominant males. For Derber, conversations are one context for the societal "pursuit of attention," through which all individuals seek recognition. He suggested that North American males are seen as more deserving of attention than females, and that this is reflected in the gender role of "attention-getter." Females, on the other hand, may be entitled to sexual attention, such as "appreciative" comments about their physical appearance, but as far as the intellectual content of conversations goes, they may be considered less capable of making a contribution. As such, they are placed in the role of "attention-giver," which complements their other traditional gender roles as care-giver and nurturer.

Derber's analysis suggests that much of the gendered order is supported in such subtle, unconscious practices. For the most part people are unaware that they reproduce these patterns. For an exercise, observe your own patterns of speech with members of your same sex, and then with members of the other sex. You may be surprised at how accurately Derber predicts these patterns. Changing these subtle tendencies first requires an honest recognition that they exist; making others aware follows. If left alone, linguistic sexism persists simply by virtue of the fact that it is almost invisible to those who participate in it.

GETTING GENDERED: THE DEVELOPMENT OF THE SELF

If there is little evidence to support the "natural" superiority of males over females, then how is it that the gendered order is structured systematically to advantage males? The answer is gender socialization, the process through which the gendered order is socially reproduced in the young. Through it, the continuity of the gendered order is ensured. Upon the birth of a child, the proclamation of the child's sex is usually the first piece of information verbalized. With the claim, "It's a boy" or "It's a girl," the process of gender socialization begins. Most people do not like to refer to a child as "it." So the establishment of whether "it" is a "he" or a "she" takes on paramount importance and sex is communicated in socially coded ways.

One common way in which sex is proclaimed is to dress babies and young children in clothing and colours considered to be sex-appropriate. It may even be difficult to purchase clothing in gender-neutral tones or styles. Parents may wait to discover the sex of their child before decorating the nursery or accumulating too many clothes, for fear of "making a mistake" by having pink in a boy's room or perhaps too much "masculine" clothing for a little girl. Hair styles also are highly gendered, with girls being encouraged to grow long, curly locks, sometimes adorned with ribbons and barrettes, while boys' hair is more often kept shorter and unadorned. Boys tend to be dressed in a way that suggests readiness for "rough and tumble" play—in rugged, hardy clothing. Girls more often are dressed in a way that suggests delicacy and a need to stay clean and out of the mud—in lighter colours, more delicate fabrics, and ribbons and bows. Why such conformity? The social disapproval that people would expect for dressing a boy in a pink dress, for example, speaks to the strength of our gender norms. The parent or care-giver who must explain to children that "boys don't wear dresses" is passing this on. Today, however, more children are being dressed in "unisex" sweatsuits and overalls, suggesting a change from the more rigid patterns of the past. Yet, a glance at any advertisement for children's clothing will also reveal that attitudes have not changed completely.

Another code applied very early to newborn children involves their naming. Parents anticipating the birth of a child usually develop two separate lists of names—one "if it's a girl," the other "if it's a boy." It is seen as socially important to convey

Young children are encouraged to behave in ways considered sex-appropriate.

sexual identity through names. There are very few truly androgynous names, that is, names that could be equally applied to a male or a female. The naming of a child in a gender-inappropriate way may lead to the child having to endure endless teasing from peers, and as we have seen, the reactions of others are important for the development of identity.

The toys chosen for babies and young children also suggest definite ideas of gender-appropriate play. A visit to a toy store will confirm that the children's toy industry remains highly gendered. Many boys continue to be offered battle-oriented toys, construction toys, cars, and trucks, suggesting socialization into instrumental traits. Girls, on the other hand, are surrounded by stuffed animals and dolls dressed in pink and lace, as well as toys pertaining to household tasks such as baking and cleaning, suggesting socialization into expressive traits. While there is some evidence of cross-over and the use of gender-neutral toys, a glimpse at Saturday morning television advertisements directed at children will confirm that even today this important source of gender socialization remains strong.

Some more subtle ways in which boys and girls are shaped for their gender include the ways in which parents convey their own expectations to children. For example, parents tend to handle children differently, from the newborn stage on, depending on their sex. Boys tend to be handled more roughly, girls more gently (McDonald and Parke, 1986). Even the tone of voice used to address newborns differs, with a softer tone for girls and a stronger tone for boys. Research indicates that mothers tend to speak more clearly to their sons than to their daughters, and tend to teach their sons more actively than they do their daughters (Weitzman, Birns, and Friend, 1985). In the same study, it was shown that even those parents who claimed to be committed to treating their boys and girls exactly the same were actively, albeit unconsciously, socializing them into different gender roles.

As seen in Chapter 4, Socialization, individuals tend to respond to the expectations and activities of significant others by repeating behaviours for which they are given approval. The most significant others in early childhood socialization belong to the immediate family. Primary socialization into gender roles is reinforced in turn by agents of secondary socialization, such as schools, the media, religious institutions, and the workplace. Consistency of expectations is thus maintained throughout the gendered order.

Through the process of gender socialization in Canadian culture, boys are consistently rewarded for emulating the "masculine," while girls are generally, if not consistently, rewarded for emulating the "feminine." Negative sanctions—for example, names like "wimp," "sissy," or "tomboy"—are given to those who deviate, suggestive of the fear of parents that their child might be homosexual. Interestingly, the least forgiving dispensers of these labels are often children's peers—evidence of the power of their own gender socialization. Gradually, children internalize the gender norms so that they are inseparable from their sense of self. Boys will come to view it as unthinkable ever to wear a dress; girls may be convinced that they cannot do math.

TRAPPED IN OUR BODIES: THE BODY AND SEXUALITY

The relationship between the gendered order and gendered identity becomes readily apparent when we examine cultural norms for physical attractiveness. All individuals are trapped in their bodies and the body becomes a very important factor in social development at an early age. Others perceive individuals according to cultural appearance norms—as cute or pretty, plain or ugly, fat or thin, tall or short. From subtle differences such as whether they have blonde, brown, or red hair, to more significant ones such as whether they are differently abled in some way, the social meanings attached to physical attributes all become early components of the self. Indeed, it would not be an exaggeration to say that the foundations of a sense of self-worth are often built on how bodies conform to appearance norms.

For the most part, ideas of beauty and attractiveness are culturally produced. The mass media and fashion industries play a large role in this process. Successfully socialized males and females internalize these norms and attempt to emulate them. One systematically consistent aspect of this is the objectification of females. Females learn at an early age that they are objects to be looked at. Long before they understand the meaning of sexuality, young girls are encouraged to emulate the seductive appearance of adult women, while young boys are encouraged to appreciate this appearance and to respond in an active way.

Indeed, historically, women's worth has been embodied in their appearance—women's assets have been culturally defined in terms of physical attractiveness and childbearing capacity. Females have been taught that it is through these means that they can achieve status in the adult world—by marrying men who will then support them through male access to the public world of work and industry.

In turn, males have been socialized to view themselves as subjects—autonomous actors whose success depends on initiative, assertiveness if not aggressiveness, and persistence. The male body should reflect this by being strong and tough. The ways in which men dress, walk, and talk all mirror these societal expectations. "Masculine" traits are applied to the pursuit of females, the objects.

Males in turn receive status from other males based on the beauty and youth of the women whom they date and marry. On this topic of youth, masculine qualities are more highly valued and may be seen to improve with age, while feminine "assets" fade over time. Women become increasingly devalued, particularly as they pass out of the childbearing years (Harman, 1986). On aging men, grey hair and wrinkles are a sign of distinction, suggesting wisdom and experience, while on women they suggest unattractiveness and diminished worth. With menopause, Greer (1992) pointed out, many women experience a kind of social "invisibility" suggesting that their value to society has vanished with their youth.

It would be wrong to suggest that, just because the body is so important for women's gendered identity, appearance norms are not oppressive for males in our society. The rigid norms governing how males and females must present themselves are oppressive to both sexes. A rugged, "masculine" body conforms much more closely to societal norms than does a smooth, soft, "effeminate" one. Sexual performance is somehow implied by how masculine one appears. Penis size, muscle development, height, and profusion of facial and bodily hair all may be criteria on which males compare themselves, and in each case bigger or more means more "manly." Penis size is mythologized to be directly related to the amount of pleasure a male can give a female in intercourse, and hence a large penis is a source of status among males, while one that "doesn't measure up" may be a source of shame. Muscular development is seen to indicate strength as well as sexual prowess. Height is significant given the cultural requirement that in heterosexual relationships males must be taller than females, or else their masculinity is called into question. Facial hair, especially among adolescent males, is seen to be evidence of virility, as is hair elsewhere on the body, particularly the chest. Balding at any age, but particularly "premature" balding, is a dreaded sign of failing virility. Young men who are chubby and smooth-skinned may be labelled "baby face," a characterization very close to "wimp" in terms of the male experience of sexuality. Any indication of impotence or lack of virility will bring shame to most males.

Although body awareness is a constant source of concern for both males and females, research has shown that females in our culture tend to be more concerned than males about their bodies, and that this concern tends to take the form of negative feelings about their bodies. Males, in contrast, tend to feel more positive about their bodies (Franzoi, Kessenich, and Sugrue, 1989). For females, the high premium placed on appearance often leads to an almost obsessive pursuit of beauty according to cultural definitions—a goal that is unattainable by most, but made to appear within reach by the cosmetics and fashion industries—and to a cultural obsession with achieving a desired weight.

Recently, sociologists and psychologists have noted the widespread occurrence of eating disorders.

Ideas of beauty and attractiveness are culturally produced, especially by the mass media and fashion industry.

Anorexia nervosa is a condition affecting mostly females that takes the form of voluntary starvation in the pursuit of thinness. The obsessive quality of this disorder leads those suffering from it to have a distorted perception of their bodies, such that they always feel fat, even when severely malnourished and underweight. Bulimia is a related condition in which sufferers alternatively binge and purge, frequently aided by the use of laxatives and diuretics. These conditions have reached epidemic proportions in North America among female high-school, college, and university students, and are severely debilitating, in some cases even leading to death. While the psychological explanations for such eating disorders are complex, many researchers attribute their massive increase to the "cult of thinness," in which women's self-worth is defined particularly through their appearance (Hesse-Biber, 1989; Wolf, 1990).

Less life-threatening, but nonetheless telling about contemporary cultural values, is the current emphasis on physical fitness for both males and females. On the one hand, some argue convincingly that fitness is important for health. On the other hand, many individuals become obsessed with fitness, suggesting that there is more to it than simply a concern for health. Indeed, the social meanings attached to fitness translate into definitions of self-worth. Individuals who "work out" regularly and are seen to be fit are somehow interpreted as being more desirable and worthy. This has allowed fitness centres and aerobics classes to become the "meet markets" of the 1990s.

Change in the arena of body and sexuality has been slow. Indeed, not only does female objectification persist, but the objectification of the male body, through the use of cosmetics and fashion, seems to be on the increase (Wolf, 1990). While many might argue that there is greater room than ever for the exercise of individual choice, for example in clothing, the high rates of eating disorders, combined with the cultural obsession with fitness, lead one to wonder whether fundamental patterns have changed at all.

THE EFFECTS OF GENDER

Work and reproduction: the gendered division of labour

Masculine and feminine roles also affect adult norms of biological and social reproduction. In the gendered order, gender differences are manifested in expectations regarding motherhood, fatherhood, and paid and unpaid labour, known as the **gendered division of labour.**

The idea that women are biologically more suited for the social role of parenting has historically led to limitations on the possibilities for both women and men. If mothering should come naturally to women, then it follows that it will be expected that all women will be mothers, willingly, lovingly, and competently. Along with these expectations go certain sanctions against those who would rather not have children, or those for whom mothering is difficult. Such women may find themselves labelled deviant, as "selfish" or "bad mothers" respectively (Schur, 1984). Yet the role is contained within a web of relations that limit women's other roles, particularly in the public sphere of paid labour. Women who wish to "have it all," for whom a complete life includes both a career and a family, may find the expectation that they will stay at home for at least the early periods of a child's life inhibiting to progress in their careers. In turn, some women may sacrifice childbearing potential in order to become established in their careers. Still, for many women, the combination of mothering and working outside the home, while stressful and trying at times, remains a satisfying combination (Crosby, 1991).

Men too are limited in terms of the expectations surrounding parenting. It is only in recent years that males have become more involved in fathering. Far more prevalent during the decades of the 1950s through to the 1980s was the model of the "absent father"—perhaps physically present in the family, but emotionally uninvolved in the expressive sphere of family life. For authors such as Miedzian (1991), the pressures placed on males to "be a man" have channelled their socialization away from nurturing. Masculinity, when rigidly interpreted, excludes warmth and caring. So it stands to reason that boys raised on such a model will not be encouraged to take an active part in parenting.

There is a tendency to associate the concept of work with paid employment, and it is only recently that distinctions have been made between paid work outside the home and unpaid work in the home (see Chapter 9, Families). Women's work in the home may be divided into three categories: "wifework," "motherwork," and "housework" (Rosenberg, 1990). *Wifework* refers to the work expected of women in their roles as wives: seeing to the emotional, physical, and sexual needs of their husbands. *Motherwork* refers to the work expected of women in their roles as mothers: seeing to the emotional as well as physical needs (feeding, clothing, and healing) of their children. *Housework* refers to the work expected of women in their roles as homemakers: cooking, cleaning, shopping, and overall maintenance of the sense of order and appearance of the home.

Within the paid workforce, there has historically been a wide disparity between "men's work" and "women's work," in terms of the perceived social value of the work and its remuneration. In keeping with their gender socialization, men have typically occupied higher status white-collar jobs or more physically demanding blue-collar jobs, while women have been relegated to the pink-collar ghetto of women's work. Indeed, women have been said to occupy a **double ghetto**: the pink-collar ghetto of paid labour and the domestic ghetto of unpaid labour. Women who work outside of the home full-time are still expected to do wifework, motherwork, and housework when they are home. They are the ones who must take time off from work if a child is sick, and they are blamed if there are problems at home (Luxton, 1990).

Women's work outside the home is frequently in low-status occupations that mirror women's training as care-givers and homemakers. The largest number of employed women continue to hold positions in the clerical field, while other "typical" female occupations include teaching, nursing, and social work. In recent years the trend has been towards greater cross-over between typical men's work and women's work. But while women's representation in traditionally male-dominated professions has increased greatly in the last decade, there is still substantial room for change (Marshall, 1990a; see Figure 6.1).

Historically, men's wages have been significantly higher than women's, even when men and women worked in the same occupation. This reflected the societal assumption that men's work was more important than women's work, and was necessary to support a family. The discrepancy between men's and women's salaries has been explained by the idea of the "family wage": historically it has been assumed that a male breadwinner would be earning the money to support an entire family (with the female staying at home, doing unpaid domestic labour). If women did work outside the home, this work was not taken seriously but treated as work for "pin money."

Objectification of women in the work world has been an unfortunate fact of life as well. Wolf (1990) chronicled how the "professional beauty qualification" has been the generally unstated, single most important factor in a woman's success in the paid labour force. There are whole categories of work in which physical attractiveness is a prerequisite for success—the so-called "display" jobs which permeate the entertainment and service industries. But women in all lines of work have experienced sexual harassment on the job—unwanted attention of a sexual nature. When this occurs in a work setting, it is experienced as a confusion between being treated as a worker and as a sex object. For women who may already have low self-esteem, the message is that their looks are more important than their brains. In addition, sexual harassment usually involves a power differential, with the majority of incidents involving males in a superior position harassing subordinate women. The fear of job loss, stalking, or other reprisal has kept women silent in the past. Recognition that sexual harassment was widespread in the workplace as well as in the educational system led to greater regulations and penalties for this behaviour. As a result, it is less threatening today for individuals experiencing harassment to come forth and seek justice.

Many women occupy the double ghetto of paid pink-collar labour and unpaid domestic labour.

FIGURE 6.1 Women's representation in Canadian occupations

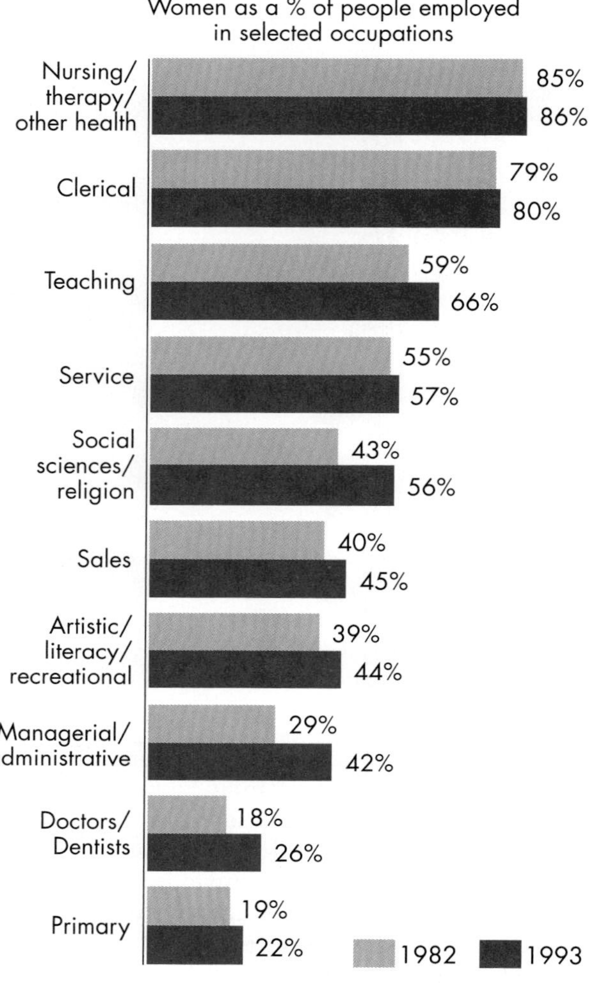

Source: *Statistics Canada, Catalogue No. 75-507E.*

Ideas concerning women's work outside the home have changed in recent years. Sixty-two percent of married women now work in the paid labour force, mostly for economic reasons (Calzavara, 1993). Yet disparities in remuneration have been slow to adapt to the changing realities. Even today, women's full-time earnings are just over 70 percent of men's (see Chapter 7, Social Stratification). Policy initiatives such as pay equity are important steps in the direction of rectifying these inequities.

Health and aging

Not surprisingly, men and women experience health and aging differently. Historically, men's life spans have been significantly shorter than women's (a topic to which we shall return in Chapter 15, Demography and Population Study). This means that women often outlive their partners, and indeed, in old age there are far more widows than widowers. Several explanations have been advanced for these differences. In keeping with the biological tendency for women to endure stress better than men, some argue that females may simply be biologically favoured for longevity. Others suggest that these differences are environmentally produced. Many of the diseases and ailments that cause an early death in males are related to the paid workforce and the stresses it produces. Cardiovascular disease, the leading killer of Canadian males aged 45 to 64, is often the result of a stressful lifestyle and not enough emphasis on proper nutrition and exercise (Parliament, 1990). Striving executives who put in many hours of overtime per week to the neglect of their physical and emotional well-being may be prime candidates for such an early death. And given the fact that, to date, women have not been employed in great numbers in the types of paid jobs that are seen to require such commitment, it is not surprising that they are less frequently casualties of such work-related diseases. Other work-related illnesses, such as cancer, may have their origins in poor working conditions associated with typical blue-collar "men's work," such as factory work and mining. Time will tell if, as more women enter the paid labour force, they will come to suffer from such work-related diseases.

Because of the dependency that many women experience in their roles in the private realm during their childbearing and childrearing years, many are ill-prepared financially and emotionally for growing old as widows. Pension plans are geared to members of the paid workforce, automatically excluding women who have devoted their adult lives to the demanding task of being a full-time homemaker. Yet it is this segment of society that lives longer. It is not surprising that a large proportion of elderly females end up in poverty, some so destitute as to make up part of the growing category of "homeless women" (Harman, 1989; also see the boxed insert on "Homeless Women"). Aged women, particularly the "older elderly" (those over 75 years of age), account for a significant proportion of Canada's poor.

Recently, the longevity gap between males and females has diminished slightly. This may be a product of both better health care for men and greater involvement in the paid labour force for women. It is interesting that, while cigarette smoking in Canada has been in an overall decline, the group in which it has been slowest to fall is women (McKie, 1990). And while mortality rates continue to drop, cancer is still the leading cause of death for women aged 45 to 64, with the percentage of female deaths due to cancer increasing (Parliament, 1990).

The feminization of poverty

One of the most profound cumulative effects of the gendered order on the life experiences of women in Canadian society is that, at all stages of the adult life cycle, women are more likely than men to be poor, and they are more likely than men to be trapped in a life of poverty. This state of affairs is known as the **feminization of poverty** (Harman, 1992). The reasons for it have to do with the blocks to opportunities experienced by women, as well as the ways in which the Canadian state operates to keep poor women in a condition of dependency on government assistance such as welfare and family benefits.

Much of this is a consequence of the broader patriarchal ideology through which females are socialized to aspire to the roles of wife and mother.

Homeless Women: A Tragic Consequence of Patriarchy

Homelessness among women has become increasingly visible in our society in recent years, and this visibility has led to a general alarm that something should be done about it. Women are generally seen to belong in homes—and within our culture, the "home" implies private property and family. Women without homes are therefore seen as deviant. In a study of homeless women in a large Ontario city, Harman (1989) found that most of those who stayed in a hostel for homeless women had in fact been "domestically fixed" at one time, and had become homeless when their ties to family and property were severed. "At least half of those seeking shelter at one hostel for women are former mental patients. Others are widows; married women escaping from violent and/or alcoholic husbands; wives left alone as a result of desertion, commitment, or incarceration of their husbands; teenage runaways; and single mothers" (Harman, 1989: 20).

To understand the feminization of poverty, look at what happens to some women when economic support is removed from their lives. Suddenly they are without income, and it is the rare homemaker who will have sufficient financial resources to continue to make mortgage payments and keep up a house. From there, the descent to poverty is a rapid downward spiral, facilitated by the stigma attached to being a female lone parent. Child care for preschool children is expensive and subsidized places are limited. Paid employment is hard to find if one is unskilled and has been out of the workforce for a number of years. Even women who have careers find it next to impossible to sustain the same standard of living on one income. Social services are inadequate and shelters are often overcrowded. Affordable housing is limited. The "Catch-22" of the welfare system—one must have a fixed address to receive welfare payments, and consequently one must have enough money to cover first and last months' rent and other related expenses such as moving costs—means that some women cannot make use of affordable housing even if it is available to them. Welfare payments may provide for a subsistence lifestyle, but certainly do little to help a woman "get back on her feet." Literally on the street, without a fixed address, without an income, and unable to acquire housing, these women join the ranks of the homeless. One woman poignantly expressed her experience of rapid loss of status and income when her husband died: "I remember waking up one morning and realizing, 'Oh God, I'm on the skids'" (Harman, 1989: 20).

Many women are ill-prepared financially and emotionally for growing old alone.

In Canadian society, these roles are devalued and provide women with a "legitimate" livelihood only when couched within a traditional nuclear family arrangement. Yet, a glance at recent statistics indicates that lone-parenting is the fastest-growing category of household arrangement in Canadian society. And within this category, 82 percent of lone-parent families are headed by females (Moore, 1990a), many of whom live in isolation, without support from their former or estranged husbands, forced to rely on government assistance.

The stereotypical "single mother" on government assistance is often a target of criticism, stigmatized for deviating from the conventional role of mother. Her morality may be called into question even if she is single as a result of leaving an abusive husband, or is alone due to the desertion of a husband. If the woman has not been educated or trained for paid employment, or is unable to secure it, she must receive some kind of financial support to provide for her family. The amounts provided are barely sufficient to cover minimal food and housing. Child care is expensive and a luxury few can afford, with subsidized day-care spots limited and waiting lists long. Thus, women in this situation are tied to the home; any work that they do find tends to be menial and low-paying. The result is often a vicious circle of poverty which is difficult to escape. The road to change must include the opening up of opportunities for education, child care, affordable housing, and decently paid labour for those who want it, and the provision of adequate support for those whose choice is to engage in full-time mothering at home.

Gender and deviance

Gender norms affect definitions of male and female deviance. In the realm of sexuality, the heterosexual assumption is predominant. Males and females who choose same-sex partners and homosexual lifestyles are labelled deviant. Individuals may also be labelled deviant for violating work norms—for example, males who choose to stay at home to care for their children while their wives work outside of the home, or those who choose unconventional occupations such as nursing or social work. More generally, males who are not "masculine" and females who are not "feminine" meet with social disapproval. Males who do not conform to the demands of "masculinity" may be labelled "wimps." After being told at a very young age that "boys don't cry," and being encouraged to be rough and aggressive, males who swim against the tide and develop their "sensitive" side often pay the heavy price of peer disapproval.

The study of gender and deviance also reveals some interesting paradoxes. The first paradox is that violence is considered normal, not deviant. It is generally agreed that ours is a culture of violence (Miedzian, 1991). Some, such as Kaufman (1993), have observed that learning to be masculine is analogous to learning to be violent. Little boys are often encouraged to fight, and are sometimes taught that violence is the swiftest form of conflict resolution.

Ruth (1990) observed that training into the Arnold Schwarzenegger mode of masculinity is similar to training into the role of soldier. Soldiers cannot do their job if they feel compassion for the persons they are expected to kill. So, cold objectification of others, including women and children, may be as "normal and natural" to a man raised to idealize the "Terminator" as any other feature of the taken-for-granted world. Indeed, in some circles using violence to control women is even celebrated. On the other hand, males who reject the association between masculinity and violence may meet with resistance from other men and even some women, for whom their choice poses a threat. It is important to recognize, however, that these traits are not natural; they are socially constructed. Present concern with the tolerance of violence in society led Miedzian (1991) to conclude that perhaps if society socialized boys to develop their nurturing side, things such as war, child abuse, and violence against women would be unthinkable. But at the moment, sensitivity among males is often considered deviant. At an early age boys learn that the full experience of human emotions is a sign of weakness and femininity.

A second paradox is that, for women, to be "normal" in our society often is to be deviant. Under patriarchy, only women who uphold the male definition of normality and who are subordinate to men are considered normal women. Women who deviate from male-established norms, such as Devor's "gender blenders," are labelled deviant. More generally, when females exhibit strength and assertiveness, their behaviour may be met with social disapproval and labelled "unladylike" or "unfeminine." Females who aspire to nontraditional occupations, who do not marry, or who opt out of the motherhood role may all experience definitions of themselves as socially unacceptable. Lesbians may be labelled deviant precisely because they refuse to accept subjugation to male dominance.

In the area of crime (discussed in Chapter 5, Deviance), males are overwhelmingly represented in violent crimes, crimes against the person, and crimes against property. Females more often commit shoplifting, and are more often charged with "morals" crimes such as soliciting, stripping, and other behaviours involving their sexuality. When women are the victims of crimes by men, most notably battering and sexual assault, too often society responds by questioning their complaints—asking what the women did to provoke the crime.

This "blaming the victim" represents a third paradox. Domestic violence has until very recently been considered a private matter of discipline and social order (men's work). If women were battered, they were probably not performing their roles adequately in some way. Regrettably, some police and judges still retain this view and act upon it. Sexual assault is another area in which females have often been blamed for their own victimization. Accusations that a woman has "asked for it" or detailed questioning of her personal morality too frequently continue to be responses to charges of sexual assault. This is particularly true of women such as prostitutes or strippers, whose occupations lead many to assume that they are always sexually available and hence cannot be "raped."

The activities that a society labels as deviant point to its normative structure. That gender norms continue to be fairly rigid and that individuals violating them continue to be stigmatized indicate that the gendered order remains intact. Only when females and males cease to be labelled deviant on the basis of their gendered activities will we be able to say that true change has come about.

WORKING TOWARDS CHANGE

This chapter has suggested that a sociological analysis of gender relations must take into account the development of the self as well as the larger gendered order that structures the experience of being male or female in Canadian society. As we have seen, the gendered order is a pervasive one. And while its existence has clearly favoured men, it must also be seen as largely oppressive of both women and men. Expectations of masculinity and femininity are both pervasive and consistent, with enormous pressure to conform and a ready-made stigma system for those who deviate. The general tendency to avoid ostracism keeps most males and females conforming more or less to the social expectations of the gendered order. And it is this very tendency to conform that inhibits social change.

But change has begun. Primarily through the efforts of the women's movement, social organizations at all levels are now forced to be aware of

Stark Data on Women: 100 Million Are Missing

Little girls in China no longer have their feet crushed by foot-binding, and widows in India are no longer supposed to be roasted alive on the funeral pyres of their husbands. But a stark statistic testifies to women's continuing unequal status: at least 60 million females in Asia are missing and feared dead, victims of nothing more than their sex. Worldwide, research suggests, the number of missing females may top 100 million.

If sex discrimination in the West means office harassment or fewer good jobs for women, in the Third World it often means death. A traditional preference for boys translates quickly—in China, India, and many other developing countries—into neglect and death for girls. While the discrimination is widely seen as a relic of outdated attitudes, in fact the problem appears to be getting worse in Asia. Recently released census data in China and India show that in both countries the sex ratio of the population became more skewed over the course of the last decade.

The tens of millions missing include females of all ages who are aborted or killed at birth, or who die because they are given less food than males, or because family members view a daughter with diarrhea as a nuisance but a son with diarrhea as a medical crisis requiring a doctor.

A Shadow on Census Data

Remarkably little research has been conducted on the plight of the missing women, and even their disappearance is discernible merely as a shadow on the census data and mortality statistics.

"It's shocking that so little is known," said Amartya Sen, a Harvard economist who has tried to call attention to the issue. Professor Sen estimates that considerably more than 100 million females are missing around the world, and he asserts that the reason the shortfall is getting worse in some areas is that girls are not allowed to benefit as much as boys from the improvements in health care and nutrition that are lowering death rates in developing countries.

Any investigation into the case of the missing women begins with one fact: 5 or 6 percent more boys are born than girls, but in normal circumstances males die at higher rates at every age thereafter. Typically in the West, where female infanticide is not considered an issue, children are disproportionately male, the number of men and women evens out by the time people are in their twenties or thirties, and the elderly are disproportionately female. In relatively advanced countries like the United States, Britain, and Poland, there are about 105 females for every 100 males. In India, however, a [recent] census found only 92.9 females for every 100 males, down from 93.4 in the 1981 census and 93.0 in the 1971 census. And in China, the 1990 census found just 93.8 females for every 100 males, compared with 94.1 at the time of the 1982 census. By a conservative calculation there are 30 million females missing in China, about 5 percent of the national total, more than are missing in any other country.

A United Nations report this summer, "The World's Women," found that other countries with very low ratios of females include Afghanistan, with 94.5 for every 100 males; Bangladesh, 94.1; Bhutan, 93.3; Nepal, 94.8; Pakistan, 92.1; Papua New Guinea, 92.8; and Turkey, 94.8.

"Millions of women have died because they're women," said Sharon Capeling-Alakija, director of the United Nations Development Fund for Women, adding that mothers as well as fathers are responsible. "In most societies, women are the bearers of tradition, and if decisions are made between boy children and girl children, women were involved in making those decisions."

The killing of newborn girls was banned in India in 1870, and was denounced and outlawed by the communists after they imposed order on the Chinese countryside after the 1949 revolution.

Nevertheless, female infanticide has deep roots in rural China—partly because infants were not always regarded as full persons until they had lived for a year or grown their teeth. An old fable recounts approvingly how a couple buried their daughter alive so they would have more food to give to the man's mother. In burying their child, the couple found a treasure and were thus rewarded for their filial piety.

The Ultrasound Option

These days, technology has presented parents with a tidier option than infanticide: ultrasound tests that determine the sex of a fetus.

"Everyone wants a son, so they get an ultrasound test and if it's a girl they have an abortion," said a businessman from a rural area in Fukian Province. Though the practice is illegal in China, the man said: "There's no law for the doctors. It's all money and connections."

In India, amniocentesis is sometimes used in the cities to determine the sex of a fetus so that it can be aborted if it is female.

The United Nations report cited 8000 abortions in Bombay after the parents learned of the sex of the fetus, only one of which involved a male. Professor Sen believes that the practice is not widespread enough through India to account for a significant proportion of the millions of missing females. In China, however, anecdotal evidence suggests that selective abortion may be having an impact on the statistics.

Chinese law prohibits doctors from telling prospective parents the sex of the fetus, but the prohibition simply raises the cost of the bribe to extricate the information from the ultrasound operator. Even official reports acknowledge the practice. "Ultrasound has brought great joy to peasants who still carry old ideas," *Science and Technology Daily* reported earlier this year. It quoted a peasant as saying: "Ultrasound is really worthwhile, even though my wife had to go through four abortions to get a son."

Source: *Nicholas D. Kristof, 1991. "Stark data on women: 100 million are missing."* New York Times, *November 5, 1991, B5–9.*

gender issues, at least nominally. Consciousness of the dangers of sexism is gradually filtering through. But feminism, and gender consciousness in general, has been disproportionately a white, middle-class, urban social movement. It is for these groups that things have improved the most. The voices of women of colour and poor women, however, are increasingly being heard. They are changing the face of feminism as it takes into account the historical tendency of the movement to ignore their issues—racism in particular.

In any event, as with all dimensions of society, any change at the structural level must be met with some comparable change at the level of individual behaviour—the gendered identity. It is necessary for all members of the society to examine ways in which they have benefited as well as ways in which they have been oppressed by the gendered order, and to begin to work for change in their own arenas.

SUMMARY

Whether one is born female or male in Canadian society will have significant implications for identity and life chances. Socialization, identity, sexuality, position in the paid labour force, longevity and general health, relative poverty, and many other variables are determined in part by sex. Gender is the socially constructed set of expectations associated with a particular sex.

Canadians live in a patriarchal society—one that generally favours males and disadvantages females. Functionalists regard the patriarchal arrangement as useful and necessary. Symbolic interactionists maintain that it is a negotiated order and one that may be changed. Marxist theorists see it as a consequence of oppressive social structures, primarily capitalism.

In addition, there are a variety of feminist perspectives. Maternal feminism views motherhood as a source of women's status; liberal feminism looks to law and policy to remedy social inequality; socialist feminism regards the combined effects of capitalism and patriarchy as constituting the basis for women's oppression; and radical feminism advocates the abolition of patriarchy. Similarly, there is no one male response to feminism. Responses range from sympathy to antagonism.

The question of biological determinism has been hotly debated. To date, studies have revealed no compelling evidence to suggest that males and females are differentially suited for social roles on the basis of biological factors alone. Yet this argument continues to be made, and is frequently used to justify social inequality.

The gendered order is structured by many invisible means, one of which is language. Linguistic sexism suggests that male experience is either universal or more important than female experience. Analysis of conversations reveals that males tend to dominate them while females tend to be more submissive. A conscious, increased use of gender-inclusive language may help to overcome some of these inequities.

Gender socialization is a powerful force in the perpetuation of gender inequality. Through this process, males learn to be masculine and females learn to be feminine. Clothing, names, toys, physical handling, and tone of voice all reflect parental and societal expectations that children will learn and conform to accepted gender norms. Deviations from these norms are heavily sanctioned.

The body and sexuality are the stage for a clearly visible gendered drama. Females and males alike find that the expectations for the shape and presentation of their bodies are difficult to ignore. Particularly for women, the body is objectified and seen to be a critical source of status, leading in some cases to obsessional disorders such as anorexia nervosa and bulimia. Conforming to rigid codes for masculinity and femininity in a structure of compulsory heterosexuality is highly restrictive.

Gender inequality is also evident when it comes to reproduction and paid labour, in the gendered division of labour. Because females are biologically equipped for reproduction and the devalued role of mother, they have also been ghettoized in devalued roles as homemaker and pink-collar worker. Males, on the other hand, have tended to have greater access to high-status positions in both the home and the workplace. While there is some evidence of change, distinctly male-dominated and female-dominated occupations persist.

Men and women experience health and aging differently in Canada. Much of this has to do with the social roles into which they are cast, and the resultant toll taken on the body. Males tend to have shorter lives than females; however, females are more likely to grow old alone and poor. As the working lives of men and women become more alike, for example when they move into occupations traditionally held by the other sex, these tendencies may even out.

The feminization of poverty is one striking consequence of patriarchy in Canadian society. Women are more likely than men to be poor during their adult lives, and to be trapped in a life of poverty. This situation is not likely to change until more opportunities are open to women in the paid labour force and programs such as universal day care are instituted to free women from domestic obligations.

Social sanctions for deviating from gender norms are strong. The heterosexual assumption makes the choice of a homosexual lifestyle a costly one. Other deviations from the rigid expectations of masculinity and femininity in the areas of the body, sexuality, reproduction, and paid and unpaid labour may lead to social stigma. Most Canadian adults find it costly to go against the grain and tend to prefer conformity. This in turn reinforces the gendered order and keeps the rate of change slow. But change is occurring, and many hope that the social basis for gender inequality may one day disappear.

QUESTIONS FOR REVIEW AND CRITICAL THINKING

1. What groups are the major sources of resistance to gender equality today and how do they benefit from their stance?

2. How might you, as an elementary school teacher, go about changing the current rigid system of gender socialization?

3. Suppose that somehow the English language could be rendered completely gender neutral. Would this mean the end of gender discrimination? If not, why not?

4. What are some of the methodological problems associated with trying to prove biological determinism when it comes to sex and gender?

GLOSSARY

double ghetto the dual segregation of women into the pink-collar ghetto of paid labour outside the home and the domestic ghetto of unpaid labour inside the home

expressive dimension the set of traits including emotionality, passivity, and weakness, seen by functionalists as associated with the female roles of unpaid wife, mother, and homemaker, particularly as limited to the private sphere

feminization of poverty the tendency in Canadian society for women at all stages of the adult life cycle to be poorer than men, and to be trapped in lives of poverty

gender a social category, either masculine or feminine, referring to the social expectations developed and placed upon individuals on the basis of their biological sex

gender norms the set of norms specifying appropriate behaviour for males and females; those who violate these norms are generally labelled deviant

gender socialization the process of acquiring a gendered identity

gendered division of labour role differentiation in which males and females are segregated, according to their sex, in the spheres of both paid and unpaid labour, according to the belief that certain tasks are more appropriate for one sex than the other

gendered identity the self as it develops in accordance with the individual's gender and the social definitions of that gender within the larger gendered order

gendered order the set of structural relations through which individual members of society are accorded differential treatment on the basis of their gender

heterosexual assumption the assumption that females and males in our society are exclusively heterosexual; those who are not are labelled deviant

ideology of gender inequality the widespread belief and understanding that males are superior to females, and that they are therefore more entitled to make decisions, to control resources, and generally to occupy positions of authority

instrumental dimension the set of traits including rationality, aggression, and strength, seen by functionalists to be associated with the male roles of breadwinner and disciplinarian, particularly as limited to the public sphere

liberal feminism the view that most structural inequality between women and men can be eradicated through the creation of laws and social policies which will alter power relationships

linguistic sexism the tendency to communicate sexist messages, such as male superiority or the assumption that certain roles must be occupied by either males or females, through the use of language

maternal feminism the view that women's real strength lies in their reproductive capacities, and that women's roles as wives and mothers are their true calling and source of status

patriarchy the system of male dominance through which males are systematically accorded greater access to resources and women are systematically oppressed

private realm the realm of unpaid domestic labour and biological reproduction, seen from a functionalist perspective as the preserve of females

public realm the realm of paid labour and commerce, seen from a functionalist perspective as the preserve of males

radical feminism the view that equality between the sexes can be achieved only through the abolition of male supremacy. Some radical feminists argue for female separatism and the abdication of women's reproductive role as the route to liberation.

sex a biological category, either male or female, referring to physiological differences, the most pronounced of which involve the reproductive organs and body size

socialist feminism the view that gender inequality has its roots in the combined oppressiveness of patriarchy and capitalism

SUGGESTED READINGS

Fausto-Sterling, Anne

1992 *Myths of Gender: Biological Theories about Women and Men*. (2nd ed.) New York: Basic Books.

A thorough analysis of prevailing myths regarding sex and biological determinism, in which the assumptions and biases behind scientific research are revealed and their social implications discussed.

Kaufman, Michael

1993 *Cracking the Armour: Power, Pain and the Lives of Men*. Toronto: Viking.

A sensitive discussion of the paradox of being male in a patriarchal society, a role Kaufman identifies as one of power and pain.

Ruth, Sheila

1990 *Issues in Feminism*. (2nd ed.) Toronto: Mayfield.

A text which provides a comprehensive examination of the history of feminism and contemporary issues, combining brief readings from notable theorists with lengthy critical commentaries.

WEB SITES

http://www.women.ca

Canadian Women's Internet

The homepage of the Canadian Womens' Internet Association, this site contains many useful links to information for and about women. Topics range from Gender and Sexuality, to Women and Technology, and Health and Fitness.

http://www.dfait-maeci.gc.ca/english/html/canada/19women.htm

Women in Canada

This site, which is maintained by the Department of Foreign Affairs and International Trade, provides a detailed overview of women's participation in Canadian society from an historical perspective.

CHAPTER

7

Social Stratification

Edward G. Grabb

INTRODUCTION

Modern societies are complex, filled with all kinds of people working at various jobs, living in different circumstances, and engaging in a wide range of activities and behaviours. Social scientists usually refer to this great diversity and complexity in social life as **social differentiation**. Of course, societies vary in the degree to which social differentiation occurs. However, it seems that, in the course of human history, social differentiation has increased.

Logically, social differentiation involves only a distinction of duties and responsibilities in a social structure. An example would be the distinction between the various jobs performed in a factory or office. In virtually all but the simplest structures, however, this *division of labour* gives rise to a difference in the ranking and evaluation of the individual tasks and those who perform them. This process by which individuals, or categories of individuals, are ranked on the basis of socially differentiated characteristics is known as **social stratification**. More simply, social stratification refers to relatively enduring structures of *social inequality* among individuals and groups.

In this chapter, we examine basic concepts and definitions, and then consider classical theories of inequality and some recent developments in the field. Subsequently, we look at the eight most important factors or patterns of social differentiation that give rise to the unequal distribution of privilege and prestige in Canadian society.

CONCEPTS AND DEFINITIONS

Power

It has been asserted that the study of social stratification is concerned mainly with who gets what and why (Lenski, 1966). In this view social stratification is a *distributive process*, in which some people receive more of the valued things in life, especially wealth and prestige, than do others. In addition, social stratification is concerned with examining the *relations between* those groups who receive different amounts of wealth and prestige. Here, we argue that **power**—the ability to command resources and thereby control social situations—is the basic concept to consider when attempting to explain both the distribution of these valued things and the relations between stratified groups in society. Hence, power is the essential determinant of social stratification.

Most sociologists are interested in studying **structured** or **institutionalized power.** Power is structured or institutionalized when it becomes a regular and recurring part of everyday existence, usually because it is established in formal laws or in accepted conventions and customs (Lenski, 1966; Grabb, 1997). We can identify three major forms of structured power in society: *economic power*, which stems mainly from control of material resources like property or wealth; *political power*, which arises largely from control over human resources or the activities of other people; and *ideological power*, which comes from control over the ideas, beliefs, knowledge, or information that guides social action (Giddens, 1981; Grabb, 1993a, 1997).

Status and stratum

How is power established or institutionalized in society? One approach to this question is to examine how power derives from the rights of individuals or groups occupying a certain position, or **status**, in the various spheres of social life. Social stratification represents institutionalized power differences in a set of these statuses. In earlier European societies, for example, the status of king had greater power than the status of duke, which in turn had greater power than the status of serf.

Sometimes those performing different functions and occupying different statuses are, nevertheless, of similar rank in terms of their command over resources. For example, carpenter, plumber, electrician, and auto mechanic are distinct occupational statuses, yet they are often considered of about equal rank in the stratification system. This cluster of occupational statuses, which we might label "skilled labourers," is an example of a **stratum**, or status category.

Obviously, every individual can and does hold many statuses simultaneously. Consider a person who is female, thirty years old, married, a high-school graduate, and a real-estate agent. These traits are, respectively, that individual's sex status, age status, marital status, educational status, and occupational status. The combination of all such statuses is a person's **status set**.

Status hierarchies and power dimensions

Those statuses that translate into significant power differences in society are the most crucial for the study of social stratification. We can isolate at least eight **status hierarchies** that seem most important in Canadian society: the three socio-economic hierarchies of wealth (including income and property), occupation, and education; race or ethnicity; region or rural–urban location; gender; age; and political status. These hierarchies represent eight power rankings that define most of the structure of stratification in Canada. As we shall see in Chapter 14, Social Movements, some of these rankings may also provide the basis for group cleavage or integration in society and, hence, for collective action.

Social stratification in Canada can thus be seen as a multiple hierarchy phenomenon (Lenski, 1966; Curtis et al., 1993; Rothman, 1993). If individuals have consistently similar status levels within all or most of these hierarchies, this is known as **status consistency**. Some individuals rank relatively high on all or most power rankings. An example might be a white, male, Ontario lawyer who earns over $100 000 per year, has a university education, and serves as a deputy minister in the federal government. A high degree of status consistency in a society tends to be indicative of a "closed" stratification system, one in which only certain groups dominate and benefit most from the society.

The opposite of status consistency is **status inconsistency**, which occurs when an individual's ranking on one status hierarchy has little or no relationship to rankings on other hierarchies. An example might be a wealthy doctor living in a large Ontario city whose parents were immigrants to Canada. A large degree of status inconsistency in a society may indicate a more "open" stratification structure in which traditionally disadvantaged groups, such as racial minorities or women, are able to achieve high status in other hierarchies, for example in the educational or occupational hierarchies.

Ascribed and achieved status

The difference between open and closed stratification systems relates to another pair of concepts: ascribed versus achieved status. An **ascribed status** is a feature assigned to an individual by circumstance rather than by accomplishment. These features tend to be characteristics an individual acquires at birth and cannot change. Race, ethnic origin, sex, and age are examples of ascribed statuses. **Achieved status** refers primarily to performance characteristics, traits attained by individual action. Perhaps the best examples in a society like ours are education and occupation. A society can be characterized as open to the extent that achieved statuses are more important than ascribed statuses in determining a person's rank in the overall stratification system. Some earlier social thinkers have argued that the modern age is one in which achievement criteria have indeed become of increasing importance (Parsons, 1951; McClelland, 1961). "What you know" not "who you know," "what you do" not "what your background is," are said to be the key factors. While there may be some evidence for this argument, we shall see that achieved statuses and ascribed statuses tend to go hand in hand. In other words, while achieved statuses play a more important part in social stratification than was the case in centuries past, the opportunity to achieve, particularly in the education (see Chapter 11, Education) and occupation hierarchies, is strongly influenced by ascribed traits such as race, sex, or inherited wealth. Hence, ascribed statuses have considerable influence in the stratification process, even in supposedly achievement-oriented societies such as Canada. A similar position was stated in Chapter 6, Gender Relations.

Social mobility

The question of an open stratification system is also relevant to the concept of *social mobility*. To the extent that a society is open, there should be considerable opportunity for individuals to change their positions over time on the important status hierarchies. Consider occupational mobility, for example. This movement can involve changes in the occupation of the same individual during his or her life, or **intragenerational mobility**. Or it may entail differences between the occupational status of child and parent, that is, **intergenerational mobility**. While we usually discuss **vertical mobility**, movement up or down a status hierarchy, as most indicative of an open stratification system, we can also examine **horizontal mobility**, movement between positions within the same rank or status category. An example would be a person who leaves a job as a government economist to teach economics in a university. Both jobs fall into approximately the same stratum in the occupational status hierarchy.

Race, ethnic origin, sex, and age are examples of ascribed statuses.

Class and social class

The final major concept to consider is class. This is probably the most frequently used term in the field of social stratification. However, because of the many different meanings attached to the concept, it is difficult to offer a single definition that is acceptable to everyone. In this chapter, we use the class concept in a way more or less consistent with its use by the two principal classical theorists of stratification, Marx and Weber. For clarity, we can distinguish between the terms *class* and *social class*. *Class* refers only to one's position in the general economic hierarchy. As discussed later in the chapter, this corresponds to Weber's view of class as position in the economic "marketplace." It also parallels approximately Marx's concept of a "class in itself." In all cases, **class** refers to a category or stratum of individuals with a similar degree of economic power, as indicated by any of the following: property ownership, educational qualifications, labour power, or occupation (see Giddens, 1973).

For a **social class** to exist, however, more than just similar economic position or market capacity is required. The individuals involved must also have a common sense of identity, an awareness of their shared characteristics and interests, and a tendency to act together as a real group. As we shall see, this definition corresponds closely to Weber's view and approximates what Marx called a "class for itself." Whereas simple economic classes are often identifiable in societies, genuine social classes rarely come into existence. Marx expected that the class of wage labourers in the capitalist system eventually would become a social class in the complete sense: a class-conscious, politically mobilized, revolutionary proletariat that would act as a group to produce fundamental change in the social structure. Our findings in Canada and other modern societies, however, suggest that this particular social class, this proletariat, has yet to take shape. Instead, the closest approximation to a real social class in modern times may be at the top of the stratification system, among an upper set of controlling élites that possess the consciousness of kind and regular interaction necessary for a real group to exist (Porter, 1965; Clement, 1975; Carroll, 1986; Francis, 1986).

Now that we have considered the key concepts and definitions, we can examine more closely the theories that sociologists have offered to explain social stratification. We begin with the classical views of Marx and Weber. Then we compare these theories with a quite different school of thought, structural functionalism. Finally, we look at some recent attempts to combine the most important ideas from these earlier approaches into new explanations.

MAJOR THEORIES OF SOCIAL STRATIFICATION

Marx: class, conflict, and the power of property

Historical roots

Marx's theory of classes and class conflict is the key starting-point for understanding structured inequality in modern societies. Both supporters and opponents alike have devoted considerable effort to a critical evaluation of his ideas.

Marx was born in Germany in 1818 and died in England in 1883. His life spanned a period of great social change and political and economic turmoil in Europe. In the first half of his life, Marx witnessed and supported unsuccessful revolts in Germany and France, events which he saw as attempts by the less privileged to achieve social justice and a more equitable share of the wealth in those societies. The latter part of Marx's life was spent in England, where industrial capitalism had developed most fully. The so-called "industrial revolution" taking place in Britain was transforming the social structure in a way that both fascinated and saddened Marx. Tremendous surplus wealth was generated by the efficient capitalist economic system, yet this wealth was largely given over to the owners of business while the great majority of working people lived in poverty. Dickens's novels, such as *Hard Times*, are perhaps the best-known illustrations of this period of British history.

It was out of this social and historical context that Marx's ideas emerged (and also the science of sociology itself, as mentioned in Chapter 1). The great gap between rich and poor in that period, and the fact that capitalism could produce such extraordinary wealth yet leave so many people impoverished, were for Marx contradictions that required explanation. Marx tried to arrive at an explanation by analyzing societies from previous ages: ancient Greece, ancient Rome, and medieval Europe, in particular. He concluded that each major societal form is characterized by a clear split between "haves" and "have-nots": master and slave; feudal lord and serf; capitalist and worker. Moreover, each of these forms of social organization is marked by struggle, either open conflict or underlying antagonism, between the two main groups.

The means of production and class structure

For Marx, what really underlies the division of societies into two opposing groups, apart from obvious differences in wealth and prestige, is the power that derives from the ownership or non-ownership of property. In particular, Marx focused on private ownership of productive property, or what he called the "means of production." Under capitalism, productive property refers to natural resources necessary to produce the essentials of life (e.g., food, material for clothing, housing, tools) and to the factories and machinery that transform raw materials into finished goods.

Marx argued that, historically, the dominant group in any society was the one that owned the means of production. It was precisely because some people could claim possession of productive property that inequality of social groups and the formation of classes occurred. Private property meant that owners could determine the distribution of all wealth. Thus, under the capitalist system in Marx's time, the propertyless majority, who owned only their own labour power, had no choice but to rely on those who owned property to employ them as wage workers, often with only sufficient income to keep themselves and their families alive.

Marx argued that the propertyless majority, who owned only their labour power, had no choice but to rely on those who owned property to employ them as wage workers.

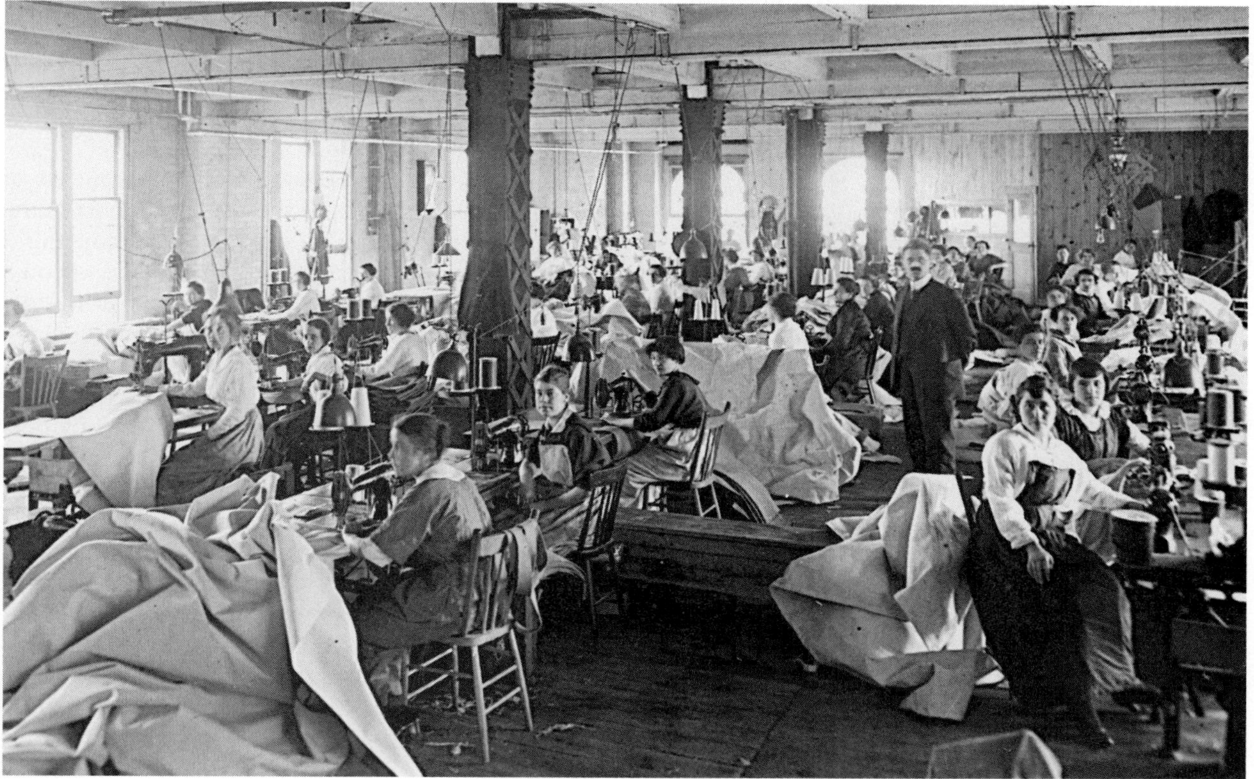

Marx believed that a basic contradiction in this system would become more and more apparent to the people as capitalism developed and expanded. The contradiction, in Marx's view, was that the mass of workers, the majority of the population, gained little benefit from the great wealth they themselves produced. In other words, those who generated the riches of the society through their labour received only a small portion as a living wage, with the remainder going to the capitalist owning class.

Marx claimed that under feudalism, the economic system that operated prior to capitalism, a similar contradiction had existed. The ruling class of feudal lords, who contributed little to the creation of wealth in their system but reaped most of its benefits, was opposed by the then new class of capitalists, a rising, dynamic force seeking social change and a new economic system. Likewise, Marx expected that the working class, or **proletariat**, would become the rising new force under capitalism, one that would oppose the now obstructive and superfluous class of capitalists, the **bourgeoisie**. Just as the bourgeoisie had triumphed over and transformed feudalism, so too would the proletariat realize its potential, overthrow the bourgeoisie, and transform capitalism into socialism.

Revolt of the working class

The change from capitalism to socialism was for Marx the culmination of this historical process of class struggle. For socialism to triumph, however, the working class would have to become more than just a **class in itself**, a category of people sharing the same economic position as non-owners of productive property. In addition, an awareness of common position and a willingness to mobilize as a force for change would be essential if the proletariat were to become a genuine **class for itself**, a group that would change society.

To achieve the mobilization of the working class, several obstacles would have to be overcome. For example, apart from their economic power, the owners of property, in Marx's view, had great influence in various ideological structures: religious institutions, the media of communication, the educational systems, and so forth. We shall return to this argument in subsequent chapters. The owning class could use each of these structures to manipulate or indoctrinate the workers and to justify its privileged position. Also, the owning class had effective control of the political structure, or state, and so could use legal, military, and police power to maintain its position if necessary.

Despite these obstacles, Marx believed that a successful revolution by the proletariat was possible, and that the circumstances necessary for this change would eventually be realized. While Marx offered no precise predictions as to how the revolution would come about, he did expect a number of processes in the development of capitalism to spur the working class to action (Giddens, 1973). To begin with, capitalism encourages the rise of urban centres, since large numbers of propertyless rural inhabitants migrate to the cities in search of employment (see Chapter 16, Urbanization). This growing concentration of urban labourers is a key initial step towards working-class awareness. A second important process in capitalism is the increasing expansion of production into large-scale factories employing many workers. This process also means a concentration of workers in close proximity to one another and a further basis for awareness of their common class position.

In addition, workers are made more aware of their common plight and their separation from the owning class by the workings of the capitalist economy. In Marx's view, capitalism is based on a rational and efficient, but relentless and self-interested, pursuit of profits by the owning class. The quest for increasing profits frequently has unfortunate consequences for the society as a whole. For example, in their desire for greater gain, owners often produce more goods than they can sell. This practice means a loss of money by the capitalist, whose most obvious recourse is to lay off workers to save money. But laying off workers means less money for the workers to purchase the capitalist's products. Hence, the demand for these goods falls and the capitalist loses even more money. In this downward-spiral fashion, economic crises tend to occur in the capitalist system: overproduction, high unemployment, and slow economic growth. After each crisis there is a period in which the economy stabilizes, but always at the expense of the lower strata.

Several additional developments occur in the stabilization period to widen the gulf between the working and owning classes. First, the smaller capitalists, or *petite bourgeoisie*, who are the most vulnerable in bad economic times, either sell out their businesses or fail, and are taken over by larger capitalists. This leads to a growing concentration of ownership by a shrinking group of large capitalists. This concentration, coupled with the gradual disappearance of the middle class of small owners, makes it more and more clear that workers and big capital are the only two classes of consequence in the system. Second, it is increasingly evident to the workers that they are the losers in economic crises, while the large bourgeoisie survive quite nicely. As capitalism matures, *absolute* living standards for everyone, even the workers, are likely to rise because of the tremendous surplus wealth that is amassed. However, in Marx's view, the *relative* difference in economic well-being between owner and worker will continue to widen. This widening gap and the realization by workers that they are the first to suffer in bad times stimulate class polarization still further.

One final factor that Marx believed would promote working-class consciousness and the polarization of the bourgeoisie and proletariat was the rise of the joint stock company. In the earlier stages of capitalism, owners do play an active role in the production process by managing operations and making administrative decisions. Under advanced capitalism, however, businesses are increasingly owned only on paper, with individuals buying shares in companies. Marx believed that, in such a system, it would become even more obvious to the workers that mere ownership is essentially superfluous to productive activity. That is, owners as shareholders control the means of production and accumulate rewards from it, but offer nothing constructive or valuable in return, not even managerial or administrative effort. Thus, the distinction between the productive proletariat and unnecessary capitalists would become increasingly clear.

Marx believed that all of these processes would produce an awareness among the workers of their exploitation and oppression by the bourgeoisie. The far greater numbers and, consequently, the potential power of the working class, coupled with its consciousness of class position and its desire to eliminate class inequalities, would set the stage for the workers to mobilize to overthrow the capitalist class. We should note that Marx did not see this revolution by the proletariat as automatic, in the sense that it would come about of its own accord. The basic conditions for the change were, in Marx's view, inherent in the capitalist mode of economic and social organization. However, the ultimate fate of the revolution depends on the actions of the proletariat and its desire and willingness to change society.

Classless society

What system would replace the capitalist order? Marx avoided specific predictions about this new system, but he generally suggested two stages would follow the revolution. First, Marx foresaw a socialist phase, a "dictatorship of the proletariat," with the leaders of the revolution heading the political apparatus of the society, the state. (We shall discuss the state more fully in Chapter 12, Political Sociology.) The state would abolish private property, thus eliminating any distinction between owning and nonowning classes. While the tremendous productive capacity of the old system would be retained, the state would ensure that the wealth created by the economy was distributed equitably to the productive members of society, to the workers themselves.

In the second stage after the revolution—communism—the state as a political force would become unnecessary and would die away, although some individuals would still be required to remain as administrators of the productive and other spheres of society. Communism would represent the first system without class distinctions, without a class structure, and without class conflict (Giddens, 1973).

Whether the classless society Marx envisioned will ever come to pass remains an open question. For many observers, the disappearance during the 1990s of communist regimes in the former Soviet Union and other countries raises doubts about Marx's projections, at least for the foreseeable future. It is also notable that, even in societies in which a socialist system has been implemented or still exists, inequality has not been eradicated. The need for a group of administrators to oversee the complex

Program for Revolution: *Key Points in* The Communist Manifesto

In 1848, Marx and Engels outlined the key changes that they believed were required in the transition from capitalism to socialism. The following passage is taken from their famous document, The Communist Manifesto.

...in the most advanced countries, the following will be pretty generally applicable.

1. Abolition of property in land and application of all rents of land to public purposes.
2. A heavy progressive or graduated income tax.
3. Abolition of all right of inheritance.
4. Confiscation of the property of all emigrants and rebels.
5. Centralization of credit in the hands of the state, by means of a national bank with state capital and an exclusive monopoly.
6. Centralization of the means of communication and transport in the hands of the state.
7. Extension of factories and instruments of production owned by the state; the bringing into cultivation of wastelands, and the improvement of the soil generally in accordance with a common plan.
8. Equal liability of all to labour. Establishment of industrial armies, especially for agriculture.
9. Combination of agriculture with manufacturing industries; gradual abolition of the distinction between town and country, by a more equable distribution of the population over the country.
10. Free education for all children in public schools. Abolition of children's factory labour in its present form. Combination of education with industrial production, etc., etc.

When, in the course of development, class distinctions have disappeared, and all production has been concentrated in the hands of a vast association of the whole nation, the public power will lose its political character. Political power, properly so called, is merely the organized power of one class for oppressing another. If the proletariat during its contest with the bourgeoisie is compelled, by the force of circumstances, to organize itself as a class, if, by means of a revolution, it makes itself the ruling class, and, as such, sweeps away by force the old conditions of production, then it will, along with these conditions, have swept away the conditions for the existence of class antagonisms and of classes generally, and will thereby have abolished its own supremacy as a class.

In place of the old bourgeois society, with its classes and class antagonisms, we shall have an association in which the free development of each is the condition for the free development of all.

Source: *Karl Marx and Friedrich Engels, 1848.* The Communist Manifesto. *New York: Washington Square Press (1970, pp. 93–95).*

operations of any advanced society is probably one major reason why the elimination of stratification has not been realized.

Weber's critique of Marx

One common criticism of Marx's theory of classes is that it paints too simple a picture of social stratification, especially in modern societies. Critics claim, first of all, that Marx concentrated too much on one source of power in society, the economic sphere. Secondly, many writers feel that Marx's split of the economic structure into two classes, the propertied and the propertyless, ignores the existence of other identifiable classes.

Multiple power sources

One of the first to raise such issues was another German thinker, Max Weber. Weber lived and wrote in a time after Marx's death and was able to observe certain developments in capitalism that Marx could not. Weber accepted Marx's emphasis on economic class and property ownership as fundamental to social inequality. However, Weber pointed out that economic class by itself was not the only source of power or criterion for ranking in the social structure. Weber noted that power or influence could also be gained from **status honour**, or prestige, deriving from membership in certain groups. Such *status groups*, which may include ethnic, religious, or similar entities, involve exclusive membership; awareness of like tastes, lifestyles, and interests; and a tendency to act and interact as a unit. Similarly, Weber discussed **party**, referring to the political sphere and political involvement, as an additional basis of power or command over resources in society. Weber was one of the first to view power in this multifaceted way. Each of the three factors—economic class, status group, and political party—serves as a source of power and a basis for group formation in society (Giddens, 1973).

Weber conceded that these three aspects of stratification are frequently closely related, so that those who dominate the economic system tend also to have considerable status honour and political control. However, he disagreed with what he believed was Marx's contention, that all power derives ultimately from the control of the economy and the production process. Weber did not accept the view of some Marxists that the political, religious, educational, and other structures of society act only to serve the interests of the ruling economic class. To Weber, each of these structures possessed some power in its own right, some recognized sphere of influence and control. In this sense, Weber's view is one of the first *pluralist* conceptions of power in social theory. Power is pluralist here in the sense that it derives from more than one single source or structure.

The existence of "middle classes"

Weber's pluralist view of power is also revealed in his discussion of class structure. Weber argued, in opposition to Marx, that there were more than just two main economic classes, the bourgeoisie and proletariat. (As discussed earlier, Marx also was aware of the existence of middle classes in capitalism, but he believed that these groups were transitional and would eventually become part of the two major classes.) In his work, Weber included a range of middle classes, people who lack the privilege of large property ownership but have more than just labour power to sell in the capitalist marketplace. These middle classes possess one or both of the following: (1) small amounts of productive property, such as shops, small businesses, or small farms; (2) valued skills, such as the special training or education of a physician, lawyer, or artisan.

Weber agreed with Marx that the small business segment of the middle classes was in decline. However, the other major segment, those people with specialized skills or training, would not decrease but expand and flourish under capitalism. Many of these people would fill positions as technical and administrative workers in the huge, developing bureaucratic structures of modern society. According to Weber, the need for managers, accountants, bookkeepers, supervisors, engineers, architects, teachers, and so on in the business, government, and educational bureaucracies would ensure that the middle classes would not be a transitional group, but a rising force in modern society.

Classless society and bureaucracy

You will recall Marx's expectation that future societies would see the end of classes and inequality. If we employ Marx's criterion for defining classes—the ownership or non-ownership of property—it is possible to envision the disappearance of classes. We need only abolish private property and the basis for class formation would not exist. This is the approach that was taken officially in socialist countries like China or the former Soviet Union. It appears, however, that the abolition of private property is insufficient to eliminate inequality between identifiable groupings in society. Whether we call these unequal groupings classes or strata, the fact of inequality persists, even with private property eliminated. In socialist societies, the bases for power differences and group formation have simply shifted from property ownership to other factors, particularly access to valued education or skills and to political power. Those who dominate these sources of power tend to dominate the society (Giddens, 1973, 1981; Parkin, 1979).

Weber's analysis of bureaucracy provides some explanation for the persistence of structured inequality in both socialist and capitalist societies. In any social structure, people in decision-making positions must have the legitimate right or power to decide, if they are to ensure that their chosen course of action will be followed by others. By definition this means that hierarchies based on unequal power and control will arise. In the modern era, these power hierarchies have increasingly taken the form of bureaucracies (to be dealt with further in Chapter 13, Formal Organizations and Work). Bureaucracies are designed for the administration and performance of various important tasks—policy-making, allocation of economic resources, health care, job placement, defence, and so forth. While socialism may attempt to remove material inequalities, it cannot eliminate the need for these administrative structures in making and implementing important decisions.

The problem of attaining individual equality and freedom in the face of bureaucratic dominance in societies of every type is probably the major dilemma facing Marxist and socialist theorists in the present day. In fact, Weber argued that bureaucracy would be even more common in socialist systems in which so many more aspects of life are regulated by government. Hence, power differences and inequality could be even greater in a socialist system than under capitalism. Certainly, the recent history of current and former communist countries points to this problem.

Weber clearly recognized the threat bureaucracy poses to equality and freedom, but believed the bureaucratic form was necessary for the efficient coordination and management of essential tasks in complex societies. Unlike another theorist, Michels, Weber did not believe that an *iron law of oligarchy* operates in social structures, in which those in power inevitably abuse their position to extract special benefits for themselves at the expense of the masses. Nevertheless, Weber believed that the potential for such abuse of power is basic to modern social organizations, whether capitalist or socialist. We shall return to these issues in Chapter 13, Formal Organizations and Work.

Structural functionalism: consensus, individualism, and pluralism

While Marx stressed conflict, group (class) action, and the singular importance of economic power in understanding social stratification, the structural functionalist school of thought emphasizes consensus, individual action, and the pluralism of power in social structures (Davis and Moore, 1945; Parsons, 1953). Let us consider these three points.

Consensus or conflict

Marx believed that conflict and struggle between groups are basic to the operation of all known societies. In contrast, structural functionalist theorists, as mentioned in Chapter 1, concentrate on what they perceive as the harmony and agreement that mark social interaction. Social groups could not survive as they do, they argue, without considerable consensus on the norms and values that govern social life. Rather than viewing structured inequality as something imposed upon the people by those in power, structural functionalists have argued that this inequality is based largely on an underlying awareness and agreement about the value put on various positions in the social structure.

The value given to each position or status depends on two factors: its functional importance for society and the relative scarcity of people with the talent or training needed for the position. Some statuses, such as doctor, scientist, or judge, are said to be both more important and harder to fill than, for example, the positions of parking lot attendant or file clerk. Hence, the rewards attached to the more crucial positions and those requiring rare skills must be proportionately greater than the rewards attached to the less valuable statuses. Otherwise, the most qualified individuals would not aspire to the key positions or, if in them, would not perform their important duties properly. The rewards used to motivate individuals in this system are of three types: (1) "sustenance and comfort," which are most readily attainable from material and economic gains such as money or property; (2) "humour and diversion," which may come from material returns but also include such benefits as extra leisure time or a flexible and varied work schedule; and (3) "self-respect and ego expansion," which tend to stem mainly from the prestige and honour accorded those who occupy important positions.

Several assumptions underlie this functionalist argument, but a central one is the presupposition

Some statuses are said to be both more important and harder to fill than, for example, the positions of parking lot attendant or file clerk.

that there is a high level of consensus among social actors: first, on the functional importance of each status—that is, on what the important jobs are; second, on what constitutes a "reward" in social life; and, third, on how rewards should be allotted to the various positions in the social structure.

The further assumption that different rewards are essential to motivate human beings leads to the conclusion that social inequality is inevitable and, in fact, performs a positive function for society by providing incentives for people to develop their talents to the full and to find their "proper" places in the stratification system. It is alleged that those who are willing to work hard and apply themselves, and who can forego present rewards to achieve special skills and training, will achieve privileged positions in the system and be rewarded with greater material benefits, prestige, and life satisfaction. It is assumed once again that there is general agreement on the importance of hard work, on the existence of opportunity for all, and on the rules that regulate the contest for success.

Individualism versus class action

The second aspect of structural functionalist thinking that distinguishes it from Marxian theory is its general avoidance of the concept of class. Rather than proposing a class or group basis for understanding inequality in societies, structural functionalists focus almost solely on individual action and individual status as the factors in social stratification. In modern societies, the most important status determining stratification position is the individual's occupational status. The functional importance of this status and not, for example, inherited wealth and privilege, indicates the stratification rank of any single individual.

Pluralism or property

While the structural functionalist analysis of social stratification differs considerably from the Weberian perspective, one view they share is that societies are pluralist or multifaceted structures. In the structural functionalist conception, social organization involves the coordination of interdependent subsystems, each with its own functions to perform if the overall system is to survive. The major subsystems, or *institutions*, of society include the economy, the polity (or political institutions), religion, education, and the agents of social control (police, military), among others. Each institution is said to operate in harmony with the others, to ensure social stability, maintenance of the system, and the general well-being of the population. The contrast between this formulation and Marx's focus on the overriding power of property ownership is apparent. For Marx, those who dominate the economy through ownership of the means of production ultimately hold sway in all other spheres and, moreover, can bring the power of the political, social control, and other structures into play to protect their domination.

Combining the major theories to explain modern stratification systems

We get very different views of social stratification depending on which theoretical perspective we consider. The differences exist primarily because each approach emphasizes different factors to explain structured inequality in modern societies. It can be argued that no major theory by itself gives a complete picture of the stratification process, and that each applies better to some situations than to others. Consider the Marxian perspective. Marxism originated in nineteenth-century Europe and seems particularly suited to describe the group struggle and class divisions of that time and setting. Since then, however, Marxism has achieved its greatest following in the less industrialized countries of the world, and may not be as applicable to industrialized societies as it once was. In the less industrialized countries of Africa, Asia, and Latin America, for example, the continued sharp contrast between rich and poor has enabled class polarization and revolutionary potential to remain strong. In the industrialized capitalist countries of North America and Europe, however, absolute living standards have risen significantly for virtually everyone, the middle strata have not disappeared, and opportunities for mobility are still at least perceived to exist by many people. Hence, complete class polarization and outright revolution seem like distant and unlikely developments in advanced capitalism at this time.

Nevertheless, many elements of Marxian theory are useful for understanding modern stratification systems. The role of conflict and struggle in human affairs and the great power invested in those who own and control property are undeniably important facets of modern life that affect social stratification. This will become more apparent in our analysis of the Canadian economic élite.

The structural functionalist view of stratification originated in the United States where, historically, such ideas as equal opportunity, free competition, and individual achievement were cherished and accepted as realities by much of the population. It is unlikely, however, that anything resembling complete equality of opportunity has existed in any known society. Discrimination on the basis of race, gender, and family background, for example, continues to play a significant role in defining stratification systems, even in nominally egalitarian societies. However, certain aspects of the structural functionalist perspective do ring true. Some consensus, not just conflict, does operate in social systems; otherwise, social organization would not be possible. In addition, the expansion of the labour forces of most modern societies has provided opportunities for individual success in the stratification system, on the basis of merit and training.

Some theorists have attempted to reconcile these disparate theoretical approaches by bringing together elements of each perspective that have the greatest merit. Dahrendorf (1959) and Lenski (1966), for example, attempted to show how both conflict and consensus operate in social systems. It is likely that a complete synthesis of theories is not possible. However, key features of the major theories can be combined to provide a more inclusive model for representing social stratification (Grabb, 1997). We suggest, first of all, that individual action, especially through educational and occupational attainment, does play a role in defining social stratification in countries like Canada. At the same time, group memberships play a major part in determining the structure of inequality. Most notable is membership in the upper class, and in that small set of élites that dominates the major institutions of society. Other group affiliations, such as race, ethnicity, and gender, also contribute to stratification position, for they represent different bases of inequality, both inside and outside the élites, and are related to differences in command over scarce resources, including wealth, education, and prestige. The recognition of individual and group factors indicates that both the structural functionalist and Marxist approaches are relevant for understanding the stratification process.

Acknowledging the existence of multiple bases for stratification is consistent with both Weberian and structural functionalist theories. Each theory stresses the pluralist nature of power in stratification systems. However, each ranking does not play an equally important role in producing the system of inequality and in the distribution of resources. Following Marx, we shall argue that control of property and wealth, particularly by large business enterprises, is the most important source of power in modern stratification systems. We shall examine Canadian research on this point later in the chapter. At the same time, following Weber, we suggest that the other two socio-economic status hierarchies, education and occupation, also are crucial in shaping the system of inequality.

Taken together, these three hierarchies have tended to promote the formation of a structure of three classes or strata in capitalist countries like Canada. This structure is made up of an upper class that dominates large property ownership; a middle class that, because of highly marketable skills, education, and training, holds the more powerful and rewarding jobs; and a working class that has few skills other than labour power and so occupies the less powerful and less rewarding positions in the labour force. Of course, within these three broad groupings, many finer distinctions could be drawn. For example, sociologists sometimes speak of the "lower middle class" or the "upper working class" as subcategories in this three-class system. Some also include in this representation of the stratification system a fourth grouping, an "underclass" of very poor and disadvantaged persons. This stratum includes people who may possess no property, education, or labour power and who may, for instance, be frequently unemployed because they cannot find work or are unable to work (Giddens, 1973; Grabb, 1993a, 1997).

In addition to the three socio-economic hierarchies discussed above, five other hierarchies contribute to the configuration of Canada's stratification system. First, political power is crucial, especially when we consider that, officially at least, the ultimate power in society, even greater than that of the economic élite, is invested in the political leadership and the state. Generally speaking, it is the interplay between those who control political power and those who dominate the economic sphere that is the key process shaping the stratification system of modern societies such as Canada. Second, differences in power and privilege between men and women are large in our society, so that gender has an important bearing on structured inequality. Age has only recently been recognized as an important factor in Canadian stratification. As for the remaining two rankings, based on ethnic and/or racial origin, and region or rural–urban location, these are of particular importance in describing Canada's stratification system, with its image as a "vertical mosaic" of diverse cultures and geographic areas (Porter, 1965).

While other possible bases of social stratification could be considered, such as religion, for example, they will not be examined here because they are less salient in contemporary Canada than are the eight hierarchies suggested above.

In the next section of this chapter we shall take a detailed look at each of the eight rankings. We shall see that there are connections in many cases between the rank of individuals and groups in one hierarchy and their ranks in others. An understanding of these interrelationships among hierarchies, taken together, should give the reader a relatively complete picture of the nature of social stratification in Canadian society.

CANADA'S STRATIFICATION STRUCTURE

Socio-economic hierarchies I: wealth, income, and property

Wealth, including various forms of income and property, plays at least two major roles in social stratification. First, wealth is clearly a result of stratification position. Wealth or income is the return people receive from their position in the economic structure. This return usually involves income from a job, but may include earnings from investments or property ownership. In all of these cases, wealth comes as a reward that can be high or low, depending on the market value of one's job or property holdings. The distribution of wealth, then, is the most direct measure or indication of how groups or individuals rank in the overall stratification system.

Nevertheless, wealth plays a second key part in social stratification, at least in capitalist societies like Canada, where private property and inheritance are protected by law. Wealth is itself a form of property that can be used through investment to acquire more wealth and property. In this sense, wealth is not only a consequence but also a cause or means by which stratification position is maintained or changed. Therefore, wealth and property ownership can be seen as two aspects of the same power source.

CBC "Portraits from a Project"

Distribution of income and wealth

How are wealth and property distributed in Canadian society? Are these sources of power widely diffused throughout the population or are they concentrated in a small group of people? There is no doubt, first of all, that people in most industrialized societies in this century have enjoyed an *absolute* increase in real wealth. In Canada, between 1951 and 1989, earned income increased by 198 percent for men and 284 percent for women, even after the effects of inflation were taken into account. It is important to note that this increase was most pronounced prior to 1980; also, during the early 1990s, growth in real income levelled off and at times declined, especially for males (Hunter, 1993: 101; Statistics Canada, 1994, *Income Distributions by Size, 1994*, Table 1).

But how this income has been distributed is really the issue. The question, in other words, is one of *relative* income, of how well certain strata have been doing compared with others. In one study of this topic, all families or individuals who earned money in a particular year were ranked by their total income for that year and then divided into *quintiles* (five strata of equal size). Results showed that the top quintile, the top 20 percent of the hierarchy, earned about 43 percent of all the income made in Canada in 1951, while the bottom quintile earned only 4 percent. By 1994, this unequal distribution of income had remained almost unchanged, with the top quintile's share at 44 percent and the bottom quintile's portion at 5 percent. In relative terms, then, the rich remained rich and the poor remained poor during this period.

These figures for Canada, which correspond approximately to those reported in U.S. studies (Edsall, 1988; Chawla, 1990), suggest that the unequal distribution of income has not changed much in recent decades. It should be noted also that various government programs to transfer and redistribute income (through taxation, pensions, family allowances, unemployment insurance, and so forth), have in total done little to make up the income deficiency in the lower strata. Evidence indicates that these programs redistribute income to the lower strata, but only modestly, and more at the expense of middle-income people than the rich (O'Connor, 1993).

To establish a more complete picture of economic inequality in Canada, we must look beyond earned income alone. It is important to consider all the accumulated assets—stocks, real estate, durable goods, and the like—that together form the total wealth of an individual or group. The available data show that, as of 1984, the top 10 percent of the Canadian population held over half of all wealth, while the top 20 percent retained about 70 percent (Davies, 1993: 108). Thus, the distribution of wealth is even more unequal than the distribution of income.

Do the Rich Really Get Richer?

The gap between the incomes of Canada's top business executives and those of other workers has grown dramatically in recent years. A study by the consulting firm KPMG looked at the Chief Executive Officers, or CEOs, of 268 major companies listed on the Toronto Stock Exchange. The study showed that, from 1992 to 1995, annual incomes for CEOs rose by 32 percent, to an average of $776,000 per year. During the same period, the average income of Canadian workers increased by less than 3 percent. The survey also revealed that pay increases for executives were not related to how well their companies had performed. In fact, the CEOs of less profitable businesses actually received bigger average raises than those running the more profitable companies. Such is an indication of how people with wealth and power in our society are able to protect and enhance their advantaged economic positions, sometimes regardless of their performance or contributions to the nation's economy.

Source: *From a Southam News story by Bertrand Marotte, published in the* London Free Press, *September 25, 1996 (p. D5).*

Distribution of property

Besides income and wealth, the other major means for achieving economic power in a capitalist society is through ownership or control of property. Under the capitalist system, large property, especially in the form of giant corporations, is rarely owned outright by one person or even a few people. Instead, corporations are owned by shareholders, each "owning a piece of the rock." This is a popular image suggesting a dispersion of economic power to the wider population. However, studies indicate that ownership tends to involve a relatively small number of shareholders in many cases. Moreover, even where ownership is dispersed, minority shareholdings rather than majority ownership are often all that is needed to achieve effective control of decision-making in the corporations. Frequently, the shares in a company are spread across a large number of isolated individuals, most of whom do not attend shareholders' meetings and some of whom may not have voting rights for electing company directors. In such instances, control of a small block of shares, perhaps only 10 or 20 percent, may be sufficient to determine how the company is run (Francis, 1986; Grabb, 1993b). Therefore, ownership or control of property, and hence economic power, can be concentrated in a small group of people.

Perhaps even stronger evidence of the concentration of property ownership has been offered by various studies of corporate control in Canada. Francis (1986) concluded that a small group of thirty-two wealthy families, along with five "conglomerates," or clusters of companies, controlled one-third of Canada's non-financial assets in 1985. Carroll (1986) has also identified a powerful set of six "cliques" that forms the inner circle of the Canadian corporate structure. It appears, then, that economic power deriving from property ownership is more highly concentrated in a smaller set of individuals than ever before.

More recent government statistics confirm this high concentration of property control and suggest that it has increased with time (Grabb, 1993b; O'Connor, 1993). By 1993, Canada's top twenty-five financial and non-financial enterprises controlled over 1200 interconnected corporations, and by themselves accounted for about 46 percent of Canada's total business assets (Corporations and Labour Unions Returns Act 1993; see also Grabb, 1993b; O'Connor, 1993).

In summary, Canada's stratification system is marked by considerable differences in economic power, in the form of wealth and property holdings. A relatively small group of people at the top possesses much of the wealth. In addition, within this "upper class," an even smaller élite, including the owners and directors of dominant corporations, controls most of the society's economic resources.

These findings are broadly consistent with a Marxist interpretation of social stratification. The continued unequal distribution of wealth, the relative decline in wealth and property holdings among the lower strata, and the concentration of economic power in a small élite all support such a view. However, these realities apparently have been insufficient to produce the class polarization and proletarian revolution Marx expected under advanced capitalism. While the explanation for this failure is complex, three possible reasons are offered. First, it may be partly because the general population has done better economically, at least in absolute terms, than Marx anticipated. Such developments as worker unionization and the institution of government social programs—health insurance, old age pensions, and the like—have meant at least modest increases in living standards for most people. Despite spending cuts by all levels of government that have weakened social programs in recent years, it may be that most workers still feel their material position is adequate. Second, those workers who are discontented may believe that they lack the power to change their situation even if they wanted to. As a consequence, rather than becoming a unified force for change, much of the working class has remained passive, accepting their disadvantaged position in the stratification system. Finally, despite the serious inequalities existing in Canada, perhaps there is sufficient real or perceived upward mobility to maintain the belief among many workers that opportunities continue to be there for those who will take them. Such optimistic beliefs would tend to reduce class polarization.

We shall consider the question of mobility later in this chapter, but whatever the opportunity structure, the inequality in economic power in Canada in recent decades has apparently not been sufficient to promote a concerted move for change among the working and middle classes. In the next section, we examine the occupation's role in the distribution of economic power, particularly for these two classes.

Socio-economic hierarchies II: occupation

Except for wealthy property holders, occupational status is the major source of economic power for most individuals. Because occupation correlates with other stratification variables—income, education, gender, ethnicity—it is sometimes viewed as the best single indicator of an individual's general stratification rank. Thus, it is useful to examine trends in the occupational composition of the labour force. In this section, we consider some of the transformations that have occurred in Canada's workforce and then look at changes in the distribution of income by occupational status over time. This will help us to assess how the market capacities of various occupations have changed in recent decades. Finally, we also look at research on occupational mobility in Canada. This will help us to evaluate the degree to which ours is an open or closed stratification system.

Occupational shifts

The first major historical development to note is the great increase in the types of jobs that exist today compared with earlier times. Nuclear physicist, computer scientist, X-ray technician, and airline pilot are some of the many jobs that have come into being in this century. The growth in the variety of occupations is a prime example of the increasing social differentiation in modern societies, a process discussed earlier in this chapter.

In addition to the greater number of occupations, there has been a notable shift in the relative size of occupational categories over time. Occupations can be divided roughly into three groups: manual or blue-collar jobs, non-manual or white-collar jobs, and agricultural or farm occupations. Manual jobs normally entail physical labour, working with one's hands, as the name implies. In social research, these jobs are sometimes equated with the working class, and include such occupations as construction

TABLE 7.1 Canadian labour force, percentage distribution by major occupational groups, 1901–1991

	1901	*1921*	*1941*	*1961*	*1981*	*1991*
All occupations:	**100**	**100**	**100**	**100**	**100**	**100**
White collar:	**15**	**25**	**25**	**39**	**53**	**57**
Managerial	4	7	5	8	9	12
Professional/technical	5	5	7	10	16	18
Clerical	3	7	7	13	19	18
Sales	3	6	6	8	9	9
Blue collar:	**45**	**42**	**49**	**49**	**43**	**38**
Manufacturing/mechanical/construction	21	16	21	22		
Labourers	7	10	6	5	29[1]	23[1]
Transport/communication	5	5	6	8		
Service	8	7	11	11	12	13
Fishing/logging/mining	4	4	5	3	2	2
Agriculture:	**40**	**33**	**26**	**10**	**4**	**3**
Occupation not stated	–	–	–	**2**	–	**2**

[1]Because blue-collar categories differ after 1981 from previous years, these three occupational categories are combined.

Source: *Kubat and Thornton (1974: 153–55); Statistics Canada,* 1981 Census of Canada, *Catalogue No. 92-917, Table 1;* 1991 Census of Canada, *Catalogue No. 93-327, Table 1.*

worker, factory labourer, miner, lumberjack, and mechanic. Non-manual jobs typically involve working with symbols and ideas, rather than with the hands. Non-manual jobs are sometimes used as an indication of middle-class position by social scientists, and include such occupations as doctor, lawyer, teacher, nurse, business manager, salesperson, accountant, and clerk.

An examination of historical shifts in these three job categories is quite revealing (see Table 7.1). First, the proportion of agricultural occupations has declined greatly, from over 40 percent in 1901 to about 3 percent in 1991. Blue-collar occupations recently have declined somewhat, but still formed close to 40 percent of the workforce in 1991. There have, however, been shifts within the blue-collar group, including a move to more service work, such as food preparation, hairdressing, and housekeeping, plus a decline in unskilled labour and primary labour, such as fishing, logging, and mining. The white-collar sector has expanded the most, from 15 percent to more than 50 percent of the Canadian workforce. Much of the white-collar growth, however, involves lower positions—sales clerks, typists, file clerks—which, in terms of income, power, and work activities, are similar to working-class occupations (see Braverman, 1974: 417–19; Lowe, 1993; Rinehart, 1996: 110–11). In this view, then, part of the non-manual expansion indicates a rising "new working class" of low-paid, semi-skilled, white-collar workers.

Occupation and income

As Table 7.2 indicates, blue-collar relative earning power has changed little since 1931, with incomes staying at about 10 percent below the national average. At the same time, white-collar incomes have declined from 2.09 times the national level in 1931 to 1.08 in 1990. On the surface, this white-collar relative decline lends some support to the new-working-class view. That is, with white-collar incomes becoming more like blue-collar incomes, we might conclude that today's non-manual employees, in their market capacity and perhaps other traits, are more like the working class than the middle class.

TABLE 7.2 Average incomes of major occupational groups (full-time employed), as a percent of the average income for all occupations, 1931–1990

	1931	*1941*	*1951*[1]	*1961*	*1971*[2]	*1981*[2]	*1990*[2]
All occupations:	**100**	**100**	**100**	**100**	**100**	**100**	**100**
White collar:	**209**	**172**	**134**	**120**	**130**	**109**	**108**
Managerial	314	253	169	184	204	179	133
Professional/technical	214	176	141	150	144	127	122
Clerical	125	112	102	92	89	72	74
Sales	140	122	107	106	108	90	94
Blue collar:	**86**	**90**	**93**	**87**	**91**	**90**	**89**
Manufacturing/mechanical/construction	101	102	106	99			
Labourers	53	61	73	60	97[3]	105[3]	95[3]
Transport/communication	115	104	100	94			
Service	97	85	84	76	80	60	72
Fishing/logging/mining	63	69	90	71	79	107	121
Agriculture:	**35**	**30**	**37**	**38**	**51**	**68**	**56**

[1]Median income 1951.
[2]Figures after 1971 exclude those with no employment income and those whose occupations were not stated or included in the major categories.
[3]Because blue-collar categories differ after 1971 from previous years, these three occupational categories are combined.

Source: *Derived from N.M. Meltz, 1965.* Changes in the Occupational Composition of the Canadian Labour Force: 1931–61. *Ottawa: Queen's Printer (pp. 64–65); Statistics Canada,* 1971 Census of Canada, *Catalogue No. 94-765;* 1981 Census of Canada, *Catalogue No. 92-930;* 1991 Census of Canada, *Catalogue No. 93-332.*

However, several points should be noted here. First, although the white-collar income decline has tended to occur in all segments of this group, as Table 7.2 indicates, it appears to be most significant for clerical workers, who now earn incomes lower than blue-collar workers as a whole. Managerial, professional, and to a lesser extent sales incomes, on the other hand, continue to be higher than those of blue-collar workers in spite of considerable recent declines. Second, the general decline of white-collar incomes is somewhat misleading, because much of this trend is due to the flow of poorly paid women into many of these positions (see Krahn and Lowe, 1993; Lowe, 1993). White-collar males outside the clerical sector have maintained a significant edge over blue-collar workers. For example, male managers and professional-technical workers earned between 60 and 70 percent more than blue-collar workers in 1990, and even male sales workers earned 20 percent higher incomes, on average (Statistics Canada, 1993, *Employment Income by Occupation*, Table 1). Finally, it should also be noted that these income figures give only a partial picture, since they do not include other economic advantages—job security, fringe benefits, and promotion opportunities—which have traditionally been more likely to benefit white-collar workers, especially those in the professional-technical and managerial categories (Krahn and Lowe, 1993: 114; Lowe, 1993: 139–41).

Occupation and social mobility

The previous discussion of middle-class expansion and the upgrading of the occupational structure leads to another important issue: the process of social mobility in stratification systems. Earlier, we described social mobility as any shift in status by an individual or group within a status hierarchy. Analyzing vertical intergenerational mobility is particularly helpful in assessing how open or closed a stratification system is. If we can show that parents' statuses do not really affect their adult children's statuses in a particular system, this would suggest the system is open. In an open system individuals are neither helped nor hindered by the power of their parents or by such ascriptive characteristics as their family's race, ethnic origin, or social-class background. On the other hand, when children do gain or lose chances for success largely on the basis of their family backgrounds, we have a more closed stratification system.

The most general approach to the study of social mobility is to take into account all of the eight major power dimensions considered in this chapter. Thus, social mobility may be defined as a change in the relative amount of all "power resources" held by a person or group. In most cases, however, social scientists have concentrated on the occupational status hierarchy alone when assessing social mobility. This is probably because, as was noted earlier in this chapter, occupation may be the best single indicator of overall class or stratum rank for most of the population.

Labour in the Working Class

In his book *The Tyranny of Work*, James Rinehart (1996) assessed the nature of labour for the modern working class. He suggested that in more and more industries the jobs of blue-collar workers have gradually undergone a significant reduction in skill requirements in this century. Due to ever-improving technology, especially computers, and an increasing division of labour, their work has become routine, easy to learn, unskilled, and repetitive. Even what was once skilled labour, such as machining, has been affected by these trends, thus blurring the previous, more clear-cut distinction between skilled and unskilled workers.

"Semiskilled and unskilled workers literally sell their capacity to work: they sell the ability to learn a specific job, any job, in a particular work organization. When they change jobs, their 'skills' are not ordinarily transferable (unlike those of crafts[people] or professionals) and they are obliged to acquire new 'skills' for new jobs" (Rinehart, 1996: 28).

Occupation may be the best single indicator of overall class position for most of the population.

One early study showed that social mobility patterns in Canada were similar to those of other industrialized nations. This analysis found a moderate relationship (a correlation of about .40) between fathers' and sons' occupational status (Goyder and Curtis, 1977: 304–308), suggesting that family class background, as measured by fathers' occupation, has a notable but not overwhelming impact on sons' adult occupational attainments. Goyder and Curtis also found that, if intergenerational mobility is traced over four generations, the association disappears. In other words, the effect of family class background on occupational attainments seems not to accumulate from great-grandfather through to great-grandson. Hence, the authors concluded that there is an "impermanence of family status over non-adjacent generations," suggesting that Canada is "an achievement society rather than an ascriptive one" (Goyder and Curtis, 1977: 316).

More recent research on occupational mobility reveals other interesting patterns. One study found that the relationship between fathers' occupational status and the occupational status of both sons and daughters declined significantly from 1973 to 1986 (Wanner, 1993: 171–74). This indicates that people are increasingly less likely to inherit occupational privileges now than in the past, suggesting some increase in overall mobility, openness, and equality of opportunity in the Canadian occupational structure in recent years. Of course, these findings do not mean that inheritance of occupational advantages has disappeared (Wanner, 1993: 175). Moreover, such research applies mainly to the broad range of individuals between the very poor and the very wealthy. Other studies show considerable immobility within these two extreme categories, so that the very rich generally stay rich and the very poor stay poor.

In conclusion, mobility does occur in our society, even though the overall opportunity structure is far from completely open. The major mechanism providing the chance for mobility across generations seems to be the education system. Especially for that large central group from middle- and working-class backgrounds, the acquisition of skills and training through the schools is probably the best bet for individual advancement. In the next section we consider just how equally or unequally educational advantages are distributed in Canada.

Socio-economic hierarchies III: education

Education is included among the set of socio-economic status hierarchies because it is closely linked to the acquisition of wealth and occupational status in modern societies. In Canada and other countries, the education system is the primary means by which most people achieve upward mobility and material success. Education has a crucial function in sustaining the belief that our stratification system is neither closed nor totally determined by ascribed status characteristics such as race, sex, or inherited wealth. If individual achievement in the education system is consistently translated into higher stratification rank, then the argument for an open, competitive, and fair system is made more convincing. (For a general analysis of this issue in Canada, see Chapter 11, Education.)

Recall that structural functionalist theory is most closely identified with the view that the stratification process is a contest in which education and training are the means to success. In Canada, there is much evidence for such an assertion. Generally speaking, higher education is related to higher income and occupational attainment. In 1990, for example, university graduates in Canada made almost twice as much in employment income as did high-school graduates, although this difference was smaller among the younger age groups (Statistics Canada, 1994, *Earnings of Canadians,* Table 2.5). As for occupation differences, 82 percent of university graduates held upper white-collar jobs (professional-technical and managerial-administrative positions) in 1986, compared with 20 percent of high-school graduates and only 8 percent of those with elementary education (Statistics Canada, 1989, *Total Income: Individuals,* Table 6). Employment data indicate that university graduates also have other advantages. Compared with non-graduates, graduates are less likely to be unemployed, less likely to remain unemployed if they lose a job, and more likely to earn higher salaries when employed (Akyeampong, 1990; Picot and Wannell, 1993; Anisef and Axelrod, 1993). Clearly, while higher education by itself may not be sufficient for success and does not guarantee a better job to everyone, it is still a necessary prerequisite in most cases.

An important question to ask when discussing education and social stratification is, who does and who does not acquire higher education, and why (Pike, 1993)? For educational attainment to be truly an achieved status, there must be equal opportunity for all citizens to acquire education, assuming they have the motivation and the ability to do so. Otherwise, education becomes much like an ascriptive characteristic, something that one possesses or lacks as a result of the inherited advantages or disadvantages of sex, race, or family-class background.

Canadian data indicate that, in the past, ascriptive traits such as class background were significantly related to educational attainment. For example, Porter's (1965: 184) early research from the 1950s showed that individuals whose families earned above average incomes and whose fathers had high status occupations were greatly overrepresented in the university student population. However, more recent studies have found increases in the proportion of post-secondary students coming from lower socio-economic backgrounds. These results indicate that Canada's educational structure has become more "meritocratic"—more accessible to people on the basis of ability rather than class background—than it was before (see for example Guppy and Arai, 1993: 220–24). Nevertheless, these studies also reveal that students from the lower strata are still underrepresented compared with their proportion of the population.

Of course, inequality of educational opportunity may not be the only reason why people from the lower strata are underrepresented in Canada's post-secondary institutions. Some studies indicate that other factors probably have an impact. Parents' and children's perceptions of the chances for education, their knowledge of educational programs, and their evaluation of the utility of education in the job market all reduce the likelihood that lower-class children will go on in school. In addition, differences in parental encouragement of children's educational aspirations may make it more likely that middle- and upper-class children will continue in the education system (see Anisef and Okihiro, 1982; Martin and Macdonell, 1982).

Even if all of these factors are taken into account, it is likely that much of the difference in education in the population is due to inequality of access. Despite the availability of government assistance and student loans, post-secondary education remains an expensive undertaking that low-income people often cannot afford. There is also reason to believe that continued government underfunding of higher education is beginning to restrict access to post-secondary education once again (Pike, 1988). All of these factors suggest unequal educational opportunity and threaten the major avenue of upward mobility for a large number of Canadians (Wotherspoon, 1991).

This completes our discussion of the major socio-economic status hierarchies. We have seen that wealth and property, occupational status, and education all play important parts in shaping the stratification system or class structure. In the remaining sections of this chapter, we examine the interrelationships between these aspects of inequality and five other key hierarchies.

Racial and ethnic stratification

Racial and ethnic origin (to be discussed in Chapter 8) are important factors distinguishing people from one another in Canada. It is also apparent that racial and ethnic diversity, or "multiculturalism," has important implications for our stratification system.

Various factors have operated to make race and ethnicity important criteria for stratification rank. First, different groups arrived in Canada at different times, so that some groups were able to make prior claims on power and property rights. Second, some cultures may put less stress than others on the importance of acquiring wealth and power; hence, differences in values may have contributed to racial/ethnic stratification. In addition, ethnic or racial background frequently has been used as a basis for favouritism or discrimination, making it difficult for some groups to enter the upper strata while allowing others ready access. These factors and others have produced in Canada what Porter (1965) called a "vertical mosaic," a social structure involving many diverse racial and ethnic groups, ranked along a hierarchy of power and privilege.

We begin our examination of the links between racial or ethnic background and stratification rank by assessing the relationship today between these factors and the three major socio-economic rankings. Then we look at the racial/ethnic composition of the economic élite. Finally, we focus on two groups that occupy unique positions in the stratification system, the French Canadians and Native peoples.

Race/ethnicity and socio-economic status

Table 7.3 shows the rankings of twenty-three self-identified racial/ethnic categories in 1991, on three socio-economic indicators: average income, the percent of each category with upper white-collar occupations, and the percent of each category with some university education. Perhaps the most surprising result is that those of British origin, while above the total population average on all three factors, rank only sixth in income, ninth in occupation, and sixteenth in education. These figures suggest that, at least in the general population, the British no longer enjoy the dominant position they once did.

Some of the ethnic groups that rank above the British on the three socio-economic indicators are other Europeans, particularly Ukrainians, Hungarians, and Poles. However, people who identify themselves as Jewish rank the highest in most cases, while several "visible" minorities, including Filipinos, Arabs, South and West Asians, the Chinese, and others, also do very well. The situation of Jews and visible minorities is notable if we consider that all of these groups have been viewed historically as victims of significant discrimination and prejudice in Canada and elsewhere. Of course, their high socio-economic rankings should not be seen as evidence that discrimination and prejudice no longer exist in Canadian society (see Henry and Ginsberg, 1993; Reitz, 1993). As well, the high position of many visible minorities partly reflects

TABLE 7.3 Socio-economic status of selected (self-identified) ethnic groups[1], Canada, 1991

Rank	Average income[2]		Percent in upper white-collar occupations[3]		Percent with some university education[4]	
1.	Jewish	($45,523)	Jewish	(52.3)	Filipino	(54.2)
2.	Ukrainian	($33,923)	Ukrainian	(36.1)	Jewish	(47.2)
3.	Hungarian	($33,072)	Arab	(36.1)	Arab	(40.2)
4.	Polish	($32,890)	Chinese	(35.6)	West Asian	(35.6)
5.	"Canadian"	($32,714)	Hungarian	(34.6)	Chinese	(35.1)
6.	British	($31,498)	German	(33.6)	South Asian	(34.5)
7.	German	($31,276)	Polish	(33.4)	Polish	(28.9)
8.	Balkan	($31,225)	Dutch	(33.2)	Hungarian	(27.8)
9.	Italian	($30,525)	British	(31.6)	Ukrainian	(27.6)
10.	Dutch	($30,377)	Filipino	(29.8)	Latin, Central, South American	(27.5)
11.	Arab	($28,656)	West Asian	(29.6)	Vietnamese	(27.1)
12.	French	($28,509)	French	(29.6)	Spanish	(25.8)
13.	Chinese	($28,099)	"Canadian"	(29.4)	German	(25.1)
14.	West Asian	($27,832)	S. Asian	(29.2)	Balkan	(23.2)
15.	South Asian	($27,580)	Black, Caribbean	(26.7)	Dutch	(22.3)
16.	Greek	($26,347)	Balkan	(26.3)	British	(22.0)
17.	Spanish	($26,316)	Italian	(25.8)	"Canadian"	(20.1)
18.	Portuguese	($26,105)	Spanish	(25.1)	Black, Caribbean	(19.4)
19.	Black, Caribbean	($25,416)	Vietnamese	(24.6)	Italian	(18.3)
20.	Vietnamese	($23,792)	Aboriginal	(24.5)	Greek	(17.8)
21.	Filipino	($23,321)	Greek	(22.5)	French	(17.2)
22.	Aboriginal	($22,242)	Latin, Central, South American	(20.8)	Portuguese	(8.7)
23.	Latin, Central, South American	($21,032)	Portuguese	(15.5)	Aboriginal	(8.6)
FULL POPULATION		**($30,157)**		**(30.4)**		**(20.6)**

[1]Total origins, including single and multiple mentions of each group.
[2]Annual employment income in 1990, full-time employed only.
[3]As a proportion of all occupations. Upper white-collar occupations include professional, technical, managerial, and administrative positions.
[4]As a proportion of the total population fifteen years old and over.

Source: *Statistics Canada,* 1991 Census of Canada, Three Percent Sample.

Canadian government policy, which did not encourage large-scale immigration of such groups until the 1960s, and which until recently has mainly allowed those with recognized skills and training into the country. As a consequence, many highly educated middle- and upper-stratum members of these groups have come to Canada (Breton et al., 1990). There is also some indication that certain visible minorities are overrepresented in lower-paying jobs (Agócs and Boyd, 1993: 337–38). This is consistent with earlier research suggesting that non-whites as a group still make lower incomes than whites in Canada (Li, 1992: 494). The 1990 data shown in Table 7.3 also suggest that visible minorities tend to be below average on income, even though many such groups rank above average on education level and on the proportion holding upper white-collar jobs (see also Hou and Balakrishnan, 1996). On balance, however, recent evidence suggests that real opportunities for socio-economic success are available to ethnic minorities in contemporary Canadian society.

Ethnic composition of the economic élite

Historically, the British dominated Canada's economy. Information from 1885 and 1910 indicates that more than 90 percent of Canada's industrial leaders were of Anglo-Saxon background (Clement, 1975: 73). French Canadians made up 29 percent of the population but only 6 to 7 percent of the élite, and other ethnic groups were virtually excluded.

By 1951, Porter's research showed almost no change from these figures (Porter, 1965). Clement's subsequent research revealed some erosion of British dominance between 1951 and 1972, with the Anglo-Canadian proportion of the economic élite dropping slightly (to 86 percent), the French rising somewhat (to 8 percent), and "other" groups, especially Jews, increasing moderately (to 5 percent) (Clement, 1975: 234). The most recent summary of evidence on this question indicates some shifts in the composition of the economic or business élite. The British still predominate, but depending on the estimate, they now form between one-half and two-thirds of the Canadian élite or upper class. The French make up another 14 or 15 percent, while other ethnic groups, especially Jews, now account for as much as one-third of the élite (Ogmundson and McLaughlin, 1992; also Francis, 1986).

Overall, then, it seems that Anglo-Saxon background remains a decided advantage in our stratification system, since this ethnic category still forms the majority of the economic élite. However, outside this upper stratum, British origin has considerably less significance, with several other groups ranking higher in socio-economic status. In contrast, French Canadians and Native peoples historically have experienced a low ranking in the stratification system. We turn now to a more detailed discussion of these two groups.

French Canadians and social stratification

Until recently the French did not occupy a particularly privileged position in the stratification system. (This issue will be discussed more fully in the next chapter). Even now, the French rank well below average on education and only in the middle on the other two socio-economic indicators (see Table 7.3). In the past, various reasons have been put forth to explain the French position. Some have said that the French needed time to recover from the initial shock of the British economic and political takeover in the eighteenth century (Milner and Milner, 1973). Others saw the past avoidance by the French of "English-style" business and economic activity as a cause of their lower socio-economic status (McRoberts, 1988: 178). Some suggested that differences in values and upbringing put French Canadians at a disadvantage in the competition for material success, especially in business careers (Harvey, 1969; Richer and Laporte, 1971). Finally, ethnic prejudice and discrimination have been cited at times as an obstacle to French progress (Archibald, 1978).

Probably a combination of these factors contributed to the historically low position of French Canadians in our society. However, in the 1960s, during the "Quiet Revolution," there was a move in Quebec towards *rattrapage*, or catching up, with English Canada. Since then the French have come to dominate the Quebec government and civil service (McRoberts, 1988). The French now form an increasing portion of both the salaried middle class and the new business class in Quebec (McRoberts, 1988; Ogmundson and McLaughlin, 1992). Evidence also suggests that the economic advantages of the English over the French in Quebec have diminished, although some differences still exist. By 1990, French Canadians who worked full-time made about 9 percent less than their British counterparts, and about 5 percent less than the overall Canadian average (see Table 7.3). On the other hand, within Quebec at least, French Canadians earned about 1 percent more than English Canadians (Canadian Press, 1994). Other recent evidence indicates that opportunities for occupational attainment, social mobility, and educational achievement have also become increasingly similar for French and English (Pineo and Porter, 1985; Agócs and Boyd, 1993; Guppy and Arai, 1993).

These developments suggest that ethnic stratification in Quebec is changing, with the English becoming less powerful than before. Nevertheless, the English, both Canadian and American, continue to hold somewhat greater economic power at the élite level in Quebec, through their positions in dominant corporations (McRoberts, 1988). For this reason and others, many French Canadians are now calling for greater economic control and political autonomy. Some favour the Parti Québécois program of sovereignty or outright independence for Quebec. Others support a new version of Canadian confederation, in which Quebec is formally acknowledged as a distinct society and French rights and powers are given greater recognition than before. Quebec's 1995 referendum, in which almost half of the province's population voted for sovereignty, is a clear indication that French Canada's position within our society is still a serious and largely unresolved issue.

Stratification and Native peoples

Native peoples also occupy an exceptional position in Canada's vertical mosaic. The erosion of their power, through the loss of land and natural resources, had a devastating initial impact on Native inhabitants. The subsequent separation of many Natives from the rest of the population, due to voluntary avoidance, geographic isolation, and the government's policies of wardship for indigenous peoples, helped sustain and institutionalize their low status (Frideres, 1988: 17–22; Ponting, 1986: 24–34; Wotherspoon and Satzewich, 1993). Such isolation may have helped to preserve Native identity, but probably at the expense of Native participation in the quest for jobs, education, and material affluence (Bienvenue, 1985). Perhaps more than any other group, Native people face a dilemma, having to choose between preserving their ethnic identities and succeeding in the larger society. Racial prejudice must also be seen as a factor, although in recent years this appears to have declined. Some Canadians still perceive Native peoples as being low in "social standing" (Pineo, 1986; Goldstein, 1985). Some Canadians also hold negative stereotypes of Native groups. However, such stereotyping is not the norm and, overall, the Canadian public has often been sympathetic towards, though poorly informed about, Native peoples (Langford and Ponting, 1992: 141).

Some recent developments suggest that the position of Canada's Native peoples may improve. Funds derived from the settlement of Native land claims, as well as the increasing political awareness of Native leaders (refer to Chapter 14, Social Movements), may provide a means for Natives to achieve greater prosperity (Wotherspoon and Satzewich, 1993). The socio-economic attainments of Natives have also improved in recent years, although serious inequalities remain (see Table 7.3). Natives increasing hold white-collar jobs, though they still rank below the general population in occupying these positions. Although their unemployment rates are far above average, among employed Natives income differences have declined somewhat. Native workers made over half the national average in 1980, compared with only a third of the average in 1971, while those employed full-time earned about 74 percent of the national average income in 1990. Some educational improvements are also evident: in 1971 only 3 percent of the Native adult population had some post-secondary education, but by 1981 this figure had risen to 19 percent (Siggner, 1986: 71–76). By 1991, about 9 percent of Native people had attained at least some university education.

Nevertheless, the prospects for Native peoples still hinge primarily on fuller acceptance of Native rights by political leaders and the general population. The effects of the 1990 confrontation at Oka, Quebec, as well as subsequent incidents at Ipperwash, Ontario and elsewhere, are still being felt. In the long run, the Native position will probably be determined by how the dilemma of identity preservation versus participation in the larger structure is resolved.

Regional and rural–urban inequalities

Regional and rural–urban differences, perhaps even more than racial and ethnic diversity, give Canada its image as a mosaic of distinct parts. Canada's variability on these dimensions is illustrated in the contrast between major urban centres like Toronto, Montreal, or Vancouver, and the less populous and more isolated areas of the Maritimes, the Prairies, and the North. (See also Chapter 16, Urbanization.)

Geographic location has an important impact on the stratification rank of Canadians. There is a sense in which location is a source of power affecting the distribution of wealth and resources. Those who live in the urbanized, strategically located centres have considerably greater opportunity to achieve a high stratification position in our society.

One theoretical approach that helps in thinking about such differences is the *metropolis–hinterland* perspective (Davis, 1971). In this view, Canada's social structure involves a complex network of regions and communities in which the rural and peripheral areas, or hinterlands, are ultimately connected by a series of intermediate links to a few major urban centres, or metropolises. The intermediate links in the system include local outposts, small towns, and middle-sized cities, all acting at different levels as depots between the outlying districts and the large population centres.

The metropolises are the focal points for industry, economic activity, politics, and education in the nation. Large-scale business enterprises, the major corporations, the seats of political power, and the largest universities are situated in the metropolitan centres. Economically, the hinterlands serve as sources of raw materials—primary resources like fish, wheat, petroleum, lumber, and ore—most of which are processed in the metropolises and then sold to hinterland inhabitants as finished goods (see Chapter 12, Political Sociology). People constitute another resource that flows out of the hinterland and into the metropolis. More and more Canadians have left the hinterland areas for jobs in the big cities, taking with them their labour power and skills, their potential political affiliations and voting power, and their intellectual abilities (see also Chapter 15, Demography and Population Study). All of this resource potential is lost by the hinterlands in favour of the large centres. Those who stay behind, near their family roots, historical heritage, and traditional communities, suffer considerably in terms of their relative power in the stratification system. The local economy typically has little industry, so that job prospects are poorer and unemployment is more prevalent. In addition, isolation from the central political power and from greater educational opportunities helps to perpetuate and accentuate this lower position.

Metropolis–hinterland disparities are illustrated by differences in average incomes by geographic location. In Table 7.4, the average family income of all Canadians in 1994 has been assigned a score of 100. The other numbers in the table represent the average income in each location as a percentage of the Canadian average. This procedure allows us to observe a number of interesting differences in income, by region and rural–urban category. First, we see that, in both Canada as a whole and in each separate region, income generally increases with an increase in community size. In other words, the most highly urbanized areas are the places in which average incomes are greatest, while rural districts show the lowest income levels. This result is consistent with the view that wealth is more highly concentrated in the metropolis. A second finding that conforms to the metropolis–hinterland argument concerns regional differences. The most economically developed and industrialized areas, particularly the urbanized areas of Ontario, British Columbia, and the Prairies, appear to provide the highest standard of living. The entire Atlantic region is below the Canadian average (Swan and Serjak, 1993; Wien, 1993). The low incomes are especially evident in the rural regions of the Atlantic provinces and Quebec, where families earn just over 75 percent of the national average.

Other evidence related to business ownership and corporate concentration indicates that the metropolitan centres of Quebec and especially Ontario form most of Canada's economic core. By the late 1980s Toronto stood as the most influential financial and industrial centre in the nation, with Montreal a distant second (Semple, 1988). In and around these cities most of Canada's major corporations are located and directed. Not only in terms of current residence, but also with respect to place of birth, urban southern Ontarians have for some time made up the large majority of the economic élite (Clement, 1978: 95; Newman, 1981; Francis, 1986).

In general, then, economic power is heavily concentrated in the established urban locations of the nation. As noted earlier, these same locations are also the seats of political power and higher education. In combination, all these factors have promoted great inequalities between metropolis and hinterland. We should note further that regional and rural–urban differences interact with and often complicate the general stratification picture. They can mean, for example, that a factory worker in Ontario will earn as much money as a white-collar professional—a school teacher or even a family doctor—in rural Newfoundland or Prince Edward Island (Forcese, 1986: 38). It is advisable to keep

TABLE 7.4 Average family income by region and community size, as a percent of the average family income for Canada, 1994[1]

	Rural areas	Urban, under 30 000	Urban, 30 000 –99 999	Urban, over 100 000	Total
Region:					
All Canada	**85**	**90**	**96**	**106**	**100**
Atlantic provinces	76	79	88	93	84
Quebec	77	83	90	95	91
Ontario	93	94	102	115	110
Prairie provinces	83	91	96	102	97
British Columbia	100	98	98	109	105

[1]Average family income for all Canada in 1994 was $54 153 and is set at 100 in this table for comparison purposes.

Source: *Statistics Canada,* Income Distributions by Size in Canada 1994, *Catalogue No. 13-207, Tables 2, 3, and 4.*

such geographic disparities in mind when making generalizations about stratification in Canadian society.

Gender stratification in Canada

In recent decades gender inequality has come to be seen as one of the major factors in social stratification. Previously, gender differences in socioeconomic rank, power, and prestige were not given a great deal of attention by students of stratification. When these topics were discussed, the analysis tended to focus on traditional female roles in marriage and family life. Marriage, rather than career, was the principal means of female social mobility, and a woman normally was assigned a stratification rank on the basis of her husband's command over resources, not her own.

The changing roles of women in modern society (recall Chapter 6, Gender Relations) have done much to shift the focus towards women themselves in current research (Mackie, 1991; Wilson, 1991). The major change in women's roles in this century has been their influx into the labour force. In Canada, women made up over 45 percent of the paid workforce in 1991, compared with only 13 percent in 1901 (Statistics Canada, *1961 Census of Canada* and *1971 Census of Canada*, Historical Tables; Statistics Canada, 1993, *Occupation*). By 1980, for the first time in Canadian history, a majority of women had officially entered the labour force (Armstrong and Armstrong, 1983: 6). This proportion reached over 59 percent in 1991 (Calzavara, 1993: 312). The great shift of women into the work world has provided society with a whole new pool of previously untapped talents and skills. However, the economic benefits gained by the average woman entering the workforce often have been limited. Female workers have consistently earned far less than male workers, even in advanced capitalist and socialist societies. In Canada, despite evidence of gradual improvement over the past few decades, full-time working women in 1993 still earned just 72 percent of the male average (Canadian Press, 1995).

Research also indicates that the lower socioeconomic rank of women cannot be fully explained by their lesser training and experience. Canadian studies have shown that, when the greater training and experience of male workers is taken into account, women still make only 80 to 90 percent of what men make (Gunderson, 1982; Calzavara, 1993: 315–16). Data for the early 1990s suggest that, among those under the age of twenty-five who have university degrees, there is little or no difference in the average wages or incomes of males and females; however, the female disadvantage is still evident among older age cohorts (Statistics Canada, 1994, *Earnings of Canadians*, Chart 2.4; Beauchesne, 1994).

In Canada, full-time working women in 1993 still earned just 72 percent of the male average.

It seems likely, then, that discrimination is a factor in the income difference, most notably outside the younger age groups.

Some writers have suggested that female subordination in the stratification system is so serious that women's position is almost like that of a minority group, such as blacks or Native peoples. You will recall, for example, that we discussed the feminization of poverty in Chapter 6, Gender Relations. While there are problems with such a claim, some aspects of women's situation do parallel that of minority groups. First, sex, like ethnicity or race, is an ascriptive trait that affects opportunities and life chances. Second, just as minorities are sometimes negatively evaluated, both by others and by themselves, so too are women (Mackie, 1991: 26–29).

There are also more objective similarities between women and minority groups. One analysis of 1985 census data showed that non-whites and women in Canada share similar income disadvantages. Annual earnings among non-whites were about $2200 less than the Canadian average, and female annual earnings were even lower, at $5600 below the average (Li, 1992: 494). In addition, women share with racial and ethnic minorities almost total exclusion from the economic élite. As Clement has argued, "women are probably the most underrepresented social type in the economic élite" (Clement, 1990: 184; also Francis, 1986; Fox, 1989). These findings suggest that many women continue to be disadvantaged in our society.

Age and social stratification

The study of age and aging has been of increasing interest to sociologists in recent years (see, for example, McPherson, 1990). Like sex or ethnicity, age is an ascribed attribute over which the individual has no control, but which has important implications for determining stratification rank in most societies.

Most research suggests that age has an up-and-down, or *curvilinear*, association with stratification position. In other words, as we move from the youngest to the oldest ends of the age spectrum, we generally find that people in the middle-age range enjoy the highest incomes and socio-economic rank, with younger and older people ranking lower in most cases (Guppy et al., 1993: 404–408). For young people, this is often because their recent entry into the labour force means they begin at lower salary or wage levels in their occupations. For elderly people, the lower economic standing is largely the result of retirement from the labour force and having to live on reduced income from pensions and savings (National Council of Welfare, 1990).

One obvious difference between young and old is that young people generally can hope to improve their stratification rank with time, as part of the normal process of joining the workforce and moving towards a future career. Most elderly people, however, must hope that their fixed incomes will not be eroded too severely over time by inflation and rising living costs.

This difference between young and old may explain why some researchers see the problems of the elderly as more serious, even though there is evidence that young people also face an uncertain economic future these days (Côté and Allahar, 1994). In fact, not all elderly Canadians live in impoverished circumstances. Although more than 40 percent of families headed by persons over age sixty-five were living below the official low-income line in 1969, by 1989 this figure had dropped to only 11 percent (Guppy et al., 1993: 409). This trend indicates the success of government programs in alleviating the economic problems of Canada's elderly. Still, evidence shows that elderly *women* in Canada, especially those living alone, continue to endure economic difficulties (see also Chapter 6, Gender Relations). In 1989, for example, half of all elderly females who lived alone were below the low-income line (Guppy et al., 1993: 409). This example illustrates how two distinct factors in stratification analysis—gender and age—can combine to produce more complicated and more acute patterns of inequality. It also reveals the important impact of age on a person's life circumstances, even in an advanced and affluent society.

Political power and social stratification

The final component to consider in Canada's stratification system is the political power hierarchy (see also Chapter 12, Political Sociology). We have saved this topic until the end because, in a sense, political power may be viewed as the ultimate manifestation of power and the ultimate determinant of structured inequality in society. In nominally democratic countries, the political structure, or *state*, is the official representative of the power of all citizens. Thus, in theory at least, the political structure can act as the key mechanism for shaping all the major forms of stratification.

The concept of the state includes numerous substructures: the political leadership and elected representatives, the courts and judiciary, the civil service, the police, the military, and so forth (see Grabb, 1997). Virtually all societies are organized around the principle that the state is the means for creating and implementing laws, and thus the sanctions and rights that define power differences in society.

The state can establish and maintain political power differences, but the state can affect the distribution of power in other realms as well. The creation of economic power advantages for the propertied over the propertyless, through the legally recognized institution of private property, would be an illustration of how the political structure can be used to affect power differences outside the political sphere itself. Of course, political power also has the potential to remove or reduce power differences, through the creation of laws prohibiting race or sex discrimination in hiring practices, for example.

In these and other ways, position in the political hierarchy can be a source of power in itself and a potential means for establishing, enforcing, or altering power relations in other spheres. This is the basis for the argument that political power is a binding element, related to and interacting with all of the power sources that form the stratification system. In addition, some observers see political power as the ultimate power source because, in theory at least, those with power in other spheres must answer to those holding political power. Of course, other analysts (as will be discussed in Chapter 12, Political Sociology) have questioned whether the full authority of the state is really exercised when it confronts those in power in other areas, particularly the economic élite.

The state and the economic élite

We have noted that the state has the legally sanctioned power to control the actions of individuals and groups, even those who dominate the other institutions of society. In the economic sphere, for example, the government has acted against large corporations found guilty of price gouging, false advertising, environmental pollution, or making unsafe or defective products. Nevertheless, while we can think of specific instances in which political leaders have opposed the economic élite for the "common good" or the "public interest," it often appears that the state favours the economic élite and makes decisions on the basis of particular, rather than general, interests (Clement, 1988).

It is from this point of view that Porter once criticized Canada's political leadership. To him, the major political parties have long engaged in "brokerage politics," making policy decisions based on what will get them re-elected rather than what is best for the nation (Porter, 1965: 373–77). This may mean advocating policies favourable to the powerful and to special interests, in exchange for the campaign funds and voting power these groups can provide.

What is the significance of this alleged tendency for the political structure to favour the interests of

Hilary Weston, recently appointed Lieutenant-Governor of Ontario, is the wife of Galen Weston, head of George Weston Ltd. It often appears that the state favours the economic élite and makes decisions on the basis of particular, rather than general, interests.

the powerful, particularly the economic élite? Most social scientists would reject the extreme view that the state is merely a tool in the hands of the economic élite, doing the bidding of big business at every turn (see Chapter 12, Political Sociology). What seems to occur instead is that both state and economic leaders agree on the general goals and values that should guide the operation of society. Among these common goals are the need for political stability, economic development, and a continued promotion of capitalist expansion. State leaders accept the idea that the economic élite should make large profits. At the same time, however, the state must try to maintain social harmony and appear not to favour the economic élite too much, at the expense of other classes. Such action would undermine the state's basis for popular support, perhaps leading to severe disruptions in both political stability and economic development (Fox and Ornstein, 1993: 52, 61).

Composition of the state élite

Our previous discussion suggested that state leaders and the economic élite have much in common, at least in regard to goals, interests, and values. Another way of assessing the links between élites is to examine the social origins of state leaders. We might expect a considerable overrepresentation of individuals from upper-class backgrounds in the Canadian state élite. Porter's early analysis in the 1950s and a subsequent study by Olsen using 1973 data did find that the upper class was overrepresented compared with its proportion of the general population (Porter, 1965; Olsen, 1980). However, the level of upper-class representation declined during the period between the two studies. Furthermore, the majority (almost three-quarters) of the state élite in 1973 was from middle-class origins. While the working-class representation was low in both cases, these findings indicate that the state leadership is clearly open to those with non-élite origins. More recent evidence shows that, while numerous political leaders in Canada have served as directors of large businesses (and vice versa) over the years, these linkages are not nearly large enough to produce corporate domination of the government (Fox and Ornstein, 1993). This suggests that there is little *direct* dominance of the political leadership by those controlling wealth and property in Canada. Instead, the state and big business are two compatible but separate forces in our society.

Political power and the individual

To this point, we have discussed political power mainly at the élite level. However, in liberal democracies, even those dominated by élites, some power exists in the hands of the people. Voting, joining political parties and other voluntary associations, and, of course, running for election are some of the ways in which the individual can exercise political power. But what groups are most likely to use these means of political expression? In particular, which social strata are most likely to participate in the political structure?

How Does Your Rank Affect You?

The importance of the study of stratification in sociology is apparent from the wide use of stratification variables as explanatory factors in social research. Each of the eight power hierarchies discussed represents a distinct variety of structured inequality that can have consequences for a whole range of social phenomena. The literature that has developed around the effects of social stratification is massive. Here, we can briefly examine some of the work that has been done, to illustrate the effects of stratification position on the lives of Canadians. We focus specifically on differences across socio-economic strata in life chances, lifestyles, values, and beliefs.

Life chances

Probably the most crucial consequence of social stratification concerns the life chances of people from different socio-economic backgrounds. Generally, the term *life chances* refers to the ability to lead a healthy, happy, and prosperous existence. Studies show consistently that life chances decline as one moves down the socio-economic ladder. As will be discussed in Chapter 15, Demography and Population Study, lower-status individuals have shorter life expectancies (National Council of Welfare, 1993). They are more susceptible to a broad spectrum of physical and mental health problems (Clarke, 1990). The poorer strata also are more likely to suffer malnutrition, are less likely to use medical facilities and services, and experience poorer and more hazardous working conditions (Forcese, 1986). All of these elements, coupled with lower economic resources and fewer educational opportunities, lessen the quality of life in the lower strata and make the chances for a satisfying and rewarding existence less likely than they are for the higher strata.

Lifestyles

Stratification position also has a bearing on lifestyle. Differing economic resources, education levels, and life experiences lead to variations in a host of phenomena: consumption habits, manner of dress, speech patterns, and leisure activities, to name just a few. Generally, life in the lower strata is more restrictive than in the upper strata: less leisure time, less freedom of action, less flexibility in daily routine, and less variety in experiences and interests. The limited activities and experiences of working-class people are revealed in a number of ways. People from the lower strata are less likely to belong to clubs and organizations, do less reading, and participate less in community life than do other people (Eichar, 1989; Kohn et al., 1990; Chui et al., 1993). Instead, home life tends to receive greater emphasis. Nevertheless, even home activities often are disrupted by the need for working-class parents to work overtime or take part-time jobs to supplement incomes (see, for example, Rinehart, 1996: 122).

Values and beliefs

Another important consequence of social stratification is the tendency for different values and beliefs to be generated within social strata. Some studies suggest that greater economic deprivation and occupational instability in the working class lead its members to place a high value on material success, good pay, and financial security (Form, 1985).

Other research indicates that differences in the nature of the jobs done by people from different classes can lead to important differences in values and beliefs. For example, studies in several countries suggest that, because members of the working class have little personal freedom at work or control over their job environment, they place a lower value on individual independence or "self-direction" than do people in middle-class occupations. It appears that working-class parents are, in turn, more likely than middle-class parents to teach their children such values as obedience and conformity, rather than self-direction or independence (Kohn et al., 1990). In a similar way, other research has revealed that people in working-class occupations may place a somewhat lower value on individual achievement or "self-actualization" than do people in other classes (Grabb and Waugh, 1987).

Given the general pattern of social stratification suggested in this chapter, it may be no surprise that individuals who are nearer the top of the various power rankings are also likely to exercise above-average political power. Research has shown that Canadians from higher socio-economic backgrounds are more likely to vote, join political organizations, and take an interest in politics (Curtis et al., 1992; Grabb and Curtis, 1992; Chui et al., 1993). Several studies have found that those with higher stratification positions are more likely to run for public office. For example, people in upper-middle-class (professional and managerial) occupations made up roughly 20 percent of the labour force in the period between 1964 and 1985, but they accounted for over two-thirds of the federal election candidates and over 80 percent of the elected MPs in the same period (Guppy et al., 1988). Individuals who are more centrally located in terms of socio-economic status, ethnicity, and region are also more likely to express a feeling of personal political power and efficacy (Grabb, 1988; Baer et al., 1990).

In various ways, then, the political power structure is closely bound up with the more general configuration of Canada's stratification system. At the élite level, and for the whole range of individual Canadians, political power is associated with the other sources of power that determine the distribution of wealth, prestige, and other resources in this country. Those who tend to dominate the other status hierarchies—especially the economically privileged, but also men, central Canadians, and those of British background—tend as well to hold sway in the political sphere (Ogmundson and McLaughlin, 1992). Although there are exceptions, the consistency in this pattern is a striking feature of social stratification in Canadian society.

SUMMARY

This chapter has introduced the reader to the topic of social stratification, particularly as it relates to an analysis of Canadian society. We looked at basic concepts and definitions in the field and discussed the major theories advanced to explain the process of stratification in modern societies. We proposed eight principal components to consider when examining Canada's stratification system: wealth (including income and property), occupation, education, race or ethnicity, region or rural–urban location, gender, age, and political status. Each of these is the basis for a status hierarchy and corresponding power ranking reflecting the distribution of resources and inequalities among people in Canada.

Our analysis indicates some fairly close linkages among the eight status hierarchies, with high status on one hierarchy often associated with high status on the others. Certain rankings seem to have a relatively greater influence on the stratification process. In particular, power deriving from wealth and property tends to have the greatest impact on the general shape of the stratification system. The group that dominates in this hierarchy, the economic élite, is the single most powerful entity in the structure. Along with the political leadership, or state élite, they make most of the major decisions affecting the operation of the country, the distribution of wealth and resources, and the extent of inequality experienced by other Canadians.

QUESTIONS FOR REVIEW AND CRITICAL THINKING

1. Structural functionalists argue that social stratification, especially inequality of rewards, is necessary to motivate the best or most qualified individuals to seek the most important positions in society. What does this view imply about the motivations or abilities of those individuals and groups that do not attain high positions? How would they respond to this argument?

2. Some have said that Marx's theory of classes and revolution is not relevant to modern societies such as Canada. Can you think of some ways in which this statement is true and some in which it is false? How might recent events in the former Soviet Union, China, and elsewhere influence your response?

3. What major proposals or programs do you believe could be instituted to eliminate or decrease inequality in Canada? In particular, discuss this question with reference to women or racial and ethnic minorities, such as Native people or French Canadians.

4. Sociologists have always debated the precise meaning of the concept of social class. Less often do they consider what people in general think about social class. What important characteristics and behaviours, in your opinion, distinguish social classes? Is there one key criterion or are there many? In a mini-research project, ask a sample of your friends or fellow students what social class means to them. See if there are any differences of opinion among them. For example, do men and women give different responses? Older and younger people? Poorer and richer people?

GLOSSARY

achieved status a position in a status hierarchy attained by individual effort or accomplishment

ascribed status a position in a status hierarchy that is inherited or assigned

bourgeoisie the capitalist class, as defined by Marx. The *petite bourgeoisie* were the small property owners, destined to be swallowed by the larger capitalists.

class a set of individuals sharing a similar economic status or market position

class for itself a Marxian category including people who share the same economic position, are aware of their common class position, and who thus may become agents for social change

class in itself a Marxian category including people who share the same economic position, but who may be unaware of their common class position

class, status, party Weber's answer to Marx concerning the bases of social inequality: class is economic, status is prestige, party is political; all three are measures of inequality

horizontal mobility movement by an individual from one status to another of similar rank within the same status hierarchy

institutionalized power sometimes called *domination*, power is institutionalized when it becomes a regular part of everyday human existence, usually because it is established in formal laws or accepted customs

intergenerational mobility movement or change between parental status and a child's status in the same status hierarchy

intragenerational mobility movement by an individual from one status to another in the same status hierarchy during a single lifetime or career

power a differential capacity to command resources and thereby control social situations

proletariat Marx's word for the working class, the non-owners of the means of production

social class a category of individuals who possess similar economic position as well as group consciousness, common identity, and a tendency to act as a social unit

social differentiation the tendency towards diversification and complexity in the statuses and characteristics of social life

social stratification the general pattern of inequality, or ranking, of socially differentiated characteristics

status any position occupied by an individual in a social system

status consistency similarity in the ranking of an individual's statuses in a set of status hierarchies

status hierarchy any one of a set of rankings along which statuses are related in terms of their power

status inconsistency dissimilarity in the ranking of an individual's statuses in a set of status hierarchies

status set the combination of statuses that any one individual occupies

stratum a set of statuses of similar rank in any status hierarchy

vertical mobility movement up and down a status hierarchy

SUGGESTED READINGS

Curtis, James, Edward Grabb, and Neil Guppy (eds.)

1993 *Social Inequality in Canada: Patterns, Problems, and Policies.* (2nd ed.) Scarborough, Ont.: Prentice Hall.

This book, a collection of articles dealing with all the major stratification hierarchies in Canada, also considers some of the important consequences of stratification for people, and policies that could be implemented to alleviate problems of inequality.

Grabb, Edward G.

1997 *Theories of Social Inequality: Classical and Contemporary Perspectives.* (3rd ed.) Toronto: Harcourt Brace Canada.

This book reviews and evaluates the major perspectives on social inequality that have emerged from classical and contemporary social theory.

Krahn, Harvey, and Graham Lowe

1993 *Work, Industry, and Canadian Society.* (2nd ed.) Toronto: Nelson.

This book reviews a range of sociological issues pertaining to the study of work and industry in Canada, including labour force trends, women's employment, the organization of work, and questions of power and control at work.

Wilson, Suzanne

1991 *Women, the Family and the Economy.* (3rd ed.) Toronto: McGraw-Hill Ryerson.

Women's experiences in family, work, and public life are reviewed in this book. This is a basic introduction to a range of material dealing with Canadian women.

WEB SITES

http://spock.plugnet.se/~vp1/internat/marxbio.htm

Biography of Karl Marx

Read more about the man and his work at this site. There is also a link to the Marx/Engels biography archive.

http://www.achilles.net/~council/facts.html

The Canadian Council on Social Development

This site provides a wealth of statistical and other data on income inequality, poverty, and welfare in Canada.

CHAPTER 8

Race and Ethnic Relations

Carol Agócs

INTRODUCTION

Canadians often describe their society as an "ethnic mosaic," a varied composition of many peoples whose distinctive cultures give colour and texture to the whole. The image of the mosaic symbolizes the reality of the ethnic and racial diversity which has been increasingly characteristic of Canadian society in recent decades.

Although census definitions of ethnic origin have changed over time, Figure 8.1 provides a rough illustration of the changes in the Canadian population that have occurred over the past 120 years. While British and French contributions to the mosaic have been dominant throughout modern history, the British share has declined from 60 to 28 percent of Canada's total population since Confederation. The population of French origin has decreased from 31 to 23 percent. By contrast, the population of ethnic origins other than British and French has grown from 8 to 31 percent of the total. Considering only persons who claim single ethnic origins, the most numerous populations other than the British and French include—in order of size—German, Italian, Chinese, Aboriginal, South Asian, Ukrainian, East Indian, Jewish, and black origin groups (Statistics Canada, *1991 Census of Canada, Ethnic Origin: The Nation*, Catalogue No. 93-315).

Canada's mosaic exists within the structure of a **pluralistic society**, a social system of coexisting ethnic groups. To some degree each group maintains its own distinctive culture and social organizations, such as clubs and religious institutions. At the same

FIGURE 8.1 Ethnic origins as a percentage of Canada's population, 1871–1991

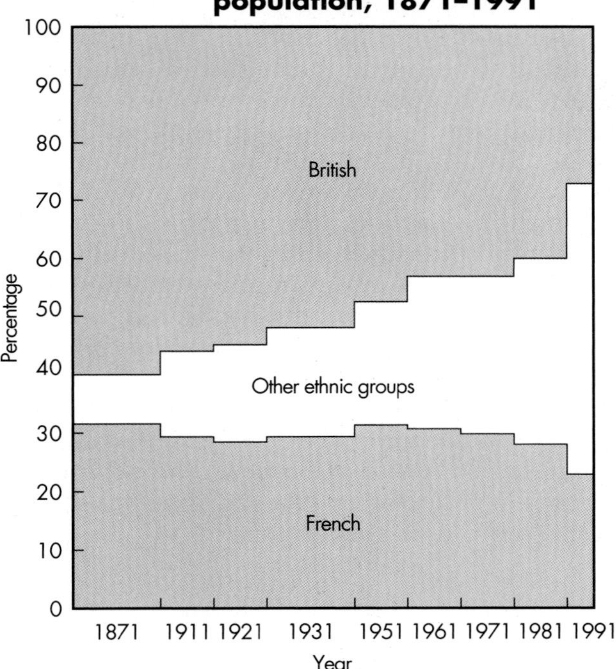

Source: *Minister of Industry, Trade and Commerce, 1974.* Perspectives Canada, *Table 13.5; Statistics Canada,* 1981 Census of Canada, *Catalogue No. 92-902, Table 1;* 1991 Census of Canada, Ethnic Origin: The Nation, *Catalogue No. 93-315 (p. 1).*

time, each participates with Canada's other ethnic groups in common cultural, economic, and political institutions.

However, ethnic populations in Canada, as in most pluralistic societies, are hierarchically ranked. Some ethnic groups, such as the British in Canada, have historically dominated positions of economic, political, and social power, while others, such as Native peoples, have been and remain relatively powerless. In referring to Canadian society as a **vertical mosaic**, Porter (1965) called attention to the fact that ethnicity is a major source of inequality, cleavage, and even conflict in Canadian society. More recent research (e.g., Agócs and Boyd, 1993) has documented the growing importance of racial diversity as a basis of inequality in this country. You will recall that we discussed such inequality in the last chapter, and we will do so again in Chapter 14, Social Movements.

We begin this chapter on race and ethnic relations in Canada with a discussion of the processes involved in the formation and development of immigrant communities. Once we have an understanding of local ethnic communities as social entities, we shall consider the meanings of the concepts of ethnic group, race, and minority group, and some of the manifestations of ethnic and racial inequality. We shall then discuss the historical processes of colonialism, conquest, and migration, forces that have created Canada's vertical mosaic. Finally, we shall examine three influential interpretations of the past, present, and future of ethnic and race relations—assimilationism, two-category perspectives, and pluralism—and consider some of the implications of each for social policy. Our concluding theme will be the continued importance of racial and ethnic pluralism and conflict in the modern world, and in Canada in particular, and the challenge this social reality poses for this generation.

THE LOCAL ETHNIC COMMUNITY: FORMATION AND DEVELOPMENT

One day in 1962, a young man stepped off a plane in Toronto, having flown all night from Rome. He had torn up roots for the promise of a steady job, a house, a good standard of living for his family, and an education for his children—things less attainable at home. He was welcomed by his uncle, who drove him to a tidy duplex in a predominantly Italian neighbourhood. There his aunt, cousins, and other relatives from his home village of Gagliano, in the barren mountains south of Naples, waited to celebrate his arrival.

His aunt and uncle had sent money for this journey, the fruit of several years of saving and planning. They had arranged for their nephew to work as a labourer for the same construction firm where the uncle worked as an equipment operator and for him to share temporarily the upstairs apartment with another young man who had arrived from Gagliano the year before. The new immigrant was to learn some English and to try in the next year or two to save enough money to repay his aunt and uncle and to buy a one-way ticket to Toronto for his wife, who was waiting in Gagliano.

The experience of this man was far from unique; after World War II approximately half a million Italians immigrated to Canada, part of a total immigration from all countries to Canada of over five million (see Figure 8.2). For all immigrants, settling in a new country means cutting ties with relatives and lifelong friends in the "old country" and trying to become part of a sometimes confusing world of strangers.

Studies of the immigration experience suggest that migration is frequently a social act, like that of our young man, with primary social relationships as strong influences upon the decision to migrate and the subsequent process of settlement. (We shall discuss the reasons for migration more fully in Chapter 15, Demography and Population Study.) The migrant's destination is often a place where relatives, friends, or others from the same town have already settled. **Chain migration** is a sequential movement of persons from a common place of origin to a common destination, with the assistance of relatives or compatriots already settled in the new location. Assistance may take the form of information helpful in weighing the decision to migrate, money for transportation, a place to stay upon arrival, job offers, or legal sponsorship.

In the years since World War II, Canadian immigration policy has encouraged family reunification

FIGURE 8.2 Immigrants as a percentage of census metropolitan areas, 1991

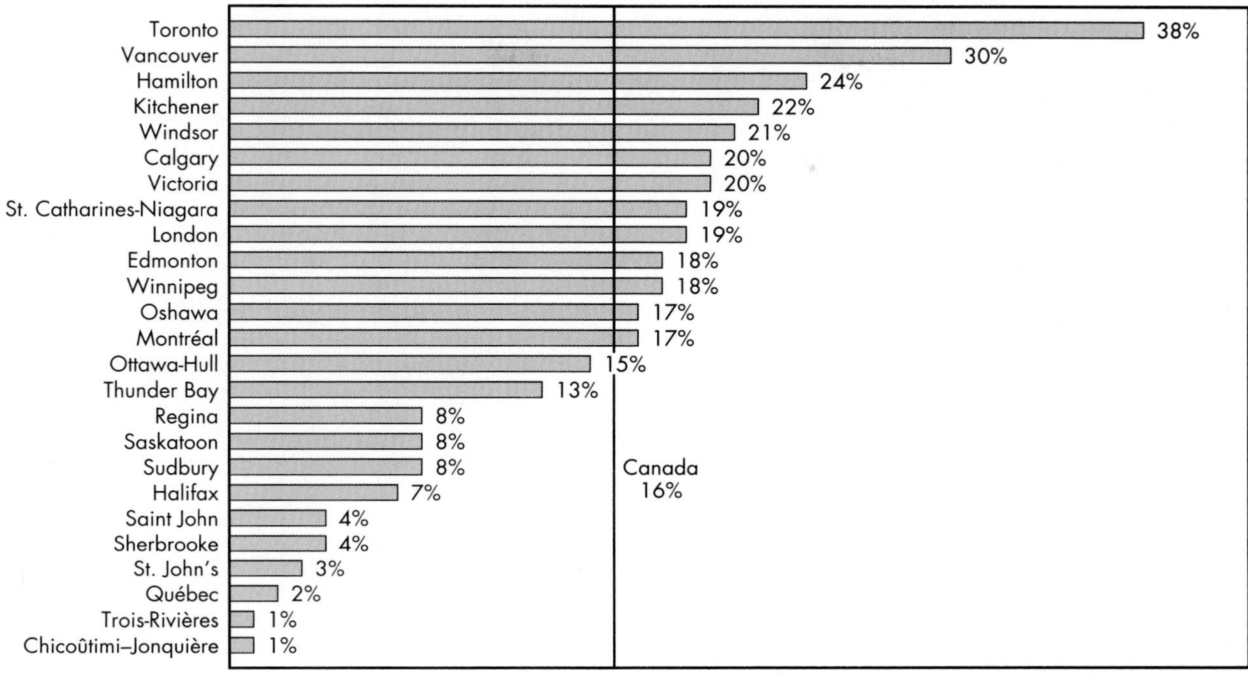

Source: *Statistics Canada,* 1991 Census of Canada; Canadian Social Trends, *Catalogue No. 11-008E, Summer 1993 (p. 10.)*

through the chain migration process by freely admitting some relatives of persons settled in Canada, and by classifying immigrants who receive legal guarantees of support from relatives or others in Canada as family class, assisted relatives, or *sponsored immigrants*. Sponsorship of new immigrants by relatives has been the characteristic pattern among some ethnic populations such as Italians, Greeks, and Portuguese. About 63 percent of newcomers to Canada from Asia, 75 percent from the Caribbean, and 71 percent from South America immigrated as members of the family class or as assisted relatives during the years 1981 through 1985 (White, 1990: Table B4).

Through chain migration, separated family members and friends may be reunited, and a supportive community is often formed which may help the immigrant to cope with the inevitable experience of alienation associated with confronting a new and strange culture. Whole families, even entire villages, have been transplanted from Lebanon, Italy, Portugal, Greece, and many other parts of the world to urban neighbourhoods in Canada (for example, see Campani, 1992).

Chain migration is an adaptation and extension of traditional kinship and friendship ties and reciprocal commitments. The new arrival from Gagliano, resettled in Toronto with his aunt and uncle's aid, paid rent to them, helped them to build an addition to their house, and was a frequent and welcome visitor for evening chats. Perhaps in time, the newcomer in turn assisted other relatives to resettle in Toronto. Around a widening network of such exchanges over a period of time, an ethnic community takes shape.

Most ethnic communities develop *institutions*—organized, patterned ways of behaving and carrying on social interaction in order to accomplish specific goals of the group and meet its collective needs. Institutions such as religious organizations, separate schools, shops and professional services, social agencies, political or advocacy organizations,

Around a widening network of chain migration, an ethnic community takes shape.

and cultural and social organizations may appear to parallel and duplicate organizations already present in the larger society. But Rosenberg and Jedwab (1992) suggested that ethnic groups develop organizations as a means of coping with community needs that are not otherwise met within the context of Canadian society. In a study of the Italian, Jewish, and Greek communities of Montreal, they found that each group developed and used ethnic organizations in different ways, depending upon how the group was treated by the surrounding Quebec society. In a 1978–79 survey of nine ethnic groups in Toronto, Breton (1990) also found considerable variation among the groups in degree of involvement in ethnic organizations. However, most groups preferred to use mainstream organizations, such as human rights commissions or unions, to deal with discrimination, rather than turn to ethnic community organizations.

The degree to which an ethnic population develops a strong sense of solidarity and ethnic identity and a self-sufficient range of ethnic institutions parallelling those of the larger society, referred to as **institutional completeness**, depends upon many factors. These may include the group's cultural values and social patterns, the treatment it receives from the society around it, the size of the city and of the ethnic population, its prosperity, and the nature of the employment opportunities offered by the region in which the community is located. If an ethnic community builds a secure niche within a local economic structure, it may grow in size and affluence, be able to support ethnic organizations, and develop common economic and political interests as well. For example, in postwar Toronto, Italian immigrants established themselves in the construction industry as labourers and craftspeople, and increasingly, as contractors and developers (Reitz, 1990). As a consequence of such occupational specialization, ethnic community members may come to share values that go beyond language, culture, and social ties, to encompass well-defined economic and political interests. Many other examples of occupational specialization within a local economy could be mentioned, including Toronto's Macedonians, who concentrated in the restaurant and catering business (Herman, 1978), postwar immigrants from the Netherlands, who have been well represented in agriculture (Ishwaran, 1977), and recent immigrants from Hong Kong, many of whom are entrepreneurs in Canada.

Perhaps to some degree occupational specialization is rooted in the desires of immigrants themselves, who may come to Canada seeking opportunities to farm, own a business, or practise a trade or profession—goals that may be difficult to achieve in their homelands. It has also been Canada's policy to encourage the immigration of experienced and trained farmers, entrepreneurs, tradespeople, and professionals.

Occupational specialization and exploitation may result in part from discrimination or limited opportunities in the local economy. Although discrimination in employment on the basis of ethnicity, race, or religion is legally prohibited in Canada, job opportunities for some racial and ethnic groups, and for immigrants in particular, may be limited. Reitz (1990: 178–79) found that, for immigrants in Toronto who had low educational qualifications, ethnic specialties provided opportunities to earn income, but in jobs of low status. For example, Portuguese women were ten times more likely than other women to work as cleaners (Reitz, 1990). At the same time, access to an ethnic labour market can contribute to the business success of ethnic entrepreneurs. For Germans, Jews, and Ukrainians, Reitz (1990: 181) found that ethnic occupational concentration had no negative effect on income or status, and for Italian men, working in an ethnic business had a positive effect on income. Thus some members of ethnic groups seem to derive benefits from ethnic specialization, but its impact on occupational status and income varies, depending on a particular group's or individual's circumstances.

There is evidence that occupational differences among white ethnic groups have declined over time (Isajiw, Sev'er, and Driedger, 1993), although some distinctive ethnic occupational concentrations persist. Thus, white ethnic groups have experienced upward mobility in the occupational structure, to the point where they have reached income equality with the majority population, provided they have adequate qualifications. A growing body of Canadian research, however, suggests that race and aboriginal status are associated with disadvantage in occupational status and income (Agócs and Boyd, 1993; Lautard and Guppy, 1990). Satzewich and Li (1987) found that immigrants who are members of racial minorities in Canada have lower incomes and occupational status than European and U.S. immigrants who arrived in Canada at the same time, even when sex, age, English proficiency, and level of education are statistically controlled. Reitz (1990: 160–61) found that in Toronto, men of West Indian and Chinese ethnicity had much lower incomes than the majority white population and the other five ethnic groups in the study, when education, work experience, and hours worked were taken into account. (Further evidence of racial discrimination in employment will be discussed later in this chapter).

We have begun our discussion of Canadian race and ethnic relations by trying to understand something of the origin, development, institutional framework, and economic base of the local community that originates as a consequence of migration. It is now necessary to address the more general questions of the meanings of ethnicity, race, and minority-group status.

ETHNIC GROUP, RACE, AND MINORITY GROUP: SOME DEFINITIONS

The ethnic group

The Turks of Germany, the Scots of Canada, the Italians of Australia, and the Kurds of Iraq all may be seen as examples of ethnic groups. They all exist within pluralistic societies in which peoples of various cultural, religious, or racial backgrounds live side by side, however uneasily, within a single social, economic, and political system. Such societies exist as a consequence of the historical processes of colonialism, conquest, and migration. Before we turn to an overview of the ways in which these processes have shaped the evolution of ethnic and race relations in Canada, it is necessary to explore the meaning of the concept *ethnic group*.

An **ethnic group** is a highly variable and complex social entity that has assumed various forms in different societies and historical eras; scholars, therefore, disagree on its defining characteristics. The influential theoretical perspectives of Weber (1946) and Barth (1969) suggest, however, that ethnicity has four major dimensions, listed in Table 8.1, with their manifestations at the individual and group levels.

Ethnicity as an ascribed status

To say that membership in a social group is an ascribed status means that it is conferred at birth, a social attribute inherited from parents and other ancestors. Ethnicity, like race, gender, and age, is not something which individuals aspire to, strive for, choose, or achieve in life, except in rare and controversial instances. Like other gifts or accidents of birth, ethnicity is a relatively enduring identity, rather than something that can be set aside or changed, as an occupation can be. It is one of those givens of social existence that become deeply embedded within individual identity. Of course, individuals will vary in the degree to which ethnicity is central in this respect.

The fact that ethnicity is ascribed means that ethnic groups are self-perpetuating, an important characteristic differentiating ethnic groups from other kinds of social groups such as religious sects or voluntary associations. The ethnic group, then, includes ancestors long dead, as well as those who are the present-day carriers of the group's culture, and probably at least some of their children as well. Because the ethnicity of parents and ancestors is visited upon their children and grandchildren, the ethnic group itself continues to exist from generation to generation, at least as a potential that may be realized under certain conditions.

To say that ethnic identity is ascribed and that ethnic groups are self-perpetuating does not mean that ethnic groups are biological entities, or that individuals inherit behaviours or cultural patterns or even combinations of physical traits. Ethnicity is not a matter of biological inheritance, but of social definition and experience.

Ethnicity as a form of social organization

From the perspective of its individual members, the ethnic group may be viewed as a set of social relationships originating within a family, and radiating outward to include primary ties with kin, friends, neighbours, and others with whom interaction is frequent. If informal interaction and communication patterns tend to be particularly intense among persons of the same ethnicity, then these relationships may be said to form an *ethnic network*. Members of a network frequently share a set of values and way of life, and individuals may identify their personal fates with these people. For some, being part of an ethnic group may meet needs for social relatedness and belonging.

TABLE 8.1 Some defining characteristics of the ethnic group

	Dimensions of ethnicity			
	An ascribed status	*A form of social organization*	*A subculture*	*A focus of identity*
Individual ethnic group members	inherit ethnic group membership	are involved in interaction and a shared institutional framework	tend to share some fundamental values	feel a sense of belonging with other members
The ethnic group as a whole	is self-perpetuating	has boundaries	transmits a culture rooted in historical experience	is recognized as a collectivity by others in the society

As one element of a pluralistic society, then, the ethnic community is a product of social interaction rather than formal organization. The ethnic community has no rules of membership, no coordinating agency, no official leadership. Yet it does have norms that regulate membership, an internal social hierarchy, and formal organizations that promote group solidarity and meet collective needs.

An important feature of the ethnic group as a form of social organization is that it has *boundaries* that include some individuals but exclude others. If a social group is to have an identity, it must have boundaries that are set and maintained by patterns of interaction. Some kinds of social interactions may be confined largely within the group while others are not.

In part, ethnic group boundaries may be culturally defined; for example, an Irish Protestant who marries a Jew may be included within the boundaries of the Jewish community by converting to its religion. Sometimes geographic concentration and isolation from other groups can contribute to the maintenance of ethnic boundaries, as among the Old Order Mennonites and Hutterites, who choose to minimize contact with others by separating their communities both geographically and socially from the surrounding population. Spatial separation or segregation may reinforce discriminatory social barriers between ethnic populations and the rest of society. The isolation of Native peoples as a result of the reserve system has helped to maintain boundaries between them and other Canadians, and has contributed to their lack of access to educational and occupational opportunities, health care, and the standard of living generally available to other Canadians.

However, the survival of an ethnic group usually does not depend upon physical isolation. An ethnic group's boundaries may persist even when its members live side by side with other groups, and participate with others in economic, social, and political activities. For example, the Jewish community retains a high degree of ethnic identity, solidarity, and community involvement within the context of a highly urbanized and cosmopolitan lifestyle (Isajiw, 1990; Breton, 1990).

Boundaries are perhaps most effectively maintained not by physical isolation or separation, but by social norms that influence behaviour in interpersonal relationships. Norms, or expectations about role behaviour, are learned during socialization within a family and community, and are continually reinforced through daily interaction and experience. While norms may regulate or restrict inter-ethnic contacts in intimate relationships, contacts that do not threaten group boundaries may be permitted more readily. In many plural societies, ethnic groups meet in the marketplace, at work, or in school. Ethnic *endogamy*—that is, marriage within an ethnic group—is perhaps the critical factor in the maintenance of ethnic group boundaries. Isajiw (1990: 77–81) found that Toronto ethnic groups differ in their emphasis on marriage within the group. For the Jewish group, endogamy remained an important value into the third generation, while for Ukrainians, Germans, and Italians, it decreased in importance with each generation in Canada.

The ethnic group as a subculture

An ethnic group as a social organization, with boundaries maintained by social norms governing interaction, has an existence of its own, independent of its individual members. It persists from generation to generation; it has a history. The sharing of experience over time gives specific cultural meanings to the social relationships that ethnic group members have with one another. These historical experiences are unique to each group, and are an important dimension of the ethnic identity that is passed down to succeeding generations during socialization. They shape understandings of what it means to belong to the ethnic group. Shared understandings, growing out of a group's historical experience, then give support to a complex of shared values as well as to personal identity.

Generally speaking, the sharing of cultural traits such as food preferences or distinctive styles of musical expression need not be a defining characteristic of an ethnic group. Italians may remain Italians even if they do not enjoy the opera, read no Italian newspapers, and belong to no church. And Poles who do these things nevertheless will not be defined as Italians. While ethnic group members may tend to share certain cultural traits and many values, it would be a misconception to define ethnic group membership in these terms.

The sharing of language is a bit different. The maintenance of language has been considered a fundamental aspect of collective existence for French Canadians and Ukrainians, but has not been as strongly emphasized by German, Italian, or Jewish Canadians (Isajiw, 1990: 51). In a 1973 survey of Canadians of German, Polish, Ukrainian, and Italian ancestry living in the largest cities, however, Reitz (1980a) found that knowledge of the mother tongue is strongly related to participation in ethnic institutions, regardless of generation. Among some aboriginal peoples, there is currently a strong interest in teaching their original language to the young as a part of cultural survival and spiritual renewal.

Ethnicity as a focus of identity

Socialization, discussed in Chapter 4, is the critical factor in the acquisition of ethnic identity. Ethnic identity is a part of self-concept. If both parents are members of the ethnic group, or if the family participates actively in the life of one ethnic community, children may form a strong identification with that group. Their individual personalities become firmly linked with the historical experience, values, way of life, and social patterns that are at the core of group life. Thus, personal identity and collective identity become intertwined (Nicks, 1985).

However, the process of acquiring ethnic identity is usually not simple in contemporary pluralistic societies. As children grow up, they typically confront many influences that go beyond the home and primary social network to include the educational, communications, government, and other institutions of the larger society, and a variety of informal social contacts. In such encounters, children may also sense that their group occupies a lower rank in the stratification system of the larger society and that social mobility or acceptance by the larger society may involve compromising their ethnic identity. An extreme example is the treatment of Native children in Canadian residential schools, where they were forced to live apart from their families and communities, and were punished for speaking their own languages or maintaining their communities' beliefs and values.

Because of such experiences—and because it may be painful to be singled out for being "different"—children may experience considerable conflict between the two worlds in which they live: the home and ethnic community, and the larger society of the school and peer group. Stonequist (1963) used the term **marginality** to describe the condition of personal identity whereby individuals function and identify themselves as members of the group into which they were born, while at the same time participating in another very different and sometimes hostile world (Streitmatter, 1988). Living on the margin between two worlds, full members of neither, they bear within themselves two competing identities.

Situations in which individuals assume a new ethnic identity represent interesting instances of marginality. The author and conservationist Grey Owl was born in 1888 in England, where he had a conventional Victorian childhood as Archie Belaney. Soon after his immigration to Canada in 1906, he settled with an Ojibway band, learned their language, married an Ojibway woman, and identified himself as an Indian for the rest of his life. Grey Owl's lectures and writings advocating the protection of Canada's wildlife commanded a large and enthusiastic following while he lived. But after he died, it was discovered that he had not been born an Indian, and there was public outrage about the fact that he had presented himself as one (Dickson, 1973).

Children of immigrants sometimes live on the margin between two worlds, bearing two competing identities that are equally important.

Race and minority group

The public reaction to the discovery that Grey Owl was really Archie Belaney suggests the power of the social meanings attached to ethnic labels. Grey Owl lived in an Ojibway community as an accepted member, yet the general public to whom he addressed his writings ridiculed him as a white man masquerading as Native, a fraud who tried to present himself as a member of a social category to which they felt he did not really belong.

Inherited features such as family surname and physical traits, such as skin colour and hair texture, in themselves have no necessary consequences for behaviour. Yet such identifying features often become *socially defined* as very significant. All individuals who have a particular characteristic, such as dark skin, may be seen by others as members of a single **social category**, which is defined as a collection of individuals all of whom share a single trait that is regarded as socially meaningful. The social meaning attached to racial or ethnic categories often includes the assignment of a rank within the hierarchy of society. This position is not necessarily subordinate; ethnicity is not always stigmatizing, nor always associated with oppression. It is quite possible for an ethnic group to occupy an élite or privileged status, as the British have done until recently in the economic life of Quebec.

Frequently, however, racial or ethnic labels become criteria for assigning individuals or groups to subordinate positions within a social hierarchy. Moghaddam and Taylor (1987) studied the effects of this process on women who had immigrated to Canada from India. These women tended to perceive themselves as "women," "individuals," and "Canadian." But they felt they were perceived by most Canadians as "Indian," "women," "immigrants," "coloured," and "South Asian"—labels associated with lower status in Canadian society.

Members of a social category may not have anything in common beyond their shared identifying features. However, if as a consequence of their treatment and position in society they become involved in social interaction with one another, and come to share values and a sense of identity and common interests, they may *become* a social group. This process of *ethnogenesis* has occurred among the First Nations of North America, who lived as separate and frequently warring groups, each with its own culture, until Europeans forced upon them a common label and identity. It was only because Columbus thought he had arrived in India that the label "Indians" was applied to aboriginal peoples of the Americas.

Race and racism

A primary example of an arbitrary social category is a **race**, which consists of persons who share inherited physical characteristics such as skin colour and facial features, characteristics charged with social meaning in some societies. Indeed, an enormous amount of scientific evidence has invalidated notions that genetically separate races of human beings exist. A population may display a number of inherited physical features that tend to be less typical of other populations, but these features "are derived from a great reservoir of genes that is the common inheritance of all mankind" (Geipel, 1969: 3). In the words of Gould (1981: 323):

> ...all modern human races probably split from a common ancestral stock only tens of thousands of years ago. A few outstanding traits of external appearance lead to our subjective judgement of important differences. But biologists have recently affirmed—as long suspected—that the overall genetic differences among human races are astonishingly small.

Moreover, research in genetics has established that the physical attributes that have been considered the markers of race, such as stature, skin and eye colour, or hair texture, are inherited quite independently of one another and are not always found together. The so-called "races" thus can best be understood as social constructs defined by dominant groups in a society (Li, 1988: 23) to justify exploitation and subjugation. "It is precisely for this reason that the term race is increasingly questioned as an appropriate analytic category in sociology just as it was earlier in biology" (Mason, 1988: 5–6).

Racism is an ideology that regards racial or ethnic categories as natural genetic groupings, and that attributes behavioural and psychological differences to the genetic nature of these groupings. Biological traits are used to label some human beings—invariably

A Comment on the Terminology of Race

The term *race* refers not to "real" social groupings whose membership can be specified objectively or empirically, but to arbitrary categories that reflect a social process of labelling and classification. The concept of race has changed through time, and has taken on various social meanings that have had profoundly negative effects upon the lives of individuals and groups of people. So while race is a product of human decisions that have no scientific basis, the reality of "race" as a social concept cannot be denied; nor can the fact that the concept of race has been used as the basis for social stratification, oppression, and the denial of the humanity of the majority of the world's people. As the sociologist W.I. Thomas pointed out: "what is perceived as real is real in its consequences" (Merton, 1957: 421).

In today's pluralistic society, a variety of terms are used to refer to the concepts of race, colour, or minority status based upon physical characteristics. It is probably true that all of these terms create discomfort and misunderstanding, especially to the degree that they are words used primarily by dominant white majorities to refer to people whom they consider to be different. For example, in Canadian legislation and government policy, the term *visible minorities* is used to refer to people who look different from the white majority in Canada because of the colour of their skin or facial characteristics, and who very often are disadvantaged in the workplace as a consequence. A great variety of peoples, including those of African, East Asian, Southeast Asian, West Asian, and sometimes South or Central American descent are lumped into the category of visible minorities. Clearly, this term does not refer to a social group. Other terms including *people of colour* and *racial minorities* are also used to refer to this category.

It should be noted that aboriginal peoples in Canada do not see themselves as a "visible minority" or an ethnic group within the multicultural population of Canada, but as Canada's First Nations—sovereign peoples whose relationship to the government and people of Canada has yet to be defined.

Deconstructing the various terms that refer to race and to aboriginal ancestry, and subjecting them to historical and critical analysis, is an important issue for interdisciplinary research. Any terminology that is imposed upon minorities by dominant majorities, rather than developed and proposed by these groups to refer to themselves, will be problematic and implicated in the structure of racism in society.

those belonging to categories other than the one doing the labelling—as inherently inferior, and therefore proper objects of exploitation and domination.

During this century, racist notions have been used to rationalize the oppression of aboriginal peoples, the Nazi extermination of Jews and Gypsies, and laws restricting the immigration of southern European and Asian peoples to Canada and the United States.

Social scientists, like others who influence public opinion, have contributed their share to racist thinking (Gould, 1981). In North America, for example, ethnic groups were called "races" throughout the early decades of this century, and Canadian political leaders and social scientists argued in favour of restricting the immigration of U.S. blacks, Chinese, and other groups, on the grounds that they were undesirables, or not biologically equipped to adapt to the Canadian climate (Krauter and Davis, 1978). The term *race* was used in the Canadian census to refer to the French- as well as the English-origin population until 1941. However, largely through the efforts of later generations of social and biological scientists and of human rights, ethnic, labour, and community organizations, racist ideas have been challenged and have weakened their hold on popular thinking in Canada, although they are far from disappearing. Indeed, racist conceptions continue to be put forward in both academic and political contexts, in Canada as in other parts of the world.

Minority groups and patterns of subordination

A **minority group** is a social category that occupies a subordinate rank in a social hierarchy; such a group is accorded unequal treatment and excluded from full participation in the life of society. The term *minority* refers not to the size of the group—a minority may outnumber dominant groups, as in white-dominated South Africa—but to its position in a context of power relationships. In post-Confederation Canada, Japanese, Chinese, Canadian Indians, Inuit, and blacks have suffered various restrictions on their freedom of access to employment, housing, education, and citizenship. The right to vote has at some time been denied to each of these groups.

In the modern world, extreme forms of social control have been used to subordinate minorities of all types. Such measures include *expulsion*, the forcible removal of a minority from its homeland—a fate suffered by Canada's First Nations during the settlement of the country, and by west coast Japanese Canadians during World War II. Soon after Canada declared war on Japan, all persons of Japanese origin living within one hundred miles of British Columbia's coastline, the majority of them Canadian citizens, were forcibly evacuated from their homes. They were stripped of their property and placed in "relocation centres" in Alberta, Ontario, and other provinces, where they lived in camps and worked as farm labourers. After the war most Japanese remaining in Canada did not return to their west coast communities, but remained dispersed in other areas.

The modern world has also seen instances of *annihilation* or *genocide*—the intentional massacre of peoples. The destruction of certain aboriginal groups as a result of the European conquest of the Americas, of European Jews and Gypsies by the Nazis, of Armenians in Turkey, and of Muslims in Bosnia-Herzegovina are but a few items in a catalogue of horrors (Chalk and Jonassohn, 1990).

Dominant groups frequently control and restrict the economic, social, and political participation of minorities by means of **discrimination**, the practice of denying to members of certain social categories opportunities that are generally available within the society. Discrimination may in some instances occur by legal means (*de jure*). For example, until 1960 an article of the Indian Act withheld the franchise from Indians in all provinces except Newfoundland. More common in Canada today is *de facto* or informal discrimination that occurs as a matter of common practice, often in violation of the law, as in the case of a landlord who, in contravention of provincial human rights statutes, finds an excuse for refusing to rent an apartment to someone who is a member of a racial group.

Canadian evidence on the prevalence of discrimination against members of minority groups is accumulating. In a 1978–79 survey of Toronto ethnic groups, Breton (1990: 207–209) found that for a majority of West Indians (57 percent), discrimination against their group in employment was a serious concern. The same was true for 37 percent of Chinese, 33 percent of Portuguese, 20 percent of Italians and 15 percent of Jews—and about the same proportions of the majority Canadian population agreed with these groups' perceptions of the discrimination they faced. Driedger and Mezoff (1981) found that two-thirds of Jewish high-school students in their Winnipeg sample had experienced discrimination, in the form of verbal abuse, ethnic jokes, language ridicule, and other acts. Almost half the Polish-, Italian-, and French-origin students also reported these experiences. Approximately two-thirds of South Asian and West Indian respondents in a 1979 Toronto survey of social agency clients reported experiences of discrimination, primarily in housing and employment (Head, 1981: 72). The same proportion of women who had immigrated to Canada from India felt they had been badly treated in Canada because of their race (Moghaddam and Taylor, 1987: 134).

Systemic or **institutionalized discrimination** is a form of discrimination that occurs as a by-product of the ordinary functioning of bureaucratic institutions, rather than as a consequence of a deliberate policy or motive to discriminate. Systemic discrimination consists of patterns of institutional practices that perpetuate majority-group privilege and create disadvantage for minorities simply by conducting "business as usual." For example, by setting a rule that recruits must be at least 1.8 m tall, a police department may effectively exclude many Chinese and aboriginal applicants, since the average height of members of these groups is less than the requirement. By means of such arbitrary criteria that have no demonstrable relationship to job performance, privileged groups may control access to employment opportunities.

There is strong evidence that minorities in Canada also face discrimination in employment, including wage discrimination. For example, in a study of sixteen Canadian ethnic populations, Li (1988: 118–19) found that Chinese and blacks had higher educational levels than the national average. But when education, age, gender, and place of birth were statistically controlled, the average incomes of Chinese and blacks were the lowest of all the groups.

Research in Toronto has demonstrated the existence of direct discrimination by employers against black job applicants. Pairs of job applicants, matched in all respects except that one was black and the other white, applied for over 430 advertised jobs. The whites received three job offers for every one received by the black applicants, who experienced many instances of discriminatory treatment (Henry and Ginzberg, 1985; 1993). Similar field trials in Washington, D.C., and Chicago found levels of discrimination comparable to those found in the Toronto study, suggesting that "discriminatory practices are not widely different in the two countries" (Reitz and Breton, 1994: 84–85).

Many other studies in Canada and the United States have shown how discriminatory employment practices restrict access to jobs, promotions, and equal pay for North American-born black and Asian minorities (for example, see Bielby, 1987; Duleep and Sanders, 1992). Analyses of data for Toronto (Reitz, 1990: 151) and Canada (Boyd, 1993; Christofides and Swidinsky, 1994; Li, 1992) demonstrate that when education and other productivity factors are taken into account, minority women face even more income disadvantage than minority men in the workplace. Women who are members of minority groups, then, are doubly disadvantaged in employment due to the effects of both gender and minority group discrimination (Das Gupta, 1996; Neallani, 1992).

Discrimination in employment is reinforced in some societies by the practice of segregation on the basis of minority status. **Segregation** is a form of social control whereby physical distance is maintained in order to ensure social distance from groups with whom contact is not wanted. Segregation involves the exclusion of ethnic, racial, or other minorities from the facilities, residential space, or institutions used by dominant groups.

For most of this century in South Africa, under an elaborate system of legislated racial segregation known as *apartheid*, or "apartness," every individual was classified by race, interracial sex and marriage were banned, and racially separate public facilities, educational systems, residential space, and work arrangements were enforced. After a struggle that lasted for generations and cost the deaths, imprisonment, and torture of thousands, the key segregation laws were repealed in 1991. Democratic elections in which all races voted were held for the first time in 1994 and Nelson Mandela was inaugurated as president, with a mandate for governance based on principles of reconciliation, democracy, and equality (Sparks, 1995).

As a consequence of the massive institutional changes resulting from the civil rights movement, U.S. blacks and whites increasingly meet in the public sphere. However, both economic inequality and

Nelson Mandela has become a symbol of determination to end institutionalized segregation in South Africa.

residential segregation have remained entrenched, despite legislation at all levels of government that forbids discrimination in housing throughout the United States. Because of segregated residential patterns and income disadvantage, over 75 percent of black students in Illinois, New York, Michigan, California, and Mississippi attend segregated schools (Hacker, 1992: 163).

Rates of residential separation among ethnic and racial groups is also high and persistent in Canadian cities, even when socio-economic status is taken into account (Kalbach, 1990; Balakrishnan, 1982). Indexes of residential segregation are highest for the Jewish and Portuguese populations and moderate for the black, Chinese, Hungarian, Russian, and Italian groups (Kalbach, 1990: 98). In Toronto, the Chinese and black populations show a pattern of scattered pockets of concentration (Kalbach, 1990: 130). Research suggests that people's desire to live near others of the same background, discrimination, and poverty may all be causal factors in ethnic and racial residential separation (Agócs, 1979).

Explaining discrimination

In their attempt to explain discrimination in modern societies, social scientists have studied various kinds of influences. Before the 1960s, there was much interest in the role of ideas and beliefs in motivating discriminatory acts against minority group members. Of special importance was the concept of **prejudice**, an attitude that prejudges individuals because of characteristics assumed to be shared by all members of their group. Those characteristics may be based on **stereotypes**—mental images that exaggerate what are usually perceived to be undesirable traits of typical members of a group, and which are applied to all of its members.

A prejudice is not a product of experience, and may persist despite contrary evidence, particularly when prejudice serves to rationalize a position of privilege. One reason prejudice is often so deeply entrenched is that it is a part of culture that is learned early, and that it is a product of negative emotions as well as mental images (cf. Sniderman et al., 1993). The teachings of parents and teachers, the nursery rhymes and stories, the television shows and movies children are exposed to all contain assumptions and evaluations concerning social groups and their attributes and social ranks. Indeed, the mass media in Canada continue to be criticized for ignoring ethnic and racial minorities and for presenting them in ways that are stereotyped, innacurate, and insulting (Fleras and Elliott, 1992: 233). (See the boxed insert on "The Mass Media and Racial Minorities.")

The connection between prejudiced attitudes and discriminatory behaviour has been the subject of a great deal of research over the past few decades. The implication of many studies is that

The Mass Media and Racial Minorities: "The Prism of Whiteness"

Few would dispute the prominence of the media in guiding, shaping, and transforming the way we look at the world,...how we understand it,...and the manner by which we experience and relate to it.... A media-dominated society such as ours elevates the electronic and print media into an important source of information on how to shape an operational image of the world... Those in control of media information define the beliefs, values, and myths by which we live and organize our lives. They impose a cultural context for framing our experiences of social reality, in the process sending out a clear message about who is normal and what is desirable and important in society...

Media values are designed around those priorities that can capture as large an audience as possible for maximizing advertising revenues.... Media messages come across as safe, simple, and predictable in order to appeal to the lowest common denominator in society. Information about the world, if it attracts a broad audience, is included. Otherwise it is excluded, especially if any potential exists to offend significant markets. Especially in advertising, the media acknowledge the necessity to cater to dominant attitudes and prejudice. The logic of these circumstances dictates media mistreatment of racial (and other) minorities as the norm rather than the exception...

The media in Canada relay information about who racial minorities are, what they want, why, how they propose to achieve their goals, and with what consequence for Canadian society. How responsibly have the media acted in this respect?...

Certain patterns can be extrapolated from media (mis)treatment of racial minorities. Minorities are defined and categorized (a) as invisible, (b) in terms of race-role stereotyping, (c) as a social problem, and (d) as amusement...

(a) Minorities as Invisible

Racial minorities are reduced to invisible status through underrepresentation in programming, staffing, and decision-making. Minorities are deemed unworthy of coverage unless caught up in situations of conflict or crisis... This marginalization continues into advertising, where they are excluded because of minimal purchasing power or low socioeconomic status and prestige... A 1987 ACTRA (Alliance of Canadian Cinema, Television and Radio Artists) study found that minority members accounted for only 3 percent of the actors on Canadian stages, less than 3 percent of those in commercials, and 5.5 percent of the actors on television. This compares with the average of 16 percent representation in American television.... Media "whitewashing" (especially in advertising) contributes to the invisibility of minorities in society. Racial minorities are restricted in [a] way that "denies their existence, devalues their contribution to society, and trivializes their aspirations to participate, as fully-fledged members"...

(b) Minorities as Stereotypes

Minorities have long complained of stereotyping by the mass media. Notwithstanding some improvements in this area, the report card on mass media stereotyping shows only negligible improvement. Race-role images continue to be reinforced, perpetuated, and even legitimized through media dissemination and selective coverage. When appearing in advertising, racial minorities are often cast in slots that reflect a "natural" propensity for the product in question. Who better to sell foreign airlines, quality chamber-maid service in hotels, or high-cut gym shoes?...

(c) Minorities as Social Problem

Racial minorities are frequently singled out by the media as a "social problem." They are described in the context of "having problems" that require solutions requiring an inordinate amount of political attention and consuming a disproportionate slice of national resources... In addition, the media are likely to define minorities in terms of "creating problems" by making demands unacceptable to the social, political, or moral order of society. For example, aboriginal peoples in Canada are portrayed time and again as "troublesome constituents" whose demands for self-determination and self-government are anathema to Canada's liberal-democratic tradition. This "us versus them" mentality fostered by the media is conducive to the scapegoating of racial minorities, who are blamed for an assortment of social ills or economic misfortunes...

(d) Minorities as Amusement

Racial minorities are often portrayed as irrelevant to society at large. This decorative effect is achieved by casting minorities in the role of entertainment by which to amuse or divert the audience. On-air television programming creates a situation where racial minorities find themselves ghettoized into roles as sit-com comedians. The restrictive effects of such an orientation serve to trivialize minority aspirations, as well as to diminish their importance as serious contributors to Canadian society...

Racial minorities are victimized by media treatment that confirms and endorses audience prejucide... Compounding the difficulties is the absence of racial minorities in creative positions, such as those of director, producer, editor, or screenwriter. Fewer still are positioned in the upper levels of management where key decision-making occurs. The experiences and realities of racial minorities are distorted by the media, largely because of the inability of largely white, middle-class media personnel to perceive and understand the world from a different point of view.

Source: *Augie Fleras and Jean Leonard Elliott, 1992.* Multiculturalism in Canada: The Challenge of Diversity. *Scarborough, Ont.: Nelson Canada (pp. 234–43). Reprinted by permission of ITP Nelson Canada.*

the relationship between attitudes and behaviour is extremely complex. A prejudiced person does not always act in a discriminatory way, and there is little evidence that discriminatory behaviour is caused by prejudiced attitudes.

Survey evidence has shown that, with the passing generations, the attitudes of U.S. whites towards minority racial and ethnic groups have become more tolerant and accepting. A U.S. report on data from national opinion polls between 1942 and 1983 showed "growing and now virtually universal verbal commitment to the principle of racial equality" (Reitz and Breton, 1994: 65). A 1990 survey by Decima found that 90 percent of Canadians and 86 percent of Americans agreed that "all races are created equal" (Reitz and Breton, 1994: 67–68). Yet African-Americans continue to suffer from disproportionate rates of poverty, unemployment, menial occupational status, and poor living conditions (Hacker, 1992: Ch. 4), and the relative disadvantage of their poorest segments has become more severe and entrenched over time (Wilson, 1987). Clearly, improvement in the attitudes of the dominant group is not in itself a solution to the problems of inequality and discrimination.

RACE AND ETHNIC RELATIONS IN CANADA IN THE TWENTIETH CENTURY: AN OVERVIEW

Inter-group relationships in Canada in this century have been shaped by the historical processes of colonialism, conquest, and migration, processes that continue to have influence generations after these events took place. Colonized groups such as the First Nations of North America became part of a plural society involuntarily, by coercion, and remain economically and politically marginal to that society. The military conquest of Canada's French by the British shaped subsequent relationships between the two majority groups. Migrating groups, such as the many of Asian, South or Central American, or European origin that now populate Canada, entered the society voluntarily, although economic need or political repression may have driven them from their homelands. The communities and institutions they have established in Canada are not transplants, but new social forms created in response to the challenges that confronted them in the new country. We shall discuss each of these historical processes in turn.

Colonialism and the First Nations

The struggles and accommodations that have characterized contacts between the First Nations—the Indians and Inuit—and the rest of Canadian society reflect a system of inter-group relations that grew out of **colonialism**. In colonial situations, whether in the Americas, Africa, or elsewhere in the world, a settler culture and society have invaded and dominated an indigenous population, controlling and exploiting the land, resources, and institutions of that population, and over time undermining or destroying its traditional culture and way of life.

In the course of colonization, the settler country generally sends out representatives to extract resources from the colonized land, establish settlements, and administer the indigenous population. As institutions of the settler country are imposed on the native population, frequently by violent means, the erosion of their cultures and economy proceeds. Thus, a social system becomes established that is characterized by external control and seizure of the indigenous population's property, and their oppression and enforced dependence—all of which is rationalized by a racist ideology.

During the earliest period in the colonization of Canada by the French and English, the First Nations provided for their own survival needs in traditional ways, through fishing, hunting, gathering, trading, and cultivating crops. But during the early sixteenth century, cooperative relationships in the fur trade were established between the Europeans, especially the French, and various First Nations. By the end of the century, the trading economy had undermined traditional subsistence activities and incited warfare among Native groups vying for exclusive trading alliances with the European powers.

Both the French and the British used trading relationships with First Nations for economic gain and to enlist them as allies against their enemies.

But as political and economic realities changed, and these alliances and trade relationships became less useful and profitable, the British increasingly made war upon First Nations. They wanted Native lands for their land-hungry settlers. Some of these white encroachments were met with armed resistance, as in the 1869 and 1885 rebellions of Indians and Métis under the leadership of Louis Riel in the Red River and Saskatchewan River regions. The first rebellion ended with limited gains for the Natives, but the second ended in complete defeat and the hanging of Riel. By 1901, wars, forced resettlement, and disease had brought an absolute decline in the size of Canada's Indian population, from an estimated 200 000 to 1 000 000 at the beginning of European settlement to not much more than 100 000 (Beaujot, 1978: 36).

The practice of negotiating treaties with individual bands, begun by the British Crown and continued after Confederation, resulted in the surrender by some First Nations of their interests in their ancestral lands in return for the right to live on reserves as wards of the state, segregated from the rest of Canadian society. Under the terms of the Indian Act (first passed in 1876 and subsequently revised), *registered* or *status Indians* are entitled to live on reserve lands and to receive certain government programs and services, such as education and health care. However, some First Nations have opted out of certain sections of the Indian Act and some are self-governing.

Since Confederation, the affairs of registered Indians have been managed by various branches, departments, and ministries of the federal government, which has administered the reserves, band funds, property inheritance, education, welfare, and the fulfilment of treaty obligations. As the reserve system became entrenched, Indians manifested the demoralization that has affected powerless colonized peoples in many parts of the world. Indian residents of reserves have had few ways to influence the paternalistic and quasi-colonial government bureaucracies. Indeed, it was not until 1960 that Indians were guaranteed the right to vote in federal elections.

Non-status Indians are those who do not meet the criteria of status Indians under the Indian Act, and are thus exempt from the Act's provisions. So too are the *Métis*, a people descended from marriages between Indian women and early settlers, traders, and trappers, mainly of French and British stock. Although these groups suffered many of the same injustices and deprivations endured by status Indians, they do not have the same entitlements.

Canada's 33 000 Inuit are also exempt from the provisions of the Indian Act. Sustained contact between Inuit and other Canadians has occurred only recently, beginning with the construction of large military installations in the North during the Second World War. Since that time, change in the Inuit way of life has been rapid and dramatic, involving impoverishment, social disorganization, and much disruption of traditional ways of life, as is usual with colonialism, when a settler society invades and dominates an indigenous population. In recent years, government policy, including the forced removal of communities, and economic change have led to the concentration of many Inuit in urban centres, where educational and social service facilities and housing are located. The rapid importation of southern workers, institutions, consumer goods, and social patterns has further transformed traditional Inuit culture, economy, and family life, and created marginality among the young.

As a result of a comprehensive land claim settlement between the federal government and the Inuit people, Canada's third territory—Nunavut—is now being created in the central and eastern Arctic. Nunavut, which means "our land" in Inuktitut, constitutes more than a fifth of Canada's land mass. In 1999, Nunavut will establish its own elected legislative assembly and government within the Canadian parliamentary system (Platiel, 1993). (See the boxed insert on "Nunavut: a Distinct Inuit Society.")

In the post-World War II years, the size of the aboriginal population increased substantially. In the years from 1961 to 1987, the registered Indian population nearly doubled, to 415 898 (Indian and Northern Affairs, 1988), in part because of a 1985 amendment to the Indian Act that ended its discriminatory impact on Indian women who had married non-Natives, and on their children. Moreover, among registered Indians the rate of population increase is about twice that of the rest of Canada, resulting in an Indian population that is younger

Nunavut: A Distinct Inuit Society

The map of Canada is being redrawn. The Inuit of the Eastern Arctic have reached a land claim agreement with the government of Canada. It is the largest and richest Native land claim ever in Canada, perhaps in the world. But it is even more than that, because tied to it is the creation of a new territory—Nunavut—Canada's third northern territory, which will be carved out of the Northwest Territories. Stretching from the Manitoba border to the northern tip of Ellesmere Island, Nunavut will be larger than any other province or territory, and twice the size of British Columbia. When the new territory is officially born on April 1, 1999, the working language of its government will be Inuktitut, since 80 percent of its 22 000 residents are Inuit....

For Canada, Nunavut represents a new relationship with an Aboriginal group. For the first time, a provincial or territorial government will speak largely on behalf of one group of Native people. While Nunavut will not mean self-government for Inuit in a constitutional sense, it will be self-government in effect because of the Inuit majority. The Inuit will acquire responsibility for a host of social, economic and political problems, and must hope that the solutions can be found with their powerful new tools of government and management. Defining how they will exercise these powers is the next major challenge facing Inuit leaders.

"Inuit will have enormous influence on issues that concern them," says John Amagoalik, who is sometimes called the father of Nunavut. He was one of a dedicated group of Inuit who devoted much of the last 20 years of their lives to the negotiations. Those issues of Inuit concern distill down to a sense of control over their own lives, and recognition of the right to self-determination. "We are very much a distinct society," he says. "The Nunavut government will have the responsibility of protecting and preserving that distinct society."

The accord gives the Inuit the same control over their affairs as other territorial governments have, and more autonomy than any other Native group in Canada. The land claim settlement gives the Inuit outright ownership of about 18 percent of the land... The remaining 82 percent...remains Crown land, but the Inuit will have joint control with the federal government over land-use planning, wildlife, environmental protection and off-shore resources. Inuit will keep the right to hunt, fish and trap throughout Nunavut. The settlement also gives them $1.15 billion, which they hope will help generate economic and social revival.

It is not a perfect deal for the Inuit. To get it, they agreed to sign away forever any future claim to Aboriginal title to the land. But to many, it was a triumph of patience and dedication, as more than a decade and a half of difficult negotiations came to fruition....

A key to Amagoalik's perseverance may lie in his own childhood experience of Inuit powerlessness. He was among the Inuit who were experimentally relocated by the federal government in 1953 from Inukjuak, in northern Quebec, to Ellesmere Island. He remains outspoken about the deception that led to his family's relocation into an area of poor hunting and wretched living conditions. The federal government, to this day, refuses to acknowledge the move was for sovereignty reasons...

For most Inuit, one appealing aspect of Nunavut is that government will be closer to the people, both physically and spiritually. But a major problem will be how to gather and hear opinions from such remote communities. A solution may lie in the fact that the North is already well linked through satellite television services. Such an instantaneous communications link could be used to connect communities to one another and the leadership forum to its people...

Today there are profound social problems in Nunavut. Jobs are scarce and Native unemployment is commonly in the 30 to 50 percent range. Only 15 percent of students complete high school... "We know that our culture is eroding, that spousal assault and drug and alcohol abuse are increasing, that the suicide rate among young Inuit is a tragedy of national importance." The detractors of Nunavut say it will be impossible to create a new government amid such social ills and low levels of education. The proponents argue that Nunavut itself is the answer to these difficulties, with its opportunities for jobs and training.

Source: *David F. Pelly, 1993. "Dawn of Nunavut." Canadian Geographic, March/April 1993 (pp. 21–26).*

than the Canadian average. Although the birth rate among Native peoples has begun to decline, Trovato (1987) predicted that it will remain high relative to that of the general population of Canada despite increasing modernization, which typically entails declines in fertility.

Today, fewer than two-thirds of registered Indians live on the more than 2000 reserves in Canada. Living conditions vary considerably from one reserve to another, but generally speaking the reserve population is impoverished and lacks opportunity for higher education and employment. Life expectancy for Indians is about eight years below the Canadian average, and infant mortality is 1.7 times the national average (*Globe and Mail*, June 14, 1990). Many reserve communities face severe environmental hazards resulting from industrial and resource development, which has polluted waterways and disrupted the fish and game stocks upon which many communities have depended for a livelihood.

Increasing numbers of Indians have been migrating to urban centres, and sizeable Native populations have settled in Vancouver, Calgary, Edmonton, Regina, Saskatoon, Winnipeg, Toronto, and Montreal, as well as in a number of smaller centres located not far from reserves (McDonald, 1991). Research on the experiences of Indians in various Canadian cities has found a pattern of stratification similar to that existing on many reserves. Most off-reserve aboriginal people live in family households, but suffer severe economic and social disadvantage. The unemployment rate for aboriginal people living off-reserve is roughly triple the rate for the Canadian population (McDonald, 1991). In many instances, life in the city appears to offer no more advantages than living conditions on reserves, and there is evidence that to many, reserve communities are more attractive than cities if some economic opportunity is available (Gerber, 1984).

For aboriginal people in Canadian society, whether living on or off reserves, the past twenty

The need to implement an alternative to the reserve system and the movement towards self-government by aboriginal peoples present a major policy dilemma for Canada's pluralistic society.

Native People in Canadian Society: A Native Woman's View

Marlene Pierre-Aggamaway, past president of the Native Women's Association of Canada, has described the relationship between Native women and the state.

In "Indian country," it is the women who pass on the ways in which we are to arrange ourselves as families, the ways in which we arrange ourselves in our communities. Passing on the ways was always our responsibility. In...a matriarchal society, it was also the women who selected the leadership. But one of the sad facts about the condition of Native women today is that, although we have the responsibility to pass on that which makes up the Indian system, we ourselves do not know our heritage... we, as Native women, have also to contend with the attitude of almost all of the Indian leadership in the country: our place is at home. We are supposed to be ten paces behind men, not beside men or in front of men, or wherever we want to be. ...

I think that Canadian society in general has been determining our needs as it has perceived them. Non-Native women's organizations do not seem interested in Native women's concerns. And Native women have had even less opportunity to express their concerns than have other women. The Indian leadership still says that it is representing the views of Native women and it is not. ...

What are the issues that we, as Native women and as Native people, must deal with in the future? Central to everything is sovereignty: the power to make decisions for ourselves, whether we are Indian or non-Indian. For many of us, the ultimate solution is the exercising of our people's sovereignty according to our culture and traditions. ... It is our belief that only with the return of our sovereignty will discrimination be lessened. We have confidence enough in our traditions and culture to know that Native women will then be able to take their rightful place in the future of our people....

If sovereignty is central to our survival, then economic development is central to the success of sovereignty. ... In the historical past, Native women had an integral part to play in economic development. Today, Native women are expected to be concerned with the family and with the social and cultural development of the community. They are not perceived as being direct and full participants in the economy; they are only adjuncts to the economic and political structures of Indian and Inuit societies. ...

The change in status of Native women began with the arrival of the Europeans and with the subsequent imposition of dependency on Indian and Inuit societies by the Canadian government. Prohibition of traditional culture and of religious rituals, alien social systems, and the introduction of non-traditional coping mechanisms such as alcohol, placed incredible pressure on the community, seriously damaged the family unit, and altered the roles of Native women. A major factor was the introduction of the wage economy. Native women's work began to resemble women's work in general. ...

We realize that our development does not depend on a return to the past or an out-of-hand rejection of non-Native technologies, but on a blending of our cultural, economic, social, and political aspirations with the appropriate tools of today. We want to take from the past, blend it with the present, and come out with something that is acceptable to and can be carried out by Native people. ...

Culture and economy are inseparable. Many people today have come to accept culture as being the music, dress, and language of a people. ... But cultures are inconceivable without an economic base. Even spiritual life revolves to a considerable extent around the ways people see their lives supported. ... One of the alarming aspects of the loss of a culture is that, in the absence of processes which meet a people's needs, social disintegration takes place. That is why acculturation can be associated with alcoholism, suicide, family disintegration, and all the other social ills for which the federal government has programs. This is a model of colonialism: first, one creates the problem through the destruction of the Native economy and then one offers welfare programs as a remedy. The logical answer to that destructive process is for the Native people to develop or re-develop their own economies. ...

To develop economic self-reliance, a people must exercise sovereignty and to exercise sovereignty, the Native nations must achieve economic self-reliance. ... Returning to Native people real control over their own lives must be the primary goal if we, as a Native people and as Native women, are to survive, and perhaps even to prosper.

Source: *Joan Turner and Lois Emery (eds.), 1983.* Perspectives on Women in the 1980s. *Winnipeg: The University of Manitoba Press (pp. 66–73).*

years have been a time of collective commitment and action directed towards change and renewal, and ultimately self-determination. Native associations, community organizations, and individuals are engaged in struggles to reclaim and strengthen their cultures, languages, religions, lands, communities, and families, which have all been profoundly damaged by the impact of colonialism and its legacy of discrimination and racism.

French and British Canadians: two majorities, two solitudes

Conquest is another historical process that brings pluralist societies into being. In Canada the British conquest of New France was followed by a series of events that established the foundations of contemporary French–British dualism. The dominant metaphors in Canadian scholarship as well as in law and popular tradition have long described Canada as a bicultural country composed of "two societies," "two majorities," "two charter groups," "two founding races"—and, some have added, "two solitudes."

The French–British relationship has distant historical roots that should be familiar to all Canadians. New France after 1663 was a French colony that was to be developed into a flourishing agricultural society resembling rural France. In 1665, when the Crown's first administrator, Jean Talon, arrived, New France held about 3000 settlers, the majority of whom were men and boys. By making land grants to discharged soldiers, offering land and free passage to new settlers from France, and importing shiploads of young French women whose orphaned or impoverished state left them few alternatives, Talon oversaw the growth of New France to 7833 French inhabitants by 1675 (Lower, 1973: 22). After that time there was very little immigration from France, and today's population of some six million Canadians of French ancestry are largely the descendants of those early settlers.

The pattern of French settlement, known as the *seigneurial system*, entailed the granting of lands by the French Crown to landowners (*seigneurs*), who declared themselves vassals to the king. *Seigneurs* were obliged to parcel out the lands under their authority to *habitants*, or permanent settlers. Small groups of *habitants* lived in parish communities, each with its Roman Catholic *curé*, who performed many essential secular as well as religious functions.

The *habitants* farmed long narrow strips of land running back from the rivers, but for the most part agriculture remained a subsistence activity rather than a profitable commercial venture. As an economic activity, farming could not compete with the fur trade, which grew in importance. The primary economic value of New France as a colony became its resource of furs, readily available through trade with Native peoples. Trade relationships between European countries and their colonies in general can be described as a mercantile system, characterized by crown control of industry and trade. Colonies were treated solely as sources of raw materials, dependent upon the parent country for manufactured goods, as well as for defence and religious and political authority.

It was primarily to control the fur trade that the British and French states struggled for possession of New France. The struggle intensified after the founding of the Hudson's Bay Company. This famous company was entitled under charter from the English Crown to exclusive trading and commercial rights, and to the rights to govern and to make war, in the lands now called northern Ontario and Quebec and in parts of Alberta and the Northwest Territories, as well as Manitoba and Saskatchewan. The Hudson's Bay Company soon established trade relations with the First Nations, who then became involved in the armed struggle between the British and French.

Not only commercial rivalry but also differences of religion, economic life, and culture figured in the British–French conflict. The large and relatively prosperous population of British Protestants, initially concentrated along the Atlantic coast, spread westward into French territory and consolidated Britain's hold upon the east. In the early eighteenth century France lost both Newfoundland and Acadia to the British, Acadia becoming Nova Scotia.

The Treaty of Paris (1763) transferred virtually all Canadian lands under French control to the British, whose empire now stretched from the Atlantic to the Mississippi. Britain then faced the problem of governing some 65 000 French-speaking Roman Catholics, who possessed a distinct way of life, history, language, and set of institutions. The British chose to deal with this challenge by establishing a policy of cultural and political pluralism that recognized the "French fact," legally acknowledging the special status of the French in Lower Canada. This recognition was embodied in the Quebec Act of 1774, which reaffirmed the religious freedom of Roman Catholics, confirmed the Church's right to tithes, recognized the seigneurial system of land tenure, allowed the trial of civil suits by French law, and provided for an appointed legislative council with French representation whose ordinances were to be published in both French and English.

For nearly all of the century that followed, the history of Canada was a story of tense British–French relationships, with recurring challenges, especially by British merchant groups and Loyalist migrants from the United States, to the rights enshrined in the Quebec Act and to customs generally followed in French-speaking parts of Canada.

With Confederation in 1867, the foundation of contemporary language rights was laid. Under Section 133 of the British North America Act,

> Either the English or the French language may be used by any Person in the Debates of the Houses of the Parliament of Canada and of the Houses of the Legislature of Quebec; and both those Languages shall be used in the respective Records and Journals of those Houses; and either of those Languages may be used by any Person or in any Pleading or Process in or issuing from any Court of Canada established under this Act, and or from all or from any of the Courts of Quebec. The Acts of the Parliament of Canada and of the Legislature of Quebec shall be printed and published in both those Languages (Royal Commission on Bilingualism and Biculturalism, 1967: 47).

The constitutional basis for Canadian bilingualism, making French an official language equal to English in federal and Quebec law, resides in this legalistic language.

The Manitoba Act, passed three years later in the aftermath of the Métis rebellion, confirmed the official equality of French and English in the public life of Manitoba. However, this important legal guarantee of French language rights outside Quebec did not survive the rapid influx of English-speaking settlers. By 1890 the French were reduced to a small proportion of Manitoba's population, and the provincial legislature, reflecting the assimilationist and anti-Catholic mood of the time, abolished separate schools and adopted the English Language Act, making English the sole language of public affairs in the province. This act was not disallowed by the federal government nor tested in court until 1979, when the Supreme Court ruled that all legislative acts of the province must be rewritten in both languages. This decision was reaffirmed in 1985.

Contemporary French–English relationships

Outside Quebec there has generally been little recognition by the other provinces of the "French fact." For example, at the present time New Brunswick, with less than 3 percent of Canada's population, is the only officially bilingual province. Federally, the Royal Commission on Bilingualism and Biculturalism was established in response to Quebec's Quiet Revolution of the 1960s, which brought rapid modernization to the economic, political, and cultural institutions of the province and stirred nationalistic and separatist currents. As a consequence of the Commission's extensive research and public hearings, the federal government enacted the Official Languages Act (1969), which sought to extend the use of French within the federal civil service and to make public services available in French wherever concentrations of francophones reside.

The fragile legal foundation of Canadian bilingualism and biculturalism is one essential ingredient of contemporary French–English relationships. Another is the territorial concentration of almost 83 percent of Canada's single-origin French ethnic population in the province of Quebec, whose population was 75 percent of French ethnic origin in 1991, according to the census. Québécois control over the province's territory and its major educational, religious, judicial, and governmental institutions is a unique resource in the struggle of French Canadians to maintain their language and culture. The victory of the Parti Québécois in the Quebec provincial elections of 1976 reflected a widespread desire to maintain and extend this control.

The first important initiative by the new government, the 1977 language legislation known as The Charter of the French Language, or Bill 101, specified that the language of Quebec's French majority would be the official language of Quebec, and the legal language of work, business, education, and all public functions within the province (*Editeur Officiel Québec*, 1978).

If we attempt to understand why the Parti Québécois government enacted such legislation as its first priority, we may gain insight into some of the dilemmas of the French position in Canada today. For French Canadians, legal guarantees and territorial concentration have not altered the fact of English cultural and economic dominance, and the erosion of the French language and culture outside Quebec. This erosion has complex sources, among them the fact that English-speaking immigrants to Canada have vastly outnumbered French-speaking immigrants; the adoption of the English language both by the French outside Quebec and by other ethnic groups in Quebec and in Canada as a whole; and the decline in Quebec's birth rate. We shall discuss each factor in turn, as well as the impact of the historical dominance of the British in the life of Quebec.

From 1946 to 1971, eleven immigrants came to Canada from Britain for every one from France (Beaujot, 1979: 17), in part because of preferential treatment accorded English-speaking and British immigrants. However, even after the law was changed to extend greater opportunities to immigrants from other parts of the world, the number of French-speaking immigrants continued to be negligible. The federal Immigration Act of 1978 acknowledged this by broadening the provincial role in the selection and integration of immigrants, resulting in some increase in the number of French-speaking immigrants to Quebec.

However, French Québécois have continuing reason to be suspicious about the adverse effects of immigration on their culture. Even in Quebec the majority of postwar immigrants adopted the English language and culture rather than the French: in Montreal prior to Bill 101, for every immigrant who acquired French, three learned English (Beaujot, 1978: 35). Quebec sociologist Marcel Rioux estimated that in his province "something like 85 percent of the children of new arrivals attended English schools in the 1970s" (1978a: 144). This was possible because, until the passage of Bill 101, English and French had equal status as languages of Catholic and public instruction in Quebec. (In other provinces provision has been made less often for the instruction of French-speaking children in their first language.)

Scholars of French Canada, such as Breton (1978) and Guindon (1977), have pointed out that French Canadians have historically responded as a collectivity to their marginal position in Canadian political, cultural, and economic life by creating a complex system of parallel institutions and informal social networks within which many community affairs and social relationships are confined. French Catholic schools, parishes, credit unions, labour organizations, communications media, voluntary associations, and a wide range of other institutions, some with government support and others operating through custom and tradition, have met the collective needs of French Canadians. British Canadians in Quebec also developed a fairly high degree of institutional completeness, and traditionally dominated the economic sector. As a result, in past generations British–French contacts in Quebec were largely confined to the public sphere, to formal bureaucratic settings such as the factory. But even within the factory the presence of occupational stratification often meant that French assembly-line workers worked and ate lunch side by side with other French workers, and were linked weakly to English-speaking white-collar workers and management by bilingual supervisors.

However, the modernization of Quebec society, the Quiet Revolution, recent language legislation, and other reflections of national consciousness and political power changed the rules of the game in Quebec by opening up mobility channels to the French and extending the control of francophones over Quebec's economic, educational, and political institutions. There is evidence that, after the passage of Bill 101, the use of French rapidly increased within business organizations. Most francophones are now able to work in their own language in Quebec, and the proportion of anglophones who are bilingual has increased greatly, according to census information. Indeed, not only did income

FIGURE 8.3 Dominant mother tongue and significant minority mother tongues for provinces and territories, 1991

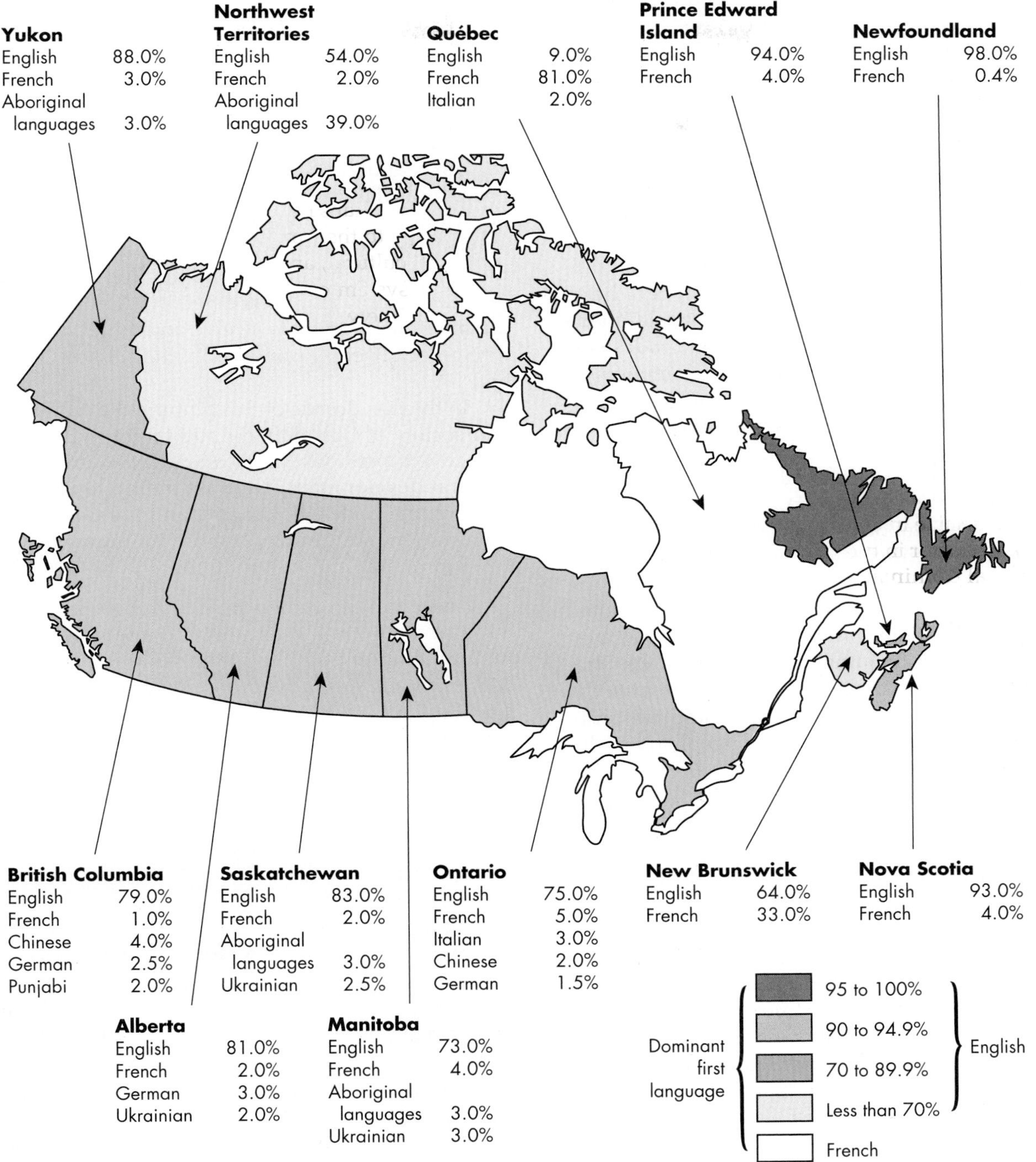

Source: *Statistics Canada,* 1991 Census of Canada, Mother Tongue: The Nation, *Catalogue No. 93-313, Table 1.*

disparities between Quebec's anglophones and francophones decline during the 1970s, but by 1980 it was more profitable in terms of income for anglophones to learn French than for francophones to learn English (Grenier, 1987: 790).

One element of this change was the out-migration of many anglophones, especially unilingual people uncertain about their future in an increasingly French Quebec. Their departure in turn heightened a trend towards polarization in Canada. With French dominant in Quebec and English in the rest of Canada, with the English minority declining in Quebec and French culture fading in other provinces, many observers have identified a social reality not of a bilingual Canada but of a Canada of two unilingual solitudes (see Lachapelle and Henripin, 1982). French immersion has been a very successful educational movement in Canada, but it has not stemmed the tide of assimilation of French as a living language and culture outside Quebec. Waddell (1986: 108) suggested that "within English Canada, French appears to be essentially a symbolic language that mingles class and national sentiments, or a souvenir of distant Quebec or Acadian origins." He argued that the federal government has adopted an institutional approach to language rights and services based on the concept of individual rights, while Quebec has endorsed a territorial principle based upon the notion of collective rights and ethnic community survival. Thus, the vision of a bilingual and multicultural Canada is in conflict with that of a francophone Quebec in a bicultural Canada.

Constitutional and political developments have accelerated the trend towards two solitudes. The 1982 Canadian Constitution was not ratified by Quebec partly because of the absence of a provision recognizing that province as a "distinct society." The failure of the federal and provincial governments in 1990 to approve the Meech Lake Accord, which contained such a clause, followed by the "No" vote in the 1992 national referendum on the Constitution, has led to a reassessment of their relationship with Canada by many Québécois. The 1993 election of the separatist Bloc Québécois as the Official Opposition federally, and the 1995 referendum which took Quebec to the brink of a victory for separation and sovereignty, illustrate that the relationship between the two majority groups in Canadian society has arrived at a critical turning-point.

The "other ethnic groups": the shaping of the Canadian mosaic

It is inaccurate to think of Canadian society as nothing but two unified ethnic blocs in confrontation, complex as the implications of such an image may be. Along with the Native presence, a history of massive immigration has created a much more complex pluralism in Canada, one marked by a high degree of ethnic and class diversity. According to official figures, roughly twelve and a half million foreign-born people came to Canada between 1851 and 1991.

In the first decade of this century, the economy and society of Canada were still largely agrarian, and government policy was oriented towards agricultural development. The vast prairie lands had yet to come under the plough, and the Canadian government sought to promote immigration to

The relationship between the two majority groups in Canadian society has arrived at a critical turning-point, as witnessed by the 1995 referendum.

"settle the empty west with producing farmers," in the words of Clifford Sifton, then Minister of the Interior and architect of Canada's immigration policy in the early twentieth century (Royal Commission on Bilingualism and Biculturalism, 1969: 22). Government sponsorship of recruitment and transportation for immigrant peasants and farmers from Europe and the United States, and the availability of free land, combined to double the foreign-born population of the prairies from 1901 to 1911. The majority of immigrants in those years, as in earlier decades, came from Great Britain and the United States. While many of the British immigrants, like the Irish settlers of the nineteenth century, gravitated towards the industrial cities, large numbers of the Americans, among them people of German, Polish, Danish, and various other ethnic backgrounds, joined the stream of new farmers to the prairies. At the same time, the first heavy wave of immigrants came from central and eastern Europe; among those were Ukrainians, Poles, Hungarians, and Russians.

Early twentieth-century rural ethnic settlements in Manitoba, Saskatchewan, and Alberta frequently took the form of isolated and homogeneous communities, described by Dawson in a classic study called *Group Settlement: Ethnic Communities in Western Canada* (1936). The bloc settlements of such groups as Doukhobors, Mennonites, German Catholics, Mormons, and French Canadians constituted "culture islands," each occupying a territorial base set off from surrounding populations by distinctive language, institutions, and religious or national identity. They were relatively successful as settlers because of their group settlement patterns and the cooperative nature of their social organization, which differed from the myth of the individualistic pioneer homesteader.

The era of the farmer-immigrant was a relatively brief one in Canada's history, for the predominant pattern of immigrant settlement has long been urban. As early as 1921, the first year for which data are available, 56 percent of Canada's foreign-born were living in urban areas, compared with only 48 percent of the Canadian-born. The transformation of Canada from an agrarian to an urban industrial society was already well under way at that time, and opportunities for industrial employment in the growing cities attracted both farm-reared Canadians and immigrants.

An era of accelerated urbanization and a second peak period of immigration followed World War II. Before the war, about 54 percent of Canada's total population and 60 percent of its foreign-born were urban dwellers, but by 1971 the proportions had reached 76 percent of all Canadians and 88 percent of immigrants (Kalbach, 1978: 99). Cityward migration of Canadians, as well as immigration, contributed to the growing ethnic diversity of the cities during the postwar years.

The heavy influx of new immigrants during the years since 1945 has also contributed to urban ethnic diversity, since the vast majority of these immigrants have settled in the seven largest metropolitan areas of Canada. For example, in 1991, 38 percent of the population of Metropolitan Toronto and 30 percent of Vancouver residents were born outside Canada. Immigrants tend to gravitate towards destinations that offer economic opportunity. In an urban industrial society, job opportunities are most plentiful in the largest cities, and the effects of chain migration are also seen in the congregation of immigrants there. By 1991, 57 percent of all immigrants to Canada were living in Toronto, Montreal, and Vancouver, compared with 26 percent of the Canadian-born population, according to the census (Statistics Canada, 1993, *1991 Census of Canada, Immigration and Citizenship: The Nation*, Catalogue No. 93-316, Table 5). Take another look at Figure 8.2, which shows immigrants as a percentage of selected city populations as of 1991.

Since World War II, the predominance of British immigrants has given way to a broader mix of peoples. While the United Kingdom and the United States have continued to contribute large numbers of immigrants, Chinese, Indians, Italians, Dutch, Vietnamese, Poles, Portuguese, and people from the Caribbean, the Philippines, and the African and South American continents have joined them (see Figure 8.4). Over 300 000 people have come to Canada as refugees since World War II, having been displaced by revolutions and political oppression in their homelands. In the 1980s, on average, slightly less than one-fifth of immigrants claimed refugee status (Badets, 1989). With the refocusing of immigration policy in the 1970s to emphasize occupational skills, educational qualifications, demands of the economy, family reunification, and refugee criteria instead of

FIGURE 8.4 Immigrants from selected places of birth, as percentage of total foreign-born, Canada, 1991

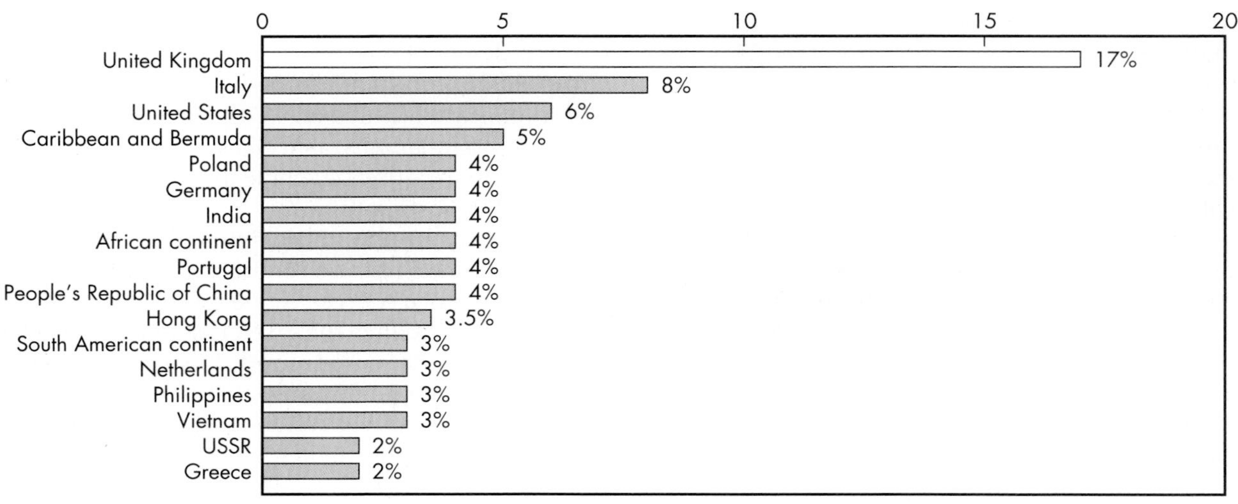

Source: *Statistics Canada,* 1991 Census of Canada, Immigration and Citizenship: The Nation. *Catalogue No. 93-316, Table 2.*

national origin, the immigrant population has become increasingly heterogeneous and representative of Third World countries. Before 1978, immigrants originating in Europe made up 70 percent of newcomers to Canada, but since that time Europeans have made up less than 30 percent of immigrants, while people born in Asia have constituted 40 percent of immigrants since 1978 (Badets, 1989).

PERSPECTIVES ON CANADIAN RACE AND ETHNIC RELATIONS

We now turn our attention to three dominant perspectives on inter-group relations within a pluralistic society—assimilationism, two-category perspectives, and pluralism. Each perspective functions in two ways at the same time. First, each describes a social reality, and second, each contains suggestions about the future of ethnic and race relations, and as a result, has implications for social policy.

Assimilationism

The interpretation of ethnic group relations that dominated North American thought for at least the first half of the twentieth century was **assimilationism**—the view that ethnic diversity gradually and inevitably declines as ethnic group members are integrated or absorbed into the general population of the society. Ethnic groups are viewed as transitory rather than central and enduring features of modern society. This is partly because of the assumed irrelevance of ethnic diversity to the political, social, and economic life of modern industrial society, which is viewed as rational, achievement-oriented, bureaucratically organized, and international in scope. Attachments of sentiment, ascription, kinship, community, and shared culture, which are fundamental to ethnic identity, are seen as survivals of an earlier stage of societal development and out of place in the modern age. This view of ethnicity is usually held by functionalists, but it could be argued that most of the great sociological theorists, from Marx to Weber to Durkheim, have reflected such a perception.

Assimilation is the process of becoming part of the larger surrounding society and culture by becoming more and more like the dominant group, so that in time Polish Canadians, for example, would be indistinguishable from the British or French Canadians with whom they live. As a group they are unique only while they are relatively recent arrivals. In time they will improve their social and economic position and disappear into the great melting-pot, in which various ethnic groups and cultures blend into a single culture and society.

The melting-pot image has been a prominent feature of national identity in the United States, but assimilationism as a description and social ideal has also had its adherents in Canada (e.g., Porter, 1980). Assimilationist assumptions were reflected in official policy towards immigrants and ethnic groups before World War II. The preference for British immigrants and the existence of severe restrictions on the immigration of racially and culturally different peoples have already been mentioned. These restrictions were based, in part, on the assumption that those peoples who are most similar to the dominant Canadian population—the British—would most readily adapt to life in Canada, cause fewest problems for the dominant group, and ultimately assimilate.

Assimilation is the process of becoming part of the larger surrounding society and culture by becoming more and more like the dominant group.

The sociological theory of assimilationism is rooted to a large degree in the work of Robert Park (1950; 1952), one of North America's first and most important sociologists, and leader of the Chicago school of urban sociology between 1915 and 1940. As we saw in Chapter 1, What Is Sociology?, Park's theories became influential in Canada through the work of Charles Dawson, a scholar and teacher in the field of Canadian ethnic group relations, who was Park's student at the University of Chicago and later founder of the first Canadian department of sociology at McGill University.

Park viewed the modern world as a melting-pot, a total system characterized by large-scale geographic and social mobility that tended to break down the isolation of local cultures, causing cultural and social patterns in the global society to become uniform and homogeneous. Park considered the breakdown of small-scale, provincial societies and cultures, with their ascribed class and status distinctions, to be a positive development. He felt it would help to liberate individuals by making status dependent upon achieved rather than ascribed criteria. (Many of Park's contemporaries, on the other hand, interpreted these same developments as signs of a decline of community and a growth of alienation in society.)

Park developed the notion of a **race relations cycle** to describe four successive stages in the relationships between dominant and minority groups in any society. These stages are contact, competition, accommodation, and assimilation. Through exploration, migration, or conquest, groups come into *contact*, beginning a process of communication that breaks down the isolation of each. If these groups begin to draw from a common pool of limited resources, *competition* ensues between them. The competitive stage may eventually be resolved through the *accommodation* of the weaker group, which adopts the language and culture of the more powerful. In time, if the distinctive external signs that differentiated one group from another are erased, *assimilation* is complete. The peoples intermingle and the offspring of inter-group unions belong fully to neither group. Ultimately, the ethnic group member becomes "a mere individual, indistinguishable in the cosmopolitan mass of the population..." (Park, 1950: 208–209).

There would, however, be instances of intergroup contact in which the race relations cycle would not run full course, for Park believed that distinctions among peoples may be maintained when ethnic or racial characteristics are highly visible. He considered physical traits such as colour to be the chief obstacles to the universal assimilation he envisioned, for these external marks cannot be changed, and constitute lightning-rods for animosities and prejudice. Their presence perpetuates an endless vicious circle of majority prejudice, and minority withdrawal and defensiveness.

Other sociologists after Park contributed substantially to assimilationist theory, among them Gordon (1964), who noted that the concept of assimilation must be broken down to reflect the many-sided nature of individual and group life. It is especially important to distinguish between cultural assimilation, or **acculturation**, and **structural assimilation**. Gordon argued that individuals may acculturate quite readily—that is, they may learn the language, values, and customs of the dominant group and make them their own. But this does not mean that they will be assimilated into the social structure—that is, accepted into intimate or primary social relationships with the dominant group. The majority group may still hold back from entering into friendship, marriage, or neighbour relationships with the minority. Thus, even though a group may acculturate, it may never succeed in assimilating into the social structure of the larger society.

Assimilationist thinkers generally hold liberal, individualistic values, and assume that it is only through individual achievement that upward mobility in the social hierarchy can occur. They further assume, as in Park's thought, that maintaining one's ethnic culture and languages will hinder upward mobility because it reduces acceptance of the ethnic group member by the majority group. Thus, ethnic group members must accept a trade-off: giving up their ethnicity in return for social acceptance, improved status, and a good standard of living.

The notion that the assimilationist perspective provides a useful interpretation of the realities of ethnic group relations is not as widely held in Canada, where the image of the mosaic has long been a national symbol of its ethnic diversity. As discussed previously, patterns of ethnic and especially racial inequality remain entrenched both for men and for women, even when level of education is controlled. The Canadian mosaic continues to be a vertical one.

As a social goal and guide to policy, assimilationism has also been subjected to damaging criticism. The assimilationist perspective suggests that, if the goal is equality of opportunity for all, then public institutions must be universalistic rather than particularistic. That is, institutions must apply the same set of rules to every individual in the same way, "regardless of race, religion, or national origin." Groups, then, are officially ignored, and only the claims of individuals are recognized by assimilationist theorists. It is assumed that, in order to be equal, people must all be alike, and that equality means treating everyone alike, regardless of their differences.

It had become apparent by the 1960s that the condition of blacks and Native peoples as groups was not improving through the process of social mobility whereby individuals play by the universalistic rules of the game. The goal of bringing these groups into the mainstream of American and Canadian societies has seemed farther and farther away as census data chart the continuing gap between the incomes and unemployment rates of blacks and Natives, on the one hand, and the rest of the population on the other. The historical legacy of slavery, colonialism, discrimination, and cultural destruction weighs heavily upon present generations.

Many thoughtful observers in academic and public life concluded that extraordinary measures have to be taken to overcome the barriers to assimilation and integration that result from long-standing patterns of discrimination and disadvantage. The application of universalistic rules and standards is resulting in what we earlier called systemic or institutionalized discrimination. Inequality is built into the occupational structure, and many minority group members are not even getting to the starting-gate in the race for advancement. The rules of the game are not fair to all, since they were established by the majority and serve to maintain their position of privilege. It follows that the rules must be changed in order to remove those barriers that have excluded minorities from access to jobs, promotions, and career advancement.

Employment equity is a broad strategy for change in the policies, practices, and culture of the workplace (Agócs, Burr, and Somerset, 1992). Its objectives are to increase the representation of disadvantaged groups at all levels of the occupational structure, to remove barriers to their career advancement, and to create a workplace culture free of discrimination. In Canada at the present time, the designated employment equity groups are Native peoples, visible minorities, women, and people with disabilities. Under the 1986 federal Employment Equity Act (as revised in December 1995), employers in the federal jurisdiction, and the federal public service, are required to implement employment equity programs and to report annually on their results. The Federal Contractors Program requires employers who sell goods and services to the federal government to implement employment equity requirements as well.

Employment equity requirements and enforcement from 1987 until 1995 were weak, and their impact on the representation of racial minorities and aboriginal people in employment was small (e.g., Leck and Saunders, 1996; Jain et al., 1997). However, there is reason to hope for greater progress under the strengthened federal requirements.

Two-category perspectives

Scholars who theorize a two-category system of race relations in North America have argued that the assimilationist perspective describes whites only. Blacks and Native peoples are in a separate category; they have not been part of the melting-pot because of the persistence of racism in society, which has its roots in the historical experiences of slavery and colonialism. They are viewed as minority groups who continue to occupy a disadvantaged position in a society dominated by whites, who constitute a single homogeneous social category. Rioux (1978b) has argued that the Québécois are also a minority group in this sense, one whose destiny is unique because of its historical position as a people conquered, colonized, and dominated by the British.

Two-category perspectives on race relations are pluralistic in the sense that they view society not as a single body, but as two separate collectivities in conflict. These two distinct social categories are hierarchically ranked, and bound together in a relationship of dominance and subordination within a single society and culture.

Examining several nineteenth- and twentieth-century societies in which the institutions of slavery and colonialism were integral parts of the development of modern capitalism, Van den Berghe (1967) developed a two-category theory of relationships between the races. According to him, liberal democratic societies such as the United States faced the dilemma of reconciling their ideals of liberty and equality with their oppression of black slaves and their extermination of Native peoples. Van den Berghe reasoned that this reconciliation was accomplished ideologically by dividing humanity into two categories: "the civilized" (the human beings) and the "savages" (the inferior beings whose humanity was denied). The application of egalitarian and democratic ideas was restricted to those defined as "the civilized," that is, the dominant white group. The result in countries such as the United States and South Africa is what Van den Berghe called a "Herrenvolk democracy"—a system that was "democratic for the master race but tyrannical for the subordinate groups" (Van den Berghe, 1967: 18).

Could such a harsh image apply in any way to Canadian reality? Although slavery did not become entrenched in Canada, it did thrive until the passage of the Emancipation Act by the British Parliament in 1833. Blacks have been subject to discrimination not only under Canadian immigration law, but also in employment, public accommodations, housing, and education. Segregated black schools existed in Ontario and Nova Scotia until the mid-1960s (Krauter and Davis, 1978: 50). However, an all-encompassing system of *de jure* racial segregation like that of the southern United States never became established in Canada. The image of a distinct, racially defined social category standing in a relationship of legalized subordination to whites apparently does not apply to blacks in Canada in the same way that it did in the United States.

However, Canada is not without its own race-relations dilemma. The reserve system has long been the principal instrument of Canadian policy towards the First Nations. It is a policy that has treated the various Indian peoples as a single social category with "special status" under the law, excluded from the larger society yet dependent upon that society, and hence subordinate to it. While keeping Indians socially, politically, and economically separate and subordinate, the reserve system and the Indian Act have been instruments of acculturation to the religions, languages, values, and traditions of the larger society, and of the destruction of First Nations' cultures and social structures.

The First Nations are not merely one of the many racial and ethnic groups in the Canadian mosaic. Because of their aboriginal rights, and because of the history of colonialism to which Native peoples have uniquely been subjected, they are fundamentally different from other groups, and require recognition as autonomous peoples equal in status to the English and French. As such, the First Nations are entitled to control over their ancestral lands, self-determination, and the right to deal collectively with the government of Canada—a right implied in the government's traditional practice of making treaty agreements with aboriginal peoples as nations. Many bands and Native organizations such as the Assembly of First Nations (representing Indians), the Native Council of Canada (representing Métis and non-status Indians), and the Inuit Tapirisat have been negotiating for many years with the government of Canada and initiating court actions in attempts to gain self-government and ownership of lands traditionally occupied and used by aboriginal peoples, and never ceded under treaties. In pressing their claims, the First Nations are attempting to ensure the survival of their peoples and cultures as distinct entities, and to improve their standard of living and access to opportunity for succeeding generations.

This perspective challenges the assimilationist assumption, explicit in federal policy since Confederation, that First Nations should be absorbed into the larger society. The need to implement an alternative to the reserve system, and the movement towards self-government by aboriginal peoples, present a major policy dilemma for Canada's pluralistic society.

Pluralism

During this generation, the worldwide rise of nationalistic movements has shaken loose historic accommodations between dominant and subordinate ethnic and racial groups, not only in Canada and the United States, but also in many parts of Africa, Europe, Asia, and even the former Soviet Union. Ethnic and aboriginal communities across Canada have sought public recognition of their distinctive aspirations and ways of life, and racial minorities have demanded an end to discrimination.

Ethnic and racial diversity are very much a part of our contemporary society, and "assimilation" seems as far away as it ever has. From Québécois, First Nations, Jews, Chinese, Haitians, and many other groups come the questions: Can't we all enjoy equal opportunities as members of one society while maintaining our differences, our identities, and our communities? Can we not coexist as equals within a single society, even though we do not all look the same, or share the same values and culture?

Pluralism, the view that ethnic diversity and conflict remain a central feature of contemporary societies, and that ethnicity continues to be an important aspect of individual identity and group behaviour, has been widely accepted in the post-World War II era. The image of the ethnic mosaic has become integral to Canadian national identity, and a feature said to distinguish Canadian from American values and culture. It is generally understood today that "Canadian culture" itself is not a homogeneous whole, but an intricate tapestry of many hues woven from the strands of many ethnic and regional subcultures.

Since Canada is a pluralistic society, both assimilation and ethnic and racial differentiation are going on at the same time. While in some respects Canada's ethnic groups become more alike as time passes, in many ways their influence brings an increasing diversity to the cultural, social, and political life shared by all Canadians. For example, immigrants, by becoming citizens and voting, may show signs of assimilation. Yet in local elections they may support candidates who represent their own ethnic group's interests, thus bringing diversity to the political spectrum.

In fact, many pluralists contend that ethnic group members make progress and improve their positions in the social hierarchy not by individual achievement and dissociation from their roots, as assimilationists would argue, but by group efforts, using ethnic solidarity as a resource. It is collective action that benefits the group, and thereby its individual members. When members of an ethnic community vote in a bloc, they force the political system to recognize and respond to their concerns. When relatives pool their resources to start a business, they not only provide jobs for their kin, but also contribute to the economic life of their community. When members of the community patronize ethnic businesses, they strengthen the community's overall business climate. When successful ethnic businesspeople are able to assist their children to attend university, they help to provide the community's next generation of leaders. In all of these examples it is the collective action of the community, rather than the efforts of isolated individuals to achieve upward mobility, that brings progress to members of the group.

Pluralism is the view that ethnic diversity remains a central feature of modern urban society, and that ethnicity is an important aspect of individual identity and group behaviour.

A study of Iranians in Montreal suggests that different members of the same ethnic group adopt varied strategies in integrating into Canadian society. In the study, those immigrants who chose a strategy of ethnic cultural maintenance were more likely to belong to Iranian organizations and to endorse collective means of getting ahead. Those who agreed with an assimilationist strategy tended not to belong to Iranian organizations and to have an individualistic view of mobility. Both groups had a high level of confidence in their ability to do well in Canada (Moghaddam, Taylor, and Lalonde, 1987). Many studies (e.g., Breton et al., 1990) have provided evidence that ethnic groups, as well as individuals, adopt a variety of different approaches as they integrate into Canadian society and improve their socio-economic position, while retaining varying degrees of ethnic identity and community solidarity.

The increasing heterogeneity of Canada's population, the growing numerical strength and voting power of ethnic groups, and the acceptance of a collectivist strategy have coincided with a shift away from the official image of Canada as a bicultural country towards a recognition of it as multicultural. In 1971, Prime Minister Trudeau, with the support of all political parties, announced a policy of "multiculturalism within a bilingual framework," under which federal recognition and support would be extended to the various ethnic groups that constitute the Canadian mosaic (Government of Canada, 1971). The Multiculturalism Act of 1988 affirms the government's commitment to the preservation and appreciation of cultural diversity, and to the promotion of the full and equal participation of individuals and communities in all aspects of Canadian society (Fleras and Elliott, 1992). However, critics (e.g., Li, 1988) have noted a lack of results and questioned the government's real commitment to these principles.

The institutions of Canadian society have begun to grapple with the fact that ethnicity is not just an individual trait, but a fundamental characteristic of the social system as a whole. Canadians now face the challenge and opportunity of learning to live in harmony and mutual respect in a society in which ethnic and racial diversity will continue to grow.

SUMMARY

Canada is a pluralistic society, a social system composed of ethnic groups that coexist in both peace and conflict within a common cultural, economic, and political framework, while maintaining cultures and social institutions that are to some extent distinctive. Canada has been called a vertical mosaic in recognition of the fact that racial and ethnic groups occupy different ranks within its stratification system.

A major form of ethnic group life in Canada, the local immigrant community, often develops through a process of chain migration, the sequential movement of people from a common place of origin to a common destination, with the assistance of relatives or compatriots who settled there earlier. In the ethnic community the newcomers find a familiar social network and an array of institutions to meet their needs. As the community grows, it establishes a place for itself within the local economic structure. Economic interests combine with cultural and social patterns to shape the community's distinctive adaptation to the new environment.

As a concept, ethnicity has several dimensions. Ethnicity is an ascribed status, a potential conferred upon individuals at birth, which becomes a part of personal identity during socialization within an ethnic community. The ethnic group is self-perpetuating and has boundaries that are set and maintained by patterns of interaction rather than by formal structures, cultural traits, or isolation. The ethnic group is also a subculture, the product of shared historical experiences that shape present understandings about values important to the group.

While members of a social group share values, interests, and patterns of interaction, a social category such as a race is a collection of individuals who share certain physical features that are charged with social meaning. Racist ideologies have rationalized the exploitation of certain categories of human beings because of inherited characteristics.

Minority groups are categories of people that are oppressed and relegated to subordinate ranks in the social hierarchy, regardless of their numbers. Various forms of social control, including annihilation, expulsion, discrimination, and segregation, have perpetuated the oppression and subordination of minority groups in modern societies.

Canadian race and ethnic relations have been shaped by the historical processes of colonialism, conquest, and migration. Colonized groups such as aboriginal peoples become part of a plural society involuntarily, often suffer long-standing and severe discrimination and disadvantage, and remain economically and politically marginal to that society. The reserve system has been the cornerstone of Canada's Indian policy, although increasing numbers of Indians are migrating to cities, where they generally experience many of the deprivations that drove them from reserve communities.

The conquest of the French by the British shaped the subsequent relationship between Canada's two founding peoples. Legal guarantees at the federal level provide for the perpetuation of the language, religion, and culture of French Canadians, and the concentration of the French within Quebec provides a powerful territorial and institutional base in the struggle of the French to perpetuate their culture. But, for a variety of reasons, the French language and culture have eroded in the rest of Canada, where English cultural dominance has accompanied the economic dominance of what was once British North America.

Immigrant groups enter a society voluntarily, although they may have been driven from their homelands by economic want or political oppression. The British and Americans have long been Canada's dominant immigrant groups, but in the post-World War II era immigrant origins have been diverse, with increasing representation of Third World peoples. In recognition of the reality of ethnic diversity, the federal government in 1971 announced a policy of "multiculturalism within a bilingual framework."

Interpretations of ethnic and race relations encompass both the task of describing social reality and the need to formulate social goals or visions of what Canadian society should be like. Assimilationism is the view that diversity declines as ethnic group members achieve economic prosperity and are absorbed into the general population and culture of the society. This view of society as a melting-pot has proven to be an inaccurate description of social reality and a doubtful guide to social policy. Two-category perspectives, applied to North America, attempt to understand the experiences of white and racial minority peoples in very different terms. Whites are seen as constituting a single social category, one into which white ethnic groups are generally assimilated. Because of the historical experiences of slavery and colonialism, and/or a legacy of racism, two-category perspective holds that racial minorities are socially defined as a separate category, whose members generally occupy a subordinate status in society and therefore remain unassimilated. Pluralism, the perspective that recognizes the central place of ethnic diversity and conflict in modern societies, has long typified Canadian thought on ethnic relations, and is expressed in the policy of multiculturalism. But inequality remains a central feature of most pluralistic societies today, including Canada, and racism and ethnic conflict continue to pose dilemmas for Canada and the modern world.

QUESTIONS FOR REVIEW AND CRITICAL THINKING

1. Compare and contrast the historical experiences of twentieth-century European immigrants to Canada with those coming today. What does this suggest concerning their positions in twenty-first-century Canada?

2. Describe the historical process of growth and development of a local ethnic community with which you are familiar. Examine the degree to which ethnicity continues to influence the attitudes and behaviours of members of this group. Compare your observations with those of students who have studied other groups.

3. Are Canadian blacks an ethnic group? Your discussion should include a thoughtful analysis of what an ethnic group is.

4. Examine the migration, marriage, and occupational patterns in the history of your family by charting your genealogy and then listing the occupations, geographic movements, and marriages of as many family members as possible. In an essay, summarize any patterns you observe, applying concepts used in this chapter such as chain migration, occupational specialization, ethnic network, discrimination, ethnic stratification, occupational mobility, and ethnic endogamy.

GLOSSARY

acculturation the learning of the language, values, and customs of a dominant group by an ethnic group; also called *cultural assimilation*

assimilationism the view that ethnic diversity gradually and inevitably declines as group members are absorbed into the general population, in the process becoming more and more like the dominant group

chain migration sequential movement of persons from a common place of origin to a common destination with the assistance of relatives or acquaintances already settled in the new location

colonialism the domination by a settler society of a native or indigenous population. The colonizing society extracts resources from the conquered land, establishes settlements there, and administers the indigenous population, frequently employing violence and a racist ideology. In time, the colonized population suffers the erosion of its traditional culture, economy, and way of life, and usually occupies a subordinate status in the pluralist society of which it has involuntarily become a part.

discrimination the denial of opportunities, generally available to all members of society, to some people because of their membership in a social category

ethnic group a people—a collectivity of persons who share an ascribed status based upon culture, religion, national origin, or shared historical experience founded upon a common ethnicity or race

institutional completeness the development of a full set of institutions in an ethnic community that parallels those in the larger society

marginality the state of having within the self two conflicting social identities; also, the social condition of a minority group that lives on the edge of a society, not treated as a full member of that society

minority group a social category, usually ethnically or racially labelled, that occupies a subordinate rank in the hierarchy of a society

pluralism the view that ethnic diversity, stratification, and conflict remain central features of modern societies, and that race and ethnicity continue to be important aspects of individual identity and group behaviour

pluralistic society a social system of coexisting and usually hierarchically ranked racial and ethnic groups, each of which to some degree maintains its own distinctive culture, social networks, and institutions, while participating with other racial and ethnic groups in common cultural, economic, and political institutions

prejudice prejudging people based upon characteristics they are assumed to share as members of a social category

race an arbitrary social category in which membership is based upon inherited physical characteristics such as skin colour and facial features, characteristics defined as socially meaningful

race relations cycle the four stages, posited by Park, in the relationship between dominant and minority groups. The cycle involves contact, competition, accommodation, and finally assimilation.

racism an ideology that regards racial or ethnic categories as natural genetic groupings, and that attributes behavioural and psychological differences to the genetic nature of these groupings

segregation the maintenance of physical distance between ethnic or racial groups. Sometimes this term is used to describe the exclusion of minorities from the facilities, institutions, or residential space used by dominant groups, as in South Africa's system of apartheid. At other times, it refers to the residential separation among ethnic or racial populations that may occur for a variety of reasons.

social category a collection of individuals who share a particular trait that is defined as socially meaningful, but who do not necessarily interact or have anything else in common

stereotypes mental images that exaggerate traits believed to be typical of members of a social group

structural assimilation acceptance of a minority group by a dominant group into its intimate, primary, social relationships

systemic or **institutionalized discrimination** discrimination against members of a group that occurs as a by-product of the ordinary functioning of bureaucratic institutions, rather than as a consequence of a deliberate policy to discriminate

two-category perspectives the view of race relations that sees two hierarchically ranked, separate collectivities in conflict, bound together in a relationship of dominance and subordination within a single society and culture

vertical mosaic the hierarchical ranking of ethnic populations in a society

SUGGESTED READINGS

Das Gupta, Tania

1996 *Racism and Paid Work.* Toronto: Garamond Press.

This Marxist analysis examines racial and gender inequality, and the dynamics of racism and sexism, in the paid workplace in Canada, with a focus on the health care and garment manufacturing sectors.

Frideres, James S., with Lilianne Krosenbrink-Gelissen

1993 *Native People in Canada.* (4th ed.) Scarborough, Ont.: Prentice Hall Canada.

A thorough look at this sensitive and important topic, it includes an examination of Native history, treaties, and land claims along with discussions of their political economy and moves towards self-determination.

Henry, Frances, and Carol Tator

1994 *Democratic Racism: Racial Inequality in Canadian Society.* Toronto: Harcourt Brace.

The authors, social scientists and long-time activists for racial equality, examine the dynamics and impacts of racism in Canadian society today.

Purich, Donald

1996 *The Inuit and Their Land: The Story of Nunavut.* Toronto: James Lorimer.

Purich, a former director of the Native Law Centre at the University of Saskatchewan, examines the social, economic, and political history of Nunavut and the Inuit struggle for self-government.

WEB SITES

http://infoservice.gc.ca:82/canadiana/faitc/fa26.html

Multiculturalism in Canada

This page, compiled by the federal government, provides useful and detailed information on multiculturalism and multicultural policy in Canada.

http://www.uarr.org

Urban Alliance on Race Relations

This site, maintained by the members of the UARR, provides information on issues and events related to racism in Canada, as well as a range of internet based resources on this topic.

PART IV

Social Institutions

Social institutions are structures organized around the performance of central activities in society. They include the beliefs, values, and norms concerning the manner in which a society's needs should be met and the groups that serve these needs. Important activities such as marriage, reproduction, and childrearing, for example, are generally conducted within families. The teaching of skills and values to the young occurs, among other places, in the schools. The acquisition of a particular sense of the meaning of life can take place within religious institutions. Finally, the administration and coordination of power and authority are found in political institutions. This next section examines these social institutions.

We introduced social differentiation by saying it was both a cause and an effect of social phenomena. The same could be said about social institutions. As causes, institutions can influence culture, norms, values, and roles. Certain institutions, especially families, religion, and education, socialize individuals to acquire culture. Institutions also define what is and what is not deviant, and affect both an individual's chances of engaging in deviance and the reactions, if any, to that deviance. Religious and political institutions may provide a basis for social movements.

In turn, institutions are affected by cultural variations and by social differentiation. For example, stratification rank and race or ethnicity affect the type of family life individuals experience, and their education, religion, and politics. Finally, institutions affect one another, as when family and religious values affect educational values, or when education and religion affect political behaviour. Thus, there is extensive interdependence among the various institutions and important links between institutions, culture, and socialization. All contribute to the structure of social life, which impinges on individuals and affects their behaviour.

Because the concept of institution entails the ideas of serving social needs, or getting the tasks of society accomplished, institutions are often portrayed as structures built upon consensus and agreement among their members. Yet, there is also conflict between and within each of these institutions, as when religion clashes with secular education, or when government agencies intervene in what some see as family decisions. As you have done elsewhere in the book, keep in mind alternative explanations when you read a functionalist, conflict, symbolic interactionist, feminist, or other explanation. Ask yourself what a sociologist with a differing perspective might say.

DDS

CHAPTER

9

Families

Roderic Beaujot

INTRODUCTION

It is already evident from the previous chapters that the study of families is an important part of the study of society. The chapter on culture introduced examples from the sociology of families: definitions of "mother," an explanation of sexual jealousy, and the appearance of incest taboos in almost all societies. It was also pointed out in Chapter 4, Socialization, that much of socialization takes place in families.

Two further points underscore the place of families in the study of society. First, families are the social arena in which most people spend most of their lives. Thus, if we want to find out how people live and how their lives are organized, it is important to know something about what happens in their families. Second, as one of the institutions of society, families affect and are affected by other social institutions. For example, an economy based on a high degree of job mobility requires the geographic mobility of families, and it may also require that individual families be more self-sufficient and less dependent on kin or relatives left behind. Thus, the economy can affect families. In turn, the actions of families can affect economic institutions. For instance, when people decide to have fewer children, consequences are soon felt in the industries that supply baby products. Much later, there will be repercussions in the housing market (less demand for housing) and on the growth of the labour force (fewer workers).

While the study of families is important for an understanding of society, at least two factors make this study difficult. First, virtually all of us have lived in families, and we are frequently too willing to make generalizations about families based on our own limited personal experience, making it difficult to take an objective look at actual family behaviour. The second difficulty is that family behaviour is generally considered private. Consequently, as researchers we are often barred from studying families in their natural settings. When we can observe them, much of normal family behaviour may be camouflaged—consciously or unconsciously altered by family members—making it hard to reach proper conclusions.

We shall begin the chapter with definitions of marriage and related family terms and then highlight some of the differences and uniformities in family patterns across societies. This will remind us of some of the variations in family behaviour and of the necessity of viewing families against the background of the larger society. In the theory section we shall concentrate on the functionalist and conflict perspectives in an attempt to understand long-term family changes. We shall consider both the changing role of families in society and the changing importance of families in individuals' lives. Since so much of family behaviour is influenced by the roles that men and women have in society, a section on gender roles follows. We shall then trace the life cycle of families, including socialization for marriage, childbearing and childrearing, and marital breakdown. We examine the latter in light of the changing role of families in society. The final section considers the general question of change and continuity in family patterns in the recent past and immediate future.

DEFINITIONS OF MARRIAGE AND FAMILY

Marriage can be defined as a commitment and an ongoing exchange. In noting that marriage includes a *commitment*, we mean that it involves a more or less explicit contract that spells out the rights and obligations between partners. The commitment can be defined at either the personal or social level. At the personal level, it means that marriage is undertaken with considerable seriousness. At the social level, it is a type of social contract, meaning that certain customs and laws govern the processes of entering into or leaving a marriage. Even the dissolution of cohabitation now involves laws concerning children and property.

In noting that marriage includes *ongoing exchanges*, we wish to stress that it involves a continuing interdependence between spouses. It is useful to distinguish two types of exchange, the expressive and the instrumental, terms we saw in Chapter 6, Gender Relations. The **expressive exchanges**, or emotional dimension of marriage, include love, sexual gratification, companionship, and empathy. The **instrumental exchanges**, or task-oriented dimension, include earning a living, spending money, and maintaining a household. In virtually all marriages, expressive and instrumental exchanges take place (Scanzoni and Scanzoni, 1988). However, in some circumstances the economic dimension may be more important (a farming couple who act as an economic unit), while in others the expressive level may be foremost (a childless working couple whose marriage involves mostly companionship).

Marriages do not just happen; they have to be maintained as ongoing exchanges. In the process, one partner may provide more of some things (e.g., income), while the other partner provides more of others (e.g., empathy). Such sharing will continue if the partners see some level of equity in the exchanges, so that each finds marriage to be rewarding. If such complementarity is not perceived, then the exchange, and in fact the marriage, may break down.

A **family** can be defined as two or more people related by blood, adoption, or marriage (legally sanctioned or otherwise), and who reside together. There are two crucial aspects to this definition of a family: the persons must be related in some way and they must customarily maintain a common residence. If they are not related, they form a household and not a family. If they are related but not living together, they are kin and not a family as defined here. Kin may live in close proximity, and there may be considerable social and economic integration among them, but they are not considered a family unless they live in the same dwelling.

VARIABILITY IN FAMILY PATTERNS

As indicated in Chart 9.1, there are considerable differences across societies in matters related to marriage and family structure. To demonstrate this variability, we shall consider three aspects of the family: number of partners in the marriage, sex codes, and emphasis on a nuclear family versus a kinship network.

Number of partners in the marriage

There are four possible compositions of the marriage group: **monogamy**, **polygyny**, **polyandry**, and **group marriage**. (For definitions of these terms, see Chart 9.1.) From anthropological data gathered in various societies, however, it is clear that historically some marital arrangements have been found with greater frequency than others.

Monogamy is without question the most prevalent marital form, representing the majority of marriages in almost all societies. At the same time,

CHART 9.1 Family terms

Family and kin	
Family	Two or more people related by blood, marriage, or adoption and residing together
Nuclear family	A family that includes only spouses, and any unmarried children
Single-parent family	A family consisting of one parent and one or more children
Common-law union	A nuclear family consisting of partners who are not legally married, with or without children
Reconstituted family	A nuclear family with children from a prior union of one of the spouses
Blended family	A nuclear family that includes children from more than one marriage or union
Extended family	A family that includes more than spouses and unmarried children (e.g., grandparents, married children, other relatives) living in the same residence
Consanguine family	A family organization in which the primary emphasis is on the biological relatedness (e.g., parents and children or brothers and sisters), rather than on the spousal relationship
Kin	People related by blood or marriage
Choice of partners	
Exogamy	Partner must be chosen from outside a defined group
Endogamy	Partners must be members of the same group
Number of partners	
Monogamy	Marriage involving only two partners
Polygamy	Marriage involving more than two partners
Polygyny	One man married to two or more women; husband-sharing
Polyandry	One woman married to two or more men; wife-sharing
Group marriage	Marriage involving two or more men and two or more women
Descent	
Patrilineal	Descent traced unilaterally through the male line; the individual is related only to the father's relatives
Matrilineal	Descent traced unilaterally through the female line; the individual is related only to the mother's relatives
Bilateral	Descent that follows both the male and female lines; the individual is related to both parents' relatives
Residence	
Patrilocal	Couple takes up residence with the husband's parents
Matrilocal	Couple takes up residence with wife's parents
Neolocal	Couple resides alone
Authority and dominance	
Patriarchal	Males are the formal head and ruling power
Matriarchal	Females are the formal head and ruling power
Equalitarian	Equal dominance of males and females

75 percent of the world's societies (but not 75 percent of the world's population) appear to accept polygyny. This figure is based on a classic study by Murdock (1957), who compiled anthropological and sociological information from 565 societies—data known as the *World Ethnographic Sample*. For

example, polygyny is quite common in West Africa and is an option in most Muslim or Islamic counties. In Senegal, about a third of married men and close to half of married women are in polygynous unions. When polygyny is common, moreover, it is associated with a wide gap in the average age at marriage. It is men who are more established and consequently older who are able to marry young women. Also, most women are married rather than single, divorced, or widowed. When doing field work in Sierra Leone, I worked with a twenty-year-old man whose father had sixteen wives in his lifetime. This man was now sixty-five and married to twelve wives, but considering marriage to two other young women. In some other countries, such as in Muslim North Africa, where polygyny is permitted, it is rather rare. Turkey and Tunisia are Muslim countries that have forbidden polygyny.

Polyandry is relatively rare. A present-day example where polyandry continues but is on the decline involves the Jaunssari of the Himalayas. As in most other cases where polyandry has been observed, it is brothers who share a wife. The prospective bride has a choice to accept one man as her husband or to accept the man and his brothers. The women largely are in charge of the agricultural activities, while the men work in surrounding urban areas. The main explanation for the practice is that it prevents the land from being subdivided into parcels that would be too small for subsistence. Polyandry enables the inheritance to stay within the male line, without being fragmented among brothers.

Group marriage is similarly rare. Although no longer the case, it was for a time practised among the Nayar in Southern India. At or before puberty each girl was given a "ritual husband," but the couple's obligations to each other were mostly of a ceremonial nature, partly because the men in this society acted as mercenary warriors for neighbouring kingdoms and were often absent. After marriage, women could receive any of the men of the neighbourhood group as sexual partners. At the birth of a child, one or more of them had to acknowledge paternity and pay for the delivery of the child. If no man came forward, it was assumed that the father was either of a lower caste or a Christian man, and the woman was put to death (Gough, 1959).

Sex codes

The regulation of sexual behaviour outside of marriage also varies. In a sample of 158 societies, Murdock (1960: 265) found that premarital intercourse was permitted in 41 percent of societies, conditionally approved in 27 percent, mildly disapproved in 4 percent, and forbidden in 28 percent. Thus, the majority of societies at least tolerated premarital intercourse. An example of a particularly relaxed attitude is that of Trobriand Islanders, the users of magic discussed in Chapter 3, Culture, among whom premarital coitus was taken for granted (Malinowski, 1929). In this group, sex was seen as a natural expression of personality, and thus it was considered natural to let children begin their sexual activities at an early age with a number of partners. After puberty each person tended to form a more permanent relationship with a person of the other sex. If the association continued, the couple was expected to marry.

In general, extramarital coitus is more stringently prohibited than is premarital coitus. However, this too varies, since it was freely allowed in 3 percent of societies, conditionally permitted in 13 percent, and socially disapproved but not strictly forbidden in 3 percent (Murdock, 1960: 265). Even where it is forbidden, many people consider adultery to be acceptable as long as its existence remains a secret. Trigg and Perlman (1983) found that 70.8 percent of married Canadians, but only 51.1 percent of single Canadians, claim that extramarital sex is "always wrong." The situation that receives the most approval is one in which the person is in love with the extramarital partner.

Consanguine versus nuclear bonds

A final type of variability in family patterns that can be highlighted is that between consanguine and nuclear family bonds. A **consanguine** family is based on extended biological relatedness, while a **nuclear** family involves spouses and any unmarried children. All societies recognize both, but vary considerably in the importance they accord blood versus spousal bonds.

In tribal societies the consanguine family is generally paramount. The kinship group is often the most important group in society. Kinship may predominate in all spheres of life: groups based on kin ties are also economic units for production and consumption, political units with regard to power, and religious units with an emphasis on ancestral worship. The Yoruba of Nigeria provide a good example of the importance of consanguine bonds in a tribal society. Communal residence and occupational cooperation would be endangered among the Yoruba if men listened to what their wives said rather than to what their brothers and fathers said:

> In fact...relationships between spouses, even in monogamous marriages, are not very strong in traditional Yoruba society and parents do not exclusively focus their attention on their biological children. Even in 1973 only one-third of Yoruba spouses slept in the same room or even ate together (admittedly indexes of affection regarded as less significant by Yorubas than by outsiders), and fewer still identified the person to whom they felt closest as their spouse, while children were commonly brought up by a number of kinsmen (Caldwell, 1976: 340).

Networks of relatives are important in this type of society. They provide economic security, increase the number of allies in the political sphere, and increase the number of people who can attend family ceremonies. Both reproduction and marriage are at a premium in such tribal societies. The advantage of having many offspring is the fact that, from a very young age and throughout the lives of their parents, children provide a variety of services. The advantage of marriage is that it increases the number of alliances with other kin groups. Since the marriages are for the benefit of the kin rather than for the couple, they are usually arranged by parents.

In the nuclear family, the kin network continues to exist but is considerably less important. The emphasis is on the spousal bond, and thus it is important that the spouses choose each other rather than become joined through a parentally arranged marriage. Relations within the nuclear family are much more important than the relations among kin. Couples are less concerned with ancestors and kin than they are with their own children. In fact, they are likely to "spoil" their children, in the sense of giving them more care and wealth than they can ever expect in return. The emphasis is also on having a smaller number of children so that each of them can have the best possible chance in life.

In the nuclear family, the kin network exists but is less important than the bond between spouses.

We could go on stressing the variability in family patterns. For instance, we could talk about the various traditions regarding who is permissible as a spouse and the various outlooks on marital dissolution. There are also subcultural variations in Canadian families—for instance, the distinctiveness of Hutterite, Inuit, French, or Chinese families. Other evidence of diversity includes the existence of common-law unions, single-parent families, blended families with children from more than one marriage or union, and gay or lesbian marriages (see the boxed insert on "Gay and Lesbian Relationships").

Gay and Lesbian Relationships

The legal definitions of marriage are largely restricted to heterosexual relationships. However, this is being challenged in various circumstances. In 1996, a legal case found that the Ontario Family Law Act is counter to the federal Charter of Rights and Freedoms when it defines marriage as involving a man and a woman. Consequently, a couple who separated after a ten-year lesbian relationship have had access to the courts in establishing support obligations.

In a book entitled Intimate Relationships, Sharon S. Brehm focuses on research evidence concerning gay and lesbian relationships:

Comparisons between heterosexual and homosexual relationships indicate that there are many similarities. [There are few] differences in adjustment or general lifestyle patterns.... If we want to describe what goes on in a relationship between two homosexual individuals—what makes for the success of the relationship and what may lead to problems—we do not have to use a different language. We can use the same terms as we would in describing a relationship between two heterosexuals. In our intimate relationships, we are all much more similar than we are different.

It would, however, be foolish to claim that there are no differences between homosexual and heterosexual relationships. Homosexual couples still face considerable social stigma and legal barriers. Legally, homosexuals are prohibited from marriage, which creates difficulties for tax returns, joint ownership of property, guardianship/adoption of children, pension plans, insurance coverage, and wills.... But for all of the distress they cause, these problems pale in comparison with the devastating effects of AIDS. On the other hand, the social psychology of AIDS may have strengthened gay men's motivation to establish enduring relationships.

Source*: Sharon S. Brehm, 1992.* Intimate Relationships. *New York: McGraw-Hill (pp. 138–41).*

We have focused on three elements of diversity: number of spouses, sex codes, and consanguine versus nuclear bonds. It is important as well to note the elements of uniformity in this diversity: (1) although polygyny is accepted in many societies, most marriages are in fact monogamous; (2) although there are different orientations towards premarital and extramarital sex, reproduction and sex are generally controlled for the benefit of families; and (3) although some societies emphasize consanguinity and others the nuclear family, both always are in existence. A number of other uniformities in family patterns also exist, as we discuss below.

UNIFORMITY OF FAMILY PATTERNS

Importance of marriage

Most societies place a high premium on marriage. Marriage is important, at least for reproduction and socialization of the young, and the majority of adults are expected to fulfil these roles. In effect, most people are motivated towards marriage as the preferred state of adult life. Other aspects of culture that imply a premium on marriage include the expectation that the parents of a newborn be married to one another, the discouraging of activities that impinge on marriage, particularly adultery and homosexuality, and the dim view taken of marital dissolution. In *Embattled Paradise*, Skolnick (1991: 220) concluded that there is now more tolerance for variation, but lifelong heterosexual marriage with children remains the preferred cultural norm in North America.

Incest taboo

The incest taboo, prohibiting sex and marriage for close biological relatives, is another feature that is almost uniform across societies. The exceptions to this rule are so rare that some have called the incest taboo a cultural universal (see also Chapter 3,

Culture). The taboo reinforces the family in two ways. First, restricting legitimate sexual activity to spouses prevents sexual rivalry from breaking up the family. Second, the requirement to marry outside of the nuclear family enlarges the kinship network through alliances with other families. Mead reported the following imaginary dialogue from an Arapesh informant whose friend wanted to marry his own sister:

What? Do you not want brothers-in-law? If you marry another man's sister and another man marries your sister, you have two brothers-in-law. If you marry your own sister, you have none. With whom will you visit? With whom will you talk? With whom will you hunt? (Mead, 1971: 52).

Importance of inheritance

Another virtual uniformity is the importance of inheritance, a fact that partly explains the premium that is put on marriage and reproduction. A marriage involves much more than the two spouses; families are also joined over generations, partially by the passing on of property. The inheritance that links generations produces social relationships that will continue into the future.

In concluding this section on uniformities in family patterns, it is important to note that there are exceptions to these uniformities. Although nearly all societies put a high premium on marriage, those undergoing extensive social change present some deviations from this pattern. In the Israeli kibbutz, for example, the family was seen as endangering communal solidarity, and was thus given little importance; the marriage ceremony was reduced to the simplest ritual and children did not eat or sleep with their parents. In revolutionary Russia, marital dissolutions became very easy to obtain and, for members of the political élite, extramarital sex was not considered a serious transgression.

Certainly, no society requires that all adults be married all the time. The incest taboo is almost universal, yet there are exceptions, and the taboo does not necessarily prevent incestuous behaviour. Moreover, while inheritance along family lines is the general rule, this practice can be interrupted in times of revolutionary change.

THEORETICAL PERSPECTIVES ON FAMILY CHANGE: A FUNCTIONALIST VIEW

Some of the theoretical perspectives used in other fields of sociology are also employed in the sociology of families. For example, structural functionalism, defined in earlier chapters, maintains that changes in any one part of society affect other parts and that each part of society serves some function for the whole.

Here we offer a functionalist argument in an attempt to understand some of the broad changes that have occurred in families. We shall consider families both at the macro-level, as a societal institution, and at the micro-level, as the social arena in which people spend most of their lives. At the macro-level we shall consider changes in instrumental exchanges, and at the micro-level changes in expressive exchanges.

The macro-level

Some functionalists argue that the factory system led to the separation of work life from family life, and encouraged a change from the larger, self-sufficient extended family to the more compact nuclear form (Goode, 1977). I would argue, however, that it is incorrect to link industrialization with the emergence of the nuclear family. At least when living arrangements are considered, the nuclear family has almost always been the predominant family form.

In addition, extended kinship relations have not disappeared; in fact, they continue to be important in modern societies. Families keep the kinship network alive through visits and mutual support, and many people see these relationships as very important to their lives, especially as they get older. A United States study (Rossi and Rossi, 1990) found that, with increasing age, adults come to feel that it is family and kin who matter most to them, on whom they can rely, and with whom they interact the most. While older parents rarely live with their children, in the majority of cases they are not far away and interact frequently (Connidis, 1989a;

1989b). What has changed with industrialization is the amount of social control that the kin group can exercise over the individual. People are less dependent on their kin for meeting everyday needs, and as a consequence are no longer forced to conform to their wishes; life is more a matter of individual choice.

Certainly, however, industrialization brought about increased structural *differentiation*. A largely accepted functionalist conclusion is that families and kin groups in the nonindustrial settings of the past had a far wider range of functions than in today's industrialized society. Nonindustrial families were the chief units of reproduction, production, consumption, socialization, education, and sometimes religious observance and political action. Individuals normally turned to family or kin to cope with the problems of age, sickness, and incapacity. In fact, it was through membership in a family that individuals had claims to membership in the broader society.

With the greater amount of specialization brought on by industrialization, families lost some of the functions they had previously performed. For instance, not only did economic production take place outside family units, but education was turned over to schools, defence to the state, and worship to religious institutions. Old-age homes and hospitals took over care of the aged and infirm.

Today, the crucial remaining functions of families are procreation and the raising of children. For a society to continue, its individuals have to be replaced by a new generation, and this largely occurs through the children born to families. These children then have to be socialized to play adult roles. Although families are not the exclusive agents of socialization, they remain very important, especially in the early years.

The micro-level

The second function that families fulfil is the meeting of family members' emotional needs. In nonindustrial societies, functionalists suggest, individuals obtained much of their emotional gratification through an involvement with religion and community. To use Durkheim's terms, these societies were held together by *mechanical solidarity*, a sense of belonging and immediate identity with the surrounding community (see Chapter 1, What Is Sociology?). In the industrial world, societies are held together more by *organic solidarity*, by a division of labour whereby individuals are dependent on each other's specialized abilities. But such societies are also competitive and impersonal, providing individuals with less psychological support and security, and less of a sense of identity. In the transition from a nonindustrial to an industrial society, families became considerably more important as sources of emotional gratification, affective involvement, and a sense of personal identity for individuals. They provide members with stable, diffuse, and largely unquestioning support, repairing whatever damage might, with industrialization, be done in the competitive struggles of the outside world. Thus, with industrialization, the importance of families has increased at the emotional level, for nurturance and affection.

The increasing importance of the expressive dimension in the family, however, has not been without costs. When a family tries to satisfy all the emotional and social needs of its members, it may fall short. Some of the major problems of family life today come from the heavy demands placed upon it by individuals who require that it be a nurturing haven and a retreat from the outside world.

Another element of stress implied in the increased importance of the expressive dimension is the breaking apart of families, when individuals no longer feel that they are receiving emotional gratification through these family relationships. As long as families are expected to provide emotional well-being for their members, individuals may try to abandon current family ties, perhaps to seek new ones, when this well-being is not satisfied. We shall return to the topic of family dissolution later in the chapter.

In summary, according to the general functionalist argument, in the last century and a half industrialization caused changes in family structure and functions. The change in structure was a subtle one, involving a difference in the enforceability of kin relations rather than a radical change from extended to nuclear families. With regard to functions, many of the family's functions were lost to the larger society, but there was also a change from meeting instrumental to meeting expressive needs. Families became more important as a source of emotional gratification for individuals. While in the past families were held together partly because people needed each other for survival, today people still say that they need each other, but now it is for the emotional gratification that marriage and family can provide. As a result, families are quicker to break apart when individual members do not find a particular arrangement to be gratifying.

UNDERSTANDING GENDER ROLES AND THE FAMILY: A CONFLICT VIEW

While the previous section emphasized broad changes in family structure from a functionalist perspective, this section will examine familial gender roles, that is, expectations regarding what is appropriate for males and females in a given society, using a conflict view. As noted in Chapter 6, Gender Relations, gender is probably the most salient of an individual's roles, since it directs a wide range of lifelong behaviour, emotions, and attitudes. In the treatment that follows, we shall argue that gender roles are to a considerable extent a conflict-related social phenomenon, arising either out of the economic relations of production or out of patriarchy. These forces affect the basic socialization process (discussed in Chapter 4, Socialization) and help determine the content of that socialization.

Spousal roles and relations of production

As discussed in Chapter 7, Social Stratification, the Marxist tradition in sociology focuses on the economic basis of social arrangements. It is concerned with social groups that arise out of economic production and with the relationships between them. For Marxists, males and females have often played different roles in the productive process. Thus, from a Marxist point of view, they may be seen as "social classes," each with a distinctive set of characteristics rooted in their respective productive roles. Let us examine these roles from a historical perspective.

In certain hunting and gathering societies, women and men were considerably more equal than today, because both were important in production. In fact, in many cases the food gathered by women was more important for survival than that hunted by men. For instance, among the Naskapi people of the Labrador Peninsula, the choice of plans, of undertakings, of journeys, of winterings, was in nearly every instance in the hands of the women. In many other hunting and gathering societies it was the women who looked after preserving and storing the food; thus, in a very real sense, they controlled the "public treasure." Household management meant much more than it does now: it meant the management of the "public economy." In addition, the women's function of childbearing was very important since children were essential to the survival of the group. In effect, producing children was equivalent to producing assets for the community. At the same time, in other hunting and gathering societies, especially if they were **patrilocal** (see Chart 9.1), women did not control the product of their labour and consequently had low status.

Women were also strongly integrated in production in agricultural societies. Besides taking care of childbearing and household management, women performed farming activities along with the men. For example, women played important roles in settling the frontier in North America. This period involved a high level of female participation in economic activity, and gave women relatively high status in the community.

Hamilton (1978) has argued, however, that the seventeenth-century transition from feudalism to capitalism entailed a decrease in women's status. As economic production was removed from the household, women and children became economically dependent on the extrafamilial occupations of husbands and fathers, and their status decreased. Women's sphere essentially shrank to the household only, and men emerged as the major participants in economic production. This gave rise to the "breadwinner" model of families, in which wives were dependent upon their husbands' income, and husbands were dependent upon wives for the care of home and children.

Factory labour laws further ensured women's dependent role. For example, Ursel's (1986) analysis of labour acts in Ontario over the period 1884 to 1913 showed how the laws increasingly limited the use of child and female labour in the paid workforce. While their stated concern was to improve the conditions of children and women, the laws also entrenched the distinctions between male and female labour, limiting the hours women could work, the places they could work, and the kind of work they could do. Thus, it became almost impossible for a female factory worker to earn a living wage. For the most part, then, women's access to subsistence was dependent on entry into reproductive (family) relations.

Only in recent years, with enhanced opportunities for women to become more self-sufficient within the paid labour force, has this state of dependency been reduced. In 1991, 71.6 percent of married women whose children were all over the age of six were in the labour force. Nevertheless, structural barriers and ideologies (for instance, regarding the primacy of women's domestic role) have prevented them from fully embracing economic opportunities. Lupri and Symons (1982: 183) concluded that "the persistence of segregation in the labor force and the privatized nuclear family remain two of the most pervasive structural barriers to gender equality." Grindstaff (1990) confirmed that childbearing and childrearing restrict women's labour-force activities and disrupt their earning continuity.

Childrearing restricts women's labour-force activities and disrupts their earning continuity.

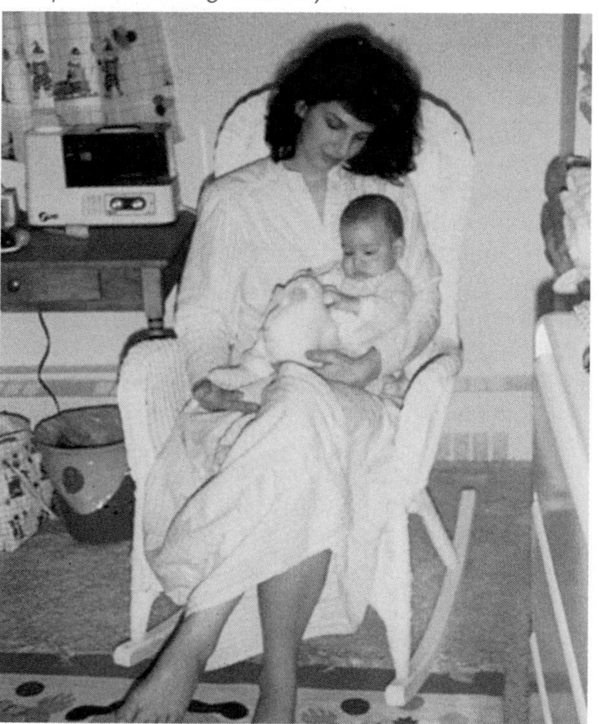

In many ways, then, marriage may still be seen in terms of a cost-benefit scale tipped in favour of men. Certainly, married women are more likely to suffer job interruptions (Robinson, 1986). Men, on the other hand, are less likely to have job interruptions once they are married. It has been argued that men profit more from marriage than women in that their life expectancy is increased by eight years when they are married, compared with a three-year increase for women (Adams and Nagnur, 1986).

Goldscheider and Waite (1986: 91) found in the United States, perhaps as a result of these differences, that while men with secure economic status are more likely to get married than poorer men, women are increasingly likely to use a higher personal income to avoid marriage, a trend not offset by an increase in cohabitation. For instance, in 1981, 45.6 percent of women aged twenty to twenty-four were either married or cohabiting, compared with 33.6 percent in 1991. For men, the parallel decline has been from 26.9 percent to 17.7 percent.

These examples indicate that decisions to marry and the relative status of spouses depend to a considerable extent on the roles that the sexes play in economic production. Economic power is translated into family decisions. As will be discussed later, it also affects the structure of marriage.

Spousal roles and culture

A second perspective on gender-role differences looks at cultural and religious norms rather than economic power. According to this view, Western civilization has a long history of patriarchy, visible in the Hebrew, Greek, Roman, and Christian traditions. These cultures gave men a considerable status advantage over women, one that persists, perhaps in weaker form, today.

For example, in the old Hebrew world males dominated all major aspects of life. They could even sell their daughters as slaves. Strict rules called for the punishment of women caught in adultery, but no such rules existed for men. The status of women was also very low in the Greek tradition. Only the men were educated. When guests came, they were visitors to the men in the household. In the Roman culture, the oldest male had power of life or death over his wife and children. Consider the following statement written by Cato, a Roman patriot and interpreter of custom:

> The husband is the judge of his wife. If she has committed a fault, he punishes her; if she has drunk wine, he condemns her; if she has been guilty of adultery, he kills her. ... If you were to catch your wife in adultery, you would kill her with impunity without trial; but if she were to catch you, she would not dare to lay a finger upon you, and indeed she has no right (Hoult et al., 1978: 33).

The Christian tradition in turn inherited many of the Hebrew, Greek, and Roman family values and customs. Just as an example, note these words from Saint Paul, sometimes read at Christian weddings:

> Wives, give way to your husbands as you should in the Lord. Husbands, love your wives and treat them with gentleness (Col. 3:18–19).

It is quite clear who is meant to be the head of the family. In addition, being loving and gentle may not be that difficult if the other person is giving way. Hamilton (1978: 73) noted that the medieval Catholic church even counselled a celibate life in order to avoid the twin evils of women and sexuality. While Protestants subsequently addressed a loving relationship between husband and wife, they also taught that the husband had the responsibility to govern while the wife had to be obedient.

Changing cultures within different historical periods have also affected spousal roles. In the Victorian period, for example, staying at home became a virtue, corresponding to the "cult of true womanhood" popular at the time (Garfield, 1990: 34). Any man who needed his wife's help in providing for family needs was viewed as incompetent or worse.

Another example of the importance of cultural norms can be seen in the emphasis placed on homemaking and child-care roles after World War II. Life was oriented towards families, families were children-centred, and men and women were relatively happy with the traditional roles for husbands (e.g., bringing home the bacon) and wives (looking after home and hearth). It was also a time of considerable hostility towards deviations from these roles. Single adults were seen as morally questionable, working mothers were considered to be depriving their children of affection, and voluntarily childless couples were considered selfish. Sentiment was strong to move women out of the labour force once their contribution to the war effort was complete. The following magazine quotation is an example of the subtle pressures put on women to return to a more traditional family form:

> What will they [women workers] demand of [postwar] society? Perhaps—and we can only hope—they'll be tired of it all [working outside the home] and yearn in the old womanly way for a home and a baby and a big brave man (*Maclean's*, 15 June 1942; as quoted in Boutilier, 1977: 23).

This trend continued during the 1950s. Skolnick (1987) called the decade a "golden age of the family," in which women were very much encouraged to fulfil themselves through their roles as wives and mothers.

During the 1960s, however, it again became acceptable for married women to work, but only as long as their employment did not interfere too greatly with family responsibilities. Thus, they could take jobs that had little prestige, made few demands on their time, and conceded authority to men. It was not until the 1970s and 1980s that women were encouraged to pursue lifestyles wherein they could devote themselves to careers as fully as men have traditionally done.

Yet, while there has been change, many Canadians still believe that the roles of men and women should remain different, and that such differences are natural and proper. For instance, people often think that the roles of men and women should be complementary rather than identical. In a 1988 poll, 28 percent of men and 23 percent of women felt that "everyone would be better off if more women were satisfied to stay home and have families" (Lenton, 1992). A popular cultural expression that reinforces this sentiment is the concept of "opposite sex." In most ways, men and women are not opposites to each other, as "up" is opposite to "down." Nevertheless, people continue to use the term.

Turning to contemporary male family roles, it is important to note that while more men are accepting of working wives, only a minority of men are willing to take an equal part in household management and family responsibilities. Lupri and Mills (1987) analyzed the time budgets of several hundred married couples in Calgary, and concluded that the conduct of husbands regarding household responsibilities does not change much in order to accommodate wives' employment. Dual-earner couples who were childless divided labour, including both paid work and housework, in a way that approached symmetry, but dual-earner couples with children had patterns that were far from symmetrical. The wife did an average of 38 percent more total work over the week. From this point of view, one might argue that "childlessness is the easiest route to equality"; in fact, in many marriages it is probably the only route. Children tend to introduce a more traditional division of labour, even to marriages that started out on a relatively equal footing.

In conclusion, we see that over time there have been important changes in the relative status of men and women, and many of these changes can be related to the roles that the sexes have played in economic production, inside and outside of families. At the same time, the cultural norms and expectations regarding the roles of men and women also affect family life.

SOCIALIZATION FOR MARRIAGE AND MATE SELECTION

Having examined the basic characteristics of families, family change, and gender roles, let us now look more closely at the marital life cycle. We start with questions of socialization for marriage and mate selection in our society. We shall then discuss dating, premarital sex, cohabitation, love, homogamy in mate selection, and age at marriage.

Socialization

To be properly socialized for any role, one needs the motivation to practise the appropriate behaviour, the ability to perform the requirements of the role, and the knowledge of what is expected. With regard to marriage, the overwhelming majority of people are motivated to perform the role of husband or wife at some stage of their lives. In terms of practice and abilities, dating provides various relevant experiences. However, unmarried individuals may have difficulty learning about what is actually *expected* of husbands and wives, insofar as other people's marriages are generally private. In addition, most people anticipating marriage are very confident, believing that their good intentions will be sufficient to ensure a successful union. As a consequence, they do not seek out information.

The problem of lack of knowledge is further complicated by the fact that, traditionally in our society, boys and girls tend to be socialized differently. Adolescent girls become adept at interpersonal communication and in the language and actions of romantic love, but they are generally not encouraged to be sexual. On the other hand, mostly through their peer groups, adolescent boys are encouraged to be sexual rather than romantic in their heterosexual relationships, and to be less communicative (Skolnick, 1987: 212–13).

Another difference between boys and girls is the fact that marriage has traditionally been more important for girls than for boys. Although the number of exceptions is growing, we can still generally say that a woman derives more of her status from marriage than does a man. Parents, especially mothers, are quite aware of the importance of marriage for their daughters, and often try to move them in this direction.

Thus, boys and girls have different stakes in entering courtship. The stakes are higher for girls, since, at least around the late teens and early twenties, marriage represents a more important life goal for them. For males, marriage becomes an important life goal at a later stage. In addition, boys and girls seek different things from courtship. One might say that boys seek physical intimacy while girls seek love and commitment. Courtship partly involves each gender training the other to be more responsive to what each wants and expects. Boys train girls to see sex as part of a relationship, while girls train boys to see love and commitment as part of a relationship.

Dating and premarital intercourse

Waller (1937) described dating on a U.S. campus during the Depression in a way that may sound slightly exaggerated, but which remains relevant today. He felt that dating was a more or less explicit (often conflictual) bargaining relationship, in which each person tried to get the best possible deal. Dating, like marriage, can thus be seen as involving exchanges. In a sense, people who are dating can bargain even harder than those who are married, since they are not formally committed to each other. For instance, if the dating partners are not equal in their desirability as dates, then the one with the higher "rating" has more power in the bargaining and can exploit the other party. Another feature of the dating process, according to Waller, is the "principle of least interest." This means that the less involved person has more power because he or she has less to lose if the relationship ends. The trick then is to remain uncommitted, but to pretend to be committed in order to get the partner committed. (The boxed insert "Bargaining for Sex" provides another example of the pressures involved in dating).

Sex before marriage, as a specific aspect of dating, has also received considerable attention from sociologists of the family. Hobart (1993) studied attitudes and behaviour regarding premarital sex of students in ten post-secondary institutions in 1988. He inquired both about attitudes (what do you think is right for males and for females?) and about behaviour (what have you done?). Table 9.1 presents some of the results. It is useful to consider the extent to which these findings support "old moralities" or "new moralities" of sexual behaviour.

There are several **premarital sexual standards** by which people judge the acceptability of premarital sex. Among these, there are two old moralities: the **abstinence standard**, which forbids premarital sex, and the **double standard**, which grants men premarital sexual licence but expects premarital virginity of women. The data show that about 10 percent of the students favoured the abstinence standard. In addition, there is very little difference in the sexual activities that a given respondent considers appropriate for males and females, indicating that the double standard is also not very prevalent.

The two new moralities of sexual behaviour receive somewhat greater approval among Hobart's respondents. The **love standard** regards sex as a physical expression of love and sees premarital sex as acceptable when love or strong affection is present. The **fun standard** views sex as primarily a giving and receiving of sexual pleasure; intercourse is acceptable as long as the partners are willing. The love standard receives the greatest support, since slightly more than half of students consider premarital intercourse to be acceptable if the partners are in love. About a third of students indicate that intercourse is acceptable even though the partners are not particularly affectionate. These respondents thus subscribe to the fun standard of sexual behaviour.

There are a few notable attitude differences between males and females in the study, with females more likely to support the love standard and males the fun standard. For instance, 42 percent of men compared with 23 percent of women subscribed to the fun standard. At the same time, little difference between males and females is in evidence when actual behaviour is concerned. Hobart showed that, between the sexes, the percentage experiencing premarital intercourse *per se* has over the years roughly equalized. The percentage of male post-secondary students who had experienced premarital intercourse rose from 58 percent in 1968 to 75 percent in 1988, while the female change was from 39 to 78 percent (Hobart, 1993: 62). Overall, more than half of young people do not have sexual intercourse until about the age of eighteen. Also, intercourse is not particularly frequent: one-third of the sexually experienced have intercourse once a month or less (Herold, 1984: 16, 165).

For women, this long-term increase in permissiveness can be related to general changes in gender roles. Various historical examples have led sociologists to conclude that premarital sex codes are more permissive when females have greater equality and

Bargaining for Sex

Based on interviews in Flin Flon, Manitoba, Luxton showed how dating and premarital sex can be described as a process of exchange and bargaining. This exchange reflects the different roles of men and women in society.

The "long arm of the job" stretches from the workplace into the bedroom and exerts its grip on the most intimate part of marriage. Sexuality is so complex that it operates on many levels and has different meanings in different situations. In some ways it is an expression of human need, of pleasure and of the social togetherness of lovers. In other ways it is an oppressive and repressive relationship which grinds the tenderness and love out of people, leaving behind the frustration, bitterness, and violence. ... On one level marriage can be understood as an exchange between wife and husband—her domestic work, including sexual access, for his economic support.

This underlying exchange becomes apparent in the prelude to marriage, the period in which women are recruited for domestic labor. The process of dating—of selecting a mate for marriage—is, of course, not experienced as an exchange by the people participating in it. The economic necessity for women and the sexual motivation for men are hidden under massive layers of ideology, propaganda, and confusion. People date and marry for many reasons, often because "that is the way things work." They are usually so caught up in the process that they do not have time to reflect on it. Although very few Flin Flon women and men had analyzed the forces that underpin their lives, they did experience the power of those forces. In dating practices, for example, women generally dated men their own age or older. Men rarely dated older women. While a couple may have agreed to share the costs on a date, men were generally expected to pay. Most significantly, women were not supposed to initiate a relationship. They had to wait until a suitable man approached them.

This means that the balance of forces in any female/male relationship is likely to be unequal. Men tend to have the advantage of being older, having economic power, and social authority. Women rarely have access to as much money and they cannot act forthrightly. They are forced to manipulate and insinuate—to set things up so that men will ask them out and, ultimately, ask them to marry.

This inequality permeates sexual activities. Whatever their real feelings (and often they do not know what their real feelings are), both women and men get involved in the process of serious dating where women trade sexual "favors" for a "good time" and economic rewards. On some level the participants are aware of this underlying exchange.

The women know that if they hold out too long, they risk losing the man to someone who is less resistant. Three young women were evaluating their relationships with their current steady boyfriends. All three men were working. One woman, age sixteen, had been out with her seventeen-year-old boyfriend six times. She commented:

> Tomorrow will be our seventh date. Last time he really wanted me to neck with him but I wouldn't. I only let him kiss me goodnight when he took me home. I don't think I can get away with that again this date. I'm going to have to let him go further or he'll never take me out again.

Her boyfriend had been working for the Company for two years. He owned a car and had sizeable savings. He had also stated publicly that when he married, as a wedding present he would give his wife the down payment for the house of her choice. Because of his resources he was considered a "good catch." Her fifteen-year-old friend replied:

> Yeah, John [age sixteen] and me were necking last weekend and we got real close. He wants to go all the way but I said no way. Not till I get married. But he laughed and said I'd be an old maid if I never made out till then. I'm afraid that if I give in, I'll get pregnant, but if I don't then I'll lose him.

The third woman, sixteen years old, agreed:

> Yeah! Boys always expect you to go all the way. And if you won't, then they go find someone else who will. Andy [her eighteen-year-old boyfriend of six months] said that it wasn't worth his while taking me out all the time, spending his money on me, if I didn't come across.

... Men try to cajole and coerce women "to go all the way." Women resist, give in a bit, resist some more....

Source: *Meg Luxton, 1980. More than a* Labour of Love. *Toronto: Women's Press (pp. 55–57).*

TABLE 9.1 Attitudes toward sexual intercourse and incidence of various sexual experiences, by sex of respondent, 1988, in percentages

	Males %	Females %
Abstinence standard	10	9
Love standard	48	68
Fun standard	42	23
Has never petted	7	8
Has experienced intercourse	74	78
Engaged to all intercourse partners	1	2
In love with all intercourse partners	26	23
Number of Respondents	940	946

Source: *Adapted from Charles F. Hobart, 1993, "Sexual behaviour" in G.N. Ramu (ed.),* Marriage and Family in Canada, *(2nd ed.) Toronto: Prentice Hall (pp. 60, 62).*

are subject to less occupational differentiation. As women become less dependent on marriage for their major source of status, it is less necessary for them to keep sex out of the dating relationship in order to exchange it for the marriage contract. Sex and marriage, then, are becoming less closely linked for women, as has long been the case for men. Reliable birth-control methods have greatly enhanced this separation, and it would appear that the fear of disease, including AIDS, has not encouraged a return to more conservative standards.

Cohabitation

Along with more liberal attitudes and behaviour regarding sex before marriage, the increasing incidence of cohabitation—marital union without religious or legal contract—can also be seen as an indication of the decreased significance of the formal marriage contract in people's lives. Cohabitation has increased greatly in recent years. In 1991, 11.3 percent of all couples were cohabiting, compared with 6.4 percent ten years earlier. Moreover, in a 1990 survey, 39 percent of women and 42 percent of men aged thirty to thirty-nine had at some point in their lives lived in a common-law union (Stout, 1991: 20).

To a certain extent, these less formal relationships are simply being substituted for marriage. Yet, in some respects, cohabitation is not a true replacement for more formal arrangements. For instance, Rindfuss and VandenHeuvel (1990) found that the cohabiting are more similar to the single than to the married. Further, common-law unions are extremely short-lived compared with marriages, and childbearing rates are low. According to the 1984 *Family History Survey*, five years after the beginning of such unions 27 percent of couples are still cohabiting, 46 percent have married their partner, and 27 percent have separated (Burch and Madan, 1986: 19).

Marriages preceded by cohabitation have higher rates of dissolution. After ten years of legal marriage, the rate of dissolution is 17 percent for those preceded by cohabitation and 10 percent for those not preceded by cohabitation (Burch and Madan, 1986: 22). One might think that experimenting with marriage-like relationships before marriage would enable people to test their long-term prospects as a couple and to make better marital choices. However, it would seem that those who are willing to be in informal partnerships are also more willing to dissolve formal arrangements. Cohabitation may provide experience at getting along together, but a marriage is different in the sense that it involves a long-term commitment. Surveys show that people who are living together do not consider themselves married, and that cohabitation is best viewed as an alternative to being single or as a prelude to marriage. However, there are increasing numbers who do consider cohabitation as an alternative to marriage, and by 1991, 42 percent of common-law unions involved children.

Love in mate selection

Love is difficult to define. In one sense, it is a rather general concept that can mean anything from *eros* or "attraction to the physical appearance of the beloved," to *agape* or the "giving of oneself." We shall not define love here except to say that it involves strong sentimental or emotional attachment. Our main concern is to look at the role that love plays in courtship and mate selection.

First, it should be noted that in many cultures love has been irrelevant to mate selection. The following statement from an anthropologist makes the point clearly:

> All societies recognize that there are occasional violent emotional attachments between persons of opposite sex.... Most groups regard them as unfortunate and point out the victims of such attachments as horrible examples. Their rarity in most societies suggests that they are psychological abnormalities (Linton, 1936: 175).

Other researchers, however, suggest that anthropologists have tended to overlook evidence of romantic love, especially when people may express their love in other ways. The Yąnomamö, for instance, do not kiss and have no word for love in their language, but there is evidence of people eloping due to mutual affection (Fisher, 1992).

In Western history, romantic love may have emerged only in the twelfth century, along with a series of other social and ideological changes (Lee, 1975). Romantic love was particularly suited to landless knights who sought spouses of higher status than those their parents could find for them. For the general population, the "romanticization of courtship" probably did not occur until the nineteenth and twentieth centuries (Shorter, 1977). The trend away from arranged marriages and towards marriages based on romantic love occurred along with the other family changes that were noted in the section on functionalism. Love became more important as the focus of marriage changed from ensuring the survival of the participants to satisfying their expressive needs.

The actual frequency with which people experience love in our society may be explained in two ways. First, the emotion of love can be generated by the blocking of sexual activity. Love as blocked sex makes sense in the context of the love standard of sexual morality. That is, in order to justify having sex, one has to conjure up sentiments of love. Second, and probably more important, love emerges because people are expected to fall in love. There are various reasons for getting married (for economic gain, to gain the status of an adult, to have children, to escape from loneliness, to get away from one's parents, for sexual gratification, because everyone else is doing it, etc.), but these reasons are generally not acceptable in our culture unless one is also "in love."

Homogamy in mate selection

In everyday conversations about mate selection, two contradictory principles often emerge: "opposites attract" and "like marries like." Clearly, most people do choose someone different from themselves in that they choose someone of the other sex. Beyond that, the idea that opposites attract receives little research support.

Support for **homogamy**, the idea that like marries like, is considerably stronger. Among marriages occurring in 1990, more than half in each of the following groups married others of the same religion: Jewish, Mennonite, Pentecostal, Jehovah's Witness, Catholic, Eastern Orthodox, and other Christian and non-Christian groups. Even those whose religion was "unknown or not stated" were more likely to marry someone who was in the same category (Statistics Canada, 1996, *Marriages 1994*: 16–17). Moreover, a study in the United States found that both the education of potential marriage partners and the social class of their parents remain important in mate selection, but that education has become more important in homogamy than social class (Kalmijn, 1991).

Love has become more important as the focus of marriage in the twentieth century, while economic considerations have lessened.

The general conclusion, then, is that most people are likely to marry someone who is pretty much like themselves in most social and economic characteristics, and who has similar things to exchange in the marriage bargain. This departs considerably from the romantic notion that love and marriage are individualistic and that everyone has an equal chance of falling in love with everyone else. Note also that this is an average tendency; obviously, some marriages involve partners who are very different from each other.

Age at marriage

One example of dissimilarity between married partners—that is, of **heterogamy**—occurs with respect to age. On average, women marry at a younger age than men. In some societies the age gap is quite large, with the ideal considered to be a five- to ten-year difference. In Canada, the difference in the mean age at first marriage is closer to two years (men 28.8, women 26.9 in 1994), having declined from a difference of about three years in the 1960s and four years in the early part of the century.

Although at two years the gap is small, it has considerable sociological relevance. A younger person is likely to be less experienced at taking responsibility and leadership, and to have achieved less in economic or career terms. Taken together, these differences mean that for most couples a wife will tend to be of lesser status than her husband, a condition known as the **mating gradient**. In the average marriage the husband will tend to earn more money, partly because he is older and more established. As a consequence, for the benefit of the total family income, his job may be given priority when some aspect of family life affects the spouses' jobs. In other words, the family is more likely to move for the sake of his job than for hers, and the wife is more likely than he to withdraw from the labour force for the sake of the children. If the wife's income is lower, which is usually the case, it often seems to make sense to proceed in this fashion. What this means, of course, is that the slight disadvantage with which the wife started, because she is younger, can become entrenched over the course of the marriage.

MARITAL AND FAMILY INTERACTIONS

Having considered socialization for marriage, premarital interaction, and mate selection, we can now move into the study of some specific aspects of marital and family interactions. We shall look first at the marital life cycle, then at the structure of marriage, single-parent families, and finally, childbearing and children.

The marital life cycle

To obtain an overview of typical marital interactions, it is useful to consider the average ages at which people pass through given stages, from marriage to the death of one spouse. Table 9.2 presents data on the mean age at various life stages for Canadian women who were born between 1841 and 1960. They are calculated using life-table techniques.

TABLE 9.2 Median age at family life course events and years spent in life stages, Canadian female birth cohorts

	Birth Cohort			
	1841–50	*1901–10*	*1931–40*	*1951–60*
Median age at:				
– first marriage	26.0	23.3	21.1	22.5
– first birth	28.0	25.0	22.9	24.5
– last birth	40.0	29.1	29.1	26.3
– empty nest[1]	60.1	49.1	49.1	46.3
– widowhood	59.5	61.3	67.2	69.9
– death of women	64.3	67.3	79.4	82.2
Years spent:				
– between marriage and first birth	2.0	1.7	1.8	2.0
– raising dependent children	32.1	24.1	26.2	21.8
– married, with no dependent children	–0.6	12.2	18.1	23.6
– in widowhood	4.8	6.0	12.2	12.3

[1] Age of mother when last child is aged twenty.

Source: *Ellen M. Gee and Meredith M. Kimball, 1987.* Women and Aging. *Toronto: Butterworths (p. 83).*

These techniques assume that events occurring over a given period, such as marriages, divorces, widowhoods, and deaths, can be summarized for a population over a hypothetical life cycle.

As we can see, important changes have occurred in the typical marital life cycle from pre-modern to modern times. The mean age of mothers at birth of their children has decreased, especially for the birth of the last child, which typically occurred at age forty in the 1841–50 birth cohort, but occurred at age twenty-six for those born between 1951 and 1960. The years of childbearing have also been reduced on average, from twelve to two years. Another important difference in the marital life cycle is the emergence of the empty nest stage, between the marriage of the last child and the death of one of the spouses. This stage did not exist for the typical mid-nineteenth-century couple, but today the couples in the youngest age cohort who remain married can expect to live together for twenty-four years after their last child reaches age twenty. Since evidence indicates that the empty nest is an enjoyable period in the life cycle, this is a happy outcome (Lupri and Frideres, 1981).

The increased life expectancy and the decreased family size of today's societies also present a very different context for family life. In earlier times family life patterns were subject to sudden changes, since death so often interfered in the family life cycle. For instance, while traditionally about 10 percent of children lost their mother by the age of ten, today only 1 percent are maternal orphans by this age (Burch and Selvanathan, 1987: 384). Orphanhood, once a common experience, is now rare. The increased rate of survival of parents means that the nuclear family can now be much more self-sufficient. Under high mortality conditions, it was very risky to depend on the nuclear family alone.

In the mid-nineteenth century, only 6 percent of couples would have celebrated their fiftieth wedding anniversary, compared with 39 percent under 1981 mortality conditions. Couples now live a longer life together, changing the meaning of "till death do us part." When romantic love was introduced into Western civilization as the basis for marriage, the promise to "love each other for life" had a vastly different time horizon. When young lovers make a similar promise today, they probably do not realize that it likely will be for almost fifty years. Even when divorces are entered into the calculation, the average duration of marriage is thirty years (Nault and Belanger, 1996: 36, 42). An unhappy marriage is probably more likely to be broken when one has the prospect of a long life to "endure." Thus, the instability caused by death has been replaced by the personal instability of the marital relationship itself.

More recent data allows us to present other dimensions of the marital life cycle. Table 9.3 provides a summary of such results for periods 1970–72 and 1991. We noted already the increase in the average age at first marriage. As achieved characteristics, particularly education and occupation, play a larger role in the lives of women, many delay marital relationships while they establish stable work careers. Women's greater economic independence allows them to search longer for an acceptable partner. As both women and men wait longer to marry, there is a higher chance that the delay will result in non-marriage, which increased from under 10 percent in 1970–72 to over 25 percent by 1991.

Another related turnaround noted in the 1986 census was the increased proportion of young people living with their parents. For instance, at age twenty-two, 48.5 percent of young people are living at home, compared with 35.3 percent in 1976 (Ram, 1990). The mean years lived in the parental family increased from 22.7 to 24.2 years.

Table 9.3 also shows that individuals can expect to spend, on average, slightly less than half of their whole life in the married state, with the average number of marriages per person being 1.3 for men and 1.2 for women. Among persons getting married in 1990, 77 percent had never been married before, 20.2 percent had been divorced, and 2.8 percent were widowed. In a third of the marriages, at least one of the partners had been married before.

Persons who divorced in 1991 did so at an average age of 39 years for women and 41.8 for men, and spent an average of 21.5 and 14.8 years respectively in the divorced state. These statistics do not include the period of separation that often precedes an official divorce. A significant change over the period 1970–72 to 1991 is the decline in the percentage of divorced persons remarrying, especially women. This probably corresponds to the lesser need for women to be married, given their greater economic independence. Divorced women are perhaps also more likely to have concluded that the relative costs of marriage may not always be to their benefit.

Couples now live a longer life together: the average duration of marriages that do not end in divorce is close to fifty years.

The average age at widowhood is 74.1 for men and 71.2 for women. The average length of time spent in this state is 8.7 and 15.1 years respectively. Widowed persons are not likely to remarry: only one in twenty-five widowed women remarry according to 1991 statistics, partly a result of the number of available men of comparable age. Projections for the generation of persons born in 1921–36 would imply that 60 percent of men will be married at the time of their deaths compared with 20 percent of women (Péron and Légaré, 1988). Since women have smaller pensions related to previous employment, and as survivor benefits from the deceased partner's pension may be low, widowed

TABLE 9.3 Summary statistics on the never-married, married, divorced, and widowed states, by sex, Canada, 1970–1972 and 1991

	Men		*Women*	
	1970–1972	*1991*	*1970–1972*	*1991*
Never-married state				
Average age at first marriage	25.0	30.2	22.8	27.7
Percentage of population never marrying	10	30	8	25
Average time spent single (for total population)	26.3	45	25.0	38
Married state				
Percentage of population marrying	90	70	92	75
Percentage of lifetime lived as married	58	45	52	43
Number of marriages per person marrying	1.3	1.3	1.3	1.2
Average age of the married population	49.2	52.6	46.3	50.2
Divorced state				
Percentage of divorced persons remarrying	85	64	79	52
Average length of a divorce	4.9	14.8	10.0	21.5
Average age at divorce	41.5	41.8	38.6	39.0
Average age of divorced population	51.5	55.4	56.8	58.3
Average age at remarriage	42.8	47.1	40.6	42.4
Widowed state				
Average time spent widowed (for total population)	2.0	3	9.7	10
Average length of a widowhood	7.8	8.7	14.5	15.1
Average age at widowhood	68.6	74.1	67.0	71.2
Percentage of widowed persons remarrying	24	11	9	4
Average age of the widowed population	72.3	76.2	73.4	76.5
Average age at remarriage	60.5	65.6	56.5	58.7

Source: *O.B. Adams and D.N. Nagnur, 1988.* Marriage, Divorce and Mortality: A Life Table Analysis for Canada and Regions. *Ottawa: Statistics Canada, Catalogue No. 84-536 (pp. 11, 14, 15); F. Nault and A. Belanger, 1996.* The Decline in Marriage in Canada, 1981 to 1991. *Ottawa: Statistics Canada, Catalogue No. 84-536-XPB (pp. 36, 42).*

women suffer economic disadvantages. While the incomes of the elderly in general have increased, women living alone have not done as well, and this has contributed to the feminization of poverty (see Chapter 6, Gender Relations).

As a consequence of the changes in the family life cycle, a larger proportion of people are living alone. Such persons make up 23 percent of households and 10 percent of all adults. It is far more acceptable to remain single than was the case in the past. In 1971, 15 percent of women at ages twenty-five to thirty-four were neither married nor cohabiting, compared with 30 percent in 1991. For men at these ages, the proportion who are not in union has increased from 21 to 39 percent. Living alone is particularly predominant among older women, including one-third of those over sixty-five (Ram, 1990: 34). While many elderly are living alone, they are not necessarily isolated. Stone (1988) found that, for the elderly in private dwellings, relatives and close friends are more important than formal support. Only some 7 to 10 percent of the elderly have no surviving children (Péron and Légaré, 1988). The evidence would indicate that, while co-residence of elderly persons with their children has declined, families do not abandon their elderly. Contact between siblings in later life is also important, especially for women, those who are not married, and the childless (Connidis, 1989b).

The structure of marriage

Just as marital life cycles differ cross-culturally and over time, so too do marital structures. Scanzoni and Scanzoni (1988) identified four historical North American **marital structures** based on the positions and roles of spouses: *owner-property, head-complement, senior partner–junior partner*, and *equal partners*.

The **owner-property marriage** is mentioned mainly for historical reasons. In this structure the man in effect owns his wife, who is legally his property; the two are one, and the one is the husband. The expressive element in this type of marriage is rather unimportant. While this marriage structure is not very equitable, it does involve clear rights and duties on the part of spouses. (See the boxed insert "What Contributes to the Relative Marital Power of Spouses?")

A **head-complement marriage** is one in which the wife is "the other half," expected to find meaning in life largely through her husband and family. In making decisions, the husband must take into account the wishes of the wife as complement. The husband has basic responsibility for earning the family income and the wife for the care of the home and family. The expressive side of marriage is important here, as spouses are expected to find pleasure in each other's company and to offer each other emotional support. While this type of marriage structure is decreasing, a significant number of marriages in Canada still fit this description. For instance, among married women aged between

What Contributes to the Relative Marital Power of Spouses?

Relative power of spouses, although very difficult to measure, is an important aspect of marital interactions, especially from a conflict perspective. The relative power of spouses depends in part on their respective interpersonal abilities, but it is also structured, largely in favour of males, by broader social factors. For example, the power of a wife is lowest when she is at home with young children and highest when she is working. When she is not totally dependent on her husband, she has more bargaining leverage and thus more power in family decisions.

The stratification in the broader society that gives advantages to men has its reflection in the family, since those who have higher status, power, and authority often use these resources to dominate and control relationships (Hutter, 1988). The patriarchal ideology that enables men to control the public world of work, politics, and religion also enables them to have the upper hand in most aspects of the marital relationship. Research indicates that there are various dimensions to marital power, but that wives have power in domains not considered very important by either themselves or their husbands (Brinkerhoff and Lupri, 1978).

It is possible that the very definitions of love that are accepted in our culture promote the power difference between men and women. Rossi (1985) proposed that our definition has been feminized—it is taken to refer to expressive questions, emotional closeness, and verbal self-disclosure, including disclosure of one's weakness. The more instrumental side of love, that is, doing things together or helping one another, is less likely to be defined as love. As an example, in one study a husband was asked to show more love for his wife and decided to wash her car. While that was instrumental help, it was not accepted as a sign of love by the wife or by the researchers. Rossi therefore concluded that the accepted definition of love tends to exaggerate women's dependency on the relationship while men's dependency is repressed. She proposed that a more androgynous kind of love, one that combines expression and practical help, would acknowledge that there is interdependence of men on women, as well as of women on men, in relationships.

twenty-five and forty-four, some 16 percent had not been part of the labour force in the year and a half before the 1991 census, compared with under 4 percent of married men in the same age group. An American poll taken in 1989 asked: "Which do you feel is more important for a family these days, to make some financial sacrifices so that one parent can stay home to raise the children, or to have both parents working so the family can benefit from the highest possible income?" Sixty-eight percent opted for the first choice, only 27 percent for the second (Footlick, 1990: 18).

A **senior partner–junior partner marriage** is a variant of the above, with the wife having more independence than in the previous case because both husband and wife are employed. However, the husband contributes the larger share to the family income and the wife has basic responsibility for the family and household. Since many women combine work and motherhood, they seek jobs that make it easier to have interruptions, to work part-time, or to combine with household duties (Desai and Waite, 1991). Over the past three decades, this senior partner–junior partner arrangement has likely become the most common of the four marital categories. While 61 percent of husband–wife families involved both spouses working in 1991 (Ghalam, 1993: 5), women largely remain the junior economic partners within the family. In 1989, wives contributed 38 percent and husbands 62 percent of the spousal earnings in dual-earner families (Chawla, 1992: 27). Some 30 percent of wives in dual-earner families work part-time, while fewer than 4 percent of husbands work part-time (Moore, 1989b). In terms of housework, married women who are employed do about 68 percent of the work while married men do 32 percent (Marshall, 1990c: 19).

Finally, the **equal partners marriage** involves spouses who are equally committed to their jobs and who share in household and family tasks equally. A small though growing minority of marriages fit this description. In fact, families where the wife earned more than the husband amounted to 25 percent of husband–wife couples in 1993 (Crompton and Geran, 1995). In a third of these cases, the husband was unemployed or looking for work sometime during the year. Harrell (1985) also found that the greater the wife's contribution to total family income, the more likely it was for the husband to be involved with cooking and cleaning the house.

It is important to note as well that, although the equal partner arrangement occurs in only a minority of families, equality of partnership rights is enshrined in law. For example, in Ontario, the Family Law Reform Act says that "it is necessary to recognize the equal position of spouses as individuals within marriage and to recognize marriage as a form of partnership" (Ontario Family Law Act, 1990). The act goes on to indicate that, as a default condition, family assets are to be divided in equal shares upon the breakdown of a marriage. Generally speaking, these conditions also hold for persons who have cohabited for three years, or for those who are cohabiting and have a child.

Single-parent families

Just as marriages can take a number of alternative forms, so too can families. The largest increases in the 1980s have in fact involved nontraditional family forms, including common-law unions and single-parent families. Together, these two forms made up 22.8 percent of families in the 1991 census.

Families with only one parent made up 13 percent of all families in 1991, but they vary considerably according to the age, marital status, and sex of the parent. In 1971 most one-parent families were led by a widowed parent. In contrast, in 1986 those with a separated or divorced parent made up 59.5 percent of the total, while another 13.4 percent had a never-married parent (Ram, 1990: 87). Only 17.8 percent of the one-parent families were led by a male parent, while the rest—the vast majority—were headed by women.

Over the course of their life, the experience of single parenthood is in fact quite common for women. In 1984, among women between eighteen and sixty-four who had ever had children, 26 percent had experienced lone parenthood. For about two-thirds of these, parenting alone had ended either through a new union (the great majority) or when the children left home (16 percent). The average duration of the lone-parenting episodes was 5.5 years, with 10 percent lasting less than six months and 17 percent lasting more than ten years. Among those

Families with only one parent made up 13 percent of all families in 1991, and over 80 percent of those were led by a female parent.

who experienced one episode, 12 percent experienced at least one subsequent episode (Moore, 1989a).

An increasingly common route into single parenthood involves births to single women. Such births have increased since the mid-1970s. The largest increases have occurred not among teenagers, whose birth and abortion rates have actually declined since the 1970s (Grindstaff, 1990), but among women over the age of thirty, again evidence of the separation between sexual activity and marriage. On the other hand, many of these women may in fact be living in common-law unions and thus may not really be single parents (Ram, 1990: 32).

Moore (1987) has analyzed female lone parenting with the help of the 1984 *Family History Survey*. Compared with currently married women of the same age, female lone parents are more likely to have lived in common-law relationships, to have had their children earlier, and to have less education. In effect, they must raise children while facing a double disadvantage of lack of support from a spouse and fewer job skills. McQuillan (1992) found that between 1971 and 1986, as participation of married women in the labour force increased, the income gap between single-parent and two-parent families grew. (See the boxed insert "What are the Challenges and Rewards of Single-parenting?") Thus, along with the greater incidence of elderly females living alone that was cited earlier, the growth in the number of young, female-led, single-parent families has contributed considerably to the feminization of poverty in Canada.

Childbearing

Childbearing is a part of marital interaction that deserves special attention, especially given the considerable changes since World War II in the ease with which couples can control their reproduction. In fact, few aspects of family behaviour have changed

What Are the Challenges and Rewards of Single-Parenting?

In 1991, 13 percent of families in Canada were single-parent families; among those, 82 percent consisted of a mother with children and 18 percent of a father with children. In 1994, the average income of two-parent families with children in Canada was $62 000, compared with $28 000 for female-led and $41 000 for male-led one-parent families. In the excerpt that follows, Cherlin notes the problems associated with the lower standard of living of single-parent families, as well as some of the non-economic rewards of single-parenting.

Saddled with sole or primary responsibility for supporting themselves and their children, single mothers frequently have too little time and too few resources to manage effectively. There are three common sources of strain. One is responsibility overload: single parents must make all the decisions and provide all the needs for their families, a responsibility that at times can be overwhelming. Another is task overload: many single parents simply have too much to do, with working, housekeeping, and parenting; consequently, there is no slack time to meet unexpected demands. A third is emotional overload: single parents are always on call to give emotional support to their children, whether or not their own emotional resources are temporarily depleted.

Moreover, divorced and separated women who are raising children often find that their economic position has deteriorated. Many of those who were not employed in the years preceding their separation have difficulty reentering the job market.

As a result of their limited earning power and of the low level of child support, single mothers and their children often experience a decline in their standard of living after a separation.

[Yet] to be sure, life in a single-parent family also has its rewards, foremost the relief from marital conflict. In addition, single parents may gain increased self-esteem from their ability to manage the demands of work life and family life by themselves. They may enjoy their independence and their close relationships to their children. Some writers argue that women are particularly likely to develop an increased sense of self-worth from the independence and greater control over their life they achieve after divorce. ...

Less is known about long-term adjustment to divorce. ... [But] the amount of contact between children and their noncustodial fathers is shockingly low. In the 1981 *National Survey of Children* [United States], half of the children from maritally disrupted homes who were living with their mothers had not seen their fathers in the last year. Just one-sixth of these children, who were then age 12 to 16, were seeing their fathers as often as once a week.

Source: *Andrew J. Cherlin, 1992. Marriage, Divorce and Remarriage. Cambridge: Harvard University Press (pp. 73–75, 79–80).*

so fundamentally as the extent and effectiveness of control over marital fertility.

Just as marriage can be regarded as involving ongoing instrumental and expressive exchanges, so too the advent of children can be analyzed through the consideration of what they bring to the marriage in terms of "values" and "costs." The value and cost of children are here considered broadly to include both economic (instrumental) and noneconomic (expressive) components.

At the economic level, children are very costly, since they are largely dependent on their parents and do not contribute to family income. Henripin and Lapierre-Adamcyk (1986) found, on the basis of the 1982 *Family Expenditure Survey*, that the average annual direct cost of the first child is slightly more than $5000 per year. The costs vary with the age of the child, from relatively inexpensive preschool years to a very expensive adolescence. There are also indirect costs or revenues foregone as a result of the lower involvement of parents, especially mothers, in the labour force. These are highest at young ages. For example, two preschool children reduce revenues by some $7000 per year. Adding these costs until the age of seventeen, Dionne (1989) found that the first child costs some $83 000 for a lower-income family, $111 000 for one with medium income, and $149 000 for a higher-income family.

In 1989, three children aged seventeen, twelve, and ten would cost $20 000 for one year and, after taking into account tax benefits, would reduce the family's standard of living by 33 percent, compared with a family with no children.

The noneconomic costs and values of children are more difficult to determine. Children are costly in the sense that parents have less time and energy for themselves. Children are sometimes emotional and psychological burdens; parents worry about them and have to put up with various inconveniences, ranging from a messy place at the table to a dented car fender. On the positive side, children do offer certain advantages: people's status as adults can be more firmly established when they are parents; having children can provide a sense of achievement, of power and influence, of continuity beyond death; children provide immediate pleasure in the form of fun, excitement, and laughter in the home.

However, the value and cost of children do not cover the whole dynamics of childbearing. People are not completely free in the decision to have children (see Chapter 15, Demography and Population Study). There are often also normative influences that encourage couples to have children. This influence can be stronger in some groups than in others. The fact that fertility in Quebec was higher than in the country as a whole until the 1960s can be partly explained by normative influences that stressed "familism" in traditional French Canadian communities. There was considerable normative pressure on parents to have large families to preserve the French fact in Canada. This changed in the 1960s as community influence, through the Roman Catholic Church, became less intense and parents became more concerned with the cost of children. French Canadians are now more likely to have fewer children in order to take advantage of the new opportunities for social mobility that have opened up for them since the Quiet Revolution of the 1960s.

Although the level of fertility in Canada has gone down, most couples want to have children. According to census data, in 1981 only 7.3 percent of Canadian ever-married women between the ages of forty and forty-four had no live births. Childlessness was higher, at 30 percent, for women aged twenty-five to twenty-nine, but these women under thirty obviously still have time to have children. Indeed, among married women who had no children at the age of thirty in 1981, 45 percent had at least one child by the age of thirty-five in 1986 (Balakrishnan and Grindstaff, 1988). For the group of women born in 1951–56, Needleman (1986: 49) estimated that 15 percent of the ever-married will have no children. Remembering that biological sterility is around 5 to 6 percent, it is clear that, while voluntary childlessness is increasing, it still represents a minority of the population (Veevers, 1980; Ramu, 1984).

Childrearing

Not only do most couples want to have children, they generally take the childrearing role seriously. But while parents want to do a good job, they are faced with the considerable difficulties inherent in the role itself, at least as it is defined in our society (LeMasters and DeFrain, 1989). For instance, the parenthood role offers no margin of error; parents are expected to succeed with every child. In addition, parents cannot easily quit. They can escape from an unhappy marriage, but not from parenthood. In other words, they are supposed to keep trying, even if they know they are failing. Another problem is that parenthood involves being totally responsible for other human beings, yet not having full authority since other agencies also have an influence on what happens to the children. Finally, although there are high standards for the performance of the parenthood role, there is no established model to follow and little training available. That is, raising children remains the preserve of the amateur.

Perhaps as a result of these difficulties, couples with young children at home are more likely to be dissatisfied with their marriages than are childless couples or those whose children have left home. Eichler (1988: 181) argued that the strain involved in raising children may have increased recently because children are dependent longer, while at the same time there are fewer adults per household, along with fewer children who can keep each other busy. Yet, while marital satisfaction is lower when there are children at home, marital stability is higher. That is, couples with young children are less likely to separate, and marriages with no children are the most prone to divorce (Waite and Lillard, 1991).

Given the difficulties of childrearing, it is predictable that many parents feel frustrated when things do not go well, and that some parents transfer this frustration on to the children in the form of child abuse. This phenomenon is by no means new, but until recently it was largely ignored, both by the public and by researchers of the family (Propper, 1984). The variables now being uncovered that seem to be related to child abuse include parental immaturity, unrealistic expectations, lack of parental knowledge, social isolation, unmet emotional needs, and the parents' own abuse as children. A precipitating crisis then sets the abuse in motion. Moreover, there is in effect a general propensity to abuse, in the sense that adults have much power over children, including the legitimate use of physical strength to impose their authority. Since, as we have proposed, most parents also have high expectations for their children, abuse can occur when these expectations are somehow frustrated, especially if violence is seen as an acceptable form of family interaction.

Family change and children

Much of the analysis of families focuses on the marital partners rather than children. In a 1984 study, Marcil-Gratton (1988) provided insights into how low fertility, labour-force participation, and increased separation and divorce are relevant to the family lives of children. In the early 1960s, 25 percent of births were first births, compared with 44 percent in the early 1980s. This means that a greater proportion of children have "inexperienced" parents. They also have fewer older brothers and sisters: half of the generation born in the early 1960s had two older brothers or sisters, compared with one-fifth of those born twenty years later. One in five had a brother or sister ten or more years older, compared with one in twenty for the later generation. Because of lower fertility and its concentration over a shorter time in the lives of adults, children today have less opportunity to interact with and learn from siblings.

The changes in the work lives of mothers also affect children, as part of the socialization function is transferred to others at an increasingly young age. In the early 1960s, only 10 percent of mothers continued to work after the birth of a first child, compared with 50 percent in the early 1980s. The proportion working right after the birth in the early 1980s is comparable to the proportion working when children were twelve years old, twenty years earlier.

The diversity of marriage behaviour is also relevant. In the early 1960s, 5 percent of children were not born in a marriage, compared with 14 percent twenty years later. Among children born in the early 1960s, 13 percent saw their parents separate by the age of ten, compared with 23 percent for those born in the early 1970s. Among the latter, half had been in reconstituted families, 20 percent had seen a second episode of single parenthood, and 10 percent a second reconstituted family, all before the age of ten. Among children born in 1961–63, 8 percent lived in a single-parent family by the age of six, compared with 18 percent of those born in 1975–77. (See the boxed insert on "Children of Divorce.")

For both children and parents, remarried families can entail significant changes (Hobart, 1988). Fathers, in particular, tend to reduce their attachments once their children are in reconstituted families. Data from the United States suggest that the majority of fathers become marginal in the lives of their children within a few years of separation (Bumpass, 1990). Compared with those still married, separated mothers also have less contact with their adult children who have left home.

MARITAL BREAKDOWN

Having considered selected aspects of marital interaction, we turn our attention in this section to marital breakdown. We have proposed that a marriage involves ongoing instrumental and expressive exchanges and that it involves a form of commitment. How can we use this recognition of exchange and commitment to help us understand divorce trends?

Decrease in instrumental functions

It should be quite evident by now that there has been a decrease in the instrumental functions fulfilled by families. Thus, families have less to hold them

Children of Divorce

This excerpt largely focuses on how children are negatively affected by divorce. What features would produce more positive outcomes for children in divorce?

While divorce may present a solution to a couple's problems, we must not forget that there is also pain associated with divorce, much of it suffered by children. In 1991, 13.8 percent of children under fifteen were living with one parent, double the 1966 figure. From observations of children in Toronto, Ambert demonstrates how bad marriages, whether they remain intact or break up, are detrimental to young people.

Personal observation of some fifty children, between five and thirteen years of age, with parents who had separated (many were also divorced) within the past three years, leads me to believe that, if there is a true victim of divorce, it is the child; indeed, I have not met one single child who had not been adversely affected, at least in the short term, by the disintegration of his or her parents' marriage. The symptoms I most commonly observed were sadness or melancholy, a desire for parental reunion (often even after remarriage or in the context of impending remarriage), a certain discomfort among peers from intact families (the need to explain the situation even if not asked about it, outright lies about parents' marital status and whereabouts or embarrassment when asked), a fear of not being loved by one or both parents, attempts to take as much advantage as possible of each parent, lack of parental guidance, and at times gross permissiveness on the part of parents who felt guilty about their children.

This last point was present in all their parents, and is an element in the post-separation parent–child relationship which has not been adequately researched. All the separated and divorced parents I observed were harboring feelings of guilt vis-à-vis their children, often disproportionate to the harm actually done to the child. This parental guilt, combined with a fear of losing the children's love, leads to various attempts to compensate for the situation that are not healthy for the child; material gifts to a child increase at the risk of passing on to the child the message that material possessions mean love.

Another common form of compensation is over-permissiveness. I did not find instances of greater restrictiveness or permissiveness in mothers or in custody fathers, but I found, typically, greater permissiveness in all the fathers who were the non-custody parent. These fathers allowed their children to do things that they would not previously have accepted, such as drinking alcoholic beverages under age, being drunk, seeing risqué films or shows, eating too much and too many sweets, rudeness to them, their mothers and other adults (including stepmothers and girl friends), lying, minor forms of vandalism, and truancy. I also observed several fathers who were "proud" of their teenage sons' sexual adventures and even exploitation of young girls; these fathers had generally been adulterous themselves. It was as if the sons' behavior helped to justify the fathers' act: the fathers felt that the sons "understood" them. In these same cases, I observed a distancing between mothers and sons.

Even though they may rationally accept divorce as necessary, as better than an unhappy intact marriage, most children never accept divorce emotionally and hope, often for many years and despite remarriage, that their parents will come together again. This is why many such children reject a remarriage and may even sabotage it after it has taken place.

The following quote, from a student autobiography, is revealing of a different attitude.

> Looking back, I just wish my parents had divorced. Rather, they stayed together for us kids. But, at night, I used to bury my head under my pillow (I still have the habit: I sleep like that even though I am now married) so I would not hear their yelling and their quarrelling. I just wished my father would leave. We would have been so much happier.

Source: *Anne-Marie Ambert, 1980.* Divorce in Canada. *Don Mills, Ont.: Academic Press (pp. 171–73).*

together. This is particularly true in the economic domain, where families now involve considerably less economic interdependence. For the wife, it is much easier to get out of an unhappy marriage if she is employed and in a senior partner–junior partner marriage than if she is in a head-complement marriage. Moreover, if she no longer receives her status from her marriage, the prospect of moving out is less negative. Stated differently, the greater independence of women makes the divorce alternative more viable.

Considering instrumental functions helps us to understand several other things about the incidence of divorce. Divorces are less likely to occur when there are young, dependent children because the family is more economically interdependent at that time. Indeed, both childless couples and those in the empty nest stage have higher risks of divorce (Rowe, 1989).

Divorce levels are also higher at lower levels of socio-economic status. A lower income means that the instrumental exchanges in the marriage are less rewarding, making the prospect of divorce less negative for working-class individuals.

Importance of the expressive dimension

We have argued that marriage now is seen much more as an arrangement for the mutual gratification of participants. Spouses now expect more from families in terms of intimacy and interpersonal affect. In addition, individual well-being and self-fulfilment are seen as important values. Families are expected to serve individual needs, rather than individuals serving family needs. Therefore, divorce may be more prevalent today because it represents a natural solution to marriages that do not serve the mutual gratification of the persons involved.

One of the most consistent findings in divorce research is that the probabilities of divorce are higher for those getting married at an early age. For women aged thirty-five to forty-nine, the probability of marital dissolution among those who married at nineteen years of age or younger was almost twice as large (26 versus 14 percent) as that for those who married at the age of twenty-five or older (Balakrishnan and Grindstaff, 1988). There are several reasons for the higher divorce levels among those marrying young; some were discussed in the previous section. The lower income associated with youth means that the instrumental exchanges may be less rewarding. Furthermore, those marrying young are more likely to be downwardly mobile, especially if the wife is pregnant at the time of marriage, because this detracts from the possibility of pursuing further education. Regarding the expressive dimension, one can hypothesize that, as these young married persons mature, they find their spouses have been poor choices and they do not receive the expected gratification. It may even be that, for persons marrying at younger ages, emotional gratification is particularly important. Early marriage may have been a way of escaping an unrewarding situation in their original families. If the expressive dimension is especially important to them, they will be more likely to separate if this dimension is not working.

The higher incidence of divorce for second marriages can be seen in this light as well. The lowest dissolution rate is for marriages involving two previously single people, while those involving a divorced woman and a single man or two divorced persons have the highest failure rates (Dumas, 1990: 28). Persons who have already divorced are more likely to see marriage in terms of mutual gratification and to leave a marriage that is not rewarding.

It is clear that the rejection of one marriage is not to be confused with the rejection of marriage *per se*. In fact, persons who are divorced are more likely to get married in any one given year than never-married people of the same age (Dumas, 1985: 17). In 1984–86, divorced persons had a 23 percent chance of marriage during the following year, compared with a 12 percent chance for single persons (Adams and Nagnur, 1988). The average duration of divorce—or the period until remarriage or death—is eight years for men and sixteen years for women. Persons getting divorced are generally not doing so because they do not want to be married; instead, they do so because they find the exchanges with a *particular* partner to be unrewarding.

Redefinition of the marital commitment

Obviously, divorce would be less common if everyone frowned on it and if the legal restrictions were formidable. But there has been a significant change in the attitudes towards divorce in Western societies. The social stigma attached to marital dissolution has lessened considerably and people now accept that divorce occurs frequently among the "normal" population. There has also been considerable change in the definition of acceptable grounds for dissolving marital commitments. Until 1968, adultery was the only grounds for divorce in Canada. The 1968 Divorce Act extended the grounds for divorce to include both fault-related grounds and marriage-breakdown grounds. Fault-related grounds include adultery and other sexual offences, prolonged alcohol or drug addiction, and physical and mental cruelty. To obtain a divorce on these grounds, there must be an injured party who brings the other spouse to trial, which then finds him or her guilty. As of 1986, divorce under marriage-breakdown grounds can occur after spouses have lived apart for one year, for whatever reason.

Figure 9.1 indicates quite clearly the jump in divorce levels with the advent of the 1968 Act. Part of this jump includes the backlog of separations that occurred before 1968. Even taking this into account, there still has been a great increase in divorce since 1968. Nault and Belanger (1996: 17) have calculated that, if persons marrying today experience the divorce rate observed in 1991, 31 percent of their marriages will be dissolved through divorce. Compared with other countries, Canadian rates are higher than in Japan, France, or Germany, roughly the same as those of Sweden and the United Kingdom, and considerably lower than in the United States.

FIGURE 9.1 Divorce rates, 1951–1994

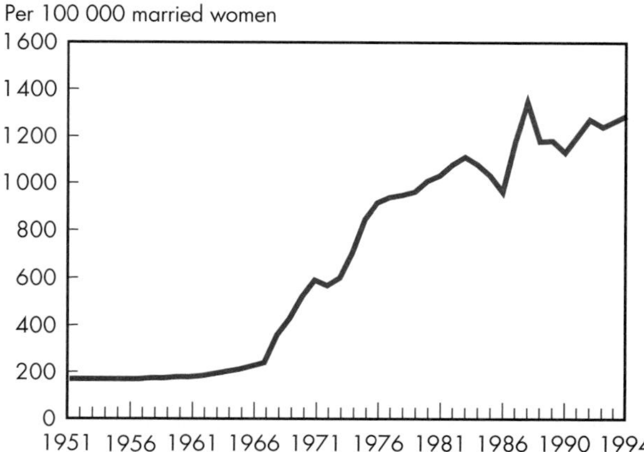

Source: *O. Adams, 1988. "Divorce rates in Canada."* Canadian Social Trends *11 (p. 19); Statistics Canada, 1996.* Divorce 1994, *Catalogue No. 84-213-XPB.*

CHANGE AND CONTINUITY IN FAMILY PATTERNS

In a sense, there has been considerable change in family patterns over the last few decades. Skolnick (1987), for example, argued that the 1950s were the "golden age of family," but this has changed over time due to the politics surrounding family life in the latter part of the century. Since the 1970s, the effects of the women's movement, especially the increasing participation of women in the labour force and the questioning of traditional gender roles, have brought about changes in families. In particular, there is a greater amount of flexibility and diversity in what is defined as acceptable with regard to marriage and family living. The less formal marital arrangement of common-law unions is something that would not have been acceptable a few decades ago. Other elements of flexibility in family living include the greater acceptability of single parenthood, childlessness, blended families with children from more than one union, and even gay marriages.

The following reflection of a minister after performing a gay marriage indicates this openness to alternate forms of intimacy:

> Gay people have the same desire for happiness and ought to have the same right to happiness in our society as heterosexuals. And one of those rights is the chance (with the same lack of guarantees of success or permanence we all struggle with) to create a marital relationship of depth and love (Strong et al., 1983: 340).

With all these changes, some have suggested that "the family" is in crisis (see the boxed insert "The Family in Crisis?"). While some may regret the erosion of traditional family values, others see these changes as liberating. For instance, living as a common-law couple is not a problem, except possibly for the old-fashioned parents of those involved; divorce is often a solution to a poor marriage; later marriage and lower fertility are liberating, for women in particular (Beaujot, 1990).

A better description of what is happening for the vast majority of people, however, is probably continuity in family patterns. There is no evidence

The Family in Crisis?

We often hear reference to the family being in a state of crisis. In a book entitled *The Canadian Family in Crisis*, John F. Conway stated his reasons for believing this is so.

Conway viewed the family as undergoing a major transition, from the traditional patriarchal family (dominant since industrialization) to an egalitarian family, and argued that, while this transition is under way, the family is in a state of serious crisis. This crisis partly involves the family's ability to do what it is supposed to do: support children, women, and men.

Recent social, economic, and technological changes have brought about this crisis. In particular, there are various contradictions between the move towards gender equality and the assumptions of the traditional patriarchal family based on complementary husband and wife roles.

According to Conway, without adequate child care we see many of the consequences of this crisis in the lives of children who are subject to the insecurity of family breakdown and absent fathers. We see the vulnerability of children in the numbers who are abused, living in poverty, or even committing suicide. In effect, the family is not providing the support that children need.

Other consequences of the crisis are felt by women who are caught in various contradictions. In particular, they are expected to be involved in the labour force, yet the work world is not ready to accept them on an equal footing with men. At home, some are abused and more are fatigued as they perform a double duty, because husbands are not taking on an equal share of housework and child care. Many women decide to move out of a marriage in order to resolve some of the conflict, but that brings the additional problems of single parenthood, especially poverty.

Conway proposed that men are also subject to some of the consequences of the crisis in the family. He said that they have a sense of unease, that is, they are not sure what is expected of them. They too are suffering from the contradictions between the traditional and the egalitarian assumptions. In some ways, they are also subject to a double burden in terms of work and family life, expected to give a hundred percent to career achievements yet also expected to do more at home. In addition, many men are separated from their children and miss the basic human interactions with children that they consider to be an important part of family life.

While Conway saw that the family is in crisis, he was optimistic because he argued that the void created by the death of the traditional family, which arose during industrialization, will be filled by an egalitarian family. While the whole book is about family difficulties, he ends with the concept of a "joyous funeral" for the family's previous form. At the same time, much social change would be needed to bring about this egalitarian family. In particular, for women there is the need for equality in the work world, that is, pay equity and employment equity. For children there is the need for support mechanisms, in particular day care, while parents are at work. For both mothers and fathers there is the need for various changes, such as parental leave and flex time, to enable a better accommodation between roles inside and outside the family.

What do you think about Conway's interpretation and propositions? Is it true that the family is in a state of crisis? Will an egalitarian family resolve the conflicts between the world of work and the private world? Will an egalitarian family be more stable?

Source: *R. Beaujot, 1995. "Review of John F. Conway, The Canadian Family in Crisis,"* Journal of Comparative Family Studies *26, 2: 284–86.*

that marriage is going out of style, since most adults continue to choose to live in families. The level of divorce has gone up drastically, but remarriage is the mode for divorced persons. It is perhaps more accurate to refer to divorce in terms of family *re*-organization rather than family *dis*organization. Although the proportion of adults living alone has increased, there is a strong preference for marriage, or at least for some form of intimate relationship. Although separation and divorce have increased, the 1984 *Family History Survey* found that seven out of ten women with children were still in their first nuclear families by the survey date. This survey also indicated that 90 percent of those who had ever married did so only once. Although the level of childbearing has gone down, there is little rejection of parenthood *per se*. Although there has been a liberation of gender roles, with more women in the labour force, wives still contribute on average one-third of the family income and do two-thirds of the housework.

It would seem, then, that the family continues to thrive as an important social institution, although in a variety of forms. Families may not play the same roles, or as many roles as in the past, and they are not as permanent, but they remain crucial to the lives of most people.

SUMMARY

A family is two or more people related by blood, marriage, or adoption, and who reside together. Marriage involves a commitment and ongoing expressive and instrumental exchanges between partners. A look at various cultures shows uniformity in family patterns in some aspects, such as the incest taboo, but variability in others, such as monogamy and polygyny. Thus, there is much variety and complexity to family behaviour, and it is necessary to view family questions against the background of the larger society. This variety is also visible when we look historically at family change. For example, the Industrial Revolution introduced a greater separation between the economic sphere of "public" activity and the "private" family sphere.

In the theory section, we attempted to understand some of the historical changes in families from a structural functionalist perspective. With regard to family structure, the functionalist approach points to a decrease in the extent of social control that kinship networks exercise over individuals. As well, families no longer perform some of the functions that they previously provided for the larger society. On the other hand, families now play a more important role in the emotional gratification of their individual members.

The section on gender roles placed the study of families within a conflict context and examined the roles that men and women typically play in society, roles that are very much affected by their respective relationships within the process of economic production. Wives' economic role decreased with industrialization, since production was moved outside of the family setting, but it is now increasing as more women have joined the paid labour force. A second consideration regarding gender roles is the fact that our cultural inheritance gives certain advantages to males. During the Victorian period, and to a lesser extent in the "golden age of the family" in the 1950s, there was considerable pressure on women to concentrate their attention on homemaking and child care. Here again, the recent period has witnessed considerable change.

In the section on socialization for marriage and mate selection, we first noted that there is little systematic knowledge available to inform people about what to expect from marriage. Also, boys tend to be socialized towards the sexual and girls towards the emotional aspect of heterosexual relationships. Dating was described as an exchange or bargaining situation in which the person with the most to offer has the most power. Within this dating "environment," moreover, there are several normative standards in existence. As we saw, the abstinence standard has decreased, while the love standard, or permissiveness with affection, is the most representative of post-secondary-school students. We saw as well how love plays an important role in mate selection in our society, partly because everyone expects to fall in love. This is certainly not the only factor operating; homogamy is also important, with similar people getting married to each other more often than those who are different in social, economic, and physical characteristics. In addition, the woman in a marriage is often younger than the man. This age gap tends to entrench traditional gender-role differences.

The section on marital interactions first considered the marital life cycle. The empty nest stage is an important and relatively new stage in this cycle. Another new stage is a premarital one involving young people living together before marriage. Considering the structure of marriage, it was suggested that an important proportion of Canadian marriages are of the head-complement type, in which the husband has basic responsibility for earning the family income and the wife for care of the home and family. The largest category is the senior partner–junior partner type, in which the wife contributes to the family income and the husband helps with home and child care.

Regarding childbearing, it was shown that children are expensive and that people are having fewer of them. There has been a weakening of the norm that childbearing is an essential part of marriage. Nonetheless, most couples have children and want to perform well in the difficult job of childrearing.

The rising level of marital breakdown was related to the decrease in instrumental functions played by the family, the increase in the importance of the expressive dimension in marriage, and the changing definition of the commitment.

Finally, while there is a larger variety of family forms today, including especially common-law unions and single-parent families, we saw how continuity is a better description of what is happening in the family patterns of the vast majority of people.

QUESTIONS FOR REVIEW AND CRITICAL THINKING

1. There are a number of alternatives to the traditional husband/wife/two-children family, e.g., homosexual union, reconstituted family, patrilocality, and polygyny. Choose several alternatives and describe the strengths and weaknesses of each.

2. Talk to your friends and try to determine how much gender-role differences affect expectations about mate selection and marriage.

3. While modern families may represent an improvement for spouses, especially wives, they are worse for children. Discuss.

4. Examine a month's copies of a daily newspaper from the Depression, World War II, the 1950s, and recent times to see if the social pages reveal differences in family structure.

GLOSSARY

expressive exchanges the emotional dimension of marriage, including sexual gratification, companionship, and empathy

heterogamy marriage between persons who are dissimilar in some important regard such as religion, ethnic background, social class, personality, or age

homogamy marriage of persons with similar physical, psychological, or social characteristics. This is the tendency for like to marry like.

instrumental exchanges the task-oriented dimension of marriage, including earning a living, spending money, and maintaining a household

marital structures the four common forms of husband–wife relationships within marriage. **Owner-property marriage** is a marriage in which the husband owns his wife; in a **head-complement marriage** the wife finds meaning in life through her husband; in a **senior partner–junior partner marriage** the wife is employed, but her job and income are less important than her husband's; and in an **equal partners marriage** both spouses are equally committed to marriage and a career.

marriage a commitment and an ongoing exchange. The commitment can include legal or contractual elements, as well as the social pressures against dissolution. The arrangement includes both instrumental and expressive exchanges.

mating gradient the lesser power of a woman in marriage, partly due to her being younger than her husband

premarital sexual standards standards by which people judge the acceptability of premarital sex. The **abstinence standard** allows no premarital sex;

the **double standard** allows premarital sex for men only; the **love standard** permits premarital sex for persons of either gender if they are in love; and the **fun standard** approves of premarital sex for either gender, even without love.

Note: Other important terms are defined in Chart 9.1.

SUGGESTED READINGS

Ambert, Anne-Marie

1992 *The Effect of Children on Parents*. New York: Harworth.

While most studies consider how parents affect children, Ambert considers the two-way relationships between parents and children, as well as the relevance of the broader social context. Children clearly have considerable effects on parents, and these are often not properly recognized.

Ariès, Philippe

1962 *Centuries of Childhood*. New York: Knopf.

Ariès has written a very readable classic on the different orientations of past generations towards children and families.

Conway, John F.

1993 *The Canadian Family in Crisis*. Toronto: James Lorimer.

This book considers how family change is having an impact on the lives of children, women, and men. Relevant public policy considerations are offered for improving people's lives in a variety of family forms.

Larson, Lyle, J. Walter Goltz, and Charles Hobart

1994 *Families in Canada: Social Context, Continuities, and Changes*. Scarborough, Ont.: Prentice Hall.

After considering theoretical, methodological, historical, and anthropological questions, this textbook takes a life cycle approach to summarize the research on Canadian families.

WEB SITES

http://www.yahoo.com/Society_and_Culture/Families

Yahoo! Society and Culture: Families

The perfect resource for anyone doing research on family issues, this site provides links to dozens of sites worldwide dealing with a range of topics, from fatherhood to dating and marriage, to parenting generally.

http://www.mts.net/callmom/

The Call Mom Line and File Folder

This page proves that mothers come in all shapes and sizes. Here, direct from cyberspace, you can read published questions and answers from clients seeking advice about the problems of day to day life.

SAINT GABRIEL OF THE SORROWFUL VIRGIN

CHAPTER 10

Religion

F.R. Westley and Fred Bird

INTRODUCTION

No one subject appears more consistently in the work of the early European sociologists than religion. Durkheim, Marx, and Weber each wrote extensively and movingly on the question of religion, and their works seem to be driven by the same basic questions. What is the source of the awesome power that religion can have over the minds of believers? What are the consequences of religion for social life? What is the origin of the inevitable tension that seems to exist between the religious and secular spheres, the sacred and the profane? What is the future of religion? All three men wrote from a deep commitment to rational thought as the way to truth and understanding. From such a perspective, religion seemed initially (and in some cases finally) the last bastion of superstition, ignorance, and darkness. And yet all three, born as they were into religious homes, expressed even in their criticisms a sense of nostalgia, as of something lost. And they were impressed by the toughness and resilience of religion, in the face of what they considered to be overwhelming odds. In the end, all three came to treat religion with a grudging respect.

Nor can contemporary sociologists ignore the importance of religion. Religious beliefs and rituals have appeared in some form in all societies and in all times. Religion as a social institution has been a powerful organizing and socializing force in many societies, and continues to be so today. Religion as a system of symbols has for centuries formed the basic fabric of culture—the ideas, values, and artifacts that reflect and support the social organization of any society. This chapter attempts to explore some of the answers that early sociologists and contemporary thinkers have given to the questions concerning the nature and future of religion.

WHAT IS RELIGION?

Confronted with a variety of religious beliefs and activities, sociologists have long debated how to define religion. Weber dodged the basic question. Instead of offering a succinct definition, he observed in passing that religions seemed to be organized around attempts to make sense of an irrational and hostile world. Marx was somewhat more straightforward when he referred to religion as the opiate of the masses. However, this seemingly disparaging statement was balanced by others in which Marx identified religions as social organizations that acted to aid the oppressed, served as vehicles for protesting against their suffering, and carried cultural information and social mores. Durkheim's view was functional. Religions were culturally transmitted systems of beliefs and rituals set forth to distinguish between sacred and inviolable objects and times, and profane realities with which people might interact casually and practically. At the same time, Durkheim regarded religions as the embodiment of ideals and social forces such as social solidarity.

Debates about what constitutes religion and about the measures of religious sentiments and practices have continued. Some have equated religiosity with specific beliefs, membership practices, nominal adherence, or particular kinds of experience. Others have argued that religious identifications and practices are multifaceted, that there are various ways of being religious, which may include asceticism, or denial of worldly pleasures, the occasional

Can Religion Make People Happier and Healthier?

A study in 1994 of university students in London, Ontario, focused on the relationship between religion and well-being. More specifically, the question was whether depth of faith and quality of religious experience had an impact on the physical and psychological health of students.

The study involved nearly 300 students at the University of Western Ontario, some of them affiliated with Christian faith groups on the campus and others not. The "affiliated" students, numbering 172, belonged to groups associated with the Anglican, Christian Reformed, Lutheran, Roman Catholic, and United churches, as well as three major interdenominational fellowships—Campus Crusade for Christ, Intervarsity Christian Fellowship, and Navigators. The "non-affiliated" students, numbering 127, were selected from undergraduate sociology classes to serve as a basis of comparison. The sample was deliberately chosen this way, not to be a representative sample of university students, but in order to ensure the inclusion of students of different faiths and varying levels of religious commitment. In addition, only Christian groups were selected, to minimize the effects of other explanatory factors, such as cultural differences, on the findings.

Using a detailed self-administered survey form, the students answered a number of questions about their physical and emotional health, stress, beliefs and values, religious practices, and faith experiences. The data revealed that both groups of students had encountered a number of stressful events in the six months prior to the study. The affiliated group, however, reported slightly fewer events and, more importantly, they experienced significantly less stress related to those events than the non-affiliated students. On a standard measure of happiness or emotional well-being, the affiliated students also scored significantly higher, and believed themselves to be healthier than their non-affiliated counterparts; they were also less likely to have visited their family physicians, walk-in clinics, or hospital emergency rooms during the six months before the study. In terms of overall life satisfaction, the affiliated students were more content with all aspects of their lives and more likely to be involved in volunteer activities, both in their church communities and in the larger society.

The affiliated and non-affiliated students were similar in self-esteem and mastery—two personality traits that help people deal with stress. What really made the difference, then, for the affiliated people? Was it simply belonging to a religious group or was it something else? Was it going to church? Prayer? Having a personal relationship with God? Having a strong spiritual orientation? Making a financial commitment to the church, either currently as a student or in the future? In fact, all of these dimensions were significantly associated with better physical and emotional health. It does seem, then, that there are important benefits to be gained from a strong faith.

The results of the study seem to reflect something about religious commitment. No direct causal interpretation that would suggest that people ought to run out and join the nearest religious organization can be made, however. Nor do the results of this study negate the general trend towards declining service attendance and religious commitment in Canadian society. The results do suggest that among the students studied, those who report more frequent prayer, regular church attendance, significant financial commitment to their churches, a sense of closeness to God, and a strong spiritual orientation are more satisfied with their lives, feel that they are in better health both physically and emotionally, and are better able to deal with stress.

Source: *B. Gail Frankel, 1993. Written for this volume.*

attendance at religious services, participation at religiously celebrated weddings and funerals, pilgrimages to venerated sites, or prayers before sporting events (Glock and Stark, 1967).

At a general level, however, we may define **religion** as any culturally transmitted system of beliefs and rituals that people use to orient themselves to their world and its meaning in relation to some reality (or realities) regarded as sacred. Yet even this rather loose definition raises concerns. One is how to distinguish between religious activities and other similar human activities; a second is how to identify what it means to be truly and intensely religious, and how to distinguish this from less pure and fervent expressions. The second question is value-laden and can really be answered only from a particular religious or anti-religious point of view. The first question is more conducive to examination by sociologists. Let us see how this examination has been attempted from the functionalist, symbolic interactionist, and conflict perspectives as found in the work of Durkheim, Weber, and Marx, respectively.

PERSPECTIVES ON RELIGION: THE WORK OF DURKHEIM, WEBER AND MARX

Emile Durkheim: the causes and consequences of religion

Durkheim's view of religion ran contrary to that of many social thinkers of his time, who thought of religion as complete illusion, a fiction sprung from human imagination, reflecting nothing but that imagination. Arguing from a functionalist perspective, Durkheim felt that since religion of some kind appeared in all times and places, it must fulfil some important social role, and its power over the minds of adherents cannot be lightly dismissed as illusion or misapprehension. On the other hand, Durkheim felt that religion is partly illusion. While religious experience is real enough, believers are confused about the origins of the experience. It is the role of the social scientist, according to Durkheim, to get beneath the surface of religious symbols and rituals in order to understand the source of the power they evoke and to get at the kernel of the reality they express.

The power of the sacred

Durkheim (1965 [1912]) began his study of religion by looking more closely at the nature of religious experience itself. He was interested in why people feel that a power exists which is both outside of and greater than themselves, a power capable of acting on them with or without their consent. He noted that this experience of an outside, superhuman power is basic to most religions, and that individuals most commonly experience this power during religious celebrations or festivals in which they are gathered together with other people. He also noted that people usually attribute the power to **sacred** objects and activities shared by the group, but set apart and treated with awe and respect.

Having discovered these recurring patterns in various religions, Durkheim then asked whether there exists an equivalent nonreligious experience that produces the same sentiments in participants. Is there perhaps a social as opposed to a supernatural explanation for religious experience? Borrowing from the work of LeBon (1960 [1895]) and his studies of crowd psychology, Durkheim noted that people behave quite differently in groups than they do alone. Crowds are capable of generating in individuals levels of excitement, panic, and ecstasy that they would be quite incapable of experiencing alone. When in any crowd, Durkheim argued, individuals may lose their distinct character and will and become part of something larger than themselves: the group. If asked to identify the source of the emotion that grips them, they will usually name the object of crowd concern, for example, "I panicked because of the fire," but, in fact, their panic might be out of proportion to the real danger of the fire. Alone, each might have responded quite differently to the fire. The real source of their panic is the group interaction. (Crowd behaviour is further discussed in Chapter 14, Social Movements.) Durkheim termed this emotional and contagious aspect of crowd behaviour *collective effervescence.*

From this comparison between religion and crowd behaviour, Durkheim hypothesized that the source of the religious experience might in fact be group life itself. Perhaps, as with crowds of any kind, religious gatherings generate a sense of excitement, awe, or terror, which the individual attributes to supernatural forces or deities that are the focus of the gathering. However, he asked, why does belief in such deities not vanish when the group disperses? And how is it possible in the first place for reasoning individuals to lose themselves so completely in the emotion of the group?

Durkheim's answer to both questions lay in the very nature of the human individual. As social beings, individuals are shaped and socialized from the very beginning by the actions and attitudes of other members of society. Society, in the form of parents and teachers, shapes in individuals a sense of duty, of obligations, and of right and wrong behaviour. As it does so, it instils in them a voice of conscience they cannot escape, even though at times it seems foreign to them and contrary to their immediate desires. In short, individuals are never free from the attitudes of their social groups. At times of collective effervescence, individuals merely succumb more completely to the group will. But even when alone, they carry with them the group will, in the form of conscience.

We can see, by following Durkheim's logic, how he came to believe that the power the sacred seems to have over the minds of individuals is really the power the *group* has over the minds of individuals. The experience of collective effervescence, which in religious gatherings is attributed to the presence of the sacred, in fact can be generated by the presence of others caught up in any common concern or activity that transcends their individual perspectives. This social experience contains the properties of the religious experience: the sense of being acted on by something outside the self and greater than the self, and the sense of being carried away. And according to Durkheim, these feelings are accurate representations of individuals' relations to their social groups. Individuals in fact are part of something larger: the social group. They are deeply affected by the collective ideals and sentiments of that group, with or without their conscious consent. The only inaccuracy is believers' perceptions that attribute power to the sacred symbol or deity, as opposed to its true source: society itself.

Durkheim also felt that a true understanding of the workings of religion can be achieved only by studying the simplest forms of religion, in the same way that a biologist begins by studying single-cell organisms. He chose totemism, the religion of the Arunta, an Australian aboriginal tribe, as the simplest form of known religion. Working secondhand from anthropological documents, Durkheim used the tribal belief system to illustrate his theory that religious experience reflects social experience, that sacred power is in fact social power.

The Arunta Totemism as a religion was based on the worship of a sacred animal or totem. Durkheim was interested in the relation between this form of worship and the social organization of the Arunta. Was there a similarity to be found there between sacred and social experience? Were they functionally related? Once again, Durkheim argued that the two were in fact the same thing.

Durkheim believed that the power the sacred seems to have over the minds of individuals is really the power the group has over the minds of individuals.

Durkheim began by outlining the social organization of the Arunta. The tribe was divided into a number of clans. These were organized on the basis of patrilineal kinship groups—an arrangement, unlike that of our bilateral descent families, which meant that all members of a group could identify a common male ancestor and trace back the history of the family as a distinct, highly coherent group, one continuous through time. All members of the Arunta identified themselves not with the tribe as a whole but with their particular clan.

The social experience of life in the clan included a sense of identification with other clan members. Participation in group activities for the Arunta meant participation in clan activities. Any feelings of collective effervescence that group gatherings produced in the individual would be centred on clan membership. Initially, Durkheim argued, the clan adopted a symbol or emblem to focus these strong emotional feelings of membership, a symbol that then served to *represent* the intense experience of group life. The obvious choice for such an emblem, according to Durkheim, was the ancestor of the group, since the ancestor represented an element that all clan members had in common. One human being looked much like another, however, and did not represent the unique and distinctive aspect of the clan. Therefore, clan members selected an animal, chosen from various animals that were part of the world of the Arunta, to represent their common ancestor. Gradually over time, argued Durkheim, the ancestor *became* the emblem, i.e., the people of the Bear clan came to see themselves as descended from a sacred bear. That being the case, it was forbidden to eat the totem animal, as it might be forbidden to eat another human being. The sacred power, which had originally been a property of the group because of their shared ancestor, came to be seen as a property of the emblem of that ancestor and, finally, as a property of all the animals of the same species as the emblematic or totem animal.

Durkheim used this insight to explain several other seemingly related aspects of the Arunta religion. For example, why were menstruating Arunta kinswomen considered taboo, shut away in menstrual huts, and seen as dangerous? Durkheim argued that, since all sacred objects are treated with respect and avoidance, perhaps there was something about menstruating kin that made them sacred. He suggested that, if the clan itself were in fact sacred, then the blood of the clan itself might also be sacred, since it was something clan members had in common (in addition to their ancestors). The blood was passed down to them from their common ancestor and linked them together. Therefore, just as the totem animal symbolic of the clan was avoided, so must the blood of kin be avoided. This would explain why menstruating kinswomen would be shut away from others.

Taking this logic one step further, Durkheim suggested that, if the blood of clan members were sacred and therefore to be avoided, then sexual intercourse between a man and a woman of the same kinship group would also have to be avoided, to protect against the possible contact with menstrual blood. Hence the Arunta always married outside their own kinship group. Durkheim argued that this was a better explanation of the rule against endogamy (see Chapter 9, Families) than an incest taboo, because an Arunta could marry his mother's brother's daughter, but not his father's brother's daughter. Both were in fact equally close, but the first was not a member of his patrilineal kinship clan group, whereas the latter was. Hence Durkheim was able to use his insight, that the real sacred object was the clan itself, to explain a number of other beliefs and practices of the Arunta.

In sum, Durkheim saw both the origins of religious experience and the source of religious power in the effects of the social group on the individual, whether in the collective effervescence of the crowd or in the socially taught, consensually supported individual conscience. He argued that individuals in a society experience these effects as coming from outside themselves, and as being greater than themselves, and that they then attribute them to deities or sacred symbols. Once this transference has been made, however, it has enormous consequences for individuals and for society. Particularly in nonindustrial or traditional societies, the beliefs and rituals that surround the sacred have an extensive impact on the daily life of individuals. This aspect of religion was for Durkheim, as a functionalist, a second central concern: the consequences or functions of religion for individuals and social groups.

The functions of religion

In his study of the Arunta, Durkheim dealt with a small, isolated, nonindustrial social group, in which all members participated in the same religious rituals and shared the same religious beliefs. In such a group, Durkheim argued, there seemed to be five social **functions of religion**: it helped to (1) *integrate* individual members into a group, (2) *regulate* their daily activities, and (3) *empower* their activities with a sense of meaning or purpose. On a cognitive level, it helped individuals to (4) *interpret* the social and natural world, and (5) *represent* or express their relation to the social group.

A more recent example, this one closer to home, of a traditional community in which religion maintained its central role and where its functions and consequences for individuals were relatively clear was the community of St. Denis, a small (pop. 700) French Canadian, Roman Catholic farming parish between Montreal and Quebec City, which Miner (1963 [1939]) studied in 1936. In this community, all five religious functions that Durkheim identified were clearly visible. We shall therefore use this example to illustrate in greater detail what Durkheim meant by the functions or consequences of religion.

The parish of St. Denis The religious beliefs of the parishioners of St. Denis, Miner said, served to *integrate* individuals into the social group. At birth, children of the parish began a series of rituals that determined their relationship to the community. Before baptism, children had none of the social rights accorded others of the parish, since they were not seen yet as members of the group. If babies died before baptism, no masses were sung and no mourning worn, and they were buried outside the consecrated cemetery ground. Not until children had received both *petite communion* and *grande communion* were they admitted as full members of the social group. The religious ceremonies of baptism, communion, and later marriage and burial, were each a step that transformed and defined the individuals' relationship to the social group, their rights and duties, and bound them to the community.

A second way in which religion functioned to integrate members into St. Denis society was by bringing them together physically in one place. Miner pointed out that the only time all the members of the community were together was at Sunday mass. The times before and after mass were important times for the exchange of information—such as announcements concerning community news, dates of council meetings, taxes due, veterinarian visits, and tuberculosis testing—and for social celebration. The religious service, by bringing members together, integrated them into a common timetable of social, business, and civic activity.

Religious rituals and beliefs also helped to *regulate* the daily life of parishioners. In his discussion of the Arunta, Durkheim noted how all aspects of a nonindustrial society's life were divided into two categories, the sacred and the profane. The sacred in general included those activities or things that individuals shared with the group as a whole, whereas **profane** things and activities typically concerned only the individual.

In the parish of St. Denis, time, space, and daily activities were silently divided into the sacred and secular spheres. Birth marked the entrance into the secular sphere; baptism and communion marked steps into the sacred sphere. Death was the final transition into a totally sacred existence. Daily life was also divided into sacred and profane time by prayers—the family prayed together morning and evening—and by small religious observances. The week was divided up further by attendance at mass and by rituals of confession and penance.

Space was also divided into sacred and secular spheres. Heaven was above; hell was below. Churches and cemeteries were built on high points of land, and sacred objects were protected from contact with the earth. The parishioners regulated their own attitudes in accordance with these divisions. Adoration was signified by looking up; submission, by kneeling and downcast eyes.

The individual had little choice about whether or not to follow these observances. From early childhood, great pressure was exerted on individuals to encourage some activities and to restrict others. For example, a child who refused to go to mass met with disapproval not only from parents and grandparents, but also from teachers and priests. No one in the community condoned this behaviour. Members could safely depend on each other to fulfil mutual obligations and to support each other's values.

From one perspective, this regulating function of religion certainly restricted individual freedom. On the other hand, the regulation provided a built-in comfort and reassurance for the individual believer in St. Denis. The picture of the community is thus one of restricted freedom based upon consensus and harmony.

Religion provided comfort in other ways to the residents of St. Denis. It *empowered* individuals, giving them a sense that their lives were meaningful despite the sacrifices and suffering they endured. As long as they participated in the appropriate rituals and received the last rites, they believed their struggles would eventually be rewarded in heaven. A pregnant mother of six, struggling against fatigue and poverty, could confess her distress to her priest and leave reassured that she would be blessed for her sacrifices and that her duties had meaning in the larger divine scheme. Thus, the religious beliefs of the parishioners of St. Denis provided comfort, hope, and meaning, and gave them the strength to endure the hardships of daily life.

Religion also helped the parishioners to *interpret* events in their lives. Unusual happenings could be explained as miracles, representing the direct intervention of saints or of God. Miner reported that, when an overheated stove caused a fire in a house and the occupants awoke in time to put it out, this awakening was attributed to the divine intervention of the Virgin Mary. Even the ordinary could be explained in terms of religious symbols. For example, the importance of family life in the parish was interpreted in religious terms. Like God, the father of the family was expected to be harsh but just, the ultimate authority. Like Mary, the mother was seen to be compassionate and concerned, with the power to appeal to the father on behalf of those she loved. (Note the presence of instrumental and expressive roles as outlined in Chapter 9, Families, and Chapter 6, Gender Relations.)

Finally, all aspects of earthly life in St. Denis were *represented* or symbolized in the religious beliefs and rituals. Each secular institution, such as the family, had its religious equivalent. Each daily action, such as the planting of the fields, was matched by some religious ceremony to ensure its success. The division of space into sacred and profane echoed the social status divisions of high and low. For all aspects of the social and emotional experience of the individuals in St. Denis, there were equivalent religious rituals, symbols, or beliefs to express them. In this way the individuals achieved a unity between experience and belief, between emotion and symbol.

This description of the community of St. Denis helps to illustrate the consequences or functions of religion as Durkheim perceived them. We can see why Durkheim concluded that religion has a vital function in society, both for the individual and for the group. At least in traditional societies, religious beliefs and rituals help to hold members of society together in a predictable and smoothly functioning unit that makes sense to them, gives their individual lives meaning, and ensures that the social order operates and remains undisturbed.

Religion in an industrial society such as Canada presents a very different picture. There are some exceptions in Canada to this rule, notably such groups as the Old Order Mennonites and the Hutterites, who live in self-enclosed, highly regulated communities. In such groups religion still functions to integrate, to regulate, to empower, and to express. It is precisely because they are not integrated with the larger society, though, that religion can function in this way. For the majority of the population in a country such as Canada, these functions have been largely, but not entirely, taken over by other institutions, such as government bureaucracies and the mass media. We shall discuss these changes further in the section on secularization. For the moment we will turn to another theorist, Max Weber, and consider the role of religion in social change and the different kinds of religious institutions that exist in our society.

Max Weber: religion and social change

Weber believed that religion was born from a need to find an explanation for suffering, as a means to escape that suffering, and to give meaning to discrepancies between the ideal and the real worlds. He noted that, for most people in most times, to live was to suffer. And despite notions of good and evil, the rain falls on the just and the unjust alike. Even the best person may suffer disease, disaster, and distress, and in the end all must suffer death. Weber viewed religions as organized attempts to make sense out of such inconsistencies, to suggest that there is a higher order in which events that seem irrational and random in fact have a purpose and a meaning (Weber, 1964).

Salvation as an escape from worldly trials

For Weber, religion can give people a means of escape from the trials of the world. He suggested that this escape has, by and large, taken one of two forms: other-worldly mysticism or inner-worldly asceticism. Both see pain and suffering as resulting from the fact that people are born into earthly bodies that decay, feel pain and die, and have appetites that may not be met. Both systems seek ways to escape such suffering, but their solutions are quite different.

Mystics reject the world that is perceived with their senses as illusory, and seek a passive endurance of earthly trials and tribulations through a learned detachment.

Other-worldly mysticism is a religious attitude generally associated with Eastern religions such as Buddhism and Hinduism. Mystics reject the world that people can perceive with their senses as being pointless and illusory. It is not a real world to them, and yet individuals cannot escape from it, except mentally. A passive endurance of earthly trials and tribulations is sought through a learned detachment; with the right kind of training people can become separated even from the pain and hunger of their bodies. In this way, individuals achieve **salvation**, which Weber defined as an escape from suffering and a way of giving meaning to human existence.

Inner-worldly asceticism, on the other hand, has quite a different attitude to the problems of pain and suffering. It is not the world which causes suffering, but the doubts and temptations that lie within individuals. The world and the body can be mastered and disciplined so that the temptations and appetites that are the source of pain are suppressed or defeated. Salvation lies in continuing to live in the world—in contrast to rejecting it as an illusion—while carefully disciplining the body and the senses so as to avoid the excess of pain and pleasure that living in this world can bring.

Weber argued that different attitudes concerning the world, such as mysticism and asceticism, result in different kinds of behaviour. Note his symbolic interactionist perspective, arguing that subjective definitions, not objective reality, are crucial in understanding behaviour. In other words, religious attitudes influence social interaction. When an entire group shares a religious attitude such as inner-worldly asceticism or other-worldly mysticism, that religious orientation affects the development and nature of the other institutions in that society. For example, for inner-worldly ascetics to maintain the rigid discipline of their faith, they need the help of other members of the society. This means that social interaction in such groups is deliberately intense and continual so that individual behaviour can be constantly observed and regulated through group pressure.

Weber further developed this theory about the relationship between religious attitudes and social interaction in *The Protestant Ethic and the Spirit of Capitalism* (1958). In this book he discussed the influence of the attitude of inner-worldly asceticism on the development of economic institutions under capitalism. Weber was intrigued to find that a strict religious ethic that preached avoidance of all earthly enjoyments could coexist with—indeed seemed to *encourage*—the capitalistic enterprise that fosters the accumulation of worldly goods.

The Protestant ethic thesis

From Weber's viewpoint, the religious impulse is to *escape* suffering, and suffering is tied inextricably to physical conditions. The economic impulse, on the other hand, stems from physical appetites and is designed to *meet* physical needs. For the religious person, therefore, economic activity means spending time on precisely those aspects of life that are the source of suffering. The religious answer is to ignore or repress physical needs; the economic answer, to cater to them. It seemed paradoxical to Weber, therefore, that the inner-worldly asceticism of the early Protestants tended to appear together with an economic ethos that favoured the accumulation of worldly wealth.

In an effort to explain the relationship, Weber traced the origins and precise meaning of the inner-worldly asceticism peculiar to early post-Reformation Protestant groups to a brand of asceticism he termed the **Protestant ethic**. This ethic, which originated in the teachings of Calvin, the sixteenth-century religious reformer who led the Protestant Reformation in Switzerland, involved a kind of worldly monasticism that accepted being *in* the world, but not *of* it. In reaction to the Catholic notion of individual control over salvation through freely chosen good or bad deeds, Calvin preached **predestination**, the notion that individuals at birth have been determined by God to be either the chosen or the damned. Unlike the Catholic Church, which held that the priesthood and especially the Pope might intercede between the average person and God, Calvinists believed that, not only were humans unable to intervene between other humans and God, they could not even presume to know whether they were among the elect, and they could not do anything to influence or even understand God's decision.

Weber suggested that this doctrine of an unknowable predestination in the long run proved difficult to live with. Few people could tolerate the tension and anxiety produced by such a situation. The early Calvinists, however, were a stern bunch. They could find comfort in faith and in hard work, which would leave little time for doubts. By working hard they also could fulfil a purpose in this life, a **calling**. They would act as tools of God to help Him achieve His great and unknowable ends.

What fascinated Weber about this particular aspect of Calvinism was its economic implications. If people worked as hard as most early Protestants did to discipline mind and body, they eventually would be successful in worldly terms. If they were farmers, for instance, they might end up in any given year with more than they could eat and be forced to sell the excess or exchange it for other goods so that it would not go to waste. Thus, they might well begin to accumulate wealth and worldly goods.

The way out of this difficulty lay, according to Weber, in defining the accumulation of wealth as acceptable, as long as it was not spent on pleasure. If pleasures were continually denied and money used simply to further God's work, then the accumulation of wealth in itself would not represent a danger. After all, the Calvinist creed meant that people had to live in the face of temptations and to maintain self-control. Those with money who did not give in to the pleasures of the world were surely more virtuous than those with none who faced no temptations.

This combination of austerity and accumulation of wealth laid the groundwork, according to Weber, for the **spirit of capitalism**, which he defined as "self-denial in favour of economic gain." The Protestant ethic did not directly cause capitalism, but rather a relationship of **elective affinity** existed between the two. By this Weber meant that there was a logical "fit" between the two: the economic system of capitalism, which depended upon the accumulation and reinvestment of surplus money, was nourished and encouraged by a religious ethic that said people must work hard and ceaselessly but not pamper themselves by enjoying the luxuries resulting from this labour. In this way a religious attitude shaped an economic attitude, resulting in the economic institutions that characterize many Western societies today.

Routinization of charisma

The process of change in religious organizations also fascinated Weber. He argued that most successful religious movements tend to lose their original religious idealism and force as their economic and social strengths increase. Over time most religious movements compromise, allowing economic concerns to become increasingly important. And so, movements that begin as opposed to the things of the world often end up, to the degree that they are lasting movements, representing the power and wealth of the world. Weber termed this process **routinization of charisma** (1946b [1922]).

By **charisma** Weber meant a kind of irrational personal authority that one individual or group exerts over another. Most "new" religions evoke in their followers an excitement and intensity of feeling that they do not find in their ordinary daily relationships or activities. This intensity and excitement do not generally endure, however, and in time the relationship becomes routine and ordinary. When this happens, Weber argued, the charisma has become routinized.

It is easy to find examples of routinization of charisma in North America. The history of North American religion is one of a continual procession of new faiths that start out as radical groups, critical of those who live self-indulgently and enjoy wealth and power, the rewards of earthly existence. Partly because of the discipline imposed on group members, and partly in an effort to ensure their own survival, these groups eventually become involved in economics and politics, and eventually may identify with the rich and powerful whom they originally despised. We shall look more closely at this process, using an example drawn from the development of the western frontier in Canada.

Routinization of charisma: a Canadian example

Canadian society was shaped by a number of processes, among them the interaction between frontier life and religious innovation. In the early part of the nineteenth century, Anglicans, Catholics, and Presbyterians were dominant in eastern Canada, but from 1850 to 1950 wave after wave of new religious groups caught the popular imagination, particularly in western Canada. They found an ideal breeding ground in the early frontier towns.

The Canadian sociologist Clark (1962) described the interaction between religion and frontier life. The people who moved westward, first to the prairies, then to the mining towns of British Columbia, were often those who could not find a place for themselves in the established towns of the east. For young people growing up in such eastern communities, it was not easy to find a place in society unless they were born into wealthy or powerful families. The political and business leaders were also the social leaders, and they and their families were the mainstays in the established churches. Thus, for those who were disadvantaged in such a community, religion did not offer an escape from suffering. Quite the contrary; for them, attendance at a church service might only serve as a reminder that they were socially marginal in that society.

But as long as the frontier remained open and unsettled (at least according to the white settler's point of view), there seemed to be another option. Such individuals could go west to seek their fortune. These frontiers were appealing not only because of economic opportunities, but because they were wild, undisciplined areas where restless individuals, frustrated by the conventions of the established society, could escape and live as they pleased.

As is often the case, however, actual life in the frontier town was not as pleasant as these settlers had imagined. Everyone wanted to get rich quickly, and most were inspired by a kind of reckless optimism, which turned to desperation and despondency when the fabled fortunes failed to materialize. Many who came west were quickly destitute, and those who did strike it rich, perhaps by finding gold, had little to spend their money on but cards, drink, and prostitutes, and often lost fortunes as fast as they had made them. Without such stabilizing influences as families, and with the ever-present temptation to squander what money was made, the general morale of such towns was low indeed. Mental breakdown, suicide, and emotional instability were common. Those who had left the established communities of the east, thumbing their noses and sure of their future fortunes, had to face both renewed failure and the loss of hope.

Such populations were ideal candidates for religious conversion, and there were those ready to reap the harvest. Just as the frontier became a haven for socially marginal individuals, so it attracted the less established religions. Some had failed to find a foothold in the eastern communities, where established churches held sway, while others crossed the border from the United States in search of new converts. Groups such as the Newlight Baptists, Methodists, the Salvation Army, Pentecostals, the

Disciples of Christ, and the Plymouth Brethren prospered in the frontier areas where social upheaval and economic disorganization prevailed.

The leaders of these groups were able to offer renewed hope to many discouraged frontier people. They preached the notion of a spiritual elect—music to the ears of individuals who had suffered partly because they could not seem to gain acceptance among the social elect. Listening to these travelling ministers, people might have felt that if they could be royalty in the Kingdom of God, what did it matter if their earthly position was less exalted? There could be great comfort in such a thought. Not only were the material possessions they lacked unimportant, but the "saved" could scorn the "unsaved," successful though the latter might be in worldly terms.

The experience of the revival meetings also offered a kind of escape. Crowds of people gave themselves up to religious frenzy, swept along by the powerful preaching and the excitement of others. They forgot about their work and their troubles, and gathered day after day to attend the revivals. The conventions and inhibitions the converted possessed were easily thrown off in the sweeping feelings of togetherness and abandon generated by the meetings. Clark (1962) noted, for example, that illegitimacy rates tended to increase at times of collective outbursts of religious sentiment. Debts went unpaid and personal swings in emotion between hope and despair grew more intense. Those unable to experience religious conversion felt a renewed sense of failure; those who achieved conversion struggled to maintain their sense of election while their personal life and economic condition disintegrated further.

These unstable and highly emotional responses among the converted were threatening, however, to the leaders of such religions. First of all, it was exhausting to maintain such a feverish level of excitement and difficult to continue duplicating the experience of mass euphoria, particularly as the audience became accustomed to an individual leader. Over time some of the mystery wore off. Second, despite promises of salvation, the audience began to see that things were getting worse and worse economically, and that they were soon not going to have enough to eat. The religious leaders personally confronted similar problems. Dedicated as they might have been to their calling, they nonetheless needed food and clothing and money to rent the meeting halls or tents. The devotion of followers was all very well, but it was not going to pay the bills. To make matters worse, revivalist leaders were often viewed suspiciously by local law enforcers as rabble rousers bent on creating social disorder.

In response to these difficulties, the new religious groups in the frontier towns began to crack down on their memberships and to impose new standards of personal conduct, often of an ascetic nature. It was soon no longer enough to have the conversion experience itself; for adherents to show that they were numbered among the saved, they also had to stop sinning. Marriage was encouraged, as were temperate drinking habits. Gambling was proclaimed as an evil that might tempt the "saved" back into lives of sin. Individuals' intense religious experiences gradually became less important, as the reputation of the group as a whole and observance of group norms became paramount. Hard work, frugality, and morality became the required attitudes of the "saved."

Such values, when coupled with rigorous community support, tended, as we saw in the case of Weber's ascetic Protestants, to produce tangible economic and social results. The communities stabilized as families were created, laws obeyed, and schools opened. And hard work and sober economic conduct produced wealth that could be reinvested to produce greater wealth. As the communities stabilized, so did the religious groups themselves. At first small and appealing mainly to marginal members of society, the new religions began to number among their members the political and economic élite of the frontier communities. Churches were built and ministers hired. In the new communities the once-marginal religions became the established religions. They had fully accommodated the secular world and had indeed become powers in that world. The routinization of charisma was complete.

Yet, even in the new communities, as in the old ones back east, there were those who did not fully fit in. There were still marginal members. These in turn often left to seek their fortunes elsewhere, and encountered yet other new religions that could not find a foothold in these newly established towns. And thus, as long as there were new frontiers, the cycle could repeat itself.

In summary, then, routinization of charisma involves the compromise of religious ideals with worldly concerns on the part of the group members and leaders. Routinization is accompanied by organizational changes, which we shall discuss in some detail in the next section. The process itself is triggered by a number of factors, each of which poses a central problem for the long-term survival of the group, including:

1. *The problem of leadership succession* Since the group was initially attracted by the personal charisma of the first leader, what will hold the group together if the leader dies, retires, or loses charisma? Members must seek a new leader on other, rational, and more pragmatic grounds.
2. *The problem of political survival* Since the movement started out opposed to the rich and powerful in society, it was in continual danger of being attacked and oppressed by these same enemies. To ensure survival, it was necessary to compromise somewhat with these authorities, to make some friendships and political alliances with the powerful in society.
3. *The problem of physical survival* The rejection of economic and family concerns in the early stages of the charismatic movement cannot be maintained for long. Members must begin to be able to work in order to eat, and renewed participation in family life helps ensure the physical survival of the group by providing a new generation of members.
4. *The problem of organization* A successful movement will attract large numbers of followers. At a certain stage the numbers will grow so large that they cannot be controlled solely by the force of the leader's personality. In the highly charged atmosphere of group meetings, individuals may become increasingly disruptive and order may break down. To keep the followers under some control, the leader needs to appoint assistants and to tone down the emotional nature of the meetings.

These problems and their solutions have a direct impact on group organization. Those groups that fail to resolve these difficulties generally break up and disappear. Most new religions change their organization, taking on the characteristics of established groups and losing some of the excitement and sense of purpose that initially characterized them. In the next section we shall take a closer look at two distinct organizational forms that represent the beginning and end points of that transformation process.

Types of religious organization

Weber realized that there are many different ways of being religious and that these differences are reflected in different types of religious organization. A contemporary of Weber's, Troeltsch (1931), further elaborated on Weber's ideas and was among the first to attempt to differentiate between different kinds of religions. Troeltsch termed his two types *church* and *sect*. Based on an awareness of the organizational differences between the Catholic Church and the "protesting" splinter groups, some of which were later to develop into the various Protestant churches, Troeltsch noted a number of differences between the two types of religious organization.

Troeltsch viewed a **sect** as a voluntary association constituted by people who consider themselves to be specially qualified by virtue of beliefs, experience, and/or behaviour. Sects tend to be radical in nature and opposed to established society. Members of sects reject worldly concerns. Membership is usually adult and voluntary; people are not born into sectarian religions, but choose to join them. Because of this self-selection and voluntary joining, sect members often have similar social backgrounds and other traits in common. They are often, for example, recruited from the underprivileged of society. They find in sect life an organization more democratic and egalitarian than they experience in the wider society. Members enjoy essentially equal status, perhaps with the exception of the leader. Sects also offer a supportive world, with communal charity a common practice. If members are in difficulty, others come to their aid. Finally, the religious experience itself is, as we have seen, highly subjective, personal, emotional, and intense, offering a direct and intimate relationship with God. A contemporary example of a sect in Canada is the Hutterites.

By contrast, Troeltsch noted that a **church** tends to be conservative and very supportive of the secular world. Membership in the church is often involuntary—that is, people are born into the church—and infant baptism is common, not the exception to the rule as it is in the sect. Members may come from widely varying social backgrounds, but those who control the church are generally from the more privileged classes of society. Life within the church has none of the informal, spontaneous, or democratic nature of the sect. The organization is hierarchical, with church officials in positions of greater power than the average layperson.

There is also a division of labour, with specially designated religious roles, absent in the informal organization of the sect. Due to the formality and the greater numbers involved in the church, this organization is much less personal than the sect. Church members are often little involved in each other's lives and may not even know the names of most of the others in the congregation. Finally, the religious experience is quite different from that of the sect. Expressions of personal emotion by the church congregation are discouraged and services are highly ritualized, and sometimes intellectual in nature. There is little of the sense of immediacy and personal relationship with God, since church officials often are more concerned with their followers' ethics than with their internal experiences. In Canada, a good example of the church form is the Roman Catholic Church in Quebec, especially prior to the Quiet Revolution.

Within an established church, religious experience is highly ritualized and almost intellectual in nature.

Troeltsch's church–sect typology may be applied to a number of religious groups that have operated in North America. In our discussion of religion and the frontier in Canada, the church organization was exemplified by the established religions that the adventurers were trying to escape, and the sect organization by the new religious movements they encountered on the frontier. For the most part, however, North American sociologists have found Troeltsch's classification scheme too simple to encompass the great variety of religions in North America today (Nock, 1993). In response, some contemporary sociologists have revised the model by splitting Troeltsch's notion of *church* in two. Unlike Europe at the time Troeltsch was writing, neither Canada nor the United States had just one church that dominated the entire country. Instead, there have existed a number of different churches, which, like sects, have had to compete for membership. Sociologists have called these competing church-like religions **denominations**. Included under this heading today are such established Protestant groups as Anglicans, Presbyterians, and Baptists. The term **ecclesia** is reserved for churches that dominate a country as the "official" religion of a society, such as Islam in Saudi Arabia or the Catholic Church in Spain. Both denominations and ecclesia share church-like qualities when compared with sects, but they differ to the extent that denominations must compete with one another and so are not allied with the state in quite the same manner as ecclesia. No denomination is as all-powerful as an ecclesia.

Another type of religious organization that sociologists have introduced into discussions of North American religions is the **cult**. In the media, this term is often used to describe any new religious movement, a classification to be discussed later in the chapter. Sociologists, however, use the term *cult* more precisely to describe a kind of religious organization related to, but different from, sects. Like sects, cults are often "new" or early forms of religion, but they are very different from sects in the demands they place on members. Cults are very loosely organized and do not demand that their members conform to strict moral and personal codes, as sects do. Cults are often quite intellectual and unemotional. Members come and go as they please, drifting out of one group and into another. In some contemporary cults, a course fee is required. In this way cults can survive financially without retaining the loyalty of their memberships. Because of the initiation fees found in many cults, they often attract a more privileged group than do sects. Like sects, however, cults usually have an adult, voluntary membership and an egalitarian organization. Contemporary examples of cults are such groups as Transcendental Meditation, Psychosynthesis, est, Arica, and Silva Mind Control.

Many groups such as the People's Temple, Hare Krishna, and the Unification Church are also called cults, but they are in fact sects, making the same kinds of demands and placing the same kinds of restrictions on members that sects have for several hundred years. It is somewhat ironic that these groups, the focus of so much fear and concern in the general population, are quite similar to the groups that shaped Canada's religious history, at least in organizational terms. Critics who accuse such groups of "brainwashing," because members sever their ties with their past, are ignoring the fact that this is characteristic of conversion to sects. Most sectarian converts withdraw from worldly things for a time after their conversion. This period does not usually last forever, and it would be difficult to see in the Methodist or Baptist denominations today the evil influence that robbed families of their beloved in the days when they were among the new religious movements of the frontiers.

In summary, building upon the work of Weber and Troeltsch, most sociologists of religion today identify four distinct organizational types relevant to North America: ecclesia, denomination, sect, and cult. It is important to remember that these categories are not static, and that all religious organizations may change over time. As mentioned, sects can and do become denominations. In other cases, cults have become sects, as in the case of Scientology, which started out with a very open, flexible organization but has become increasingly strict and demanding with members. Denominations rarely become sects, but they do produce sects by alienating some of their membership or by becoming too impersonal or status-conscious.

Marx: religion as ideology

In contrast to Durkheim's functionalist view and Weber's symbolic interactionist perspective on religion, Marx's writings on religion flow from a conflict orientation. Basically, he viewed religion as a kind of **ideology**, a belief system used by a group to justify its worldly activities. Marx felt that gods and religious ideals were social inventions which people forgot they had invented, and to whom they therefore mistakenly attributed powerful and independent existences. People allowed this process to happen for different reasons. For the oppressed, religion provided some comfort, but of a dangerous kind. Religion was the "flowers on the chains" that bound this group in servitude. It prevented them from seeing that the social system was really responsible for their condition. Marx felt great compassion for those who needed religion to reduce their suffering. He wrote: "Religion is the sigh of the oppressed creature, the sentiment of a heartless world and the soulless condition. It is the opium of the people" (1964 [1843]). However, Marx also felt a particular anger about religion, precisely because, through comforting, it deceived; for it was only by seeing the depth and the source of suffering, he argued, that the common people could change their lot.

The élite, on the other hand, blatantly used religion for social control, to justify their position of power and their disproportionate wealth, and to protect their privilege by insisting that their power was part of a divine plan. Marx drew this conclusion in part from observing English society in 1855. Here he saw what he considered to be many examples of church and ruling class uniting to oppress the poor. In June 1855, for example, the Sunday Trading

Feminism and Religion

Recent years have witnessed a virtual explosion in research attempting to understand and interpret the world from the perspective and experiences of women. With the rise of the second wave of feminism in the 1960s and the maturing of the women's movement in the decades following, feminist scholars have begun to revise, reformulate, and reappropriate the knowledge base of the Western world. Not only has this been true in the realm of work in the domestic sphere, and in reclaiming of history, but it has also occurred in the religious and spiritual realms as well.

One of the first tasks of religious feminists has been to argue that religion treats women poorly and to suggest that the Judaeo-Christian tradition is sexist. For Mary Daly (1968; 1973), since God is male, then the male is god. We need to move beyond the concept of God the Father, she contended. "A woman's asking for equality in the church would be comparable to a black person's demanding equality in the Ku Klux Klan" (Daly, 1975: 6). Other feminist theologians disagree. Trible (1979) and Fiorenza (1979) argued for the liberating potential of biblical faith: for them, the essential message is not the sanctity of patriarchy but liberation for men and women through a sense of relatedness to God. Building on the theme of the exodus of the children of Israel, the prophetic plea for justice or the concern Jesus expressed for the poor and oppressed, Fiorenza (1985) contended that feminist "herstorians" can rediscover in the Judaeo-Christian tradition the theme of liberation.

For Fiorenza and a host of other feminist theologians and Christian writers, there is sufficient ground to hope and work for the repentance and reform (Christ and Plaskow, 1979). From this perspective, the task of feminist theology is to "uncover Christian theological traditions and myths that perpetuate sexist ideologies, violence and alienation. A Christian feminist spirituality thus has as its theological presupposition...the Christian community's constant need for renewal and conversion" (Fiorenza, 1979). Fiorenza argued that such can be accomplished only when women are granted full spiritual, theological, and ecclesial equality.

Yet, it is important to see that concern with the language and message of Scripture to women is not new. Almost 100 years ago, in 1895, Elizabeth Cady Stanton succeeded in publishing what she called *The Woman's Bible*. Based on her belief that the language and interpretation of passages dealing with women in the Bible were a major contributor to women's inferior status, she mounted an effort to write commentaries on passages from both the Old and New Testaments (Stanton, 1895). Today, many religious groups are attempting to re-think the language of their sacred books, their liturgy, and their hymnals.

Source: *N. Nason-Clark, 1993. "Gender relations in contemporary Christian organizations." In W.E. Hewitt (ed.),* The Sociology of Religion: A Canadian Focus. *Toronto: Harcourt Brace (pp. 224–25).*

Bill prohibiting commerce on Sundays was passed by the English government. While supposedly protecting religious values (such as a day of rest on the sabbath), this bill in fact made life more difficult for the poor and protected the interests of the ruling class. Marx noted that it was only small businesses that stayed open on Sundays, to cater to the working people, who usually received their pay late on Saturday. The larger businesses, which catered to the ruling classes, did not need Sunday commerce to survive (Marx and Engels, 1964).

Marx's image of religion perhaps seems best suited to countries dominated by ecclesia. One of the characteristics of an ecclesia, as pointed out, is that it has no competition; there is no religious alternative for someone in a country dominated by one. However, as illustrated in the preceding section, in much of Canada religion was historically represented not by an ecclesia but by a number of sects, which became competing denominations and later spawned new sects. Moreover, participation in sectarian belief systems, as previously mentioned, often helped the adherents to advance socially and economically. This fact would seem to contradict Marx's theory, at least in the North American context. However, Marx might well have argued that not all sectarian groups improved the economic lot of members, but almost all did discourage active political participation, leaving the workings of the world to secular forces. In this sense even sectarian religion oppressed its adherents, causing them to accept social and economic conditions that they could potentially have changed if they had employed political activism instead of religious withdrawal.

SECULARIZATION AND THE DECLINE OF RELIGION?

The secularization process

By **secularization** sociologists mean that process by which traditional religious beliefs and rituals lose their hold over society as a whole, and other institutions take over the functions of religion. Secularization seems to accompany industrialization and urbanization, and most sociologists agree that it is a gradual but continuous process in technological societies.

There are a number of reasons why the control and importance of religion seem to lessen as societies become industrialized. One of these is that industry demands increasing division of labour; this in turn means *specialization*. In traditional societies, such as the parish of St. Denis, the church dealt with problems ranging from social concerns to illness. However, as social groups grow in size and complexity, completely different institutions take over the different functions that were once solely the responsibility of religion. This is particularly true of the integrating, regulating, and interpreting functions.

Doctors take over the function of interpreting and dealing with illness, formerly the priest's role. Scientists take over the function of explaining natural phenomena and prescribing techniques for farming, and educators take over the function of interpreting social phenomena to society's members. Big business and mass media take over the function of integrating members into the social order. Lawyers and politicians take over the regulation of people's behaviour. Slowly, organized religion loses its powerful role as integrator, regulator, and interpreter of social life.

In an effort to survive, some religious groups seem to hasten the secularization process through their own activities. In a situation of declining commitment to and interest in religion, denominations find that they need to compete for members. To do this, some compromise even further with secular society, for example sponsoring nonreligious youth groups, using "folk" as opposed to traditional music, or trying to turn religious services into discussion groups. In the process, they abandon the few distinctly religious functions they may still possess (discussed further below), becoming secular organizations and competing with other secular organizations.

Another response to the general secularization trend has been the emergence of reinvigorated conservative religious groups, which are confessedly anti-secular. These have arisen among Protestants, who have especially voiced opposition to scholarly analyses of Scripture and liberal social-action programs. They have also emerged among revivalist Catholics, who have rallied not only against more liberal attitudes towards contraception and abortion, but also against the more ecumenical orientation of the Canadian church hierarchy (Cuneo, 1989). Tradition-oriented Jewish practices have enjoyed a partial revival in the midst of continuing secular developments, as the more regular observance of the sabbath and religious holidays has served as a vehicle for strengthening the sense of ethnic cohesion and family solidarity.

Secularization: a two-way street

Contemporary sociologists are somewhat divided in their assessment of the extent and nature of the actual secularization process. Some feel that religion will continue to become increasingly irrelevant for humanity. Others suggest that religious institutions, now that they are no longer responsible for integrating society and maintaining law and order, will be able to perform their remaining functions better. These include giving meaning to life, or *empowering* individuals, and *expressing* individuals' relationship to their society.

Both Durkheim and Weber suggested that some aspects of religion might become more important in modern society. Durkheim thought that as science and social science took over much of the explanatory and interpretive role of religion, people would still need religion to empower and motivate them, and more importantly, perhaps, to express their relation to society or to demonstrate what people in a given society had in common. In modern, diversified societies, such a sense of unity would be even more precious, since it would be harder to achieve. But even when people had very little in common in terms of jobs or lifestyles, they would continue to share their common humanity. As mentioned previously, people hold sacred what they share or have in common, and Durkheim argued that, in the society of the future, people would hold sacred their common humanity, holding out ideal human virtues as something for which to strive. He termed this hypothesized religion of humanity the **cult of man** (Durkheim, 1969 [1898]).

Weber's definition and view of religion led him to related but slightly different conclusions about its ultimate fate (Weber, 1946a [1922]). As mentioned, Weber felt that religions draw their power from their ability to provide an escape from suffering, and from their ability to explain that suffering. Religion does this best, from Weber's point of view, to the extent that it is *rationalized*, that is, made internally consistent and logical on an intellectual level. In other words, Weber felt that religion would allow an escape from suffering and provide meaning best when it became a carefully thought-out and systematic philosophical position focused on achieving its goals, as opposed to a collection of haphazard rituals and beliefs.

While Weber was a great believer in rational thought and the advance of science, he also felt that something is lost when all irrationality is removed from religion—a process he termed **the disenchantment of the world**. At the same time, Weber thought it possible that human beings would always need an outlet for their mystical and emotional sides. Both Durkheim and Weber, therefore, suggested that traditional religions supplied an important source of meaning and an outlet for emotions, and that some form of religion might continue to exist in modern society to meet these needs.

Bibby and secularization in Canada

A series of studies by Bibby (1979; 1987; 1993) explored the question of whether Canadians are

Christianity and the Confrontation with Modernity in Canada

Since the advent of the twentieth century and the decline in popular adherence to things religious, Christian churches throughout the Western world have made a concerted effort to make centuries-old religious teaching speak with greater authority to the problems of modern life. Some observers of these efforts have argued that the response to modernity has ultimately been driven by a narrow preoccupation with institutional survival. Others see church adaptation as motivated by more genuine concern for the salvation of humankind. Regardless of motive, however, there is little question that the innovations in church thinking and action in recent years—such as those apparent within the Catholic Church in the wake of the Second Vatican Council (1962–65)—signal a dramatic change from traditional church postures.

The confrontation with and reaction to modernity by the Christian churches has been as much apparent in Canada as elsewhere. Here, the significant changes in society and politics since Confederation have been coupled with a dramatic decline in many forms of church participation—most notably attendance at religious services. In Quebec, especially, the traditionally high church-attendance rates for the predominantly Roman Catholic population have eroded markedly, with the most visible drop occurring in the aftermath of that province's "Quiet Revolution."

continued

In response to this new reality, many Canadian churches have moved gradually, but with determination, to reassert their place within Canadian society. For some, this has meant reaffirming and advertising a fundamentalist agenda, based upon a more literal interpretation of the Bible, in order to attract those who may feel adrift in the societal milieu of today and desire a return to more traditional forms of religion. The Pentecostal churches in particular have benefited from this approach. Even within Catholicism, the rapid growth of the conservative charismatic movement, with its emphasis upon direct personal contact with the spiritual, has raised more than a few eyebrows.

Still other churches, especially those larger institutions within the mainstream of the religious market, have moved to adapt to the new Canadian reality in a more "liberal" fashion, choosing to focus on the injustices of modern capitalism. As early as the 1930s, in fact, a concern for social justice appeared on the agenda of several Protestant church groups in western Canada. This "Social Gospel" was influential in the formation of the CCF, the forerunner of the NDP. Today, many of the Protestant churches carry on this tradition, speaking out on controversial social issues such as unemployment, Native rights, and, most recently, the environment.

In the Catholic Church as well, an intensive campaign has been under way since at least 1970 to make Canadians more aware of the problems faced by the socially disadvantaged. In a series of statements released by the Canadian Conference of Catholic Bishops, the Church has soundly criticized capitalist economics, and spoken out strongly in favour of affordable housing, the right to employment, and a more just distribution of income.

There is no question that the more liberal position adopted by those churches has attracted a new following and won much applause. Nevertheless, in some respects, the new focus on social justice issues has had some unanticipated and largely undesired results. For example, the decision taken by the leadership of the United Church of Canada to support the ordination of gays and lesbians precipitated an unprecedented exodus of church members—many of whom were already dissatisfied with the organization's liberal politics. Informal estimates suggest that upwards of forty congregations and some 10 000 members had left the church by 1990. Some of the Catholic bishops' more controversial statements, such as their 1983 statement "Ethical Reflections on the Economic Crisis," have consistently drawn criticism from a number of Catholic and non-Catholic economists, politicians, and theologians. Moreover, the concern for social justice within the institutional church has hardly met with overwhelming enthusiasm among laypeople—so much so that there is today increasingly a turn to more moderate political commentary on the part of Canada's bishops.

Whether or not the churches' innovations—conservative or liberal—manage to reaffirm the relevance of the spiritual in modern Canadian society remains to be seen. For the time being, however, as Bibby's (1993) research has shown, many Canadians simply may remain content to relegate faith-related matters of whatever quality to the periphery of their daily lives, and turn to religion only when necessary to mark important events in the life cycle, such as marriage or the birth of children.

Source: *W.E. Hewitt, 1993. Written for this volume.*

becoming more or less interested in religion and whether some are searching for a new religion. Overall, he noted that in terms of traditional measures of religiosity, such as belief in God, belief in life after death, and attendance at weekly services, there has been a marked decline. In 1950, 95 percent of Canadians polled by the Gallup organization stated that they believed in God. In 1990, 82 percent made the same statement. Belief in life after death dropped even more sharply, from 78 percent in 1950 to 68 percent in 1990, and attendance at religious services dropped from 67 percent in 1946 to 23 percent in 1990.

In his later studies, Bibby (1987; 1993) changed somewhat his interpretation of these data. It seems that Canadians continue to maintain, at least officially, a religious identification with the faith of their parents. After a brief period in young adulthood when some may list their religious affiliation as "None," many return to listing it as Catholic, Protestant, etc. However, this has little to do with faith or with rediscovering religious doctrine and finding it a satisfying response to questions of meaning; in fact, only about 25 percent of the population is highly involved in religious organizations (Bibby, 1993: 169). Rather, it seems that Canadians assume the label of commitment but in fact select only fragments of beliefs, practices, and knowledge, to be used and discarded as they are needed. We shall return to Bibby's notion of fragmented or consumer religion later in the chapter.

Thus, few Canadians today have the kind of involvement with religion that characterized the daily lives of the parishioners of St. Denis, or even the lives of their own grandparents. They may ignore largely the questions of suffering, of salvation, of purpose, or of identity that Weber argued were at the heart of the religious impulse. However, while it is clear that secularization is an important trend in Canada today, the fact that many Canadians are still in fact "religious" should not be ignored. According to Bibby (1993: 132, 154) the great majority—82 percent—of the population still answers affirmatively to questions concerning a belief in God. Only 12 percent of people polled by Bibby in 1990 listed their religion as "no religion." In addition, the decline in religious affiliation has not affected all denominations equally (see Table 10.1). The Roman Catholic Church has maintained its following in relation to the general population over the last hundred years, and in fact has increased it slightly. United Church affiliation has declined markedly, as has that of other mainstream denominations such as the Anglicans, but some small groups are actually growing.

Hinduism and Islam are currently among the fastest-growing religious groups in Canada. Other rapidly growing groups are the Jehovah's Witnesses and Pentecostals (see Table 10.1). Among indigenous peoples, traditional religious beliefs and practices have also become increasingly important (Lewis, 1993).

Some of this rapid growth is due to a high birth rate; such is the case for the Hutterites. Others, such as the Jehovah's Witnesses, grow by recruitment. Finally, immigration of ethnic groups affiliated with certain religious sects and denominations may account for some growth. It should be noted, however, that stated affiliation is not always a valid measure of religiosity, and that growth may be more apparent than real. Indeed, many people may have indicated a religious affiliation when asked to do so on a census, yet have told Bibby that religious questions and questions of meaning do not have a central role in their lives.

Canadians continue to maintain, at least officially, a religious identification with the faith of their parents.

REDEFINING THE RELIGIOUS LANDSCAPE

New religious movements

Along with change, growth, and decline in the traditional religious market, there has appeared in recent years a tendency towards **new religious movements**, especially among middle-class youth in Canada and the U.S. (Kent, 1993). These movements include both cults and sects. Some are Eastern imports, such as Divine Light Mission, Hare Krishna, and Zen Buddhism; others are neo-Christian movements, such as The Way and The Children of God; and still others are "human potential" movements, such as est and Silva Mind Control, which grew out

TABLE 10.1 Percentage of population for selected religious groups in Canada, 1871–1991

	1871	*1881*	*1901*	*1921*	*1941*	*1961*	*1981*	*1991*
Roman Catholic	43	42	42	39	42	46	47	45
United Church	na	na	na	na	19	20	16	11
Anglican	14	14	14	16	15	13	10	8
Conservative Prostestant	8	8	8	8	7	7	7	7
Baptist	7	7	6	5	4	3	3	2
Mennonite[1]	*	*	0.6	0.7	1	0.8	0.8	0.8
Pentecostal	*	*	0.0	0.1	0.5	0.8	1.4	1.6
Salvation Army	*	*	0.2	0.3	0.3	0.5	0.5	0.4
Lutheran	1	1	2	3	3	4	3	2
Presbyterian	16	16	16	16	7	4	3	2
Other	1	1	2	5	6	7	7	4
Eastern Orthodox	*	*	0.3	2	3	1	1	1
Jewish	0.0	0.1	0.3	1	1	1	1	1
Jehovah's Witness	*	*	*	0.1	0.1	0.4	0.6	0.6
Mormon	0.0	*	0.1	0.2	0.2	0.3	0.4	0.4
Hindu	*	*	*	*	*	*	0.3	0.6
Muslim	*	*	*	*	*	*	0.3	0.9
Sikh	*	*	*	*	*	*	0.3	0.5
Buddhist	*	*	0.2	0.1	0.1	0.1	0.2	0.6
None	0.0	0.0	0.0	0.2	0.5	1	7	12

*= Not available; na = Not applicable

[1]Mennonites included with Baptists in 1871 and 1881; Hutterites included with Mennonites for all years.

Source: *R. Bibby, 1987.* Fragmented Gods. *Toronto: Irwin, 1987 (p. 47); R. Bibby, 1993.* Unknown Gods: The Ongoing Story of Religion in Canada. *Toronto: Stoddart (p. 154); Statistics Canada, 1993.* 1991 Census of Canada: Religions in Canada, *Catalogue No. 93-319.*

of therapeutic philosophies and the encounter-group movement of the 1960s to become pseudo-religions (Robbins, 1988).

It is difficult to find precise data on Canadian participation rates in new religious movements. Bibby's data, drawn from a national sample of rural and urban communities across Canada, suggest that only 5 percent of the population are even "strongly interested" in new religious movements. But the figure may be higher in certain areas, and a much larger number have at least tried (and then dropped out of) a new religion.

Why do young people from middle-class homes choose to participate in new religious movements that seem deviant by many standards? This question has puzzled and disturbed many people, particularly the parents of children who have joined such movements as Hare Krishna and the Unification Church and who have rejected their family and past life.

Sociologists have given various explanations for the growth of and interest in new religious movements (Kent, 1993). They have argued that the moral confusion of today causes young people to turn to the relatively authoritarian leaders of such groups for guidance. This argument is based in part on the finding that many participants in such movements originally came from relatively authoritarian and conservative families. In their teens, they rebel against these families by becoming involved in a counterculture and in drugs. For some such people, a new religious movement offers a return to the relatively strict values of their childhood (many new religious movements require conservative dress and strictly control sex, drugs, and alcohol), but in a form which bears some resemblance to a counterculture of anti-materialism, mysticism, and Eastern influence.

A second interpretation of the appeal of these movements focuses on their emphasis on ritual and experience instead of doctrines or ideas. Adherents claim that what attracts them is the experience of participation, and this experience seems linked to rituals and group practices. The efforts of traditional denominational groups to secularize their rituals seem to be related to a decline in intense emotional or expressive experience provided by such rituals. It is possible that people turn to new religions because they fulfil those expressive and empowering functions that remain the special domain of religion.

A third explanation of the appeal of such movements lies in their emphasis on magical techniques. Many middle-class individuals today experience powerlessness, a sense of being at the mercy of the huge international economic and governmental conglomerates. Nor is it clear how social power may be recaptured. As will be discussed in the next chapter, standard middle-class success routes such as education no longer seem to ensure a secure place in society. The values of material wealth and personal happiness still motivate middle-class youth, but they no longer know how to achieve them. Such a sense of powerlessness and lack of clear social rules of procedure have been linked in nonindustrial societies to the appearance of witchcraft (Malinowski, 1954), and it may be that the magic orientation of new religious movements is a response to similar confusion in middle-class youth today.

A last interpretation of new religious movements focuses on the individualistic or private nature of participation in many such movements, particularly those of the human potential variety. This argument suggests that these groups may in fact be expressive of modern society because their focus is not so much on group life but on self-realization. As Durkheim predicted, in a specialized, diversified society, people worship an idealized version of the human individual.

Does worship of the individual and secularization mean that religion is dying in contemporary Canadian society? Perhaps religion as we have known it. But it is possible—as some theorists have argued—that we are looking in the wrong place for modern religion. Although it is no longer found in places of worship, it may resurface in other aspects of people's lives. Before concluding our discussion of religion, it is worthwhile examining two contemporary theories that suggest a fundamental redefinition of religion. They are Bellah's (1970) notion of civil religion and Bibby's (1993) concept of consumer religion.

New definitions of religion

Civil religion

An alternative to traditional religion as a force that functions to empower, express, regulate, and integrate is presented by the political systems of modern nations, particularly those systems supported by a considerable degree of patriotism. Bellah (1970) employed the term **civil religion** to describe public ceremonies that are in fact celebrations of a way of life, sacred to a national group. Civil religion transcends denominational and faith divisions, and serves to legitimize the political structure and to inspire a sense of commitment to society.

In Canada, manifestations of civil religion are seen in our attitude towards national symbols, such as the Canadian flag. These objects are treated with reverence and are often the focus of religious rituals. When the national anthem is sung, men uncover their heads as they would in a church. For many, it is close to sacrilege to fly a flag that has been worn or damaged.

In addition, civil religion, according to Bellah, legitimizes the political authorities of a country, who are treated as almost sacred. Until recently Canadians promised to do their best "for God and the Queen," and *God Save the Queen* was commonly sung at public events. The Queen is also the head of the Anglican Church, and it is through the mainstream Protestant churches such as the Anglican, Presbyterian, and United churches that symbolic support of the sovereign is given in the form of prayers. These prayers are also, of course, for the government of the country, and "for its success in securing order and justice" (Fallding, 1978: 143).

In sum, the notion of civil religion suggests that, if more traditional expressions of religion are on the decline, people may turn to national symbols and

Civil Religion: Canadian Jewry

Most Canadian Jews, like members of many other religious groups in Canada, practise a form of consumer religion. Some norms, concerning such matters as resting on the sabbath, are not widely honoured, nor are kosher dietary laws, requirements for daily prayer and study of the Torah (the Jewish scriptures), and so forth.

For all this selectivity, however, Jews are generally consistent in the parts of their traditional faith to which they do adhere. For example, most Jews marry within the fold. Such endogamy was mentioned in Chapter 9, Families. Prayer services on the New Year (Rosh Hashanah) and Day of Atonement (Yom Kippur) are heavily attended, and many people fast on the latter. Friday-evening special meals ushering in the sabbath are common, and the festival of Hanukkah also retains a considerable following.

These selections are not made arbitrarily. Much, if not all, of what Jews today practise stresses the importance of Jewish identity, akin to ethnic identity (discussed in Chapter 8, Race and Ethnic Relations), and, within that context, the importance of the family. Festivals celebrating the deliverance of their people, "the Passover seder, marrying within the 'faith,' family meals on Sabbath eve—in all this, Jewish peoplehood and its component element, the family, are offered and reinforced as principal values" (Lightstone, 1986).

Within the last half century, two powerful symbols have been etched into the minds of Canadian Jews. One is the Holocaust—the near destruction of the Jews in Europe—and the other is the emergence of the nation-state of Israel. Indeed, it can be argued that Israel and the Holocaust have, for many Jews, displaced the Torah as the main symbol of Jewish identity. Together, they communicate the idea that Jews are "outsiders," who, when persecuted, "miraculously survive and are even renewed" (Lightstone, 1986). Thus, religious festivals like Hanukkah and Passover have come to symbolize the centrality of Jewishness, resistance to forces of assimilation, and vigilance against anti-Semitism.

Canadian Jews have set up distinctive institutions within society, such as synagogues and Jewish community centres, while continuing to participate in the larger social, cultural, and economic milieux. More than that, however, they have adapted their faith. Judaism has become a civil religion—a celebration of the vitality of the Jewish people, and a way to preserve their identity.

For more on this topic, see J. Lightstone, 1986. "Mythe, rituelles, et institutions de la religion civil de la communauté juive canadienne." Religion et culture au Québec: figures contemporaines du sacre, *Y. Desrosiers et al. (eds.). Montreal: Fides.*

public ceremonies to express and experience their relation to their society. Certainly, around the world, nationalistic movements such as that found in Quebec are increasing in popularity, and perhaps such nationalistic movements are related to the decline of traditional religion. The images of Queen and maple leaf may not express the French Canadian experience, but St-Jean Baptiste Day, originally a religious *fête*, has become a secular celebration honouring the Quebec nation. Participation in such movements may well offer individuals the sense of integration, expression, and collective effervescence traditionally provided by religion, and may be seen as a celebration of what individuals in society have in common—in the case of Quebec, the French language and culture. Similarly, Blumstock (1993) has seen Canadian nationalism as filling a moral vacuum within academia. Nationalist ideology, he argued, has in fact been elevated to the status of religion among Canada's intellectual élite.

Bellah's notion of civil religion suggests that religion may be found in contexts quite distinct from traditional places of worship. In the face of considerable evidence pointing to the slow decline of such religion, it may be necessary to redefine religion, as Bellah has done, to understand the increasing variety in the ways Canadians are religious.

Consumer religion

In *Fragmented Gods,* Bibby (1987) analyzed the present state of religion in Canada. Developing a line of argument first suggested by Berger (1969), he examined how religion is both marketed and consumed in Canada today. He noted the continued dominance of four large "companies"—a multinational organization centred in Rome (the Roman Catholic Church), a multinational company centred in England (the Anglican Church), a national corporation (the United Church), as well as a collection of organizations that together represent the Conservative church. He argued that religion in Canada today is **consumer religion**—that Canadians largely seem to consume in fragments what these companies offer, to pick and choose the parts they like. Many utilize rites of passage for birth, death, and marriage; a decreasing number regularly attend services; many identify with fragments of beliefs; some associate with interest groups or social programs that have little religious content but which are sponsored by the churches and take place on church premises. The movement from commitment to consumption of fragments of beliefs, practices, and services is most prevalent with younger Canadians and thus may represent the wave of the future, Bibby asserted. He demonstrated that, while Canadians are drifting away from traditional forms of commitment, they are not abandoning their religious traditions altogether. There is little or no evidence of any sizeable increase in the attachments to new religions, to evangelical conservative religion, to invisible religion, or even to no religion. In terms of religious preferences, Canadians seldom move away from the affiliations of their parents.

Keeping the Customers

Despite difficulties...menu diversification has had the effect of allowing the country's religious groups to cater to a wider range of people. But it has done more than facilitate fragment selection. It has also served to keep membership stable. ...

Today's diversification makes...switching largely unnecessary. Roman Catholic, Anglican, United Church, or Conservative Protestant members now have the choice within their own denominations of being evangelical or agnostic, charismatic or formal, detached or involved, socially concerned or pietistic.

The failure of alternatives—the Conservative Protestants, the new religions, invisible religion, and no religion—to recruit Canadians who appear to be "churchless" is therefore not surprising. All the major religious groups are capable of providing a wide range of content and functions. As a result, the vast majority of affiliated Canadians can readily make functional shifts within their own religious groups, without having to go elsewhere.

If an Anglican, for example, wants to be more deeply committed, he or she can become an evangelical Anglican, rather than defying conventionality...and joining the Baptists. The capacity of established groups to accommodate functional shifts has intensified affiliational stability.

...Academics like Stark and Bainbridge are misreading the Canadian religious scene when they suggest the country is ripe for the invasion of new religious movements. Evangelistically minded church leaders, such as Atlantic Baptist executive Dr. Eugene Thompson and the Ontario Baptist executive Donald Hill, likewise make a serious error in equating irregular attendance with nonaffiliation. Referring to recent Gallup polls, Thompson comments, "Every Sunday there are 16 113 856 Canadians who do not attend any church. Canada is a mission field."...

The Canadian religion market is anything but open...[It] is very tight. Fragment-minded consumers continue to identify with the historically dominant groups that are serving up religion *à la carte* across the country.

What is at issue is not so much group selection as menu selection. Canadians are still eating in the restaurants. But their menu choices have changed. Roman Catholics, for example, continue to dine out. What is disconcerting to many leaders and observers is that many Catholics are opting only for the appetizers, salads, or desserts, rather than full-course meals. Even more upsetting to some people is that the minimum charge has been lifted—it is now possible to skip the entrée page altogether.

Source: *Reginald Bibby, 1987.* Fragmented Gods. *Toronto: Irwin (pp. 131–34).*

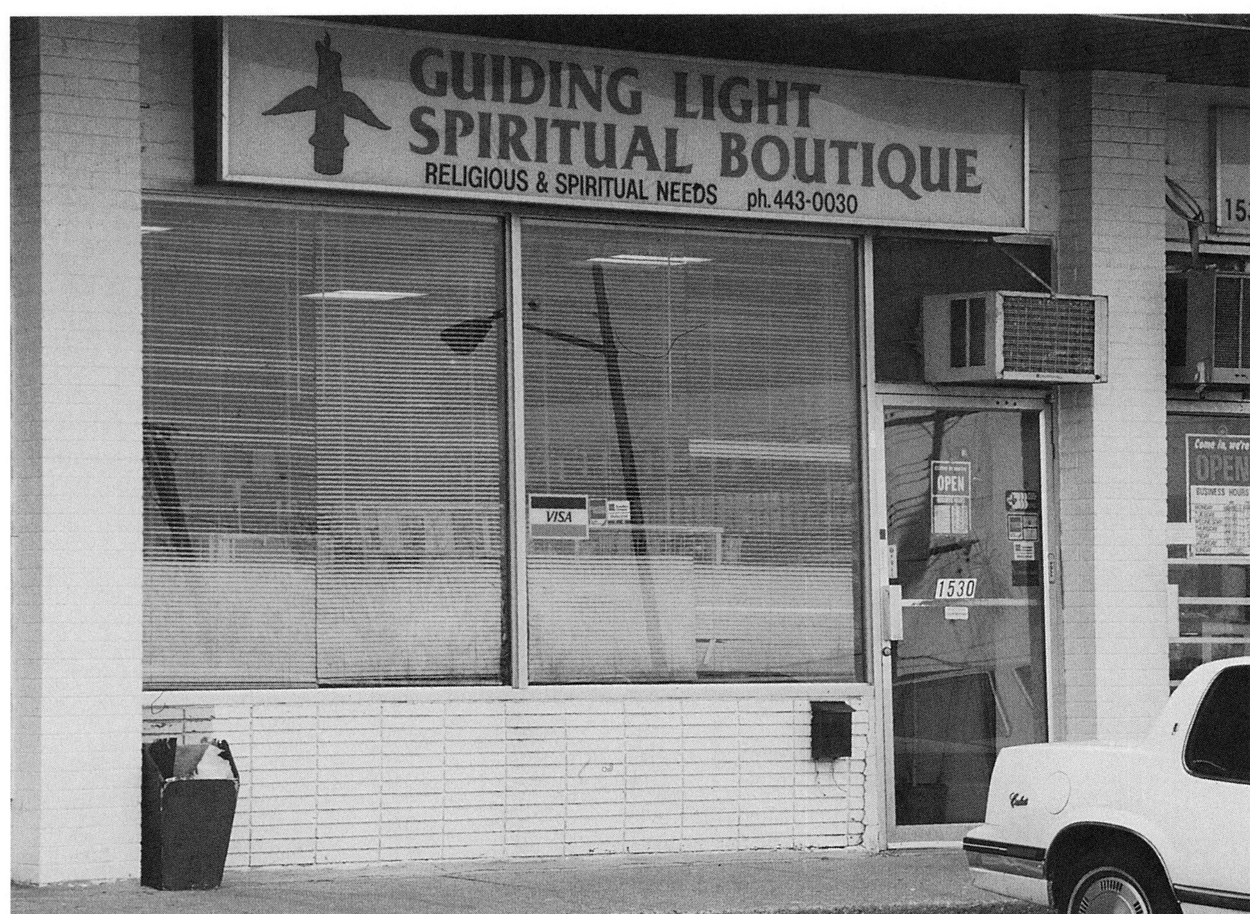

According to Bibby, Canadians are now likely to treat religion as an assortment of consumer items from which they can choose at will.

The character of the preference, however, has changed. Canadians are now more likely to treat religion as an assortment of consumer items from which they can choose at will. This attitude originates in the actions of the churches themselves, as well as in the changing expectations and orientations of participants. Churches, in an attempt to compete in a declining market, no longer insist on certain norms or behaviours as a condition of membership. They no longer demand a total commitment to a way of thinking or a way of life. Rather, they seek to attract audiences to a series of events (such as concerts, at which the regular congregation gets no preferential treatment over non-members for seats) or participation in (often) nonreligious interest or activity groups. This suits the fragmented, consumer-oriented lifestyle of many people today, but it weakens the churches' traditional claim to be reality-defining institutions.

Bibby continued this line of argument in his *Unknown Gods* (1993). He suggested that Canadian churches have largely failed to meet the spiritual needs of Canadians. They have failed to define culture as they once did—they are now increasingly defined by it. They have failed to *reconnect* God with self, with the nature of interpersonal relations, and with life in other societal institutions. As a result, Bibby concluded, the gods of the future will continue to be fragmented and places of worship will represent little more than another stop in a cosmic shopping centre.

SUMMARY

According to Durkheim, the power of religion is really the power of society. Religion, particularly in traditional societies, has important social functions: it interprets, regulates, integrates, and empowers individuals and social groups, and it represents society through religious rituals, myths, and dramas.

For Weber, religion's important purpose lies in its meaning for adherents. Religion provides interpretations of reality and holds out the possibility of escape from suffering. As a meaning system, for example, the religious ideas of the early Protestants led to behaviour that encouraged profitable economic activity in the form of capitalism. Finally, while it is possible to distinguish distinct types of religious organization—ecclesia, denomination, sect, and cult—religious organization evolves continually in response to social changes within and outside the organization.

The work of Marx reflects a conflict theory of religion. Marx argued that religion is used as an ideological tool by the upper classes to justify their monopoly of power and wealth. While the oppressed may find some comfort in religious beliefs, these beliefs serve to blind them to the sources of injustice in this world, and so prevent them from taking action to eliminate them.

Since the time when Durkheim, Weber, and Marx wrote, religion has been generally declining in influence. This process of secularization seems related to increasing specialization, the tendency for other institutions to take over the functions of religion, and religions' efforts to adapt to the change by transforming their rituals and beliefs to make them less purely "religious." Religious attendance has declined, and many people no longer experience the meaning of their lives in religious terms.

Both Durkheim and Weber predicted the secularization process. However, Durkheim suggested that people would still need religion to empower and motivate them. In a very specialized and individualistic society, he predicted, religion too would become specialized and individualized. Weber also felt that, as the world became increasingly rationalized or disenchanted, people might still need an outlet for the mystical and emotional aspects of their personalities. Because of these irrational needs, new charismatic movements might continue to arise.

Available data suggest that religion is indeed becoming less important to many Canadians. Church attendance has declined, as have religious explanations for life's difficulties. However, membership in some denominations is not declining, and some sects and cults are even growing in membership. In particular, middle-class youth have turned to a variety of new religious movements. Some explanations for this trend include a search for moral clarity, a desire for greater social and personal control, a need to represent or embody the conditions of modern life in an ideology of some kind, and a search for intense emotional experience. Canada has always been more resistant than the United States to such movements.

Finally, two contemporary theories of religion suggest that, in the future, religion may have to be redefined. Bellah argued that in modern times public ceremonies have taken on religious overtones. This civil religion celebrates a way of life sacred to national groups. Bibby's concept of consumer religion, on the other hand, looks at the fragmentation of religion and growing Canadian consumer orientation towards religious consumption.

QUESTIONS FOR REVIEW AND CRITICAL THINKING

1. Charismatic leaders are found not only in religions but also in politics. Think of a national leader who could be called charismatic, particularly a leader who appears to head a charismatic movement. Does or did he or she face the problems of routinization of charisma as discussed in this chapter?

2. Can you apply Durkheim's idea that the sacred is really a reflection of the social to your religion, showing, as among the Arunta, that the religious experiences may have social origins?

3. What examples may be drawn from Canada today to show that religion is still the opiate of the masses, as Marx suggested?

4. Have you noticed any of your friends and relatives returning to religious services? Ask them where and why they have gone back, and compare the reasons they give with those given in the text to explain growth in religious groups.

GLOSSARY

calling a purpose in life. In a religious context, it is a belief that people are born with certain abilities in order to fulfil God's will on earth through their life's work.

charisma the recognition and acceptance of authoritative claims based not on traditions, rational argument, or accepted procedures, but on the person or group of persons and their personal messages

church a type of established religious organization usually characterized by membership by birth. It often represents the only religion of a given society.

civil religion the common beliefs and rituals of a political community that interpret political activity in religious or quasi-religious terms

consumer religion Bibby's idea that religious beliefs and services are increasingly treated by people as consumer items to be chosen or discarded at will

cult a type of non-established religious organization characterized by voluntary membership. It is often highly intellectual and features a loosely knit organization that makes few claims on members.

cult of man Durkheim's term for the religion of the future that he believed would hold the idealized human individual as sacred

denominations competing church-like religious organizations

disenchantment of the world the process by which the world is perceived as losing its magical, religious, and nonrational attributes

ecclesia another term for *church*, used by sociologists to describe the dominating or sole religious order of a society, as opposed to *denomination*

elective affinity the parallel development of two distinct social phenomena that serve to reinforce each other

functions of religion the social role of religion in traditional society, as defined by Durkheim. Its functions are to empower, to integrate, to interpret, to regulate, and to represent.

ideology a relatively well-articulated statement of beliefs and objectives that can be used to justify patterns of conduct, especially worldly activities; used by Marx to describe religion

inner-worldly asceticism a religious attitude that offers salvation through self-discipline and accepts the world as an arena for religious activity

new religious movement a generic term used to describe a range of new religious groups, typically of the cult or sect variety

other-worldly mysticism a religious attitude that rejects the world as illusion and offers salvation through detachment from the physical world

predestination the belief that an individual's spiritual salvation is determined before birth by divine plan

profane those objects and activities seen by a society as devoid of supernatural power or significance, of concern only to the individual

Protestant ethic a directive for inner-worldly asceticism attributed by Weber to early Protestant groups

religion any culturally transmitted system of beliefs and rituals to which people orient themselves in order to understand their world and its meaning in relation to some reality(ies) regarded as sacred

routinization of charisma the process of organizational change whereby, for purposes of group survival: 1) authority is transferred from a personal charismatic leader to non-charismatic officials; 2) spontaneous patterns of group organization become fixed and ritualized; and 3) the members and leaders experience reinvolvement with the secular world

sacred those objects and activities set apart by society and treated with awe and respect

salvation according to Weber, a way of giving meaning to one's existence; a way of escaping pain and suffering

sect a type of non-established religious group characterized by voluntary membership, a radical social outlook, and rigorous demands

secularization the process by which traditional religious beliefs and rituals lose their hold on society and other institutions take over their functions

spirit of capitalism an attitude of self-denial in favour of economic gain

SUGGESTED READINGS

Bibby, Reginald W.

1993 *Unknown Gods: The Ongoing Story of Religion in Canada*. Toronto: Stoddart.

This is a comprehensive diagnosis of religion in Canada today, based on several national and local surveys. The study reveals a continuation in the trend towards declining church attendance and consumer-oriented religion. At the same time, Canadians exhibit a strong desire for meaning in life, which to date the established churches have failed to address.

Durkheim, Emile

1965 [1912] *The Elementary Forms of Religious Life*. New York: Free Press.

This classic study of the origins of traditional tribal belief and ritual is highly detailed, with a lengthy introduction and conclusion that are particularly informative and helpful in understanding Durkheim's general theory of religion.

Hewitt, W.E. (ed.)

1993 *The Sociology of Religion: A Canadian Focus.* Toronto: Harcourt Brace.

This is an edited volume with contributions by some of Canada's best-known sociologists of religion. The book deals not only with the principal theoretical issues within the field, but offers detailed descriptions of the state of religion in Canada today.

Weber, Max

1958 [1904–5] *The Protestant Ethic and the Spirit of Capitalism*. New York: Scribners.

One of the more accessible of Weber's works, this book documents his controversial thesis concerning the relationship between one religious tradition (Protestantism) and the economic ethos (capitalism) on which much of Western society is based.

WEB SITES

http://www.religioustolerance.org/var_rel.htm

Descriptions of 57 Religions, Faith Groups and Ethical Systems

The title says it all. Along with better known faith groups, you will also find information about Eckancar, Macumba, and Satanism, and other religions.

http://churchonline.com/index.html

Church Online!

This page provides links to the web pages of religious organizations worldwide, as well as links to various internet based resources. You will also find copies of archived sermons.

CHAPTER

11

Education

Alan Pomfret

INTRODUCTION

By virtue of their clientele, staff, size, activities, and relationships to other social institutions, schools are quite complex. They are characterized by considerable diversity, ambiguity, and numerous contradictions. Consequently, it is a difficult and often humbling task to obtain an accurate picture of what actually happens in schools. It is the job of the sociologist to sift carefully through the complex phenomena surrounding schooling to discover the enduring structures and relationships that characterize the field. Investigators, however, in response both to the complexity of schools and to their own personal and disciplinary interests, often tend to focus on only one part of the picture, at the expense of other parts or the whole.

At the most general level, sociologists of education are interested in describing ways in which schools are related to other social institutions such as families and the workplace, and explaining why such relationships exist. For example, what is the relationship between class background or gender and level of educational attainment? Do schools treat all students fairly? What is the relationship between educational and occupational attainment? Do schools prepare students for adult work, love relationships, and political roles? Does more accessible schooling result in a more open society? As we can see, the sociology of education shares many of the central concerns discussed in Chapter 7, Social Stratification, and Chapter 13, Formal Organizations and Work.

In this chapter, we shall examine two main topics of inquiry within the sociology of education: (1) the role of education in society, and (2) education and equality. The first topic deals with the manner in which schools as institutions relate to other societal institutions such as the economy, the labour market, families, and the social stratification system. Here, we shall look at the various theories about the origin and subsequent growth of modern educational systems. The second topic, education and equality, deals with individuals, and emphasizes the relationship between their social environment and their educational performance. Here, we shall focus on the effects of gender and social class on educational opportunity. We begin our discussion with a description of the Canadian educational system and its development.

THE EXPANSION OF EDUCATION IN CANADA

Virtually all Canadian post-secondary students have already spent a considerable amount of time in various educational settings. Yet there was a time—not so very long ago—when there were no schools as we know them. Although some urban centres started to build modern school systems as early as the 1850s, many parts of Canada did not acquire even the most basic systems until the turn of the twentieth century and even later. As recently as the early 1950s, only about 50 out of every 100 people in Canada between the ages of fourteen and seventeen were in school. By 1990 the figure had risen to approximately 90 out of every 100. Today, one in three Canadians is either a student, a teacher, or a school administrator. Within a century education has moved from a relatively minor cottage industry to become a major economic concern and social institution. In the next section some of the main characteristics of this expansion will be described.

TABLE 11.1 Full-time educational enrollment in Canada, by level, 1951–1994

	Year		
	1951	*1971*	*1994*
Elementary/ secondary	2 541 300	5 466 400	5 022 300
Post-secondary (full-time)			
Non-university	27 600	173 800	376 800
University	63 500	323 000	574 300

Source: *Statistics Canada, CANSIM cross-classified table 00570202.*

Educational expansion: a description

Educational expansion in Canada can be divided into three phases. The first, which began in the mid-nineteenth century, witnessed the rise of mass, compulsory, state-funded elementary school education. In the early part of the twentieth century, during phase two, the secondary school system started to expand. Finally, in the early 1960s or phase three, the post-secondary sector grew tremendously. There were, of course, exceptions to this general trend. Since education is a provincial responsibility, the system has always varied somewhat from region to region. For example, Quebec did not pass compulsory attendance laws until 1943. Even today, the Northwest Territories lack a fully effective system of compulsory elementary education. Overall, though, the pattern of expansion has been relatively uniform throughout the country.

In quantitative terms, the growth in Canadian education during the 1950s and 1960s was particularly dramatic. Table 11.1 shows that elementary and secondary school enrolment, for example, increased markedly between 1951 and 1971. This is partly attributable to the now-famous "baby boom" that occurred in the wake of World War II. The baby boom also subsequently affected post-secondary school enrolment rates, which show similar gains over the same period.

Since World War II, we have also seen an increase in the *participation rate*, especially at the secondary and post-secondary levels. Between 1951 and 1971, the number of persons in Canada aged fifteen to nineteen increased 90 percent, from about 1.1 million to 2.1 million. During the same period, however, the number of secondary school students grew by 333 percent. In 1951 only about five out of every ten people between the ages of fourteen and seventeen were attending secondary school; by 1961 just under eight out of every ten people in the same age group were in school. Today the participation rate is about nine in ten, or 90 percent.

At the post-secondary level, a similar pattern emerged (see Table 11.2). In 1951 only 7 out of every 100 Canadians between the ages of eighteen and twenty-one were enrolled full-time in a university. By 1981 the figure had almost tripled, to just over 18 out of every 100. By 1991, over half a million full-time students were attending Canada's seventy universities, twenty-four of which had been built between 1961 and 1971. Moreover, more and more women entered the universities (see Table 11.3). The percentage of women among all students enrolled full-time in universities increased from 26 percent in 1961 to well over 50 percent in 1994. Universities increased their part-time enrolments as well. In 1962, part-time students accounted for 23 percent of the total university undergraduate enrolment; by 1990, they accounted for 40 percent. In fact, all levels of the educational system offering various forms of credit and non-credit continuing and part-time education have experienced considerable growth

TABLE 11.2 Full-time post-secondary enrollment as a percentage of the relevant age groups, by level

	Non-university	University		Total post-secondary
Year	(as percent of population aged 18–21)	Undergraduate (as percent of population aged 18–21)	Graduate (as percent of population aged 22–24)	(as percent of population aged 18–24)
1951	3.2	7.0	0.6	6.0
1961	5.3	11.9	1.1	10.6
1971	11.2	18.5	3.2	18.5
1981	13.8	17.9	3.3	19.8
1991	20.8	30.1	5.3	30.9

Source: *Statistics Canada, 1990.* Education in Canada: A Statistical Review, 1988–89, *Catalogue No. 81-229, Table 25; Statistics Canada, 1992.* Education in Canada: A Statistical Review, 1990–91, *Catalogue No. 81-229.*

TABLE 11.3 Female enrollment as a percentage of full-time post-secondary enrollment, by level

	Non-university	University			Total Post-secondary
Year		Undergraduate	Graduate	Subtotal	
1961	69.1%	26.2%	16.4%	25.7%	38.4%
1971	45.9	37.7	22.6	36.0	39.5
1977	50.5	44.4	31.9	43.0	45.9
1990	53.9	51.3	41.4	50.2	51.6
1994	54.4	53.8	42.5	52.3	53.1

Source: *Statistics Canada, 1980.* Perspectives Canada III, *Catalogue No. 11-511, Table 4-11; Statistics Canada, 1989.* Advance Statistics of Education, 1989–90, *Catalogue No. 81-220, Tables 7, 8; Statistics Canada, 1993.* Advance Statistics of Education, 1993–94, *Catalogue No. 81-220, Tables 7, 8.*

since 1970, particularly at the secondary level. As a result, the median years of schooling completed has increased dramatically in the second half of this century.

The rate of growth in the community college sector was even greater, increasing its share of the 18- to 21-year-olds from 3.2 percent in 1951 to 20.8 percent in 1991. From 1961 to 1971, the number of community colleges increased from 29 to 133, with a 1991 enrolment of 324 400 full-time students in 198 institutions. The rapid expansion of the community college sector gave many individuals access to an alternative, shorter-term, more vocationally oriented form of post-secondary education. In 1990, however, about one-third of community college students were in programs that would eventually enable them to transfer to a university. This large percentage partly reflects the situation in Quebec, where, unlike other provinces, students usually have to attend a CEGEP (*Collège d'enseignement général et professionnel*) for two years before they are eligible for university.

EXPLANATIONS OF EDUCATIONAL EXPANSION

There are a number of theories that attempt to explain the expansion of the educational system since the late nineteenth century. These include functionalist theory, capital accumulation theory, cultural markets theory, and process model. Let us examine the major assumptions of each.

Functional explanations

To a functionalist, societies such as Canada need schools. Gone forever are the technologically simpler times when relatively unchanging occupations and social positions could be passed from parent to child. This state of affairs enabled most youngsters to learn all they needed to know about work and life through apprenticeship and interaction with their peers, parents, and other adults in their community. The demand for formal education that did exist was met by the small number of church-run or private schools and colleges. Indeed, the word *school* itself comes from the Greek word "leisure," a derivation reflecting both the scarcity of schools and the privileged background of those who attended them.

Industrial technology changed all of this in Canada in the last century, just as it is changing life in today's developing countries. It eliminates some existing occupations while simultaneously creating new ones. Technology creates a more complex and ever-changing division of labour, one increasingly dependent for its efficient operation upon large numbers of people with highly developed expertise in an ever-expanding variety of areas. Contrary to the nonindustrial practice of allocating jobs to people on the basis of ascriptive criteria, people in industrial societies are more likely to be allocated to jobs on the basis of achieved ability and expertise. This is as it should be, argue functionalists; otherwise society would be courting disaster.

A technological change poses such challenges for both parents and school-age children. The **functional theory of education** holds that education exists to meet these challenges and thus to fulfil the ever-changing array of functions within society; specifically, its role is to provide skilled workers, to determine ability and commitment for job selection, to legitimize social position, to establish core values for society, to provide moral education, and to teach citizens about government and how to acquire information. The precise nature of these challenges may be summarized as follows.

1. *The problem of skill acquisition.* Parents can hardly be expected to prepare their children adequately for occupations and ways of living that the parents themselves have never experienced. Where, then, are young people going to learn the skills needed to operate the new technology? From a societal perspective, individuals possessing such skills are needed to keep the society productive and growing. Where are such people to be found?
2. *The problem of selection.* Different jobs require different skills, and some require more complex skills than others. Obviously, if a job should be matched with a person's ability and motivation, how is a person's competence and commitment to be determined? And how can the entire pool of talent be tapped to ensure that the best people are being selected?
3. *The problem of legitimacy.* Skill requirements are not the only way to distinguish among jobs. Some jobs pay more than others, some have more power associated with them than others, and some are more prestigious than others. Not everybody can have a top job, since there are only a limited number of positions available in each occupational category. This means that some people have to settle for less than others. In a society in which birth is no longer acceptable as a way of determining adult status, what does it take to get people to accept their own positions in that system?
4. *The problem of core values for a cohesive national society.* A more complex division of labour, whatever its economic benefits, is potentially socially divisive, given that the labour force is now divided into so many different types of occupations. Moreover, for Canada as for many other nations, increased immigration accompanied the advent of urbanization and industrialization. Increased

Functionalists claim that education exists to meet the challenges posed by technological change, and thus to fill the ever-changing array of functions within society.

immigration means that many ethnic groups, each possessing a unique culture, tradition, social network, and language, reside within a country's boundaries. How can a nation united by a set of core values be produced out of such seemingly diverse and potentially antagonistic cultural and social elements?

5. *The problem of moral education.* Moral education or socialization also becomes a problem, as work, family, and education—once so closely united in nonindustrial times—become increasingly separated and differentiated from one another. As work becomes increasingly differentiated from the home, parents experience greater difficulty in exercising moral authority and control over their children. The father, and often the mother, works away from the home. Children can obtain jobs and income independent of their parents. Parents thus have less to pass on to their children in terms of skills and property. The resulting shift in family authority patterns means that the family can no longer be counted on to function effectively as the only socializing agent for the young. Yet the young have to be properly socialized. How is this to be done? Who will supplement the family's function as a socializing agent?

6. *The problem of democratic citizenship.* The problem of citizenship is twofold. One aspect involves providing people with more information about the structure and workings of government. But more than this is required. Given the ever-changing nature of the environment, people also have to learn *how to learn*—how to acquire and examine new information. Where are people to acquire such skills?

Functionalists claim that the school system was started and expanded because people at the time saw it as one solution to the problems of skill, selection, legitimacy, values, moral education, and citizenship confronting a modernizing Canada. Schools would (and still do) train young people in the necessary skills and allocate their students to jobs on the basis of ability and motivation. Schools would (and continue to) produce order out of potential chaos by instilling core values in all students, foreign and native-born. Compulsory, universal attendance ensures that all youngsters are exposed to the school's moral authority and skill training. By including all youngsters in the school's selection process, society also attempts eventually to acquire the best people for its various occupations. Thus, schooling means efficient and effective human-resource development. Moreover, including everyone in the sorting process undermines any claims that the selection process is unacceptable because some are unfairly excluded. Equality of educational opportunity promotes equality of social opportunity. In this way, equality of opportunity then legitimizes inequality of results. Finally, through schooling, people learn how to be useful and effective democratic citizens.

The general assumption of functionalist theorists is that certain functions or tasks must be performed if society is to survive. Schools perform some of these functions. If societies become increasingly structurally differentiated—that is, if the family becomes increasingly separated from the work setting—schools can carry out the functions of socialization, selection, and training that the home can no longer perform. Functionalists feel this claim is as true of the present as of the past. They see today's schools as continuing to perform the functions that originally necessitated their expansion.

Problems with functional explanations

You will recall the functionalist claim that advances in industrial technology result in a need for more complex skills and abilities, which can be acquired only in schools. Braverman (1974) and especially Collins (1979) admitted that industrial technology obviously creates some jobs requiring more complex skills than many nonindustrial jobs require. But, they contended, the number of such jobs, especially in early industrial periods, is not nearly as great as functionalist imagery implies. If anything, many early industrial jobs are less complex than nonindustrial jobs, and historically, some argue, the general trend has been towards an occupational structure consisting of increasingly simple jobs. In other words, a measure of "deskilling" has occurred. Moreover, the skills needed to perform these jobs are learned mainly at work, not at school.

Still, functionalists are correct in pointing out that the level of schooling individuals require to be able even to apply for most jobs has risen, sometimes dramatically. Although greater job complexity may account for some of the rise, some of the increase has been for jobs that have experienced little or no change in the complexity of the skills required to perform them. The result is that individuals now need more schooling than their parents simply to be considered eligible for jobs requiring the very same skills. If the need to acquire new skills does not account for the increase in educational requirements for jobs, what does? We shall return to this question later.

Critics of the functionalist theory also point to significant features of schools that functionalists completely ignore. For example, Hurn (1993) wondered how functionalists, given their emphasis on the relationship between skill training and the rise of schooling, can explain the continued existence in schools of a liberal arts curriculum that includes such subjects as Latin and ancient history—seemingly quite irrelevant to the effective performance of most jobs outside of schools. Cultural markets theory, to be discussed later, offers us one way of explaining such a curriculum. But first let us turn to conflict theory explanations of educational expansion, to those theories that most directly oppose functionalist explanations.

Capital accumulation explanations

Capital accumulation theory, a conflict theory that draws heavily on the ideas of Marx, identifies social control as the prime mover behind educational change. To Marxists, the most distinguishing aspect of capitalism is that it must expand through innovation in order to survive, and to expand it must accumulate capital for reinvestment. To acquire profits, employers must pay workers less than the value of what the workers produce, a practice workers may resist as exploitive. Thus, the employer–worker relationship is inevitably antagonistic. (We discussed this idea in Chapter 7, Social Stratification.) To capital accumulation theorists, schools neither start in response to the needs of society in general nor operate to benefit everyone. Instead, schools are started by employers as one way of rendering harmless the potentially explosive class (e.g., worker versus employer) antagonisms that accompany the spread of capitalism in the form of the factory system.

This explanation of schooling in capitalist society is one illustration of the more general concept of the **correspondence principle**, which states that educational systems correspond to the society's mode of production. For example, in examining the origins of the American school system, Bowles and Gintis (1976) noted that, wherever factories were built, school construction soon followed. To explain this, they argued that new factories recruited workers from either the surrounding rural areas or from immigrants who also had rural origins. These workers were not familiar with factory life and work routines, and many were away from their parents for the first time. Moreover, there was a natural class conflict between employers, who wanted to maximize profits, and workers, who wanted to maximize wages and optimize working conditions. The employers, to turn their new recruits into a dependable and productive workforce, established schools that would prepare working-class children for their future jobs as factory workers. Changes in both secondary and post-secondary education, it was argued, were thus related to changes in the needs and functioning of capitalism. Bowles and Gintis acknowledged that there was also considerable public demand for more schooling, but argued that the capitalist élite treated those demands by selectively implementing only those changes that did not disturb its needs.

Problems with capital accumulation explanations

Collins (1977: 20–21) identified a number of weaknesses in the capital accumulation model. To begin with, he pointed out that England established its school systems after, not at the same time as, industrialization; Denmark, Prussia, and Japan developed theirs before industrialization. Second, Collins disagreed that the school systems were designed to create a class of factory workers: "mass, compulsory education was first created not for industrial, but for military and political discipline." Third, the capital accumulation argument "does not fully explain why some industrial societies have large mass-education systems and why some have small ones." And fourth, it cannot explain the educational expansion of the 1960s, an era not marked by a correspondingly dramatic increase in capitalism or in worker agitation, which capitalists might have perceived as being in need of control.

In Canada, the capitalist accumulation model has also not been well received. Most analysts now agree that the movement to establish a system of mass education in this country, particularly in Ontario, consisted not of the capitalist élite, but of *middle-class*, urban social reformers concerned about the socially disruptive potential of the "lower orders" of society. A further problem with applying the capital accumulation model to Canada is the fact that in Canada, including areas such as Toronto, the movement to establish mass elementary education began before industrialization (Houston and Prentice, 1988). Moreover, in Montreal, unlike their English-Canadian Protestant counterparts, the French-Canadian Catholic élite remained aloof from efforts to establish a system of mass elementary education (Copp, 1974). In addition, a collection of articles on the origin of education in Western Canada identified a number of different factors, including religion, that influenced the early development and growth of provincial school systems there (Sheehan et al., 1986).

The cultural markets explanation

Obviously, many differences exist between functionalist and capital accumulation theory. However, both tend to see educational change as an essentially rational process: functionalists see schools performing certain critical functions for society in general; capital accumulation theorists see the school system meeting the needs of the capitalist élite by serving as a key component in the larger system of worker control. The **cultural markets theory**, drawing on Weber, rejects this assumption of rationality and argues that school change is more complex than either the functionalist or the capital accumulation theory maintains. You will recall from Chapter 7, Stratification, that Weber also rejected Marx's unidimensional view of social stratification, arguing instead that class, status, and power are each important unidimensional aspects of inequality.

For Collins (1977; 1979), the cultural market for schooling consisted of various types and combinations of groups fighting each other in a variety of ways for various types of education. Among the groups operating here are, first of all, *material interest groups,* which value getting a job above all else and may push for practical vocational education. Second, *status groups,* concerned with cultural survival, may demand that schools concentrate on language and other forms of cultural education. (We mentioned this idea with respect to Quebec, in Chapter 8, Race and Ethnic Relations.) Third, *power groups*, preoccupied with controlling others, may insist upon having highly bureaucratized school systems.

Although at one time secondary schools were an important battleground for this struggle, the main contest has shifted to the post-secondary arena. Groups compete not only over the type of education they want, but also over the amount. In the case of modern schooling, credentials such as degrees, diplomas, and certificates—not necessarily education and training in themselves—are the key goods sought. This is because school credentials act as a kind of cultural capital or symbolic wealth, which credential holders can use to purchase other goods. Possessing credentials entitles individuals to other valuable cultural resourses such as jobs, income, status, power, even social relationships. Let us illustrate with an example specifically how this works.

Historically, lawyers, doctors, and employers have been responsible for the rise in educational requirements for law, medicine, and business administration, respectively. A functionalist would say this was done to provide potential recruits with much-needed training as the demands of these professions grew. Cultural markets theory suggests two additional purposes. First, increasing the educational requirements of an occupation increases its status. Doctors, lawyers, and business executives have high status in our society, because high-status occupations have more autonomy, control, and security to define their role than do low-status occupations. High-status occupations also have more power to define what constitutes a fair income. Governing bodies such as the Canadian College of Family Physicians, the Canadian Bar Association, or the Canadian Institute of Chartered Accountants perform these functions for their members. In sum, the cultural markets theory would suggest, additional schooling is less relevant to the skill acquisition needed to perform work roles than to self-promotion of the occupation in question.

Second, increasing an occupation's educational requirements facilitates occupational closure. For reasons that will be discussed at length in the next section, many types of people will be unlikely to acquire the necessary qualifying school credentials even though they may have the ability to do the job. This tends to limit competition for available positions. Moreover, when lower-status groups in the cultural market for schooling purchase more schooling for their children in a bid to better their position, the already dominant groups respond by increasing the requirements and then purchasing even more schooling for their own children, in order to maintain their relative advantage in the market.

In sum, then, part of the dramatic increase in education in the 1950s and 1960s may have been due to self-serving credential inflation; another part was probably due to pressures by the new middle-class groups, created by the postwar economic expansion, for more education for their children as a way to ensure the passing on of their new relative affluence. Unlike functionalism and capital accumulation theory, the cultural markets perspective also argues that the main forces affecting schools may be found both outside and *inside* schools. In fact, professionals inside the school are, as a group, one of the key contenders in the market; for however closely schools may have been linked to other groups in the beginning, once established they take on a life of their own. In other words, the people who staff schools exercise some control over what happens in them. Like other contenders in the market, they will promote arrangements that enhance their own autonomy and security.

The cultural markets perspective argues that professionals inside the schools exercise some control over what happens in them.

To Hurn (1992), the cultural markets notion of school autonomy accounts for one aspect of schooling that neither functionalists nor capital accumulation theorists can explain: why so much of the school curriculum remains so remote from the work world. From the perspectives of both societal needs and capitalist domination of labour, the study of Shakespeare, colonial history, Latin, and many other disciplines is irrelevant and irrational. Hurn suggested that at one time these were high-prestige subjects, which only people of leisure—namely, high-status, wealthy people—could afford to pursue. They were the mark of cultivated, civilized minds. Teachers based their jobs and careers, then, not on knowledge of occupationally relevant skills, but on these prestigious liberal-arts disciplines. Where public acceptance was low or slow in developing, school professionals *imposed* a liberal arts education upon students. This was possible because, as schools became increasingly organized into one comprehensive elementary-to-university system, school professionals were able to strengthen their control over the curriculum. University teachers made a liberal arts education a university entrance requirement. And as professional faculties such as law schools joined the university, their students generally were required to obtain a liberal arts degree before entering professional education.

Thus, according to cultural markets theory, schools reflect the outcomes of struggles involving many conflicting interests. Consequently, it is impossible to see in the resulting diversity a rationally constructed system dedicated entirely to meeting the needs of either a society undergoing industrialization (the functionalist view) or capitalist élites (the capital accumulation view).

The process model of educational expansion

Although the preceding theories of educational expansion overlap in many ways, they do not directly compete with one another on all issues at once. Different theories attempt to describe and explain different aspects of the origins and subsequent expansion of the system of mass, state-supported schooling. Some stress structural factors; others, group factors; and others, cultural or ideological factors.

Acknowledging this complexity and the difficulty associated with resolving some of the contrasting claims, Smelser (1991) has recently proposed a *process model*—a method of analyzing educational change designed to identify the distinctive results and direction of change during a given historical period. The model requires identifying the beginnings and endings of certain periods of educational change. Among other things, it takes into account how politics affects and is affected by educational change. It also examines the effects of education on class structure, the two-way relationship between society and education, and the growth and impact of the independence of the educational system. This model implies that there may be few, if any, universal laws associated with educational change and, therefore, that any one approach may apply only in certain circumstances. For example, the relationship between the development of capitalism or industrialization, on the one hand, and educational systems, on the other, may differ from location to location, depending on local circumstances. Given this possibility, the most prudent course of action would be to identify the key concepts and issues relevant to the period being studied, on which analysts should then focus. Applying this model to nineteenth-century Britain, Smelser (1991: 30) concluded, for example, that if "a connection between industrial/urban development and mass education existed, it was based less on economic demands in the early phases of urban/industrial development than on the dynamics of class, community, religion, and polity that were associated with that development." We shall see later that similar theoretical contradictions in the study of school- and classroom-level processes have also led to the development of a process model of schooling.

The Social Construction Approach to Studying Classroom Dynamics

The social construction approach to studying classroom dynamics examines classroom- and school-level processes from a Marxist perspective. One proponent of this model, Apple (1986), argued that all levels of teaching are undergoing processes of deskilling similar to that occurring in many other occupations in advanced capitalist systems. This deskilling results from a growing reliance upon curriculum packages and computers at the elementary and secondary level, from increasingly close ties to business—especially in community colleges (Muller, 1990)—and from increasingly large classes due to cutbacks in government funding at the university undergraduate level. The overall impact is a growing reliance upon standardized forms, teaching practices, and testing procedures. These in turn contribute to the sense of an increasingly rigid and authoritarian learning environment in the classroom. Apple acknowledged that many people in schools—teachers as well as students—actively try to oppose these trends.

Aronowitz and Giroux (1985) have criticized the social construction approach. The main thrust of their criticism is that the approach fails to recognize sufficiently the complexity of classroom and school processes. In particular, they argue that too much emphasis is placed on the structures (e.g., curriculum, teaching methods) and too little on the ability of people to oppose these structures. For example, they suggest the approach insufficiently recognizes the efforts of teachers to overcome the effects of deskilling and other changes affecting the classroom. They also point out that reform efforts in Canada from the late 1950s to the early 1970s were designed to change student–teacher relationships in the direction of increased student autonomy.

Reform efforts in Canada from the late 1950s to the early 1970s were designed to change student–teacher relationships in the direction of increased student autonomy.

DEFINING, DESCRIBING, AND EXPLAINING INEQUALITY

Expansion, reform, and equality

We began this chapter with a brief description of the main features of the growth of the school system in Canada. We examined several theories that attempt to explain, in general terms, the *causes* of educational expansion. We turn now to a consideration of its *consequences*. Most of the sociological research concerned with the impact of the expansion of education focuses on the educational boom period following 1950. Of necessity, then, the following discussion will focus on Canada since that time.

In any assessment of the consequences during this period, it is essential to keep in mind that the expansion of the system was accompanied by unprecedented pressures for, and attempts at, change. Reform and expansion were virtually synonymous terms describing education after the 1950s. As much as, and perhaps more than, the actual expansion of the system, the reform movement raised expectations about what education should, could, and would do for individuals and for society.

Educational reform efforts in Canada from the late 1950s to the early 1970s were led by professional educators who generally favoured student autonomy. Plans for community schools, free schools, team teaching, child-centred teaching, and open-concept schools all identified an increase in student participation as a key objective. Teachers would be less directive and more facilitative—that is, rather than teaching *at* passive students, they would create a climate that *enabled* the students to learn through greater participation. A classroom climate of commitment, cooperation, and support would replace one of apathy, competition, and mistrust. Such a change would enable students from all groups to develop their potential and do better academically. Yet, by the 1970s, in the minds of many of its proponents, the educational reform "movement" failed. Teachers were still directive, and structured inequality of educational opportunity, along lines of ethnicity, gender, race, and social class, persisted.

During the 1980s and 1990s a new and considerably more diversified range of attempts at changing various aspects of the educational system began to appear. On the one hand, educational "insiders" continued to extend and refine the changes started by the earlier reform movement. On the other, various educational "outsiders," including many parent groups, started arguing for a reversal of these changes and a return to the basics, and for increased accountability of educators. Still others, including labour and business representatives, argued that Canada and the world had changed so much since the 1960s that it should forget the old battles and get on with developing a system that would respond to new social, economic, and political trends of the 1990s. As a group, the outsiders also identified a set of factors that they believed blocked effective reform, among them too much power in the hands of educational professionals; a lack of vision concerning the goals and direction of education; lack of accountability by educators, reflected in the absence of standardized tests that would allow a direct comparison of the effectiveness of different educational methods; faulty teaching and curriculum fads, such as "whole language teaching" and "spiral" mathematics; and unwarranted arrogance and defensiveness on the part of professional educators.

Equality of educational opportunity

One of the pillars of the earlier reform movement—and one that persists today despite current controversy—is the desire for educational policy that seeks to achieve equality of opportunity. Sociologically speaking, equality of educational opportunity is usually said to exist when success in school depends upon achieved rather than ascribed criteria. Equality of educational opportunity is seldom taken to mean that schools must ensure that all students perform in exactly the same way or receive identical rewards. Many consider it obvious that not everyone does or can do equally well in school—some students are more intelligent and motivated than others. Most people would argue also that the school's academic teaching and evaluation procedures should detect and differentially reward such individual differences in ability and motivation. In Canada's competitive and achievement-oriented school system, inequality, regardless of its drawbacks, appears to be an unavoidable and pervasive fact of life.

Working within such a definition, one of the school's main responsibilities is to provide an equal opportunity for students to develop to and perform at the level of their potential abilities, and then to reward them accordingly. Two equally intelligent and motivated students should achieve equally well in school regardless of any other differences between them, especially ascriptive ones, such as gender, region of birth or residence, ethnicity, or social class position. In other words, the differences or inequalities in students' educational attainments are justified only to the extent that the competition producing them is fair. The competition is fair, and equality of educational opportunity exists, only to the extent that students are judged on achievement rather than on ascriptive criteria.

Persisting patterns of inequality

What happens to students in schools? For some students, education represents the first rung on the ladder of success. For others, it represents an insurmountable obstacle unfairly condemning them to a life they would rather avoid. Some see schools as forums in which to display their accomplishments, to acquire cherished rewards, or to develop otherwise ignored abilities. Others see schools as hostile, alien, punitive, and threatening environments that are constantly making senseless and unpleasant demands, and passing unfair and insensitive judgments. To still others, schooling is an irrelevant experience to be endured, then quickly forgotten when they finally and thankfully enter the real world. Partly in response to these varying perceptions and beliefs, some students perform better than others at school. While some tend to be ignored or criticized, others receive help and praise; while some leave school as early as possible, others continue for as long as they can.

What accounts for such noticeable variations in student perception and performance? Why do some people seem to benefit more from schooling than others? Two general kinds of responses to this question are possible. The first suggests that such differences result mainly from differences in individual temperaments, abilities, motivations, and other uniquely individual dispositions, traits, and characteristics. In short, some people have what it takes and others do not. The second response, which comes out of sociologically oriented investigations, suggests that these perceptions are not individual but *social* in nature—in the sense that social context influences the kinds of experiences students have. There are patterned or structured relationships among students' social roles (e.g., gender, ethnicity, religion, social class) and certain school experiences (e.g., grades and grade levels achieved, courses and programs taken, interactions with teachers, perceptions and beliefs of teachers and students). All in all, what this second, sociological response suggests is that equality of opportunity is not a reality in Canadian schools. In the following sections, we shall examine disparities in two areas—gender and social class—and the reasons for the persistence of these disparities.

Dropping Out and Unemployment: Is Apprenticeship the Answer?

Despite its growing educational participation rates, Canada is exploring ways of using the school system to respond to the twin issues of high teenage-dropout rates and youth unemployment. Some suggestions for dealing with these problems come from Stephen Hamilton, who based his recommendations upon his examination of Germany's apprenticeship system at the upper-secondary-school level. In this system, most Germans between the ages of sixteen and eighteen participate in a dual system of apprenticeship and part-time vocational schooling. Hamilton's suggestions represent an attempt to adapt the German system to North American conditions. Do you find the suggestions convincing? How could we overcome the fact that in Germany the system is of more benefit to males than to females?

We need a coherent system with a sequence of steps through which young people can move. Building on existing programs and practices, our communities could offer a range of opportunities such as these:

Exploratory apprenticeships. Community service work is especially appropriate for middle-grade youth who are not ready to make vocational choices. Unlike the situation with traditional apprenticeship, there is no presumption that the student will continue in this line of work. And unlike the usual teenage jobs, service programs may give young volunteers chances to plan projects themselves and to take on higher levels of responsibility.

School-based apprenticeships. In addition to...cooperative education programs and academies..., some schools run their own enterprises, ranging from restaurants to day-care centers. School-based programs protect the young person's principal role as student and emphasize that the lessons to be learned are primarily general academic ones; job skills and occupational choice are less critical.

Work-based apprenticeships. A particularly promising form of work-based apprenticeship combines schooling with apprenticeship over a period spanning two years of high school and two years of technical college. Upon completion of such a "2+2" program, an apprentice has earned a high school diploma, an associate's degree, and qualification for employment as a technician, a promising occupational category with career potential.

Clearly, this goes far beyond the agenda of the usual school–business partnership. Expanding apprenticeship will require changes in the ways both schools and workplaces deal with young people. Schools, for example, must become more flexible. The idea that students can learn some things most effectively outside the classroom entails loosening rigid schedules and abandoning the practice of awarding credit primarily on the basis of hours spent in the classroom.

Shifting toward performance-based accreditation will...provide a means of assessing the quality of instruction in the workplace, a serious issue.

But, most important, cooperation must flow from agreement on the fundamental goals of education. The schools must serve the needs of a democracy for an educated citizenry, not just the needs of industry for prepared workers.

This is a promising moment for new forms of collaboration between schools and business precisely because new technology, new styles of management, and the growth of service employment are enlarging the common ground for employers' needs and the goals of democratic education. Many employers now describe their ideal employee in terms that fit the traditional well-educated person: someone who is able to communicate clearly, perform basic math, think critically, solve problems, work cooperatively, and behave responsibly.

By inventing an apprenticeship system whose primary purpose is general education, achieved by means of instruction and experience in school and workplace, we can more effectively educate youth who do not enroll in university. Ultimately, we can prepare them for employment, for further education, for citizenship, and for fuller, more satisfying lives as well.

Source: *Stephen F. Hamilton, 1990. "Is there life after high school?: Developing apprenticeship in America."* The Harvard Education Letter *4, 4 (pp. 1–5).*

To what extent does equality of educational opportunity exist in Canada?

Gender inequalities

Concerns about gender equality in education focus partly on the relative participation and performance of men and women in various educational programs, and partly on the quality of women's experiences in these programs. Concerning the former, a number of discrepancies in female–male participation and performance patterns in Canadian post-secondary schools are apparent. Data from 1991 show that, at community colleges, 54 percent of full-time and 63 percent of part-time students are female; at universities, 53 percent of full-time undergraduates and 64 percent of part-time undergraduates are female. At both types of institution, moreover, gender separation is evident. In the community colleges, only 16 percent of the full-time students in engineering and applied sciences are female, whereas 84 percent of the students in the health sciences, including nursing, are female. Females make up 61 percent of the full-time business and commerce enrolment, including 53 percent of management and administration students, but also 97 percent of secretarial science students. University enrolments and graduation rates (see Table 11.4) reveal a similar trend. Female students dominate nursing, pharmacy, rehabilitative medicine (85 percent), humanities and arts (62 percent), and social sciences (53 percent), especially psychology (76 percent) and sociology (71 percent). Economics, geography, and political science are male-dominated. Yet it is worth noting that 43 percent of business, management, and commerce students are female. Males also predominate in engineering (85 percent) and math and physical sciences (71 percent), especially physics. In this last area, however, female participation rates are increasing, if slowly. While between 1987 and 1991 the absolute numbers of both females and males in these programs decreased, the

TABLE 11.4 Women as a percentage of graduating students, full time and part time, in major fields of study and by degree level, 1994

Field of Study	
Education	70.0
Fine and Applied Arts	66.6
Humanities	63.5
Social Sciences	55.9
Agricultural and Biological Sciences	57.2
Engineering and Applied Sciences	18.3
Health Professions	71.4
Mathematics and Physical Sciences	29.9
Total Graduations	**57.1**

Degree Level (all fields)	
Bachelor's	57.4
Master's	48.4
Doctoral	31.8

Source: *Statistics Canada, CANSIM cross-classified table 00580602.*

proportion of females in undergraduate sciences rose from 27 to 29 percent. In addition, women science students have as good (or poor) a chance as their male peers of completing a science program once they start it (Grayson, Pomfret, and Gilbert, 1993). In some subject areas, females are slightly more likely than men to complete the program, to complete it faster, and with slightly higher grades (Pomfret and Gilbert, 1991).

At the graduate level, 1991 figures reveal that females make up 41 percent of the full-time and 48 percent of the part-time graduate enrolment. Full-time male students outnumber females in all fields except education (74 percent female), fine and applied arts, and humanities. Only 14 percent of graduate engineering students are female, as are 22 percent of mathematics and science students. This pattern is repeated for part-time students, except in the case of the health professions, where the majority of students are female. In law and medicine, females have reached near parity with males, making up 51 and 45 percent of the student cohort, respectively.

Along with participation and performance, the quality of women's experiences in education is a major area of concern. Many question whether current educational structures and practices place unnecessary and unfair constraints on women's opportunities to learn. Women may be placed in situations where they either feel or actually are excluded and unwelcomed, or even threatened, by males. Teaching practices may be male-biased in terms of content, approach, and style, and thus incompatible with females' preferred learning styles, perhaps especially in the sciences (Human Resources Committee, National Advisory Board on Science and Technology, 1993; Rosser, 1990). Belenky et al. (1986) proposed an instructor–student "connected teaching" model as more consistent with women's preferred ways of knowing.

In summary, more women than ever before are entering post-secondary education. They make up either an equal number or the majority of students in a growing variety of university programs. Yet, in other programs such as engineering and science, participation has increased little, resulting in very noticeable gender differences. The differences become more noticeable the higher up one moves in the educational system. Questions remain as well about the quality and appropriateness of women's educational experiences. Despite occasionally

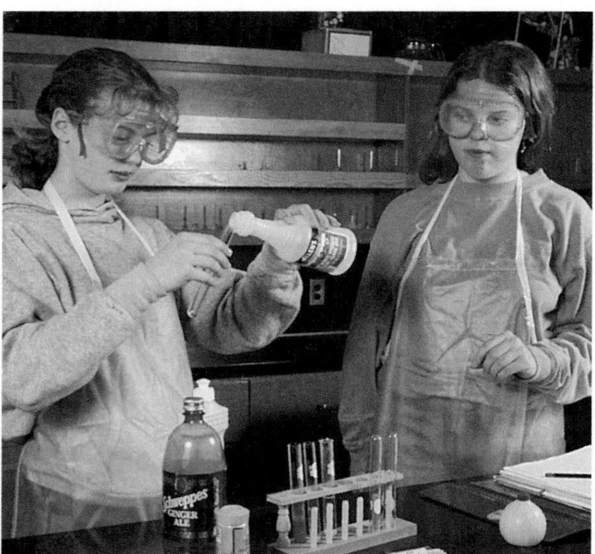

Though these courses are compulsory in elementary school, females are less likely than males to take secondary school maths and sciences.

impressive gains in areas such as law and medicine, and more modest gains elsewhere, women have by no means achieved full equality of educational attainment with men (see the boxed insert on "Computers and Gender Differences in the Classroom").

Class inequalities

In terms of group scores, students from working-class families tend to perform less well academically in school than students from middle-class families. This does not mean that every working-class student performs less well than every middle-class student. It does mean that, if a child is born into a working-class family, he or she is *more likely* than a middle-class child to receive lower grades, to enrol in non-university programs, or to quit school as soon as possible, even when both have equal levels of ability and motivation (Curtis et al., 1992). The fact that almost everyone has access to schools at the elementary and secondary levels does not, of itself, ensure equality of educational attainment for members of different social classes.

At the post-secondary level, class inequality becomes especially noticeable. Despite the fact that educational expansion has slightly lessened class as a barrier, university students are still more likely to come from middle-class than from working-class families (Guppy and Arai, 1993: 223). This middle-class advantage progressively decreases, however, as one moves to part-time university, to full-time community college, and to part-time community college attendance. Community colleges, in fact, appear to draw their students fairly equally from across class categories.

Computers and Gender Differences in the Classroom: A Solution or a Problem?

The International Association for the Assessment of Educational Achievement recently examined computer usage in Austria, Bulgaria, Germany, Greece, India, Japan, Latvia, Netherlands, Slovenia, and the U.S. (Pelgrum et al., 1993). The findings with respect to gender were not comforting. In all countries females knew less than males about information technology, enjoyed using computers less, and reported more software problems. The possible causes cited for these gender differences were degrees of parental support, less female access to computers (in terms of availability and use), and the scarcity of female role models.

It is important to recognize that gender differences were found both inside school and at home. Yet few of the schools surveyed had policies concerning the gender issue, and the policies that existed were formulated without parental input. Concerning teachers, a majority of schools did encourage female role models, and a few made both female and male teachers aware of the gender differences between male and female students.

How well do these findings correspond to your own experiences with using computers in the classroom? What other difficulties or problems have you encountered? What do you think should be done about them?

Because of their greater inclusion of working-class students and an emphasis on vocational education, community colleges have been characterized as "a proletarian alternative to the university" (Nock, 1983: 364) by some Canadian observers. Certain "mass" universities (e.g., York, University of Alberta) may also be seen as falling within this category. Compared with "élite" universities such as Toronto, McGill, and Queen's, which historically have enrolled a disproportionate number of offspring from élite families, many of these generally newer mass universities place more emphasis on vocationalism. As such, they may represent the "proletarianization of the university system" (Nock, 1983: 361).

Explaining inequality

The preceding section described some of the patterns of gender and class inequality in education. We now turn our attention to an explanation of these patterns. First of all, to illustrate some of the reasons for continuing gender inequality, we shall focus on explanations of both the quantitative and qualitative aspects of women's under-participation in science and mathematics programs.

Explanations of gender inequalities

At one time it was common to locate the source of women's under-participation in mathematics and science programs in biological differences. It was claimed that, for genetic reasons, women were less spatially and mathematically able than men (Maccoby and Jacklin, 1974). These deficiencies led to poor performance by women and thus to low participation in math and science programs. However, as we saw in Chapter 6, Gender Relations, recent research has discredited the notions of significant spatial and mathematical gender differences, the genetic basis for such presumed differences (Fausto-Sterling, 1992), and the notion that spatial ability affects mathematical performance (Ethington and Wolfe, 1984).

Consequently, researchers are focusing more on participation, rather than ability, as a key issue. Why do fewer women than men participate in science and math programs, even when they have the ability to do well in such programs? Researchers using this approach stress the social determinants of participation. Some claim that men may possess negative stereotypes and prejudicial attitudes about women, which result in discriminatory practices inside and outside the classroom (Dagg and Thompson, 1988). For example, focusing on the participation and performance of eighth-grade mathematics students, Baker and Jones (1993) documented considerable variations in females' participation and performance over time and from place to place. They concluded that this variation is a response to the perceived opportunity structure for women after graduation. Women's math participation rates and performance patterns equal male patterns in those nations with more equal gender opportunity structures for adults. Women are less likely to take and do well in math in those societies where the genders are less equal. As Baker and Jones (1993: 99) put it: "Parity in opportunities for adults yields parity in preparatory performance." They cautioned that it remains an open question as to whether and how this early educational equality translates into other forms of gender equality later in life.

Another general argument is that science is more than a cognitive process: it is a way of life, and its practices are closely tied to ideas of self and relationships to others, and hence to people's moral and ethical senses (Lengermann and Niebrugge-Brantley, 1990). The usual conduct of science stresses the autonomy of the self and emphasizes limited and clearly defined reciprocal relationships with others. However, many people, including those with the academic ability to study science, also have a view of self that stresses a care and response orientation to others. Although the behaviour of both men and women may be guided by both orientations, women more than men prefer the care and response orientation (Gilligan, 1982). More generally, it is also suggested that the double burden many women carry (family as well as occupational demands) makes advanced scientific study impractical for them, especially given the demanding nature of scientific careers. For this reason, many women find that the educational and occupational worlds of science do not express or satisfy their emotional and ethical preferences. What this means is that, given a choice, even when they are academically competent, many women (and men as well) will choose to go into educational programs in which they may feel less emotionally and ethically uncomfortable (Grayson, Pomfret and Gilbert, 1993). One policy implication of this attitude is that it may be necessary to change the way science and math are taught if society is sincere in its wish to attract women and to retain them in science programs.

This may be more easily said than done. One study of a grade nine science classroom focused on the efforts of a specially trained teacher to encourage students to participate more actively in class and to feel confident about their ability to do science (Eccles and Blumenfeld, 1985). Two observers concluded that the teacher did treat female and male students in the same way. However, at the end of the year the researchers discovered that, while these techniques did increase male confidence, they did not have a similar impact on females. The reason was that females and males interpreted the teacher's behaviour differently. Males reasoned that the teacher was reacting positively to their responses because they were doing well. Females reasoned that, since their responses were not that good, the teacher must be reacting positively to them in order to encourage them to participate more and to feel good about their contributions. Equality of treatment did not produce equality of outcomes because students' interpretations of the situation differed systematically by gender.

Along similar lines, Holland and Eisenhart's (1990) study of peer culture at two universities concluded that the peer culture on university campuses orients women's energy and attention to an ideology of romance and attractiveness which assumes male privilege and dominance. Increasing involvement in the peer culture leads to greater acceptance of the ideology of romance during the women's undergraduate careers. Peer culture rather than academic culture encourages women to downgrade the importance of school and career in their lives, and to raise doubts about the purpose of school, and it can potentially function as a pathway to marginal careers. Both this study and the grade nine science study suggest that simply treating females and males equally will not produce equal outcomes because of the different meanings students give to their lives. Any program committed to equality must take into account how students interpret their situations. These perceptions, it would appear, are a crucial determinant of how students react to the program.

Explanations of class inequalities

Student resources A major approach to explaining the weaker performance of working-class students involves looking at the students' homes and communities, and at personal traits such as attitudes, aspirations, and expectations—all presumably produced and maintained by such environments. A major focus within this approach is the relationship between students' educational aspirations and social class. Numerous studies have found that, in any group of students with similar I.Q. scores but differing social-class backgrounds, working-class students will tend to have lower educational aspirations than middle-class students (Heyns, 1986). The usual assumptions are that: (1) the lower aspirations and expectations account for the lower school performance; and (2) the aspirations and expectations are the result of working-class experiences and conditions, such as poverty, malnutrition, and lack of parental and peer-group encouragement. These assumptions strike many people as reasonable and thus are widely accepted. But should they be? Increasingly, researchers are saying no to this kind of thinking, but their findings are contradictory.

The main difficulty with the student-trait approach to explaining unequal school performance is that it assumes that we already know what it takes to produce school success. It takes motivation, ability, confidence, ambition, and so on. Those who have these traits do well, those who lack them do not do well. As reasonable as this may sound, is it true? To what extent are these traits important determinants of school success? And how do they work? How does an aspiration get expressed behaviourally in student–teacher interaction, classroom work, studying, and writing tests? The answer may lie in the school setting itself.

School structures and streaming Streaming—allocating secondary school students to different academic levels on the basis of perceived ability and vocational objectives—is a common practice in Canada. Figures on the proportion of students allocated to individual streams are generally not available, but a 1987 Toronto survey indicated that 64 percent of Toronto students were in the advanced stream (up from 52 percent in 1980) while 10 percent were in the basic stream (down from 19 percent in 1980). Once placed, students seldom switch streams. Although in theory students can take courses at any level, most tend to take courses at one level only.

Many argue, however, that streaming contributes to inequality. To begin with, initial stream placement may be unfair. Class, along with ethnic or racial background, often acts as a key criterion, and it may account for the disproportionate number of working-class students in less challenging streams (Curtis et al., 1992). School systems may allocate fewer resources to the lower stream, with, for example, students in lower streams being taught by less experienced teachers using inadequate resources. Lower stream students then learn less, get less support from teachers, get lower grades, drop out of school, and are less likely to go on to a post-secondary institution. Thus, streaming actually widens the initial achievement gap between various social groups. In at least one province—Ontario—concern over this issue led the government to stop streaming its grade nine students in basic, general, and advanced levels as of the 1993–94 school year; streaming now takes place in grade ten.

Nevertheless, researchers using large-scale surveys have generally found little support for these criticisms of streaming, as such surveys consistently identify students' individual and background characteristics as the key sources of educational attainment (Hurn, 1985). Moreover, students' academic ability and past school performance are considerably more important than class background in determining their stream placement. Using these results, it is difficult to conclude that secondary school practices and structures increase social inequality. However, they do not lessen it.

Social class in the classroom If school resources, student resources, and school structures do not account for the relationship between social class and educational attainment, what does? Increasingly, sociologists argue that the answer to this question is to be found in only one place: the classroom itself. In particular, researchers increasingly suspect that elementary school classroom practices may increase (rather than merely pass on) social class inequality (Bidwell and Friedkin, 1988). While information about secondary schools tends to come from large-scale surveys, elementary schools are more commonly studied using direct observational methods.

However, classroom processes are also very difficult to study, and this probably explains why there are so few classroom studies. But investigators are increasingly coming to believe that the costs associated with studying classroom processes are trivial when compared with the potential increases in our understanding of the relationships among students, schools, and society.

In his four-year observational study of six Ottawa kindergarten classrooms, Richer (1988) found that, in addition to the explicit curriculum, there was an unstated, and often unrecognized and unsanctioned, hidden classroom curriculum, also being transmitted to students. Richer described the hidden curriculum as consisting of cognitive and social dimensions. At the societal level, the hidden curriculum teaches children to value (1) competing with others; (2) material possessions and private property (e.g., show-and-tell sessions); (3) work over play; and (4) obeying authority or submission of self. At the school level, students are supposed to learn (1) attentiveness; (2) the proper way to seek attention; and (3) docility.

Richer (1988) argued that success in school depends more upon the extent to which students conform to the expectations of the hidden curriculum than upon their ability or willingness to master the formal curriculum. In particular, middle-class children and females, because of the "cultural capital" they possess, are better able to meet these hidden expectations than are working-class students and males. For example, girls are better able to meet the submission-of-self requirement because they tend to be less aggressive and more passive and compliant, to adults at least, than males. On the other hand, middle-class children tend to be more individually competitive than their working-class counterparts. Therefore, females and middle-class children generally do well in school because, although for different reasons, they are more comfortable there. To illustrate this point further, Richer showed that teachers tend to discipline males much more than females.

On the basis of his study Richer proposed a conception of equality better suited to Canadian conditions than the more common definition developed earlier in this chapter. He termed it "equality to benefit" and claimed it "exists when salient sub-groups in a society can convert their own cultural heritage into educational success" (Richer, 1988: 341). This necessitates shaping the learning process (e.g., teaching and/or learning methods, curricula) to enable groups to translate their differences into educational benefits. Thus, it is not desirable for schools to ensure that all students are treated in the same way, since students from different salient groups (e.g., male and female, working and middle class) will respond differently to the same treatment. Thus, apparently fair, equal treatment turns out to be quite unfair.

Studies by Richer and others support the claim that classroom practices increase social class inequality, especially in the early grades. In particular, these studies suggest that the relationships among teacher classifications, curriculum organization, student–teacher interaction, and various social inequalities vary from school to school and classroom to classroom. A major source of the variation is the socially constructed meanings teachers and students give to their everyday educational activities.

Synthetic approaches to explaining inequality
Perhaps more than any other individual, Bernstein (1973) developed an explanation of the relationship between social and educational inequality that combines the main concerns of the newer classroom studies and the more traditional student-environment studies. Bernstein claimed that social class influences inequalities in school performances in two ways: through its impact on the student and through its impact on the school. These two separate factors then combine in a way that perpetuates existing inequalities. Let us examine the student first.

Bernstein argued that social class affects people's language skills, and thus the way they articulate their thoughts. For reasons related to the conditions and experiences of their respective social class positions (e.g., differences in wealth, family authority patterns, social networks), middle-class people learn how and when to use what Bernstein calls an elaborated code; working-class people rely more extensively upon a restricted code. A formal or **elaborated code** is necessary when the speaker cannot assume that the listener will understand what is being said; thus it is necessary to be fairly explicit and specific. The resulting complex and subtle language makes it easier to communicate abstract and symbolic ideas and concepts. By way of contrast, a **restricted code** can be used if the speaker is certain the listener will understand potentially confusing references, for example, to whom a particular pronoun refers. Restricted codes are more oriented to the here and now. Thus, the language is less explicit, the sentences shorter, and the grammar simpler for restricted codes than for elaborated ones. It is also harder to communicate general concepts and ideas using a restricted code. The main thrust of Bernstein's argument is that, although both middle- and working-class people can and do use both types of codes, middle-class people are more likely than working-class people to encounter and to recognize the formal situations, such as a white-collar job interview, that require the use of an elaborated code. Middle-class people are also more likely to feel comfortable with the impersonal social relationships that exist within such situations.

The catch is that success in school depends upon mastery of an elaborated code. This is the second part of Bernstein's analysis of the impact of social class upon inequality in schools. In a variety of ways, success in school is based upon mastery of middle-class social relations and skills, such as knowing how and when to use elaborated codes. It would be illogical to conclude from Bernstein's work that working-class students are linguistically deficient, deprived, or inferior to middle-class students in any absolute sense—although some have drawn just such a conclusion. Bernstein argued instead that the school must change its practices in order to meet the needs of working-class children. In a related vein, Karabel and Halsey (1977: 67) noted that middle-class children bring more "cultural capital" to school than working-class children, mainly because the middle class has managed to define such "capital" as important. The result is that working-class students perform poorly in school because they do not have the linguistic competence that the middle-class-dominated school system requires for success.

Bernstein argued that success in school is based upon mastery of middle-class social relations and skills.

Bernstein's notion of linguistic codes has come under attack, however. In a review of research relating to Bernstein's theory, Stubbs (1983) pointed out that the real issue in terms of linguistic skill appears to involve *preference*, or at least frequency of use, rather than ability. Even Bernstein's data show both working- and middle-class youngsters using both elaborated and restricted styles of language. It is just that working-class students use elaborated speech less frequently than middle-class students, at least under the experimental conditions used by Bernstein's researchers to collect linguistic data. Accordingly, Stubbs (1983: 63, emphasis in original) argued that "What has to be explained is why [working-class] children do not frequently *use* linguistic forms they quite clearly *know*" and more generally "...why different social groups *use* different forms of language in different contexts."

More than a decade after Bernstein's study, Wells (1986) conducted a study of 128 British children, 32 of whom were followed intensively for seven years, from the age of three to ten. The linguistic data were naturalistic in that they consisted of randomly collected audiotape-recorded conversations from home and video and audio recordings from school. Wells argued that:

1. working- and middle-class children start school at the age of five with similar linguistic competence;
2. differences in the everyday linguistic environments (e.g., use of words, questions, etc.) of home and school have been greatly exaggerated; and
3. differences in linguistic styles are not related to educational achievement.

The factor most strongly related to educational achievement at age ten is literacy. It is not that schools reward one way of speaking over another (e.g., elaborated over restricted), but that they reward written rather than oral uses of the language. He stressed that oral and written competence are not necessarily related, that both are equally valid ways of learning, and that having stories *read* to you is the best way to become familiar with the forms and uses of written language. However, middle-class children have greater exposure to the written forms of language, and are more aware of and comfortable with its uses and value by the time they reach school. Contrary to Bernstein's claims, Wells (1986: 87) concluded that schools contribute to this imbalance. The relationship between social class and performance on "cognitive competence" measures was weak prior to the children entering school, but increased considerably once students were at school, because the preschool tests rely on oral competence and the school tests rely on literacy skills.

A more recent attempt to discover the link between students' social class background and their educational attainment examined students' grade one experiences. In a large-scale, longitudinal study of students in Boston, Alexander et al. (1993) focused on the novel, transitional aspects of grade one. They found, somewhat disturbingly, that grade one experiences can affect performance throughout the subsequent school careers. Three grade one practices appear to have the most lasting impact on students:

special education classification and placement, grade retention (being held back), and ability grouping (a more informal and less uniform version of secondary school streaming). Of the three, special education placement and grade retention are the most directly related to social class, with working-class males most likely to be placed in special education classes and to be retained there.

The third practice, ability grouping, appears to be linked to students' social class characteristics insofar as teachers may rely more on perceived potential, and less on students' standardized test scores or assigned grades, in forming reading ability groups (Bidwell and Friedkin, 1988). Students classified by teachers as low achievers find it difficult to escape this classification in subsequent years. The authors also argued that ability grouping affects the expectations and perceptions of significant others towards students. This further benefits the already favoured and disadvantages at least some in the lower-class groups classified as "less able" (Pallas et al., 1994). Overall, if the initial findings from this type of research stand up to further scrutiny, it will give renewed importance to the need for reform in the early grades to decrease inequality, and will also explain why it has been so difficult to discover social class bias in secondary school structure and practices.

Another area of emergent research focuses on the symbolic and interactive nature of educational processes in classrooms and schools. People do not necessarily respond in predictable ways to what others do; rather, they first interpret what others are doing and then respond on the basis of these interpretations. Gardner (1991) pointed to the need for educators and researchers to pay more attention to children's interpretations of their world. He argued that children develop powerful intuitive theories, or symbolic understandings, about the physical and social world, including theories of mind and self. These symbolic understandings come from their everyday experiences and are practical working theories that help kids make sense of their everyday life. However, schools tend to stress academic, or *disciplinary*, understanding and are often unaware of children's *symbolic* understandings when they construct educational experiences for children. The focus on disciplinary understanding begins to intensify considerably around grade seven. By the time students reach university, disciplinary understandings are almost the exclusive mode of transmitting knowledge. Often the requirements of disciplinary understanding conflict with the requirements of symbolic understanding. Most children experience this conflict as a sense of the growing irrelevance of school knowledge to their everyday lives, and hence as a source of frustration. Gardner believed that this conflict accounts for the academic malaise that seems to set in, for most of those students who experience it, around grade seven and increases thereafter. Bidwell and Friedkin (1988) argued that students from middle-class backgrounds have more resources than working-class students to cope with the onset of this and other school-related frustrations. Thus, they do better in school.

In conclusion, these attempts to explain social class inequality illustrate the difficulty of trying to determine the effects of schooling on student achievement and growth. They point also to a number of features of education that need to be taken into account in any attempt to determine the effects of schools on students. One is the interactive nature of classroom and school life. Different students may respond very differently to fairly similar learning conditions because of their definitions of the situation. Of particular interest to sociologists is the extent to which these differences are structured along lines of social groups, such as class, ethnicity, gender, and race.

The second thing that must be taken into account is the implication that the relationship between key variables may vary from setting to setting. For example, the relationship between social class and school grades, or gender and science attainment, or ethnicity and self-esteem may be strong in one classroom but weak or absent in others. The task is not to find out what the relationship is in each case, but to discover the conditions (e.g., the size, structure, or physical location of the school) that produce these different relationships. In addition, in examining the effects of schools on students, it may be more useful at times to determine the impact of learning conditions on the overall distribution of a given outcome, such as grades or satisfaction, *within* a group rather than to focus on average increases *between* groups (Byrk and Raudenbush, 1992).

Third, there are many levels in the school system. Decision-makers at each level decide how to distribute the scarce resources at their disposal. Their decisions often have important implications for what those in the lower levels may be able to accomplish. Thus, although decisions at certain levels may not affect student learning directly, they do have indirect effects (Byrk and Raudenbush, 1992). For example, classroom characteristics (such as size) may not affect individual learning directly, but rather influence the formation of instructional groups. These groupings may in turn affect learning (Barr and Dreeben, 1983). Raudenbush and Byrk (1988) hypothesize that reducing class size—a school-board decision—may not affect the overall achievement levels of students, but it may affect the *distribution* of achievement by reducing the gap between ability groups, depending on how teachers decide to organize their classrooms and use their time.

The overall hope is that, by taking into account the above key features of schooling, we can eventually arrive at a better understanding of how schooling affects students in general, and especially of how it affects equality of educational opportunity for key social groups in particular.

SCHOOLING, MOBILITY, AND SUCCESS

In our discussion of inequality in the last section, we focused on how gender and social class affect what happens to students in school. But what impact does schooling have once students leave school? In particular, how do one's school experiences and performance affect one's work experiences and performance? What is the relationship between educational and occupational attainment? As a point of departure, we begin our consideration of these questions with a brief discussion of some of the issues presented in Chapter 7, Social Stratification.

The relationship between school success and status attainment is complex. Schooling, as measured by the number of years spent at school, certainly is related to both occupational status and income, i.e., the greater the education, the greater the status and income. At the same time, the relationship between schooling and earnings is generally weaker than that for schooling and occupational status. Moreover, family background remains important in determining both earnings and occupation, primarily through its direct effect on educational attainment. In the end, then, as noted in Chapter 7, both status attainment and social mobility may be affected more by economic than by purely educational factors (Creese et al., 1991). Nonetheless, education remains a critical factor in mobility. While a university degree does not guarantee getting and keeping a job, university graduates are more likely to be employed at more interesting and better-paying occupations than community college and high-school graduates. This is especially true for women.

Recent developments in transition patterns from school to work in Canada illustrate this theme. In Canada, the lines between school and work are not as distinct as in some other countries. Some students leave school to work for a while, then return to further their education. Others hold jobs and attend school at the same time. Increasingly, many enter and re-enter the educational and labour-market systems a number of times. These patterns hold true for both secondary and post-secondary students. On the other hand, post-secondary students, especially university students, are more likely to be employed in more secure and better-paying work once they graduate (Krahn and Lowe, 1991). In general, Canadians tend to use education as vocational and career training, and for good reason: employers rely heavily upon educational credentials in their initial screening of potential employees.

By way of contrast, let us look at the situation in other countries. In Great Britain, the boundary between work and education, and between education and vocational training, is much sharper. Considerably fewer students go on to university. Those not attending university enrol in vocationally oriented apprenticeship programs and are encouraged by potential employers to leave school at age sixteen. Few secondary school leavers desire to return for further education, even when economic conditions produce high unemployment (Bryner, 1991). In Japan, post-secondary vocational and career education is funded mainly by the private corporate sector and functions as part of their lifelong employment system, a pattern that is being strengthened in response to global competition. Consequently, vocational training is organized to meet the needs of corporations rather than the needs of individuals (Ueda, 1990). Acceptance at a prestigious university is also a guarantee of an attractive job in a major corporation (Stevenson and Baker, 1992). For one final example, West Germany has an extensive apprenticeship system for potential manual and most non-manual workers. Since it is assumed by employers that students in this system acquire relevant job-related skills and norms, students' achievement in the apprenticeship system strongly affects their subsequent job placement, pay, and promotions (Heinz, 1991) (see also the boxed insert on "Dropping Out and Unemployment").

In Great Britain, Japan, and Germany, university graduates are more likely to obtain appropriate employment than in Canada or the United States. In Canada and the United States, the link between educational credentials and the acquisition of job-relevant characteristics is less direct. Consequently, while educational credentials affect the ability to seek and obtain initial employment, subsequent pay and promotions depend much more upon actual job performance.

The continuing loose link between education and work in Canada and the United States has led some employer groups to criticize the school system for failing to produce students with the skills and attitudes needed to be effective workers. However, Ray and Mickelson (1993: 15) argue that low work motivation and commitment may be an unfortunate but realistic response on the part of non-university students to their job prospects, not to their educational experience. They speculated that vocational "school reforms of any kind are unlikely to succeed if non-college-bound students cannot anticipate opportunity structures that reward diligent efforts in school." Krahn and Lowe (1991: 168) reported that in Canada the "problem is certainly not one of work values and attitudes. [Canadian students have] a high level of commitment to work, a willingness to learn about new technologies, and a very strong belief in the value of higher education." However, they worry about the possible effects of "current trends towards more part-time job creation in lower level service sectors" and the resulting lower chances of "entering a rewarding career path." In summary, then, economic policies and trends rather than educational practices may be the main cause of the poor link between educational credentials and the acquisition of job-relevant characteristics in Canada.

THE FUTURE OF SCHOOLING

Given our past experiences with reforming education, it seems safe to say that schools will continue to change, but probably not in ways anticipated by any one group of reformers. Two trends will likely have a significant impact on the future of schooling in Canada. First, continued economic stagnation and inadequate job creation will result in considerable uncertainty about the future and the kind of public support appropriate for education. Second, Canada's population will continue along the path of increasing diversity. In 1991, 15 percent of Canadians reported neither English nor French as their first language. In Canada's major urban centres, the figure is much higher. Immigrants, anti-poverty groups, and collectivities representing blacks, Natives, and other minority groups are increasingly demanding more of a voice in Canadian education.

The main impact of this economic and demographic situation will be an increase in the number and kinds of interest, bureaucratic, and status groups contending in the cultural market for the future of Canadian education. New business, labour, political, minority, community, gender, professional, parent, religious, teacher, and student groups will become increasingly active as advocates of various educational reforms. Inevitably, many of these advocates will be from outside the educational establishment. This will force both insiders and outsiders to confront the complexities of the schooling process as outlined in this chapter. Dominant groups of the past will no longer be able to impose their definitions and policies so easily. Armed with their socially constructed problems and solutions, different groups will compete for their fair share of the scarce resources in the expanded cultural market for schooling (see the boxed insert on "Does Anyone Know What Our Educational System Should Be Doing").

Does Anyone Know What Our Educational System Should Be Doing?

Education, like every other social institution, is reeling under the impact of globalization. Some in government and business argue that the educational system must change drastically to meet the evolving demands of today's global economic society. Canadians, they say, need national curricula and standardized assessment criteria, up-to-date basic as well as advanced technology-driven curricula, and greater centralized control and local accountability to produce a workforce that will allow Canadians to prosper economically. They complain that professional educational and school administrations have become too bloated and complacent, and must be reduced to save money and move the system forward.

Defenders of existing arrangements argue that it is the responsibility of government and business leaders to solve many of the problems the critics are currently attempting to blame on schools. They argue that schools are in fact doing a good job of what they were built to do, namely, providing a sound basic and advanced education. It is inadequate political and economic policies and conditions that result in economic problems. If Canada is not performing well enough in the global economy, it is up to corporate and political leaders rather than the schools to do better.

This debate reflects the lack of consensus about what it is schools should be doing. Schools have never been expected to do just one thing. The debate also reflects the different emphasis placed by different constituencies on school resources. Some stress jobs and economic development, while others stress citizenship and personal development. Where do you stand on these issues? Do you see any end to this disagreement? Does this debate mean that schools no longer have an agreed-upon social purpose? How might this debate affect the curriculum, students, and teachers? How has it affected you (hint: think about issues such as your tuition, course availability, and class size)?

The political and social need to achieve temporary resolutions to the resulting conflicts will accelerate at least one contemporary trend: the proliferation of programs recognizing the needs of special groups. The major educational forces in Canada are decentralizing as groups demand increased responsiveness to their concerns. As the gap between educational professionals and the various publics widens, we shall likely see a proliferation of home study, private schools, and publicly funded, independent schools. Even within the present educational system, given available resources, we are most likely to see the intensification of a dual public and Roman Catholic system in Ontario, and the increased growth of French immersion, heritage language programs, schools for the arts, high school academies, gifted programs, and single-sex programs.

System insiders are likely to focus on developing innovations such as cooperative work-study programs, integrated curricula, and international education programs. Outsider groups will argue for a more national, centralized, and accountable school system in order to build a cohesive national identity and to compete effectively in an increasingly centralized, interdependent, and global economy. Although such groups will have an impact at the legislative level, their efforts will coexist with and be modified by the demand from local groups for education reflecting local standards. It is likely that some groups, such as corporate leaders, will end up establishing their own special institutions—possibly with public support, given Canada's traditional loose linking of economy, society, and schooling. We will then end up with a considerably more differentiated educational system, requiring renewed efforts by researchers at understanding its dynamics and effects.

Functionalists are likely to have a mixed reaction to these developments, seeing some as potentially undermining education's ability to foster a cohesive society. Capital accumulation theory suggests that the main outcome of such developments will be to strengthen the status quo, as already advantaged groups increase their influence on the school system. A cultural markets perspective suggests that, while considerably greater equality of educational opportunity is possible, it is unlikely to occur unless there are radical shifts in the balance of power among the key contending groups in the market. More likely, there will be relatively minor shifts as some groups gain a slight competitive advantage while others lose some ground. These shifts will eventually be reflected in educational participation rates, as these groups turn to education to acquire for their children the credentials they feel are necessary to secure their advances. This in turn will affect the meaning attached to various educational credentials in Canadian society.

Taken individually, however, these approaches offer only a partial understanding of the changes to come. The social constructionist, classroom-level studies in particular point to this conclusion (see the boxed inserted "The Social Construction Approach to Studying Classroom Dynamics"). Those investigating classroom processes claim that our knowledge of the educational system, based as it is upon these three large-scale, macro-structural approaches, is very incomplete. Such perspectives tend to treat the school and classroom as black boxes, with mysterious and hidden workings. Sociologists must continue to attempt to open up these boxes for investigation, to gain a greater understanding of what goes on in the schools. Thus, although new contenders in the cultural market for schooling may win the political and policy battles and establish new educational offerings, the impact on student learning depends in part on how students and others actually respond to their new situation. Past research suggests that the actual results may be very different from those intended. Still, only with all possible insights—both macro and micro—is a useful assessment of education's current status and future prospects possible.

SUMMARY

This chapter began with a description of the growth of education in Canada. Demographic trends were used as one explanation of the recent educational expansion, as were a number of theoretical perspectives, including functionalism, capital accumulation theory, cultural markets theory, and the process model approach. Functionalists claim that a general consensus exists within society that schools ought to expand, and that the expansion of schools generally benefits everyone by fulfilling important societal functions in an age of technological change. By way of contrast, both capital accumulation and cultural market theorists stress the importance of conflict, and interest-group competition for power. Capital accumulation theory portrays schooling as yet another weapon invented by capitalists to dominate and exploit workers. Without denying the existence of the capitalist–worker conflict, cultural market theorists see schools being used in a variety of ways for numerous purposes by many different types of competing power, status, and economic groups. Finally, the process model attempts to take into account the main features of a number of perspectives.

The second major section of the chapter examined equality of educational opportunity. With respect to educational attainment and gender, first of all, differences between males and females in terms of school participation and performance were noted. While female participation seems to be growing in many areas, women are still underrepresented in math and science, and in the higher levels of graduate studies. With regard to class, students from middle-class families do better in school than students from working-class families.

A number of explanations for these patterns were also discussed. In the gender area, no one factor accounted fully for the differences observed. As for class, a number of explanations were put forward. The first was the school: we argued that both the literature on educational innovations and the research on the relationship between school resources and educational attainment suggest that altering school characteristics is either ineffective or difficult to achieve in terms of promoting equality of educational opportunity. Another explanation examined student social environments and their effect upon aspirations, motivation, and the like. Research into these issues does not always uncover very strong associations between environmental features (e.g., parental support), student traits (e.g., ambition), and educational attainment. Moreover, this approach assumes that we know what factors actually determine success and failure in school. A third explanation looked directly at what happens in the classroom. While nothing conclusive has emerged from this research, the studies suggest ways in which a student's social class background is translated (e.g., through streaming) into inequality of educational opportunity and attainment.

The section ended with a general model of the key factors needed for a study of the impact of schools on class inequality, including patterns of language use and the grade one experience.

In the third section, on schooling and social mobility, it was suggested that, even if equality of educational opportunity were achieved, equality of social opportunity would not necessarily follow. These themes were illustrated through a discussion of the recent research on the transition from school to work. It was also shown that, in Canada, distinctions between school and work are not clear cut; for example, many return to school after some years in the workforce. In addition, Canadians tend to use vocational training to obtain necessary credentials. Finally, inequality is not necessarily the fault of the education system; economic policies and trends may be responsible for producing graduates without necessary skills.

The chapter concluded with a brief discussion of the future of schooling from the perspective of the functionalist, capital accumulation, cultural markets, and classroom studies perspectives. The overall theme of the chapter was that educational processes are extremely complex and there is much we do not know. Consequently, it is important to keep an open mind about schooling and to use existing perspectives, not as definitive statements of the way things are, but as guides in determining what questions to ask, how to go about answering them, and how to evaluate the questions and answers of others.

QUESTIONS FOR REVIEW AND CRITICAL THINKING

1. What is your preferred learning style? Describe your various professors' teaching styles. How closely do they match your learning style? Does it matter?

2. Talk to several students to whom you are close, and who are members of the other sex. In what ways are your views of university or college similar to theirs? In what ways do you differ? To what extent do the differences represent gender differences and to what extent do they reflect unique individual differences or other kinds of structured social differences (e.g., ethnicity, class)?

3. Recall your elementary education. How much truth is there for you in the title of Fulghum's book *All I Really Need to Know I Learned in Kindergarten* (New York: Ivy, 1989)? Which of the theories explained in this chapter best explains that formative experience?

GLOSSARY

capital accumulation theory the theory of education that argues that capitalists use schools to defuse class antagonism and to make workers docile, cooperative employees

correspondence principle applied to education, it means that educational systems correspond to society's economic mode of production. More generally, it is the Marxist view that social institutions mirror the mode of production.

cultural markets theory an alternative to functionalist and capital accumulation theories of education, it stresses the competition among different types of groups for varying kinds and amounts of schooling

elaborated code a language code that is relatively formal, does not depend on the listener knowing the speaker's situation intimately, and facilitates discussion of symbolic and conceptual issues

functional theory of education explains education in terms of the functions it serves: skill acquisition, preparation for job selection, legitimizing social position, and passing on core values, moral education, and the essentials of good citizenship

restricted code a language code that is relatively informal and depends upon the listener understanding the context, and that is expressed through short sentences and simple grammar; useful for communicating immediate experiences to friends and others familiar with a situation

SUGGESTED READINGS

Anisef, Paul, and Paul Axelrod (eds.)
1993 *Transitions: Schooling and Employment in Canada.* Toronto: Thompson Educational Publishing.

A representative collection of essays on one of the major current concerns in Canadian education.

Curtis, Bruce, D.W. Livingstone, and Harry Smaller
1992 *Stacking the Deck: The Streaming of Working-class Kids in Ontario Schools.* Toronto: Our Schools/Our Selves Educational Foundation.

A critique of the persisting patterns of social class inequalities in Ontario elementary and secondary schools, with some prescriptions for reform.

Gaskell, Jane, and Arlene McLaren (eds.)
1991 *Women and Education: A Canadian Perspective.* (2nd ed.) Calgary: Detselig.

Does gender matter in education? Are our schools "gender blind"? Should they be? This collection of sixteen articles (half of them by sociologists) presents a diversity of "post-sex-role" feminist perspectives on elementary, secondary, and post-secondary schooling in Canada as well as on more general educational issues.

Stevenson, Harold W., and James W. Stigler
1992 *The Learning Gap: Why Our Schools are Failing and What We Can Learn from Japanese and Chinese Education.* New York: Summit Books.

One of the more specific research studies on the potential relevance of Japanese and Chinese childrearing and educational practices for North American schools.

WEB SITES

http://www.ccn.cs.dal.ca/~aa331
Schoolfinder Online

This page provides easy asscess to a large number of universities and colleges in Canada, as well as information about funding, programs and various other aspects of university/college life.

http://www.flora.ottawa.on.ca/homeschool-ca/
Canadian Homeschool Resource Page

At this site, learn about alternatives to conventional education in Canada.

NO TO WELFARE CUTS!
LET THEM
FOR MASS LABOUR
NONSENSE
Common Sense Revolution doesn't add up.
WORKFARE COSTS MORE THAN WELFARE.
OPPOSE THE ANTI-SOCIAL TREND!
the ANTI-SOCIAL TREND!
350%

CHAPTER

12

Political Sociology

David MacGregor

INTRODUCTION

Questioned about liquor smuggling across the Canadian border, Chicago mobster Al Capone reportedly scoffed, "I don't even know what street Canada is on!" Actually, cross-border commerce in illegal spirits during the U.S. Prohibition era (1920–1933) helped make Capone one of the world's richest men. Al Capone's booze empire was sheltered by differences in the social climate on either side of the Forty-ninth Parallel. The Temperance movement sputtered in Canada in the early 1920s, and with U.S. distillers forced out of business by Prohibition, Canadian spirits flowed across the border into gangland outlets.

A half century later, the crime boss's free trade vision was seized with extraordinary fervour by President Ronald Reagan, who wanted to abolish economic barriers between Canada and the United States. President Reagan and his successor, George Bush, worked with Prime Minister Brian Mulroney to establish both the 1989 Free Trade Agreement (FTA) and the 1993 North American Free Trade Agreement (NAFTA), which would dissolve tariff barriers between Mexico, Canada, and the United States. Before he was elected in October 1993, Liberal Prime Minister Jean Chrétien said that he would refuse to sign NAFTA. Once he became prime minister, however, Chrétien became an enthusiastic free trader and sought to extend the agreement to Chile and other countries in South America. Yet, unlike Capone's free trade in liquor, the FTA and NAFTA may entail reduction of cultural differences between Canada and its neighbours. Thus, public discussion on the issue has been, and will likely continue to be, heated.

While it concerns economic arrangements, free trade—in either spirits or automobiles—is also a hotly contested *political* issue, as are questions of environmental protection, Canadian federalism, and gender equality. This chapter will examine these and other issues in the context of political sociology. The main goal of political sociology is to encourage critical thinking about Canadian politics from a sociological perspective. The chapter begins with a look at the nature of authority in the state.

AUTHORITY AND THE STATE

Prime Minister Brian Mulroney left an astonishing legacy. While his free trade policy, Goods and Services Tax (GST), cuts to unemployment insurance, broken promises on a national child-care program, threats to medicare, and other controversial measures caused considerable anguish among Canadians, they also sparked various forms of popular protest. In mid-May 1993, for example, a national convoy of political dissidents converged on Parliament Hill in Ottawa to denounce Conservative policies. "I haven't seen this level of organizing since the 1960s," said Judy Rebick, then head of the National Action Committee on the Status of Women. "It's incredible" (*Globe and Mail*, May 14, 1993). Subsequently, when Premier Mike Harris came to power in Ontario in June 1995, a similar series of actions was launched by labour and social justice groups against his government. Mass demonstrations against the Ontario Tories took place in London and Hamilton. In October 1996, the largest protest march in Canadian history filled the streets of Toronto with hundreds of thousands of middle- and working-class people, the unemployed, students, gay rights groups, teachers, and industrial workers.

Mass public protests like those sparked by Conservative governments in Ottawa and Toronto are a feature of relations between dissenting groups and the state in most countries. In response, states may spend millions on anti-terrorist squads and on security guards to keep protesters at bay. They may hire agents to watch and inform on "subversives," and may authorize police to bug telephones, open mail, and harass people suspected of anti-government activities. This use of force in the interest of self-preservation forms a central aspect of sociological definitions of the state. Weber, for example, described the **state** as an organization that successfully "claims the *monopoly of the legitimate use of physical force* within a given territory" (1978: 78, emphasis in original). As he pointed out, however, the state rarely resorts to the bare exercise of violence, and political struggles are usually more or less peaceful. States generally are based on a belief in legality and on the readiness among the populace "to conform with rules which are formally correct and have been imposed by accepted procedure" (Weber, 1964: 131)—a condition sociologists refer to as the *legitimacy* of the state.

A state that enjoys legitimacy has little need of force; people will obey without violent confrontations. It is usually only when its legitimacy is in question that the state resorts to the use of armed might. In October 1970, for example, members of the Front de la Libération du Québec (FLQ) kidnapped a British diplomat and murdered a Quebec cabinet minister. Fearing the state was losing its legitimacy in Quebec, Prime Minister Pierre Trudeau and his cabinet ordered the Canadian Armed Forces into the province. Tanks and troop carriers streamed into Montreal; Ottawa became an armed camp as young soldiers brandishing machine-guns were posted around government buildings. Early the next morning, the War Measures Act was invoked, suspending civil liberties. More than 500 people were arrested without warrant, including "poets, artists, professors, teachers, doctors, lawyers, workers, taxi drivers, students and technicians. ..." Quebec sociologist Marcel Rioux observed at the time that "only businessmen seem to have been spared" (1971: 142–43).

The use of force in the interest of self-preservation forms a central aspect of sociological definitions of the state.

A Weberian perspective would interpret Trudeau's actions in the light of external geopolitics. **Geopolitics** involves relationships of power and prestige among nation-states. The legitimacy of a state is dependent on its power and prestige on the international stage. In turn, a state's legitimacy in domestic politics rests on its success on the global scene. "The ability of internal political factions," wrote Collins (1986: 147), "to dominate a state depends considerably on the position of the state in the transnational situation, or...on its place in the world system." By sending in the troops and arresting suspected dissidents, Trudeau sent a message to the international community: the **government**, that political organization in charge of the state, had the will and determination to prevent the breakup of Canada. "The national stage," said Collins (1986: 147), "is the stage on which the drama is played, but the international arena writes the plot."

In defining the state, Weber also made an important distinction between power and authority. Weber (1954: 323) defined **power** as "the possibility of imposing one's will upon the behavior of other persons." The ability to make others do as one wishes could be based on a wide variety of circumstances, including physical force, possession of a weapon, strength of character, or even personal charm. By contrast, **authority** refers to a particular type of power, which may take two forms. The first form is derived from ordinary marketplace relationships, and is based on a voluntary contract. For example, a deposit with a bank gives the bank authority over that money in exchange for payment of interest to depositors. Depositors not satisfied with the arrangement are free to withdraw their deposits. The second form, which we are primarily concerned with here, is that held by the state. Weber defined this type of authority as "the probability that certain specific commands (or all commands) from a given source will be obeyed by a given group of persons" (1964: 324). State authority involves, on the one hand, a ruler or group of rulers, and on the other, a group that is ruled. It also normally requires an administrative staff of reliable persons to execute the commands of the ruler(s). For example, the Canadian Parliament has passed laws directing citizens and residents of Canada to complete tax forms and pay taxes if they earn more than a certain minimum income. Compliance with the Income Tax Act is compulsory and there is a staff of bureaucrats to make certain that people pay the taxes they owe.

Weber further identified three types of formal authority as exercised by the State: charismatic, traditional, and rational-legal authority. Pierre Trudeau's term of office may be used to illustrate the sources of each type (to be discussed more fully in Chapter 13, Formal Organizations and Work). The Trudeau government was lifted into power in 1968 by a tide of public adulation for Trudeau himself, which many journalists of the time attributed to his charisma. Charismatic leaders, according to Weber, attract followers by the force of their personalities, which are seen to possess a unique, almost supernatural quality. This *charismatic authority* is usually short-lived and not extendible much beyond the life of the charismatic personality. Moreover, it is constantly threatened with disruption and caprice; the need for order and continuity eventually replaces charismatic authority with ritual, bureaucracy, and discipline. Similar points were made in Chapter 10, Religion, concerning the routinization of charisma.

At the same time, Trudeau was never a charismatic leader in the full Weberian sense; nor was his government based on *traditional authority* rooted in time-honoured attitudes or practices, such as a succession of kings or emperors. Ultimately, his authority derived from the victory of his party in electoral contests. Like all leaders in contemporary industrial countries, Trudeau's power rested on the third form of authority identified by Weber, *rational-legal authority*. This is authority based on law, on rationality, and on efficiency. Personality has very little to do with this type of authority, which instead is based on "rationally established norms...enactments, decrees and regulations" (Weber, 1978: 299).

The specific form of rational-legal authority operative in Canada and other Western states is called **liberal democracy**. When we say that Canada is a liberal democracy, we mean that the government in control of the state is chosen by periodic elections in which every adult citizen has the right to vote for one or another competing political party. The right to vote is made effective by certain civil liberties, like freedom of speech and of assembly, and protection from arbitrary arrest and imprisonment. Every Canadian is formally equal before the law, and minority groups are given some special protection. The freedom of individuals to do as they choose is guarded to an extent consistent with the freedom of others.

The next sections of this chapter focus on the debate about the nature of political power or authority in liberal democracies. Pluralist, élitist, Marxist, postmodern, dependency, and Hegelian theoretical perspectives are briefly considered, with special reference to their contribution to an understanding of the relationship between social classes and the structure of governance in Canada. The nature of the welfare state, federal–provincial relations, and the relationship between class, gender, and political participation are then examined in the light of these perspectives.

THEORIES OF STATE CONTROL

Pluralist theory

Recent political sociology has focused almost exclusively on the question of who has power in society, and has tended to polarize around pluralist and élitist views. **Pluralism**, to begin with, is the view that modern democratic societies are governed by competing interest groups, each having the power to veto proposed policies considered harmful to its position. (We discussed this idea in the section on the origin of norms in Chapter 5, Deviance).

For pluralists, modern democracies are characterized by the diverse character of leadership groups, by egalitarian recruitment to positions of power and influence, and by responsiveness of government and industry to the demands of a variety of citizens and consumers. As a result of this dispersion of power in modern society, no single leadership group or élite can dominate or control the state. For example, Parsons (1968) argued that, although a big-business élite exists, it does not totally rule society because its power is challenged by, and thus must be shared with, other leadership groups, such as the political élite and government bureaucracy. Moreover, business leadership itself is divided into various competing factions that undermine its ability to present a united and powerful front.

A key assumption of the pluralist model is that in all liberal democracies there is a broad consensus of values and beliefs. No bitter and irreconcilable conflicts permanently divide individuals and groups from one another. Most people respect others' property rights and individual freedoms. They believe that government is generally fair and impartial, and that the various power blocs try to give members of competing groups a square deal. There is popular agreement that all can achieve success provided they are capable and willing to work hard. (Similar tenets were expressed in the functionalist explanations of stratification and education cited in previous chapters).

Élite theory

The pluralist notion of a basic societal consensus is rejected by élite theorists. If such a consensus can indeed by demonstrated, they argue, the identity of values and beliefs in society is merely "an ideological deception created and manipulated by those in power" (Forcese, 1978: 303). **Élitism**, as espoused by theorists such as the U.S. social critic Chomsky (1989), is the notion that the ideas and values people are exposed to in our society are actually selected and controlled by a single exploitative and powerful élite. Through its influence in the mass media and the educational system, this élite can ensure that information and knowledge counter to its interests do not reach the great majority of people. As a result, the authority and power of the ruling élite is never *fundamentally* challenged in the political system.

The conflict arguments of élite theorists derive from an imposing tradition of political theory led by Pareto (1935), Mosca (1939), and Michels (1958). These individuals, whose ideas were formed by their experience with Italian democracy around the beginning of the twentieth century, argued that the notion of mass participation in democratic society is a myth. All political institutions, even the most democratically organized political parties, inevitably degenerate into narrow, self-perpetuating cliques.

Pareto was the first sociologist to develop systematically the notion of a ruling élite and to examine the role of élites in history. Despairing of real change in the governance of society, he argued that political history proves that élite rule is inevitable. "Pareto argued that it mattered little what the declared principles of government might be—democratic, socialist, or liberal—the effect was the same: the exploitation of the poor for the benefit of whoever was in power" (Bellamy, 1988: 19). Further, Pareto's principle of the **circulation of élites** holds that the decline of one ruling group merely prepares the way for domination by another. According to Pareto, a ruling élite appears in the form of either the "lion" or the "fox." *Lions* are radical élites, who seize and hold power by force; *foxes* are older ruling groups, who use persuasion and craft to neutralize their enemies and win over the masses. Lions start out as popular challengers of the existing system, but successful lions often mellow into scheming foxes, who eventually risk losing their power to a new group of angry lions (Bellamy, 1988: 27–28).

Mosca centred his studies on the working of parliamentary bodies, and found that political power tends to accumulate in the hands of a few. All societies, he declared, contain only two classes: a class that rules and a class that is ruled. Mosca fully realized that modern mass politics differed in many ways from earlier forms of domination; but the difference was reflected in a change in "legal and political superstructures of power" rather than in actual political control by ordinary people. "The reality was still rule by an elite" (Bellamy, 1988: 40).

Following the lead of Pareto and Mosca, Michels applied the concept of ruling élites to the leadership of socialist political parties and trade unions. These organizations professed to be highly democratic, but Michels discovered that each was actually controlled by a tiny conservative-minded group that worked behind the scenes to serve its own interests. Michels' experience led him to formulate the **iron law of oligarchy**. However democratic its initial values might be, Michels contended, every organization develops a form of élite manipulation and control because of its need for discipline and continuity in leadership. (Michels' work will be discussed in more detail in Chapter 13, Formal Organizations and Work.)

C. Wright Mills is perhaps the most influential of the more modern élite theorists in the tradition of Pareto, Mosca, and Michels. Writing in the late 1950s, he argued that the U.S. was ruled by a small, interacting élite composed of business leaders, top politicians, and the upper echelon of the military. This **power élite**, as Mills (1956) called it, emerges from the similarity of interests that characterizes the ruling economic, political, and military institutions in modern society. For Mills, the bloated U.S. military budget that benefited all three of the constituents of the power élite provided the best example of élite power and arrogance in a liberal democracy.

According to Mills (1956), the élite-controlled mass media and political parties cut off channels of dissent to encourage unanimity of opinion in the general populace. He doubted the possibility of any fundamental challenge to the power élite from traditional centres of opposition such as labour unions. The workers, Mills suggested, have accepted the values of consumer society and wish nothing beyond the offerings of shopping plazas and suburbia. The only hope for recovery of democratic values in contemporary society rests with the intellectuals—students and others concerned with ideas—who would link social problems and the forces available for their solution with the everyday concerns of ordinary people.

In summary, while pluralists base their perspective on the cornerstones of leadership variety and consensus of beliefs, élite theorists, such as Mills, suggest that there is no real competition and variety in leadership, as the various powerful groups in society tend to have similar interests and to manipulate consensus itself to their own advantage.

Élites in Canada

Porter took up Mills's notion of the power élite and applied it to Canadian society. As discussed previously, his classic *The Vertical Mosaic* (1965) ultimately rejected the theory of a unitary power élite in favour of a modified pluralist model. Porter found much evidence supporting the view that a highly integrated group of wealthy persons controlled the dominant institutions in 1950s and 1960s Canadian society. Nevertheless, this group made up no single élite, but instead was divided into a pluralist system of competing élites, including economic, political, bureaucratic, mass media, and military leadership groups. Each of these groups had its own interests, based on the functions of the respective institutions it represented. For example, in its search for the kind of exciting news material that sells newspapers and magazines, the media élite sometimes found itself at loggerheads with the interests of the business

Élite theorists suggest that there is no real competition and variety in leadership, as the various powerful groups in society tend to have similar interests.

community. Similarly, when the Liberal government unified the armed forces in the 1960s, it provided an illustration of conflict between the political and military élites in Canadian society.

The Marxist view

While his own work indicated that a single ruling group does not exist in Canada, Porter did not deny that further empirical investigation might uncover forces leading to a power élite. Clement (1975) claimed that, in fact, there is compelling evidence to indicate that a unified business-based élite presently dominates Canadian politics and government. The economic or corporate élite appears to have grown even more exclusive and tightly integrated than it was in the late 1950s, when most of Porter's data were collected. Clement argued further that "élite switching"—the interchange and sharing of members between élites—has increased so that the Canadian corporate, bureaucratic, and political élites are blending into one single group, with the corporate élite dominating the others.

Clement's research led him to reject both the pluralist and élitist conceptions of political power. Instead he adopted a Marxist standpoint, which emphasizes the role of social class in the framework of power and authority. In this view, the corporate élite is synonymous with the *bourgeoisie* or capitalist class, the class that owns and controls most productive land and capital. The great majority of people belong to the working class or *proletariat*, the class that works for wages or a salary but has little or no share in the nation's productive resources.

The Marxist argument from which Clement's work derives disputes the pluralist claim of representative power-sharing. It states that there can be no real consensus in society so long as people are divided by class relationships of ownership and non-ownership, as they are in virtually all liberal democracies. Marxists contend that élite theorists ignore the social class basis of political power by concentrating on the activities of real or imagined leaders instead of the actual economic and social structure of modern capitalism.

As discussed in Chapter 7, Social Stratification, Marx believed that the development of capitalism ultimately would bring large masses of people into direct political activity. He expected the working class would become increasingly conscious of its own interests and would fight to have these interests reflected in the political arrangements of society. The proletariat would then seize power and install a communist form of government, which would destroy class divisions and allow all individuals to develop their human capacities to the fullest degree.

Thus, Marx understood politics in terms of the potential it offers for the freedom and happiness of the individual, rather than just as an arena for power struggles. Yet, despite his optimistic view of the nature of politics, Marx was convinced that the governments of his time were dominated by the capitalist class. The class that controls the economy, he contended, also rules the state.

Today, thinkers in the Marxist tradition hold that the state in liberal democratic society continues to reflect the social and political interests of the bourgeoisie. Given this assumption, the analytical problem for Marxists is to discover how the capitalist class maintains its domination of the state. According to the Marxist framework, in liberal democratic society the state acts on behalf of the bourgeoisie while remaining relatively autonomous of this class. That is, the state does not merely do whatever capitalists tell it to do; at least to a certain extent, state personnel decide for themselves what policies to follow. Nevertheless, this process results in decisions that are in the *interests* of the capitalist class.

According to Miliband (1985), there are several reasons for the pro-business character of the state. First, those who wield authority in the state also act as agents of large, private economic interests. Government cabinet ministers and senior public servants are often also business leaders or members of business families. The 1993 Canadian federal election, for example, was fought with both dominant political parties led by people drawn from the boardrooms of big corporations. Moreover, even where such direct ties do not exist, state leaders and bureaucrats are likely to share the basic values and ethics of the capitalist class and to act in accordance with them. Finally, noted Miliband, the working class in capitalist society has failed so far to grasp its own real interests because capitalist control of the mass media and government prevents the formation of working-class consciousness. Ideas and opinions expressing the viewpoint of the working class, he wrote, are drowned out by those that help maintain the status quo.

Other writers in the Marxist tradition underplay empirical studies of élite family background and behaviour, and abandon theories that attempt to explain how people are fooled by their leaders. Instead, they view capitalism as a structure, that is, as a system of activities and institutions that operates independently of the ideas and purposes of individuals. *Structuralist Marxists* argue that government cannot help becoming an instrument of the bourgeoisie, simply because the state must allow the economy to run as smoothly and efficiently as possible. To accomplish this, government has to obtain the cooperation and good will of the capitalist class, and refrain as far as possible from interfering with market forces. The structuralist Marxists also claim that the very operation of the capitalist economy and the state tends to block or turn aside effective working-class political action.

Postmodernism

The future of Marxist sociology looked bleak in the early 1990s. Breathtaking changes in Eastern Europe and the collapse of the U.S.S.R. in 1991 suggested that Marx's vision of communism was only a vague dream. At the same time, the free market thrust initially orchestrated at the global level by politicians including British Prime Minister Thatcher and U.S. Presidents Reagan and Bush was gathering steam.

As Marxism's attraction waned, sociologists and other social scientists were increasingly drawn to *postmodernism*. This movement, which started originally as a new approach in art and architecture, spread to the social sciences in the 1980s. French thinkers such as Derrida turned away from the study of history and social structure, and advocated the importance of language and textual analysis. Culture rather than economics was the dominant paradigm.

Postmodernists distrusted the idea of progress that was so important for Marx, and adopted the critical and despairing view of modernity associated with the German philosophers Nietzsche and Heidegger. They replaced Marx's class-struggle perspective with a focus, suggested by Foucault, on the identities between power and knowledge. (For an example of an analysis inspired by Foucault, see the boxed insert "Government at a Distance: Official Graffiti."). Delight in the play of illusion and reality represented by advertising and popular culture pushed aside the Marxist themes of ideology and capitalist control.

At first, the implications of postmodernism for political theory were unclear. Gradually, however, a pattern began to emerge. Key features were scepticism about any form of utopia; a radical dislike for science and technology; openness to spirituality and faith—except that offered by established religions; warmth towards minority ethnic and cultural traditions, and hostility towards the dominant white/Western heritage; and, most significantly, a profound suspicion of the state. Postmodernists tend to be blind to the private exercise of power, such as that exerted by transnational corporations, but hypersensitive about perceived intrusions by government. They advocate politics based on new social movements, including ecologism, feminism, and anti-racism. They feel that the state is now "decentred," impotent to effect real change in a "globalized" society. Instead, politics must be fought out in a multitude of "political spaces" by a wide assortment of social groups.

Postmodernism, as we have seen, was a product of boom-time capitalism and the failure of socialism and communism in Europe. The political constellation changed suddenly, however, in the mid-1990s, with possibly fatal consequences for postmodernist social theory. The recession in the world's advanced industrial nations continued, as small advances in growth were not matched by an increase in jobs. At

Government at a Distance: Official Graffiti

Michel Foucault argued that modernity is characterized by the effort of government to control the actions and behaviour of ordinary persons. According to Canadian sociologists Hermer and Hunt, governments and private organizations increasingly rely on "official graffiti" to carry out this task. In its ordinary use, graffiti refers to defacement of public property by individuals or groups who wish to transgress or subvert the social order. By contrast, official graffiti denotes "official regulatory signs" that "mark, scar and deface public spaces." Forms of official graffiti include the ubiquitous road traffic signs, *Entry* and *Exit* (or *In* and *Out*), along with "that most invasive and emblematic piece of official graffiti, the prohibition circle with its diagonal red slash across the circle warning, for example, No Smoking."

Official graffiti involves the paradox that, although people experience such regulation as an intrusion, they also rely on regulatory intervention to get on with their lives. They are resentful when a *No Parking* sign denies them a spot, but also "curse the illegal parker" and demand tighter enforcement of parking laws.

Icons and messages on consumer products are another type of official graffiti. The user of these products is usually assumed to be incompetent. Thus plant poisons are labelled "Not to be Taken Internally"; a fast-food styrofoam coffee cup is labelled "Attention: Hot"; a shampoo label contains detailed instructions about how the product should be used.

Finally, official graffiti may rely on shared understandings of morality and public good. "These contexts characteristically construct some social risk or danger. They constitute an implied audience that is warned of the risk; for example, the risks of smoking, from using drugs or alcohol."

Official graffiti makes us pawns in the hands of remote authority and absent experts. Its deep and unquestioned penetration into the everyday world threatens individual autonomy and democracy. Thus, official graffiti is often the target of unofficial or street graffiti. Parking signs are defaced, for instance. A *No Pets* sign might be changed to *Pets Welcome*. *Post No Bills* signs are often surrounded by unauthorized posters.

Source: *Adapted from Joe Hermer and Alan Hunt, 1996. "Official graffiti of the everyday."* Law and Society Review *30, 3 (pp. 455–80).*

the same time, the transition from socialism to capitalism in Russia and Eastern Europe looked increasingly difficult. In the former Soviet Union, the fall of the commissars sparked the rise of mafia groups and widespread gangland violence. Some argued that the solution to the problems of post-communist societies lay not in the free market but in a strong, interventionist state. Government could foster the growth of private industry while limiting the impact of imported goods and domination by foreign capital. Democratic politics could be nurtured in a state-protected environment, whereas a continuing, unregulated free-market invasion might destroy the new democratic structures that emerged from the fall of communism (Burawoy and Krotov, 1993).

Postmodernism's lean towards culture and away from economics meant that the movement could not comprehend this abrupt transformation of politics. To some extent, the changes suggested the relevance of a renewed Marxism, sensitive to the possibilities and challenges of democratic politics.

Dependency models

Innis and the staples approach

From within Canada, another challenge to Marxist conceptions of state control came from Harold Innis, a pioneer of Canadian sociology and **political economy**, the interdisciplinary blend of political science, history, sociology, and economics. Innis argued that political economy must consider Canada's position within the global network of nations. This section will present Innis's theory and show its relationship to two important themes in Canadian politics, United States–Canada relations and environmentalism.

According to Innis, Canada has been a dependent hinterland or periphery successively to three great metropolitan powers: France, England, and the United States. Originally a colony of France, Canada became a British territory, and then a junior partner of the United States. These dependent relations have affected Canada's economic development, as well as its political structure and culture.

Innis's **staples approach** pointed to many important issues in Canadian development. The country, he noted, "has never been self-sufficient, and its existence has depended primarily on trade with other countries" (1956: 11). Canada's exports have mainly been staple products (raw materials such as furs, fish, timber, and wheat) bound for manufacturing centres located elsewhere—particularly the United States. Staples production led to neglect of manufacturing in Canada and slowed the growth of an urban consumer market for Canadian products.

Dependence on a staples economy has implications not only for sovereignty and state control, but for resource management as well. Marchak's (1983) prize-winning study of the B.C. forest industry, *Green Gold*, outlined the connection between dependence on a staples product and environmental concerns. She showed how the province's reliance on export of forest products jeopardized its economy and devastated the environment. Unregulated

Canada's dependence on a staples economy has led to unregulated corporate exploitation of products such as minerals, and has had significant environmental costs.

corporate exploitation of staples products like timber or minerals has significant costs, Marchak argued. It "steadily decrease[s] the earth's resources, pollute[s] the environment, and destroy[s] the habitat of the earth's creatures" (1983: 379–80). Ten years after Marchak's study, environmental concerns remained at the forefront of B.C. politics. In a move that angered local environmentalists, the provincial NDP government approved timber cutting in Clayoquot Sound, the largest remaining temperate rainforest on Vancouver Island.

In other parts of Canada the story is similar. Ralph Klein followed in the footsteps of previous Alberta premiers by compromising environmental standards in the interests of business, handing over much of Alberta's forests to timber production and "open[ing] the doors to the importation of hazardous waste from other provinces" (Harrison and Laxer, 1995). In Ontario, Premier Mike Harris relaxed anti-pollution laws and cut more than a third of employees of the Ministry of Environment and Energy.

Dependency theories

Since the appearance of Innis's staples argument, more comprehensive forms of **dependency theory** have emerged. In Canada, advocates of the dependency view have noted that this country leads the world in the proportion of its economy owned by foreigners. The reasons for this were first fully explored in Levitt's influential classic *Silent Surrender: The Multinational Corporation in Canada*, which documented "Canada's slide into a position of economic, political, and cultural dependence on the United States" (1970: 1). Levitt's study pointed to some disturbing facts. Although extensive American ownership of Canadian industry was widely believed to have provided Canada with much-needed capital for development, she showed that U.S. investment was actually financed with profits earned in Canada or with loans from Canadian banks.

According to Levitt, crucial decisions about investment and employment in Canada's branch-plant economy were often made outside the country. Instead of supporting a strong research establishment in Canada, with its attendant boost for professional and university employment, American branch plants preferred to rely on research and development done by parent firms in the United States. As a result, investment in industrial research and development lagged well behind that in other advanced economies. American economic dominance brought a decisive bias in politics as well, so that Canadian domestic and foreign policy were heavily influenced by U.S. political currents. Finally, warned Levitt, distinctive Canadian culture was jeopardized by an overwhelming invasion of U.S. print and electronic media. On average, Canadians were likely to know more about U.S. politics and history than about their own social and political heritage, and of course their knowledge of the U.S. was in deep contrast with U.S. ignorance of Canada.

Levitt's book reflected and encouraged a dramatic shift of opinion in Canada. The country embarked in the 1970s on an ambitious program of Canadianization in industry, media, the arts, and education. Government intervention helped reduce foreign ownership and stimulated home-grown enterprises. As we shall see in a later section, however, this movement was reversed somewhat in more recent years.

Laxer's (1989) study *Open for Business* is another example of the dependency approach. Laxer compared Canada with other "late developer" countries such as Sweden and Japan, which began to industrialize at the close of the nineteenth century. According to Laxer, linguistic divisions between English Canada and Quebec in the nineteenth century weakened the Canadian state. These conflicts prevented the emergence of a strong, activist government that could have accelerated Canada's economic growth. Instead, the country found itself dependent on American and European investors. By contrast, Sweden built an interventionist state that aided rapid industrialization and maintained the country's economic autonomy.

Hegel's political theory

In 1989, a bureaucrat in the U.S. State Department stirred up the mass media when he predicted "the end of history." According to Fukuyama (1989), the struggle between the superpowers had ended, with the United States as victor. The big world conflicts were over, he claimed. All that remained for history was the spread of the liberal democratic form of government.

Fukuyama based his ideas on those of the nineteenth-century German, Hegel, who was the first to contend that liberal democratic government might be the final and ultimate achievement of world history. Hegel offered an interesting and fruitful way to think about politics and state control. He divided society into three parts: the family, civil society, and the state. Each of these, Hegel argued, can become dominant and rule over the rest.

In the early stages of human life, according to Hegel, the family was the organizing principle of society. Family relationships of love and mutual support brought people together. Communities and nations were made up of clans or kin groups. Rulers came from high-status families. Later, with the Greeks and Romans, the family principle became weak, and two new forms appeared, those of civil society and the state. These subsided somewhat during the subsequent feudal period, but re-emerged with renewed force by the sixteenth century.

Civil society involves a market principle of individual self-interest and personal gain. A passion for liberty and a profound belief in the rights of private property are also characteristic of this stage. The U.S. government is based on the principle of civil society. According to Bell (1989: 48), "the United States has been the complete civil society...perhaps the only one in political history." Bell's idea of the United States as civil society conformed closely to pluralist theory. Government is a marketplace, he said. Here different "interests [contend] (not always equally)" and political deals take place. Basing its decisions on the U.S. constitution, the Supreme Court acts as the "final arbiter...and the interpreter of rules that [allow] the marketplace to function" (Bell, 1989: 50).

The *state* principle, on the other hand, involves taking into account the interests of others, regardless of family ties or personal satisfaction. According to Hegel, the principle of the state must dominate the market. Moreover, the **ideal state** unites the ideas of love and mutual protection, which guide family life, with the idea of civil society, or the principle of individual liberty. It is marked by the caring for others. Ideally the family should be a form of communism (from each according to ability, to each according to need). So if this (family) principle were imported into government, as Hegel recommended, then something like Marx's communism would be the result.

What brings about the change from family to civil society, and from civil society to state? According to Hegel, it is the human mind. Each succeeding type of society further develops the power of human consciousness, or the capacity for freedom. When people feel the old system can no longer offer them a good life, they turn against it and create a new one. Of course, this is a simplified version of his theory. Hegel connected changes in consciousness to material conditions, as did Marx. For both Hegel and Marx, however, social conditions themselves are the result of conscious human activity.

Hegel's political theory offers a way to think about Canadian politics that is explored further in later sections. If the United States is the complete civil society, then Canada is a nation in which the state principle is more prominent. Canadians have developed a unique set of federal institutions and programs, including medicare, the CBC, the Canada Council, bilingualism and multiculturalism, and regional development. Despite government cutbacks, which accelerated dramatically under the Chrétien Liberals, these state activities still differentiate the country from the American model.

The universal class

There is another aspect of Hegel's political theory with special relevance to Canadian politics: his idea of bureaucracy or the universal class. Hegel's theory of social class resembles and also contrasts strongly with that of Marx. Marx's theory centres on the ownership or non-ownership of the means of production. Capitalists own the means of production, and employ workers, who have no property. Hegel agreed with this, but added a third group, the class of state workers or the **universal class**. Today this class would include municipal, provincial, and federal public servants. Teachers, nurses, social workers, and many other professional groups linked with government would also belong to the universal class.

Hegel used the term *universal class* for several reasons. Workers and capitalists are connected to a particular firm or industry only; the universal class works for the welfare of a region, province, or an entire nation. Moreover, the power of the universal class lies not in property ownership, but rather in its superior knowledge. Finally, because of its wide interests and its combination of knowledge and power, the universal class can unite with diverse groups and classes in the struggle for social justice. The environmental movement, for example, has many connections with researchers in government, and is a coalition of the universal class and other social groupings.

While Marx's theory involves conflict between capitalists and workers, Hegel suggested that there may be battles and alliances among all three classes. The largely middle-class environmental movement in British Columbia, for example, wants to preserve the nation's forests. It is fighting not only big pulp and paper firms, but also some B.C. forestry workers. Similarly, recent efforts by business-dominated governments to cut spending by firing public servants are justified as prudent fiscal policy; actually, they are a means of waging war against the universal class. In a penetrating analysis of politics in Alberta, Harrison and Laxer (1995: 115) write that

> The ethic of the private sector, to maximize profits, is not always appropriate to the delivery of public services.... There is often a conflict between the demands of the privatization businesses for high profits and the need for universal coverage of all citizens at the lowest prices. The best way to resolve such conflicts is often public ownership or public delivery of services.

Writers with a view similar to Hegel's have started a challenging new sociology of politics. Gouldner (1979) and others argued that future society may be ruled by "this New Class, in which domination is based not on ownership of wealth but on monopoly of knowledge" (Szelenyi and Martin, 1988: 647). Lipset (1985) contended that the main vehicle for social change in advanced capitalist countries is a new oppositional intelligentsia. Reform of "postmaterialist" (social) issues requires well-educated and affluent groups, including students, civil servants, and professionals.

THE WELFARE STATE

It is often said that Canada, along with most of the other Western liberal democracies, is a welfare state. What does this term mean? A common definition is that a welfare state assumes responsibility for the basic well-being of its citizens. Esping-Anderson (1989) proposed a more adequate definition. He wrote that a **welfare state** does two things: first, it protects citizens from market forces; second, it treats individuals equally, regardless of their class position.

To perform the first task, the state must allow individuals to leave their jobs without fear of losing income or seniority. People must be able to take a leave of absence for reasons of "health, family, age or even educational self-improvement; when, in short, they deem it necessary for participating adequately in the social community" (Esping-Andersen, 1989: 20). Few welfare states offer this amount of protection, but some are better than others. On this basis, the Canadian welfare state lags behind the welfare states of Sweden or Norway.

Esping-Andersen's second criterion involves the ways in which a welfare state dispenses services or financial aid to the population. Some provide the same benefits to all individuals, regardless of their income. Others use means tests or income cutoffs to determine benefits. For example, the Mulroney government linked Old Age Security benefits to income and abolished universal family allowance benefits in favour of income supplements to poor families. By doing so, it replaced universal programs with ones based on earnings. At the same time, the federal government has resisted pressures to introduce income criteria for provision of medicare to Canadians. Thus, a broad range of medical services is available to individuals in Canada whatever their income.

Why are the criteria of both market protection and universality so important? Without market protection, for example, welfare programs might be used by government to promote the interests of the rich against those of the poor. A program that requires the unemployed to accept any available job or face penalties (such as Quebec's 1990 Welfare Reform Law) really enforces the preferences of employers. Similarly, a welfare scheme based on income rather than universal criteria may be attacked by those who receive no benefit from it. Ottawa's abolition of the Family Allowance Program, and its replacement with a non-taxable supplement to low-income earners with children, is an example. By contrast, universal programs like medicare and secondary schooling come to be viewed by the electorate as social rights, and efforts to reduce them meet with strong resistance.

Neoconservative threats to the Canadian welfare state

During the 1960s and early 1970s, Canada experienced a virtual legislative revolution in the role of the state. The federal government introduced many welfare programs, including the Canada Pension Plan, the Unemployment Insurance Act, and the Canada Assistance Plan. Canada was a leader in the area of hospital and medical insurance programs and education. Compared with the United States, Canada developed a generous welfare system. Nevertheless, in relation to other advanced industrial countries, Canadians did not enjoy good protection against unemployment and poor people received inadequate benefits (O'Connor, 1989).

A 1993 United Nations report strongly criticized Canada's lack of progress in limiting poverty. U.N. officials noted that Canada had allowed the gap between rich and poor to grow wider during the 1980s and early 1990s, in part by cutting spending on social programs. This trend, some have noted, points to a general and progressive weakening in Canada's comprehensive social safety net. Between Mulroney's Tories and Chrétien's Liberals, tens of billions of dollars were withdrawn from federal health, education, and welfare spending. The shrinking federal presence suggested to many that the Canadian political union was in jeopardy. A diminished government in Ottawa was no match for strong regional forces, such as those represented by Quebec sovereigntists, which were pulling Confederation apart.

Pressure to reduce or dismantle the Canadian welfare state has come from a number of sources in recent years. The most salient factor, however, is **neoconservatism** (sometimes also called *neoliberalism*), a political ideology emphasizing the need for less government interference in the marketplace in order to stimulate economic growth and prosperity. Elements of the neoconservative agenda include free trade among nations, zero inflation, a reduction or elimination of government deficits and debt, and lower taxes on business enterprise. Let us examine each of these goals and assess their effects on the Canadian welfare state in recent years.

Free trade

Established after World War II, the General Agreement on Tariffs and Trade (GATT) has worked to lower tariff barriers worldwide. By reducing tariff walls, the GATT brought national economies closer, as part of a process generally referred to as *globalization* (see the boxed insert on "Child Labour"). Computers and improved communications and transportation further stimulated this trend. Bankers can now make huge international financial transfers in a few seconds, and manufacturers can use plants in several countries to assemble single items, such as automobiles or undershirts. These developments are now enhanced through regional trade agreements such as NAFTA.

Enhanced international economic integration has affected domestic policy in the area of social welfare. For example, in the 1960s Mexico sought U.S. investment by establishing a *maquiladora* program on its northern border. The program was designed to attract jobs to Mexico by allowing U.S. companies to operate in Mexico without paying duty on goods entering or leaving the country. As part of its incentive package to U.S. companies, Mexico adopted a neoconservative stance, suspending many domestic regulations on labour, such as hours of work, and rules in collective contracts. As a result U.S. companies now take advantage of cheaper Mexican labour, much to the chagrin of U.S. labour unions. According to Kopinak (1996), the opening of the Mexican economy has lowered wages throughout Mexico and put pressure on labour income across the North American continent.

Freer trade has also been associated with a move towards corporate monopoly rights over intellectual property. This too has served to threaten the welfare state. Monopoly rights are important for leading-edge technological industries, including pharmaceuticals, electronics, publishing, and agribusiness. In 1992 the Mulroney government extended patent protection for transnational drug firms, and severely reduced the ability of Canada's thriving generic drug industry to offer low-priced copies of name-brand pharmaceuticals. This move, which anticipated NAFTA's provisions on intellectual property rights, will increase provincial medicare costs by hundreds of millions of dollars every year.

Child Labour: The Price of Globalization

The worst factory fire in history occurred in 1993 in a toy factory in Bangkok, Thailand. A blaze grew rapidly in the large industrial complex that lacked fire safety standards common in the West. Workers were locked inside to ensure that they kept at their machines, and didn't steal the toys. Bodies of hundreds of girls and women were found by fire fighters in large heaps around the locked doors of the factory. Hundreds more suffered serious back and head injuries when they leaped from factory windows.

Thailand is one of the success stories of globalization, a term used to describe increased trade, investment, and financial dealings in the world economy. The main agents of globalization are huge transnational corporations that spread their operations across the world. Transnationals often locate their plants in countries where labor is cheap, and health and safety standards are low. To remain competitive, compliant governments abolish or relax regulations and taxes that might annoy far-flung private empires.

Another country deeply affected by globalization is Bangladesh, which has a thriving textile industry. Workers there make pajamas, blouses, shirts and other clothes for consumers in Canada, the United States and Europe. Many textile employees are children, some as young as five, who work the same hours as adults. Often the work day is 12 hours long, and workers are lucky to get one day off a week. Government statistics reveal that children under 14 make up at least 15 percent of the work force.

Bangladesh is the ninth largest supplier of clothing to Canadians, and seventh largest for the United States. Protests about child labor from North America and Europe are rejected as "protectionism." Bangladeshi officials, and those in other Third World countries, defend child labor as a traditional part of their culture.

World-wide, tens of millions of little children are working long hours in manufacturing industries, but this has little to do with cultural traditions. Child labor in the Third World repeats the familiar pattern of early Victorian England, where most textile operatives were female, and almost half were children under 14. Victorian factory masters argued that child labor laws would make their industry uncompetitive in the world market. They fought the Factory Acts for decades, and child labor was not eradicated anywhere in the West until the early twentieth century.

Marx is considered out of date in this post-Communist era, yet much of his great work *Capital* deals with the epic struggle against child labor and exploitation of women and men workers that convulsed England throughout the nineteenth century. Capitalist exploitation of child workers and young women in the Third World suggest that Marx will remain relevant for a long time yet.

Source: *Adapted from Robert A. Senser, 1992. "On their knees."* America, *September 1992 (pp. 166–73).*

Zero inflation

Unemployment steadily increased during the 1970s, along with record rates of inflation. Neoconservative governments chose to concentrate on fighting the latter at the expense of the former, and a number of zero inflation policies, including high interest rates, high currency exchange rates, and reduced social spending, were put into place during the 1980s. The result was a large reduction in the inflation rate, but persistently high unemployment rates.

Some have pointed out, however, that high unemployment has far more severe costs for society than moderate inflation. Following the work of John Maynard Keynes, a number of economists have argued that neoconservative policies are self-defeating, requiring increasing levels of unemployment for small reductions in inflation. They suggest that governments use the powerful tools of monetary and fiscal policy to ensure both full employment and inflation reduction, and thus preserve the welfare state (see Osberg and Fortin, 1996).

Deficit reduction

During the last decade, neoconservative governments across the world have also sacrificed important social programs to reduce growing fiscal deficits.

Given the endemic yearly budget gap between income and expenditure, and the resulting debt load, many in Canada are concerned that governments can no longer afford welfare state cornerstones such as medicare, unemployment insurance, and the Canada Pension Plan.

In response, the federal government has tried to solve its deficit problem since the early 1980s by restricting social spending and reducing transfers to the provinces for education, health, and other social items. This strategy has produced a reduction in the federal deficit, but has also tended to shift the deficit crisis to the provincial and municipal levels, part of a process known as "downloading."

Many economists argue, however, that the deficit crisis is exaggerated. For example, while neoconservative economists claim that every Canadian owes, say, $15 000 because of the deficit, they forget to add that this amount is matched by $15 000 worth of government bonds or other securities mostly held by Canadians. It is important to note as well that debt service charges in Canada amount to just 5 percent of all the goods and services Canada produces (its Gross Domestic Product, or GDP)—far from crisis levels. They add that continued government spending on social programs should not be seen as a liability, but as an investment in human capital. Investment by government and business, combined with proper economic planning, can reduce unemployment, increase output, and thus eventually solve the deficit dilemma itself.

Reduction in corporate taxes

Shifting taxes from corporations to individuals has also been part of the neoconservative fiscal program. Ostensibly the objective is to make industries more competitive on the domestic and world stage by lowering their costs. Since the 1970s tax rates on corporations have dropped to very low levels; many countries have reduced income taxes for high-income earners; and some, like Australia and Canada, have abandoned lucrative inheritance taxes. Few follow the example of Japan, which has inheritance taxes and an annual levy on net wealth. In many advanced capitalist countries, wealthy taxpayers have access to a myriad of tax deductions that are unavailable to ordinary-income earners. At the other end of the scale, neoconservative administrations have increased income tax rates for low- and middle-income earners, and established regressive consumption taxes, such as Canada's GST. As a result of the shifting tax burden, the government has had less to spend on social programs and thus on the maintenance of the welfare state.

The policies discussed above have all contributed to a reduction of the welfare state in Canada. Whether or not the system survives will largely depend on who holds power in the Canadian state in years to come, and whether future governments continue with neoconservative policies or adopt a more proactive, interventionist stance. At the same time, economic and social welfare difficulties are only one set of problems facing Canadian governments. Another set of challenges, having to do with national survival itself, appears equally important, as we shall see in the next section.

CANADIAN FEDERALISM AND POLITICAL CRISIS

In the first half of the 1990s, Canada's political system suffered a sustained crisis. Provincial premiers and the prime minister, Brian Mulroney, revived the 1987 Meech Lake constitutional proposals with an agreement reached in Charlottetown during the summer of 1992. After an intense and divisive debate, the Charlottetown Agreement was overturned in a historic national referendum in October 1992. Surprisingly, opposition to the referendum united English Canadians who disliked Meech Lake with *Indépendantistes* who saw Charlottetown as a sell-out of Quebec sovereignty. In the sovereignty referendum of late 1995, Quebeckers narrowly voted against independence, saving the country on the strength of a few thousand votes. Let us review recent Canadian political history to uncover the origins of this crisis.

Canada is a unique union of ten provinces and two territories, two major cultural and language groups, and the first inhabitants of the country, the aboriginal peoples. Along with Switzerland, Canada is probably the most decentralized nation in the world. The country's founding document, the 1867 British North America (BNA) Act, outlined the division of governmental responsibilities between provinces and federal administration. However, it was a British law, not a Canadian one. The Trudeau government repatriated the Act (now called the "Constitution Act") from Great Britain in 1982 and added a Charter of Rights and Freedoms.

Why did Canada take so long to proclaim its own constitution? In 1927, Prime Minister Mackenzie King tried to bring back the constitution, but the federal government and the provinces were not able to agree on a formula for changing it in future. By the 1960s, the main roadblock to an amending formula was the province of Quebec, which wanted to reduce federal jurisdiction over its affairs.

Over the next twenty years Ottawa's efforts to satisfy Quebec's nationalist desires were complicated by the ambitions of other provincial governments. They demanded similar concessions in many areas, including ownership of natural resources, taxing powers, and control of culture and communications. A deliberate decentralizing policy by the Trudeau government allowed federal authority to wane while that of the provinces increased. To protect regional interests, provincial administrations passed legislation blocking trade and labour mobility between provinces. A significant shift in power away from Ottawa benefited rich provinces, but poor ones suffered as the federal ability to redistribute income declined. Still, the government's bilingualism policy enjoyed some success: many young anglophone Canadians learned French; bilingual signs and packaging became common.

With the repatriation of the BNA Act in 1982, the Trudeau government achieved a victory of sorts. Yet, Quebec had refused to sign the agreement and used Section 33 of the Charter—known as the "notwithstanding clause"—to exempt its French-only language and culture legislation. Also, Alberta and Manitoba resisted bilingualism and tried to restrict French language rights. But the Quebec government continued to be the key violator in the 1980s of the individual rights laid out in the Charter. Not surprisingly, most of Quebec's infringements of these rights were aimed at supporting French language and culture. While many English Canadians welcomed constitutional protection of individual rights, the Québécois came to view it as a danger to their sense of identity.

After the demise of the Charlottetown Accord, tensions between Quebec and the rest of Canada appeared to recede. However, in the 1993 federal election Quebeckers were faced with a choice between the Bloc Québécois, which advocated separation from Canada, and the Liberals of Jean Chrétien, not a popular politician in the province. In many cases they opted for the Bloc, thus contributing to an increase in national political tension once again. In Quebec, the newly elected Parti Québécois government announced a referendum on sovereignty. The Chrétien government mishandled the run-up to the 1995 Quebec referendum, lost an initial lead in the polls, and very nearly caused the partition of the country.

Who speaks for Canada?

Is Canada merely a weak union of consenting provinces, or is it based on the general will of the Canadian people? "Who speaks for Canada?" asked Prime Minister Pierre Trudeau. "Is it the provinces or the national government?" (quoted in Behiels, 1990: xxii). This question has haunted the country for the past thirty years.

Resnick argued (1990) that two contradictory views of the state divide Canada. French-speaking Québécois have used their provincial government to further the aims of a rich Québécois culture. English Canadians, on the other hand, have constructed their national vision around a strong federal government and national institutions like the railroad and the CBC. French Canadians are confident of the unique and brilliant character of Quebec society. Because of the influence of the U.S., English Canadians are far less certain of their own national identity.

At the same time, demographic factors have produced in Quebec a sense of national peril. Relative to the rest of Canada, particularly Ontario, Quebec is falling behind in population (see Chapter 15, Demography and Population Study). "Geopolitically, the most obvious consequence of the present situation is a weakening of Quebec's political weight within Confederation" (Caldwell and Fournier, 1987: 34). Quebec's stagnant population growth is accompanied by concentration in urban areas, while the vast countryside of the province empties. Although feared less intensely in Quebec than in

"Who speaks for Canada?" This question has haunted us for the past thirty years.

English Canada, Americanization also poses a threat to French Canadian culture, especially as the traditional influences of Church and large families recede. Pluralist values in the province have been undercut by population decline, and narrow ethnocentrism may grow.

Former prime minister Trudeau gambled that repatriation of the constitution and a national Charter of Rights and Freedoms would reduce discord between English Canadians and French-speaking Québécois. The 1982 Constitution Act granted Quebec the chance to be an equal partner in a federal system. It was Trudeau's reply to René Lévesque's Parti Québécois goal of a sovereign state for Quebec. However, Trudeau's Constitution Act ran into immediate problems with the provinces. These difficulties have continued into the 1990s.

One of Trudeau's main goals—reform of the process for amending the constitution—was left unfulfilled. At first, provincial premiers rejected his proposal that important changes should be decided by a national referendum; they wanted to retain sole right to decide on constitutional amendments. However, the 1992 Charlottetown referendum implied acceptance by the premiers of the amendment process recommended by Trudeau. Although he was dismissed as "yesterday's man" by the media, Trudeau played a key role in defeating Charlottetown. A series of strategically timed speeches and publications, which denounced the "blackmail" of Quebec nationalists and mocked the doomsday scenarios of bankers and other capitalists, mobilized public opinion in English Canada against the agreement.

Recent constitutional negotiations have followed an élite model that would have impressed the Italian theorists discussed at the beginning of this chapter. Mosca, Pareto, and Michels would feel very much at home watching a select group of political insiders make policy for the rest of the country. Even the title of "first ministers" adopted by the ten premiers and the prime minister has an élitist flavour. During negotiations on the 1982 Act, for example, the rights of minorities did not receive unanimous support. Moreover, the ten provincial premiers insisted on adding Section 33 to the Charter, which gave legislatures the right to override certain basic freedoms. Premier Lévesque's refusal to sign the 1982 Act left his province symbolically outside the constitution—although, like any other province, Quebec was subject to the constitution as long as it remained in Canada.

The purely élite style of negotiations was disturbed by opposition from excluded groups. Lobbying by women's and Native peoples' groups reinstated guarantees for women and aboriginal peoples in the 1982 Act. The Charter ensured that every Canadian had a right to use and be educated in either official language, English or French. No federal or provincial statute could infringe upon a person's rights on grounds such as sex, religion, colour, ethnic origin, and physical or mental ability. The multicultural heritage of Canada was to be respected and preserved.

Ten years later, the debate around the Charlottetown referendum appeared to weaken the élite monopoly on constitutional change. The "Yes" side was supported by established élites such as large corporations and the leadership of almost every political party. Most of the media, labour leaders, some English Canadian nationalists, and aboriginal leaders also favoured the huge package of constitutional reforms. Yet the television commercials and dire warnings of the "Yes" side could not prevail against the grassroots organizing of the opposition. Supporters of the "No" side, which included a diverse range of groups including the Reform Party and the National Action Committee on the Status of Women, helped to turn it back. Although Charlottetown was defeated by the people, Chrétien's Liberals proceeded to put into place some of the key decentralizing elements it contained. Élite rule was maintained, despite the democratic process.

CLASS, GENDER, AND POLITICS IN CANADA

Class and political participation

Globally, the spread of universal suffrage has dramatically altered the nature of political parties, from exclusive institutions representing a few men of property to mass organizations (Weber, 1978: 102–103). Universal suffrage itself, however, has a rather short history. Manhood suffrage without property qualifications was not introduced in Canada until 1920, although it existed in some provinces as early as 1876. Women finally obtained the vote in 1918, but Indians living on reservations were denied the franchise until 1960. While in the United States white manhood suffrage was in effect from the mid-nineteenth century, universal suffrage was delayed until well into the twentieth century and the civil rights movement of the 1960s. Only in the last generation has the right to vote been extended to Canadian men and women between the ages of eighteen and twenty-one. Individuals under eighteen, along with incarcerated criminals, the insane, and permanent residents lacking citizenship are still excluded from the franchise.

Expansion of the franchise throughout the nineteenth century was thought by many theorists of the time to herald the rise to power of the working classes. Marx himself was convinced that universal suffrage would place the reins of government in the hands of the proletariat, especially in such countries as the U.S. and Great Britain (Miliband, 1977: 79). Yet, in all liberal democracies the coming of universal suffrage failed to alter fundamentally the structure of power, just as the élite theorists like Pareto and Michels predicted. In fact, the Canadian Parliament is almost a living model of élite rule. A recent study showed that over the period 1940 to 1984 the economic background of MPs actually became less representative of the general population. Now almost 90 percent of MPs come from high-status occupations, compared with only 20 percent of all Canadians. Indeed, Parliament—and most political parties—might well be characterized as an upper-class men's club of professionals and businesspersons.

Working-class political parties, for their part, have had a limited impact on the political system. The working class and the poor in Canada are more likely to vote Liberal and Conservative than they are to vote NDP, the political party that appeals most directly to workers and low-income groups. Thus the New Democratic Party usually collects 15 to 20 percent of the national vote, while the Liberals and Conservatives share most of the remainder. In part this is because the working-class electorate is left with a choice between voting for the NDP, which supports its interests but is unlikely to form a government, or voting for the least objectionable of the two dominant parties.

A sophisticated voting analysis by Brym, Gillespie, and Lenton (1989) suggested that workers are more likely to vote NDP where there is a strong working-class presence in the community, such as a powerful union movement. Where such institutions are weak or absent, working people tend to support non-socialist parties. They argued that this "power resource" pattern persists everywhere except Alberta and Quebec, primarily because movements for separatism and autonomy in these provinces have attracted support from working-class voters who might otherwise have gone to the NDP.

Women and politics

Perhaps the greatest failure of mass political parties is their underrepresentation of women. Traditionally, women have made up less than 5 percent of MPs in the Canadian Parliament. Moreover, when women do succeed politically, it is often by cutting themselves off from other women and gaining recognition from men in power. This appears to be true in the case of Brian Mulroney's successor Kim Campbell, the first female Canadian prime minister. While claiming status as a feminist, she was not a fervent supporter of women's issues. Her record on abortion rights was ambiguous, and she refused to drop a very expensive Armed Forces helicopter purchase while claiming that a national day-care initiative was too expensive. Intriguingly, Campbell won the Conservative leadership almost by default, as most of the heavyweights from Brian Mulroney's cabinet refused to run, probably because they feared defeat in the forthcoming election. The only serious contender was Jean Charest, a 34-year-old cabinet minister from Quebec, who came very close to upsetting Campbell in the leadership race.

In more recent years, however, women's representation in the federal Parliament has increased significantly. The 1984 election resulted in a stunning increase in the number of women MPs, from less than 5 percent to almost 10 percent of Members of Parliament. Prime Minister Mulroney named six women to cabinet posts, including the Employment and Immigration ministry and the Energy portfolio. In 1988 the participation of women in the House of Commons was larger than ever, at around 15 percent. In 1993 Audrey McLaughlin of the New Democrats, the first woman to head a national political party, was joined by Tory leader and prime minister Kim Campbell. In the October 1993 election, however, Kim Campbell led the Conservatives to a devastating defeat and Audrey McLaughlin's NDP was also badly hurt. Moreover, Prime Minister Jean Chrétien severely reduced the proportion of women in senior cabinet positions. Nevertheless, women took fifty-three, or 18 percent, of the seats in Parliament.

In sum, the influence of this new female presence on national political issues has not been overwhelming. To date, women have yet to gain in a whole string of areas, including day care and funding for women's organizations. Overall, moreover, women MPs are even more likely than their male counterparts to come from the ranks of wealthy Canadians. "This finding appears to reflect a double standard wherein women must demonstrate greater achievement than men in the economic arena before they can succeed at the polls" (Guppy, Freeman, and Buchan, 1988: 420–25).

Such trends continue largely because men have more social and economic power than women. This basic difference shows up at the highest levels of government, where issues important to women are not given full prominence. Male political leaders also are able to deflect public attention from women's concerns during periods of economic uncertainty. "The main business" of the ruling male power structure, wrote Smith (1989: 48–50), "defines the central position from which topics introduced by feminism are marginalized." Child care and family responsibilities are not part of the "organizing career processes in government and economy." Consequently, for example, neoconservative leaders are able to frame the "budget deficit" as the chief political issue of the day, freezing out initiatives in day care and other "non-essential" areas. During their second term, from 1988 to 1993, the Conservatives' first move was to abandon a national day-care program they had promised in the election campaign. "Child care is not a luxury, it is a necessity," wrote Judge Abella in her landmark 1984 Royal Commission Report on women's equality in employment (quoted in Bishop, 1989). Most women of childbearing age were in the Canadian workforce by 1989, yet few public spaces were available for the millions of children who required them.

Sexual Politics in Quebec

When delegates to the 1993 Progressive Conservative leadership convention met in Ottawa, many were impressed by the family life of Kim Campbell's leading challenger, Jean Charest. Unlike the twice-divorced Campbell, Charest was happily married, with children. Still, a few English Canadian delegates couldn't figure out why Charest's wife "kept her own name."

Many of the struggles of the modern feminist movement are aimed at freeing women from traditional patriarchal authority so that they can be recognized as citizens with the same rights and obligations as men. In Weber's terms, the battle involves a shift from traditional patterns of authority to rational-legal ones. Although there is no law requiring them to do so, wives have traditionally adopted the surname of their husbands, a custom historians have traced back to the seventeenth century. Until our own century marriage symbolized a property relationship, in which a wife and children were the property of the husband. The wife's change of name signalled her transfer from the ownership of her father to that of her husband.

In the province of Quebec this social custom has been abolished. Perhaps because it represents a fundamental challenge to patriarchal authority, the Quebec law on marriage has been little noticed or discussed elsewhere in Canada. (This, in fact, may explain the puzzlement of English Canadian delegates at the 1993 Conservative leadership convention!) Article 442 of the Civil Code of Quebec reads: "In marriage, each spouse retains his surname and given names and exercises his civil rights under this surname and these given names" (Eichler, 1983: 275).

Defenders of the practice of a woman dropping or modifying her name once she takes the vows of marriage argue that after all "a name isn't that important," and that no inequality is involved, merely convenience. Moreover, they contend, what difference does it make whether a woman carries her husband's name or that of her father—they're both men! Feminists respond that a name is of utmost importance because it is the foundation of an individual's identity. After all, a woman's name is what marks her achievements and her relationships to others in the first twenty or thirty years of her life. It is what she is; that is the nature of a name—anyone's name. Thus, when a married woman takes on her husband's name, she also very often shares his social identity as well.

As far as convenience is concerned, it is far easier to keep one's name than to change it. A new bride is required to alter all her identification papers, including driver's licence, social insurance numbers, and so on. After she is married, a woman can be identified in telephone books and other sources only under her husband's name.

"This has ramifications," wrote sociologist Eichler, "not only for one's own self-perception and the way one is perceived by others, but also for identification over time. For instance, someone who knew a woman before marriage but did not know her married name might find it difficult or impossible to locate her if a marriage had taken place in an interval of no interaction" (1983: 276).

It is true that a woman who decides to keep her own name after marriage is most likely choosing to keep her father's surname, since almost everyone in our society is named after her or his father. But if a woman keeps her name, she at least has the option of passing it on to her children. Article 56.1 of the Civil Code of Quebec finally makes it possible for a woman, who must endure the long rigours of pregnancy and the reality of childbirth, to name her children after herself rather than (or in addition to) her husband. "A child is assigned, at the option of his father and mother, one or more given names, and the surname of one parent or a surname consisting of not more than two parts taken from the surname of his mother and father." Thus a family of four might include as many as four surnames, a change that will complicate life for bureaucrats!

The new Quebec law, said Eichler, ensures "that women will no longer have to change a fundamental aspect of themselves upon marriage, and for men it will symbolize that marriage no longer means the acquisition of a wife as property" (1983: 276).

Source: *Adapted from Margrit Eichler, 1983.* Families in Canada Today: Recent Changes and Their Policy Consequences. *Toronto: Gage.*

At the municipal level, knowledge about women in contemporary Canadian politics has been advanced by Kopinak's (1985; 1987) studies of local female–male differences in political attitudes. Focusing on the southwestern Ontario city of London, Kopinak found that women have made large gains in municipal politics since the beginning of the modern feminist movement. During the period 1966 to 1982, women advanced from holding fewer than 5 percent of seats on councils, boards, and commissions to a total of 25 percent; however, the most significant increase occurred between 1969 and 1971. Kopinak showed too that women in London's municipal politics were far from marginal. They succeeded in obtaining "high-status offices such as alderman, controller, and mayor," and they usually took progressive stands. Their approaches to policy-making, however, appeared to contrast with those of men, in that the women were somewhat less likely to make decisions beneficial to one group at the exclusion and/or expense of another. Women's policies generally reflected a community orientation while men's policies often had a business orientation. Yet, although they performed very well at the municipal level, women rarely moved up to positions in provincial or federal governments. In contrast, many men who succeeded in municipal politics later pursued careers as provincial or federal MPs.

Kopinak's research has also shown important differences in male–female political attitudes. Women have been characterized as more politically conservative than men, but Kopinak showed that in Canada at least "there is no support for women's greater conservatism" (1987: 29). Women are more likely than men to favour social welfare programs and they want more democracy in the workplace. Surprisingly, women's progressive leanings increased with income, while men's support for liberal causes declined at higher income levels. "[M]ore liberal ideology in women is reproduced not through women's higher education, but by the resources (e.g., family income) afforded by a privileged class position." While women are more liberal than men, the difference is not great enough to justify belief in "separate male and female cultures.... [T]here are more similarities than differences in the patterning of men's and women's political ideology" (1987: 34).

In conclusion, universal suffrage and mass political parties have not fulfilled their early promise of carrying the interests of working people and women directly into the state. Instead, as we have seen, they have tended to concentrate power in a narrow, business-oriented, mostly male party élite. Thus, the liberal democratic state falls short of the ideal. Far from promoting the interests and self-realization of each citizen, it often blocks the development of the majority in order to perpetuate the power of a relatively restricted élite.

SUMMARY

This chapter outlined some of the major arguments about the nature of the state in liberal democracies, and applied these arguments to the Canadian state. We found that, despite the apparent pluralist character of the Canadian state, élite theory has much to contribute to an understanding of government in Canada, as does, to a limited extent, the ruling-class model of Marxism. Postmodernism was seen as less applicable. Postmodernists, for their part, downplay the power of the state in favour of a view that sees an increased role for emergent social movements in policy-making. Staples and, related to these, dependency theorists have documented the crucial nature of the Canadian state's relationship to external powers. In particular, Canada's subordinate relationship to the United States continues to be an important factor in the nation's political and economic life, and significantly influences the options available to federal and provincial governments. Finally, the Hegelian approach throws new light on the class structure of liberal democratic society, showing the functional importance of the universal class of state employees. The bureaucracy, allied with state clients and public-interest groups, has its own class interests that set it in opposition to the dominant groups of civil society, and that are reflected in the organization of government. These interests have become more apparent as the health, education, and social services apparatus of the welfare state has established its predominance over the traditional military and economic concerns of the state.

The chapter also examined a number of political issues facing Canada, including the fate of the welfare state and problems with Canadian federalism. The chapter closed with an examination of the relationship between social class, gender, and political participation in Canada. Here the examination revealed that universal suffrage had not, generally speaking, ensured the full participation of the poor and women in the political process.

QUESTIONS FOR REVIEW AND CRITICAL THINKING

1. What strategies might be used to ensure greater participation of women and the poor in Canadian politics?

2. Can you find lions and foxes in the administration of your university or college, or in any group to which you belong? Which factors allow foxes to keep lions at bay?

3. How is Innis's staples approach useful in explaining Canada's environmental problems?

4. In the final analysis, who do you think controls the state in Canada? Have élite theorists gone too far in their assessment of the structure of governance in Canada?

GLOSSARY

authority according to Weber, power that is seen as legitimate by those subjected to it

circulation of élites Pareto's conception that the decline of one élite prepares the way for domination by another; *lions* seize power, become *foxes*, and are in turn replaced by new lions

civil society Hegel's market system of industry and exchange; its principle is individual self-interest and personal gain

dependency theory the idea that a country's economic development is dependent upon decisions and policies made elsewhere

élitism the notion that power in all forms of society is inevitably held by a small ruling group

geopolitics the relationships of power and prestige between nation-states that determine a nation's legitimacy at home

government the political party or group that controls the state

ideal state Hegel's notion of the state that unites the principle of the family with the idea of civil society

iron law of oligarchy Michels' idea that the leadership of democratically run organizations becomes élitist and tends to seek power for its own ends

liberal democracy government characterized by free elections contested by competing political parties and guaranteed by effective civil liberties

neoconservatism the view that government's role in the economy and society should be severely restricted; sometimes also referred to as neoliberalism. Neoconservatives generally believe in free trade, zero inflation, deficit reduction, shifting the tax burden away from corporations and the rich, and reducing the welfare state.

pluralism the view that power in modern society is shared among competing interest groups

political economy the interdisciplinary blend of economics, political science, history, and sociology. It argues that economics makes sense only within the framework of politics and history.

power the ability to command resources, both material and human; the possibility of imposing one's will upon the behaviour of others

power élite Mills's concept for the combination of business, political, and military leaders that he saw as ruling the United States

staples approach Innis's view that Canada's economic well-being is heavily dependent upon the export of staples or raw materials. This in turn compromises Canadian political sovereignty.

state an organization that successfully claims the monopoly of the legitimate use of physical force within a territory

universal class Hegel's class of government or state-sector workers

welfare state one that protects citizens from the excesses of market forces and treats every person equally

SUGGESTED READINGS

Allen, Robert C., and Gideon Rosenbluth

1992 *False Promises: The Failure of Conservative Economics*. Vancouver: New Star Books.

This critique of neoconservatism is probably the best introduction to Canadian economics available today.

Conway, J.F.

1992 *Debts to Pay: English Canada and Quebec from the Conquest to the Referendum.* Toronto: James Lorimer and Company.

In a study of the conflictual relationship between Canada's two solitudes, Conway analyzes the failure of the Charlottetown Accord and referendum.

WEB SITES

http://www.usask.ca/library/gic/

Government Information in Canada

GIC is an electronic journal with numerous articles on various aspects of government in Canada.

http://home.istar.ca/~unitylink/index.html

The Unity Link

This site provides up to date information on the state of Canada's unity debate. You can access the resources, or contribute to the debate yourself online.

PART

V

Social Organization

This last section focuses on social organization in its various aspects. Types of organizations, their sources, and their impact on society are discussed in Chapter 13, Formal Organizations and Work. As we shall see, organizations, whether they be formally or bureaucratically structured, as in the case of educational, religious, and political institutions, or based upon a more informal structure, as are families, have an especially important influence on human behaviour.

Chapter 14 examines social movements. Their origins are attributed to various sources, including subcultural groups wanting a better position in society, religions trying to create a different social order, political groups seeking power, or members of certain social strata hoping to change the distribution of power and privileges. Collectively, however, social movements share a desire to achieve their goals through change. If successful, most will end up looking like the bureaucracies described in Chapter 13. Some may even become conservative oligarchies, with leaders more interested in maintaining their power than in achieving the original goals of the movement. In both instances, new social movements may emerge and the process may be repeated once more.

Demography, examined in Chapter 15, looks at the factors that determine the size and composition of the population of a society, including social institutions, social differentiation, even cultural values. For instance, religious and political values have been important in Quebec's encouragement of population growth, which is seen as a means of maintaining the size of the francophone population in Canada. Population variables in turn affect most other areas of society. As an example, population size partly determines stratification patterns, since it influences chances for mobility. Population change also affects the education system, since it determines the demand for education, the availability of classrooms and other facilities, and hence the opportunities for individuals to receive higher education.

Probably the most obvious consequence of population growth is increased urbanization, the last topic covered in this book. As it will be discussed in Chapter 16, how cities grow and the different effects of urban and rural life on individuals are the principal concerns of urban sociologists. The distinctions between city, town, and rural areas are many and they affect a whole range of social phenomena, from crime to how people relate to one another.

This examination of social organization completes your introduction to sociology with a Canadian focus. Although presented last, it is a most important area of concern. As you read the chapters, note how the forces discussed are important determinants of the social structure that in turn influences and shapes the behaviour of individuals.

CHAPTER 13

Formal Organizations and Work

Bernard Hammond

INTRODUCTION

Most of us were born and will die in a hospital, one example of what sociologists call an organization. Between birth and death, in each day of our lives, we are touched by the products and influences of still other organizations, such as schools, factories, and clubs.

This chapter begins by clarifying exactly what sociologists mean by the term *organization* and its subcategories *formal organization, bureaucracy,* and *informal organization*. We then examine some of the historical factors that have led to the development of formal organizations—the most pervasive type of organization found in society today. In the next section, we look at the theories that have attempted to explain formal organizations and their societal role during the past century. Finally the chapter looks at the organization of work in contemporary society.

What is an organization?

When you think of some specific organization with which you are familiar, say, your high school, college, or university, what comes to mind? Most people think of a building, a specific physical structure. Others think of individuals who are part of the organization: friends, the person or persons in authority, a favourite teacher or professor. Neither the individuals alone nor the physical structures, however, constitute the essentials of what sociologists mean by organization. Both the people and the buildings can be replaced and the organization will go on.

What is left if both physical structures and specific individuals are removed from the picture is a certain acknowledged pattern of relationships, certain regular, rule-governed ways of behaving that are at once both stable and fluid. It is this patterned set of reciprocal relationships that sociologists refer to as an **organization**.

On the one hand, to the extent that they are rule-based and prescriptive, and thus have the power to shape behaviour, organizations are like objects. On the other hand, they are constantly reshaped by the conscious human activity that constitutes them, and therefore they are subjective creations. As symbolic interactionists point out, actors who participate in organizations are engaged in a "social construction of reality," a process in which these individuals not only create organizations, but are in turn shaped by them.

In addition, organizations are historical entities and must be understood as part of the broad sweep of social influences that shape society as a whole. Our approach, therefore, stresses the need to be mindful of both the subjective and objective aspects of organizations, as well as the historical context in which they exist.

Before we proceed, it is necessary to refine our language somewhat so that we can make the necessary and sometimes subtle distinctions required in sociological analysis. Just as the Inuit have many different words to describe snow (see Chapter 4, Socialization), sociology has many words to describe organizations. The newcomer to either culture must begin by learning the native dialect.

Formal organizations, bureaucracies, and informal organizations

Sociologists define **formal organizations** as social groups with a relatively complex division of labour that are deliberately and consciously created in order to achieve some specific goals. Thus, a business, a school, or a political party is an example of a formal organization. Collectively, formal organizations are the most common forms of organization found in many societies.

A **bureaucracy** is a special type of formal organization characterized by a rigid hierarchy of command, and is particularly characteristic of the modern world. The work of Weber remains the touchstone for contemporary sociological analysis of bureaucracy. We shall return to his work and a more specific conception of bureaucracy later in the chapter.

Informal organization, finally, arises within the structure of formal organizations. Because the principles and rules of formal organizations are stated very generally to cover a broad range of activities, inevitably such formal rules cannot resolve all of the specific and unexpected problems that may arise. Conflicts of interest, new situations for which no formal rules exist, and a less-than-perfect consensus may each challenge the formal organization. Since problems must be solved and decisions made, informal rules and patterns of behaviour emerge to handle these situations. For example, according to the formal rules of colleges and universities, course selection should be based on brief calendar descriptions of courses. In practice, however, these are often inadequate, and students depend heavily on the word-of-mouth reputation of courses and professors to make their choices. In so doing they are creating an informally organized pattern of behaviour, to manage a problem left unresolved by the formal organization.

Of the two basic organizational types, formal and informal, the first has attracted the most attention within the sociological literature. Consequently, the formal organization—and its subtype, the bureaucracy—will command much of our attention in the remainder of the chapter. We shall begin our examination with a discussion of the factors that have led to the historical development of formal organizations.

HISTORICAL DEVELOPMENT OF FORMAL ORGANIZATIONS

It is impossible to know exactly when and how someone discovered that formal organizations would allow complex tasks to be accomplished more efficiently. We do know, however, that very early civilizations undertook large-scale, long-term projects that could not have been managed without a high degree of coordination. The pyramids of ancient Egypt and the temples of the Incas, Aztecs, and Mayas, for example, all would have required the existence of highly developed organizational structures to assure their completion.

In many cases the impetus to develop larger and more sophisticated organizations came from military needs. As ancient Rome extended its influence into the furthest reaches of the known world, for example, a highly sophisticated military-political organization was created to ensure centralized control over its far-flung territories. Religion also provided an impetus to the development of formal organizations. Here an example is provided by the Roman Catholic Church. Although the early organization of the Church was sometimes quite ambiguous, it moved significantly towards formalization when Christianity was adopted as the state religion of Rome in the fourth century by Constantine. And from the beginning the mandate to evangelize the world implied an increasing need for organization. Today, two thousand years after its inception, the Roman Catholic Church represents

It is impossible to know exactly when and how someone discovered that formal organizations would allow complex tasks to be accomplished more efficiently.

one of the most enduring and extensive formal organizations ever devised.

Certain social structural developments have also contributed to the historical emergence of formal organizations. First, the simple increase in population and its shift from rural to urban centres necessitated growth in formal organizations to coordinate the concentration of larger numbers of people more efficiently (see Chapter 16, Urbanization). Second, the invention of a money economy, the growth and centralization of capital, and the creation of increasingly larger businesses (and unions) went hand-in-hand with the development of formal organizations. Finally, the rise of formal organizations has been associated with the emergence of the contemporary nation-state in the late Middle Ages and early days of industrialism. Today, in many countries, whether socialist or capitalist, "big government" has become a fact of life. We saw something of this in Chapter 12, Political Sociology. The growth of the welfare state in the twentieth century has absorbed many of the functions once performed by other organizations, such as religious groups or private charitable concerns. This and other factors have led to the creation of governments of massive scope, requiring very extensive coordination. Despite downsizing, the federal, provincial, and municipal governments still employ hundreds of thousands of people.

THEORETICAL PERSPECTIVES ON FORMAL ORGANIZATIONS

The bases of formal organizations

Durkheim on the division of labour

Formal organizations are characterized by an aspect of the societal process that sociologists call the **division of labour**. Durkheim popularized this term, and while not a student of formal organizations *per se*, his work in this area helps us to understand how these phenomena are possible.

One of the key questions of interest to Durkheim was one that had occupied many social theorists before him, namely, what holds society together? The answer provided to this question by earlier social philosophers like Hobbes, Locke, and Rousseau was the **social contract**. Briefly and simply stated, social contract theory held that at some point in early history, to prevent total chaos, people came together and made a rational agreement to cooperate. This social contract checked the unbounded selfishness that would otherwise have destroyed them all.

Durkheim, however, rejected this argument. With Comte, an earlier French sociologist whom he greatly admired, Durkheim believed that the basis of social order is essentially a moral one—shared sentiments, beliefs, and values. This moral order constitutes a "precontractual solidarity" and precedes any rational agreements to cooperate that people may enter into. Durkheim called this body of shared moral feelings the *collective conscience*—defined in Chapter 5, Deviance, as a source of legal norms. He believed the collective conscience to be stronger in certain types of societies than in others.

In one of his most famous works, aptly entitled *The Division of Labor in Society* (1893), Durkheim made a distinction between different types of societies. He began by looking back to societies earlier than his own late nineteenth-century industrial society. He felt that these earlier, simpler, and smaller societies possessed a greater moral consensus, or shared sentiments and values as might be found in a common religion. In such societies there was a high degree of similarity in terms of occupational possibilities, insofar as economies were relatively undifferentiated. For example, if the economy of a community was based on fishing, most people fished together and shared similar activities and interests. In other words, the division of labour was not highly differentiated.

These societies, Durkheim felt, are characterized by **mechanical solidarity**; almost all people were, by virtue of their membership in the community, automatically integrated into a common morality. As in all societies, some deviance did occur, but it was met with harsh punishment. The punitive, repressive nature of the laws that such societies enacted, often demanding death for what we would consider minor forms of deviance, reveals the strength of the common morality or collective conscience.

In modern societies that are very large and complex, however, the division of labour is much more differentiated. Instead of each worker or family producing all its own necessities, specialization develops. The diversity created by such specialization may lead to strong divisions among different segments of the society. In such a situation, the moral consensus of simpler societies may break down, especially if strong religious beliefs no longer seem able to bind people together. However, these complex societies are not simply reduced to warring factions. Rather, a highly differentiated society produces its own type of integrity or solidarity based upon the mutual interdependence of the various groups involved: the capitalist needs the labourer, and both capitalist and labourer need the services of the carpenter, the butcher, and the clothier. As in human or other organisms, the various parts work together to constitute the whole. Durkheim called this kind of integration **organic solidarity**. In this more complex society, the collective conscience is weaker, because the constituent groups, only loosely united, share few common interests and moral sentiments.

Evidence of these weaker bonds can be seen in the laws enacted under organic solidarity that are geared towards civil and/or administrative ends. Deviance from these laws does not evoke the same harsh punitive response evident in a society highly integrated by mechanical solidarity. Restitution, not punishment, is the goal.

This brief and limited examination of Durkheim's work sensitizes us to the major driving forces underlying all forms of social organization in contemporary society, namely, the division of labour and the trend towards increased complexity and "rational" organization. As industrialization developed and the occupational and social world became more specialized, formal organizations became more and more the tool by which modern societies were managed, organized, and integrated.

In modern societies, specialization in the division of labour has produced what Durkheim called organic solidarity, *with the various parts working together to constitute an efficient whole.*

Cooley and group life

Writing in the early part of this century, the American sociologist Cooley (1864–1929) contributed an analysis of group life somewhat similar to that of Durkheim. He distinguished between primary and secondary groups as embodying different qualities of human relationships (1956 [1909]).

Primary groups are characterized by emotion, warmth, cooperation, and face-to-face interaction. Families and friendship groups are examples. Primary groups are very important for forming and maintaining an integrated self, and it was Cooley who wrote about the looking-glass self (see Chapter 4, Socialization). This integration of self results in the strong sense of identity that group members have with one another. Cooley felt that primary groups are ideal social forms, but, like mechanical solidarity, they are threatened in contemporary urban societies. Instead, more and more human associations are carried out in secondary groups.

Secondary groups are characterized by relationships that are goal-oriented, impersonal, rational, and efficient. As a group, city shoppers relate to one another and to the supermarket cashiers in this way. Similarly, commuters on buses and subways typically maintain a cool, distant, and limited relationship with one another and with their conductors. Formal organizations are excellent examples of such secondary-group relationships.

The work of Durkheim and Cooley gives us some idea of the underlying basis for formal organizations in contemporary society. By contrast, the Weberian and Marxian traditions provide a much more explicit treatment of this topic. It is to the Weberian formulation that we turn first.

Weber on bureaucracy

Weber devoted a good part of his life to understanding and explaining the increasing influence of formal organizations in Western society. Weber's primary concern was with an *ideal type* of formal organization he called *bureaucracy*. He saw it as a manifestation of a much broader historical process of *rationalization*, and as a particular form of *authority*. Each of these terms has a special meaning that must be clarified.

The concept of the **ideal type** was a central device in Weber's method of analysis. Constructing an ideal type involves extracting the most prominent features of a social phenomenon. Ideal types do not exist in reality, but are mental constructs that help us understand the essential features of the phenomenon under study. One of the principal applications of this technique of analysis is found in Weber's work on bureaucracy.

By **rationalization** Weber pointed towards what he sometimes called the progressive "disenchantment of the world," the movement away from magical or sacred interpretations of the world (see Chapter 10, Religion). In their place, a broad-ranging systematization of human knowledge in its various spheres, such as science, music, and even art, emerges. Weber saw the development of rationalization as being particularly far advanced in the Western world—as evidenced by the growth in rule-based and highly structured bureaucracies.

Bureaucracy for Weber was also associated with a particular form of authority (see also Chapter 12, Political Sociology). In essence, authority is simply the exercise of power made acceptable to the members of a society through a process Weber called **legitimation**. Throughout history, three principal ways of legitimating power have successively emerged, resulting in three ideal types of authority. **Charismatic authority** is based upon the perception that a leader has special qualities and therefore should be obeyed. It is effective only so long as that belief exists; if the relationship of faith between followers and leader is broken, charismatic authority collapses. **Traditional authority** exists when "legitimacy is claimed for it and believed in on the basis of the sanctity of the order and the attendant powers of control as they have been handed down from the past..." (Weber, 1964 [1947]: 341). A certain amount of discretion is accorded leaders with traditional authority, but tradition also puts limits upon the degree to which their free personal decisions will be tolerated. The patriarchal family, in which the father is the undisputed head of the household, is often cited as an example of traditional authority.

Rational-legal authority is that which underlies modern bureaucracy. This authority type "rests on a belief in the legality of patterns of normative rules and the right of those elevated to authority under such rules to issue commands" (Weber, 1964 [1947]: 328). The essence of rational-legal authority is subservience to rules. Thus, obedience is owed to the impersonal, legally constituted order, not to the person occupying a particular office as in the case of traditional authority.

As the quintessential form of rational-legal authority, bureaucracies for Weber are guided by six basic principles:

1. there is the principle of fixed and official jurisdictional areas, which are generally ordered by rules, that is, by laws or administrative regulations;
2. the principles of office hierarchy and of levels of graded authority mean a firmly ordered system of super- and subordination in which there is a supervision of the lower offices by higher ones;
3. the management of the modern office is based upon written documents;
4. office management...usually presupposes thorough and expert training;
5. when the office is fully developed, official activity demands the full working capacity of the official;
6. the management of the office follows general rules which are more or less stable, more or less exhaustive, and which can be learned. Knowledge of these rules represents a special technical learning which the officials possess.

(Gerth and Mills, 1946: 196–98)

Weber both admired and feared the advance of bureaucratic structures in society, and indeed the two faces of bureaucracy are clearly evident today. On the one hand they are highly efficient tools, which permit the accomplishment of exceedingly complex tasks. As such, they can be of great service to humanity. On the other hand, contact with formal organizations is often frustrating, impersonal, and alienating for clients. Individuals become standardized, programmed, powerless victims of a new kind of tyranny. There is also a tendency for bureaucracy to perpetuate itself and to begin to serve its own survival goals rather than those of the people to whom it owes its existence (see the boxed insert on "Does Bureaucracy Always Mean Efficiency?"). For a nation, bureaucracies can assume tremendous power, often with negative consequences. The Canadian government's organizational apparatus, for example, is so complex and sometimes so poorly understood that serious questions may be raised about its "accountability." Control of the organization of government is removed from ordinary Canadians and becomes problematic even for their elected representatives. Excessive power is also revealed in the case of multinational corporations, which can threaten the autonomy of independent states. In recognition of these kinds of dangers, and in spite of his admiration for this modern form of organization, Weber glumly predicted that bureaucracy would be "the iron cage" of the future.

Marx on the state and worker alienation

In the Marxian tradition, the analysis of formal organizations has two main concerns: first, it focuses on the state as a bureaucratic structure; second, it is concerned with the implications of formal organizations for work as a human activity. Let us examine each of these concerns in turn.

Does Bureaucracy Always Mean Efficiency?

As suggested in this chapter, Weber was ambivalent about the role of bureaucracy in contemporary society. This ambivalence is shared by the modern functionalist Merton. In an article entitled "Bureaucratic structure and personality" (1957), Merton argued that bureaucratic practices often contradict organizational goals. Trained to adhere strictly to the rules, bureaucrats may, for example, be inflexible, timid, and unable to adapt and innovate when confronted with new situations. Inflexible adherence to rules and career incentives like promotion may also take a higher priority than organizational goals. Further, Merton noted a tendency for conformity to official regulations to become an end in itself rather than a means to an end. By losing sight of organizational goals, bureaucrats may reduce organizational effectiveness while generating "red tape," which simply frustrates potential clients. Finally, bureaucratic impersonality can serve to alienate and frustrate clients, who are meant to be helped. Patients in a hospital who are awakened from a sound sleep only to be asked to take their sleeping pills find themselves victims of bureaucratic routine that lacks compassion and caring.

The bureaucratic state, to begin with, is seen by Marx as a creation and tool of the capitalist class—the bourgeoisie—through which its interests are served (see Chapter 12, Political Sociology). The state is thus not an independent entity acting on its own behalf; nor does it act impartially on behalf of all its constituents. Even in democracies like Canada, orthodox Marxists would argue that the federal government and provincial governments reflect and defend capitalist principles—the principles of "big business." With the coming of the proletarian revolution and the inevitable fall of the bourgeoisie, however, Marx predicted that the state would eventually "wither away." In a society of equals, the bureaucratic state would no longer be necessary as a tool of domination by one class over another.

This analysis of state bureaucracy was continued by Lenin and Trotsky. A major concern of both was the apparent flaw in Marx's theory exposed by the fact that the bureaucratic state did not disappear following the Russian Revolution of 1917. In the end, they responded by arguing that the Revolution in fact had not immediately created a communist society. Rather, the society that had emerged out of the Revolution was socialist, with socialism a transitional stage between capitalism and communism. In this period a bureaucratic state still persists because conditions are not developed to the point where its elimination is possible. For example, the education of the masses, necessary for the further development of the productive forces, requires a bureaucratic structure and must be accomplished before administration can be assumed by the people themselves. Thus, until the coming of the fully developed communist state, a measure of bureaucracy has to be tolerated and, along with it, career bureaucrats who often serve their own needs and those of the bureaucracy before those of the people.

The series of political revolutions in the communist bloc that began at the close of the 1980s have renewed and intensified this debate. First, in Poland the workers' movement Solidarity clashed with the bureaucratic state, making transparent the lack of identification between the interests of the labour movement and those of the state. In country after country, as the winds of change transformed communist governments, it became increasingly apparent how vast bureaucracies supported rule by an élite few who lived in luxury while the majority suffered poor living conditions and shortages of vital necessities.

The unfolding of these events has placed a heavy burden of proof on the Marxist camp and lends weight to the arguments of Weber. In contrast to the Marxian tradition, Weber ascribed a much more independent role to bureaucracies. He did not see bureaucracies as identified with the capitalistic state, nor as destined to wither away with its demise. Rather, he considered them to be even more necessary in a socialist than in a capitalist state

Is Bureaucracy Inevitable?

A contemporary and friend of Weber's, Michels is remembered mainly for his concept of the *iron law of oligarchy.* In his book *Political Parties* (1915), Michels was concerned with what he felt is the very strong tendency for formal organizations, whether of the capitalist or socialist variety, to be bureaucratically ruled by an élite few (an oligarchy), who occupy positions in the upper ranks of the hierarchy. Michels felt that this tendency towards oligarchy is a threat to democracy because it happens even if the leaders are initially elected, as in political parties. Two main factors are responsible for the tendency towards oligarchy: the psychological needs of the leaders to maintain power ("every private carries a marshal's baton in his [or her] knapsack...") and the need of the public to be guided. Though pessimistic about the possibility of democracy, Michels was not without all hope. He believed that a continual critical examination of the dangers of oligarchy would help minimize these dangers, though not remove them.

Like his friend Weber, Michels was critical of the Marxist notion that socialist societies would not require bureaucratic administration. The organization of a complex society cannot be accomplished without rational organization, and along with rationalization comes hierarchy and a class of administrators, he argued. Eventually the iron law of oligarchy reasserts itself and again the majority submits to the élite few.

The startling degree of oligarchic repression that had become commonplace in Eastern European state bureaucracies after World War II would have come as no surprise to Michels or Weber. Against Marx's claim that socialism would eliminate the need for bureaucracy, they maintained that the real threat to human freedom is not capitalism but bureaucracy and the tendency to élite rule. Many who lived in these countries would agree with their viewpoint.

(Weber, 1964 [1947]: 339), and argued that the *Communist Manifesto*, which predicted the "dictatorship of the proletariat," was wrong. Instead of control passing to the workers, Weber saw more and more power in his day being assumed by a class of bureaucratic administrators unsympathetic to workers' interests (see the boxed insert on ("Is Bureaucracy Inevitable?").

The second concern of the Marxist tradition is the organization of work in a capitalist society. This concern grows out of Marx's conviction that alienation of the worker is widespread in capitalist relations of production (Marx, 1932 [1864]), with the means of production owned by the capitalists, and the workers owning nothing but their labour power. This structure of domination gives rise to four main forms of **alienation**.

First, workers under capitalism are alienated from the productive process. The capitalists purchase the labour of workers and decide how it is to be used. The workers work for wages, not to fulfil their own creative human needs. Second, workers are alienated from the product of their labour. They have no control over the objects they produce. These are owned by the capitalists, who sell them for a profit. A third form of alienation under capitalism is the workers' alienation from others. Workers are alienated from capitalists, whom they see as hostile masters of the products of their labour. But they are also alienated from their fellow workers, with whom they frequently find themselves in competition for survival. Finally, the structure of capitalism forces workers into an alienated relationship with their humanity, their capacity to express their essential human nature. The ability to act freely, spontaneously, and creatively is what most securely distinguishes humans from other animal species. When loss of control over the process and products of their work cuts workers off from their fellows, they are also robbed of that special masterful and creative relationship to nature that makes them truly human.

Thus, the very organization of work in capitalism results in a situation of objective alienation. For humans, to be without control of the creative capacity in work is to be alienated. This loss of control by workers is aggravated by capitalism's increasing tendency to fragment, specialize, and allocate tasks that were all once performed by the

Marx argued that alienation of the worker is endemic in capitalist society.

same worker to several workers on an assembly line. Marx was very aware of this tendency, which had already widely established itself in his time. This tendency had also been described by Adam Smith (1977 [1776]) in his *Wealth of Nations*. Smith used the manufacture of pins as an example of how specialization can increase production. He reckoned that ten workers independently producing pins could each produce fewer than 20 pins per day. But if pin-making were broken down into stages, with each worker performing only one stage, ten workers could produce over 48 000 pins per day. In *Capital*, Marx illustrated the same point using the manufacture of glass bottles as an example (1977 [1867]: 481).

Although Smith was aware of the numbing effects of such specialization on a worker, he accepted it as inevitable in every "improved and civilized society." Marx, however, condemned it as a specific type of alienation associated with capitalist production, one that turns the worker into a "crippled monstrosity" (1977 [1867]: 481).

A good deal of study has been devoted to the existence of alienation in modern organizations. Much of this study, however, has departed from Marx's conception of alienation as an objective reality stemming from the workers' separation from the process and product of their labour under capitalism. Instead, alienation is examined as a subjective category—questionnaires are often used to measure workers' perceptions of their work environment. However, in a review of such studies, Rinehart (1996) pointed out that attitude questionnaires capture neither the complexities of worker alienation nor the attempts of workers to humanize the workplace. Rather, feelings of alienation are most often expressed in behaviour such as strikes, restriction of output, industrial sabotage, and humorous horseplay on the job (Rinehart, 1996). Alienation at work can also result in physical or mental illness for workers "including death, disease, disability, dissatisfaction, anxiety, stress, and unease" (Navarro, 1982: 18). Highly automated, repetitive, and monotonous jobs take an especially high toll on workers' health. In a study of postal workers in Edmonton, it was shown that those employees who code mail using modern automated letter-sorting machinery have more health problems than those who sort mail by hand. These health problems take the form of "eye and vision problems, hearing loss, and psychophysiological problems such as fatigue, loss of appetite, irritability, sleeplessness, dizziness, and headaches" (Lowe and Northcott, 1986: 70).

Two further historical developments in organizational theory help bridge the gap between the classical perspectives of Weber and Marx, and current attempts to understand the growth and functioning of formal organizations. These are the Scientific Management and Human Relations schools. We examine these in the next section.

Scientific management

In his 1911 book *Scientific Management*, an engineer by the name of Taylor outlined a set of ideas on how to achieve maximum productivity in industry. The most notable aspect of this approach—known generically as the **scientific management** perspective—is that it sees workers basically as economic individuals who are successfully motivated by monetary rewards. The task for scientific management, therefore, becomes one of matching the work task, through a consciously organized division of labour, as closely as possible to the economic incentive.

At a practical level, the scientific management approach gave rise to a number of organizational practices, especially the now-famous "time and motion studies." These analyses require that every action needed to perform a task be carefully scrutinized and broken down into its component parts. Subsequently, as part of an effort to enhance overall efficiency, all non-essential motions are eliminated, while performance of essential ones is regulated by time standards.

The time and motion study eventually came to form the basis of piece-work, assembly line production in the early part of this century. Each worker is assigned a small part of the complete task to perform over and over again, while co-workers are assigned others. The completed product emerges only after passing through the whole assembly line. Workers are paid, at least partially, on the basis of the number of pieces produced in a given period of time. The object of a production process organized in this way is to combine the most effective reward system with the most efficient division of labour in order to extract the maximum output physically possible from each worker. Marx's nightmare of the inhumanity of the production process is thereby conceptualized as a formal organizational goal.

The theory of scientific management attracted many adherents during the early part of the century, and although severely criticized on both empirical (the data were faulty) and humanitarian grounds, it continues to exert its influence today in a variety of forms. Its advantages to employers and administrators are obvious; even some workers can be convinced that this type of incentive system is worth the costs it exacts in terms of monotony and boredom on their part.

The distinctive feature of scientific management theory and policies based on it is the almost sole concentration on formal organizational principles. Those who apply the theory wish to establish rules and regulations to cover all possible work situations. The underlying assumption is that human nature is machine-like and thoroughly rational, motivated by simple, uncomplicated economic needs. In fact, human nature is more complex, and people are capable of exercising much more control over their environment, even under oppressive conditions, than they are sometimes given credit for. This observation became the basis for the school of thought we shall examine next.

The human relations school

The human relations school emerged from attempts by Mayo and his associates at Harvard's Department of Industrial Relations to test certain propositions derived from the scientific management perspective. This research was carried out from 1927 to 1932 in Western Electric's Hawthorne Works in Chicago.

The authors of the Hawthorne Studies, as the project came to be known, made their first contribution to a new perspective on organizational behaviour following a test of a basic scientific management idea—that increased illumination of the workplace would result in increased production. To their surprise they found that production increased not only when lighting was increased, but even when lighting was decreased. Similarly, in a set of experiments using rest periods of varying lengths, the researchers found that production rates increased uniformly whether breaks were long, short, or eliminated altogether.

The general conclusion reached by the researchers was that the attention the workers received as experimental subjects, and the generally changed social situation and patterns of interaction resulting from the experimental situation, were responsible for the increased output. In fact, the observation that simply putting people in an experimental situation will change their behaviour has become widely known in the social sciences and is often referred to as the "Hawthorne effect."

In a later study, in which employees worked in groups to wire telephone switchboards known as banks, the researchers uncovered another significant finding. They showed that, contrary to the assumptions of scientific management, social factors and not economic incentives are the most important determinants of production rates. In fact, they revealed, workers set and, through labelling, informally enforce norms for what they consider reasonable quotas. Those who deviate from these norms by producing less are chided as "chiselers"; those who deviate by producing more are labelled "rate busters."

As the studies inspired by the human relations perspective accumulated, additional insights were gained concerning the informal aspects of organizations. For example, a democratic style of leadership, which gives workers a say in production decisions, rather than the authoritarian style of supervision advocated by scientific management, results in a higher-quality product and more independent and contented workers. Human relations studies concluded that communication between ranks, especially in matters that affect workers, is a good management practice.

The **human relations school**, then, contradicted several fundamental assumptions of scientific management, and in the process contributed to the discovery and appreciation of the informal structure of formal organizations. It revealed that people, even within the limits imposed by a rule-governed, hierarchical, and bureaucratic organization, seem to be able to assert themselves and pursue their human needs through a variety of informal adaptations. At the same time, the ultimate concern of the human relations school is with productivity enhancement. Thus, though it represented advance over the cruder postulates of scientific management, it has remained, as Rinehart (1996) pointed out, a *managerial* science.

The structuralist approach

The structuralist approach comprises a diverse set of theories that encompasses much of the present work being done in the field of organizational analysis. Just as the human relations school developed as a reaction to scientific management theories, this approach first developed from a series of criticisms of earlier models. Structuralists have criticized scientific management theories, first of all, for being biased in favour of employers and administrators, for being excessively concerned with economic factors, and for simply being inhumane in their application of rules and procedures intended to maximize production regardless of human costs. The structuralist approach also sees the human relations school as biased in favour of management, insofar as it is also oriented towards production, albeit in a less obvious way. The human relations adherents express a management position, not through advocacy of piece-work and the stopwatch, but by stressing open communication between managers and workers, and by attempting to give the workers a feeling that they are a part of the decision-making process. Structuralists feel that this attempt to create an impression of the organization as "one big happy family" is misleading. It glosses over certain real conflicts of interest among different groups within the organization, particularly between managers and workers. Dissatisfaction among workers is often a reflection of these real and inevitable conflicts of interest, and attempts to convince them that their dissatisfaction is due to faulty communication and misunderstanding merely deceive them.

Generally speaking, **structuralism** claims to be a synthesis and development of the two earlier approaches. To begin with, structuralists feel that both informal and formal structures are important in their own right, and that more should be done to study the relationship between the two levels of organization. They tend to recognize both social and economic rewards as important motivational factors for organizational employees. They also broaden the scope of their analysis to include such organizations as hospitals, schools, prisons, churches, colleges, and mental institutions. Finally, structuralists believe that important factors in the environment affect what happens inside the organization. For example, decisions about the internal organization of colleges and universities—such as their admission policies, program development, and the numbers of students and faculty to be recruited—depend on external environmental factors. The state of the economy, political priorities, and demographic trends are only a few of many such factors that help shape their internal organization.

Structuralists believe that it is important to examine the relationship between the formal and informal levels of social organization.

Symbolic interactionist perspectives

The organization as negotiated order

The attempts that we have encountered thus far to understand organizations can be criticized for emphasizing almost totally the static aspects of organizations. Whether focusing on the formal structure or the informal structure, the attempt is usually to discover the regular *stable* patterns that constitute the organization. Just how these patterns are built and rebuilt in the daily activities of the members who participate in the organization is overlooked, or at least not emphasized. It is precisely this process that is the central focus of **negotiated order theory**—the process by which the organization is socially constructed day by day, through conflicts of interest, dialogue, and negotiation on the part of its participants (Corwin, 1987: 107–8).

The theoretical foundation of negotiated order theory is found in symbolic interactionism. For our purposes, one fundamental assumption of the school is critical: specifically, that social order is constantly evolving. In attempting to explain social order and the maintenance of stability in society, symbolic interactionism looks neither to the notion of social contract nor to Durkheim's belief in a moral order. For symbolic interactionists, social order is not a once-and-for-all static structure. These theorists draw upon the work of Mead, one of the founders of symbolic interactionism you encountered in Chapter 4, Socialization. They see social order emerging from the interaction among persons guided by agreements and understandings that are not permanently fixed, but are always themselves under negotiation. Hence, social order is an ongoing process requiring participants to work at the necessary bargains, contracts, and arrangements through which this order is produced and reproduced. Thus, social order is an "emergent" product, one that arises out of the meaningful actions of its participants and that is always being constructed.

Negotiated order theorists take this fundamental principle of symbolic interactionism and apply it to the study of organizations. They point out that organizational actors rely upon informal understandings and tentative agreements to get on with their work, rather than turning to a fixed set of rules to solve internal conflicts and tensions, as would be predicted, for example, by Weber's model of bureaucracy. In fact, they argue that the formal rules found in organizations are not very extensive or explicit, and that organizational personnel frequently do not know all the rules, or how and in what situation to apply them. Consequently, the rules are treated as general understandings, the specific meaning of which must be worked out in concrete situations. This is the principal task of the negotiation process. For example, doctors, nurses, social workers, psychologists, and many other professional and nonprofessional groups who work in hospitals often have different understandings of the same illnesses. Therefore, agreement upon treatment programs and patient care is not predetermined by a set of formal rules; rather, it is always an achievement, something to be accomplished through a continuing process of conflict and negotiation.

Ethnomethodology

Sometimes the unwritten agreements arrived at in this process of negotiation become accepted and even, in some cases, taken for granted by the personnel of an organization. The analysis of these taken-for-granted assumptions and bargains that we often rely upon in our own everyday lives has given rise to a school of thought that is related to symbolic interactionism and yet quite different from it. Called *ethnomethodology*, this perspective explores the fundamental and perennial sociological problem of how social order originates and is maintained.

While negotiated order theory concentrates upon the *explicit* activity of conflict, bargaining, and tentative agreements that characterize organizational life, **ethnomethodology** emphasizes the *implicit*, taken-for-granted, embedded rules that informally underlie organizational life. Its task is to uncover these rules, to reveal the role they play in maintaining social order, and to analyze their relationship to the formal, explicit rules and agreements, negotiated or not.

Ethnomethodology has shown that taken-for-granted, informal agreements sometimes even contradict the formal rules of an organization. Sudnow (1967) used this method in his classic exploration of the dying process in modern hospitals. He uncovered many personnel practices that serve the needs of the formal organization rather than those of dying patients. In one case Sudnow observed that organizational personnel may begin to treat dying patients as if they were already dead, for example by initiating proceedings to obtain permission for autopsy and organ transplants before the patient has died. In another case Sudnow observed a nurse closing the eyes of a comatose patient so that the body would be easier to prepare for the mortuary. Overall, he found such practices—which he collectively dubbed "social death"—to be based on widespread and agreed-upon informal procedures that had no foundation in the formal structure of the organization.

In another study it was shown that the formal expectations of workers in a bureaucracy do not adequately describe the actual behaviour of the individuals who occupy different positions in the structure. Rather, informal practices, in which the lines between managerial and clerical skills overlap substantially, can come to be taken for granted. Cassin (1980), in her analysis of civil service workers in British Columbia, examined discrepancies between job descriptions and the actual work carried out by different levels of workers, and discovered that female secretaries often performed managerial work. In screening communication and allocating priorities to certain tasks for their bosses, they were exercising executive judgments. At a formal level these skills are neither acknowledged nor rewarded, but at an informal level secretaries often jokingly claim credit for teaching their bosses all they know. While the boss is rewarded with promotion, secretaries are given symbolic rewards such as flowers on their birthday or during "secretaries' week." Informal practices can thus become a routine part of everyday life in the organization, and can determine individual behaviour as strongly and as surely as formal bureaucratic rules.

In discussing symbolic interactionist perspectives on formal organizations, we have presented brief examples of analyses from both negotiated order theory and ethnomethodology. These perspectives have contributed greatly to our understanding of social life generally and social organizations in particular, and their applications provide fascinating reading. Every perspective in science has its limitations, however, and these are no exception. Both perspectives have been justly criticized, for two reasons especially.

First, their concentration on the internal dynamics of organizations ignores the societal context in which organizations exist. They do not take into account the fact that what happens internally is often the result of major societal shifts that form the environment for and impinge upon organizations.

A second, related criticism is that concentration on a micro-level of analysis tends to overlook the fact that organizations develop in and are shaped by the broad historical forces to which they owe their birth and to which they remain subject. For example, due to restraints upon government spending, Canadian hospitals are sometimes forced to eliminate beds and reconsider programs. This leads to a great deal of conflict and negotiation among hospital personnel and administrators concerning which programs are most necessary. A sociologist studying only these types of negotiations would learn a great deal about the internal dynamics of hospitals, but little about the external, historical, and economic developments that make spending restraints a government policy in the first place. Such external considerations are not usually an explicit part of the internal negotiation process. This external, developmental aspect of organizations is a matter about which earlier theorists, such as Weber, were acutely aware, but one that has typically been neglected by negotiated order theorists and ethnomethodologists. We now move to consider one theory that does take greater account of these types of external factors.

WORK AND THE NEW INDUSTRIAL SOCIOLOGY

Along with alienation, discussed earlier, the concept of the "labour process" held a central and closely related place in Marx's *Capital*. In the **new industrial sociology**, the Marxian concept of alienation remains central, but the analysis goes further to revive Marx's concern with the organization of the workplace itself. It sees the history of formal organizations as the history of capitalist control of workers, and looks at how increasing specialization, subjugation to the machine, technological innovation, and hierarchical bureaucratic management have affected the alienation process.

In examining this broader mix of social and historical factors, the new industrial sociology embraces a much wider field than the study of formal organizations alone, and is sometimes located within the more general category called the sociology of work. Here, however, we shall limit our discussion to the ways in which the new industrial sociology evaluates work in formal organizations.

Though agreeing that formal organizations should be seen as arenas for the control of workers by capitalists, the new industrial sociology is careful not to suggest that workers are totally passive in the face of the techniques of control devised by owners and managers. In his *Contested Terrain*, for example, Edwards (1979) saw control in the firm not as simple domination by management, but as more of a contest between employers and managers on the one hand and workers on the other. He saw systems of control in the firm as having changed since the nineteenth century, partly as a consequence of changes in firms' "size, operations, and environment but also as a consequence of workers' success in imposing their own goals at the workplace" (Edwards, 1979: 18).

Edwards saw the emergence of three distinct types of control in history (1979: 18–22). The first type, which characterized the nineteenth century, he called *simple control*. Here a single entrepreneur, alone or with a small group of supervisors and managers, ruled the firm. The ruler(s) exercised arbitrary power with the ever-present option of terminating uncooperative workers, which left the workers relatively powerless.

As firms grew in technological complexity, towards the end of the nineteenth century, the distance between entrepreneurs and workers was expanded by additional levels of supervisors, giving rise to a second type of control. *Technical control*, Edwards argued, found its classical form in the assembly line, piece-work, and scientific management, discussed earlier. Here, machinery set the pace of work and directed the labour process, which gave a double advantage to employers. Mechanization strengthened the hand of employers because it reduced jobs, thus increasing competition within the potential labour pool. Also, inside the firm, it reduced workers to the status of machinery attendants.

A third form of control discussed by Edwards is *bureaucratic control*, based on the principle of hierarchical power. In the past half century, employers have turned the principle of hierarchy into a further form of control by linking it to a stratification of work. Each job is given a distinct description, title, and level

The new industrial sociology focuses on the occupational structure and the development of organizational and administrative devices designed to control workers and the labour process.

of pay; and the worker is offered the promise of a "career" in exchange for adherence to company policy. It represents, therefore, yet another manifestation of the employer's control of the work process.

Although Edwards saw these three techniques of control as developing in a historical sequence, all three methods are evident in factories and firms today due to uneven capitalist development. And in response, workers have fought back. In addition to unionization and collective bargaining, they have lobbied for reduced hours of work and more control over decision-making. The story of labour's response to industrialization in Canada, its organizational forms, and the management techniques of employers has been documented by Lowe and Krahn (1984).

This battle for workplace control goes on, new industrial sociologists suggest, because it reflects the fundamental contradiction of capitalism: the class struggle between owners and non-owners of capital. Moreover, it reflects the struggle of workers against the objective alienation implied in that structure. It is also, however, a contest in which workers are at a distinct disadvantage. Even apparent successes, such as the concessions accorded by the application of human relations policies, often represent thinly disguised efforts to increase production and profit. Or, having gained a degree of autonomy in decision-making (Rinehart, 1996), workers cannot rest on their laurels, because employers often attempt to move back to more direct forms of control.

The impact of Japanese management styles and worker control

More recent developments in North America and elsewhere—developments that ostensibly give workers more control over their work life through the reorganization of the workplace along the lines of Japanese industry—have received a great deal of attention by sociologists and managers alike. In many respects these efforts are modern-day applications of the human relations school discussed earlier, and consequently share many of their liabilities, especially in that they hold the promise of sharing control with workers but in the end act primarily as production-enhancement mechanisms.

One of the strategies employed by Japanese management has been the **quality circle**, a small group of employees who meet periodically to discuss how to improve quality. Quality circles have an interesting history, which actually began in the U.S. After World War II, American experts visited Japan as part of the postwar effort to help the Japanese learn American industrial standards. Quality control for Americans involved having middle managers and engineers apply statistical principles to all stages of the production process. The Japanese added a simple but revolutionary twist to this practice. Instead of involving only a minority of engineers and managers, they taught quality control techniques to all employees, from top management to rank-and-file workers. This responsibility was exercised in "circles," or study groups of about five to ten persons under a supervisor. The practice spread quickly throughout Japanese industry. Management uses successful participation in quality circles as a criterion for promotion and salary increases. Honorific rewards such as recognition and a feeling of contributing to the group seem to be the most effective motivating factor for workers, a finding consistent with the human relations school and contradictory to the principles of scientific management.

It wasn't until 1967 that the idea of Japanese-style quality circles was introduced to the United States (Armour, 1987: 180). The first American company to introduce the concept into its organization was Lockheed Missile and Space Company, in 1974. Since then the practice has been widely adopted across the United States and Canada (Rinehart, 1996). Quality circles on this continent, however, have met with much greater scepticism and resistance than they have in Japan.

It is possible to identify at least three sources of resistance to the concept. One has been middle-level managers who may feel threatened by the participation of workers in production decisions (Armour, 1987: 183). A second source of resistance is cultural. Japanese culture prepares workers to accept cooperation and participation with management more readily than is the case in North America. More importantly, Japanese culture encourages the identification with collective goals that is inherent in the concept of quality circles. Morgan (1986: 114) provided an excellent summary of these differences between Japanese and North American cultural values. Briefly, he found that Japanese organizations give employees a sense of belonging and not just a place to work. An emphasis on interdependence, shared concerns, and mutual help give the organization the collaborative spirit of a village or commune. Employees see fellow workers as an extended family, and although authority relations are paternalistic, traditional, and deferential, they frequently make for lifelong commitments to the organization. Employers are aware that the welfare of the individual, the corporation, and the state are closely linked. Morgan contrasted this cultural context with the ethic of competitive individualism prevailing in American corporations. He saw many American corporations and their workers as preoccupied with "the game," in which winning and the rewards and punishments associated with success and failure are all-important. Organizational managers "set objectives, clarify accountability, and kick ass or reward success lavishly and conspicuously" (Morgan, 1986: 119).

A final source of resistance to quality circles in North America comes from organized labour. At face value, *quality circles* imply movement away from the typical top-down management style to a more egalitarian style, in which workers are given a chance to participate in decisions concerning their work in "partnership" with management. But in reality, quality circles can be seen as only a contemporary version of the human relations approach to management. Critical evaluation of that approach has taught unions to interpret these initiatives as attempts to co-opt workers for the purpose of increasing production, lowering costs, and increasing profits. While quality circles lead to some greater degree of working-life autonomy, the real management decisions remain firmly in the hands of top management. Decisions concerning job security, development of product lines, plant closures, and

The Matsushita Electric Company is guided by the collective values that transform Japan's industries into communities.

investment policies are not viewed as legitimate concerns of workers (see the boxed insert on "The Canadian Auto Workers' Statement on the Reorganization of Work").

Still, Japanese-style management initiatives in Canadian industry will continue to have an impact on Canadian workers in a variety of ways. Japanese investment in Canada has increased significantly in recent years. In Central and Western Canada, investment has been concentrated in forestry and coal production, while in Eastern Canada cars and electronics have been the focus (Walmsley, 1992: 17–27), including many Japanese– North American joint ventures, usually Japanese-managed, such as the Toyota–General Motors CAMI plant in Ingersoll, Ontario.

Some degree of culture clash between the Japanese style of management and broader Canadian cultural values is evident, leading to efforts, sometimes unsuccessful, to blend Canadian and Japanese work styles. The Japanese custom of encouraging workers to stay after work to socialize over drinks in order to promote team spirit and company loyalty does not appeal to Canadians, who typically maintain more rigid boundaries between the world of work and the home world—a value raised to the level of a virtual necessity in a society where dual-earner families predominate. Similarly, Japanese efforts to give the appearance of reducing the status difference between workers and management by paying workers a salary has not met with wide acceptance in Canada, where the hourly

The Canadian Auto Workers' Statement on the Reorganization of Work

The workplace is changing. We have never been and are not now opposed to positive changes in the workplace—we want to use our experience, knowledge, and skills to produce good quality products and quality services in well-designed workplaces equipped with the proper tools and equipment. And we want to insure that this production does not ignore our rights and entitlements.

The initiative for the recent change is, however, coming from an aggressive and determined management with its own agenda. Management is proposing a variety of programs under different names (team concept, employee involvement, quality of worklife, quality networks, total quality control, socio-technical systems). But whatever the current title, the selling point is both the stick and the carrot: the threat of competitiveness and the promise of a new "partnership" between workers and management, a partnership allegedly leading to greater worker control, greater security, and more enjoyable work.

As a union, we need to look behind the surface of "partnership" and ask ourselves what it really means and what the result will be. Workers belong, and pay dues, to our union because they want to improve their standard of living through collective bargaining, and to improve their workplace conditions through strong union representation in respect to grievances, health and safety, human rights, and equitable treatment.

False Promises

This "partnership" and its promises are false. For all the talk about jointness and worker control, employers are certainly not putting true equality between themselves and their employees on the agenda. Management will continue to jealously guard the management's rights and to unilaterally decide when to modernize, how much to invest, what to produce, with what kind of technology, and so on. The truth is that management's agenda is not about surrendering its power, but about finding more sophisticated ways to extend it.

CAW Guidelines

The workplace is changing, but the outcome of the changes is not predetermined. Much is new in the workplace but what is not is that management has its agenda and we have ours. Management has articulated its program—packaged as the team concept—as empowering workers and reforming the workplace. This theme of industrial democracy is not new to us. Our union was born out of, and continues to be built on, demands for a more democratic workplace. And the barrier to workplace democracy continues to be management. Its obsession with getting more with less subordinates workers' rights and working conditions to a narrow preoccupation with reducing costs, reducing staff, and eliminating any free time.

We reject managerial efforts, under whatever name, which jeopardize workers' rights, undermine workplace conditions, and erode the independence of the union.

1. We reject the use of Japanese production methods which rigidly establish work standards and standard operations, thereby limiting worker autonomy and discretion on the job.
2. We reject the use of techniques such as Kaizening (pressure for continuous improvement) where the result is speed-up, work intensification, and more stressful jobs.
3. We oppose workplace changes which limit mobility, weaken transfer rights, and erode seniority provisions.
4. We reject the introduction of alternative workplace structures and employee-based programs which purport to represent workers' interests while circumventing the union.
5. We reject efforts to shift compensation from wages to incentives and [the allocation] to individuals [of] the rewards of productivity improvements.
6. We oppose the process of union nomination of joint appointees to new jobs created to perform company functions.
7. We oppose initiatives which undermine worker solidarity—structures which require conformity to company-determined objectives and which divide workers into competing groups internally, nationally, and internationally.

8. We oppose the use of peer pressure in company campaigns to discipline and regulate the behaviour of workers.

9. We reject workplace reorganizations which threaten job security by subcontracting or transferring work outside the bargaining unit.

10. We oppose efforts to render workplaces so lean that there is no place for workers with work-related, age-related, or other disabilities.

11. We oppose efforts to involve and reward workers in the systematic elimination of jobs or the disciplining of other workers. We support efforts to involve and empower workers, to increase worker dignity, to produce quality products with pride, to make jobs more rewarding and workplaces more democratic. These objectives will be achieved through our own agenda for change, our own demands around training, technology, improving jobs, improving the work environment, guaranteeing health and safety, strengthening mobility rights, strengthening affirmative action, and strengthening the union.

Source: Canadian Dimension, *March 1990 (pp. 23-25).*

wage, not to mention hours of overtime, are significant markers of the value placed on work in most manufacturing, non-management positions.

Other aspects of Japanese management have been more successfully transplanted. For example, Canadian workers can, more or less, see with conviction the logic and practical benefits in the Japanese prescriptions for cleanliness and order learned by all school children as the five S's: *Seiri*—"arrange things properly"; *Seiton*—"keep things in their proper place"; *Seiso*—"clean the workplace"; *Seiketsu*—"maintain the above three principles"; and *Shitsuke*—"practice self-discipline and respect for fellow workers."

On the whole, these practices have been successfully transplanted to the Canadian context, with impressive results in terms of production quality. As an example, the Toyota plant in Cambridge, Ontario, has won an award for producing the highest-quality car in North America, based on a survey of 33 000 new-car owners (Walmsley, 1992: 18). In the U.S., a major study of Japanese "transplants" to the United States has shown that Japanese production methods have been successfully implemented there as well (Florida and Kenney, 1991). A more critical appraisal of this transfer process, however, must raise questions about the cost to labour, particularly given the Japanese aversion to unions, in the long-term struggle between labour and capital for control of the workplace.

Clearly, in the view of the new industrial sociology, control over the labour process is a constant struggle in which workers remain at a disadvantage. Improvements in technology and automation pose increasing challenges to control of the labour process, as do innovative management styles such as that of the Japanese. It is the position of the new industrial sociology, in keeping with its Marxist vision, that the ultimate battle for control between employers and workers will not be won on the shop floor or in the bureaucratic and automated firm. Rather, it will be won in the broader historical struggle in which capitalist relations of production are modified to give a real measure of control to the worker in the form of ownership of the means of production.

In Canada, the prospects for such a victory in the near future are not great. In addition to Japanese corporations taking on an increasingly important role in the auto industry, and the threats that their management style brings to union strength, the larger political and economic context is encouraging for neither workers nor the union movement. Major shifts in certain industries have already taken place, with a loss of jobs to the U.S. and Mexico, where labour is cheaper. Including Mexico and potentially even Central and South America in a "free trade" bloc opens North American industry to an even greater supply of inexpensive labour. Hence, unions are becoming increasingly worried not only about loss of membership but about the threat that foreign labour poses to past gains in terms of wages and benefits. The extraordinary mobility of capital that can see North American plants moved, it seems, almost overnight to more lucrative environments where labour is cheaper, is an even greater threat to the strength of the labour movement in North America than new styles of management. The effects of these changes in the structure of global capital are compounded by innovations in technology that improve productive efficiency while being less dependent on labour. Sustained record rates of unemployment are thus symptoms of a further weakened labour movement.

SUMMARY

We began this chapter with a brief statement on the importance and pervasiveness of organizations in contemporary society. We then discussed the historical development of formal organizations, showing the role of military, religious, economic, demographic, and political factors in their origins and growth.

In the second section we turned our attention to theoretical perspectives on formal organizations. We began by looking at the early work of Durkheim and Cooley, and their examinations of those societal features, such as the division of labour, that have rendered formal organizations possible. Next we discussed the work of Weber on bureaucracy as a specific ideal type of formal organization, and as a particular rational form of authority representing one manifestation of the broader historical process of rationalization in the Western world. We then introduced the Marxian tradition of analysis and its tendency to identify bureaucracy with the state and to believe that both would gradually disappear with the coming of communist society. We also introduced Marx's concept of alienation, a structurally

The More Things Change...

In addition to threats to workers that may result from freer international trade and the movement of capital to countries where labour is cheaper, there are important dynamics taking place within the labour force which have equally serious implications for conditions of work in Canada. This is especially true for women, who are entering the labour force in ever-increasing numbers. In 1991, 58 percent of all women participated in the labour force, compared with 41 percent in 1975 (Ghalam, 1993: 2).

As was pointed out in Chapter 6, Gender Relations, women have made moderate gains in managerial, administrative, and professional jobs. Yet some still do not receive equal pay for work of equal value, and many still encounter the so-called "glass ceiling" that forms an effective barrier to advancement. Moreover, many women are still entering relatively low-paying clerical, service, and sales positions or the traditional "female" positions of teaching, nursing, or related health occupations. In 1991, 71 percent of women in the labour force could be found in one of these occupations—a moderate decrease since 1982, when 77 percent of women were so employed. In 1991, 29 percent of women in the labour force were occupied in clerical jobs, making this the single most popular occupational category for women. Only 6 percent of men held such positions (Ghalam, 1993: 6).

The expansion of the service sector, where wages are generally lower than in industry, and the increase in part-time employment are two other trends in the labour force that have significant implications for Canadian labour. Once again, women are disproportionately affected by these trends (Shea, 1990: 22). In 1989, 59 percent of service workers were women. In addition, more women than men are working part-time, and thus are less likely to be protected by strong union representation and more prone to lay-off and dismissal.

Overall, the general impact of these shifts in the Canadian labour market has been to weaken rather than strengthen the position of labour versus capital. This will likely further delay any real autonomy on the part of the majority of Canadian workers, especially women.

induced condition resulting from capitalist ownership of the means of production, and workers' consequent lack of control over the process and product of their work.

We then looked at early modern views of formal organizations. We began with a discussion of scientific management, which was developed to achieve optimal production rates, especially from industrial workers. On the basis of the simple assumption that individuals are primarily motivated by economic incentives, application of this approach led to the introduction of an increased division of labour and, in particular, the assembly line method of industrial production. Following this, we looked at the chief early critic of scientific management, the human relations school. Its researchers showed that people are motivated by social as well as economic rewards, and that production can be increased by recognizing this broader spectrum of human needs in the organization.

In the last part of this section we looked at modern theories of formal organizations. We first discussed contemporary structuralist approaches to formal organizations, and then focused our attention on negotiated order theory, ethnomethodology, and the new industrial sociology. All concentrate on the process aspects of organizations. The first approach, based upon the symbolic interactionist school, sees formal organizations as emergent structures, always in process and dependent upon the continual bargaining and meaningful dialogue of their participants. Ethnomethodology, on the other hand, represents a more radical departure from conventional sociology. To an ethnomethodologist, all social organization becomes an occasion to uncover the taken-for-granted assumptions, rules, and practices by which social order is constructed and society is made possible. Formal organizations provide yet another such opportunity.

In the last part of the chapter we examined the new industrial sociology, which focuses on the labour process and how historical changes in technology and organization are but variations of the basic condition of alienation of the worker under capitalism. It shows too how workers have continued to struggle to achieve some measure of control over the labour process, and thus have attempted to redeem their most basic need to express their humanity through work. A look at Japanese quality circles and other features of Japanese management styles accompanied the discussion.

Probably more than any other area, organizational analysis remains underdeveloped in Canadian sociology. Indeed, an overarching characteristic of the work in this area is the lack of a comprehensive theoretical model of formal organizations. Such a model would help us draw together in one analysis the historical context of organizations, their subjective and objective dimensions, formal and informal structures, internal micro-level processes, and macro-level structures and links to the broader society. Given the signs represented by at least some of the work presented here, however, this situation may change in future.

QUESTIONS FOR REVIEW AND CRITICAL THINKING

1. Examine the key features of bureaucracy as cited by Weber. How many of these do you see operating at your college or university? At your place of work?

2. To what extent do formal organizations reflect male authority patterns? Do you see changes occurring in the basic structure of authority in organizations as more and more women take up positions of responsibility?

3. You are about to start a new business with fifty employees. What style of management, in terms of the degree of control over the productive process given workers, would you adopt?

4. You are a worker in a new business. Under what style of management would you prefer to work?

GLOSSARY

alienation according to Marx, a distortion built into the structure of capitalism, in which workers are put into conflict with others and lose control of creative capacity, the productive process, and the product of their labour

bureaucracy a special type of formal organization characterized by centralized, hierarchically organized authority. It emphasizes impersonal work relationships, technical knowledge, and rationality.

charismatic authority according to Weber, authority that rests upon the belief that a leader has special qualities and therefore should be obeyed

division of labour an interrelated set of occupational roles or other specializations within a group or society

ethnomethodology as applied to organizations, the theory that examines their taken-for-granted, informal, often unconscious rules

formal organizations social groups with a high division of labour, deliberately and consciously created to achieve specified goals

human relations school the approach to studying organizations that stresses informal work practices and holds that workers are motivated more by social than by economic rewards

ideal type a research strategy that extracts the most prominent or essential features of a social phenomenon. Ideal types in their pure or abstract form are not found in reality, since no one individual case perfectly embodies all essential features.

informal organizations spontaneous interaction usually emerging within formal organizations, based upon unofficial and often implicit rules or understanding

legitimation in Weber's view, the process of rendering power acceptable to those affected by its exercise

mechanical solidarity Durkheim's notion of social integration based on a homogeneity of values and behaviour, characteristic of societies marked by a simple division of labour; similar to precontractual solidarity

negotiated order theory the theory of formal organizations that focuses upon the process by which an organization is socially constructed, through conflicts of interest, dialogue, and regular negotiation on the part of its participants

new industrial sociology the study of formal organizations in which the Marxian concept of alienation remains central. It sees the history of formal organizations as the history of capitalist control of workers and their subsequent alienation.

organic solidarity Durkheim's conception of social integration based on mutual interdependence of social roles; characteristic of societies marked by a highly differentiated, complex division of labour

organization a relatively stable, patterned set of reciprocal relationships and expectations (social roles and norms) that creates the possibility of predictable behaviour

primary group a social group in which relationships are characterized by emotion, warmth, cooperation, and, usually, face-to-face interaction

quality circle a small, voluntary work group that meets periodically to discuss work-related problems and recommend solutions

rationalization Weber's idea that there existed a historical tendency to bring more and more aspects of social life under the rule of rational, efficient, scientific thought

rational-legal authority according to Weber, authority that rests on a belief in rules and the legality of norms

scientific management the theory of organizations stressing economic needs of individuals and workplace organization. Efficiency is believed to result from providing proper economic incentives to workers.

secondary group a social group in which relationships are instrumental, impersonal, rational, and efficient

social contract the idea that society is held together by a rational agreement to cooperate. This contract prevents the chaos of war of all against all.

structuralism the theory that recognizes formal and informal organization, and their relationship to each other. It also looks at the effects of the environment upon the organization, and at economic and social rewards within the organization.

traditional authority according to Weber, authority based upon the conventions of past generations

SUGGESTED READINGS

Hall, Richard

1987 *Organizations: Structures, Processes and Outcomes.* (4th ed.) Englewood Cliffs, NJ: Prentice Hall.

A good contemporary analysis of division of labour, formal structure, and hierarchy in organizations, the book, as the title implies, is sensitive to the need to study structure, process, and outcomes in organizations.

Krahn, Harvey, and Graham S. Lowe (eds.)

1993 *Work, Industry and Canadian Society.* (2nd ed.) Scarborough: Nelson.

A comprehensive introduction to the sociology of work and industry from a Canadian perspective.

Rinehart, James

1996 *The Tyranny of Work.* (3rd ed.) Toronto: Longman.

A concise Marxist analysis of alienation in contemporary work organizations and workers' attempts to assert themselves.

Scott, W. Richard

1987 *Organizations: Rational, Natural and Open Systems.* (2nd ed.) Englewood Cliffs, NJ: Prentice Hall.

An evaluation of the state of organizational analysis, it uses a systems approach to understand the structural features of organizations, and their relationship to their immediate environments and to the larger society.

WEB SITES

http://www.web.net/caw/

Canadian Auto Workers Home Page

This page provides news and views from the point of view of one of Canada's largest and most influential unions.

http://www.palantir.ca/the-alliance/default.html

Alliance of Manufacturers and Exporters Canada

Canada's major business organizations are represented at this page, which provides information on programs, services, trade, and business activity, along with links to other business related sites.

CLEARCUTTING =
ANCIENT TREES SACRIFICED
+ SOIL RUINED
LAND IS LIFE
SAVE TEMAGAMI!
Wilderness Society

CHAPTER

14

Social Movements

Samuel Clark

INTRODUCTION

When we employ the term *social movement*, we are usually referring to a large group of people trying to bring about or resist social change. They may want to make a small change, such as diverting an expressway that threatens an old residential community; or they may want to make a very large change, such as dismantling the existing political system or transforming the established economic order. They may, like pro-lifers or members of the anti-pornography movement, be concerned with values and morals; or they may, like the Social Credit and CCF, be concerned primarily with economic issues.

The first part of this chapter reviews the various ways in which sociologists have studied social movements and related kinds of social behaviour. In it we shall outline five different theoretical approaches to the subject. In the second part we shall turn to an analysis of several specific Canadian social movements, adopting a more descriptive and less theoretical tone.

FIVE THEORETICAL APPROACHES

Collective behaviour

One way of approaching the subject of social movements is to include them in a broader category of human activity known as **collective behaviour**. As sociologists use this term, collective behaviour occurs when a large number of people do not accept some of the prevailing values, norms, and/or leaders in a society. They are unwilling to tolerate things the way they are, or they do not follow normal routines and may even try to persuade others not to follow them as well. They advocate or engage in activities that sociologists would call less "institutionalized" or structured, when compared with conventional, routine behaviour.

As we shall see, sociologists differ widely over the kinds of activity that should be grouped together under the heading of collective behaviour. The most common practice, however, has been to include such diverse phenomena as panics, crowds, fads, crazes, and publics, along with social movements, on the grounds that they are all relatively unconventional. Let us examine these types of behaviour. We will begin with the least institutionalized form of collective behaviour—the panic—and then return to a discussion of social movements, the most institutionalized form.

A **panic** occurs when people are overcome by fear or apprehension, and try to save themselves or their possessions by taking immediate action. The term usually implies that such action is rash and impulsive, and that it involves a flight or withdrawal from a situation perceived to be dangerous. People rush to escape from a burning building; they hurry to remove their savings from a bank that appears to be on the verge of collapse. In most panics there is little if any social control. As a rule, no leaders emerge to direct the collectivity, and there are no generally accepted norms about how people should conduct themselves.

A **crowd** is a temporary grouping of people in physical proximity. No sociologist would claim that all crowds should be placed in the category of collective behaviour. Many crowds are conventional, or casually emerge in the course of conventional behaviour. People waiting for a bank to open or watching a street performer are examples. But some crowds depart sharply from the routine, as when fans pour onto the playing field in the closing moments of a football game, or demonstrators are attacked by a group representing an opposing viewpoint. Many people regard such crowds as highly emotional, irrational, and fickle, but sociologists are no longer happy with such assumptions.

A **fad** is an unconventional practice that spreads rapidly and is adopted in a short period of time by a large number of people. A fad is essentially a social norm, but one that is to some degree unusual and departs from the widely accepted norms in a particular society. The best-known kinds of fads are clothing fashions; but furniture styles, varieties of food, and types of leisure activities may also become fads. By definition, a fad is temporary. If it persists for more than one or two years, we no longer call it a fad, but refer to it as conventional behaviour.

A **craze** is a special kind of fad, one that involves unusually intense commitment and enthusiasm, and is inevitably regarded as very strange and perhaps offensive by other people. Some crazes consist of outlandishly unconventional acts, for example running naked through spectator events (popular in the 1970s), while other crazes involve a commonplace pattern of behaviour carried to excess, such as marathon dancing (popular in the 1930s). In either case, a craze requires a level of commitment that is not necessary for most fads.

A **public** is a large and usually dispersed group made up of persons who share an interest in the same thing. They may hold similar views or they may sharply disagree. Those Canadians who are concerned about the dangers of nuclear energy constitute a public in Canada today, as do those interested in professional hockey, the depletion of the ozone layer, Madonna, poverty, the government deficit, solid waste disposal, drug addiction, or the health-care crisis. We can learn about the views of publics by studying public opinion polls, the results of political elections, calls to phone-in shows, letters to newspapers, media interviews, etc.

Finally, a **social movement**, as we have said, is a large collectivity of people trying to bring about or resist social change. Sociologists generally assume that it is the best organized and most institutionalized type of collective behaviour. Whether or not this is true, social movements are certainly more likely to have associations that coordinate the activities of their supporters. Sociologists now refer to these as SMOs (social movement organizations). The degree of participation of members in SMOs is the most important characteristic that distinguishes social movements from other forms of collective behaviour. These SMOs may even possess a formal or semi-formal structure consisting of leaders, a division of labour, and rules that regulate the conduct of members. Often we find that a large social movement is promoted by a number of SMOs. This has been the case with the women's movement, both in its early phase before and after the turn of the century and in the more recent phase since the 1960s (Prentice et al., 1988: 170; Adamson, Briskin, and McPhail, 1988: 7–8).

A social movement is a large collectivity of people trying to bring about social change. The environmental movement is one prominent example of recent years.

A number of different versions of the collective behaviour perspective have emerged over the years, successively building on one another. We shall discuss several of the most influential theories within this tradition, taking them in order of their appearance in the literature.

Blumer and social contagion

One of the earliest proponents of the collective behaviour approach was Blumer, whose classic statement appeared in 1939. He was largely concerned with the behaviour of unconventional crowds, which he saw as driven by social contagion—a concept previously used by the French writer LeBon (1960 [1895]). In Blumer's words, **social contagion** refers to "the relatively rapid, unwitting, and nonrational dissemination of a mood, impulse or form of conduct" (1951 [1939]: 176). An idea, belief, or perception (often a fear) spreads through a group of people much like an epidemic. This happens as a result of a special kind of social interaction in which human responses become magnified as they move back and forth between interacting persons. You start getting nervous; that makes people standing beside you nervous; this in turn makes you more nervous; and so on.

Blumer called this interstimulation **circular reaction**. He contrasted it with "interpretative" behaviour, in which people do not allow themselves to become excited by one another, but instead thoughtfully interpret the actions of others before acting upon them. Circular reaction, as opposed to interpretative behaviour, generally arises when something (e.g., a natural catastrophe, such as a flood or earthquake) has disturbed the established ways in which people are accustomed to doing things. Or it may occur during those periods of history when people acquire new desires or impulses that cannot be satisfied through conventional behaviour.

Blumer's work has had enormous impact on the subsequent study of collective behaviour, but it has also evoked considerable criticism, especially in recent decades. Two objections in particular stand out. First, there is insufficient empirical evidence to demonstrate that circular reaction is more characteristic of collective behaviour than it is of routine behaviour, or even that such a process really exists. No one has yet developed a means of identifying and measuring circular reaction. Second, the idea of contagion exaggerates the unanimity of collective behaviour; it implies that participants are swept up in a common mood and respond similarly. Many writers have called this assumption into question, suggesting that, even within the same crowd, people may vary in both their attitudes and their behaviour.

Smelser's theory of collective behaviour

Without a doubt, the most ambitious work on collective behaviour in American sociology is Smelser's classic *Theory of Collective Behavior* (1962). While most sociologists influenced by Smelser have not been willing to accept his comprehensive and systematic theory in its entirety, many of Smelser's specific concepts and arguments have proven useful.

For Smelser, collective behaviour is essentially an attempt to alter the social environment. More precisely, he argued that we should apply this term when we find people trying to change their environment on the basis of a special kind of perception called a **generalized belief**. Generalized beliefs are oversimplified notions; like magical beliefs, they portray the world in terms of omnipotent forces, conspiracies, or extravagant promises. For example, a radio broadcast in 1938 called *The War of the Worlds* incited a serious panic in the New York area by creating a generalized belief that the earth was being invaded by beings from another planet.

There are a variety of changes that people might want to make in their social environment. Smelser used this variety to distinguish among different types of collective behaviour, such as panics, crazes, and social movements. He also made a distinction between two types of social movement: "value-oriented" movements that try to change values, and "norm-oriented" movements that seek to change social norms. According to Smelser, whether or not collective behaviour occurs—and if so, what type—depends on a number of conditions, including the strains or problems plaguing a society, the nature of the generalized belief, and the factors that precipitate or provoke the collective behaviour.

Two principal kinds of criticism have been levelled at Smelser's book. The first claims that his theory is little more than a set of concepts related to one another by definition. He does not, critics point out, get very far by defining a value-oriented movement as one in which people seek to change values, and then hypothesizing that a generalized belief among people that a certain value should be changed will give rise to a value-oriented movement. Yet this kind of circular logical deduction forms the bulk of Smelser's theory. The second criticism, which focuses particularly on the notion of generalized beliefs, takes Smelser to task for claiming that the motivations and aims of those who engage in collective behaviour are the illusions of irrational minds. In actual fact Smelser did not take such an extreme position, but it is certainly true that his concept of generalized belief implies a measure of irrationality. Although critics have often distorted Smelser's argument, they have nevertheless identified some serious weaknesses in it.

Emergent norm theory

This theory was developed by Turner and Killian (1957) and deals principally with crowd behaviour, as did Blumer's work. Unlike Blumer, however, they argued that there is a great diversity among those who participate in a crowd. Not all members of a crowd, for example, do the same thing, nor do they all think the same way. Indeed, in many cases a large portion of a crowd has serious doubts about what it is doing, and some might even disagree. And yet they frequently go along, or at least stand back and let the crowd carry on. Why?

The answer, if you accept **emergent norm theory**, is that they are under the impression that most others in the crowd are in agreement. They perceive, rightly or wrongly, that a consensus exists about a specific action that should be taken—for example, that an accused rapist should be lynched, that police arresting a man should be resisted, or that a university building should be occupied. As a result, they may conform to what the crowd is doing. Indeed, sanctions might even be imposed on those who *fail* to do so. When this happens—that is, when people start to conform to the apparent will of the crowd—then we can say that a new norm is emerging.

Game theory

The propositions of game theory are similar to those of emergent norm theory. Again the focus is on crowds, which are presumed to be highly diverse, and to consist of many members who are hesitant to participate (Berk, 1974a; 1974b; Granovetter, 1978). Yet there is a difference in emphasis between these two theories. Those who take a game theory approach are critical of the notion of emergent norms; they claim that it assumes people conform automatically and without thinking. **Game theory**, in contrast, assumes that people behave rationally in crowds. Members of a crowd conduct themselves on the basis of the relative pay-offs and costs of an activity.

According to game theory, the effect of a crowd on an individual is not that it induces an irrational hysteria or euphoria (as most earlier writers implied), but that it alters the pay-offs and costs of certain kinds of behaviour. A crowd can make it easier to do something that is usually costly. The probability, for instance, of getting arrested for breaking into a store, for attacking an immigrant, or for running naked through a classroom is greatly reduced if you are not the only person doing it. Indeed, it is even possible that in the presence of a crowd normally costly activity may be rewarded. One's status in a group could be raised if one were the first to charge a police blockade or to throw a punch at an opposing demonstrator. In extreme cases there might be penalties imposed on those who do *not* follow the crowd. We should not underestimate how often people may go along with collective behaviour out of fear that otherwise they might lose status among their friends, or perhaps even be attacked themselves.

Legacy of the collective behaviour approach

The theories of collective behaviour just discussed have become less acceptable in the past twenty years. Many sociologists are now quick to point out the weaknesses of this tradition. One repeated objection is that most writings on collective behaviour give insufficient attention to **social structure** and the particularities of social structure. They convey the impression that what is important about collective behaviour is much the same in all societies, in any historical period, regardless of differences in social structure.

Second, this theoretical interpretation pays little attention to interest groups and to conflict among such groups. Some sociologists argue that much of what is called collective behaviour is simply the activity of people in conflict; and yet the concept of conflict almost never appears in the collective behaviour literature.

Finally, a number of critics object to the argument that collective behaviour is non-institutionalized. They point out that people may participate in collective behaviour in order to defend values they have held for years, and they may do so in a relatively conventional manner. This is often true of social movements. We shall discuss a good example of this in the second part of this chapter when we look at the historical roots of French Canadian nationalism. Other examples include the pro-life and anti-pornography movements. Even crowds can acquire a conventional character. Rioting can become a tradition, such as the storming of a football field after the final game of the year, or clashes with police stemming from yearly marches or festivities. An example frequently cited by critics of the collective behaviour approach is the food riot that was common in Western Europe during the late eighteenth and early nineteenth centuries. Typically, these rioting crowds followed well-established norms and sought to defend time-honoured values (Rudé, 1964; Thompson, 1971) (see boxed insert on "Orderly Riots"). Cases such as these have led many writers to question the fundamental assumption of this approach: that the distinguishing feature of collective behaviour is its relative non-institutionalization.

Social breakdown

There is a widespread supposition in sociological writings that social unrest occurs when established institutions are disrupted or weakened. As a consequence, the argument goes, people are left "uprooted" and become susceptible to the appeal of a social movement. This notion pervades many different theoretical approaches to our subject, including the collective behaviour tradition just discussed. But we shall treat it separately and call it the **social breakdown approach**.

This theoretical perspective owes a considerable debt to Durkheim's notion of **social integration**, the attachment of individuals to social groups or institutions. We saw in the introductory chapter how this concept could help explain suicides. Durkheim also used it to account for economic conflict in Europe at the turn of the century (Durkheim, 1949: 2). Breakdown arguments may be formulated in several ways. Most common in sociology are the following sorts of assumptions.

1. The probability of social unrest is greatest in those places or countries where intermediate institutions (educational institutions, political parties, trade unions, etc.) are either absent or not functioning properly. These institutions integrate people into society and thus restrain rebellious behaviour. For example, perhaps the reason more social unrest is found in many Latin American countries than in Denmark or Switzerland is that intermediate institutions are stronger in Denmark and Switzerland.
2. The probability of social unrest is high during periods of rapid social change (especially during rapid industrialization and urbanization) because such change disrupts and weakens traditional institutions. This kind of argument has been used to explain political turmoil in many developing countries and former Soviet-bloc countries today.
3. The people most likely to participate in social unrest are those who are relatively alienated, uprooted, or socially maladjusted. They are individuals who, for some reason, are poorly integrated into social institutions, perhaps even dismissed by others as misfits. Activists in the women's movement have been regarded this way, both in its first phase and in the more recent phase. Cartoons at the turn of the century portrayed feminists as unseemly and offensively self-assertive.

It is best to postpone some of the criticisms of this approach until we discuss the remaining theoretical perspectives. At this point we can simply offer one general remark. Although it is true that intermediate institutions may restrain rebellious behaviour, it is also possible for them to promote social unrest. Think of the role that universities, political parties, and labour unions have played in promoting the separatist movement in Quebec.

Orderly Riots

It is now recognized that crowds are not as wild and senseless as was once thought. There is often a logical pattern to their activities, including the choice of victims for their violence. In some cases the behavior of the crowd can be highly structured. E.P. Thompson has argued that English food rioters in the late eighteenth century were following the values and norms of a traditional "moral economy," which dictated that the food requirements of the local population be met before grain could be exported from a district. The conduct of many such crowds could be highly restrained and was often perfectly legitimate within the traditional social order.

It is the restraint, rather than the disorder, which is remarkable; and there can be no doubt that the actions were approved by an overwhelming popular consensus. There is a deeply felt conviction that prices *ought*, in times of dearth, to be regulated, and that the profiteer put himself outside of society. On occasion the crowd attempted to enlist, by suasion or force, a magistrate, parish constable, or some figure of authority to preside over the *taxation populaire*. In 1766 at Drayton (Oxon.) members of the crowd went to John Lyford's house "and asked him if he were a Constable—upon his saying 'yes' Cheer said he sho'd go with them to the Cross & receive the money for 3 sacks of flour which they had taken from one Betty Smith and which they w'd sell for 5s a Bushel"; the same crowd enlisted the constable of Abingdon for the same service. The constable of Handborough (also in Oxfordshire) was enlisted in a similar way, in 1795; the crowd set a price—and a substantial one—of 40s a sack upon a waggon of flour which had been intercepted, and the money for no fewer than fifteen sacks was paid into his hands. In the Isle of Ely, in the same year, "the mob insisted upon buying meat at 4d per lb, & desired Mr Gardner a Magistrate to superintend the sale, as the Mayor had done at Cambridge on Saturday sennight." Again in 1795 there were a number of occasions when militia or regular troops supervised forced sales, sometimes at bayonet-point, their officers looking steadfastly the other way. A combined operation of soldiery and crowd forced the mayor of Chichester to accede in setting the price of bread. At Wells men of the 122nd Regiment began by hooting those they term'd forestallers or jobbers of butter, who they hunted in different parts of the town—seized the butter—collected it together—placed sentinels over it—then threw it, & mix't it together in a tub—& afterwards retail'd the same, weighing it in scales, selling it after the rate of 8d per lb...though the common price given by the jobbers was rather more than 10d.

It would be foolish to suggest that, when so large a breach was made in the outworks of deference, many did not take the opportunity to carry off goods without payment. But there is abundant evidence the other way, and some of it is striking. There are the Honiton laceworkers, in 1766, who, having taken corn from the farmers and sold it at the popular price in the market, brought back to the farmers not only the money but also the sacks; the Oldham crowd, in 1800, which rationed each purchaser to two pecks a head; and the many occasions when carts were stopped on the roads, their contents sold, and the money entrusted to the carter.

Source: *E.P. Thompson, 1971. "The moral economy of the English crowd in the eighteenth century."* Past and Present *(pp. 112–13).*

Relative deprivation

This is the simplest and most straightforward theoretical approach to social movements, and probably comes closest to your own common-sense explanation. It says that people will turn against existing social arrangements when they are most unhappy with them. Concepts such as *discontent* and *dissatisfaction* have been used to describe popular feelings of this kind. According to this point of view, if the level of discontent rises in a society, people are more likely to rebel.

Numerous reasons can be given for increases in discontent. The most generally accepted in sociology is that they occur when people are experiencing **relative deprivation**, or a gap between what people believe they have a right to receive (their expectations) and what they actually receive (their achievements). A popular view today is that people are most likely to participate in social unrest when their expectations for advancement are frustrated. This situation is even more likely to generate unrest than one in which their welfare is actually deteriorating.

The idea of rising expectations has been around for a long time. It is probably most often associated with the French statesman and historian Alexis de Tocqueville, who wrote a famous study on the origins of the French Revolution (1955 [1856]). De Tocqueville's explanation of the Revolution consisted of several different lines of argument, but he is most remembered for his claim that the Revolution occurred when economic conditions were relatively better and political repression less severe than in earlier periods. He also pointed out that support for the Revolution was greatest in comparatively prosperous parts of France. He suggested that prosperity and political freedom, far from satisfying people, simply raise their expectations further. And then he drew the conclusion so often quoted: "Thus the social order overthrown by a revolution is almost always better than the one immediately preceding it, and experience teaches us that, generally speaking, the most perilous moment for a bad government is one when it seeks to mend its ways" (1955 [1856]: 176–77).

In spite of its intuitive appeal, some serious questions can be raised about relative deprivation theory. Again you will find it easier to understand them after we have discussed the collective action approach. Nevertheless, we can make a preliminary observation here. The relative deprivation approach makes the mistake of focusing primarily on the conditions that immediately precede a social movement or a revolt. There is an assumption that, if we can identify and understand discontent just before an uprising, then we can explain the uprising itself. Relative deprivation explanations of the French Revolution concentrate on social conditions and the popular mood as they emerged in the late 1780s. But what if people had been just as dissatisfied in earlier years and yet did not rebel? If this were true, relative deprivation theory might be doing little more than identifying precipitating factors.

Collective action

The fourth theoretical approach contrasts sharply with the first three. It conceives of social movements in a very different way. To begin with, it rejects the concept of collective behaviour and the whole idea that a social movement is relatively non-institutionalized. Instead, it argues that social movements (as well as crowds and many other forms of social unrest) belong to an even broader category of human behaviour called *collective action* (Tilly, Tilly, and Tilly, 1975; Tilly, 1978).

It is necessary to define this term carefully, since it can easily be confused with collective behaviour, which has quite a different meaning. Collective *behaviour* refers to relatively non-institutionalized conduct, that is, conduct that departs from the ordinary and routine. In a Canadian neighbourhood, a group of young people wearing rings in their tongues is collective *behaviour*. In contrast, **collective action** covers both institutionalized and non-institutionalized activity. It can best be defined as the pursuit of a goal or set of goals by a number of persons. Thus it includes a wide range of social phenomena. A terrorist organization kidnapping a diplomat, a group of neighbours cleaning a park, the members of a trade union seeking to raise their wages, a group of students doing a class project—all are examples of collective action.

Collective action is always occurring. Every day people participate in collective efforts of some sort, within their family, at their place of work, or in a voluntary association. But not all collective action is the same. Its character varies tremendously, and this variation is what we should study, according to this theoretical perspective. Each of the preceding theoretical approaches was developed essentially to explain variations in the *amount* of social unrest. Collective action theorists suggest that we can understand much more by studying and explaining variations in the *character* of social unrest. How does collective action differ from one society to another? How does its character change over time within the same society?

Let us take an example. Suppose we are doing a study of the Native peoples' movement in Canada during the 1990s. If we were to adopt one of the theoretical approaches described above, we would ask ourselves why protest among Indians and Inuit increased during this period. We might look for rising expectations in the Indian and Inuit population, or a breakdown in their traditional institutions, or perhaps the emergence of a new norm or generalized belief.

If, on the other hand, we were to adopt a collective action approach, we would be inclined to see the recent movement as part of a tradition of collective action by Native peoples in Canada. We would emphasize that this movement was by no means their first effort to defend their interests. We would point out that Native peoples have a significant history of collective action, especially in the western provinces. We would insist on asking, therefore, how the recent movement differed from earlier movements. How did collective action by Native peoples change in terms of numbers and kinds of people participating, in terms of goals, and in terms of methods used to achieve those goals? In answering these questions we would discover, among other things, that a much younger and generally more educated Native population has become involved, and that the objectives and strategy of collective action have become less defensive and more offensive. We would learn that Natives have developed more skilled leadership, which is able both to organize Indians and Inuit and to defend their legal rights. And we would see that the movement has become more unified across Canada, though many divisions persist.

The rise in collective action by Canada's Native population can be interpreted in many ways. Does it relate to a breakdown in traditional Native institutions? Or to the emergence of more skilled leadership in the Native community? Or is there some other fundamental cause?

In addition to describing changes in the character of collective action, those who adopt this theoretical perspective also try to explain why such changes occur. To do this they examine the underlying social bonds and divisions in the society, and endeavour to understand how these structural conditions change over time. For each historical period one needs to determine the particular combinations of people that are likely to engage in collective action. The job is to identify two kinds of factors: first, *cleavage factors*, which tend to separate people from one another or set them at odds; and second, *integrating factors*, which pull people together in social groups so that they can engage in collective action, whether or not collective action actually occurs. A basic argument of the collective action perspective is that both cleavage and integrating factors are necessary conditions for social movements to occur.

Notice in this regard that the collective action approach has borrowed a concept from the breakdown perspective—the concept of integration—but has broadened its application. When breakdown theorists talk about integration, they mean integration into established groups and institutions that support the status quo. Integration, as far as they are concerned, always impedes social unrest. Advocates of the collective action approach, however, are referring to integration into any kind of group or institution, whether or not it supports the established order. In other words, they assume that social integration forms the basis for any kind of collective action, radical or conservative, rebellious or loyalist. This assumption challenges the basic tenets of the breakdown approach.

The collective action approach also runs counter to relative deprivation theory. Collective action theorists are extremely critical of the emphasis placed on discontent as a condition for social unrest. They insist that discontent, though perhaps a necessary condition, is not a sufficient condition for social unrest. In other words, its presence alone does not ensure that social protest will occur. Even a very high level of discontent is not, by itself, enough to generate protest. Discontent must be mobilized. The people who are dissatisfied have to come together and get organized to act collectively. Their goals must be defined; they must be persuaded to join forces; and their activities have to be coordinated.

The weakness of the discontent approach, according to this alternative line of reasoning, is that it treats mobilization as non-problematic. It assumes that people will automatically mobilize if their level of dissatisfaction is high. The collective action perspective firmly rejects such a supposition, and argues, on the contrary, that mobilization *is* problematic, indeed far more problematic than discontent. Reversing the emphasis, collective action theory claims that enough dissatisfaction is generally present in any society to cause social unrest, provided it can be mobilized. But the mobilization of discontented populations is extremely difficult. Consequently, the argument goes, when protest does materialize, often it is not because the level of dissatisfaction has risen, but rather because conditions for the mobilization of discontented people have improved.

Resource mobilization

An important body of literature within the collective action perspective focuses on the means by which people are mobilized in collective action. The concept of mobilization may be familiar to you. The word is frequently used outside sociology. One often speaks of mobilizing people to fight wars, vote for certain political candidates, search for lost children, collect donations for charity, clean up the environment, and so forth. In all of these contexts one is describing the commitment of resources to a goal or objective to which they were not committed before. At a particular time, people are organized to engage in a specific collective activity. The term **mobilization**, it is essential to understand, is not meant to denote the *creation* of new resources but rather the *transfer* of resources from one kind of collective action to another. A fundamental assumption of the resource mobilization approach is that getting resources transferred is an organizational problem, and as such should be studied using concepts developed for the analysis of social organizations in general.

Let us now identify some more specific conditions that assist mobilization. One is an appropriate *ideology*, or **frame**, that is, a set of beliefs which helps people to interpret and explain their world and which provides the basis for collective action. The term was developed by Goffman (1974), but adapted for the study of social movements by Snow and others (Snow et al., 1986; Snow and Benford, 1988 and 1992). In resource mobilization theory the function of a frame is to identify a problem, diagnose it, attribute blame, and offer a solution. Common perceptions among members or potential members of a movement also facilitate the coordination of their activities and direct them towards a common goal.

An underlying frame can emerge spontaneously (that is, without anyone trying to create it) in a culture, but frames are usually brought to bear on a specific issue consciously and intentionally by social movement leaders. These leaders usually have to struggle against alternative frames promoted by the dominant institutions in a society or by the leaders of opposing groups. The gay and lesbian movement has had a particularly difficult time in struggling with opposing frames in society.

The success of any organizational activity also depends on whether or not members possess an *effective means of communicating* with one another. People have to become aware of their common interests or goals, to agree on action to achieve these goals, and to coordinate their efforts. Discontented groups that possess or are able to acquire channels for communication (particularly access to mass media) are more likely to become mobilized than those without such channels.

A network of *cooperative relationships* serves a similar purpose. A cooperative relationship is a normal social relationship involving some kind of cooperative activity. Examples might be people working as a team on a job, spending free time together in a voluntary organization or social club, or participating in the same youth gang, trade union, church, or political party. If relationships of this kind exist among discontented people, communication is greatly facilitated. Cooperative relationships can also serve as the basis for persuasion and influence. None of the other theoretical approaches gives sufficient attention to the question of how people become involved in a social movement. The answer is that they typically join through the influence of a friend or acquaintance.

Those who have studied resource mobilization have come to place considerable emphasis on the effects of **selective incentives**. The term refers to the benefits that a person can derive from belonging to an association or joining a social movement. These incentives are what motivate people to pay the costs of joining the movement. Generally, the most common selective incentive is fellowship with other activists. In some cases the prestige of a position of leadership in a social movement and the media publicity that may go with it can also be rewarding to participants. Some movements are also able to offer more material rewards, such as salaries, travel expenses, insurance discounts, or appointment to government office.

A social movement is easier to organize if leaders have *financial resources* to promote its activities. Money can buy media time, pay for members to travel, provide compensation for the work that members devote to the cause, and meet other expenses of collective action. Many social movements collapse simply because they run out of money. Those movements that have access to funds, particularly a relatively affluent body of supporters or potential supporters, will survive longer. In Canada, government grants have been an important source of funds for some movements, such as the women's movement and the environmental movement.

As a result of the need for framing, leadership, a means of communicating, cooperative relationships, and financial resources, social movements are much more likely to mobilize successfully if they can build on existing groups, organizations, or institutions. Literature on the emergence of political movements in Western Canada between the wars has generally emphasized this point (Thompson and Seager, 1985: 231, 234; Finkel, 1989: 30). The organizational base of urban movements in Montreal in the 1960s, like most other urban movements in North America, consisted of existing neighbourhood organizations (Hamel, 1991: 101–102). The women's movement that emerged in the late 1960s and early 1970s built on a range of existing or developing organizations. On the more conservative side, the movement built on established organizations, such as the National Council of Women, the Canadian Federation of Business and Professional Women's Clubs, the Canadian Federation of University Women, the National Council of Jewish Women, and the YWCA; on the more avant-garde side, the movement built on the new left movement and student radicalism, including student separatist

Contemporary women's organizations, like the National Action Committee on the Status of Women, build on already existing or developing organizations. Joan Grant-Cummings (centre) is shown here celebrating her victory to become the Committee's new President.

bodies in Quebec (Prentice et al., 1988: 331–34, 346, 354–56; Adamson, Briskin, and McPhail, 1988).

Populations vary in the resources to which they have access. Some social groups lack resources of their own and can only be mobilized if leaders and resources come from the outside; that is, they depend on external resources. Other groups have more of their own internal resources. In the course of its history a movement may develop its own resources and thus become more independent (Pichardo, 1988). Although the Native movement in Canada obtains funds from the government, it has also developed more internal resources as a result of successful land claims.

Again, let us note the difference between this line of reasoning and a breakdown argument. Theories of breakdown, if you recall, assert that a social movement is most likely to occur when social institutions are weak; breakdown theories also claim that those who participate are, as a rule, socially isolated. The collective action literature, in contrast, emphasizes the need for organizational structures to furnish leadership and framing, and to provide channels for communication and a network of co-operative relationships. According to writers on collective action, the breakdown of institutional structures will decrease rather than increase the probability of social unrest, and those who are socially isolated are least likely, not most likely, to participate.

It is also interesting to see differences in the way collective action theory and relative deprivation theory explain the fact that it is not usually the most disadvantaged groups in society that engage in social movements. Relative deprivation theory obviously solves this puzzle by saying that it is relative rather than absolute deprivation that makes people angry. Collective action theorists, in contrast, argue that only people who are better off have the resources to organize a social movement and impress their demands on authorities. This is why the poorest do not rebel.

The Marxist explanation of social movements

The collective action perspective has been significantly influenced by Marx and Marxist writers. Long before sociologists began to talk about collective action or resource mobilization, Marxists had taken what we would now call a collective action approach. During the period in which collective behaviour, breakdown, and relative deprivation were the dominant approaches in North America, Marxism was more influential in Europe.

Marxists have never been interested in all social movements. They like to study revolts that could lead to major overhauls in the whole way in which political and economic functions in a society are carried out—that is, the entire existing order. According to Marxists, such revolts fall into two categories.

The first consists of revolts that lead to the overthrow of feudalism. These are called *bourgeois revolts*. The major two in which Marxists have been interested are the English overthrow of Charles I in the seventeenth century and the French overthrow of Louis XVI in the eighteenth century (in which each king lost his head). Although the French revolt is, of course, called the French Revolution, the English do not like to call theirs a revolution; it is known as the English Civil War. Both revolts supposedly undermined the political power of the feudal lords and increased the political power of a rising bourgeois class. Some Marxists argue that this transfer of political power was a consequence of economic and structural changes taking place in the society, while other Marxists argue that this transfer of political power facilitated the economic structural changes. Neither argument has received much support from non-Marxist historians.

The second category of social movements includes those that Marx hoped would eventually lead to the overthrow of capitalism. These are primarily the labour and socialist movements of the nineteenth and twentieth centuries. As mentioned in Chapter 7, Social Stratification, Marx identified two underlying causes of these movements. First, the capitalist system creates increased exploitation, which intensifies discontent among the mass of the population and opposition to the capitalist system. Second, the capitalist system polarizes classes, bringing workers together physically in crowded urban centres and in factories, providing improved means of communication among them, and in other ways creates better conditions for the mobilization of workers in collective action, including the development of class consciousness. It is this part of the Marxist thesis that has had considerable influence on the collective action approach.

More recently, many Marxists have been influenced by the writings of an Italian communist of the early twentieth century, Gramsci, who spent many years in prison jotting ideas down on paper, which were subsequently published as his *Prison Notebooks*. Gramsci argued that the proletariat needs, even before the fall of capitalism, to build a new order in which it establishes proletarian **hegemony**. The term hegemony refers to the domination of a class or alliance of classes over others, not only economically but politically and culturally. A precondition for the revolution of the working class, in Gramsci's view, is the replacement of bourgeois hegemony with proletarian hegemony. For example, the high value placed on profit and economic growth would have to be replaced by other values in order to undermine bourgeois hegemony. He referred to the achievement of prerevolutionary proletarian hegemony as a "war of position," as opposed to a direct attack on the capitalist system, which he called a "war of movement." One of the significant contributions of Gramsci has been to persuade Marxists of the importance of noneconomic struggles, including ideological struggles, against the existing order.

The collective action approach has called attention to deficiencies in some of the earlier schools of thought. However, it is itself by no means safe from criticism. Not surprisingly, it has been chastised for ignoring discontent or motivation, or for taking them for granted. It is frequently claimed that it over-emphasizes calculating, strategic, instrumental, rational, goal-oriented action, to the neglect of non-calculating, expressive, emotional, impulsive, or passionate human behaviour. It has been lambasted for neglecting culture and psychological forces, and for ignoring the role of social movements in giving people a collective identity and meaning to their lives. And it has been criticized for giving insufficient attention to non-political movements. More surprisingly, it has also been accused of neglecting ideology, major social changes, and structural conditions. (One or more of these criticisms can be found in Scott, 1990; Canel, 1992; Gamson, 1992; and McAdam et al., 1996b.) An important part of the collective action literature could also be accused of taking a functionalist cookbook approach to social movements; for some sociologists, studying social movements has become primarily a matter of developing a list of conditions for their emergence, continuation, spread, and success.

The Marxist perspective on social movements has been criticized primarily on two grounds: first, for over-emphasizing the importance of economic factors in social processes; and second, for neglecting movements that are not based on class. There has been a tendency among Marxists to focus almost all of their attention on working-class movements.

Postmodernism and the new social movements

The first three approaches (collective behaviour, breakdown, and relative deprivation) sought to develop generalizations about social movements that would be valid in most times and places. The collective action perspective generally gives more attention to differences in time and place. Without rejecting generalizations altogether, the fifth approach we shall discuss is also more interested in understanding social movements in a particular time and place.

The particular time and place is the last half of the twentieth century in Western Europe and North America. This approach is based on the assumption that society in this time and place has changed significantly from what it was like in the nineteenth century and the first half of the twentieth. The earlier period is often referred to as "industrial" or "modern" society, while the more recent period is called "post-industrial" or "postmodern" society. This new society has given rise to "new social movements"—movements that result from new conflicts, new problems, or new forces (Touraine, 1971; Luke, 1989; Hamel, 1991). The major new social movements are the student, urban, feminist, environmental, and gay and lesbian movements.

This approach emerged primarily in Europe in reaction to the Marxist approach. It rejected the earlier emphasis on class-based movements, or at least the Marxist emphasis on the working class as the only class that could bring about fundamental change. Thus, this literature was reacting against the previously dominant approach in Europe just as in North America the collective action approach was reacting against the previously dominant approaches—collective behaviour, breakdown, and relative deprivation theory.

The new social movement approach is based on two overlapping bodies of literature regarding the nature of late twentieth-century society: (1) the postmodern literature, and (2) the post-industrial literature.

Postmodernism means a lot of different things to different people, but in sociology it means primarily a rejection of all the scholarship that has sought to explain "modernity" (that is, Western Europe and North America in the nineteenth and twentieth centuries). The scholarship that is rejected includes the major sociological theorists—Marx, Weber, and Durkheim—and all those who have been influenced by their work. Postmodernists focus on differences and discontinuities; they denounce positivism and stress indeterminacy; and they reject large, all-embracing theories, interpretations, or explanations—what they call "metanarratives" or "totalistic" theory, theories that try to explain everything.

This literature is highly diverse, encompassing a large number of contradictory claims about what postmodern society is like. It is possible to find postmodern writers asserting that postmodern people are cynical, sceptical, amoral, individualistic, spontaneous, selfish, self-gratifying, relaxed, and/or light-hearted. Gone is the serious, committed, ideologically motivated class warrior of Marxism; in

TABLE 14.1 Dominant perspectives on social movements in Europe and North America, 1950s to 1990s

	Dominant perspectives in the 1950s, 1960s, and early 1970s	Dominant perspectives in the late 1970s, 1980s, and 1990s
Europe	Collective action, especially Marxism	New social movements
North America	Collective behaviour, breakdown, and relative deprivation	Collective action, especially resource mobilization

postmodern society we have less confidence in the superiority of our convictions. Class, some postmodernists insist, is no longer the principal basis for collective action.

In addition, people who were formerly ignored, who were "voiceless," come to be heard, or should come to be heard, in a postmodern society. There is a rejection of authority and of the separation that has been made between high arts and mass culture. Some postmodern writers suggest that struggles over culture have replaced the struggles over production that dominated modern or industrial society. There is general agreement that postmodern society is disconnected and fragmented (Huyssen, 1986; Connor, 1989; Rosenau, 1992).

According to the *post-industrial* literature, during the last half of the twentieth century there has been a shift in the centre of production from resource extraction (agriculture, mining, lumbering, and so forth) and heavy manufacturing (for example, building trains) to light high-tech industry, communications, and information-based production. The manufacturing working class plays a less important role, white-collar workers and the middle class a more important role in post-industrial production. Growth depends on science and other kinds of knowledge more than on capital accumulation and investment. Domination is achieved not through economic and political repression, but through hyperconsumption, technological progress, seductive integration, and mass manipulation. The mass media and the advertising industry are the major instruments of this post-industrial integration and manipulation (Marcuse, 1964; Touraine, 1971; Luke, 1989).

What all these arguments lead to is the assertion that the distinctive characteristics of post-industrial or postmodern society have created distinctive characteristics in the social movements that have emerged in this society. The new social movements are more concerned with values and culture than were the old working-class movements. Counterculture and opposition to the conventional is praised in a "romance of the marginal" (Connor, 1989: 228). The pop art movement sought to collapse the distinction between high and low art, and between art and everyday life (Huyssen, 1986). Most new social movements are anti-authority. Although there is considerable disagreement on this point, some have argued that new social movements are less political than the old movements. There is more agreement that they are less economic. New social movements represent the formerly unrepresented, often involving a variety of groups and issues. The middle class plays a greater role than the employed working class. New social movements are characterized by spontaneity, fragmentation, decentralization, and discontinuity. These characteristics are well illustrated in the Montreal urban movements studied by Hamel (1991 and 1995).

The most common criticism of the new social movement approach is that the so-called "new social movements" are not so new. Feminist movements, youth movements, and even the environmental movement can be found in earlier periods. Many writers have pointed out as well that not all movements in the nineteenth and early twentieth centuries were working-class movements; there is nothing new about non-class movements. It has also been claimed that new social movements are not, in general, less political than earlier social movements. Critics have also charged that differences among new social movements have been disregarded. And the new social movement literature has been attacked for ignoring class (Scott, 1990; Canel, 1992; Adam, 1993; Stanbridge and Clark, forthcoming).

A major criticism of both postmodernism and the new social movement literature is that it is ethnocentric, specifically Eurocentric, and that it is fixated on middle-class experiences (Gamson, 1992). Both journalistic and academic literature on the fact of tattooing, for example, have been castigated for ignoring class differences in tattooing and for being taken in by the promoters of middle-class tattooing, who pretend that respectable and artistic tattooing is replacing ugly and offensive "biker" tattooing (DeMello, 1995).

A final word in defence of each approach

Like the people they study, sociologists are prone to fads and fashions. As already indicated, some of the above approaches are now out of favour. This is not to be deplored so long as their contributions are not cast aside. It would be a mistake, for example, to dismiss the abundant research carried out by students of collective behaviour just because we cannot accept certain parts of their argument. In particular, it would be a serious error to throw away the concept of institutionalization just because we find some collective behaviour that seems not to be less institutionalized than routine behaviour. Social behaviour does in fact vary in its degree of institutionalization. Panics, crowds, and social movements may not always be less institutionalized than the behaviour we encounter daily, but most often they are. What we need to do is study the degree of institutionalization of any social activity in which we are interested, whether it has generally been classified as collective behaviour or not. Institutionalization should be taken, not as a given, but as a variable that we want to measure and explain, and whose consequences we need to understand. Whatever its errors and omissions, collective behaviour theory does make a contribution to our knowledge on the subject.

Similarly, theories that explain social movements as a result of social breakdown should not be totally rejected. This literature is not so much incorrect as incomplete. It is perfectly reasonable to assume that social disorganization or breakdown raises the probability of protest or rebellion, so long as we specify the social ties that are breaking down. If people are well integrated into institutions that support the established order, then there is indeed little chance that they will engage in movements that challenge that order; and the likelihood that they will rebel against established institutions does increase if their integration into these institutions weakens. What breakdown theory has ignored, as we have seen, is that people have to be integrated into groups of some kind in order to be mobilized for collective action. People who are wholly disorganized, completely uprooted, and alienated may engage in anti-social behaviour, but they will not form social movements. Thus, the ideal condition for rebellious action is the integration of a large number of people into strong institutions or structures that are themselves "alienated" from the established order (Pinard, 1968).

Although relative deprivation cannot alone account for the rise of a social movement, we must somehow explain motivation. Motivating factors are more diverse than most sociologists have recognized. We need to take into account not only relative deprivation, but also other factors that could motivate a person to join a movement, such as moral outrage, an expectation that the movement will be a success, and selective incentives. We must above all explain what makes people angry, because anger is usually the major reason that people engage in protest activities. This is what relative deprivation theory tried to do, and to a considerable extent it succeeded, if at the expense of ignoring much else.

Many of the criticisms that have been made of the collective action perspective apply primarily to the resource mobilization approach, not to the collective action perspective as a whole. This is true of the claim that the approach over-emphasizes calculating, strategic, and instrumental action, that it neglects ideology, macroprocesses, and structural conditions, and that it takes a functionalist cookbook approach to social movements. Many of the criticisms of the collective action perspective can be overcome, and some are being overcome. There is an increasing recognition in the resource mobilization literature of the importance of motivation and culture (McAdam et al., 1996a).

The major strength of the collective action perspective is that it gives more emphasis to the uniqueness of societies than do the theoretical orientations to which it was reacting. It seeks most of all to identify and explain what is dissimilar about collective action at different times and in different places. Writers in this perspective would insist that most of what is significant about collective action varies from one society to another.

In an important respect this is the major strength of the new social movement approach as well. It is true that the writers in this school have ignored movements outside Western Europe and North America, but at least they have never claimed that they are explaining all social movements. What they have wanted to do is to develop a perspective that would help them best understand the movements that were emerging in the society in which they lived. They believed this could not be done with general theories.

CANADIAN SOCIAL STRUCTURE AND COLLECTIVE ACTION

The remainder of this chapter is devoted to social movements in Canada and the social conditions underlying them. We shall not endeavour to apply or test the theoretical approaches discussed above. We shall, however, adopt the general framework provided by the collective action approach. To help understand the conditions that have given rise to social movements in Canada, we shall look for sources of integration and cleavage in the social structure. A **social cleavage** is a division based on age, class, ethnicity, etc., that may result in the formation of distinct social groups. An effort will be made to explain how the social structure has provided certain groups in the Canadian population with the solidarity and resources necessary for building and maintaining collective action.

Although similar social cleavages can be found in many societies, every society is unique in two ways. First, the relative importance or intensity of different types of cleavage varies from one society to another. In some societies, class cleavages are more divisive than ethnic cleavages, while in others the reverse is true. Second, the relationship among cleavages differs from one country to another. In some societies, people who belong to the same social class may be opposed to one another because they belong to different ethnic groups. In other societies, ethnicity may coincide with class divisions and serve to reinforce them. The final "topography" that emerges from these patterns will be unique to a particular society and will determine the character of its collective action.

In Chapter 7, Social Stratification, we listed a number of patterns of differentiation that underlie Canadian social structure and give rise to unequal ranking or status hierarchies. Some of these same patterns of differentiation also divide Canadian society into identifiable groups on which collective action has been based. We shall outline, very briefly, those patterns of differentiation that have had the most effect on collective action.

Age In virtually all societies, profound differences exist in attitudes, lifestyle, social relationships, and access to resources between the young and old. This is no less true in Canada. Indeed, age differentiation may be more pronounced in an advanced industrial society such as ours than in other types of societies as a result of changes in family structure and the expansion of educational institutions that intensify and prolong differences between youth and older members of the population. These educational institutions also serve to increase the integration of young people as a group by helping to bring them together and providing a milieu for the development of youth cultures. This integration in turn can provide the basis for the mobilization of collective action by young people, and on their behalf. A consequence, most obvious in the 1960s and 1970s, has been the appearance of a variety of youth movements in Canada and in several other industrialized societies. Movements by the elderly have been less common, but are not unknown. An illustration in Canada was the mobilization of large numbers of people against the de-indexing of the Canadian old-age pension in 1985. As their proportionate size in the population grows, we may see more political activity by senior citizens, but thus far collective action by the elderly has been limited.

Class In Canada, as in most societies, class has a significant effect on collective action. This is especially the case whenever people of the same class position have developed integrative structures that help to mobilize their collective activities. Labour unions can provide such integration. The long and bitter history of labour strife is indicative of the great impact of class differentiation on collective action in this country. Also important is the influence that class has on collective action when it coincides with other major sources of social differentiation. The labour movement in Quebec, for example, owes much of its strength to a special combination of ethnic, regional, and class solidarities.

Ethnicity In Chapter 8, Race and Ethnic Relations, we discussed in detail the numerous and often deep racial and ethnic divisions found in Canadian society. It is frequently the case that people who belong to different ethnic groups also differ in attitudes, interests, and social relationships, while those who belong to the same ethnic group often share these attributes. The result, as we shall see in a moment, can be an extremely effective social base for the organization of collective action.

Region A number of factors have served to create deep regional divisions in Canada. The vast geographical expanse of the country, the fact that different parts of it were settled at different times, and the economic disparities that exist among regions have all promoted regional cleavage. Modern means of communication and considerable mobility in the population serve to mitigate these divisions to a degree, but there remain sharp social and cultural differences from one part of the country to another. In some cases there is also, within a particular region, a strong measure of social cohesion and group feeling. Collective action in Canada has repeatedly shown signs of these regional divisions and solidarities.

Rural or urban residence The cleavage between rural and urban groups usually diminishes in advanced industrial societies as the two sectors become culturally and economically assimilated. There always persists, however, a fundamental opposition in interests between rural and urban populations. That division remains especially pronounced in Canada as a result of our tendency to exploit or abandon rather than transform many of our rural areas as the country becomes more industrialized. One can find large rural areas in Canada that are economically depressed, relatively depopulated, and socially isolated from the larger urban society. Inevitably, rural–urban differences have had an impact on collective action in Canada.

Gender This is the most unpredictable of these six patterns of differentiation. On the basis of their sex, women are assigned separate roles in our society, most obviously those of housekeeper and child-raiser. On the same basis, they were once denied equal political and economic rights. On the other hand, men and women typically share attitudes, interests, and social bonds through the marriage and kinship structure. These have served to mitigate the gender cleavage, and at the same time to undermine the integration of women as a group by creating strong cross-gender ties. Consequently, in spite of the feminist movement, women are far from united in collective action.

We shall now provide a further discussion of two of the above patterns, the regional and ethnic divisions. We shall consider the way in which these sources of integration and cleavage have shaped the character of collective action in Canada.

Regional cleavage

Geographical disunity in Canada has resulted not only from the vast distances that separate people living in different parts of this country, but also from the fact that, for various reasons, regional variations have tended to coincide with other kinds of differences.

Most obviously, regional diversity coincides with economic functions. Some parts of the country are manufacturing centres; others are largely agricultural; and still others supply natural resources. In addition, and partly as a consequence, there are substantial inequalities in wealth and income from one province to another, particularly between the West and the Atlantic region (see Chapter 7, Social Stratification). Further, ethnic groups are not evenly distributed throughout the country. The most obvious concentration is that of French Canadians in the province of Quebec, but we can find other patterns of variation. For example, outside of Quebec, the percentage of persons claiming British ancestry varies widely, from close to 90 percent in Newfoundland and Prince Edward Island to about half in Manitoba and Saskatchewan. The regional cleavage is also associated with rural/urban differences; certain provinces are much less urbanized than others. In 1991 the percentage of the population living in rural areas ranged from 63 percent in the Northwest Territories, 37 percent in Saskatchewan, 41 percent in the Yukon, and over 40 percent in each of the Atlantic provinces to only 18 percent in Ontario and 22 percent in Quebec (Statistics Canada, 1992, *1991 Census of Canada*).

Given this variation, it is not surprising that values and attitudes have differed from one province to another. Public opinion surveys have routinely shown significant differences among provinces on a wide range of issues. A poll conducted in 1992 indicated that the percentage of persons favouring a decrease in immigration ranged from 58 percent in the Atlantic provinces to 35 percent in Quebec (Canadian Institute of Public Opinion, 1992).

These and other differences among regions have had a profound impact on the character of collective action in this country. Social cleavage between regions, combined with social integration within regions, has resulted in collective action that tends to be weak and divided nationally, while often strong regionally. Canadians have considerable difficulty getting together and doing things as a nation. Most organizations to which they belong, whether political, economic, or social, are geographically disconnected. Inevitably, social movements tend to attract support from specific parts of the country. Even a national movement, such as the women's movement, can vary greatly from one province to another (Adamson, Briskin, and McPhail, 1988: 8, 28). And many social movements in Canada have directly reflected the grievances and animosities that some areas have felt towards others.

Prairie movements

The best-known regional movements in Canadian history are those that appeared primarily in the Prairie provinces between the two world wars. They are by no means the only movements with a regional basis, but since they have received the most scholarly attention, we shall illustrate the effect of regional cleavage on collective action by briefly describing these movements.

The Prairie movements emerged on a social foundation that was formed by divisions of both class and region. A highly diversified population settled in the Prairie provinces in the late nineteenth and early twentieth centuries; yet out of it there soon developed a remarkably unified social group loosely based on agriculture. We must be careful, however, not to overstate this point. In addition to conflicts of interest between farmers and other sectors, there were significant divisions among farmers themselves, most notably as a consequence of differences in the size of their farms, type of agriculture, and their ethnic origin. We should also recognize that other social groups contributed to Prairie movements besides farmers. Still, farmers were critical and, in comparison with most other groups in Canadian society, those in the Prairies possessed considerable solidarity and cohesion. They were brought together by common problems and a common position in the social structure. The majority were engaged in the production of the same crop, namely wheat, and were therefore simultaneously affected by its success or failure. Their fortunes rose and fell collectively, and this served to integrate them as a group, facilitating their political mobilization.

At the same time, other factors divided them from the rest of the country. No doubt the great physical distances that separated Prairie people from those living in other parts of Canada helped to alienate them. More important, however, was a fundamental opposition of interests. Western farmers were pushed, as a result of tariffs, to buy expensive goods manufactured in Eastern Canada, yet they had to sell their wheat on an unprotected international market. Furthermore, the marketing of this wheat was, in their perception at least, controlled by urban and eastern business interests, and the terms of trade were maintained in favour of those business interests.

The first significant collective effort by western farmers was the struggle against the grain elevator companies. The Territorial Grain Growers' Association was formed just after the turn of the century and became the Saskatchewan Grain Growers' Association in 1905. This body, along with other cooperative organizations established in this period, formed an effective base for increased political activity by farmers, which accelerated around 1910 and was directed primarily against tariffs. One of the most active new political associations was the United Farmers of Alberta, which brought together two smaller bodies in 1909. There was also the Canadian Council of Agriculture, which pressed the federal government for tariff reform.

The Progressives The war effort helped to restrain the call for tariff reductions, but Prairie residents expected that, once the war was over, substantial reductions would be legislated. When this did not occur, a new wave of agitation developed. A dissatisfied group of politicians formed the National Progressive Party, which shocked the nation in 1921 by capturing sixty-five seats in the House of Commons.

Nationally, the Progressive movement did not survive long as an independent political force. Part of the explanation usually given for this decline

There is a long history of collective action on the Canadian Prairies. The general strike that shut down the city of Winnipeg for six weeks in 1919 was one of the most dramatic instances.

emphasizes two factors: the Progressives were split into two groups, known perhaps simplistically as the "Alberta faction" and the "Manitoba faction." While this lack of unity is certainly part of the story, we should not overlook the fact that the Progressives, though by no means restricted to one region of the country, drew their strength primarily from the Prairie provinces. In British Columbia, Quebec, and the Maritimes, the Progressives had little support; in Ontario the movement's objectives were different from those in the west (Thompson and Seager, 1985: 31–34). They could, and in fact did, win some significant concessions from the major parties; but—given the regional distribution of their support—they could not themselves become a major national party. By 1926 the National Progressive Party largely had been absorbed into the Liberal Party.

At the provincial level the situation was altogether different. Within certain provinces farmers and their allies were able to dominate politics and elect governments generally committed to representing their interests. This became true in all three Prairie provinces in the 1920s: farmers' parties were elected in Alberta and Manitoba and a Liberal government sympathetic to agrarian interests held power in Saskatchewan. As a consequence, while considerable dissatisfaction with the federal government persisted, western farmers were less discontented with their own provincial governments in this period. They remained so until the Great Depression.

Social Credit In 1935, under the leadership of former preacher William Aberhart, a new political party—the Social Credit Party—took power in the province of Alberta. It is not hard to understand why a movement of this kind should find support among self-employed farmers, particularly during a severe economic depression. Obtaining credit—always a serious problem for farmers—was especially difficult at this time, and it was primarily this difficulty that Aberhart's movement promised to solve. The theory of social credit assumes that economic stagnation results from a shortage of credit in an economy, and that this shortage can be overcome by the distribution of monthly cash dividends to all citizens. The program appealed as well to other classes in western society, particularly the urban working class, whose members were also suffering from the Depression (Bell, 1990).

Aberhart charged that eastern business élites were controlling and manipulating the economy to serve their interests. They tried, he claimed, to restrict the supply of money and to create a dependence on credit institutions from which they profited. As fashioned by Aberhart, social credit ideology was unmistakably anti-establishment (Finkel, 1989: 34–35). It appealed to western farmers and workers who wanted to believe that their troubles resulted from the control of the economy by eastern financial interests.

CCF At approximately the same time as Social Credit, a very different kind of movement also appeared in the west. The Co-operative Commonwealth Federation (CCF) was founded in the 1930s and eventually won a provincial election in Saskatchewan in 1944.

The surprising thing about the CCF is that its official platform was socialist, which seems a curious ideology with which to seek the support of self-employed farmers. And yet a socialist wing had been active within the farmers' movement in Saskatchewan well before the arrival of the CCF, so the CCF did not come to Saskatchewan as a foreign import. Moreover, the CCF carefully presented its program to appeal to farmers. It de-emphasized those parts of socialism that would offend their sense of free enterprise, while it stressed aspects that were plainly in their interest. The party was forced, for example, to moderate and eventually abandon its call for land nationalization, but most farmers were not put off by the idea of state regulation of the marketing of their produce, or by the nationalization of transportation and natural resources.

We should be careful not to attach too much significance to ideological differences between the Social Credit party and the CCF. Though these differences were real, in each case the program was moulded to suit the interests and demands of western farmers. Moreover, sharp differences in the ideologies of two new parties formed in two western provinces do not necessarily mean that there were great ideological differences between the people of each province. To argue, for example, that most people in Alberta were further to the right than those in Saskatchewan is to ignore the fact that many of these same Albertans voted for a radical farmers' party (the United Farmers

Regina Manifesto

One of the most interesting and significant documents in Canadian history is the CCF program adopted at the First National Convention in Regina, July 1933. Here are the opening paragraphs of that declaration.

The CCF is a federation of organizations whose purpose is the establishment in Canada of a Co-operative Commonwealth in which the principle regulating production, distribution, and exchange will be the supplying of human needs and not the making of profits.

We aim to replace the present capitalist system, with its inherent injustice and inhumanity, by a social order from which the domination and exploitation of one class by another will be eliminated, in which economic planning will supersede unregulated private enterprise and competition, and in which genuine democratic self-government, based upon economic equality will be possible. The present order is marked by glaring inequalities of wealth and opportunity, by chaotic waste and instability; and in an age of plenty it condemns the great mass of the people to poverty and insecurity. Power has become more and more concentrated into the hands of a small irresponsible minority of financiers and industrialists and to their predatory interests the majority are habitually sacrificed. When private profit is the main stimulus to economic effort, our society oscillates between periods of feverish prosperity in which the main benefits go to speculators and profiteers, and of catastrophic depression, in which the common man's normal state of insecurity and hardship is accentuated. We believe that these evils can be removed only in a planned and socialized economy in which our natural resources and the principal means of production and distribution are owned, controlled, and operated by the people.

The new social order at which we aim is not one in which individuality will be crushed out by a system of regimentation. Nor shall we interfere with cultural rights of racial or religious minorities. What we seek is a proper collective organization of our economic resources such as will make possible a much greater degree of leisure and a much richer individual life for every citizen.

This social and economic transformation can be brought about by political action, through the election of a government inspired by the ideal of a Co-operative Commonwealth and supported by a majority of the people. We do not believe in change by violence. We consider that both the old parties in Canada are the instruments of capitalist interests and cannot serve as agents of social reconstruction, and that whatever the superficial differences between them, they are bound to carry on government in accordance with the dictates of the big business interests who finance them. The CCF aims at political power in order to put an end to this capitalist domination of our political life. It is a democratic movement, a federation of farmer, labor, and socialist organizations, financed by its own members and seeking to achieve its ends solely by constitutional methods. It appeals for support to all who believe that the time has come for a far-reaching reconstruction of our economic and political institutions. ...

Source: *Walter Young, 1969.* The Anatomy of a Party: The National CCF, MCMXXXII-LXI. *Toronto: University of Toronto Press (pp. 304–5).*

of Alberta) in the early 1920s, when the Liberal Party still held power in Saskatchewan. And there is certainly no compelling reason to believe that Saskatchewan voters were indeed endorsing socialism when they voted for the CCF in 1944.

The significance of these movements does not lie in their respective ideologies; it lies in their relationship to the social groups on which they were based. Both Social Credit and the CCF, as they took shape in Western Canada, should be seen as collective efforts by members of a particular region to find political formations that represented their special needs. These needs were markedly different from those of most other Canadians and were not—at least in their eyes—being met by the national political parties.

This same sentiment was responsible for the emergence of a new political force in the west during the late 1980s. Under the leadership of Preston Manning, the Reform Party of Canada was founded to give westerners an alternative to the major political parties. As long as the Liberals under Trudeau formed the government in Ottawa, westerners could vote for Progressive Conservatives in order to express their dissatisfaction with Ottawa. When, however, the Conservatives assumed office in Ottawa and took actions that were unpopular in the west, such as introducing the Goods and Services Tax and supporting demands of Quebec, some westerners turned to the Reform Party. Its first major breakthrough was the election of Deborah Grey to the House of Commons in a March 1989 by-election, followed later in the year by the success of Stanley Waters in a poll to choose a nominee for a Senate appointment. The founders and early supporters of the movement espoused an unmistakably right-wing ideology, but the party has broadened its policies in an effort to attract voters further to the left, including discontented supporters of the NDP. In the federal election of 1993, the Reform Party won fifty-two seats, all but one of them in Western Canada.

Ethnic cleavage

Ethnic diversity in Canada coincides with many other kinds of differences. We have already discussed in Chapter 7, Social Stratification, variations in socio-economic status found among ethnic groups. We have also observed a tendency for ethnic groups to be distributed unevenly among provinces. And in Chapter 8, Race and Ethnic Relations, we saw that, even within the same city, considerable ethnic residential concentration is likely. These differences in socio-economic status and residential patterns would alone be enough to create social distances between members of distinct ethnic groups. But additional factors, particularly dissimilarities in values, have served to intensify ethnic cleavages in Canadian society.

The consequences of ethnic divisions for the character of collective action in Canada are evident at almost every level. The country abounds in ethnic institutions—schools, religious groups, clubs, and other voluntary associations. Many social movements are affected by ethnic diversity. For example, the current women's movement has not overcome divisions between French-speaking and English-speaking women, and separate organizations have been formed for some minorities, such as Native women and black women (Prentice et al., 1988: 355–56, 396–98, 405).

In addition, a number of social movements in Canada have arisen from ethnic divisions. The largest and most successful are nationalist movements in the province of Quebec. We have already mentioned some of the most important differences (in education, occupation, and income) that have helped to reinforce divisions between French- and English-speaking Canadians. We could add to this list differences in language, religion, and values.

Native peoples

Great as the cleavage is between the French and the English in Canada, it is less than the cleavage that isolates the Indians and Inuit from the rest of the society. Almost whatever variable is being considered—cultural values, income, occupation, or geographical separation—differences between Native peoples and other Canadians are no less, and indeed are often greater, than differences separating the French and the English.

The history of collective action by indigenous peoples is, as noted earlier, much longer than is often assumed. It is important not to underestimate the courage and sophistication of Native leadership in the past. Still, all things considered, what is perplexing is the weakness and ineffectiveness of Native movements until the 1990s. Why was this the case? Why did the English–French cleavage generate more significant collective action than the much greater cleavage between Native peoples and other Canadians?

Part of the answer is simply numbers. When the British took control of Quebec in the eighteenth century, the Native population vastly outnumbered the French in the territories that now make up Canada. Since then, however, the French have generally enjoyed strong population growth, while Native peoples have, until recently, suffered a serious demographic decline. As a result, the French have had the benefit of much greater numerical strength than the Native population.

Yet the French have had other advantages as well. We need to think back to the theoretical approaches discussed earlier and recall the factors that underlie collective action. These include not only cleavage factors, but also integrating factors, which pull people together and make it possible for them to organize in collective action. If people are to engage in collective action, it is not enough for them to be separated by cleavage factors from other members of society; they must also be united among themselves. Only in this way can they be mobilized.

The main obstacle to collective action by Indians and Inuit was a distinct lack of such integrating factors. Separated and alienated from other Canadians as they have been, they did not themselves form a cohesive group. They were subdivided most obviously by language and cultural differences, but also by geographical dispersion and artificially imposed administrative distinctions (e.g., status versus non-status Indians, and treaty versus non-treaty Indians). Until the 1990s, considerable factionalism characterized collective action by Indians and Inuit in Canada. Put together with several other organizational weaknesses (the absence of a large educated middle class to provide leadership, a lack of material resources, and political apathy within the indigenous population), this factionalism allowed other Canadians, until lately, to rule the Indians and Inuit without serious opposition.

Gradually, however, the organizational basis for Native collective action has improved. Ironically, the assimilation of Native peoples into Canadian society has promoted integrating factors. Linguistic and cultural differences within the Native population have declined. More advanced means of communication and transportation have made it easier for Native peoples in different parts of the country to coordinate activities. National conferences of Native peoples have become more common. As already noted, a more educated and more effective leadership has emerged. The financial resources of Natives have increased through state assistance and favourable land claims. And Native peoples have more and more come to see themselves as a unified group, even though historically that had not been the case. Native peoples were just as discontented fifteen years ago, thirty years ago, and even sixty years ago as they are now. What has changed is their organizational capacity to engage in more aggressive and national collective action than they could have in the past.

Nevertheless, the social conditions for collective action have been more favourable for French Canadians for most of this century, and to a large extent remain so. Whereas Native peoples are dispersed across the country, most francophone Canadians live in one province. Whereas Native people comprise a great many cultural groups, francophones generally belong to a single cultural group, which has its own historical tradition, a unifying religion, and a common language. And whereas Native peoples are separated into a great number of different communities with unconnected institutions, francophones possess numerous unifying institutional structures, including their own provincial government. To be sure, major sources of cleavage exist within Quebec society, most notably class and generational divisions. However, there has always been sufficient cultural and structural integration to facilitate the mobilization of effective collective action.

Quebec nationalism

There is a widespread misconception among English-speaking Canadians that nationalism in Quebec is something new. Unless defined very narrowly, French Canadian nationalism can be traced back to before Confederation. The movement for responsible government that emerged in Upper and Lower Canada in the first half of the nineteenth century was, for French Canadians, both a campaign for reform and a struggle against British political domination. Although Confederation tied French Canadians to the rest of British North America, it also gave them a separate province in which they constituted the majority, and in which, it was assumed, they would be able to protect their distinct culture. Indeed, the participation of francophones in Confederation can legitimately be interpreted as an expression of French Canadian nationalism, albeit a nationalism based on totally different premises than that found in Quebec today.

Confederation certainly did not mean a decline in the determination of French Canadians to protect their society from assimilation into the larger English-speaking culture. Almost throughout the period since Confederation, nationalism as an ideology has been popular among the Québécois. It has been articulated and advanced by countless French Canadian intellectuals, and has been espoused, in a diversity of forms and with varying degrees of emphasis, by most Quebec politicians. Until the 1950s, Quebec nationalism tended to be conservative and at times oriented towards preserving the past. Although the

Henri Bourassa was an ardent dual nationalist. He believed strongly in both provincial autonomy and Canadian independence from Great Britain.

material benefits of industrialization were welcome, ***la survivance***—the survival of French Canada as a distinct society—was to be achieved primarily by keeping people loyal to traditional values. It was assumed that support of the traditional culture was the best way to maintain a distinct French Canadian society. It was also generally assumed that this survival could be guaranteed within Confederation simply by guarding the provincial rights that Confederation had granted.

Throughout this period, the majority of French Canadian nationalists hesitated to advocate separation from the rest of Canada. Many were "dual" nationalists, who stood for both provincial autonomy and the dissociation of Canada from Great Britain. The most representative advocate of this brand of nationalism was Henri Bourassa. Although Bourassa was not opposed to the industrialization of Quebec, the underlying theme of his politics was the preservation of traditional French Canadian culture, in particular its religion. At the same time, he was an ardent Canadian. In 1903 his adherents organized the *Ligue nationaliste*, with the double objective of promoting the independence of Canada and safeguarding the rights of French Canadians.

Language, Guardian of the Faith

Henri Bourassa is widely regarded as the greatest nationalist leader in the history of French Canada. His nationalism emphasized the importance of preserving traditional Quebec culture, above all its religion. In La langue, gardienne de la foi, *he asserted that the French language embodies the Catholic religion more than does any other language and that this gives French Canadians a unique mission in the world.*

Our special mission, we French Canadians, is to carry on in America the struggle of Christian France, and to defend against all opposition, if necessary against France herself, our religious and national heritage. This heritage does not belong to us alone: it belongs to the whole of Catholic America, and constitutes a centre from which radiates inspiration and light; it belongs to the entire Church, for which it is the principal source of strength in this part of the world; it belongs to all of French civilization, for which it is the only port of refuge and mooring place in this immense sea of Saxon Americanism.

We are the only ones, let us not forget, who are capable of fulfilling this mission in America. French Canadians and Franco-Americans represent the only large group, the only nation of the French race and language outside Europe. ...

But if we want to defend our intellectual and national heritage, which belongs to French people everywhere, we must do so without disturbing the harmonious relationship between our social duties and our divine calling.

Let us fight not merely to preserve our language, or to preserve our language and our faith; let us fight for our language in order better to preserve our faith.

Source: *Henri Bourassa, 1918.* La langue, gardienne de la foi. *Montreal: Bibliothèque de l'Action française (pp. 49–51).*

Writers such as Jules Paul Tardivel and Lionel Groulx were representative of a more separatist brand of nationalism. Abbé Groulx was the most influential nationalist intellectual after Henri Bourassa. A historian at the University of Montreal, he articulated a nationalism that was conservative and religious. He extolled the destiny of the French Canadian "race," stressing the importance of their traditional culture and calling on his people to resist the forces of modernization that were threatening them.

Yet, as Abbé Groulx himself came to realize, it was not in fact possible for French Canada to insulate itself from the forces of modernization. During the very years in which he lived and wrote, the kind of society he lauded was being undermined as a rural decline and growing urbanization seriously threatened the traditional nationalist strategy. In various ways, modernization brought French Canadians into greater contact with Anglo culture. It also created monstrous pressures on them to assimilate into the English-speaking world, at least if they wanted to enjoy the material benefits of industrial society.

Although this process actually began around the turn of the century, the nationalist strategy for keeping French Canada distinct did not reflect the change until much later. Even when nationalist leaders became conscious of the seriousness of the threat—and they certainly were conscious of it by the time of the Depression, if not earlier—they were still reluctant to alter their approach to *la survivance*. In the 1930s and 1940s they experimented with various ideas, but they did not come up with a realistic solution to the danger that urbanization and industrialization posed.

The reasons for the lag in the development of their thinking are complex, but certainly a major factor was the conservatism of French Canadian élites, even while urbanization and industrialization were taking place in their province. Members of the élite continued to look to the past for the model of the ideal society, and they generally opposed any significant expansion of the public sector, particularly if it threatened to interfere with the traditional functions of the Church in spheres such as education and welfare. This "anti-statism" is most often associated with the Union nationale government of Maurice Duplessis, premier of Quebec from 1936 to 1939 and again from 1944 to 1959. More than any other individual, Duplessis symbolizes the era of conservative nationalism in Quebec.

Meanwhile, changes in the social structure in Quebec continued to undermine the traditional culture. By 1961 the number of people of French origin who could be classified as rural had fallen to 29 percent, and only 13 percent were living on farms (Posgate and McRoberts, 1976: 48). As the economy of Quebec developed along the same lines as the economy of the rest of North America, the traditional basis for distinctiveness in Quebec was eroded. French Canadian leaders began to realize that they were going to have to fight even harder to prevent Quebec from melting into the larger society that surrounded it. At the same time, urbanization and industrialization were gradually creating a new French élite in the province, whose members rejected the basic premises of conservative nationalism. New leaders emerged who did not idealize the past and were unwilling to accept the traditional opposition to the expansion of the public sector. This new élite has appropriately been called the "bureaucratic middle class" (Guindon, 1964). It was composed of educated employees in both private and public bureaucracies, most notably in state organizations and educational institutions. These bureaucracies had grown substantially in number and size after World War II to meet the needs of urban Quebec, but their power and further expansion were being frustrated by those who clung to the old nationalism. The closing years of Duplessis's premiership saw increasing opposition to his government and ideological ferment in the province (Coleman, 1984).

When Duplessis died in 1959, he was followed by premiers who were prepared to make greater concessions to this new bureaucratic middle class. Paul Sauvé, who succeeded Duplessis as leader of the Union nationale, and Jean Lesage, who headed a Liberal government from 1960 to 1966, oversaw a dramatic shift in the orientation of politics in Quebec. They led governments that were not so reluctant to expand the role of the state in the lives of the people of the province. The educational system was reorganized to train French Canadians better for participation in an advanced industrial society and to reduce the power of the Church; the delivery of social services was rationalized and expanded, and again the power of the Church was curtailed; new institutions to define French Canadian culture were established; state control over natural resources was increased; and the labour code was overhauled.

The **Quiet Revolution**, as this new approach came to be called, had profound implications for the character of Quebec nationalism. A basic assumption of French Canadian nationalism had always been that only French Canadian leaders—be they religious or political—could be trusted to look after the interests of their people and to safeguard their distinct culture. So long as a relatively minor role was assigned to the state, the best strategy was simply to maintain tight control over the provincial government while resisting any encroachments by the federal government. This had been the course pursued by the majority of French Canadian intellectuals and politicians until the Quiet Revolution.

But when a new attitude towards the state began to win acceptance, the basic principles of *la survivance* inevitably underwent a change. Nationalists who believed in the Quiet Revolution felt it imperative to do more than just protect the existing powers of the provincial government; *la survivance* now appeared to depend on an extension of these powers. Within Quebec, the new nationalists sought to expand the powers of the provincial government at the expense of other institutions, most notably the Church. Within the larger political framework, they tried to expand these powers at the expense of the federal government. Unavoidably, the Quiet Revolution gave rise to increased conflict between the governments of Ottawa and Quebec City. During the Duplessis years federal–provincial conflict had been largely avoided by Duplessis's simple refusal to cooperate with federal programs. Under Lesage and his successors (Johnson, Bertrand, and Bourassa) an intense struggle developed between federal and provincial politicians over the powers of their respective governments.

This new nationalist orientation also provided the basis for the rise of the separatist movement in Quebec. Indeed, it has been argued that separatism is simply a logical extension of the Quiet Revolution, carrying its philosophy a step further to the conclusion that the expansion of the power of the state in Quebec cannot be achieved within Confederation. To obtain the powers needed to modernize Quebec—and to keep this modernization under French control—almost complete autonomy is necessary.

As always, a stimulus for Quebec nationalism is fear of assimilation. French Canadians were adopting the individualism, pragmatism, and materialism of the North American economy and society. Through educational institutions and the media, North American culture was reaching almost all parts of the province. Ironically, the very policies and programs of the Quiet Revolution contributed to this threat. They promoted the integration of the economy of Quebec with that of North America. They standardized education in Quebec so that it looked more like education elsewhere on the continent. As the reforms of the Quiet Revolution were introduced and the Church relinquished many of its traditional functions, only language remained to distinguish French-speaking society from the larger society that surrounded it. Many Québécois turned to separatism out of fear that French Canada would not survive (Coleman, 1984).

They also turned to separatism as a result of the relative deprivation they felt in the 1960s and 1970s. The Quiet Revolution raised expectations that could not be fulfilled. In particular, French Canadians resented the fact that the business élite in Quebec continued to be largely English-speaking and that, when they talked to English-speaking people, they still had to do so in English. It was they, the francophones, an overwhelming majority in the province, who had to speak the other language.

Although the Parti Québécois won provincial elections in 1976 and 1981, their goal of sovereignty association—which would have effectively given Quebec political independence while retaining economic and other ties with Canada—was defeated in the referendum of 1980. Subsequently, support for separatism declined until 1990, when it experienced a major revival. Many French Canadians were horrified when some municipalities in Ontario passed English-only resolutions for their jurisdictions and when members of the Association for the Preservation of English in Canada trampled on a Quebec flag.

And the struggle over the Meech Lake Accord made many in Quebec feel rejected by the rest of Canada. They had little sympathy with English-speaking Canadians who opposed Meech Lake because it weakened the central government in Canada. They also could not understand the concern of English-speaking Canadians over the treatment of anglophones in Quebec. The majority of Québécois still believed their language and culture were in peril and that they had to secure the political power necessary to defend them against the vastly greater numbers of anglophones in North America.

In the federal election of 1993 the Bloc Québécois won fifty-four seats in the House of Commons and became the Official Opposition. In 1994 the Parti Québécois became the provincial government of Quebec. This set the stage for the Quebec referendum on sovereignty in October 1995, in which the voters rejected sovereignty by a narrow margin: 50.6 to 49.4 percent. In other words, the 1995 referendum was a tie game. Precisely for that reason, however, it has come to mark the beginning of a new phase in the struggle over Quebec. The province is now clearly split in half. On the one side are French Canadians living outside the Montreal and Ottawa regions; they are predominantly in favour of greater sovereignty for Quebec. On the other side are the anglophones, allophones (those of neither French nor British ancestry), and French Canadians living in the Montreal and Ottawa regions, most of whom are opposed to greater sovereignty for Quebec, or at least believe that voting Yes in the referendum would have led to total independence, even though the referendum did not in fact put the question of total independence to the voters. Whether or not this means that the rural–urban cleavage in Quebec is now shaping the independence struggle, it is clear that separatism is no longer based primarily on the Quebec urban middle class.

Although nationalist sentiment in Quebec is not a new phenomenon, it has repeatedly changed in character. Its social basis, its ideology, and its objectives have gone through a number of transformations. Many francophones in Quebec no longer see themselves as an ethnic minority, but rather as a nation that, like other nations, is entitled to its own state (du Pays, 1996). "French Canadian nationalism" has given way to a more territorially based "Quebec" nationalism, in which the ideal is to build a new nation in North America embracing all Quebeckers (Rocher, 1996).

As Parti Québécois premier of Quebec, Lucien Bouchard works closely with the separatist Bloc Québécois, the federal party of which he was once leader.

SUMMARY

The first part of this chapter examined five different theoretical approaches to the study of social movements. It began with the collective behaviour perspective, which was long the dominant theoretical school in North American sociology. This approach assumes that social movements are less institutionalized than ordinary behaviour, and it studies them along with other types of relatively less institutionalized events, such as panics, crowds, and crazes. Several different versions of this perspective were examined: an early statement of the argument by Blumer, Smelser's theory of collective behaviour, emergent norm theory, and game theory.

The discussion then turned to the breakdown theory that social unrest occurs when institutions which normally control and restrain human behaviour are weakened. The third theoretical perspective presented was the relative deprivation approach. It makes the intuitively appealing argument that social unrest is most likely to erupt when a sharp increase develops in the difference between what people receive and what they think they have a right to receive.

The fourth approach takes a different tack by placing social movements in a broad category of events called collective action. Most advocates of this position emphasize the need to study how social unrest—indeed, how any kind of collective action—varies from one society to another, and how it changes in character over time. They also attempt to explain these variations in terms of the structural conditions that underlie and shape collective action, particularly those conditions that facilitate mobilization. This theoretical approach is critical of other perspectives for giving insufficient attention to how people acquire the capacity to act collectively.

Finally, postmodernism and the new social movement approach sought to explain the particular movements that have emerged in postmodern or post-industrial society in Western Europe and North America, placing more emphasis on the importance of culture than other perspectives.

The second part of the chapter shifted to a general, and necessarily brief, examination of collective action in Canada. A very short outline was given of the principal cleavages and integrative bonds that have shaped the character of collective action in this country. Movements in Western Canada were then described as examples of collective action built on regional cleavage, and the unrest among Native peoples and Quebec nationalism were discussed as examples of collective action resulting from ethnic cleavage.

QUESTIONS FOR REVIEW AND CRITICAL THINKING

1. Many studies have shown that the level of social unrest usually increases in a society during the transition from a nonindustrial to an industrial social organization, and then declines thereafter. But there are a number of different explanations for this pattern. Given what you have just learned about theories of relative deprivation, breakdown, and collective action, how do you think each approach would explain this phenomenon?

2. Attend the meetings of a radical left organization, a right-to-life association, a feminist group, or a gay-rights body, and attempt to assess the types of people who are active in these movements. Are they alienated, uprooted, and poorly integrated into social institutions, as the social breakdown approach suggests?

3. The collapse of communism in Eastern Europe has led many people to believe that Marxism is dying both as a basis for organizing political, economic, and social structures and as an intellectual tool for understanding society. Is Marxism still useful for understanding social movements?

GLOSSARY

circular reaction a special type of social interaction in which responses are reinforced among people. The behaviour of one individual stimulates a response in another person, which in turn reinforces the tendency of the first person, and so on.

collective action the pursuit of goals by more than one person. As an explanation of social movements, this perspective looks at integration and cleavage factors and seeks to explain what is dissimilar about collective action at different times and in different places.

collective behaviour activity in which a large number of people reject and/or do not conform to conventional ways of acting. Behaviour of this kind is often described as less "institutionalized" than ordinary behaviour.

craze an unconventional practice that is adopted by a large number of individuals but is regarded as strange by most people in the society. Crazes are generally more outlandish than fads, and therefore require greater personal commitment.

crowd a temporary group of people in reasonably close physical proximity. Only unconventional crowds are included under the heading of collective behaviour.

emergent norm theory an explanation of crowd behaviour that stresses diversity of membership but a perception of consensus, which leads to a new norm expressing the apparent will of the crowd

fad an unconventional practice that spreads rapidly and is adopted in a short period of time by a large number of people. Fads are generally less outlandish than crazes, and therefore require less personal commitment.

frame a set of beliefs that helps people to interpret and explain their world and that provides the basis for collective action

game theory an explanation of crowd behaviour similar to emergent norm theory, except that it assumes that people conduct themselves in a "rational" manner and on the basis of relative costs and pay-offs

generalized belief oversimplified notions that, according to Smelser, give rise to collective behaviour. Generalized beliefs portray the world in terms of omnipotent forces, conspiracies, or extravagant promises.

hegemony the domination of a class or classes over others, not only economically but politically and culturally

mobilization the transfer of resources, particularly human resources, from the pursuit of one goal or set of goals to the pursuit of another goal or set of goals

panic a rapid and impulsive course of action that occurs when people are frightened and try to save themselves or their property from perceived danger

public a large and dispersed group made up of persons who share an interest in the same thing. They may hold similar views or they may sharply disagree.

Quiet Revolution a movement in the 1960s in Quebec to expand governmental powers, decrease Church power, modernize Quebec, and fight vigorously for *la survivance*

relative deprivation the difference between what people believe they have a right to receive (their *expectations*) and what they actually receive (their *achievements*)

selective incentives the individual benefits that a person can derive from belonging to an association or joining a social movement. Selective incentives help motivate people to join social movements.

social breakdown approach an approach to collective behaviour that argues that social unrest occurs when established institutions are disrupted or weakened

social cleavage a division (based on age, class, ethnicity, etc.) that may result in the formation of distinct social groups

social contagion the rapid and uncontrolled spread of a mood, impulse, or form of conduct through a collectivity of people

social integration the attachment of individuals to social groups or institutions. Integration depends on a set of sanctions that rewards conformity to the group and punishes nonconformity.

social movement a large collectivity of people trying to bring about or resist social change

social structure a pattern of relationships among individuals or groups in a society that usually changes only slowly. For example, the kinship structure of a society refers to the most commonly found relations among relatives and married persons in a society. Social stratification is the structure of inequality in a society.

la survivance survival of French Canada as a distinct society

SUGGESTED READINGS

Carroll, W.K. (ed.)

1992 *Organizing Dissent: Contemporary Social Movements in Theory and Practice: Studies in the Politics of Counter-Hegemony.* Toronto: Garamond.

An excellent collection of articles on social movements. While all articles discuss social movements in general, some include an analysis of a specific Canadian movement.

McRoberts, Kenneth

1988 *Quebec: Social Change and Political Crisis.* (3rd ed.) Toronto: McClelland and Stewart.

The book is one of the better introductory surveys of society and politics in Quebec.

Prentice, Alison, Paula Bourne, Gail Brandt, Beth Light, Wendy Mitchinson, and Naomi Black

1988 *Canadian Women: A History.* Toronto: Harcourt Brace.

A good history of women in Canada, covering both the changing role of women in our society and collective efforts by women to improve their condition.

Tilly, Charles

1978 *From Mobilization to Revolution.* Reading, MA: Addison-Wesley.

Tilly is the leading exponent of the collective action approach. This book is not easy reading, but it is important for anyone interested in the study of social movements.

WEB SITES

http://www.FreeNet.Calgary.ab.ca/populati/communit/ncc/ncitizen.html

The National Citizens' Coalition

Social movements come in a variety of forms and are oriented to numerous causes. At this site, learn about the NCC, a group of citizens with a neoconservative orientation.

http://evergreen.ca/home.html

The Evergreen Foundation

Dedicated to the cause of environmentalism, the EF homepage provides information on how to make Canada a greener place.

CHAPTER 15

Demography and Population Study

Carl F. Grindstaff

INTRODUCTION

Demography is the science of human numbers and comes from the Greek *demos*, meaning people. It is concerned with the study of population size, distribution, composition, and change. Demography's primary variables are: (1) fertility—births in a population; (2) mortality—deaths in a population; and (3) migration—movements of population across significant boundaries. The purpose of this chapter is to define and examine these three basic variables of population study and to illustrate the importance of population size, distribution, composition, and change as both cause and effect of societal structure and social processes.

The first section of the chapter presents a brief history of world population and some of the explanations for the current trends and patterns of global population growth. The remainder of the chapter focuses on Canadian mortality, fertility, and internal and international migration. Here, information is presented regarding measurement, numbers, trends, variations, causes, and consequences of population factors in Canada.

HISTORY OF WORLD POPULATION GROWTH

Prior to the eighteenth century, the earth's population had increased very slowly. From 8000 B.C. to about 1700 A.D., the population grew to less than three-quarters of a billion people, at a rate of 0.00005 percent per year. Shortly after 1800, after hundreds of thousands of years, the planet attained a population of 1 billion. The 2 billion mark was reached at the beginning of the Great Depression, around 1930. Thus, a billion more had been added in slightly more than one hundred years. The 3 billion figure was reached in 1963, some thirty-three years later, and currently the world is adding nearly 1 billion people to the population every twelve years. The 6 billion number will be attained in approximately 1999, going up to between 10 and 14 billion sometime in the next hundred years. In the mid-1990s alone, approximately 140 million people were born and 50 million died each year on average, for a **natural increase**—the excess of fertility over mortality—of some 90 million per year. This figure represents about 7 million per month; over 220 000 a day; 9000 per hour; 150 a minute—more than 2 people every second—being added to the world's population. And it appears that these increases will continue through the 1990s. Thus, today the growth rate is approximately 1.5 percent per year, 30 000 times as fast as the rate up to 1700. In fact, 25 percent of all human beings who have ever been born have been born since 1700, and over 5 percent of all the people ever born are living today. Humanity needs to explore and understand the implications of this growth.

Obviously this increase in the world's population cannot continue indefinitely. Sooner or later, the growth must stop and a condition of stability begin. The major questions are when, and how, and under what conditions. Since population growth on a world scale is a function of the relationship of fertility and mortality (not migration, for this can only redistribute population), for a reduction of growth only two alternatives are possible: (1) either the fertility rate must come down; or (2) the mortality rate must go up.

Ehrlich and Ehrlich (1990) argued that control of global population growth is second in importance, in terms of world problems, only to the avoidance of nuclear war (see the box "How Does Population Affect the Environment?"). Population growth is particularly important in terms of its effects, among them pollution and destruction of natural resources.

How Does Population Affect the Environment?

What is the relationship of population growth in both developing and developed countries to environmental pollution? What other factors might be involved in environmental pollution in addition to larger and larger numbers of people on earth?

Global warming, acid rain, depletion of the ozone layer, vulnerability to epidemics, and exhaustion of soils and ground water are all related to population size. They are also clear and present dangers to the persistence of civilization. Crop failures due to global warming alone might result in the premature deaths of a billion or more people in the next few decades. This would constitute a harsh "population control" program provided by nature in the face of humanity's refusal to put into place a gentler program of its own.

Of course, the environmental crisis isn't caused just by expanding human numbers. Burgeoning consumption among the rich and increasing dependence on ecologically unsound technologies to supply that consumption also play major parts. This allows some environmentalists to dodge the population issue by emphasizing the problem of malign technologies. And social commentators can avoid commenting on the problem of too many people by focusing on the serious maldistribution of affluence.

But scientists studying humanity's deepening predicament recognize that a major factor contributing to it is rapidly worsening overpopulation. The Club of Earth released a statement in September 1988 that said in part:

Arresting global population growth should be second in importance only to avoiding nuclear war on humanity's agenda. Overpopulation and rapid population growth are intimately connected with most aspects of the current human predicament, including rapid depletion of nonrenewable resources, deterioration of the environment (including rapid climate change), and increasing international tensions.

When three prestigious scientific organizations co-sponsored an international scientific forum, "Global Change," in Washington in 1989, there was general agreement among the speakers that population growth was a substantial contributor toward prospective catastrophe. Newspaper coverage was limited, and while the population component was mentioned in *The New York Times*, the point that population limitation will be essential to resolving the predicament was lost. The coverage of environmental issues in the media has been generally excellent in the last few years, but there is still a long way to go to get adequate coverage of the intimately connected population problem.

Source: *P. Ehrlich and A. Ehrlich, 1990.* The Population Explosion. *New York: Simon and Schuster (pp. 17–18).*

While it may be that problems of environmental deterioration are related more to people's behaviour than to their numbers, clearly the depletion of resources and the gap between wealthy and poor nations are accelerated by the continuing rapid population growth in the world, particularly in the developing nations.

How to deal with this issue of population growth is certainly one of the most important questions facing people in the world today. But first, in order to understand the policies and programs being developed to combat high population growth, an understanding of how this increase came about is essential.

THEORIES OF POPULATION CHANGE

There have been several general theories as to how and under what conditions populations change. Following are outlines of two of the best-known positions, demographic transition theory and Malthusian demography.

The demographic transition

Demographic transition theory sees population growth occurring in stages. Until the seventeenth and eighteenth centuries, most societies were essentially agricultural and characterized by both high fertility (births) and high mortality (deaths). Generally, both birth rates and death rates were between 35 and 40 per 1000 people. This balance between fertility and mortality resulted in low or no population growth, a condition of equilibrium known as Stage I of the demographic transition.

As industrialization progressed in the Western world between the eighteenth and twentieth centuries, improvements in technology led to medical advances, and ultimately to lower mortality. But while mortality declined, fertility remained high, owing to pressures from a whole range of social institutions: religion, kinship networks, economics, politics, and women's traditional sex roles. In fact nearly every organizational element of society stressed high fertility, reflecting the continued influence of agrarian values even after the Industrial Revolution.

Thus, in nineteenth-century Western society, the emerging demographic picture was one of traditional values supporting high fertility, coupled with technologies that permitted a lower mortality. Birth rates approximately twice death rates and a rapidly expanding population characterized probably the total Western world in the nineteenth and early twentieth centuries. This is Stage II of the demographic transition: the period of high natural increase, where births outnumber deaths.

As industrialization spread, however, desires for improved standards of living and the more individualized value systems inherent in the industrialization process clashed with the values supporting high fertility. Religion, family values, gender roles, and economic needs were all affected by industrialization. Changes in these spheres then affected the number of children people desired. As a result, fertility slowly declined. This shift from a high fertility to low fertility took place over 150 to 200 years, and the change really did not make its effects felt until well into the nineteenth century. Thereafter, fertility continued to decline slowly in the Western countries until, by the 1980s, with some temporal fluctuations, the levels of fertility and mortality were once more in balance, a situation that continues today. In this latter time period, however, the balance was achieved through low fertility and low mortality. This is Stage III of the transition: the new balance of low fertility and low mortality. Birth and death rates are in the range of 10 to 15 per 1000.

When Stage III has been reached in a society, the **demographic transition** has been completed. The entire process can be summarized as follows:

Stage I: High Fertility + High Mortality
= Low Increase

Stage II: High Fertility + Falling Mortality
= Rapid Increase

Stage III: Low Fertility + Low Mortality
= New Balance, Low or No Increase

How likely is this pattern to be repeated in currently developing areas, where industrialization is still in its earlier stages? In Europe, the transition took place over a 200-year period. Thus there was time for adjustments. Mortality declined gradually and emigration to North American drained any accumulating

In the Western world of the nineteenth and early twentieth centuries, birth rates were approximately twice death rates: stage II of the demographic transition.

surplus population, relieving the European industrializing nations of the burdens of too many people. The countries now going through the modernization process face different conditions.

First, the technology capable of reducing mortality is already invented, available, and being applied, having been imported from industrialized nations. Thus, in the developing world, mortality reduction often took place within a few years rather than the centuries that were necessary in the Western societies. This is not enough time for a corresponding reduction in fertility to match that reduced mortality. As a result, the population in some of these areas is increasing remarkably quickly, with growth rates of 2 or 3 percent per year. In the Western world, fertility was reduced only after widespread industrial development—and where the norms and values associated with high fertility slowly changed along with other changes in society. In the nonindustrialized world, that time is a luxury that cannot be afforded. Second, there are no "new worlds" opening, and existing countries increasingly limit immigration.

There are only two possible outcomes of the current rapid population growth trends in developing countries. (Table 15.1 is an excerpt of the World Population Data Sheet showing differences between developing and more developed nations.) According to one scenario, the demographic transition model will be followed and the fertility rates of 26 per 1000 will begin to fall and approach the death rates of 9 per 1000. This would have to happen relatively quickly, within the next generation, or the population increase would severely retard any sustained industrial development. A second possibility is that the birth rates will remain high, but a balance will

TABLE 15.1 Excerpt from 1996 World Population Data Sheet

Region or Country	Population Estimate mid-1993 (millions)	Birth Rate (per 1,000 pop.)	Death Rate (per 1,000 pop.)	Natural Increase (annual, %)	Population "Doubling Time" in Years (at current rate)	Population Projected to 2010 (millions)	Population Projected to 2025 (millions)	Infant Mortality Rate	Total Fertility Rate	% Population Under Age 15/65+	Life Expectancy at Birth Total/Male/Female (years)	Urban Population (%)	Data Availability Code	% Married Women Using Contraception (Total/Modern)	Government View of Fertility Level (H = too high, S = satisfactory, L = too low)	Per capita GNP 1991 (US$)
WORLD	5,771	24	9	1.5	46	6,974	8,193	62	3.0	32/6	66/64/68	43		57/50		4,740
MORE DEVELOPED	1,171	12	10	0.1	501	1,231	1,268	9	1.6	20/14	74/70/78	75		—/57		18,130
LESS DEVELOPED	4,600	27	9	1.9	37	5,743	6,925	68	3.4	35/5	64/62/65	35		54/48		1,090
LESS DEVELOPED (Excluding China)	3,383	31	10	2.2	32	4,356	5,533	73	4.0	38/4	61/60/63	38		42/35		1,320
NORTH AMERICA	295	15	9	0.6	114	331	372	7	2.0	22/13	76/73/79	75		71/66		25,220
Canada	30.0	13	7	0.6	116	33.6	36.6	6.2	1.6	21/12	78/74/81	77		73/69	S	19,570
United States	265.2	15	9	0.6	114	297.7	335.1	7.5	2.0	22/13	76/72/79	75		75/71	S	25,860
LATIN AMERICA	486	26	7	1.9	36	584	678	43	3.1	35/5	69/66/72	71		63/53		3,290
CENTRAL AMERICA	127	28	5	2.3	30	162	197	37	3.4	37/4	71/68/74	65		61/52		3,310
Belize	0.2	38	5	3.3	21	0.3	0.4	34	4.5	44/4	72/70/74	48		47/42	H	2,550
Costa Rica	3.6	26	4	2.2	31	4.6	5.5	13.0	3.1	34/5	76/74/79	44		75/65	H	2,380
El Salvador	5.9	32	6	2.6	27	7.4	9.2	41	3.8	40/4	68/65/70	45		53/48	H	1,480
Guatemala	9.9	36	7	2.9	24	13.4	17.0	51	5.1	45/3	65/62/67	39		31/27	H	1,190
Honduras	5.6	34	6	2.8	25	7.6	9.7	50	5.2	45/3	68/66/71	47		47/34	H	580
Mexico	94.8	27	5	2.2	32	119.0	142.1	34	3.1	36/4	73/70/76	71		65/57	H	4,010
Nicaragua	4.6	33	6	2.7	26	6.7	9.1	49	4.6	44/3	65/62/68	63		49/45	H	330
Panama	2.7	22	4	1.8	39	3.2	3.8	18	3.0	33/5	73/71/75	55		58/54	S	2,670
CARIBBEAN	36	23	8	1.5	45	41	47	42	2.8	31/7	69/67/72	60		60/56		—
Antigua and Barbuda	0.1	18	6	1.2	58	0.1	0.1	18.0	1.7	25/6	73/71/75	31		53/51	S	6,970
Bahamas	0.3	18	5	1.3	52	0.3	0.4	23.4	1.9	29/5	72/68/75	84		62/60	S	11,790
Barbados	0.3	14	9	0.5	133	0.3	0.3	9.1	1.6	24/12	76/73/78	38		55/53	S	6,530
Cuba	11.0	14	7	.7	102	11.8	12.4	9.4	1.5	22/9	75/73/77	74		88/85	S	—
Dominica	0.1	20	7	1.3	55	0.1	0.1	18.4	2.1	32/10	78/74/80	61		50/48	H	2,830
Dominican Republic	8.1	29	6	2.3	31	9.9	11.7	52	3.3	37/4	68/66/71	61		56/52	H	1,320
Grenada	0.1	29	6	2.4	29	0.1	0.2	12.0	3.8	43/5	71/68/73	—		54/49	H	2,620
Guadeloupe	0.4	18	6	1.2	56	0.5	0.5	10.3	2.0	26/9	75/71/78	48		—/—	—	—
Haiti	7.3	35	12	2.3	30	8.8	11.2	74	4.8	40/4	57/55/58	32		18/14	H	220
Jamaica	2.6	24	5	1.8	38	2.9	3.3	24.0	3.0	34/7	74/71/76	53		67/63	H	1,420
Martinique	0.4	15	6	.9	75	0.5	0.5	6	1.7	24/10	76/73/79	81	B	—/—	—	—
Netherlands Antilles	0.2	20	7	1.3	53	0.2	0.3	6.3	2.2	26/7	75/72/78	92		—/—	—	—
Puerto Rico	3.8	17	8	1.0	71	4.0	4.3	11.5	2.1	27/10	74/70/79	73		70/62	—	7,000
St. Kitts—Nevis	0.04	22	9	1.3	54	0.1	0.1	24.0	2.4	32/9	69/66/71	42		41/37	H	4,760
Saint Lucia	0.1	26	6	2.0	35	0.2	0.2	23.0	3.1	37/7	72/69/75	48		48/47	H	3,450
St. Vincent and the Grenadines	0.1	25	7	1.8	38	0.1	0.2	17.0	3.1	37/6	73/71/74	25		58/55	H	2,120
Trinidad and Tobago	1.3	18	7	1.2	60	1.3	1.4	12.2	2.2	31/6	71/68/73	65		53/44	H	3,740
SOUTH AMERICA	323	25	7	1.8	39	380	434	46	3.0	34/5	68/65/71	75		65/52		3,360
Argentina	34.7	20	8	1.2	58	40.9	46.5	22.9	2.7	31/9	72/69/76	87		—/—	S	8,060
Bolivia	7.6	36	10	2.6	27	10.2	13.1	71	4.8	41/4	60/59/62	58		45/18	S	770
Brazil	160.5	25	8	1.7	41	181.9	202.3	58	2.8	34/4	66/64/69	76		66/56	S	3,370
Chile	14.5	21	6	1.6	45	16.5	18.1	13.1	2.5	30/7	72/69/76	85		—/—	S	3,560
Colombia	38.0	27	6	2.1	33	45.9	52.7	28	3.0	33/4	69/66/72	67		72/59	S	1,620
Ecuador	11.7	29	6	2.3	31	14.9	17.8	40	3.6	36/4	69/66/71	59		57/46	H	1,310
Guyana	0.7	25	7	1.8	39	.8	.8	48	2.6	38/4	65/62/68	33		—/—	S	530
Paraguay	5.0	34	6	2.8	25	7.0	9.4	38	4.5	42/4	69/66/71	50		51/41	S	1,570
Peru	24.0	29	7	2.1	33	29.4	33.9	60	3.5	36/4	66/64/68	70		59/33	H	1,890
Suriname	0.4	23	6	1.6	43	0.5	0.6	28	2.4	35/5	70/68/73	49		—/—	S	870
Uruguay	3.2	18	10	0.8	84	3.5	3.7	20.1	2.3	26/12	73/69/76	90		—/—	L	4,650
Venezuela	22.3	26	5	2.1	33	28.7	34.8	23.5	3.1	38/4	72/69/75	84		—/—	S	2,760

Definitions

More developed regions: These, following the UN classification system, comprise all of Europe and North America, plus Australia, Japan, New Zealand, and the republics of the former USSR. All other countries are classified as less developed.

Mid-1996 Population: Estimates are based on a recent census or on official national data or on UN, U.S. Census Bureau, or World Bank projections. The effects of refugee movements, large numbers of foreign workers, and population shifts due to contemporary political events are taken into account to the extent possible. Such events can introduce a high degree of uncertainty into the estimates.

Birth and Death Rate: The annual number of births and deaths per 1000 total population. These rates are often referred to as "crude rates" since they do not take a population's age structure into account. Thus, crude death rates in more developed countries, with a relatively large proportion of older population, are often higher than those in less developed countries.

Rate of Natural Increase (RNI): Birth rate minus the death rate, implying the annual rate of population growth without regard for migration. Expressed as a percentage.

Population "Doubling Time": The number of years until the population will double, assuming a constant rate of natural increase. Based upon the unrounded RNI, this column provides an indication of potential growth assuming that the RNI will not change. It is not intended to forecast the actual doubling of any population. Projections for 2010 and 2025 should be consulted for a plausible expectation of future growth.

Population in 2010 and 2025: Projected populations based upon reasonable assumptions on the future course of fertility, mortality, and migration. Projections are based upon official country projections, or upon series issued by the UN, the U.S. Census Bureau, World Bank, or PRB projections.

Infant Mortality Rate: The annual number of deaths of infants under age one year per 1000 live births. Rates shown with decimals are completely registered national statistics, while those without are estimates from sources cited above.

Total Fertility Rate (TFR): The average number of children a woman will have assuming that current age-specific birth rates will remain constant throughout her childbearing years (usually considered to be ages 15–49).

Population under Age 15/Age 65+: The percentage of the total population in those age groups, which are often considered the "dependent ages."

Life Expectancy at Birth: The average number of years a newborn can expect to live under current mortality levels.

Urban Population: Percentage of the total population living in areas termed urban by that country. Typically, the population living in places of 2000 or more is considered urban.

Contraceptive Use: The percentage of currently married or "in union" women of reproductive age who use any form of contraception. "Modern" methods include clinic and supply methods such as the pill, IUD, condom, and sterilization. Data are the most recent available from sources such as the Demographic and Health Survey programs, data files of the Monitoring Report of the Population Division of the UN, or national reports. Data refer to some point from 1986 through 1992.

Government View of Current Fertility Level: This population policy indicator presents the officially stated position of country governments on the level of the national birth rate. Most indicators are from the United Nations Population Division, *Global Population Policy Database, 1991*, supplemented by recent reports from individual countries.

Per Capita GNP: Gross National Product includes the value of all domestic and foreign output. Estimates are from the *World Bank Atlas*, 25th Anniversary edition (1992).

Source: World Population Data Sheet, 1993. *Washington, D.C.: Population Reference Bureau, Inc. 1996. Used by permission—may not be reproduced without written permission.*

be achieved through an increase in mortality. That option obviously appeals to no one. It is a truism, however, that in a closed system (without migration) populations can only stabilize through the interplay of fertility and mortality. Thus, if through refusal or inability the rapidly increasing populations of the world do not reduce fertility, the demographic balance will be obtained through an increased mortality.

One of the major problems with the demographic transition model is its almost exclusive emphasis on economic and industrial development. Thus the demographic transition is only one possible framework for analyzing population change. Other approaches may be just as relevant. For example, in the modern context, Caldwell (1987) argued that the industrialized world exported not only technology to the developing countries but also the concepts of the nuclear family and alternatives to the maternal role for women. He argued that fertility will begin to decline in the developing world as these cultures accept the changing role of women and focus on the "quality" rather than "quantity" of children, independent of economic modernization. From this perspective it would seem that fertility decline will precede rather than follow economic development because of the force of these social variables. The next generation in the developing world will provide the evidence to test this hypothesis.

Malthusian theory

Thomas Malthus wrote his famous treatise *An Essay on the Principle of Population* in England in 1798, and in some respects the issues he raised are still being debated today. Malthus was writing in reaction to European utopians who argued that nineteenth-century Europe was the best of all possible worlds and that increases in population were fundamental to the further progress of the human race. Malthus, more of a pessimist, wrote that people were victims of passion and that progress would suffer by the addition of large numbers of people.

Malthus based his ideas on the relationship of population to the social and economic world on several propositions:

1. Sexual passion is a powerful human characteristic that cannot be modified. The gratification of this uncontrollable desire results in children.
2. People need food in order to exist.
3. The need for food and the need for sexual expression are inescapably in conflict, in that the satisfaction of the latter drive ultimately requires more food—to support the added population.

Malthus's basic thesis was that human populations tend to increase at a more rapid rate than the food supply needed to sustain them. In fact, in the second edition of his essay he said that, when unimpeded, populations grow in a geometric (doubling) fashion—2, 4, 8, 16, 32, 64, 128, etc.—while the food supply most likely would increase in an arithmetic (adding) way— 1, 2, 3, 4, 5, 6, 7, etc.

From these ideas Malthus came to several conclusions:

1. Population is necessarily limited by the means of subsistence or growing food.
2. Population invariably increases where the means of subsistence increase, unless prevented by some very powerful and obvious checks.
3. These checks, which keep the effects of population growth on a level with the means of subsistence, include moral restraints, vice, and misery.

For Malthus those elements in society that produce vice and misery are called **positive checks**. Wars, plagues, and famines are examples. In essence, these are checks that limit population by raising the death rate. There are also **preventive checks**, those that lower the birth rate. Malthus's preferred means here were abstinence from sex and late marriage. This is because Malthus was also an ordained minister, and he defined "artificial" birth control—the widespread contemporary preventive check—as sinful and beneath human dignity. He objected to birth control on moral grounds, saying that people would be giving in to their sexual urges, rather than taking personal responsibility to overcome them. In addition, he wanted some increases in population, for he felt that people were by nature lazy and that having some children would keep them working for progress. With no children as a "push," no progress of any kind would happen.

Some of the criticisms of the Malthusian theory are fairly obvious. First, Malthus failed to appreciate the full possibilities of the Industrial and Agricultural revolutions, which were beginning to expand productive capacities to an extent previously unknown. In fact, in the industrialized world the standard of living has increased dramatically since he wrote. The life expectancy (the number of years any person at birth can expect to live) in such countries has more than doubled in that period of time. Second, Malthus did not define specifically what he meant by the level of subsistence. Generally, it refers to the level of food supply, along with shelter and clothing, necessary to keep people alive. However, these basics may no longer be the minimum criteria. Cars, TVs, schools, recreation—all are perceived as necessities in industrialized nations. In this sense, many people may be living at a subsistence level, but now that level of subsistence is culturally and not biologically defined. Third, Malthus could not

Malthus felt that, if populations always increase to the ultimate point of subsistence, progress can have no lasting effects.

foresee the possibility of birth-control technology and its widespread application. Birth rates have in fact been declining for the past 100 years almost everywhere in the industrialized world. Thus, Malthusian arguments are most applicable today in the developing countries of Asia and Africa, where the population growth rates may in fact be detrimental to social and economic advancement. It is there where positive checks are most likely to occur. Finally, Malthus blamed the poor for the problem of poverty, and thus (some conflict sociologists would say) never got to the heart of the so-called "overpopulation problem": the selfishness of capitalists. A better sharing of wealth and resources could have alleviated some of the problems of overpopulation.

In general terms, through his formulation of positive and preventive checks, Malthus was stating that people will, one way or another, be restrained from their full reproductive capacity, but that restraint can be brought about, to a large extent, by human judgment and motives. For his time, this was not so simple nor so obvious a point.

THE GROWTH OF CANADA'S POPULATION: AN OVERVIEW

Canada is the second-largest country in the world in terms of geographic area (over four million square miles) and ranks thirty-first in population with a total number of inhabitants in 1996 of 30 million. Given its area, Canada is sparsely populated and always has been. At the time of the European colonization of North America in the early 1600s there were only an estimated 200 000 to 1 million Native people in the land that is now Canada. The European settlement grew slowly, and by the time of the Peace of Paris in 1763 there were still probably only about 100 000 non-Native inhabitants in the country (Beaujot, 1978).

In the next century Canada's population grew rapidly until, by the time of Confederation, the number of people in the country was over 3 million. The average growth rate over that hundred years was nearly 4 percent per year, an increase greater than any of today's rapidly growing developing countries. After Confederation Canada's population continued to grow, but at the more moderate rate of about 1 percent per year on the average, thus doubling about every thirty-five years. Currently, the Canadian population is growing at slightly more than 2 percent per year, with about half of that increase accounted for by natural increase and half by net international in-migration. In 1995, for the first time in Canadian history, there was more growth accounted for by net in-migration than by natural increase. This is a result of continuing low levels of fertility, a small increase in numbers of deaths due to an aging in the overall population, and larger numbers of immigrants coming to Canada in response to changes in government policy, now encouraging immigration to a level close to 1 percent of the total population of Canada (over 200,000 immigrants per year).

Indeed, it is part of Canada's identity that it is a nation of immigrants from various lands all over the world. From one perspective, this analysis is accurate: few Canadians, except for the Native peoples, would be here if it were not for the fact of immigration, on the part of themselves or their ancestors. However, it should also be noted that most of Canada's population growth is due to the fertility of these immigrants and their descendants, and not to immigration *per se*. In general, there were about three births for every one immigrant during the 1851–1996 time period of the nation's history.

In fact, Table 15.2 shows that in every decennial (ten-year) period, natural increase accounted for at least half of the population change, and in five periods it accounted for all of the growth that took place, since in these periods migration added nothing, there being a larger flow of emigrants out of Canada than immigrants into the country. On the other hand, data for the ten-year interval 1986–1996 show that there has been a substantial decrease in the importance of natural increase, with immigration a greater factor in population growth for that period.

While the components of growth that determine the size of a population are important, the distribution of that population within a country is also crucial for an understanding of society. In terms of geographical location, the numerical centre of the population of Canada has been shifting slightly to the west through the twentieth century. In 1900 about 10 percent of Canada's population lived west of Kenora (in northern Ontario, near the Manitoba border); today that figure is over 25 percent. Despite this shift, approximately 60 percent of the country's population still live in Ontario and Quebec, and this was true in 1900 as well as today.

Perhaps the most important factor relating to the distribution of Canada's population is its concentration in a relatively small part of the country. First, the population remains heavily concentrated along the U.S.–Canada border. In fact, about 55 percent of Canadians live in a 250-kilometre-wide corridor, from Windsor to Quebec City. Second, more than 70 percent of the population west of Ontario lives in the metropolitan areas of Winnipeg, Regina, Saskatoon, Edmonton, Calgary, and Vancouver. Overall, about 70 percent of its population resides on something less than 1 percent of the land area of Canada. Thus, although the population of the country is relatively small, especially in relation to geographical size, the people are heavily concentrated and urban in character. (We shall discuss urbanization in Chapter 16.)

Now that we have a general picture of Canada's population, let us look more specifically at its growth and composition.

VARIABLES OF POPULATION GROWTH

Mortality

Mortality was the first variable to undergo dramatic change in the demographic transition, and thus it will be the first major demographic process discussed in this chapter. But first it is important to

TABLE 15.2 Components of population growth in Canada: 1851–1995

Census year	*Total population (000s)*	*Change since preceding census*				
		Natural increase[1] *(000s)*	*Net migration*[2] *(000s)*	*Ratio of natural increase to total growth*	*Ratio of net migration to total growth*	*Average annual growth rate*
1851	2 436	–	–	–	–	–
1861	3 230	611	182	77.0	23.0	2.9%
1871	3 689	610	–150	132.6	–32.6	1.3
1881	4 325	690	–54	108.5	–8.5	1.6
1891	4 833	654	–146	128.7	–28.7	1.1
1901	5 371	668	–130	124.2	–24.2	1.1
1911	7 207	1 025	810	55.9	44.1	3.0
1921	8 788	1 270	311	80.3	19.7	2.0
1931	10 377	1 360	230	85.5	14.5	1.7
1941	11 507	1 222	–92	108.1	–8.1	1.0
1951[3]	14 009	1 972	169	92.1	7.9	1.7
1961	18 238	1 675	482	77.7	22.3	2.5
1971	22 226	1 090	463	70.2	29.8	2.1
1981	24 900	978	310	75.9	24.1	1.2
1991	28 120	1 000	850	54.1	45.9	1.4
1995	29 606	739	747	49.7	50.3	2.2

[1] Births minus deaths

[2] Immigrants minus emigrants

[3] Newfoundland included as from this year

Source: *Beaujot (1978); M.V. George, 1976.* Population Growth in Canada, 1971 Census of Canada Profile Studies. *Ottawa: Statistics Canada, Catalogue No. 99-701 (pp. 5 and 7); Statistics Canada, 1977.* Estimates of Population for Canada and the Provinces, *Catalogue No. 91-201; Statistics Canada,* Quarterly Demographic Statistics, 1992; Health Reports, 1990–91; Vital Statistics, Births and Deaths, 1986–1991; *Statistics Canada,* Annual Demographic Statistics, 1995, *Catalogue No. 91-213-XPB (1971 and subsequent years are based on revised estimates of the total population of Canada).*

know how mortality rates are measured, because certain techniques are more refined and can provide more insight and information than others.

Measures of mortality

Crude death rate This is the mortality figure often referred to in the mass media, and it is the measure used in the World Population Data Sheets shown in Table 15.1. The **crude death rate** is defined as the number of deaths in any particular population in one year per 1000 people at the mid-year point. It is called a crude death rate because it does not take age into account, and age is an important factor in death rates. Thus the crude rate, although easy to calculate, is useful mostly as a first impression, For example, Table 15.1 shows that Guatemala and Canada have the same crude death rates of seven deaths per thousand. This is so only because, overall, Guatemala has a very young population in comparison with Canada (45 percent of Guatemala's population is under 15 compared with 21 percent for Canada), and people at young ages have lower death rates. But when age is made comparable, Guatemala's rate is much higher at every age. Some of the crude death rates in the industrialized countries of Europe are relatively high in comparison with some developing nations as well. This is again due to the fact that European countries have relatively old populations. Canada's crude death rate will undoubtedly begin to rise in the next generation due to an increase in the average age of its population; it will not be because Canadians are less healthy, but because they are older.

Age-specific death rates Just as the title implies, this measure of mortality takes age into account. The **age-specific death rate** is the number of deaths during a year per 1000 people in a particular age group. Table 15.3 shows the age-specific mortality rates for Canadian males and females in 1994. Mortality is relatively high in the first year of life (6/1000); reaches its lowest point in the age group 5–14; and increases gradually, until by ages 55–59 the rate is approximately what it was in the first year. From 60 onward the mortality rate increases sharply as degenerative diseases begin to take their toll.

TABLE 15.3 Age-specific death rates (per 1000 population) Canada, 1994

	All causes	
	Male	*Female*
All	7.6	6.6
Under 1 year	6.9	5.5
1–4	0.4	0.3
5–9	0.2	0.1
10–14	0.2	0.2
15–19	.8	0.3
20–24	1.0	0.3
25–29	1.1	0.4
30–34	1.3	0.5
35–39	1.7	0.8
40–44	2.3	1.2
45–49	3.1	2.0
50–54	5.1	3.2
55–59	8.7	5.2
60–64	14.8	8.0
65–69	23.7	12.8
70–74	37.2	20.5
75–79	60.1	34.5
80–84	96.4	59.2
85-89	149.4	103.4
90+	230.1	197.8

Source: *Statistics Canada 1994,* Births and Deaths, *Catalogue No. 84-210-XPB (pp. 58–59).*

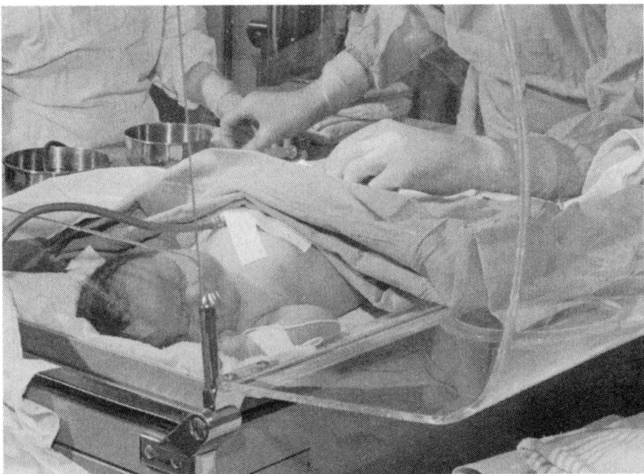

Substantial improvements in medical care since the late 1950s have helped to reduce Canada's infant mortality rate.

Infant mortality rate The **infant mortality rate** is an age-specific death rate for infants who die within the first year of life. It is defined as the number of deaths of infants under one year of age in any particular year, divided by the number of live births in that year. Some view the infant mortality rate as the single most important index of modernization in society, in that low rates are indicative of sophisticated medical, prenatal, and nutritional systems. In the late 1950s, Canada's infant mortality rate was about 28 infant deaths for every 1000 live births. Through substantial improvements in and increased availability of medical care, and through increased knowledge on the part of prospective parents, by 1996 that rate had been cut to 6 deaths per 1000 live births. Further improvements in infant mortality in Canada will probably be minimal because deaths that occur in the first month of life compose about 75 percent of all infant deaths in Canada, are due to genetic or medical difficulties, and thus are somewhat difficult to prevent.

Causes of mortality

Before the Industrial Revolution, high mortality rates were caused by famine, disease, plague, and inadequate sanitation. Better agricultural techniques and increased production, social reforms in working conditions, better shelter and clothing, improvements in public sanitation, more widespread and better personal hygiene, and, in general, a higher standard of living allowed the rates to drop.

Beginning in the late nineteenth and early twentieth centuries, advances in medicine and public health, in terms of both curing and preventing illness, further reduced levels of mortality. As mortality was brought under greater control, the causes of death and the age at which death occurred changed dramatically. In general, at the beginning of the twentieth century in Canada, infectious or **acute diseases** (illnesses passed along from person to person) became the major cause of mortality. Pneumonia and tuberculosis accounted for nearly 25 percent of all deaths in North America at the turn of century.

Today, because of improvements in treatment and inoculation, deaths due to infectious diseases are rarer. In North America today, TB and pneumonia account for less than 5 percent of all mortality. Currently, the major causes of death are what are called degenerative or **chronic diseases**. These are diseases that generally increase with age—basically problems of middle and old age—and that relate to the body simply wearing out. Cancer and cardiovascular–renal diseases, for example, account for 65 to 70 percent of all the deaths that occur in the country.

Mortality differentials

One of the most interesting areas in the study of mortality is the varying death rates among different groups of people. Mortality varies along several dimensions, and it is worthwhile to examine some of the most pronounced differentials. It is clear that certain groups of people are disadvantaged in regard to mortality.

Age **Life expectancy** is defined as the average number of years any individual can expect to live upon reaching a certain age. It is usually given as of birth, but there are life expectancies at any and all ages. Life expectancy at birth in Canada in 1850 was probably around 45 years. By 1921 that figure had increased to about 61 years, and by 1991 a newborn baby could expect to live nearly 78 years on average. It has been argued that future increases in life expectancy will be minimal unless qualitatively different types of medical advances lead to a lengthening of the life span for the whole species. But this is one of the few areas in mortality control in which there has been little or no historical change. The life span has always been 100 years, and that level has remained constant throughout a long period of reduced mortality levels.

Mortality levels are at their lowest for the age group 5–14, and then rates begin to increase slowly. Rates of accidental death and suicide are comparatively high in the 15–29 age categories. Overall, the three leading causes of death for both male and female young adults are auto accidents, other accidents, and suicide, in that order. After age 35, mortality rates begin to increase more quickly. The causes change too as cancer and cardiovascular–renal diseases increasingly take their toll.

Gender In 1991 (the latest available year of life expectancy statistics) women in Canada outlived men by as much as seven years on average, and reliable data from sixty countries around the world reveal a similar advantage for women in mortality. In Canada overall, male death rates are equal to or greater than female rates at every single age (see Table 15.3) and for nearly all causes. At the ages of 20 to 24, while there are relatively few deaths for either sex, the male rate is more than three times the female. Even at the ages of 60 to 64, the male death rate is nearly twice the female—fifteen per thousand compared with eight per thousand. Moreover, women's advantage generally has been increasing over the course of the century. In 1921 life expectancy at birth for males was 59 years and for females it was 61 years, while in 1991 it was 74.6 for males and 80.9 for females.

What accounts for these differences? The fact that the **sex ratio**, defined as the number of males per 100 females, at birth is 105 (and even higher at conception) and that males have relatively higher infant mortality rates than females lend credence to a biological explanation. It seems that, in terms of susceptibility to disease and death, females are biologically stronger. However, as indicated, the differentials have increased in the twentieth century, and it is unlikely that biological factors alone would be involved in the increasing divergence between

On average, women in Canada outlive men by about seven years, and female rates of mortality are less than male rates at virtually every age.

male and female rates. Explanations of this differential would probably be more social and cultural in character, and relate to women taking better advantage of health systems and also generally paying more attention to their everyday well-being. It may also be that women are involved in less hazardous occupations, both physically and emotionally, and take part in less dangerous recreational activities. In addition, there may be early childhood socialization patterns that promote more risk-taking on the part of males. For example, even though the number of men and women in Canada is approximately equal, more than twice as many males as females die from accidents. In summary, there is undoubtedly an interplay between biological and social factors that relate to these differentials, with lifestyle risk factors perhaps the major variable. But whatever the causes, with respect to mortality, females are superior to males at virtually every age.

There are some recent data from industrialized countries that indicate that gender differences in mortality may be narrowing. For example, in Canada between 1971 and 1991, the mortality difference by gender decreased from slightly over seven years to approximately six and one-half years (Trovato and Lalu, 1995). While life expectancy improved for both males and females, the improvement over this twenty-year period was greater for males. One explanation is that women are becoming more involved in the industrialized occupation structure, with a concomitant increase in mortality. It may be that role equality between the genders will result in a narrowing of the current differential, and women really will be "dying to be equal."

However, it is probable that the biological-social component will remain and female death rates overall will continue to be lower.

Race and ethnicity For the registered Aboriginal population of Canada, the age-specific death rates in 1990 were higher than the Canadian population for every age. For example, in 1990, while the infant mortality rate was approximately 7 in Canada generally, for Aboriginals it was 19. The average life expectancy for Native people is currently around 65. In fact, it is clear from all available data that the Aboriginal population in this country remains substantially disadvantaged compared with other Canadians (Statistics Canada Demography Division, *1984 Population Projections of Registered Indians*). These differentials are probably not due to race or ethnicity *per se*, but rather to a lack of access to the modern facilities responsible for mortality reduction, to discrimination against Native peoples of Canada, and to other social, cultural, economic, geographical, and medical circumstances. We discussed some of these problems in Chapter 8, Race and Ethnic Relations.

Marriage In all industrial countries where mortality is reasonably well under control, married people have lower death rates than do the single and the divorced or widowed, and this is true for both males and females at all ages. Generally it is hypothesized that married people have less stress and receive more social support from various kinship networks, lead more ordered and regulated lives, have others closer at hand for assistance, and make better use of medical facilities and nutritional aids. Of minor significance is a selection factor—that the least healthy, those most likely to die early, do not marry as frequently as their healthier counterparts.

For Canadian males, mortality rates are approximately 50 percent higher for the unmarried, and this trend is fairly constant across all age groups. The female mortality figures are not as divergent across the various marital status groups, but married women do have somewhat lower rates. Being married is thus more advantageous for males than for females.

Social class Differential mortality by social class is primarily associated with differing standards of living and lifestyles of the people involved. Generally, the highest levels of mortality are associated with unskilled jobs and the lowest rates with professionals. The published Canadian data on mortality are not categorized by social class, so we do not know what the exact relationship looks like in this country. In a study undertaken by Health and Welfare Canada, however, Wilkins et al. (1989) used income as a measure of social class and found that the difference in life expectancy between the highest and lowest income categories in 1971 was 6.3 years for men and 2.8 years for women. By 1986 these differences had declined somewhat, to 5.6 years for males and 1.8 years for females. Just as research in other areas of North America and Europe has revealed, various measures of social class are negatively correlated with mortality in Canada too.

Social relationships and mortality A recent approach to understanding mortality differentials relates more to psychosocial life satisfaction and to people having support networks among important significant others (partners, family, close friends). A recent evaluation of a wide range of research indicates that there is a consistently higher risk of mortality among people with both a low quantity and quality of human social networks (House et al., 1988). The specific links and mechanisms of the support–mortality relationship have yet to be explored, but it is clear that close social relationships are important for reducing mortality risk. Lynch (1979), in a book called *The Broken Heart*, stated: "We must either learn to live together or increase our chances of prematurely dying alone."

Fertility

Models of fertility

The changes, determinants, and consequences of fertility are tied to nearly all of society's institutional and organizational systems. Thus, fertility behaviour provides a basic blueprint for a society, one that can shed light on its economic, educational, social, and political evolution. The number of children born to any given group of people, the timing and spacing of that childbearing, and changes in these patterns all provide information about the basic organization of the social group.

The complex nature of reproductive behaviour and the large number of factors associated with it led in the 1950s and 1960s to attempts to develop frameworks that could encompass all the variables involved in fertility. Generally, the basic determinants of fertility consist of (1) socio-economic structural variables, (2) demographic and biological factors, (3) psychological factors, and (4) contraceptive factors. Of major importance are the structural factors, including stratification variables such as occupation, income, and education; family structure variables; technological factors; non-familial institutions; and other characteristics of social and economic organization. Then there are the "proximate determinants" that stand between social organization and social norms on the one hand and fertility on the other. These include variables such as age at entry into unions, extent of celibacy and periods of exposure to risk, contraceptive use, extent of infecundity (inability to bear children), and the practice of abortion (Bongaarts, 1982). The effect of these proximate determinants is to produce the actual reproductive level.

Recognizing the influence of this large number of factors, most researchers understandably have concentrated on a smaller part of the whole, with the result that there is no unified body of explanatory factors that can be called a theory of fertility. Generally, explanations have been influenced by the orientations of the investigators. Sociologists have concentrated on the relationship between socio-economic or other structural variables and fertility. Characteristics such as religion, ethnicity, first language, rural or urban residence, educational and labour-force composition, and occupational and income distributions are important to sociologists since they all affect fertility; so also are family-size ideals and desires, and both norms concerning and ability to control fertility.

Psychologists and social psychologists, while recognizing the importance of examining the relationship between structural variables and childbearing, suggest that any complete theoretical explanation would need to explore the actual decision-making processes in childbearing. These decisions depend on personality and psychological variables, such as need for ego support, communication between spouses, need for nurturance, marital adjustment and husband–wife dominance, and the emotional satisfaction derived from having children or not having them. This approach, rich in potential, has not been very satisfactory in the past, primarily as a result of methodological problems in measurement of personality and psychological characteristics.

A more recent approach to the study of fertility is that of the microeconomists. Based on the assumption that individuals try to maximize utility, fertility behaviour is explained in terms of costs and benefits derived by having a specified number of children. The number of children desired by a couple hypothetically is determined by their preferences for children as compared with other goods and services under the constraints imposed by costs and available income. This type of utility analysis has been criticized, primarily by sociologists. The fact that children are different from consumer durable goods and that the noneconomic dimensions of family and kinship relations are not amenable to the usual utility analysis is stressed by such people as Beaujot (1986). Social norms play an important role in childbearing decisions, and couples really do not have all the options available to the "rational" person of economics.

Measures of fertility

Measuring fertility is somewhat more difficult than measuring mortality, because of its greater complexity. Mortality happens just once and to everyone, whereas only women can bear children and they can give birth more than once in a lifetime, even to several children at the same time. Most measures of fertility focus on women and examine the frequency of births in a population at any point in time. Those measures for which the unit of time is one year are called calendar-year rates, while the few measures that examine a longer time period, often a lifetime, are called cohort rates. We shall provide some examples of calendar-year rates.

Crude birth rate The **crude birth rate** is the simplest calendar-year measure of fertility, and is defined as the number of registered births per year per 1000 people in the mid-year population. This measure is analogous to the crude death rate. It is called crude because it does not take age or sex into account, and thus many people—children, post-menopausal women, men—who generally cannot bear a child are included in the "per 1000 people" denominator. It is, however, a useful statistic in that it does not require sophisticated data and is easy to calculate. It provides a starting-point for an analysis of fertility and in fact is the measure employed for the data in Tables 15.1 and 15.4. Note in Table 15.4 that from 1971 to 1986 the number of births in Canada had been remarkably stable, at around 370 000 per year. However, in 1991 the number of births increased to over 400 000, and some of the age-specific fertility rates even went up slightly (see Table 15.5). The major reason for this small change is some older women "catching up" in the fertility they delayed while they were acquiring education and labour-force experience. It was predicted that the number of births would decline after this group moved through the later stages of the childbearing years; and in fact the latest fertility statistics available show that the number of births in Canada declined to 383 145 in 1995 and the crude birth rate was under 13 for the first time in Canadian history.

Age-specific birth rate The **age-specific birth rate** is defined as the number of births to women of a particular age divided by all the women of that age (sometimes restricted to the married women of that age, since about 80 percent of the children born in Canada are born to married women). While the age-specific rates can be calculated for single years, for convenience and presentation they are usually measured in five-year age groups. They are then shown as rates per 1000 women of specific age cohorts, e.g., women aged 20–24 in 1981 would have been born between 1956 and 1961. The data presented in Table 15.5 provide information on age-specific fertility rates in Canada beginning in 1921, the first year in which such data were collected nationally. The table reveals that women had fewer children in the 1970, 1980s, and 1990s than previously, with ages 25–29 the major reproductive years and 20–24 ranking second. However, in the 1990s there were more children born per 1000 women in the 30–34 age group than in the 20–24 category. This shows a 1990s pattern of fertility in which fewer children are born to younger than older cohorts, with a result that the average age of mothers at childbirth is increasing.

TABLE 15.4 Crude birth rates for Canada, 1851–1995

Year	*Population of Canada*	*No. of births*	*Crude birth rate per 1000*
1851[1]	2 312 919	112 400	48.6
1871	3 689 257	166 200	45.0
1891	4 833 239	172 700	35.7
1911	7 206 643	248 200	34.4
1921	8 788 483	264 879	29.3
1931	10 376 786	247 205	23.2
1941	11 506 655	263 993	22.4
1951	14 009 429	381 092	27.2
1961	18 238 247	475 700	26.1
1971	22 026 421	362 187	16.4
1981	24 899 999	371 346	14.9
1991	28 120 065	402 535	14.3
1995	29,606,097	383,145	12.9

[1]1851 includes only the four original provinces of Ontario, Quebec, Nova Scotia, and New Brunswick. Succeeding years include population of Canada and its territories.

Source: *Henripin (1972: 364); Kalbach and McVey (1971: 71, 21); Statistics Canada,* Census of Canada 1921, *1 (p. 4);* Census of Canada 1971, *1 (p. 1-1);* Vital Statistics Quarterly, *25, 2, and 24, 2;* Canadian Statistical Review, *53, 1, Section 2;* Vital Statistics, 1981, *1.* Births, *Table 1;* Vital Statistics Quarterly, *34, 1987;* Quarterly Demographic Statistics, *Cat. No. 91-002, 6 (p. 16);* Annual Demographic Statistics, 1995, *Catalogue No. 91-213-XPB (revised population and birth rate figures from 1971 to 1995).*

TABLE 15.5 Age-specific fertility rates for Canada (selected years)

Fertility rates per 1000 women by age groups

Year	*15–19*	*20–24*	*25–29*	*30–34*	*35–39*	*40–44*	*45–49*
1921	38.0	165.4	186.0	154.6	110.0	46.7	6.6
1931	29.9	137.1	175.1	145.3	103.1	44.0	5.5
1941	30.7	138.4	159.8	122.3	80.0	31.6	3.7
1951	48.1	188.7	198.8	144.5	86.5	30.9	3.1
1959	60.4	233.8	226.7	147.7	87.3	28.5	2.7
1971	40.1	134.4	142.0	77.3	33.6	9.4	0.6
1981	26.4	96.7	126.9	68.0	19.4	3.2	0.2
1991	27.3	82.6	128.4	88.0	29.2	4.0	0.2
1994	25.1	72.2	114.0	86.0	30.4	4.7	0.1

Source: *Statistics Canada,* Vital Statistics, 1976, *Catalogue No. 84-204, 1, Table 6;* Vital Statistics, 1981, *Table 5;* Vital Statistics, Births and Deaths, 1984, *Table 5;* Health Reports 1989, *1, 2, Table 3;* Health Reports, Births, 1991, *Catalogue No. 84-210;* Births and Deaths, 1994, *Catalogue No. 84-210-XPB.*

Trends in Canadian fertility

In general, fertility in Canada has been declining for more than a century, similar to the trends in other industrialized countries. Still, fertility has been an important component of population change in Canada's past. From a high of nearly 50 births per 1000 people in 1851 (few countries even in the developing world have a birth rate of that magnitude today), Canada's crude birth rate fell steadily until the middle of the Great Depression (1937), when the birth rate was down 60 percent from the 1851 levels to a rate of 20 per 1000 (see Table 15.4). The birth rate in that eighty-year period thus had responded to the industrial and economic changes that had taken place in Canada. In the 1940s and 1950s Canada experienced what has been called the "baby boom," with a 40 percent rise in births, until by 1956 the rate was 28 per 1000. This increase was related to changes in the age at marriage (decreasing), economic upturn, and shorter intervals between births. In 1961 a steady drop in the crude birth rate began, reaching a low today of approximately 13 per 1000. Even compared with 1981, the average number of children born to women in the childbearing ages (15 to 44) in 1994 declined by 10 percent. For the oldest childbearing ages (35 to 44), the decline was even greater over the 1981–1994 period, at 20 percent. This is by far the lowest birth rate in Canadian history, and recent trends show little sign of any substantial increase. The factors associated with this large decline in birth rates are increasing age at marriage, economic difficulties, more effective contraception, abortion, and the changing role of women in all areas of Canadian society.

The proportion of people who are 65 years and older, currently about 12 percent, is more than double that of fifty years ago.

This dramatic and massive decline in fertility in Canada over the past generation has important social and demographic consequences. For example, with decreasing fertility, the average age of the Canadian population has been increasing over time (see the box "How a Population Ages or Grows Younger"). A smaller proportion of children in the population automatically means a larger proportion of older people, if mortality rates are relatively constant. This aging of the population is manifested in the increasing proportion of people who are 65 years and older, currently about 12 percent, more than double that of fifty years ago. This trend will persist as long as fertility continues to decline or if it stabilizes at lower levels. Also, the decreasing number of children has and will continue to have an impact on enrolment throughout the educational system, a point made in Chapter 11, Education. The age composition of the labour force is likely to undergo important changes under the impact of the continuing fertility decline as well, as there will be fewer people available to move into the labour market as the years go by. This declining fertility, however, provides women with more opportunities to pursue a career outside the home. In turn, the increasing role of women in the formal economy may then affect the patterns of childbearing, both in terms of numbers and spacing.

At the same time as Canadian fertility rates are at their lowest levels in history, there is substantial evidence that almost all Canadian women desire to have children at some point in their lives, usually more than a single child but seldom more than two or three. Indeed, Canada remains a strongly pro-fertility

How a Population Ages or Grows Younger

What are the major factors in explaining the age of a population as a collectivity?

Whether a national population is young or old is mainly determined by the number of children women bear. When women bear many children, the population is young; when they bear few, the population is old....

A young population can only be maintained through premature death, and prolonged life is only compatible with older populations. What are the major arguments relating to this contention?

Most of us would probably guess that populations have become older because the death rate has been reduced, and hence people live longer on average. [However,] mortality affects the age distribution much less than does fertility, and in the opposite direction from what most of us would think. Prolongation of life by reducing death rates has the perverse effect of making the population somewhat younger. The (historical) reason that the reduced death rates, which prolong life, make the population younger is that typical improvements in health and medicine produce the greatest increases in survivorship among the young rather than the old.... Just as it is not possible for a population to maintain for long a birth rate much below its death rate, because such a population would shrink to extinction, it is not possible to maintain for long a birth rate much above a death rate, because then the population would grow to a physically impossible size.... In short, the present combination of a high world birth rate and a moderate and rapidly falling death rate can only be temporary. The only combinations that can long continue are birth and death rates with the same average levels.... The human population must become an old one, because only a low birth rate is compatible in the long run with a low death rate, and a low birth rate produces an old population.

Source: *Ansley J. Coale. 1963. "Population and Economic Development" in Philip M. Hauser (ed.),* The Population Dilemma. *Englewood Cliffs, NJ: Prentice Hall, pp. 46–69.*

society if that norm is defined in terms of wanting children in the family; it is only the timing of births and the size of the family that have changed. There is a definite trend towards having children later in life, even beginning childbearing after the age of 30 (see Table 15.5), in order for women to take advantage of educational and labour-force opportunities. If the appropriate societal supports are in place (day care, employment equity, parental leaves), it is likely that even larger numbers of those women who have avoided childbearing in their twenties will begin having children in their thirties. It is also likely that the average number of children for married women will be very close to two, and it is unlikely to be much higher for the near future. The real future depressant in terms of fertility may be marriage avoidance (Grindstaff et al., 1989).

Fertility differentials

Generally, the earlier a woman marries and the longer she is married, the more children she has in her lifetime. Of all variables, age at marriage and marriage duration are the most important explanatory factors in variations of number of children born. However, when marriage duration is controlled, other variables also emerge as important in fertility variation. Historically, higher fertility levels have generally been found among rural women, those with low levels of education, those with Catholic and/or French backgrounds, those with no employment outside the home, and those having low family incomes. In the past, there has been a definite inverse relationship between social class and numbers of children born.

In 1984 the Canadian government commissioned a national fertility survey to analyze fertility behaviour in relation to sociological, psychological, contraceptive, and microeconomic models of fertility; census data can also provide some insights into the variables related to fertility. The data used to examine recent levels and differentials presented in this section are based on the number of children ever born to any particular woman or group of women in a specific cohort, e.g., women born between 1931 and 1935 or 1936 and 1940 who have ever been married.[1]

Marital status In the 1960s, 95 percent of all births were to married mothers. In the 1990s, however, about 25 percent of all births are to unmarried women, including women who are in cohabiting situations. A generation ago fertility was examined only for married women, but today it is also necessary to examine the fertility patterns of women who have never been married. In 1991, for young women 20 to 24 years of age in Canada, about 65 percent were never married, 35 percent were ever-married or cohabiting (21 percent married and 14 percent living common law). By 1991 there had been 280 645 children ever born to this cohort, and nearly half (127 415) were born to never-married or cohabiting women. It is clear that, especially among young women, childbearing is no longer confined to those women who are "officially" married.

Residence Generally across the age cohorts, rural–urban differences are substantial, with rural women having more children. Women from large urban centres have 2.3 children on average, while rural farm women have 2.9. However, this association was historically more important than it is today. While young women (under 30) who now live in rural areas have more children than urban women, the differences are relatively small.

Religion Historically, religion was one of the most important variables in explaining fertility differentials. It is less significant today, and is more important for older women than for women under 30. The major distinction for purposes of classification of religion is between Protestant and Catholic, and while Catholics still have more children, the differences for the young women are very small and are sometimes even slightly in the opposite direction. For example, at the ages of 25 to 29, recent Catholic fertility is 1.33 children, and Protestant, 1.38. In the age groups over 45, Catholic women on average often had one to two more children than Protestants.

[1]Most of the data presented in this section are derived from the 1984 *Canadian Fertility Survey* and from the *1991 Census of Canada, Fertility*.

One final illustration is to compare Quebec, over 80 percent Catholic, with British Columbia, where only about 20 percent of the residents are of the Catholic faith. In Quebec, among women who have just completed their childbearing years (age 40 to 44), the average number of children ever born is 1.8; in British Columbia the number is 1.9. The same convergence is found among the other younger age groups as well, providing more evidence on the declining importance of religion as a differentiating factor in fertility. We noted the general decline in the importance of religion earlier in Chapter 10.

Education This is one of the more important variables for fertility, and it shows a consistent inverse relationship. In 1991, for all ever-married women 15 years of age and older, the number of children ever born ranged in a linear fashion from 3.6 children for women with Grade 8 or less education to 1.5 children for women who have a university degree. Those women with higher levels of education are more likely to be in the labour force and therefore less likely to have as many children. Generally, the more education a woman completes, the smaller the family size: women with higher levels of education tend to both marry later and to have more information about contraception (Balakrishnan et al., 1993).

Nativity With few exceptions across the age cohorts, foreign-born women have only slightly more children than those women born in Canada. This finding is less consistent in older compared with younger cohorts, but overall the pattern of marginally higher fertility for foreign-born women is stable. For example, foreign-born, ever-married women 15 to 44 years of age had on average 1.7 children, compared with 1.6 for native-born Canadians. The similar levels of fertility probably relate to recent immigration policies that favour applicants with high educational and occupational attainment, factors which in turn are associated with low levels of childbearing, making the fertility of immigrants comparable to Canadian-born women.

Labour-force participation From nearly every analytical perspective, labour-force participation is the most important socio-economic variable in current fertility analysis for women under 35. Whether the variable described is current labour-force participation, period last worked, or number of weeks worked, women involved in the labour force have substantially fewer children than those women who are not. Often, the average number of children born to women who are in the labour force (again, especially to young women in the prime fertility ages) is about half those born to women who are not participating in work outside the home. In 1991, for example, for ever-married women between 25 and 29, those who were not working had on average approximately two children, while for those women who were employed the figure was less than one child. Probably labour-force activity leads to fewer children and fewer children lead to labour-force activity. The differential is proportionately smaller for older women, but even at these ages the variance is significant. Overall, those women whose main work is in the home had on average two children more (4.0 to 2.0) than women who worked outside the home for more than a year before the census was taken.

Ethnicity Although there are some problems with its definition, ethnicity is important for fertility analysis. For young women, fertility is low for Jewish and Asian groups, intermediate for French- and British-origin and other European groups, and very high only for First Nations women. Women over 45 years of age display different patterns, with Asian and French women having higher fertility (although still lower than Native peoples). The English and Jewish women in that age category have among the lowest levels. Comparisons of the two major cultural groups, French and English, show a now-familiar pattern. For young women there are no English–French differences in fertility. In 1991, for ever-married women aged 30 to 34 of British ancestry, there were on average 1.7 children born. A similar number, 1.8, is found among women in Canada with a French background in the same age group. The older French women, however, had significantly more children than their English counterparts. Thus, much of the major variation in childbearing among ethnic groups is historical, with the exception of Aboriginals. In general, especially at the younger ages, Native women have about twice the number of children compared with all women in Canada.

Family planning In the early 1990s, over 90 percent of Canadian women in the childbearing ages had used some form of contraception. Of course this figure varies according to age, marital status, and sexual activity. In the *Canadian Fertility Survey* (1984), over 80 percent of all women, both married and single, had used birth-control pills at some point during their reproductive ages. However, the pill is a method employed primarily by women under the age of 30. The contraceptive of choice among older women in Canada is sterilization. A vast majority (72 percent) of women between the ages of 35 and 39 practising birth control used sterilization as their procedure for preventing pregnancy. It is estimated that more than half of Canadian women (or their partners) who have two or more children are sterilized, giving Canada the highest sterilization rate in the world, one-third higher than the United States. It would appear that older women do not want to use the pill for a permanent birth-control procedure and they are unwilling to depend on less effective methods.

Even though Canadian women are effective users of contraception, there are many accidental pregnancies, as evidenced by the approximately 100 000 therapeutic abortions performed annually in Canada in the mid-1990s. Abortion is a heated topic, with pro-choice and pro-life advocates often in both political and even physical confrontation. But as long as there are failures in the family planning system, with some women lacking access, knowledge, or interest in effective, reliable, and inexpensive contraception, some may choose that alternative.

Implications

What are the levels of fertility likely to be in the future? Such predictions are risky at best, and assume whole sets of "if…then" statements. But most current research indicates that low fertility will continue to prevail in Canada, at least in the near future. Old patterns and sequences of marriage, children, and homemaking have dissolved into a more diverse life path. Women choose various combinations of education, career, family, serial monogamy, and spacing and numbers of children (Grindstaff et al., 1989). For increasing numbers of women, then, higher educational levels and labour-force participation will be reflected in continuing low fertility.

Currently, low levels of fertility have been "blamed" for the economic downturn, low school enrolment, weak housing markets, even the potential for a bankrupt pension system. It has even been suggested that governments pay women to have children so that nations can get back on the right economic path. Such recommendations are probably ill-advised. It is not the levels of fertility *per se*, whether high or low, that create difficulties, but rather the relatively wide fluctuations in fertility that have occurred in the past forty years. Canada is going through a difficult adjustment period, changing from the high fertility of the 1950s and 1960s to the low levels of the 1970s, 1980s, and 1990s. Provided these currently low rates remain relatively constant—and, as mentioned, there are indications that the rates will be more stable in the future—the pains of accommodation will ease through the 1990s, and a rationally planned socio-economic order will be more possible.

Migration

Human **migration**, the third major demographic process, can be defined simply as the movement of people across significant boundaries for the purpose of permanent settlement. The key words in this definition are *boundaries* and *permanent*. In modern societies the boundaries are usually political in nature, and permanency refers to residence for a significant period of time.

Migration differs in several important respects from mortality and fertility. First, from what scientists have been able to determine, the migration of individuals or groups has no biological component. In this sense it is a more distinctly social human activity than either fertility or mortality, and is perhaps more subject to normative, social, economic, and political conditions. In addition, the motives and conditions under which people migrate may be more varied than those related to the other demographic processes.

While there are several theories about the factors associated with migration, the basic causes resolve themselves into what have been classified as *push* and *pull* factors. *Push* signifies conditions of undesirability at the place of origin, while *pull* refers to attractions at the place of destination. The implication is that people do not move unless induced to do so by some outside force.

All migrations have both positive and negative motives as well as intervening obstacles (for example, distance or immigration restrictions) between origin and destination, and together all of these factors are taken into account in any migration decision. Positive motivations to move may include economic advantages, greater social opportunities, a better physical or political climate, better recreation, the desire to follow friends, and so on. There are also certain disadvantages to any migration: the breaking of routines and friendship patterns, and the leaving of familiar surroundings, residence, and the whole array of ties to a social context. Any advantages of migration must be balanced against these disadvantages, and when there remains a sufficient residue of advantage, the migration is most likely.

Human migration, however, often does not occur in such a straightforward way. The decision to move is rarely completely rational, and for some subjective evaluations (e.g., it is always better "over there"), transient emotions (e.g., fights with loved ones), accidental occurrences, and personal idiosyncrasies relating to housing or shopping may complicate, even overwhelm, the rational decision-making model.

Another approach to the study of migration emphasizes those life-cycle events that occur in the lives of most people on a fairly regular basis. The beginning or completion of education; marriage and divorce; a change in occupation; a death in the immediate family; the birth of a child; children leaving home; retirement—all of these stages in the life cycle may well be associated with movements, regardless of the particular motivations or evaluations of positives and negatives at origins and destinations. At particular junctions in most people's lives, migration is likely to occur. The task in this framework is to examine migration differentials between people undergoing similar life-cycle events, and to explain why some of them move and some do not move given certain conditions and happenings in their lives.

Internal migration[2]

Migration within Canada is defined as a change in residence across a municipal boundary. Thus, a

[2]Much of the data used in this section were developed from Statistics Canada, *Mobility and Migration: The Nation*, Catalogue No. 93-322, May 1993.

person who moves from one Winnipeg address to another is not considered a migrant, but rather a mover. The actual move must be across a municipal boundary, for example from Winnipeg to Calgary, to be counted as a migration. Although there are several ways to measure this migration, the data in this chapter are derived from a measure used by the Canadian census, called a five-year interval measure. (Canada does not collect migration statistics on a year-to-year basis.) In 1991 the Canadian census asked the question, "Where did you live five years ago, on June 4, 1986?" A similar question was asked in the 1971 and 1981 census. Those who had changed residences between municipalities were counted as migrants.

Examination of these data reveals that Canada's population is extremely mobile: nearly half (47 percent) of the population five years of age and older changed residence between 1986 and 1991. Approximately 50 percent of these 13 million movers were migrants; that is, they moved across municipal boundaries. About the same levels of movement occurred between 1971 and 1981, and in general, for the past generation, Canadians have been one of the most mobile peoples in the world. However, certain types of people are more likely to migrate than others.

Age Mobility is concentrated among young adults aged 20 to 34. About 69 percent of those people moved between 1986 and 1991, in comparison with about 47 percent for the total Canadian population. Generally, much of this movement is related to the life-cycle events of marriage and labour-force entry.

Gender Overall, the patterns of migration for men and women are similar. Men tend to predominate in interprovincial migration, but the differences are small. Males 25 to 34 are more likely to migrate than women of that age, and females are more likely to migrate at ages 20 to 24, but these differences can partly be attributed to variation in age of marriage: women marry younger, and proportionately there are more married women than men in the 20 to 24 age category.

Education Various studies have shown that education is an important determinant of mobility. An examination of 1991 Canadian data on interprovincial migration indicates that people with at least some university education have the highest rates (62 moves per 1000 people) while those with less than Grade 9 education have the lowest rates (14 per 1000). There were over 800 000 interprovincial migrants 15 years of age or older, and one-third had some level of university training, compared with about 20 percent in the overall population. Male and female rates are virtually identical. Thus, the higher the education, the more likely one is to be mobile, and this undoubtedly is related to age (younger people have higher levels of education) and to more and diverse occupational opportunities for the better educated.

Occupation While there are some difficulties in ranking occupations from high to low, this general pattern is clear: the higher the occupational position, the greater the level of migration. Professionals are more than twice as likely as unskilled labourers to migrate, and again the factors involved in this differential probably relate to job demands and opportunities. It may also be that those people higher in the occupational structure have the financial resources that allow them to migrate when opportunities present themselves.

In summary, a composite picture of the likely mobile Canadian is a person of either gender, recently married, between the ages of 25 and 29, with some university training, working as a professional. Most of these same characteristics describe Canadian migrants for the period 1976–81 and in fact those of the past generation (Stone and Fletcher, 1977).

Rural–urban migration

At the time of Confederation, over 80 percent of Canada's population lived in rural farm areas. By 1921, only about half of its population resided in rural areas, and today Canada is one of the most urban countries in the world. We shall have more to say on that topic in the next chapter. For now, let us say that this urbanization occurred quickly and was brought about mostly through migration, both from other countries and from Canadian rural areas, and not through fertility, in that urban fertility rates have always been lower than rural rates. However, in the past two decades the pace of this migration to urban areas has slowed. While still larger growth is recorded in the urban sectors, the difference is smaller in historical comparison. For example, the rural population in Canada increased by over 1.2 million or 24 percent between 1971 and 1991, while the urban increase was only 4.5 million, about 27 percent. There has also been some migration from the cities to rural areas, especially to fringe areas near large metropolitan centres. It is too early to predict a trend from these data, but some of the Canadian population may be "returning to the land." This slow-down from the nineteenth- and twentieth-century rural-to-urban pattern may well be related to desires for changes in lifestyle and to economic uncertainty. Whatever the cause, such a change would have important social and economic consequences, and rural growth and its ramifications require further study.

Interprovincial migration

Over 20 percent of all internal migration in Canada occurs between provinces. The province of destination is generally determined by a combination of economics and proximity, with economics appearing to be the major factor. The wealthiest provinces have in the past attracted migration from their poorer neighbour provinces. Thus, between 1986 and 1991 (and also between 1976 and 1981) Ontario was the major recipient of Quebec and eastern provincial out-migration, while Alberta, Ontario, and British Columbia were frequent destinations of Manitoba's and Saskatchewan's migrants. Between 1986 and 1991 the largest single group of interprovincial migrants was from Alberta to British Columbia (over 92 000), while the Quebec-to-Ontario flow was second (72 000) and the Ontario-to-British Columbia third (68 000). The population continues to move westwards. British Columbia had the largest net interprovincial gain of 125 000, followed by Ontario with less than 50 000. Saskatchewan continued as a major net loser of population through migration, over 60 000.

While the largest numbers of migrants, both into and out of provinces in Canada, are associated with Ontario and British Columbia, the rates of migration are highest for the western provinces and for the Maritimes. The rate of change, even though the numbers involved are small, can also influence local populations, especially where the base is not large, as in the Maritimes. From a turnover perspective, the impact of migration on the Maritimes might well be more profound than the large numbers that come into Ontario. Thus it is important to examine both absolute and proportional change in order to assess the impact of internal migration.

International migration

From 1851 to 1996, over 13.5 million immigrants entered Canada, most of them from Western Europe, particularly Great Britain. In fact, of the total European emigration during that time period, nearly one in six came to Canada to live. This immigration has continued up to the present time, and the 1996 census showed that 16 percent of the Canadian population is foreign-born. This amount is one of the highest proportions of foreign-born people living in any country in the world, and double that of the United States.

The government has also recently begun to collect information on those people who leave the country, providing, for the first time, accurate basic statistics on emigrants from Canada (*Annual Demographic Statistics*, 1995). From 1990 to 1995, the six-year total of immigrants was nearly 1.4 million, while 270 000 left the country to take up residence elsewhere in the world, especially the U.S. During the twentieth century, only in the Depression decade of the 1930s did Canada lose more people than it gained in the immigration–emigration exchange, and this was due mainly to restrictive immigration laws during that period.

During the 1960s and 1970s Canada's immigration policies were substantially amended in a more liberal direction, and immigrant applications came to be judged more and more on the basis of skills and economic qualifications (including entrepreneurship) and less on country of origin. In 1977 and again in 1993, Canada adopted new immigration acts (the first large-scale change since 1952), which state that potential immigrants will be judged on the basis of their acquired qualifications, such as education and occupation, and not on the

The 1991 census showed that 16 percent of the Canadian population is foreign-born.

basis of sex, race, ethnicity, religion, colour, or national background. In the new immigration policy, vague reasons for exclusion, such as "moral turpitude," are eliminated; current grounds for exclusion relate more to serious health problems and serious criminal records. This system, although not perfect, less frequently excludes any national group in a systematic and biased way. In the first years of the 1990s, 5 percent of the immigrants were from the U.K. or the U.S., 20 percent from other European countries, 55 percent from Asia, and the remaining 20 percent from other areas of the world, mainly Africa, Central America, and the Caribbean (Statistics Canada, *Annual Demographic Statistics*, 1995.) Once an important stream of immigration, the interchange between Canada and the United States in the early 1990s was quite small.

The new acts also provide for substantial consultation with the provinces in order to determine the level and distribution of immigration that would be most advantageous to them, the country, and the immigrants. In the early 1990s the number of immigrants was set at about 1 percent of the Canadian population (around 250 000 people) yearly, the actual figure to be adjusted each year to achieve a desired population growth (given the current rate of fertility) and to take into account existing economic conditions. For the 1995 immigration year, the actual figure was about 215 000 immigrants, somewhat below the desired number, but the growth in the 1990s from immigration approximated the government's desires.

The types of people who are likely to become immigrants and their destinations tend to share certain characteristics. Historically, the number of males immigrating to Canada exceeded the number of females, with sex ratios often over 110. This differential reflected social roles and the greater acceptance of males going out into the world. In the last quarter of the twentieth century this situation has changed, and the number of males and females in the immigration streams are now approximately the same (in 1995, 52 percent women), reflecting perhaps more family movement (about 50 percent of the immigrants in the early 1990s are married) and the greater number of females who can achieve immigration status through their own economic accomplishments.

Immigrants to Canada are predominantly young adults between the ages of 20 and 34. In the 1990s, over 35 percent of the people who came to Canada were in this age group, about twice the proportion of any other fifteen-year age category. Between 1992 and 1995, 25 percent of all immigrants into Canada who were in the labour force were professionals, a result of a policy based primarily on the point system of admission, which stresses economics. Still, most recent immigrants are members of families coming to join relatives who had migrated previously, and not independent applicants. Finally, more than half of the total immigration over the past decade had Ontario as the provincial destination (116 761 in 1995), and it is estimated that nearly 90 percent of immigrants settled in the urban areas of the country, especially the major metropolitan centres of Vancouver, Montreal, and Toronto (recall Figure 8.2).

SEX AND AGE COMPOSITION OF THE POPULATION

A knowledge of age and sex composition in a society is essential if comparisons between different populations are to be made and understood. In Canada, nearly 60 percent of all deaths occur to males and over 75 percent of the mortality occurs to people over the age of 45. In India the death rates by sex are about equal, and 75 percent of mortality occurs to people under the age of 45. The age and sex structures affect all basic demographic processes—fertility, mortality, and migration—and accordingly they have a direct relationship to the rates of natural increase in a society.

Until 1981 the sex ratio in twentieth-century Canada had always been over 100 (that is, more males than females), and this occurred in spite of the differential mortality favouring women (McVey and Kalbach, 1995). The highest sex ratio was in 1921 (107). The greater number of males historically was due to differential migration (more males coming to Canada), but in the 1970s this factor was no longer significant. In the 1990s, unless there is a great influx of male immigration or emigration of females from Canada, the sex ratio will stay under 100, given the trends in mortality rates. In 1995 the overall sex ratio was 98, while for ages 65 and over it was 73. In that the average age of the Canadian population is increasing (see below), this decline in the sex ratio will undoubtedly continue.

With some minor fluctuations, Canada's population has shown an increase in median age throughout the twentieth century as well. Figure 15.1 shows six population pyramids for Canada, beginning in 1881 and ending with a projection for the year 2001. A **population pyramid** graphically depicts the age and sex structure of a population, with males arranged on the left side of centre and females on the right. The ages are arranged on the horizontal axis, usually in five-year age groups, and the percentage of people in each age group by sex is presented at the bottom of the pyramid. The 1881 pyramid of Canada (see Figure 15.1) is typical of a "young" population, with a broad base indicating a large proportion of children under the age of 15, and each subsequent age group progressively narrowing, indicating fewer people throughout the advancing age structure. This type of population results from a high crude birth rate, and it is this fertility rate (once mortality is beginning to be controlled) that determines whether the population is young or old (see the box "How a Population Ages or Grows Younger"). The pyramids for 1941 and 1971 show populations with a declining fertility (notice the smaller proportion of people 0 to 4 and 5 to 9 years of age in comparison with those 10 to 14 and 15 to 19) and an overall age structure that is typical of a "middle-aged" population. The projected pyramid for the year 2001 shows the early stages of an "old" population, in which the proportion of people aged 45 to 49 is about the same as that found for the five-year age groups for people under 20 years of age. Contrast this with the 1881 pyramid, in which the proportions of young people in each five-year age category are two to three times those of the people in the age groups 40 to 60. The same patterns affect median age.

In the late 1880s less than 4 percent of the population of Canada was over 65 years of age. By 1991, the proportion was 12 percent. With current fertility actually at or below replacement levels, by the year 2001 that proportion will be approximately 15 percent. If zero population growth (with the average woman having 2.1 children) is maintained for the next fifty years, the proportion of Canada's population over 65 will level out at over 20 percent (see Figure 15.2). This dramatic change in age structure,

FIGURE 15.1 Age-sex pyramids for the census populations of Canada, 1881, 1911, 1941, 1971, 1991, with projection for 2001

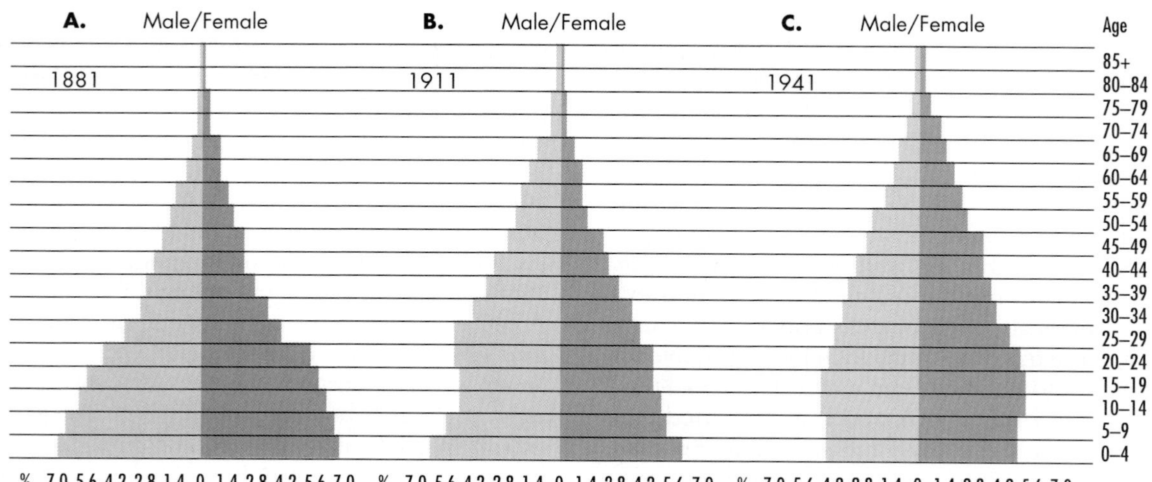

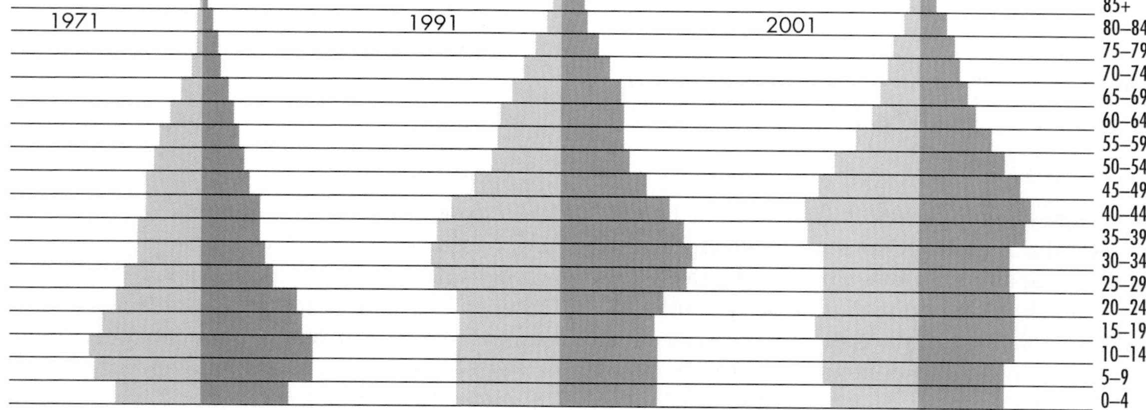

Source: *Joseph A. Norland, 1976.* The Age-Sex Structure of Canada's Population, 1971 Census of Canada, *V (part 1), Catalogue No. 99-703 (p. 57); Statistics Canada, 1974.* Population Projections for Canada and the Provinces, 1972–2001. *Catalogue No. 91-514. Ottawa: Information Canada; Statistics Canada, 1985.* Population Projections for Canada and the Provinces and Territories: 1984–2006. *Catalogue 91-520. Ottawa: Minister of Supply and Services; Statistics Canada, 1992.* Age, Sex, Marital Status and Common Law Status. *Catalogue No. 92-325E. Ottawa: Minister of Industry, Science and Technology.*

FIGURE 15.2 Projected population, by age group, 1992–2036

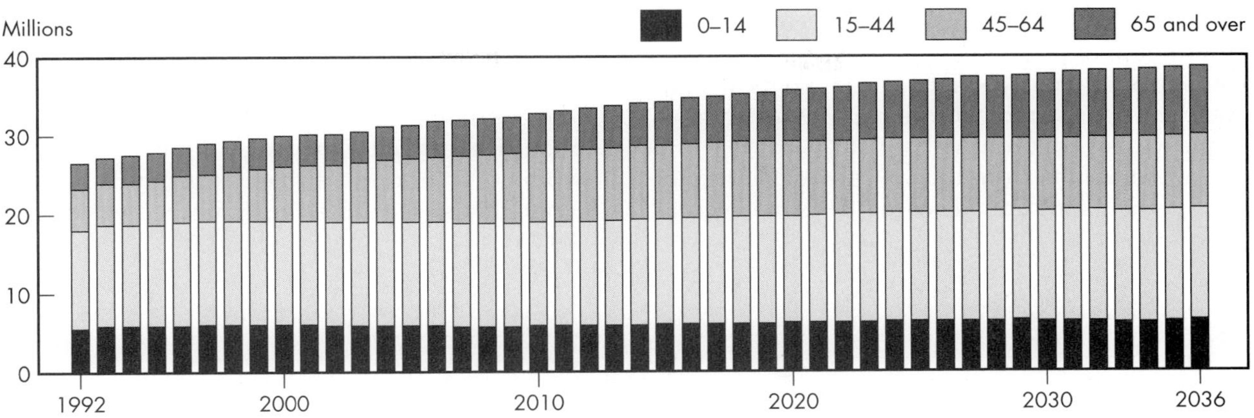

Source: *Statistics Canada, Demography Division, unpublished data, projection 3 modified to use Total Fertility Ratio of 1.84, annual immigration of 250 000, annual emigration of 86 886.*

coupled with a relatively small proportion of the population being under 15 years of age, will have important consequences for resource distribution in terms of medical care, old-age pensions, recreational facilities, educational development, transportation, housing, etc. (Foote and Stoffman, 1996). At the same time it should also be observed that changes in immigration policy could have a major impact on this scenario.

SUMMARY

Worldwide, population growth is an important issue, one that will shape the direction of the world in the foreseeable future. Some authorities argue that the impact of the birth-control policies of the 1970s and 1980s is about to be felt in the high-fertility countries, and that the social, economic, and political mechanisms necessary to bring about population stabilization are in place. It is just a matter of time, they argue, until fertility decreases to a point where there is a manageable growth rate. In fact, the world population growth rate has declined from approximately 2 percent in the 1960s to 1.5 percent in the mid-1990s. Other experts, however, feel that only drastic action to control fertility can reduce the growth rate sufficiently and quickly enough to allow for any significant improvement. Thus, while the world growth rate has declined, the number of people added each year is still close to 100 million.

In effect, then, the world is in a race between economic development, broadly defined, and a population growth that can literally eat away any possible economic improvement. Ultimately, as has been stressed in this chapter, birth rates and death rates must come into balance; it is simply a question of how, when, and under what conditions. The only really acceptable long-run alternative is for fertility rates to come down to match the lowered mortality levels; if not, the potential always exists that death rates will rise to match the high levels of fertility. This is the Malthusian dilemma of preventive and positive checks, and the reality is that one of these checks must occur. It will take a great deal of planning, foresight, organization, and cooperation to achieve a population balance in which birth rates and death rates are both at low levels. In the industrialized world—and this chapter has focused primarily on Canada—the demographic transition is all but completed. Mortality is under control, birth rates are low and at or under replacement figures, and immigration policies reflect governmental estimates of population needs. Thus its problem is less immediate.

But demographic issues are still important for Canadians. Population variables affect social and economic factors, and are in turn affected by them, and changes in one area of society have a rippling effect throughout the social structure. For example, declining fertility has an important effect upon the educational system, housing needs, recreational facilities, support for the aged, etc. In turn, economic conditions, attitudes about marriage and the family, and the work status of women have important consequences for childbearing.

If Canadians from the 1890s were suddenly transported to the Canada of the 1990s they would not recognize it, and the population component, one of the most important changes that has occurred over the last hundred years, would be a significant reason. In the next century there will undoubtedly be as many or more technological, social, and economic differences, and it is certain that the population size, distribution, composition, and change will have an important role to play in the formation of that society of the next hundred years.

QUESTIONS FOR REVIEW AND CRITICAL THINKING

1. Assume that for the next two generations (forty years or so) Canada's level of natural increase and immigration result in a zero population growth rate. What are the consequences of this condition in terms of the aging of the population, education, economic development, medical care, recreation patterns, transportation needs, pension issues, and so forth?

2. Examine your family tree, as far back as you can, noticing fertility and mortality patterns, causes of death, and migration, and compare what you find with the generalizations made in this chapter.

3. Alternatives to traditional family norms and childbearing practices have allowed Canadian women to have fewer children. At the same time there are concerns that the level of fertility in Canada today is below replacement. What policies are possible to reconcile this inconsistency?

4. The world's population is approaching 6 billion people. Assume that the world's level of resource and technological development were stable. What would be the effect on the world and its population if the numbers increased to 12 billion people in the next two generations? How and where would these people live?

GLOSSARY

acute diseases also called infectious diseases, these are illnesses communicable from person to person; the major causes of death prior to the twentieth century

age-specific birth rate the number of births to women of a particular age divided by the total number of women of that age

age-specific death rate the number of deaths to people of a particular age divided by the total number of people of that age; usually arranged in five-year intervals

chronic diseases also called degenerative diseases, these are illnesses usually found in middle and old age and related to the body wearing out; the principal cause of death in industrial societies

crude birth rate the number of births per year per 1000 people

crude death rate the number of deaths per year per 1000 people

demographic transition a model of population change that describes the movement of a society from relatively high fertility and mortality levels to relatively low ones

demography from the Greek *demos*, meaning *people*, it is the science of human numbers in terms of size, distribution, composition, and change

infant mortality rate the age-specific death rate for infants who die in the first year of life

life expectancy the average number of years individuals of a given age can expect to live in the future

migration the movement of people across a significant boundary for the purpose of permanent settlement

natural increase the increase in population occurring when fertility exceeds mortality

population pyramid a graphic representation of the age (usually in five-year intervals) and sex composition of a population

positive checks checks to population growth that raise the death rate, such as war, famine, disease; posited by Malthus

preventive checks checks to population growth that prevent the birth of children, such as abstinence and later marriage; posited by Malthus

sex ratio the number of males in a given population per 100 females in that population. For example, the sex ratio at birth around the world is approximately 105.

SUGGESTED READINGS

Beaujot, Roderic

1991 *Population Change in Canada*. Toronto: McClelland & Stewart.

A systematic discussion of population processes and policies that examines the major variables of population change, including mortality, fertility, migration, aging, and the family. A readable book with an excellent review of the important literature in the field of population change and policy.

Ehrlich, Paul R., and Anne H. Ehrlich

1990 *The Population Explosion*. New York: Simon and Schuster.

A systematic, if polemic, discussion of the problems of world population control, it ends with a recommendation for a maximum of two children per family. This monograph is a must for students interested in the relationship between population growth and environmental destruction.

Foote, David K., and Daniel Stoffman

1996 *Boom, Bust & Echo: How to Profit from the Coming Demographic Shift*. Toronto: Macfarlane Walter & Ross.

A best-selling, popularized account of the importance of the Canadian age structure and demographic patterns (fertility, migration, aging) for various social and economic trends that are taking place in the 1990s. This is a well-written account of the importance of population patterns and trends for the future of Canadian society, with some recommendations on investments such as real estate and travel.

Trovato, Frank, and Carl F. Grindstaff

1994 *Perspectives on Canada's Population*. Toronto: Oxford University Press.

This up-to-date collection of readings on Canada's population, written by Canadian demographers, presents information from a wide range of scholarly approaches. The central areas of demography are investigated, including family formation and dissolution and urbanization.

WEB SITES

http://www.un.org/

The United Nations Homepage

At the UN site, you will find a wealth of information on all aspects of population and population growth through a variety of information sources and databases.

http://www.statcan.ca

Statistics Canada

Canada's premier source of statistical information provides a host of resources for learning more about the Canadian population.

CHAPTER 16

Urbanization

Leslie W. Kennedy

INTRODUCTION

The study of urbanization, or the growth of cities, has a long history in sociology, one that can be traced to the pioneering work of Park (1952) and other "human ecologists" in 1920s Chicago. Since Park's time, however, the issues to be studied and the ways in which these issues should be approached have evolved considerably, due to the changing character of urban settlements and to alterations in society's views of cities as viable places to live.

It is the role of urban sociology to isolate those factors that affect urbanization and to identify those features cities share in common. This is not an easy task, given the range of historical incentives to urbanization and the resultant differences among cities. For example, cities vary in the kinds of people who live in them. They also have different economies and different types of employers. Moreover, they may differ because local governments have varying ideas of the services and facilities that cities should provide. If they differ in so many ways, then, can sociologists succeed in describing how cities change and how they function? How can what they learn in one city be generalized to others?

One factor frequently used to examine city life and change is population size. On the one hand, large city size allows for economies and efficiencies that benefit urban residents. On the other hand, large size can lead to a need for standardization and for complex bureaucratic administration. In addition, the city is a competitive forum in which people struggle for improved opportunity, status, and recognition. Generally, the larger the city, the greater the stakes and rewards, and the greater the competition for scarce resources. The gaps between social groups may widen, and those left behind may become disenchanted with both their social rank and the services that are available to them. Such competition—if only for space—may be increased as well by higher population density, another variable affecting city life.

Other than size and density, increases in the mix of social groups can also affect the urban environment. For example, new immigrants to cities are often faced with language difficulties and culture conflicts. At the same time, more established city residents may have to accommodate these newly arrived minorities. This mix of old and new has often resulted in major political struggles over how services and resources should be allocated to meet the different needs of diverse groups.

The demographic composition of the population is still another factor affecting city life. For example, many metropolises in Latin America, Africa, and Asia, where close to half of the population may be less than fifteen years of age, must struggle to provide shelter and employment opportunities at an ever expanding rate to a younger and highly dependent population. North American and European cities, meanwhile, are faced with different but related problems. As these societies have reduced their birth rates, a relatively large dependent older population has emerged, fuelling demands for age-appropriate shelter, transportation, and social services—in turn requiring a massive reallocation of city resources.

When urban sociologists examine cities in systematic terms—in all of these and other areas—they attempt both to isolate and explain repetitive patterns of behaviour. How, for example, does a large increase in immigrants affect the social life within inner-city neighbourhoods? How do large cities compare with small in terms of the amounts of crime that occur within their boundaries? Does high-density living lead to juvenile delinquency? To psychological stress? These are questions that need answers.

In their search for explanations, urban sociologists have developed a number of theoretical perspectives. Each offers a conceptual framework that outlines how research into a particular set of urban problems should proceed. These perspectives are the focus of this chapter. Before presenting them, we shall look at conditions that led to the origins and growth of cities, especially technological and demographic factors. We shall then examine the social changes that accompany urbanization. These include the movement from rural to urban settings, and the development of suburbs. Finally, we shall briefly examine factors affecting the quality of life in contemporary cities.

THE ORIGIN AND DEVELOPMENT OF CITIES

In early human history, when agricultural surpluses were combined with population increases, substantial numbers of people were released from food production. Many became involved in non-agricultural activities such as manufacturing, trade, administration, and even war, which subsequently generated the beginnings of urban settlements. Another direct consequence of the food surplus was a concentration of economic power in the hands of the small élite that controlled it. This élite attracted full-time specialists in crafts, government, and economy, who then required one another's services. Thus, early settlements soon began to operate as a crossroads of skills and goods, attracting further migration and even greater urban growth (Lapidus, 1986).

The first cities formed in this way were found in early societies located in the Nile Valley, Mesopotamia, and Mesoamerica, where the ecology and the climate combined to provide inhabitants with the ability to create food surpluses. In Mesopotamia, for example, communities formed around religious sites, and acted as economic agencies for the mobilization and exchange of surplus material and labour. These activities then attracted a population of managers, priests, craftspeople, and workers (Lapidus, 1986).

Over time, technological advances and increased agricultural efficiency, including the cultivation of grain, gave birth to the feudal society, with its well-defined and rigid class structure, and clear-cut division of labour according to age, sex, and occupation. Within feudal society, cities were home to political, educational, and religious élites and those who served them, including artisans, servants, and the military. For the most part, however, the population remained in rural areas.

In the modern, industrial era, the nature and function of cities has changed once more. Not only is industrial society more advanced technologically, but social power is tied to the possession of certain skills and becomes more diffused throughout the society than is the case in feudal societies, in which ascriptive criteria determined power. Geographic and social mobility then create competition for space and resources in cities. Cities subsequently become the central focus of modern society, with the majority of the population living in or near these settlements for the first time in history.

One of the most enduring features of the city in the modern era is its tendency to rapid growth. Davis (1967) pointed to three specific principles of demographic change leading to **urbanization**, or the growth of cities. First, the proportion of people living in cities may rise (that is, new cities may develop) because rural settlements grow larger and are reclassified as towns or cities. Second, natural increase—the excess of births over deaths—may be greater in the city than in the country, causing city populations to swell. Third, people may move from the country to the city and thus cause urban growth.

Davis claimed that the first factor, the growth of rural settlements, usually has only a small influence on urbanization. Nevertheless, through annexations, some small towns are absorbed by cities and subsequently redefined as urban. The second factor, natural increase, is also insignificant in bringing about urbanization, as cities rarely have higher rates of natural increase than rural areas. In fact, Davis argued, a chief obstacle to the growth of cities in the past has been their excessive mortality (1967: 11). In Canada, for example, death rates in cities have remained significantly higher than in villages or hamlets. The main source of growth in urban areas, claimed Davis, is rural–urban migration, which in turn is driven by technological change. As a nation's industrial productivity grows, more workers are required in the manufacturing and service industries, which are typically located in cities. People are thus attracted from rural areas, where the mechanization of agriculture reduces the demand for labour, to cities, where jobs are available and wages are generally higher.

Canadian urban settlement

McGahan (1995) identified four main types of settlement that have appeared in Canada since the time of the European conquest. The *colonial entrepôt*, first of all, was a dependent community founded by the metropolitan European colonizers as a garrison or administrative centre for trade. The *commercial centre* was a hub for gathering staples, such as timber, lumber, potash, and wheat, for shipment to Europe. The growth of this type of settlement, claimed McGahan, "was directly linked to the ability of its merchants to exchange primary resources for British manufactured goods" (1995: 47). The *commercial industrial city* grew up with the coming of manufacturing and the location of plants in specific locales. These supply areas and markets were tied together through sophisticated transportation networks. Finally, the *metropolitan community* emerged as urban areas began to dominate whole regions by concentrating financial and political power and transportation in one area (McGahan, 1995: 53).

The history of Canadian urban settlement can be understood by examining the evolution of these various types of settlement. The first step in this direction took place in 1600, through the formation of a colonial entrepôt—a wintering fur depot and trading post—at Tadoussac in New France. By 1663, New France had only 2500 colonists, half of them living in Quebec, Montreal, and Trois-Rivières. By 1698 these three towns constituted 22 percent of the population of 15 355 in New France (see Nader, 1975: 156ff.). Because of its role as the political, cultural, institutional, and military capital of a colony with a highly centralized bureaucracy, Quebec City attracted the largest population and was a commercial centre, but Canada in general could hardly be described as urbanized at this time.

With the transition from French to English rule in Canada after 1760, the focus of the economy turned from the fur trade to agriculture, and a number of new agricultural settlements emerged—made possible by immigration from Britain and the United States. With the expansion of agriculture inland, Montreal replaced Quebec as the preeminent Canadian city, and by the early 1800s was the main commercial centre of Canada. Here were located the principal wholesalers and importers for both the fur trade and the growing agricultural settlements in Upper Canada and the Eastern Townships.

After the designation of Upper Canada as a separate colony in 1791, a need arose to choose an administrative capital and military base for Lake Ontario. Niagara was first considered, but its proximity to the United States made it vulnerable to attack. London and Kingston were also considered, but after much deliberation by the English military, York (present-day Toronto) was selected as the new capital, partly because of its good harbour and easy access to Georgian Bay and Lake Huron. Toronto's ascendancy as the metropolitan centre of Upper Canada was assured from that point onward.

The settlement of the Canadian West did not begin until the early nineteenth century, when a hundred settlers arrived in Point Douglas (now part of Winnipeg) to found the Red River colony. Around this same time a string of colonial entrepôts arose, such as Fort Garry and Fort Edmonton, which facilitated the fur trade in the region. Later, the trans-Canada railway brought new farmers and goods to the west, and settlements began to appear near railway stations. The railway also tied Pacific coastal settlements, previously isolated, to the emerging Canadian urban system.

Despite the growth of urban settlements and their importance as commercial, military, and political centres, Canada remained a predominantly rural society until the middle of this century. By 1930, almost 50 percent of Canada's population still lived in rural areas. Since 1950, however, Canada's population has become increasingly urban. In 1991, three-quarters of Canadians lived in cities. In fact, since the end of World War II, Canada's rate of urban growth has been greater than world averages. Projecting to the year 2001, demographers have estimated that 80 to 85 percent of Canada's population will be urban. It should be noted that these trends hold true most for Ontario and least for the Atlantic provinces.

Along with rural–urban migration, a major factor contributing to urban growth in Canada is immigration (see Chapter 8, Race and Ethnic Relations, and Chapter 15, Demography and Population Study), as new Canadians have tended to choose cities rather than rural areas as their primary destination (refer back to Figure 8.2, p. 203). The major recipients of this immigration flow have been Toronto followed by Montreal and Vancouver.

The concentration of population in these and other Canadian cities is illustrated in Figure 16.1, which displays the 1991 population distribution. For example, the heavy population concentration

FIGURE 16.1 Population distribution, 1991, by census division

Source: Statistics Canada, 1991 Census of Canada. *Produced by the Geocartographics Division of Statistics Canada.*

in the industrial corridor between Montreal and Toronto, compared with smaller population concentration in the cities in the west, is dramatically illustrated in this map.

THE URBAN TRANSFORMATION

The effects of the urbanization process have long interested researchers. As mentioned at the beginning of this chapter, much of the original research on cities was done in Chicago during a time of rapid urban expansion. Along with their study of simple demographic changes, the Chicago researchers were particularly concerned with analyzing the way in which population shifts contributed to major changes in society. In the following section, we shall examine two such movements—rural to urban, and urban to suburban and rural—and the role they have played in shaping Canadian cities.

The rural–urban shift

Historically, population shifts from rural to urban areas have been both large and frequent. This move to the city can disrupt traditional family ties and lead to aimlessness and unhappiness for migrants who come from rural areas and small towns. One major concern of sociologists who examine urban–rural movements is to identify those unique features of cities that often produce these effects. Five major factors differentiating urban from rural life have been identified as significant in this regard (Poplin, 1979).

First, urbanites enjoy greater anonymity than ruralites, who are rarely free from the scrutiny of family and neighbours. While this anonymity can be liberating, urbanites may have to pay a cost in greater loneliness or lack of social support. Second, differences exist in the occupational structure of rural and urban communities, with urban areas characterized by a greater division of labour. This tends to be divisive, as manufacturing and service industries create many occupations not found in a predominantly agricultural, rural society. Third, urban communities are generally more heterogeneous than rural communities. A large percentage of the population of a small rural community may belong to the same political party, worship together, and share the same ethnic background. In cities, however, people encounter others of all types and from all walks of life. The urban community is also characterized by a multitude of organizations and associations. Fourth, in contrast to rural areas, impersonal and formally prescribed relationships are likely to flourish in the urban setting: "certainly it is not possible to develop primary relations with all people with whom [urbanites] come into contact. On the other hand, ruralites may know most of the people with whom they interact. Even when they do run across strangers, ruralites may feel quite free to greet them, offer them assistance..." (Poplin, 1979: 34). Finally, in cities people frequently judge others' status based on the neighbourhoods in which they live, the type of cars they drive, and the clothes they wear. In rural communities, on the other hand, people tend to know each other more intimately, and therefore are better able to judge, rank, and evaluate others on the basis of their personal characteristics.

Despite their intuitive logic, difficulties emerge in applying these rural–urban distinctions to contemporary cities. This is because communication and transportation networks have progressively tied urban and rural areas more closely together. As a result, many of the attributes of urban living can now be found in rural settlements (McGahan, 1995). Thus, while some qualitative differences between cities and rural areas remain, with resultant effects on the quality of life in each, these are increasingly narrowing.

Suburbanization and rural renaissance

A second type of migration to change the urban landscape—suburbanization—began on a large scale in the 1950s. This process largely resulted from the combined effects of several factors: a large increase in the number of young families with children (the baby boom), immigration, and migration to the city from rural areas. These factors led to a demand for more space, both inside and outside of residences, which could be found only on the fringes of the cities.

Suburbanization began on a large scale in the 1950s, through the combined effects of the baby boom, immigration, and migration from rural areas.

Over the years, suburban life has come to be the preferred choice of Canadian city dwellers. Some Canadians have even moved beyond city limits, to rural areas and small towns near larger centres. In the eight-city Urban Canada Study conducted in 1991, the majority of respondents indicated that they would prefer living away from the downtown areas of their city. Those preferring the suburbs ranged from a low of 70 percent in Ottawa to a high of 89 percent in Edmonton (Patterson, 1991b: 5).

For some observers there are real concerns about this suburban and rural growth, particularly in Canada's largest census metropolitan areas (CMAs). Between 1981 and 1991 the population in the urban "fringe" area increased 49 percent in Toronto, Montreal, and Vancouver. In other CMAs it increased less than 30 percent (Patterson, 1992: 2). These developments create problems related to continued dependence on automobiles, inefficiencies in service delivery, and the destruction of agricultural land. In response, city planners talk increasingly of developing "sustainable cities," where densities are set to provide environmentally sensitive solutions to urban problems, including the extension of mass transit systems, garbage recycling, water conservation plans, and so on. Future plans for cities will incorporate these ideas and will pay close attention to the settlement patterns that offer the most cost-effective way of meeting the goal of sustainability.

Perhaps not surprisingly, these movements out of the city to the suburbs or rural areas have traditionally been associated with a drop in the inner-city population of Canada's major metropolitan areas. Toronto's inner city decreased from 37 percent of the total metropolitan area population in 1961 to only 16 percent of the total in 1991. For the same time period, the numbers for Vancouver show a decline from 49 percent to 29 percent, and for Montreal the decline was from 57 percent to 33 percent (McVey and Kalbach, 1995: 165).

Despite these trends, inner city areas have seen major changes as a result of what has been called the "back to the city movement," characterized by the "gentrification" of older, run-down inner city neighbourhoods. For some this has been cause for concern, as gentrification has often resulted in the elimination of affordable housing and the displacement of lower-income residents. In defence of the process, however, it is argued that gentrification saves older neighbourhoods that might otherwise disappear and become commercial. Recent research by Bourne (1993) suggests that gentrification of lower-income areas is only a small part of the overall regeneration of inner city areas. More important, he said, is the social and economic upgrading of middle-class and élite neighbourhoods and new condominium construction on redevelopment sites, such as old warehouses or factories.

Having looked briefly at the movements from rural to urban, and from urban to suburban and rural areas, let us now look at three theoretical perspectives that try to make sense of the urban development process in general. The first perspective, the theory of human ecology, concentrates on the effects of the forces of competition on urban change.

We mentioned human ecology in Chapter 1 and noted there its strong influence on early Canadian sociology.

THEORIES OF URBAN DEVELOPMENT

Human ecology and competition

Early concepts

Based upon their research in Chicago in the 1920s and 1930s, Park and Burgess (1967) observed that urbanization and industrialization lead to a complex division of labour and to a multiplication of the means of transportation. These in turn are conducive to greater social heterogeneity and social mobility, both associated with urban growth. This growth, in turn, leads to social changes in urban areas. One such change is a decline in community cohesion. The old forms of social control represented by the family, the neighbourhood, and the local community are undermined, and their influence is greatly diminished. New communities do emerge, however. These are what Park and Burgess called **natural areas**, communities resulting from the competition for space in cities, characterized by populations having homogeneous social characteristics.

For Park and Burgess, the conceptualization of these processes was based partly on ideas borrowed from the **human ecology** school, which sees changes in the structure of cities as based on the principle of competition for scarce resources and land. This competition results in a number of processes, including centralization, decentralization, concentration, deconcentration, segregation, invasion, succession, and the overriding process, competition.

Centralization refers to the tendency for selected institutions and services to cluster near the city's focal points of transportation. The central business district (CBD), for example, becomes the focal area of the city's business. *Decentralization* refers to the tendency to move away from the central focus of

The human ecology theory of urban development sees changes in the structure of cities as based on competition for scarce resources and land.

the city, so that activities and buildings are spread throughout the urban area. *Concentration* is the massing of people in an area, as in the case of a high-rise development project. *Deconcentration* is the outward movement from existing clusters. An example of this is the population movement to the suburbs.

Segregation, the primary factor leading to the development of natural areas, is the tendency for various groups and institutions to locate in separate and distinct parts of the city. Ecologists use the concept of segregation in several ways. First, the idea of segregation is used to highlight the fact that various parts of the city are characterized by different patterns of land use, for example residential, business, and industrial areas. Second, it refers to the tendency for similar ecological units, such as ethnic groups, to cluster near one another. We discussed this idea in Chapter 8, Race and Ethnic Relations. Segregation brings together people who are racially, economically, and socially homogeneous, who also tend to share common interests, bonds, and needs. Within natural areas, then, we see groups with common interests and needs emerging.

Competition sorts out these various groups. On the one hand, the wealthy become isolated from the poor because of their greater ability to command and control choice residential sites. On the other hand, some minority groups are less able to compete and therefore forced to take up residence in the less desirable sections of the city. The competition never stops, and the organization of the city is constantly in a state of flux and change.

Invasion refers to a situation in which one group or institution encroaches on the territory held by another group or institution. For example, invasion occurs when the CBD expands into immediately adjacent areas. The movement of middle-class families into inner city neighbourhoods to renovate old houses is also a case of invasion. The arrival of a new immigrant group into a neighbourhood and its gradual pushing out of the resident immigrant group is a third example.

Succession refers to the completed process of invasion, in which an area is completely converted from one use to another. The idea of succession is temporal as well as territorial. It entails the replacement of old population groups by new ones and the appearance of new institutions in a given area. Thus, succession may require years of continuous and steady change.

Although these ecological concepts are useful for describing changes that occur in urban areas, critics have pointed out that they do not provide hypotheses that can be empirically tested. To overcome this problem, some ecologists have integrated these concepts into theories of ecological development, which they then use to describe the growth and development of cities.

Theories of human ecology

Perhaps the best-known model of urban development is the **concentric zone theory** proposed by Burgess (1925). He argued that a city grows outward in circles from the central business district (CBD), the location of the highest land values. The land use most typically found adjacent to the CBD is a zone of transition, including light manufacturing plants and rooming-houses for factory workers and transients. Outside this zone are single-family working-class homes, including second-generation immigrant settlements. Further out from the CBD is a zone of more expensive residences. Finally, at the borders of the city and furthest out from the CBD, is the commuter zone (see Figure 16.2). Immigrant groups tend to settle first in the zone of transition and then, as they prosper, move outwards, some eventually landing in the commuter zone.

Although the concentric zone theory was an adequate explanation for the development of some cities, for others it was not. Pineo (1988) and Balakrishnan and Jarvis (1991) did find some support for it in that socio-economic status, especially income, increases with distance from the city core. Nevertheless, in Pineo's sample of twenty-two Canadian cities, residential location was more closely associated with stage in the family life cycle than with income, with the central areas likely to be populated by singles, childless couples, and widows. While none of the relationships was particularly strong, this finding receives support from recent demographic data cited earlier, which show a slight increase in the populations of inner cities across Canada (except Montreal), with these locations especially attractive to better-educated people, single people, childless or single parents,

FIGURE 16.2 Three theories about the growth of cities

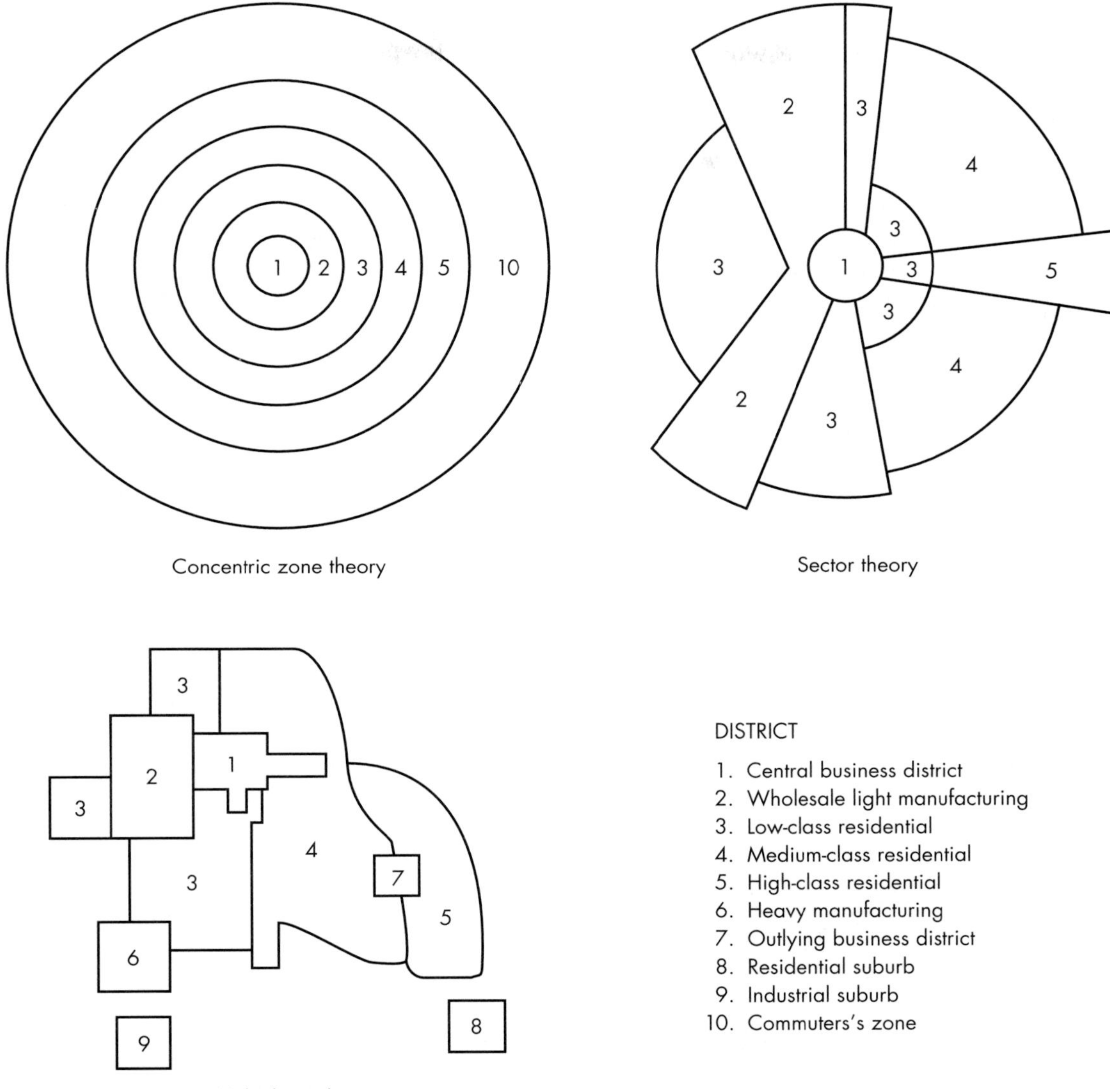

Source: *Chauncy D. Harris and Edward L. Ullman, "The nature of cities,"* Annals of the American Academy of Political and Social Science *242, November, 1945, (p. 12).*

the elderly, and immigrants (*Canadian Social Trends*, 1990).

An alternative to Burgess's explanation is **sector theory**, developed by Hoyt, who argued that most residential developments in urban areas of the United States are distributed relative to commercial and industrial districts of the city (Hoyt, 1939). Hoyt argued that the general spatial pattern of American cities thus should be considered in terms of sectors rather than concentric zones (see Figure 16.2). These sectors resemble wedges that radiate out from the CBD along transportation routes that are the locations of commercial and industrial districts. He argued, further, that the placement of high-rent *residential* areas, rather than the CBD, provides the most important organizing factor for urban growth; their location attracts certain developments (for example, shopping centres) and repels others (for example, heavy industry).

A third perspective on urban development using ecological principles is **multiple nuclei theory**, developed by Harris and Ullman (1945), who proposed that land-use patterns in many cities focus on a number of centres throughout the city. These centres or multiple nuclei (see Figure 16.2) come about for several reasons. First, similar activities that involve specialized facilities, for example those in the transportation industry, tend to group together to form a nucleus. They do this for the same reason that other like activities, such as businesses in a shopping centre, come together—because they all profit from concentration. Second, certain unlike activities tend to repel one another and are therefore kept separate, such as industrial and residential areas. They then form exclusive nuclei. Finally, activities unable to afford the high rents of more desirable sites in the city, such as specialty stores, concentrate in less costly nuclei (see also the boxed insert on "Testing Urban Ecology Models").

Social choice theories

Ecologists generally study the evolution of urban structure that results from migration into the city and the economics of land use. The question that they raise but fail to answer concerns the effect of this structure on people in terms of their relationships with friends or relatives, their recreational pastimes, their work, and so on. How do people live in cities? A second theoretical perspective, social choice, examines these questions.

Theories of social choice focus on shared values, based on a similar cultural heritage, religion, or socialization. These shared values inform the choices that people make with respect to housing arrangements, recreational pursuits, or employment patterns. It is on this choice of lifestyles that we shall focus in our discussion. In so doing we leave the macro-focus of the ecological school and turn to individuals.

Values and urban lifestyles

Wirth (1938) argued that the continued growth of American cities, their increasing density, and their increasing mixture of ethnic, occupational, and income groups would combine to create social environments in which there would be loneliness, alienation, and social deviance.

Testing Urban Ecology Models: How Good Are They Today?

Murdie (1969) examined the evolution of the City of Toronto from 1951 to 1961. He found that changes in the city incorporated the characteristics identified by the concentric zone, sector, and multiple nuclei theories. Together, these three theories provided an integrated view of Toronto's development at that time.

Murdie's findings permit a refinement of the ecological explanation of urbanization. Household attributes and family status were arranged concentrically, as suggested by Burgess. As a result, towards the centre of the city, buildings were older, densities were higher, there was a greater concentration of multiple-unit projects, less private ownership and more rental accommodation, more women employed, and there was a greater proportion of older families and fewer children (cf. Pineo, 1988).

Economic status and social rank had a sectorial distribution, in accordance with Hoyt's model. The lower the incomes, the closer the homes were to places of work. Poorer neighbourhoods tended to be located in poor-quality sections, along industrial and transportation zones. High-income areas followed the placement of amenities suitable for higher-quality housing, such as golf courses and open spaces.

Finally, segregation on an ethnic basis cut across both the concentric zones and the transportation routes. The ethnic clustering was based on concentration of schools and ethnic-based facilities and institutions, thus leading to a multiple nuclei arrangement.

Want to Live Longer? Head for the City

The average Canadian life span, according to Statistics Canada, is 75.1 years for men and 81.1 years for women. Those living in cities, however, can expect to live at least one year longer than those residing in rural areas. The Statistics Canada study also found that residents of Western Canadian cities outlive their Eastern counterparts. British Columbians live longest of all, largely due to the higher incomes enjoyed by residents of that province.

Popular mythology has long suggested that people who live in the country can expect greater longevity, due to the pureness of country air, the low-stress quality of rural life, and other factors. The fact is, however, that those variables most likely to contribute to a longer life—education, economic well-being, and close proximity to medical care—are more likely to be available to city dwellers than to their rural counterparts.

So far, claims Statistics Canada, this finding has not led to any acceleration in Canada's urbanization rates. Many of those living in the country appear to be in no hurry to trade in the joys of country living—the non-polluted environment, the breathtaking views, and the sense of solidarity with nature—simply to add one year to their lives.

Source: *Based upon a story appearing in the* London Free Press *(9 January 1997: A3).*

Gans (1970: 78) disagreed. He stated that Wirth's picture of city life is applicable only if city residents lack the ability to make choices. If people have options, they will make choices that enable them to meet their own needs, which typically vary according to the social class or age-related characteristics of the individuals involved. Depending on the way people vary according to these characteristics, Gans argued, they will adopt different values and ultimately different styles of living in the city.

The social homogeneity that emerges within class- or age-based lifestyle groups is then a critical factor in the creation of communities and the maintenance of social relationships. The differences between single-family and high-rise dwellings, or between urban and suburban locations, *per se*, do not affect social relations. A sense of community arises where people share similar characteristics; this is true for ethnic groups in cities as well. For these groups urbanism is heavily influenced by the cultural norms and values of the collectivity. Individual migrants need not feel alienated, and need not fend for themselves without the assistance of ethnic organizations to make their adaptation easier (Driedger, 1989: 144). We discussed this idea in Chapter 8, Race and Ethnic Relations.

Research in Toronto (Wellman and Wortley, 1990) used social networks as a way of defining community structure. It looked at differences between relationships among friends and relatives versus contacts with casual acquaintances, shopkeepers, etc., and confirmed the view that networks are in place to provide everyday as well as emergency support to individuals living in cities. Further, Campbell and Lee (1992) showed that both men and women interact with neighbours, although women generally maintain larger contact networks than do men. Moreover, while those in higher economic classes tend to have broader social networks in neighbourhoods, the economically disadvantaged still are able to rely on their more limited neighbourhood contacts for friendship and support.

Community size and social choice

Fischer (1995) accepted Gans's view that the values of the subgroup to which people belong determine their behaviour. At the same time, he saw the opportunities offered by large community size and structural differentiation in encouraging the development of these subcultures. The increases in size, density, and heterogeneity talked about by Wirth are not constraints on choice, forcing people into alienating and monotonous environments. Rather, the diversity afforded by large cities creates the opportunity to pursue lifestyles not available in

Social choice theories stress people's ability to choose between options about how they wish to live within an urban environment. Whether in Montreal, New York, or Sydney (pictured here), individuals will to a large extent choose the lifestyle they wish to follow.

smaller, more homogeneous environments. The simple fact that the wide range of opportunities allows particular subgroups to follow their interests argues for the possibility that subcultures can grow and flourish in cities. This does not mean social breakdown. Rather, a new social order arises to accommodate these new interests. The impersonality of city life breeds its own tolerance for the private lives of individuals. Individuality and eccentricity can, in fact, flourish in cities more than in small towns, insofar as an acceptance of deviant lifestyles is more readily obtained. This deviance is even sometimes promoted by the protection that comes with the concentration of large numbers of people who share a deviant lifestyle (cf. Tittle, 1989).

Social power and the allocation of resources

A social power perspective focuses attention on the fact that many decisions about the distribution of people and goods in cities now rest in the hands of planners, government officials, and politicians, all of whom are influenced by individual interest groups. Here we examine the bases upon which these allocation decisions are made in cities, and the consequences they have for urban social structure.

Quality of Life and Social Choice: How Do Canadian Cities Rank?

An important aspect of urban choice stems from the assessment of the quality of life that people experience in their cities. In the *1991 Urban Canada Study*, twelve dimensions of quality of life were measured. These included: the economy; physical environment; social harmony; crime and safety; cultural and recreational amenities; downtown; housing; transportation; services and infrastructure; municipal politics; stress; and city attachment.

The responses to these questions, presented in Tables 16.1 and 16.2, illustrate a wide variation in the living experiences of urban Canadians.

While Vancouver residents are positive about their scenery and climate they express dissatisfaction with traffic congestion. Toronto residents are positive about the city's cleanliness but concerned about crime-gangs and drugs. Montrealers like all the things there are to do there but find the city polluted and dirty.

The overall quality of life index, created by calculating the average ranking across cities and then calculating the relationship of each on the selected items, is presented in Table 16.3. The results show that Calgary has the highest composite index at 70 points and Montreal has the lowest at minus 55 (Patterson, 1991a).

This form of analysis illustrates a way of assessing how city dwellers view their environment and the types of concerns that they express about it. The results provide an interesting indicator, as well, of the types of amenities that people may look for when choosing a city in which to live. The value that people place on the quality of their living environment can provide an important incentive for moving or staying in a particular environment. This can have important consequences for the overall structure of our urban system.

TABLE 16.1 Perceptions of city's best qualities

	Urban Canada	*Van*	*Cal*	*Edm*	*Wpg*	*Tor*	*Ott*	*Mtl*	*Halifax*
(Weighted Base)	*(4018)*	*(679)*	*(305)*	*(329)*	*(286)*	*(1097)*	*(300)*	*(867)*	*(155)*
(Unweighted Base)	*(4014)*	*(504)*	*(500)*	*(500)*	*(500)*	*(503)*	*(500)*	*(501)*	*(506)*
	(%)	*(%)*	*(%)*	*(%)*	*(%)*	*(%)*	*(%)*	*(%)*	*(%)*
Scenery/Surroundings	19	62	23	14	2	4	22	13	10
Cleanliness	15	11	20	13	8	22	30	9	10
Variety of things to do	15	10	5	10	8	18	8	23	8
Parks/Recreational activities	12	14	10	12	7	7	30	12	6
Friendly people	11	9	25	17	24	7	7	9	13
Climate/Weather (general)	11	41	24	6	10	1	1	2	2
Racial groups	11	7	1	4	4	16	4	19	1
Size/Population	8	5	11	13	18	3	24	3	21
Convenience	8	4	7	3	2	12	6	8	12
Cultural activities	7	2	1	2	5	8	2	19	2
Arts and entertainment	7	3	2	3	2	16	6	7	2
Good transit system	7	2	2	2	3	14	3	10	2
Low crime rate	7	3	5	6	7	12	8	4	6
Shopping	7	2	2	10	3	10	3	9	5
Easy to travel around	6	3	6	11	8	5	6	6	6
Restaurants/Nightlife	5	2	2	2	2	3	2	14	2

Source: *J. Patterson, 1991. "Things that matter to urban dwellers." Institute of Urban Studies Newsletter, 37 (pp. 1–4).*

TABLE 16.2 Perceptions of city's worst qualities

	Urban Canada	Van	Cal	Edm	Wpg	Tor	Ott	Mtl	Halifax
(Weighted Base)	*(4018)*	*(679)*	*(305)*	*(329)*	*(286)*	*(1097)*	*(300)*	*(867)*	*(155)*
(Unweighted Base)	*(4014)*	*(504)*	*(500)*	*(500)*	*(500)*	*(503)*	*(500)*	*(501)*	*(506)*
	(%)	*(%)*	*(%)*	*(%)*	*(%)*	*(%)*	*(%)*	*(%)*	*(%)*
Crime gangs, drugs	20	15	10	13	9	37	4	19	10
Traffic congestion	20	31	10	9	6	27	6	19	18
Pollution/Dirty	12	11	3	3	5	11	3	27	7
High cost of living	8	7	4	1	2	19	4	4	3
Overdevelopment/Crowded	8	11	8	4	2	14	1	4	3
Municipal gov't/Politicians	7	4	3	10	12	4	24	6	4
Winters	6	1	11	23	31	2	7	2	1
Climate/Weather (general)	6	5	14	17	15	2	8	2	4
Condition of streets	6	4	4	14	8	1	3	11	3
Economy/Lack of jobs	5	2	3	2	7	4	2	12	5
Taxes	4	1	2	4	13	4	4	5	3
Racism/Racial tensions	4	2	2	1	2	3	0	9	5
Homeless people	4	2	1	1	1	2	2	12	1
Rain	3	17	0	0	0	0	0	0	0

Source: *J.Patterson, 1991. "Things that matter to urban dwellers."* Institute of Urban Studies Newsletter, *37 (pp. 1–4).*

TABLE 16.3 The urban Canada quality of life index

(Base)	Van *(500)*	Cal *(500)*	Edm *(500)*	Wpg *(500)*	Tor *(500)*	Ott *(500)*	Mtl *(500)*	Halifax *(500)*
The Economy	+5	+8	+3	−5	−2	−2	−6	−2
Physical Environment	+6	+7	−4	−7	−7	+5	−10	+8
Social Harmony	−4	+6	+4	+5	−9	+4	−10	+5
Crime & Safety	−1	+5	+1	−4	−3	+2	−2	−2
Cultural/Recreational Amenities	−1	+6	+2	−2	+7	0	−7	−8
Downtown	0	0	−5	−8	+6	+2	0	+1
Housing	−6	+1	0	+10	−7	+5	+2	+1
Transportation	−6	+4	+2	−1	+4	+2	−4	−4
Services & Infrastructure	0	+6	−3	−5	+5	+2	−6	+2
Municipal Politics	+9	+6	−2	−13	−2	−2	+6	+1
Lack of Stress	−10	+11	+2	+6	−11	+3	−8	+7
Attachment to City	+4	+10	+2	−1	−11	−1	−10	+6
Overall Quality of Life Index	−4	+70	+2	−25	−30	+20	−55	+15
Overall Quality of Life Ranking	5	1	4	6	7	2	8	3

Source: *J.Patterson, 1991. "Things that matter to urban dwellers."* Institute of Urban Studies Newsletter, *37 (pp. 1–4).*

Special interests and urban gatekeepers

Neighbourhoods have been treated by ecologists as geographical areas where people with similar characteristics live in similar types of dwellings. In contrast, researchers more concerned with the values and sociocultural relations of urban residents have treated neighbourhoods as areas where urbanites interact and find mutual support. The social power perspective, for its part, focuses on the neighbourhood as an area in which special interests develop and whence the power to affect the distribution and allocation of municipal resources derives.

For Pahl (1969), it is the pattern of *constraints* rather than opportunities that operates differentially in urban decision-making contexts. The basic propositions used by Pahl in his argument are the following. First, there are fundamental spatial constraints on access to scarce urban resources and facilities. These constraints are generally expressed in terms of time and distance. Second, there are fundamental social constraints, because of differing political power, on access to scarce urban facilities. For example, residents of affluent neighbourhoods may be more likely to obtain branch libraries or quick repairs to roads than residents of poorer neighbourhoods. Third, conflict in the urban system is inevitable. The more the resource or facility is valued by the total population in a given locality, or the higher the value and the scarcer the supply in relation to demand, the greater the conflict. Pahl (1969: 149) argued that the crucial power brokers are those who control or manipulate the scarce resources and facilities. This includes property developers, local government officers, social workers, and city councilors. It is the decisions made by these "gatekeepers" that influence the social and physical landscape of the city.

The social control exerted over individual behaviour by these gatekeepers, or special-interest groups seeking to dominate urban society has been discussed in relation to both public safety issues by Smith (1989) and to the eradication of street crime by Lowman (1989). At issue, Lowman stated, is the power to make law, the power to enforce it, the power to avoid criminal prosecution, the power to avoid victimization, and the power to affect our underlying notions of what is wrong in the first place. For example, in response to concerns about social disorder, urban gatekeepers campaigned to remove slums through urban renewal programs. Many such programs were implemented in North American cities in the late 1960s and early 1970s.

Early urban renewal efforts initially concentrated on removing "blighted" areas from inner cities and attempted, through orderly planning, to provide decent, safe, and sanitary housing. Some researchers believed that by improving the physical environment of certain neighbourhoods, living conditions for city dwellers would be much better. This perspective identified specific physical factors, such as overcrowding and physical deterioration, as having major negative effects on the social life of the city. "To remove slum areas is to remove social problems" is the general point of view adopted by this school of thought.

Other urban researchers felt uncomfortable with this simple solution. They argued that such things as differences in age, sex, and social relations—factors that make some people living in slums happier with their environments than others—were being ignored. They pointed out that many of the people who are displaced by slum-clearing programs become very disgruntled with their new and physically better environments, and express great loss at having to leave their former homes (Fried, 1973). Whereas they had friends and neighbours on whom they could rely in their older neighbourhood, in the process of urban renewal these friends have often been moved too far away to be relied upon for support on a day-to-day basis. Thus, although there is a change for the better in the physical environment, there is a change for the worse in the social environment.

Fighting back: citizen participation strategies

The negative effects of urban gatekeeping, as seen in the example of urban renewal discussed above, have often led to an increased political awareness on the part of those being displaced. Such awareness has been translated into attempts to gain greater power through citizen participation in planning decisions affecting their homes and neighbourhoods. This grassroots approach to planning and urban redevelopment has been advocated in many areas of

Urban renewal efforts date back to the 1920s. Here, health inspectors visit a home in a poor area of Toronto.

Canada, although in some cases popular organizing has come too late to stop community destruction, as was true in the Africville area of Halifax, a predominantly black residential neighbourhood of the city that was destroyed by urban renewal. Some social agencies and political groups have also provided technical and organizational expertise to citizen groups to help them combat developers and city hall more effectively.

Such popular organizing, Pahl (1989) suggested, reveals a tendency to define citizen–developer power struggles in terms of service consumption (or lifestyle). Traditional struggles in society—based on occupational or employment background—have been replaced by conflict based on lifestyle. People with similar lifestyles join together to gain concessions for their group when city developers are making choices. For example, groups who would use recreational facilities might support municipal subsidies, while others would advocate a system funded by user fees. This change in orientation brings the social power perspective more closely in line with the social choice model. What is added is the importance of control over resources leading to political power and, hence, to influence over the urban institutions that dispense these resources.

As a result of these changes in citizen–developer relations, planning and city politics are increasingly products of compromise. Whether the results are considered successes or failures depends on whose interests are being served. Overall, however, the value of maintaining neighbourhood integrity and community solidarity is tipping the scale in the direction of the people living in the affected communities. Fighting environmental decay (including poor housing conditions and crime) is now often thought of in terms of *rehabilitation* of existing areas; such activity maintains the unique social and physical character of these areas (e.g., Historic Properties in Halifax and Rossdale in Edmonton), instead of redeveloping them by tearing down and replacing existing structures.

Urban planners must thus consider the interpersonal relations of citizens as well as the physical structure of the city. Alternative forms of planning of social and physical structures in today's urban environment are developing from the struggles of the 1970s and 1980s. The redistribution of decision-making power will reflect the changing demands of the new lifestyle groups forming in modern Canadian cities. We can see these points further illustrated in two specific areas: housing and crime.

URBAN SOCIAL ISSUES: HOUSING AND CRIME

The relationship between the social and physical aspects of urban life discussed above can be used to enhance our understanding of specific issues and problems encountered in Canadian cities. We shall begin with the basic concern of providing suitable accommodation for urban residents, followed by a discussion of urban crime.

Urban shelter

Although the majority of Canadians still dream of owning their own house, increased costs have made this dream unattainable for many. In 1991, only 64 percent of Canadians owned their own home (Law, 1992), and in cities over 500 000 the figure is even less (Che-Alfred, 1990). In recent years increased numbers of multiple-family condominium units have been built. This growth in owner-occupied apartments signals an important change in housing in Canada. Interestingly, however, condominiums represent the most expensive form of housing, costing more per unit on average than single-family homes. Rental housing is often expensive too. In 1986, 36 percent of all renter families paid 30 percent or more of their income on shelter, while only 13 percent of owners paid this proportion (Bird, 1990).

Certain groups are particularly vulnerable to the problem of housing costs. As Bird (1990: 10) indicated, 56 percent of female-headed, lone-parent households paid 30 percent or more of their income on shelter. Among young families renting in census metropolitan areas, 72 percent with the principal earner aged between fifteen and nineteen had problems affording housing, as did 46 percent with a principal earner aged between twenty and twenty-four.

To respond to needs of low-income earners, governments began in the 1970s to build subsidized housing projects, such as Regent Park in Toronto. A more recently adopted strategy has been to provide assisted housing, where tenants pay rent according to their incomes, with the majority in any rental project paying market rents (McMillan, 1987: 29). Assisted housing programs rely on the marketplace to provide sufficient housing to meet the needs of low-income tenants. Implicit in this strategy is the hope that middle-class values will be transmitted to the poorer neighbours. While the success of this attempt at social engineering has not yet been demonstrated, the practice can reduce the stigma attached to living in low-income projects. Still, there is the possibility of resentment directed towards subsidized families from those paying full rent. Also, when housing is scarce, only less desirable living units are available for assisted housing.

Non-profit organizations have also been involved in constructing low-cost housing, even serving as landlords. Typically, the government guarantees their mortgage loans and subsidizes rents for those living in the project. This process of handing the control over low-cost housing construction and maintenance to low-income groups has been lauded in Canada and elsewhere as an effective means of providing shelter for the poor (*Los Angeles Times*, 1992).

At the extreme end of the continuum in the housing market are the homeless. The homeless are likely to be people with substance-abuse problems, who are out of work, and/or out of money. Often they are former residents of state-sponsored institutions, such as psychiatric hospitals (Jencks, 1994).

Understanding Crime in Canadian Cities: A Human Ecology Approach

Over the years an important focus of ecological theory has been the explanation of the socio-spatial dimensions of deviant behaviour. A recent application looks at how routine activities of urban residents make them more or less vulnerable to crime. Based loosely on the works of ecologists Hawley (1950) and Shaw and McKay (1942), routine activities theory proposes that the convergence in space and time of motivated offenders, suitable targets, and the absence of capable guardians increases the probability of crime (Felson, 1994). Routine daily activities affect the likelihood that property and personal targets will be visible and accessible to those planning illegitimate activities. Using data from the Canadian Urban Victimization Survey, Kennedy and Forde (1990) reported findings related to property and personal crime that consider the degree of exposure that individuals experience through following certain lifestyle patterns. They found that the group most vulnerable to assault is comprised of young, unmarried males who frequent bars, go to movies, go out to work, and spend time out of the house walking or driving around. It appears that it is this public lifestyle that increases risk.

Kennedy and Forde reported a similar pattern for robberies. Young, unmarried males who frequent bars and who are out walking or driving around are more likely to be victims of this crime. This type of lifestyle presents offenders with opportunities to commit crime. And just as age and sex affect the likelihood of one becoming a victim, Sampson and Wooldredge (1987) also concluded that variations in demographic and structural characteristics such as age, sex, and urbanization play a part in the committing of a crime.

This work on routine activities brings some of the ecological ideas into contemporary focus, making the link between characteristics of the urban environment and exposure to risk. The strength of this work lies in its ability to use the different lifestyles of urban residents to explain other urban phenomena.

However, care must be taken in using human ecology perspectives, as they rely on information about social aggregates rather than studying the individuals themselves. While individuals interact symbolically and define their own communities, these definitions tend to be ignored by ecologists. The communities of ecologists are real only as they are defined by the census groupings used in the analysis of data. This type of analysis leads to the problem of the *ecological fallacy*, which involves making inferences about the characteristics of individuals based on the characteristics of an area or group. For example, we cannot assume that all people living in high-crime areas are criminals. Also, the assumption in ecology that cities evolve according to some natural order ignores the effects of deliberate urban design and planning in bringing about certain urban forms and settlements.

The actual extent of the homelessness problem in Canada is yet unmeasured, partly because household surveys are used to determine population counts. In the U.S., however, where homelessness has risen to epidemic proportions, the Census Bureau has made a special effort to track homeless individuals through a special census.

Overall, Canadians are finding that housing choices are changing in the 1990s. Higher costs, innovations such as cooperative housing (Burke, 1990), new directions in the government role in providing housing assistance, and increasing concern with homelessness point to some major differences in living styles that we can expect in the next decade.

Community reactions to crime

Crime is an enduring concern of urban Canadians. Fear of crime may be a consequence not only of actual crime, but also of lack of confidence in police, concern about newcomers to the city whom people may label as potential criminals, media impressions of increases in crime rates, and personal precautions taken to ensure safety (Krahn and Kennedy, 1985).

Evidence of lack of social control in the physical environment also increases fear of crime. Wilson and Kelling (1982), using the analogy of the broken window, argued that public disorder is a progressive state encouraged by signs within the community that there is an acceptance of such disorder. When one window is broken, it provides encouragement to break others. The same idea applies to graffiti. Skogan (1990) reported that perceptions of social disorder are most strongly associated with fear in the neighbourhood in which respondents are most aware of aspects of "incivility." This incivility can include abandoned buildings, loitering teens, and broken windows. These incivility factors create a sense of unease and a feeling that informal social control of criminal behaviour does not exist.

The progressive decay of the constraints on behaviour that encourages this general state of decline provides the breeding ground for criminality. One way of preventing this from occurring is through the development of neighbourhood foot patrols—by taking police officers out of their cars and putting them back on the beat. The most important task of the police is to strengthen the informal social control mechanisms of natural communities that exist in urban areas so as to minimize fear in public places. This process allows the public to become less alienated from the problems on the street and to become involved with the police in crime prevention.

Sherman and colleagues (1989) claimed that there are "hot spots" for crime, that is, locations where a large number of offences occur. These include public places, such as bars, and private locations, such as homes where the police are repeatedly called to deal with family problems. They suggested that the police target these hot spots, either through increased vigilance or through their removal altogether. This, they say, will reduce the possibility that crime will occur at these locations.

The idea of physical structure affecting social relationships, and thereby affecting crime, has also become a popular one among law-enforcement agencies, urban physical planners, and architects. The concept of **defensible space** is the idea that crime can be prevented by constructing neighbourhoods in such a way that interaction between residents is increased and neighbourhood surveillance is facilitated, for example through the installation of good dead-bolt locks and ensuring that windows of adjacent houses face on parks for surveillance (Krupat and Kubzansky, 1987).

More work has to be done to identify additional areas of concern and to suggest ways of correcting social problems in cities. The research agenda that faces the urban sociologist is challenging, and it may play an important role in determining the future of urban settlements in Canada.

Urbanization in the Developing World: Wrestling the Tiger

While cities in the developed world fret over issues such as sustainable development, contracting out of services, and core revitalization, developing world cities are concerned with much more basic dilemmas—most related to their phenomenal growth in recent years. The number of developing world cities with over one million population is expected to double during the last two decades of this century, from 118 to 284, while the population of these cities is expected to triple, from 339 million to 931 million. By the year 2000, twenty-one of the world's thirty largest metropolitan areas will be in developing countries (Rondinelli, 1988: 22).

Consider the case of São Paulo, Brazil, the largest city in South America, and projected to be the world's largest by the year 2000. Between 1961 and 1993 the municipality of São Paulo tripled in size, from 3.7 million to nearly 10 million, while the greater São Paulo region increased from 4.7 million to over 15 million. And while municipal growth has stabilized somewhat overall (at about 1 percent per year), newer (and generally less affluent) areas on the city's southern and eastern peripheries continue to expand at an annualized rate of between 2 and 3 percent (EMPLASA, 1993: II.2.49–50). Interestingly, this pattern of growth reflects an inversion of Burgess's concentric zone model, insofar as the wealthier residential areas of the city are located closer to the city centre.

The social problems made worse by São Paulo's rapid growth are many. One of the most serious of these is poverty. As an industrial and financial centre, São Paulo is the wealthiest city in Brazil (if not all of Latin America). Yet many of its residents survive on very meagre incomes. The median income of male wage-earners, for example, is less than $3600, as compared with approximately $29 000 for larger cities in Canada. Some 35 percent of all families subsist on less than $4500, and about 10 percent on less than $1800 per year.

Another problem is housing. Not only is household occupant density higher in São Paulo than it is in most Canadian cities, but substandard housing is a serious problem in many areas. In the city core, some 3 million residents known as *cortiços* reside cheek by jowl in decrepit factories and old mansions converted to tiny flats. Another 800 000 inhabit precarious shacks in sprawling *favelas* spread throughout the city (PMSP, 1992: 34–36).

Basic services for the majority of the municipal population are also seriously lacking. In some areas of the city, especially on the periphery, streets are unpaved and neighbourhoods frequently lack schools and parks. Commuting from outer areas to the city centre and industrial nuclei is also a challenge. The public transportation system is both inexpensive and extensive—well over 3 billion passengers ride the bus or subway in the municipality of São Paulo each year, compared with about 420 million in Toronto. Service, however, is often sporadic, uncomfortable, time-consuming, and sometimes unsafe.

The quality of policing represents still another concern. Municipal and especially state military police maintain a high visibility, but the crime rate remains staggering. From January to November of 1996, police registered 7171 homicides, 101 700 robberies, and 103 200 auto thefts ("*Grande SP registra*," 1996).

Health care, finally, is seriously inadequate, as indicated by São Paulo's infant mortality rate of 31 per thousand—five times the Canadian rate. Along with a general lack of free public facilities, hospitals and health centres tend to be concentrated in the city core. With only 14 percent of the total population, the downtown region is home to nearly half of São Paulo's 167 health facilities. By contrast, the eastern periphery, with 28 percent of the population, has less than 1 percent of all facilities (EMPLASA, 1993: II.2.50, III.2.23). A lack of sanitary sewers in many regions compounds health problems. In the absence of septic tanks or other waste treatment strategies, sewage on many streets simply flows down open drainage ditches and eventually into nearby streams and rivers.

Source: *W.E. Hewitt, 1997. [Written for this volume.]*

TABLE 16.4 The World's Largest Cities, 1991

	Population in Millions		Population in Millions
Tokyo-Yokohama, Japan	27.2	Delhi, India	8.8
Mexico City, Mexico	20.9	Paris, France	8.7
São Paulo, Brazil	18.7	Karachi, Pakistan	8.0
Seoul, South Korea	16.8	Lagos, Nigeria	8.0
New York, USA	14.6	Essen, Germany	7.5
Osaka-Kobe-Kyoto, Japan	13.9	Shanghai, China	6.9
Bombay, India	12.1	Lima, Peru	6.8
Calcutta, India	12.0	Taipei, Taiwan	6.7
Rio de Janiero, Brazil	11.7	Istanbul, Turkey	6.7
Buenos Aires, Argentina	11.7	Chicago, USA	6.5
Moscow, Russia	10.4	Bangkok, Thailand	6.0
Manila, Philippines	10.2	Bogota, Colombia	5.9
Los Angeles, USA	10.1	Madras, India	5.9
Cairo, Egypt	10.1	Beijing, China	5.8
Jakarta, Indonesia	9.9	Hong Kong	5.7
Tehran, Iran	9.8	Santiago, Chile	5.4
London, UK	9.1	Pusan, South Korea	5.0

Source: *Adapted from Nancy Kleniewski, 1997.* Cities, Change and Conflict. *Belmont, CA: Wadsworth (p. 77).*

SUMMARY

We began with a historical overview of the origins and development of cities, with particular emphasis on Canada. We then considered the urban transformation process, focusing on the rural-to-urban population shift and suburbanization. In the following section a range of theories of urban development was examined, including the human ecology approach, which considers the evolution of urban structures resulting from population shifts and the economics of land use; social choice theories, which consider how values shape urbanites' choices with respect to housing, recreation, employment, etc.; and the social power perspective, which views urban change as a function of élite or special-interest-group directives. We concluded the chapter with a brief overview of two common urban problems in Canada: housing and crime.

The increasing complexity of urban environments requires that even more research be done, research that can help in planning better cities. But does planning mean regimentation? There are those who argue that it is exactly the diversity of urban life that makes cities unique. These admirers of city life use the adjectives "vibrant," "exciting," "unpredictable," and "colourful" to describe city life. It is this sense of place and the spice of diversity, the argument goes, that make modern cities attractive to many and put them in place as the centres of contemporary culture.

Certain trends in other world cities, however, particularly in the United States, should be taken into account in our assessment of the future of the city in Canada. Gordon (1985) presented a sobering assessment of the decline and ever-increasing crime rates in American cities. Racism and related problems in inner cities have caused residents to flee to places (e.g., suburbs) where these problems can be avoided or ignored, justifying their flight in the name of pursuing individual goals. In these actions there is a stated refusal to confront the inevitable conflict of divergent interests. This undermines the need to deal with the unfortunate consequences of urban conflict, which stems from the frustration of poverty or the friction between racial or ethnic groups.

The conflict is left to those who have few resources to cope with it, to those in neighbourhoods where escape from racial tension is made difficult by low incomes or scarce affordable housing. Accompanied by short-term planning and political non-accountability, these trends pose major threats to viable urban living environments. Canadians would do well to take heed of these problems in the United States. Long-range planning that attends to concerns about racial and ethnic tensions, problems of poverty and homelessness must be a high priority on our social agenda for cities in the twenty-first century.

QUESTIONS FOR REVIEW AND CRITICAL THINKING

1. Recall the bases for the origins of cities, focusing specifically on the Canadian experience. What factors figured prominently in the historical growth of your home city or town?

2. Despite the influences of the mass media and improved transportation, what differences remain between rural and urban areas? Are some increasing? Are there some not listed in the text?

3. Take a walking or automobile tour of your city or town. Does the concentric zone model describe what you find? The sector model? The multiple nuclei model?

4. How does your city compare on the quality of life index? Do you agree with others' assessments of your city?

5. Identify the "hot spots" for crime in your city or town.

GLOSSARY

concentric zone theory the theory of urban growth proposing that a central core, a zone in transition, and increasingly affluent neighbourhoods radiate from the centre of the city outward

defensible space building and neighbourhood construction that has been designed to discourage crime by increasing interaction between residents and, consequently, public surveillance

human ecology a theoretical perspective developed to explain changes in the social structure of the city based on the principle of competition for scarce resources and land. This competition results in a number of processes, including centralization, concentration, segregation, invasion, and succession.

multiple nuclei theory a theory of urban development that sees a number of centres developing in the city around specialized facilities

natural areas communities that emerge from the competition for space in cities, characterized by populations having homogeneous social characteristics

sector theory the theory of urban development that sees city land-use patterns characterized by wedge-like sectors, which begin at the centre of the city and follow transportation routes outward

urbanization the growth of cities, due to reclassification of rural areas as urban, natural population increase, and/or movement from rural areas to cities

SUGGESTED READINGS

Driedger, Leo

1991 *The Urban Factor*. Toronto: Oxford University Press.

This book provides a contemporary view of Canadian urban settlements with an emphasis on the human ecology perspective.

Fustel de Coulanges, Numa Denis

1956 *The Ancient City*. New York: Doubleday/Anchor.

Originally published in 1864, this classic work examines city life in ancient Greece and Rome.

McGahan, Peter

1995 *Urban Sociology in Canada*. (3nd ed.) Toronto: Harcourt Brace.

This book presents a thorough review of urban theory (with a special emphasis on ecological, aggregate models) as it applies to Canadian cities.

WEB SITES

http://www.city.net/

City Net

City Net is your gateway to the urban world. Choose a city and explore.

http://www.cip-icu.ca/eng/intro.html

Canadian Institute of Planners

This site provides information on dimensions and benefits of urban planning in Canada. There are links as well to other related planning sites worldwide.

Glossary

acculturation the learning of the language, values, and customs of a dominant group by an ethnic group; also called *cultural assimilation* (p. 228)

achieved status a position in a status hierarchy attained by individual effort or accomplishment (p. 169)

acute diseases also called infectious diseases, these illnesses are communicable from person to person; the major causes of death prior to the twentieth century (p. 424)

age-specific birth rate the number of births to women of a particular age divided by the total number of women of that age (p. 428)

age-specific death rate number of deaths to people of a particular age divided by the total number of people of that age; usually arranged in five-year intervals (p. 423)

alienation according to Marx, a distortion built into the structure of capitalism, in which workers are put into conflict with others and lose control of creative capacity, the productive process, and the product of their labour (p. 364)

altruistic suicide according to Durkheim, the suicide caused by the excessively strong integration found in some groups (p. 4)

anomic suicide according to Durkheim, the suicide caused by feelings of being without limits or of boundlessness, a result of the relative lack of regulation found in some groups (p. 4)

anomie theory the explanation that views the widespread discrepancy between a society's goals and the legitimate means it provides to achieve those goals as leading to normlessness and eventually to deviance (p. 116)

anticipatory socialization the learning of attitudes, beliefs, and behaviours that will be required for those new roles individuals expect to play in the future (p. 78)

ascribed status a position in a status hierarchy that is inherited or assigned (p. 168)

assimilationism the view that ethnic diversity gradually and inevitably declines as group members are absorbed into the general population, in the process becoming more and more like the dominant group (p. 226)

authority according to Weber, power that is seen as legitimate by those subjected to it (p. 333)

axiomatic logic the making of connecting links between related statements for deriving hypotheses (p. 23)

bourgeoisie the capitalist class, as defined by Marx. The *petite bourgeoisie* were the small property owners, destined to be swallowed by the larger capitalists. (p. 172)

bureaucracy a special type of formal organization characterized by centralized, hierarchically organized authority. It emphasizes impersonal work relationships, technical knowledge, and rationality. (p. 358)

calling a purpose in life. In a religious context, it is a belief that people are born with certain abilities in order to fulfil God's will on earth through their life's work. (p. 281)

capital accumulation theory the theory of education that argues that capitalists use schools to defuse class antagonism and to make workers docile, cooperative employees (p. 306)

chain migration sequential movement of persons from a common place of origin to a common destination with the assistance of relatives or acquaintances already settled in the new location (p. 202)

charisma the recognition and acceptance of authoritative claims based not on traditions, rational argument, or accepted procedures, but on the person or group of persons and their personal messages (p. 282)

charismatic authority according to Weber, authority that rests upon the belief that a leader has special qualities and therefore should be obeyed (p. 362)

chronic diseases also called degenerative diseases, these are illnesses usually found in middle and old age and related to the body wearing out; the principal causes of death in industrial societies (p. 424)

church a type of established religious organization usually characterized by membership by birth. It often represents the only religion of a given society. (p. 285)

circular reaction a special type of social interaction in which responses are reinforced among people. The behaviour of one individual stimulates a response in another person, which in turn reinforces the tendency of the first person, and so on. (p. 383)

circulation of élites Pareto's conception that the decline of one élite prepares the way for domination by another; *lions* seize power, become *foxes*, and are in turn replaced by new lions (p. 335)

civil religion the common beliefs and rituals of a political community that interpret political activity in religious or quasi-religious terms (p. 293)

civil society Hegel's market system of industry and exchange; its principle is individual self-interest and personal gain (p. 341)

class a set of individuals sharing similar economic status or market position (p. 170)

class for itself a Marxian category including people who share the same economic position, are aware of their common class position, and who thus may become agents for social change (p. 172)

class in itself a Marxian category including people who share the same economic position, but who may be unaware of their common class position (p. 172)

class, status, party Weber's answer to Marx concerning the bases of social inequality: class is economic, status is prestige, party is political; all three are measures of inequality (pp. 170, 168, 175)

cluster sampling a series of random samples taken in units of decreasing size, e.g., census tracts, then streets, then houses, then residents (p. 27)

collective action the pursuit of goals by more than one person. As an explanation of social movements, this perspective looks at integration and cleavage factors and seeks to explain what is dissimilar about collective action at different times and in different places. (p. 387)

collective behaviour activity in which a large number of people reject and/or do not conform to conventional ways of acting. Behaviour of this kind is often described as less "institutionalized" than ordinary behaviour. (p. 381)

collective conscience Durkheim's term for the set of agreed-upon standards of society assumed to have arisen out of consensus (p. 104)

colonialism the domination by a settler society of a native or indigenous population. The colonizing society extracts resources from the conquered land, establishes settlements there, and administers the indigenous population, frequently employing violence and a racist ideology. In time, the colonized population suffers the erosion of its traditional culture, economy, and way of life, and usually occupies a subordinate status in the pluralist society of which it has involuntarily become a part. (p. 215)

concentric zone theory the theory of urban growth proposing a central core, a zone in transition, and increasingly affluent neighbourhoods radiating from the centre of the city outward (p. 450)

conflict theory the sociological model that portrays society as marked by competition and/or exploitation. Its three major concepts are power, disharmony, and revolution. (p. 8)

consumer religion Bibby's idea that religious beliefs and services are increasingly treated by people as consumer items to be chosen or discarded at will (p. 295)

content analysis a method of analysis that extracts themes from communications, including letters, books, and newspapers (p. 31)

contraculture a way of life in opposition to, not merely distinct from, the larger culture; also called *counterculture* (p. 118)

control variables variables included in a model of behaviour that are neither independent nor dependent variables. They are controlled or held constant to check on apparent relationships between independent and dependent variables. (p. 30)

correlation a statistical demonstration that changes in one variable coincide with changes in another variable. Correlation is not to be confused with *cause*. (p. 35)

correspondence principle applied to education, it means that educational systems correspond to society's economic mode of production. More generally, it is the Marxist view that social institutions mirror the mode of production. (p. 307)

craze an unconventional practice that is adopted by a large number of individuals but is regarded as strange by most people in the society. Crazes are generally more outlandish than fads, and therefore require greater personal commitment. (p. 382)

critical school (also **radical school**) the view that the economic élite is the single major force behind definitions of what is and what is not deviant (p. 105)

cross-sectional research the type of research that takes place at one point in time as opposed to **longitudinal research**, which can detect change and demonstrate cause because it takes place over a period of time (p. 34)

crowd a temporary group of people in reasonably close physical proximity. Only unconventional crowds are included under the heading of collective behaviour. (p. 382)

crude birth rate the number of births per year per 1000 people (p. 427)

crude death rate the number of deaths per year per 1000 people (p. 422)

cult a type of non-established religious organization characterized by voluntary membership. It is often highly intellectual and features a loosely knit organization that makes few claims on members. (p. 285)

cult of man Durkheim's term for the religion of the future that he believed would hold the idealized human individual as sacred (p. 289)

cultural element anything that (1) is shared in common by the members of some social group; (2) is passed on to new members; and (3) in some way affects their behaviour or their perceptions of the world. Three of the most important elements are values, norms, and roles. (p. 45)

cultural integration the interrelationship of elements in a given culture such that a change in one element can lead to changes, sometimes unexpected, in other elements (p. 57)

cultural markets theory an alternative to functionalist and capital accumulation theories of education, it stresses the competition among different types of groups for varying kinds and amounts of schooling (p. 308)

cultural materialism a theoretical perspective in which cultural elements are explained by showing how they are pragmatic and rational adaptations to the material environment (p. 65)

cultural universals elements of culture found in all known societies (p. 56)

culture the sum total of all the cultural elements associated with a given social group (p. 45)

deductive logic the derivation of a specific statement from a set of more general statements (p. 23)

defensible space building and neighbourhood construction that has been designed to discourage crime by increasing interaction between residents and, consequently, public surveillance (p. 461)

demographic transition a model of population change that describes the movement of a society from relatively high fertility and mortality levels to relatively low ones (p. 415)

demography from the Greek *demos*, meaning *people*, it is the science of human numbers in terms of size, distribution, composition, and change (p. 413)

denominations competing church-like religious organizations (p. 285)

dependency theory the idea that a country's economic development is dependent upon decisions and policies made elsewhere (p. 340)

deviance a condition or behaviour perceived by society as not normal and at least somewhat disvalued, and thus an acceptable target for social control (p. 103)

deviance amplifying process an argument stating that punishing individuals for minor forms of deviance may backfire and encourage them to take up deviant careers (p. 127)

differential association a theory that sees deviance as learned in small-group interaction, wherein an individual internalizes pro-deviant perspectives (p. 126)

discrimination the denial of opportunities, generally available to all members of society, to some people because of their membership in a social category (p. 211)

disenchantment of the world the process by which the world is perceived as losing its magical, religious, and nonrational attributes (p. 289)

division of labour an interrelated set of occupational roles or other specializations within a group or society (p. 359)

double ghetto the dual segregation of women into the pink-collar ghetto of paid labour outside the home, and the domestic ghetto of unpaid labour inside the home (p. 155)

dramatization of evil the calling of attention to minor acts of deviance that could encourage more major forms of deviance (p. 127)

dysfunctions the occasional minor, temporary disruptions in social life, as defined by functionalists (p. 8)

ecclesia another term for *church*, used by sociologists to describe the dominating or sole religious order of a society, as opposed to *denomination* (p. 285)

ectomorphs, endomorphs, mesomorphs body types (thin, fat, and muscular, respectively) tested for their relationship to personality and then to crime and delinquency (p. 113)

egoistic suicide according to Durkheim, the suicide caused by weak interpersonal ties, a result of the lack of integration found in some groups (p. 4)

elaborated code a language code that is relatively formal, does not depend on the listener knowing the speaker's situation intimately, and facilitates discussion of symbolic and conceptual issues (p. 320)

elective affinity the parallel development of two distinct social phenomena that serve to reinforce each other (p. 281)

élitism the notion that power in all forms of society is inevitably held by a small ruling group (p. 334)

emergent norm theory an explanation of crowd behaviour that stresses diversity of membership but a perception of consensus, which leads to a new norm expressing the apparent will of the crowd (p. 384)

equilibrium envisioned by functionalist sociologists as the normal state of society, marked by interdependence of parts and by harmony and consensus (p. 8)

ethnic group a people—a collectivity of persons who share an ascribed status based upon culture, religion, national origin, or shared historical experience founded upon a common ethnicity or race (p. 206)

ethnocentrism seeing things from the perspective of one's own culture. It includes the belief that one's own culture is superior to others and the belief that what is true of one's culture is true of others. Two of its major variants as they affect the study of culture are *androcentrism* and *Eurocentrism*. (p. 59)

ethnomethodology as applied to organizations, the theory that examines their taken-for-granted, informal, often unconscious rules (p. 369)

experimental group the group of subjects in an experiment that is exposed to the independent variable, as opposed to the **control group**, which is not exposed (p. 28)

expressive dimension the set of traits including emotionality, passivity, and weakness, seen by functionalists as associated with the female roles of unpaid wife, mother, and homemaker, particularly as limited to the private sphere (p. 139)

expressive exchanges the emotional dimension of marriage, including sexual gratification, companionship, and empathy (p. 240)

external validity the generalizability of research results beyond the artificial laboratory experimental situation to the real world (p. 29)

fad an unconventional practice that spreads rapidly and is adopted in a short period of time by a large number of people. Fads are generally less outlandish than crazes, and therefore require less personal commitment. (p. 382)

fatalistic suicide according to Durkheim, the suicide caused by a decrease in options and feelings of being trapped, a result of the overregulation found in some groups (p. 4)

feminization of poverty the tendency in Canadian society for women at all stages of the adult life cycle to be poorer than men, and to be trapped in lives of poverty (p. 157)

folkways those norms that when violated do not provoke a strong reaction on the part of group members (p. 47)

formal organizations social groups with a high division of labour, deliberately and consciously created to achieve specified goals (p. 358)

frame a set of beliefs that helps people to interpret and explain their world and that provides the basis for collective action (p. 389)

functional theory of education explains education in terms of the functions it serves: skill acquisition, preparation for job selection, legitimizing social position, and passing on core values, moral education, and the essentials of good citizenship (p. 304)

functionalism a) the sociological model which portrays society as harmonious and as based on consensus. Its three major concepts are function, equilibrium, and development; b) applied to culture, the theoretical perspective that explains cultural elements by showing how they contribute to societal stability (pp. 7, 62)

functions of religion the social role of religion in traditional society, as defined by Durkheim. Its functions are to empower, to integrate, to interpret, to regulate, and to represent. (p. 278)

game theory an explanation of crowd behaviour similar to emergent norm theory, except that it assumes that people conduct themselves in a "rational" manner and on the basis of relative costs and pay-offs (p. 384)

gender a social category, either masculine or feminine, referring to the social expectations developed and placed upon individuals on the basis of their biological sex (p. 138)

gender norms the set of norms specifying appropriate behaviour for males and females; those who violate these norms are generally labelled deviant (p. 138)

gender socialization the process of acquiring a gendered identity (p. 138)

gendered division of labour role differentiation in which males and females are segregated, according to their sex, in the spheres of both paid and unpaid labour, according to the belief that certain tasks are more appropriate for one sex than the other (p. 154)

gendered identity the self as it develops in accordance with the individual's gender and the social definitions of that gender within the larger gendered order (p. 138)

gendered order the set of structural relations through which individual members of society are accorded differential treatment on the basis of their gender (p. 138)

generalized belief oversimplified notions that, according to Smelser, give rise to collective behaviour. Generalized beliefs portray the world in terms of omnipotent forces, conspiracies, or extravagant promises. (p. 383)

generalized other the conception of what is expected, of normative behaviour; individuals' unified conception of how the world views them (p. 92)

geopolitics the relationships of power and prestige between nation-states that determine a nation's legitimacy at home (p. 332)

government the political party or group that controls the state (p. 333)

grounded theory explanations that arise from the data collected and which are thus grounded in reality rather than in deductive logic (p. 31)

hegemony the domination of a class or classes over others, not only economically but politically and culturally (p. 392)

heterogamy marriage between persons who are dissimilar in some important regard such as religion, ethnic background, social class, personality, or age (p. 255)

heterosexual assumption the assumption that females and males in our society are exclusively heterosexual; those who are not are labelled deviant (p. 141)

homogamy marriage of persons with similar physical, psychological, or social characteristics. This is the tendency for like to marry like. (p. 254)

horizontal mobility movement by an individual from one status to another of similar rank within the same status hierarchy (p. 169)

human ecology a theoretical perspective developed to explain changes in the social structure of the city based on the principle of competition for scarce resources and land. This competition results in a number of processes, including centralization, concentration, segregation, invasion, and succession. (p. 449)

human relations school the approach to studying organizations that stresses informal work practices and that holds that workers are motivated more by social than by economic rewards (p. 367)

hypothesis a statement of a presumed relationship between two or more variables (p. 23)

I and Me the two aspects of Mead's conception of the self. The **I** is the impulsive, creative aspect; the **Me** is the reflective aspect that evaluates actions of the I. (p. 92)

id, ego, superego the major components of Freud's model of personality. The **id** is that aspect of personality which is impulsive, selfish, and pleasure-seeking. The **ego** includes the intellectual and cognitive processes that make individuals unique. Most of the ego is conscious, and it is guided by the reality principle: ideas and actions are modified to fit the real world, dependent on actual experiences. The **superego** consists largely of what is generally called "conscience." (pp. 87–88)

ideal state Hegel's notion of the state that unites the principle of the family with the idea of civil society (p. 391)

ideal type a research strategy that extracts the most prominent or essential features of a social phenomenon. Ideal types in their pure or abstract form are not found in reality, since no one individual case perfectly embodies all essential features. (p. 361)

ideology a relatively well-articulated statement of beliefs and objectives that can be used to justify patterns of conduct, especially worldly activities; used by Marx to describe religion (p. 286)

ideology of gender inequality the widespread belief and understanding that males are superior to females, and that they are therefore more entitled to make decisions, to control resources, and generally to occupy positions of authority (p. 138)

inductive logic the construction of a generalization from a set of specific statements (p. 31)

infant mortality rate the age-specific death rate for infants who die in the first year of life (p. 423)

informal organizations spontaneous interaction usually emerging within formal organizations, based upon unofficial and often implicit rules or understanding (p. 358)

inner-worldly asceticism a religious attitude that offers salvation through self-discipline and accepts the world as an arena for religious activity (p. 280)

innovation, ritualism, retreatism, rebellion Merton's four deviant adaptations to the problems created when society provides insufficient means to achieve its goals. Innovators find illegitimate means, ritualists water down goals, retreatists give up goals and means, and rebels seek both new goals and new means. (p. 117)

institution a specific set of norms and values that the members of a society use to regulate some broad area of social life (p. 49)

institutional completeness the development of a full set of institutions in an ethnic community that parallels those in the larger society (p. 204)

institutionalized power sometimes called *domination*, power is institutionalized when it becomes a regular part of everyday human existence, usually because it is established in formal laws or accepted customs (p. 167)

instrumental dimension the set of traits including rationality, aggression, and strength, seen by functionalists to be associated with the male roles of breadwinner and disciplinarian, particularly as limited to the public sphere (p. 139)

instrumental exchanges the task-oriented dimension of marriage, including earning a living, spending money, and maintaining a household (p. 240)

intergenerational mobility movement or change between parental status and a child's status in the same status hierarchy (p. 169)

intragenerational mobility movement by an individual from one status to another in the same status hierarchy during a single lifetime or career (p. 169)

iron law of oligarchy Michels' idea that the leadership of democratically run organizations becomes élitist and tends to seek power for its own ends (p. 335)

labelling theory the explanation of deviance that argues that societal reactions to minor deviance may alienate those labelled deviant and may cut off their options for conformity, thus leading to greater deviance as an adaptation to the label (p. 127)

legitimation in Weber's view, the process of rendering power acceptable to those affected by its exercise (p. 362)

liberal democracy government characterized by free elections contested by competing political parties and guaranteed by effective civil liberties (p. 333)

liberal feminism the view that most structural inequality between women and men can be eradicated through the creation of laws and social policies which will alter power relationships (p. 143)

life expectancy the average number of years individuals of a given age can expect to live in the future (p. 424)

linguistic empiricism the view that language is learned by reinforcement from others who already speak that language (p. 81)

linguistic nativism the view that children have an innate ability to learn a language and do so as a function of natural maturation (p. 81)

linguistic relativism the perspective that language determines and limits thinking and perception (p. 82)

linguistic sexism the tendency to communicate sexist messages, such as male superiority or the assumption that certain roles must be occupied by either males or females, through the use of language (p. 149)

linguistic universalism the view that language is a reflection of cultural experiences and that language does not affect thought patterns in any unalterable way (p. 82)

looking-glass self Cooley's expression for people's perceptions of how others see them (p. 90)

marginality the state of having within the self two conflicting social identities; also, the social condition of a minority group that lives on the edge of a society, not treated as a full member of that society (p. 208)

marital structures the four common forms of husband–wife relationships within marriage. **Owner-property marriage** is a marriage in which the husband owns his wife; in a **head-complement marriage** the wife finds meaning in life through her husband; in a **senior partner–junior partner marriage** the wife is employed, but her job and income are less important than her husband's; and in an **equal partners marriage** both spouses are equally committed to marriage and a career. (pp. 259–60)

marriage a commitment and an ongoing exchange. The commitment can include legal or contractual elements, as well as the social pressures against dissolution. The exchange includes both instrumental and expressive exchanges. (p. 240)

material culture the physical objects manufactured or used by the members of a society or subculture (p. 49)

maternal feminism the view that women's real strength lies in their reproductive capacities, and that women's roles as wives and mothers are their true calling and source of status (p. 143)

mating gradient the lesser power of a woman in marriage, partly due to her being younger than her husband (p. 255)

mechanical solidarity Durkheim's notion of social integration based on a homogeneity of values and behaviour, characteristic of societies marked by a simple division of labour; similar to precontractual solidarity (p. 360)

migration the movement of people across a significant boundary for the purpose of permanent settlement (p. 433)

minority group a social category, usually ethnically or racially labelled, that occupies a subordinate rank in the hierarchy of a society (p. 210)

mobilization the transfer of resources, particularly human resources, from the pursuit of one goal or set of goals to the pursuit of another goal or set of goals (p. 389)

moral entrepreneurs people who seek to influence the making of rules and definitions of deviance (p. 105)

morality of constraints the stage of moral development in which children believe that ethical rules are absolute, coming from some higher external authority; sometimes called *moral realism* (p. 89)

morality of cooperation the stage of moral development in which children see rules as products of deliberation and agreement rather than as absolute; sometimes called *moral autonomy* (p. 89)

mores those norms that when violated provoke a relatively strong reaction on the part of other group members (p. 47)

multiple nuclei theory a theory of urban development that sees a number of centres developing in the city around specialized facilities (p. 452)

natural areas communities that emerge from the competition for space in cities, characterized by populations having homogeneous social characteristics (p. 449)

natural increase the increase in population occurring when fertility exceeds mortality (p. 413)

nature versus nurture the debate over the extent to which human behaviour is affected by biological and genetic factors as opposed to social or environmental ones. Currently both factors are seen as contributing to the development of personality and the shaping of behaviour. (p. 76)

negotiated order theory the theory of formal organizations that focuses on the process by which an organization is socially constructed, through conflicts of interest, dialogue, and regular negotiation on the part of its participants (p. 368)

neoconservatism the view that government's role in the economy and society should be severely restricted; sometimes also referred to as neoliberalism. Neoconservatives generally believe in free trade, zero inflation, deficit reduction, shifting the tax burden away from corporations and the rich, and reducing the welfare state. (p. 343)

new industrial sociology the study of formal organizations in which the Marxian concept of alienation remains central. It sees the history of formal organizations as the history of capitalist control of workers and their subsequent alienation. (p. 370)

new religious movement a generic term used to describe a range of new religious groups, typically of the cult or sect variety (p. 291)

norms relatively precise rules specifying the behaviours permitted and prohibited for group members (p. 45)

operational definition the actual procedures used to measure a theoretical concept, as in I.Q. scores being an operational definition of intelligence (p. 24)

organic solidarity Durkheim's conception of social integration based on mutual interdependence of social roles; characteristic of societies marked by a highly differentiated, complex division of labour (p. 360)

organization a relatively stable, patterned set of reciprocal relationships and expectations (social roles and norms) that creates the possibility of predictable behaviour (p. 357)

other-worldly mysticism a religious attitude that rejects the world as illusion and offers salvation through detachment from the physical world (p. 280)

panic a rapid and impulsive course of action that occurs when people are frightened and try to save themselves or their property from perceived danger (p. 381)

participant observation a research strategy wherein a researcher becomes a member of a group in order to study it, and group members are aware that they are being observed (p. 31)

patriarchy the system of male dominance through which males are systematically accorded greater access to resources and women are systematically oppressed (p. 143)

pluralism a) the view that ethnic diversity, stratification, and conflict remain central features of modern societies, and that race and ethnicity continue to be important aspects of individual identity and group behaviour; b) the view that power in modern society is shared among competing interest groups. With respect to deviance, it means that definitions of deviance arise not from consensus, nor from any one group, but from a diversity of sources. (pp. 105, 230, 334)

pluralistic society a social system of coexisting and usually hierarchically ranked racial and ethnic groups, each of which to some degree maintains its own distinctive culture, social networks, and institutions, while participating with other racial and ethnic groups in common cultural, economic, and political institutions (p. 201)

political economy the interdisciplinary blend of economics, political science, history, and sociology. It argues that economics makes sense only within the framework of politics and history. (p. 339)

popular culture those preferences and objects that are widely distributed across all social classes in a society (p. 49)

population pyramid a graphic representation of the age (usually in five-year intervals) and sex composition of a population (p. 437)

positive checks checks to population growth that raise the death rate, such as vice, war, famine, disease; posited by Malthus (p. 419)

positivism the application of natural science research methods to social science (p. 21)

power a differential capacity to command resources and thereby control social situations (pp. 167, 333)

power élite Mills's concept for the combination of business, political, and military leaders that he saw as ruling the United States (p. 335)

praxis Marx's concept that research should not be *pure*, conducted just for knowledge's sake, but *applied*, undertaken to improve society (p. 37)

predestination the belief that an individual's spiritual salvation is determined before birth by divine plan (p. 281)

prejudice prejudging people based upon characteristics they are assumed to share as members of a social category (p. 213)

premarital sexual standards standards by which people judge the acceptability of premarital sex. The **abstinence standard** allows no premarital sex; the **double standard** allows premarital sex for men only; the **love standard** permits premarital sex for persons of either gender if they are in love; and the **fun standard** approves of premarital sex for either gender, even without love. (p. 251)

preventive checks checks to population growth that prevent the birth of children, such as abstinence and later marriage; posited by Malthus (p. 419)

primary group a social group in which relationships are characterized by emotion, warmth, cooperation, and, usually, face-to-face interaction (p. 361)

primary versus **secondary deviance** the former includes deviant acts committed prior to any social reaction. These acts arise from a variety of sources. Secondary deviance is that which arises out of the anger, alienation, limited options, and change of self-concept that may occur after a negative social reaction or labelling for primary deviance. (p. 128)

primary versus **secondary sources** the former are records produced by contemporaries of an event, the latter interpretations of primary sources made by others not immediately present at the event (p. 37)

private realm the realm of unpaid domestic labour and biological reproduction, seen from a functionalist perspective as the preserve of females (p. 139)

profane those objects and activities seen by a society as devoid of supernatural power or significance, of concern only to the individual (p. 278)

proletariat Marx's word for the working class, the non-owners of the means of production (p. 172)

Protestant ethic a directive for inner-worldly asceticism attributed by Weber to early Protestant groups (p. 281)

public a large and dispersed group made up of persons who share an interest in the same thing. They may hold similar views or they may sharply disagree. (p. 382)

public realm the realm of paid labour and commerce, seen from a functionalist perspective as the preserve of males (p. 139)

quality circle a small, voluntary work group that meets periodically to discuss work-related problems and recommend solutions (p. 372)

Quiet Revolution a movement in the 1960s in Quebec to expand government powers, decrease Church power, modernize Quebec, and fight vigorously for *la survivance* (p. 406)

quota sample a selection of people that matches the sample to the population on the basis of certain selected characteristics (p. 27)

race an arbitrary social category, membership in which is based upon inherited physical characteristics such as skin colour and facial features, characteristics defined as socially meaningful (p. 209)

race relations cycle the four stages, posited by Park, in the relationship between dominant and minority groups. The cycle involves contact, competition, accommodation, and finally assimilation. (p. 227)

racism an ideology that regards racial or ethnic categories as natural genetic groupings, and that attributes behavioural and psychological differences to the genetic nature of these groupings (p. 209)

radical feminism the view that equality between the sexes can be achieved only through the abolition of male supremacy. Some radical feminists argue for female separatism and the abdication of women's reproductive role as the route to liberation. (p. 143)

random sample a sample in which every member of the population is eligible for inclusion and individuals are selected by chance (p. 26)

rationalization Weber's idea that there existed a historical tendency to bring more and more aspects of social life under the rule of rational, efficient, scientific thought (p. 361)

rational-legal authority according to Weber, the authority that rests on a belief in rules and the legality of norms (p. 362)

relative deprivation the difference between what people believe they have a right to receive (their *expectations*) and what they actually receive (their *achievements*) (p. 386)

reliability the degree to which repeated measurements of the same variable, using the same or equivalent instruments, are equal (p. 24)

religion any culturally transmitted system of beliefs and rituals to which people orient themselves in order to understand their world and its meaning in relation to some reality(ies) regarded as sacred (p. 275)

replication repeating a research project in an attempt to verify earlier findings (p. 34)

resocialization the replacing of old attitudes, beliefs, and behaviours with new ones (p. 78)

restricted code a language code that is relatively informal and depends upon the listener understanding the context, and that is expressed through short sentences and simple grammar; useful for communicating immediate experiences to friends and others familiar with a situation (p. 320)

retrospective interpretation applied by society to those actors it considers deviant, it is the redefinition of their past behaviours as deviant as well (p. 128)

role a cluster of behavioural expectations associated with some particular social position within a group or society (p. 47)

role conflict a situation in which the behavioural expectations of one role are inconsistent with those of a concurrent role (p. 48)

role engulfment a process whereby an individual's deviance becomes a master status. Good traits are ignored or misinterpreted, while bad ones are magnified out of proportion. (p. 128)

role taking Mead's term for individuals' attempts to put themselves in others' places and to imagine what these others are thinking, so as to make interaction with them easier (pp. 11, 91)

routinization of charisma the process of organizational change whereby, for purposes of group survival: 1) authority is transferred from a personal charismatic leader to non-charismatic officials; 2) spontaneous patterns of group organization become fixed and ritualized; and 3) the members and leaders experience reinvolvement with the secular world (p. 282)

rule breakers those who commit deviant acts but to whom no one responds as if they have done so, either because they are not caught, or if caught, because they are excused for some reason (p. 107)

sacred those objects and activities set apart by society and treated with awe and respect (p. 275)

salvation according to Weber, a way of giving meaning to one's existence; a way of escaping pain and suffering (p. 280)

scientific management the theory of organizations stressing economic needs of individuals and workplace organization. Efficiency is believed to result from providing proper economic incentives to workers. (p. 366)

secondary analysis the examination by a researcher of someone else's data (p. 38)

secondary group a social group in which relationships are instrumental, impersonal, rational, and efficient (p. 361)

sect a type of non-established religious group characterized by voluntary membership, a radical social outlook, and rigorous demands (p. 284)

sector theory the theory of urban development that sees city land-use patterns characterized by wedge-like sectors, which begin at the centre of the city and follow transportation routes outward (p. 451)

secularization the process by which traditional religious beliefs and rituals lose their hold on society and other institutions take over their functions (p. 288)

segregation the maintenance of physical distance between ethnic or racial groups. Sometimes this term is used to describe the exclusion of minorities from the facilities, institutions, or residential space used by dominant groups, as in South Africa's system of apartheid. At other times, it refers to the residential separation among ethnic or racial populations that may occur for a variety of reasons. (p. 212)

selective incentives the individual benefits that a person can derive from belonging to an association or joining a social movement. Selective incentives help motivate people to join social movements. (p. 390)

sex a biological category, either male or female, referring to physiological differences, the most pronounced of which involve the reproductive organs and body size (p. 138)

sex ratio the number of males in a given population per 100 females in that population. For example, the sex ratio at birth around the world is approximately 105. (p. 424)

significant other any intimate personal acquaintance or specific prestigious person whose attitudes and opinions count for a great deal. Individuals take significant others into account when evaluating their own actions. (p. 92)

social breakdown approach an approach to collective behaviour that argues that social unrest occurs when established institutions are disrupted or weakened (p. 385)

social category a collection of individuals who share a particular trait that is defined as socially meaningful, but who do not necessarily interact or have anything else in common (p. 209)

social class a category of individuals who possess similar economic position as well as group consciousness, common identity, and a tendency to act as a social unit (p. 170)

social cleavage a division (based on age, class, ethnicity, etc.) that may result in the formation of distinct social groups (p. 396)

social contagion the rapid and uncontrolled spread of a mood, impulse, or form of conduct through a collectivity of people (p. 383)

social contract the idea that society is held together by a rational agreement to cooperate. This contract prevents the chaos of war of all against all. (p. 360)

social differentiation the tendency towards diversification and complexity in the statuses and characteristics of social life (p. 167)

social facts social sources or causes of behaviour; used by sociologists to explain rates of behaviour in groups as opposed to individual behaviour (p. 3)

social integration the attachment of individuals to social groups or institutions. Integration depends on a set of sanctions that rewards conformity to the group and punishes nonconformity. (p. 385)

social movement a large collectivity of people trying to bring about or resist social change (p. 382)

social stratification the general pattern of inequality, or ranking, of socially differentiated characteristics (p. 167)

social structure a pattern of relationships among individuals or groups in a society that usually changes only slowly. For example, the kinship structure of a society refers to the most commonly found relations among relatives and married persons in a society. Social stratification is the structure of inequality in a society. (p. 384)

socialist feminism the view that gender inequality has its roots in the combined oppressiveness of patriarchy and capitalism (p. 143)

socialization the complex set of processes by which infants become distinct and unique individuals as well as members of a society (p. 73)

society a group of people who reside in the same geographical area, who communicate extensively among themselves, and who share a common culture (p. 46)

spirit of capitalism an attitude of self-denial in favour of economic gain (p. 281)

spurious relationship the appearance that two variables are in a causal relationship, when in fact each is an effect of a common third variable (p. 35)

staples approach Innis's view that Canada's economic well-being is heavily dependent upon the export of staples or raw materials. This in turn compromises Canadian political sovereignty. (p. 339)

state an organization that successfully claims the monopoly of the legitimate use of physical force within a territory (p. 332)

status any position occupied by an individual in a social system (p. 168)

status consistency similarity in the ranking of an individual's statuses in a set of status hierarchies (p. 168)

status hierarchy any one of a set of rankings along which statuses are related in terms of their power (p. 168)

status inconsistency dissimilarity in the ranking of an individual's statuses in a set of status hierarchies (p. 168)

status set the combination of statuses that any one individual occupies (p. 168)

stereotypes mental images that exaggerate traits believed to be typical of members of a social group (p. 213)

stratum a set of statuses of similar rank in any status hierarchy (p. 168)

structural assimilation acceptance of a minority group by a dominant group into its intimate, primary, social relationships (p. 228)

structuralism the theory that recognizes formal and informal organization, and their relationship to each other. It also looks at the effects of the environment upon the organization, and at economic and social rewards within the organization. (p. 367)

subculture a subset of individuals within a society who are characterized by certain cultural elements that set them apart from others in the society (p. 48)

la survivance survival of French Canada as a distinct society (p. 404)

symbolic interactionism the sociological model that argues that individuals subjectively define and interpret their environments, are not fully constrained, and act from reasons, not causes (p. 9)

systemic or **institutionalized discrimination** discrimination against members of a group that occurs as a by-product of the ordinary functioning of bureaucratic institutions, rather than as a consequence of a deliberate policy to discriminate (p. 211)

techniques of neutralization rationalizations that allow deviants to define their behaviour as acceptable (p. 126)

theory a set of interrelated statements or propositions about a particular subject matter (p. 23)

traditional authority according to Weber, authority based upon the conventions of past generations (p. 362)

triangulation the application of several research methods to the same topic in the hope that the weaknesses of any one method can be compensated for by the strengths of the others (p. 36)

two-category perspectives the view of race relations that sees two hierarchically ranked, separate collectivities in conflict, bound together in a relationship of dominance and subordination within a single society and culture (p. 229)

universal class Hegel's class of government or state-sector workers (p. 341)

urban legends oral stories of the recent past, which, although believed to be true, are actually false and reflect unconscious fears (p. 49)

urbanization the growth of cities, due to reclassification of rural areas as urban, natural population increase, and/or movement from rural areas to cities (p. 444)

validity the degree to which a measure actually measures what it claims to (p. 24)

values relatively general beliefs that define right and wrong, or indicate general preferences (p. 45)

variable a characteristic, such as income or religion, that takes on different values among different individuals or groups. Causes are generally called **independent variables**, and effects are usually called **dependent variables**. (p. 23)

verstehen the *understanding* of behaviour as opposed to the *predicting* of behaviour (p. 11)

vertical mobility movement up and down a status hierarchy (p. 169)

vertical mosaic the hierarchical ranking of ethnic populations in a society (p. 202)

vicarious punishment the negative consequences individuals observe happening to others (especially a model) and that they expect will follow their own similar actions (p. 86)

vicarious reinforcement the positive consequences individuals observe happening to others (especially a model) and that they expect will follow their own similar actions (p. 85)

welfare state one that protects citizens from the excesses of market forces and treats every person equally (p. 342)

Bibliography

Adam, B.A.

1993 "Post-Marxism and the new social movements." *Canadian Review of Sociology and Anthropology* 30: 316-36.

Adams, O.B. and D.N. Nagnur

1986 "Marriage, divorce and mortality: a life table analysis for Canada and regions." Paper presented at the meetings of the Canadian Federation of Demographers, Ottawa.

1988 *Marriage, Divorce and Mortality*. Statistics Canada, Catalogue No. 84-536. Ottawa: Minister of Supply and Services Canada.

Adamson, Nancy, Linda Briskin, and Margaret McPhail

1988 *Feminist Organizing for Change: The Contemporary Women's Movement in Canada*. Toronto: Oxford University Press.

Agnew, Robert

1992 "Foundation for a general strain theory of crime and delinquency." *Criminology* 30: 47–87.

Agócs, Carol

1979 "Ethnic groups in the ecology of North American cities." *Canadian Ethnic Studies* 11: 1–18.

Agócs, Carol and Monica Boyd

1993 "The Canadian ethnic mosaic recast for the 1990s." Pp. 330–352 in James Curtis, Edward Grabb and Neil Guppy (eds.), *Social Inequality in Canada: Patterns, Problems, Policies*. (2nd ed.) Scarborough, Ont.: Prentice Hall.

Agócs, Carol, Catherine Burr, and Felicity Somerset

1992 *Employment Equity: Cooperative Strategies for Organizational Change*. Scarborough, Ont.: Prentice Hall.

Akerlind, I. and J. Hornquist

1992 "Loneliness and alcohol abuse: a review of the evidence of interplay." *Social Science and Medicine* 34: 405–14.

Akyeampong, E.K.

1990 "The graduates of '82: where are they?" *Perspectives on Labour and Income* 2: 52–63.

Alder, Christine

1992 "Violence, gender, and social change." *International Social Science Journal* 44: 267–76.

Alexander, K.L., D.R. Entwisle and S.L. Dauber

1993 *On the Success of Failure: Effects of Retention in the Primary Grades.* New York: Cambridge University Press.

Amato, Paul R. and Bruce Keith

1991 "Parental divorce and the well-being of children: a meta-analysis." *Psychological Bulletin* 110: 26–46.

Anisef, Paul and Paul Axelrod (eds.)

1993 "Universities, graduates, and the marketplace: Canadian patterns and prospects." Chapter 6 in P. Anisef and P. Axelrod (eds.), *Transitions: Schooling and Employment in Canada*. Toronto: Thompson Educational Publishing, Inc.

Anisef, Paul and Norm Okihiro

1982 *Losers and Winners*. Toronto: Butterworths.

Apple, Michael

1986 *Teachers and Texts: A Political Economy of Class and Gender Relations in Education*. London: Routledge and Kegan Paul.

Archibald, W. Peter

1978 *Social Psychology as Political Economy*. Toronto: McGraw-Hill Ryerson.

Armour, Lisa K.

1987 "Quality circles: implications for American management." In Ronald M. Glassman, William H. Swatos, Jr., and Paul L. Rosen (eds.), *Bureaucracy Against Democracy and Socialism*. New York: Greenwood.

Armstrong, Pat and Hugh Armstrong

1983 *A Working Majority*. Ottawa: Minister of Supply and Services Canada/Canadian Advisory Council on the Status of Women.

Aronowitz, Stanley and Henry A. Giroux

1985 *Education Under Siege: The Conservative, Liberal and Radical Debate over Schooling*. Hadley, MA: Bergin and Garvey.

Avison, William R. and Donna D. McAlpine

1992 "Gender differences in symptoms of depression among adolescents." *Journal of Health and Social Behavior* 33: 77–96.

Badets, Jane

1989 "Canada's immigrant population." *Canadian Social Trends* 14: 2–6.

Baer, Douglas, Edward Grabb, and William Johnston

1990 "The values of Canadians and Americans: a critical analysis and reassessment." *Social Forces* 68: 693–713.

1993 "National character, regional culture, and the values of Canadians and Americans." *Canadian Review of Sociology and Anthropology* 30: 13–36.

Baker, David P. and Deborah Perkins Jones

1993 "Creating gender equality: cross-national gender stratification and mathematical performance." *Sociology of Education* 66: 91–103.

Balakrishnan, T.R.

1982 "Changing patterns in ethnic residential segregation in the metropolitan areas of Canada." *Canadian Review of Sociology and Anthropology* 19: 92–110.

Balakrishnan, T.R. and Carl Grindstaff

1988 *Early Adulthood Behaviour and Later Life Course Paths.* Health and Welfare Canada: Report for Review of Demography.

Balakrishan, T.R. and George K. Jarvis

1991 "Is the Burgess concentric zonal theory of spatial differentiation still applicable to urban Canada?" *Canadian Review of Sociology and Anthropology* 28: 526–539.

Balakrishnan, T.R., K. Krotki, and E. Lapierre-Adamcyk

1993 *Family and Childbearing in Canada.* Toronto: University of Toronto Press.

Bandura, Albert

1973 *Aggression: A Social Learning Analysis.* Englewood Cliffs, NJ: Prentice Hall.

1986 *Social Foundations of Thought and Action.* Englewood Cliffs, NJ: Prentice Hall.

Barr, Rebecca and Robert Dreeben

1983 *How Schools Work.* Chicago: The University of Chicago Press.

Bart, Pauline and Linda Frankel

1984 *The Student Sociologist's Handbook.* New York: Random House.

Barth, Fredrik

1969 "Introduction." Pp. 9–38 in F. Barth (ed.), *Ethnic Groups and Boundaries: The Social Organization of Culture Difference.* Bergen-Oslo: Universitets Forlaget.

Beauchesne, Eric

1994 "University degrees put women on equal footing with men." *London Free Press,* October 5: A3.

Beaujot, Roderic P.

1978 "Canada's population: growth and dualism." *Population Bulletin* 33: 1–48.

1979 "A demographic view on Canadian language policy." *Canadian Public Policy* 1: 16–29.

1986 "Dwindling families." *Policy Options* 7(7): 3–7.

1990 "The family and demographic change: economic and cultural interpretations and solutions." *Journal of Comparative Family Studies* 21: 25–38.

Becker, Howard S.

1973 [1963] *Outsiders. Studies in the Sociology of Deviance.* New York: Free Press.

Behiels, Michael

1990 "General introduction." In Michael Behiels (ed.), *The Meech Lake Primer.* Ottawa: University of Ottawa Press.

Beisner, M. and W. Iacono

1990 "An update on the epidemiology of schizophrenia." *Canadian Journal of Psychiatry* 35: 657–68.

Béland, Francois and André Blais

1989 "Quantitative methods and contemporary sociology in francophone Quebec." *The Canadian Review of Sociology and Anthropology* 26: 533–556.

Belenky, M. et al.

1986 *Women's Ways of Knowing: The Development of Self, Voice, and Mind.* New York: Basic Books.

Bell, Daniel

1989 "'American exceptionalism' revisited: the role of civil society." *The Public Interest* 95: 38–56.

Bell, Edward

1990 "Class voting in the first Alberta Social Credit Election." *Canadian Journal of Political Science* 23: 3.

Bellah, Robert

1970 *Beyond Belief. Essays on Religion in a Post-Traditional World.* New York: Harper and Row.

Bellamy, Raymond

1988 *Modern Italian Social Theory.* Cambridge: Polity Press.

Berger, Peter

1969 *The Sacred Canopy: Elements of a Sociological Theory of Religion.* New York: Doubleday.

Berk, R., A. Campbell, R. Klap, and B. Western

1992 "The deterrent effects of arrest: a Bayesian analysis of four field experiments." *American Sociological Review* 57: 698–708.

Berk, Richard A.

1974a "A gaming approach to crowd behavior." *American Sociological Review* 39: 355–73.

1974b *Collective Behavior*. Dubuque, IA: Brown.

Bernstein, Basil

1973 *Class, Codes and Control*, Vol. 1. London: Routledge and Kegan Paul.

Bibby, Reginald

1979 "Religion in Canada." *Journal for the Scientific Study of Religion* 18: 1–17.

1987 *Fragmented Gods*. Toronto: Irwin.

1993 *Unknown Gods*. Toronto: Stoddart.

Bibby, Reginald W. and Harold Weaver

1985 "Cult consumption in Canada: a further critique of Stark and Bainbridge." *Sociological Analysis* 46: 445–60.

Bidwell, Charles E. and Noah E. Friedkin

1988 "The sociology of education." Pp. 449–471 in Neil J. Smelser (ed.), *Handbook of Sociology*. Newbury Park, CA: Sage Publications.

Bielby, William

1987 "Modern prejudice and institutional barriers to equal employment opportunity for minorities." *Journal of Social Issues* 43: 79–84.

Bienvenue, Rita

1985 "Colonial status: the case of Canadian Indians." Pp. 199–214 in R. Bienvenue and J. Goldstein (eds.), *Ethnicity and Ethnic Relations in Canada*. (2nd ed.) Toronto: Butterworths.

Bird, T.

1990 "Shelter costs." *Canadian Social Trends* 16: 6–10.

Bishop, Patricia

1989 "Child care." In Patricia Bishop (ed.), *Social Action Series*. Toronto: Canadian Mental Health Association.

Bland, Roger, Stephen Newman, and Helene Orn

1988 "Age of onset of psychiatric disorders." *Acta Psychiatrica Scandinavica* 77 (supplement 338): 43–49.

1990 "Health care utilization for emotional problems: results from a community survey." *Canadian Journal of Psychiatry* 35: 397–400.

Bleier, Ruth

1987 "A polemic on sex differences research." Pp. 111–130 in Christie Farnham (ed.), *The Impact of Feminist Research in the Academy*. Bloomington, IN: Indiana University Press.

Bloch, Herbert and A. Niederhoffer

1958 *The Gang: A Study in Adolescent Behavior*. New York: Philosophical Library.

Blumer, Herbert

1951 [1939] "Collective behavior." Pp. 167–222 in A.M. Lee (ed.), *Principles of Sociology*. New York: Barnes and Noble.

Blumstock, Robert

1993 "Canadian civil religion." Pp. 173–194 in W.E. Hewitt (ed.), *The Sociology of Religion: A Canadian Focus*. Toronto: Harcourt Brace.

Bongaarts, John

1982 "Fertility determinants: proximate determinants." Pp. 275–279 in *The International Encyclopedia of Population*, Vol. 1. New York: The Free Press.

Bourne, L.

1993 "The myth and reality of gentrification: A commentary on urban forms." *Urban Studies* 1: 183-189.

Boutilier, Marie

1977 "Transformation of ideology surrounding the sexual division of labour: Canadian women during World War Two." Paper presented at the Second Conference on Blue-Collar Workers, London, Ontario, May. Basic Books.

Bowles, Samuel and Herbert Gintis

1976 *Schooling in Capitalist America: Educational Reform and the Contradictions of Economic Life*. New York: Basic Books.

Boyd, Monica

1993 "Gender, visible minority and immigrant earning inequality: reassessing an employment equity premise." In Vic Satzewich (ed.), *Deconstructing a Nation: Immigration, Multiculturalism, and Racism in the '90s in Canada*. Toronto: Garamond Press.

Bozinoff, Lorne and André Turcotte

1993 "Canadians split over effects of working moms." *The Gallup Report*, Sunday, January 24.

Brabant, S. and L. Mooney

1989 "Him, her, or either: sex of person addressed and interpersonal communication." *Sex Roles* 20: 47–48.

Brannigan, Augustine and Sheldon Goldenberg

1986 "Social science versus jurisprudence in Wagner: the study of pornography, harm, and the law of obscenity in Canada." *Canadian Journal of Sociology* 11: 419–31.

Braverman, Harry

1974 "Labor and monopoly capital: the degradation of work in the twentieth century." *Monthly Review* 26: 1–134.

Breton, R., W. Isajiw, W. Kalbach, and J. Reitz

1990 *Ethnic Identity and Equality: Varieties of Experience in a Canadian City*. Toronto: University of Toronto Press.

Breton, Raymond

1978 "The structure of relationships between ethnic collectivities." In Leo Driedger (ed.), *The Canadian Ethnic Mosaic*. Toronto: McClelland and Stewart.

1989 "Quebec sociology: agendas from society or from sociologists?" *The Canadian Review of Sociology and Anthropology* 26: 557–70.

1990 "The ethnic group as a political resource in relation to problems of incorporation: perceptions and attitudes." Pp. 196–255 in Raymond Breton, Wsevolod Isajiw, Warren Kalbach, and Jeffrey Reitz (eds.), *Ethnic Identity and Equality*. Toronto: University of Toronto Press.

Brinkerhoff, Merlin and Eugene Lupri

1978 "Theoretical and methodological issues in the use of decision making as an indicator of conjugal power: some Canadian observations." *Canadian Journal of Sociology* 3: 1–20.

Brody, N.

1992 *Intelligence*. San Diego, CA: Academic Press.

Brooks, N. and A. Doob

1990 "Tax evasion: searching for a theory of compliant behavior." Pp. 120–64 in M. Friedland (ed.), *Securing Compliance*. Toronto: University of Toronto Press.

Broude, Gwen and Sarah Greene

1983 "Cross-cultural codes on husband-wife relationships." *Ethnology* 22: 263–280.

Brown, M. and B. Warner

1992 "Immigrants, urban politics, and policing in 1900." *American Sociological Review* 57: 293–305.

Brownfield, D. and K. Thompson

1991 "Attachment to peers and delinquent behavior." *Canadian Journal of Criminology* 33: 45–60.

Brunvand, Jan Harold

1989 *Curses! Broiled Again!* New York: W.W. Norton.

Brym, Robert J., Michael W. Gillespie, and Rhonda L. Lenton

1989 "Class power, class mobilization, and class voting: the Canadian case." *Canadian Journal of Sociology* 14: 25–44.

Bryner, John

1991 "Transitions to work: results from a longitudinal study of young people in four British labour markets." Pp. 171–195 in David Ashton and Graham Lowe (eds.), *Making Their Way: Education, Training and the Labour Market in Canada and Britain*. Toronto: University of Toronto Press.

Bumpass, Larry L.

1990 "What's happening to the family? Interactions between demographic and institutional change." *Demography* 27(4): 483–498.

Burawoy, Michael and Pavel Krotov

1993 "The economic basis of Russia's political crisis." *New Left Review* 198: 49–70.

Burch, Thomas K. and Ashok Madan

1986 *Union Formation and Dissolution: Results from the 1984 Family History Survey*. Statistics Canada, Catalogue No. 99–963. Ottawa: Minister of Supply and Services Canada.

Burch, Thomas K. and K.E. Selvanathan

1987 "Orphanhood in Canada, 1985." Pp. 377–407 in Department of Sociology (ed.), *Contributions to Demography in Honour of K.J. Krotki*. Edmonton: University of Alberta.

Burgess, Ernest W.

1925 "The growth of the city." In R.E. Park, E.W. Burgess, and R.D. McKenzie (eds.), *The City*. Chicago: University of Chicago Press.

Burke, M.A.

1990 "Cooperative housing: a third tenure form." *Canadian Social Trends* 16: 11–14.

Byrk, Anthony S. and Stephen W. Raudenbush

1992 *Hierarchical Linear Models: Applications and Data Analysis Methods*. Newbury Park, CA: Sage Publications.

Byrne, C., M. Velamoor, Z. Cernovsky, L. Cortese, and S. Loszatyn

1990 "A comparison of borderline and schizophrenic patients for childhood life events and parent-child relationships." *Canadian Journal of Psychiatry* 35: 590–95.

Caldwell, G. and D. Fournier

1987 "The Quebec question: a matter of population." *Canadian Journal of Sociology* 12: 16–41.

Caldwell, John C.

1976 "Toward a restatement of demographic transition theory." *Population and Development Review* 2: 321–66.

1987 "Toward a restatement of demographic transition theory." Pp. 42–69 in S. Menard and E. Moen (eds.), *Perspectives on Population: An Introduction to Concepts and Issues*. New York: Oxford University Press.

Calzavara, Liviana

1993 "Trends and policy in employment opportunities for women." Chapter 22 in J. Curtis, E. Grabb, and N. Guppy (eds.), *Social Inequality in Canada: Patterns, Problems, Policies*. (2nd ed.) Scarborough, Ont.: Prentice Hall.

Campani, Giovanna

1992 "Family, village, and regional networks and Italian immigration in France and Quebec." Pp. 183-207 in Vic Satzewich (ed.), *Deconstructing a Nation: Immigration, Multiculturalism and Racism in '90s Canada*. Halifax: Fernwood Publishing.

Campbell, Douglas F.

1983 *Beginnings: Essays on the History of Canadian Sociology*. Port Credit, Ont.: Scribbler's Press.

Campbell, K.E. and Barrett A. Lee

1992 "Source of personal neighbor networks: social integration, need, or time?" *Social Forces* 70: 1077–1100.

Canadian Press

1994 "Study urged of income disparity." *London Free Press*, March 24: A10.

1995 "Wage gap unchanged for men and women." *London Free Press*, February 8: A1.

Canadian Social Trends

1990 "The inner city in transition." *Canadian Social Trends* 16.

Canel, Eduardo

1992 "New social movement theory and resource mobilization: the need for integration." Pp. 22-51 in W.K. Carroll (ed.), *Organizing Dissent: Contemporary Social Movements in Theory and Practice: Studies in the Politics of Counter-Hegemony*. Toronto: Garamond.

Carroll, William

1986 *Corporate Power and Canadian Capitalism*. Vancouver: University of British Columbia Press.

Cassin, A.M.

1980 "The routine production of inequality: implications for affirmative action." Unpublished paper. Toronto: Ontario Institute for Studies in Education.

Chalk, Frank and Kurt Jonassohn

1990 *The History and Sociology of Genocide*. New Haven: Yale University Press.

Chawla, Raj K.

1990 "The distribution of wealth in Canada and the United States." *Perspectives on Labour and Income* 2(1): 29–41.

1992 "The changing profile of dual-earner families." *Perspectives on Labour and Income* 4(2): 22–29.

Che-Alfred, J.

1990 "Home ownership." *Canadian Social Trends* 16: 2–5.

Chodorow, Nancy

1978 *The Reproduction of Mothering*. Berkeley, CA: University of California Press.

Chomsky, Noam

1989 *Necessary Illusions: Thought Control in Democratic Societies*. Toronto: CBC Enterprises.

Christ, Carol and Judith Plaskow (eds.)

1979 *Womanspirit Rising*. San Francisco: Harper and Row.

Christie, Nils

1993 *Crime Control as Industry: Towards Gulags, Western Type?* London: Routledge.

Christofides, L. N. and R. Swidinsky

1994 "Wage determination by gender and visible minority status: evidence from the 1989 LMAS." *Canadian Public Policy* 20: 34-51.

Chui, Tina, James Curtis, and Edward Grabb

1993 "Who gets involved in politics and community organizations?" Chapter 36 in J. Curtis, E. Grabb, and N. Guppy (eds.), *Social Inequality in Canada: Patterns, Problems, Policies*. (2nd ed.) Scarborough, Ont.: Prentice Hall.

Clark, Peter and Anthony Davis

1989 "The power of dirt: an exploration of secular defilement in Anglo-Canadian culture." *Canadian Review of Sociology and Anthropology* 26: 650–73.

Clark, S.D.

1948 *Church and Sect in Canada*. Toronto: University of Toronto Press.

1959 *Movements of Political Protest in Canada, 1640–1840*. Toronto: University of Toronto Press.

1962 *The Developing Canadian Community*. Toronto: University of Toronto Press.

1975 "Sociology in Canada: an historical overview." *Canadian Journal of Sociology* 1: 225–34.

Clarke, Juanne

1990 *Health, Illness, and Medicine in Canada*. Toronto: McClelland and Stewart.

Clement, Wallace

1975 *The Canadian Corporate Elite*. Toronto: McClelland and Stewart.

1978 "A political economy of regionalism in Canada." Pp. 89–110 in Daniel Glenday, Hubert Guindon, and Alan Turowetz (eds.), *Modernization and the Canadian State*. Toronto: Macmillan.

1988 "The state and the Canadian economy." Chapter 31 in J. Curtis, E. Grabb, N. Guppy, and S. Gilbert (eds.), *Social Inequality in Canada: Patterns, Problems, Policies*. Scarborough, Ont.: Prentice Hall.

1990 "A critical response to 'Perspectives on the class and ethnic origins of Canadian elites.'" *Canadian Journal of Sociology* 15: 179–185.

Clinard, Marshall and P. Yeager

1980 *Corporate Crime*. New York: Free Press.

Cloward, Richard and L. Ohlin

1960 *Delinquency and Opportunity*. New York: Free Press.

Cockerham, William C.

1996 *Sociology of Mental Disorder*. (4th ed.) Englewood Cliffs, NJ: Prentice Hall.

Cohen, Albert

1955 *Delinquent Boys: The Culture of the Gang*. New York: Free Press.

Coleman, W.D.

1984 *The Independence Movement in Quebec, 1945–1980*. Toronto: University of Toronto Press.

Collins, Randall

1977 "Some comparative principles of educational stratification." *Harvard Educational Review* 47: 1–27.

1979 *The Credential Society: An Historical Sociology of Education and Stratification*. New York: Academic Press.

1986 *Weberian Sociological Theory*. Cambridge: Cambridge University Press.

Comack, Elizabeth and Steven Brickey

1991 *The Social Basis of Law*. (2nd ed.) Toronto: Garamond.

Combes-Orme, T., J. Helzer, and R. Miller

1988 "The application of labeling theory to alcoholism." *Journal of Social Service Research* 11: 73–91.

Condry, J. and S. Condry

1976 "Sex differences: a study in the eye of the beholder." *Child Development* 47: 812–19.

Connidis, Ingrid

1989a *Family Ties and Aging in Canada*. Toronto: Butterworths.

1989b "Contact between siblings in later life." *Canadian Journal of Sociology* 14: 429–42.

Connor, Steven

1989 *Postmodernist Culture: An Introduction to Theories of the Contemporary*. Cambridge: Blackwell.

Cook, Cynthia and Rod Beaujot

1996 "Labour force interruptions: the influence of marital status and the presence of young children." *The Canadian Journal of Sociology* 21: 25-42.

Cooley, Charles H.

1956 [1909] [1902] *Human Nature and the Social Order*. Chicago: Free Press.

Copp, Terry

1974 *The Anatomy of Poverty: The Conditions of the Working Class in Montreal, 1897–1929*. Toronto: McClelland and Stewart.

Corwin, Ronald G.

1987 *The Organization-Society Nexus: A Critical Review of Models and Metaphors*. Westport, CT: Greenwood Press.

Coser, Lewis

1964 *The Functions of Social Conflict*. New York: Free Press of Glencoe.

Côté, James E. and Anton A. Allahar

1994 *Generation on Hold*. Toronto: Stoddart.

Creese, G., N. Guppy, and M. Meissner

1991 *Ups and Downs on the Ladder to Success: Social Mobility in Canada 1986*. Ottawa: Statistics Canada.

Crompton, Susan and Leslie Geran

1995 "Women as main wage-earners." *Perspective on Labour and Income* 7: 26-29.

Crosby, Faye J.

1991 *Juggling: The Unexpected Advantages of Balancing Career and Home for Women and Their Families*. New York: Free Press.

Cuneo, Michael W.

1989 *Catholics Against the Church: Anti-Abortion Protest in Toronto, 1969–1985*. Toronto: University of Toronto Press.

Curtis, B. et al.

1992 *Stacking the Deck*. Toronto: Our Schools/Our Selves.

Curtis, Bruce

1992 "Pre-sociological observation? Maria Edgeworth, Elizabeth Hamilton, and A.A. de Saussure Necker." *Society* 16: 10–19.

Curtis, James, Edward Grabb, and Neil Guppy (eds.)

1993 *Social Inequality in Canada: Patterns, Problems, Policies.* (2nd ed.) Scarborough, Ont.: Prentice Hall.

Curtis, James, Ronald Lambert, Steven Brown, and Barry Kay

1989 "Affiliating with voluntary associations: Canadian-American comparisons." *Canadian Journal of Sociology* 14(2): 143–60.

Dabbs, James

1990 "Testosterone, social class, and antisocial behavior in a sample of 4462 men." *Psychological Science* 1: 209–11.

Dagg, Anne Innis and Patricia J. Thompson

1988 *MisEducation: Women and Canadian Universities.* Toronto: Ontario Institute for Studies in Education.

Dahrendorf, Ralf

1959 *Class and Class Conflict in Industrial Society.* Stanford, CA: Stanford University Press.

Daly, Mary

1973 *Beyond God the Father: Toward a Philosophy of Women's Liberation.* Boston: Beacon Press.

1975 *The Church and the Second Sex: With a New Feminist Postchristian Introduction.* London: Colophon Books.

Das Gupta, Tania

1996 *Racism and Paid Work.* Toronto: Garamond.

Davies, James B.

1993 "The distribution of wealth and economic inequality." Chapter 8 in J. Curtis, E. Grabb, and N. Guppy (eds.), *Social Inequality in Canada: Patterns, Problems, Policies.* (2nd ed.) Scarborough, Ont.: Prentice Hall.

Davis, Arthur K.

1971 "Canadian society and history as hinterland versus metropolis." Pp. 6–32 in Richard J. Ossenberg (ed.), *Canadian Society: Pluralism, Change, and Conflict.* Scarborough, Ont.: Prentice Hall.

Davis, Kingsley

1937 "The sociology of prostitution." *American Sociological Review* 2: 744–55.

1947 "Final note on a case of extreme isolation." *American Journal of Sociology* 52: 432–37.

1949 *Human Society.* New York: Macmillan.

1967 "The urbanization of the human population." Pp. 3–24 in Scientific American (ed.), *Cities.* New York: Alfred A. Knopf.

Davis, Kingsley and Wilbert E. Moore

1945 "Some principles of stratification." *American Sociological Review* 10: 242–49.

Dawson, Charles

1936 *Group Settlement: Ethnic Communities in Western Canada.* Toronto: Macmillan of Canada.

Dawson, D., B. Grant, S. Chou, and R. Pickering

1995 "Subgroup variation in U.S. drinking patterns: results of the 1992 National Longitudinal Alcohol Epidemiologic Study." *Journal of Substance Abuse* 7: 331–44.

DeKeseredy, Walter S.

1992 "Wife assault." Pp. 278–312 in Vincent Sacco (ed.), *Deviance: Conformity and Control in Canadian Society.* (2nd ed.) Scarborough, Ont.: Prentice Hall.

DeMello, Margo

1995 "'Not just for bikers anymore': popular representations of American tattooing." *Journal of Popular Culture* 29: 37-52.

Derber, Charles

1979 *The Pursuit of Attention: Power and Individualism in Everyday Life.* Toronto: Oxford University Press.

Desai, Sonalde and Linda J. Waite

1991 "Women's employment during pregnancy and after the first birth: occupational characteristics and work commitment." *American Sociological Review* 56: 551–566.

Devor, Holly

1989 *Gender Blending: Confronting the Limits of Duality.* Bloomington, IN: Indiana University Press.

Dickson, Lovat

1973 *Wilderness Man: The Strange Story of Grey Owl.* Scarborough, Ont.: New American Library of Canada Ltd.

Di Leonardo, Micaela

1991 "Contingencies of value in feminist anthropology." Pp. 140–158 in Joan E. Hartman and Ellen Messer-Davidow (eds.), *(En)Gendering Knowledge.* Knoxville, TN: University of Tennessee Press.

Dionne, Claude

1989 *"Le choix d'avoir un enfant."* Paper presented to ASDEQ Conference, April.

Dobasch, R.E. and R.P. Dobasch

1992 *Women, Violence, and Social Change.* London: Routledge.

Dohrenwend, B., I. Levav, et al.

1992 "Socioeconomic status and psychiatric disorders: the causation-selection issue." *Science* 255: 946–52.

Downing, Christine

1989 *Myths and Mysteries of Same Sex Love*. New York: Continuum.

Driedger, Leo

1989 *The Ethnic Factor: Identity in Diversity*. Toronto: McGraw Hill Ryerson.

Driedger, Leo and Richard Mezoff

1981 "Ethnic prejudice and discrimination in Winnipeg high schools." *Canadian Journal of Sociology* 6: 1–17.

Duleep, Harriet and Seth Sanders

1992 "Discrimination at the top: American-born Asian and white men." *Industrial Relations* 31(3): 416–32.

Dumas, Brigitte

1987 "Philosophy and sociology in Quebec: a socio-epistemic inversion." *Canadian Journal of Sociology* 12: 111–33.

Dumas, Jean

1985 "Mariages et remariages au Canada." *Cahiers québécois de démographie* 14: 209–30.

1990 *Report on the Demographic Situation in Canada 1988*. Statistics Canada, Catalogue No. 91-209. Ottawa: Minister of Supply and Services Canada.

du Pays, Jean

1996 "Les lendemains qui grincent." In Marc Brière (ed.), *Le goût du Québec: l'après référendum 1995*. La Salle: Hurtubise.

Dupré, John

1993 *The Disorder of Things: Metaphysical Foundations for the Disunity of Science*. Boston, MA: Harvard University Press.

Durkheim, Emile

1949 [1893] *The Division of Labor in Society*. New York: Free Press.

1951 [1897] *Suicide: A Study in Sociology*. Translated by J. Spaulding and G. Simpson. New York: Free Press.

1965 [1912] *The Elementary Forms of the Religious Life*. New York: Free Press.

1969 [1898] "Individualism and the intellectuals." *Political Studies* 17: 14–30.

Dyck, Ronald and Stephen Newman

1988 "Suicide trends in Canada, 1956–1981." *Acta Psychiatrica Scandinavica* 77: 411–19.

Eccles, Jacquelynne S. and Phyllis Blumenfeld

1985 "Classroom experiences and student gender: are there differences and do they matter." Pp. 79–115 in Louise Cherry Wilkinson (ed.), *Gender Influences in Classroom Interaction*. Greenwich, CT: JAI Press.

Edgerton, Robert B.

1985 *Rules, Exceptions, and Social Order*. Berkeley, CA: Univ. of California Press.

Editeur Officiel Québec

1978 *Charte de la langue française* (Bill 101). Quebec City.

Edsall, T.B.

1988 "The return of inequality." *The Atlantic Monthly* (June): 86–94.

Edwards, Richard

1979 *Contested Terrain: The Transformation of the Workplace in the Twentieth Century*. New York: Basic Books.

Eichar, Douglas

1989 *Occupation and Class Consciousness in America*. New York: Greenwood Press.

Eichler, Margrit

1983 *Families in Canada Today: Recent Changes and Their Policy Consequences*. Toronto: Gage.

1984 "Sexism in research and its policy implications." Pp. 17–39 in Jill McCalla Vickers (ed.), *Taking Sex into Account*. Ottawa: Carleton University Press.

1988 *Nonsexist Research Methods: A Practical Guide*. Boston, MA: Allen and Unwin.

Eichler, M. with R. Tite

1990 "Women's studies professors in Canada: A collective self- portrait." *Atlantis* 16: 6–24.

Eliany, Marc

1991 "Alcohol and drug use." *Canadian Social Trends* 20: 19–26.

EMPLASA—Empresa Metropolitana de Planejamento da Grande São Paulo

1993 *Metrópole Eletrônica: Dados e Informações sobre a Grande São Paulo*. Verso 1.0. São Paulo: Emplasa.

Engels, Friedrich

1972 [1884] *The Origin of the Family, Private Property, and the State*. Edited by Eleanor Burke Leacock. New York: International Publishers.

Erikson, Erik

1963 *Childhood and Society*. New York: W.W. Norton.

Erikson, Kai

1966 *Wayward Puritans*. New York: Wiley.

Esping-Andersen, Gosta

1989 "The three political economies of the welfare state." *Canadian Review of Sociology and Anthropology* 26: 10–36.

Ethington, Corinna A. and Lee M. Wolfe

1984 "Sex differences in a causal model of mathematics achievement." *Journal for Research in Mathematics Education* 15: 361–77.

Evans, John and A. Himmelfarb

1987 "Counting crime." Pp. 43–73 in Rick Linden (ed.), *Criminology: A Canadian Perspective*. Toronto: Holt, Rinehart and Winston.

Fallding, Harold

1978 "Mainline Protestantism in Canada and the United States: an overview." *Canadian Journal of Sociology* 3: 141–60.

Fausto-Sterling, Anne

1985 *Myths of Gender: Biological Theories about Women and Men*. New York: Basic Books.

1992 *Myths of Gender: Biological Theories about Women and Men*. (2nd ed.) New York: Basic Books.

Feeley, M. and D. Little

1991 "The vanishing female: the decline of women in the criminal process, 1687–1912." *Law and Society Review* 25: 719–57.

Felson, Marcus

1994 *Crime and Everyday Life*. Newberry Park, CA: Pine Forge Press.

Finkel, Alvin

1989 *The Social Credit Phenomenon in Alberta*. Toronto: University of Toronto Press.

Fiorenza, Elisabeth Schussler

1979 "Women in the early Christian movement." In Carol Christ and Judith Plaskow (eds.), *Womanspirit Rising*. San Francisco: Harper and Row.

1985 *In Memory of Her: A Feminist Theological Reconstruction of Christian Origins*. New York: Crossroads.

Fischer, C.

1995 "20th year assessment of the subcultural theory of urbanism." *American Journal of Sociology* 101: 543-577.

Fisher, Helen

1992 *Anatomy of Love: The Natural History of Monogamy, Adultery, and Divorce*. New York: Norton.

Fleras, Augie and Jean Leonard Elliott

1992 *Multiculturalism in Canada: The Challenge of Diversity*. Scarborough, Ont.: Nelson Canada.

Florida, Richard and Martin Kenney

1991 "Transplanted organizations: the transfer of Japanese industrial organizations to the U.S." *American Sociological Review* 56: 381–398.

Foote, David K. and Daniel Stoffman

1996 *Boom, Bust & Echo: How to Profit from the Coming Demographic Shift*. Toronto: Macfarlane Walter & Ross.

Footlick, Jerrold K.

1990 "What happened to the family?" *Newsweek*, Special issue on the twenty-first-century family. (Winter/Spring): 14–20.

Forcese, Dennis

1978 "Elites and power in Canada." Pp. 302–22 in John H. Redekop (ed.), *Approaches to Canadian Politics*. Scarborough, Ont.: Prentice Hall.

1986 [1980] *The Canadian Class Structure*. (3rd/2nd eds.) Toronto: McGraw-Hill Ryerson.

Form, William H.

1985 *Divided We Stand*. Urbana, IL: University of Illinois Press.

Fox, Bonnie

1989 "The feminist challenge: a reconsideration of social inequality and economic development." Pp. 120–67 in R.J. Brym with B.J. Fox (eds.), *From Culture to Power*. Toronto: University of Toronto Press.

Fox, John and Michael Ornstein

1993 "The Canadian state and corporate elites." Chapter 34 in J. Curtis, E. Grabb, and N. Guppy (eds.), *Social Inequality in Canada: Patterns, Problems, Policies*. (2nd ed.) Scarborough, Ont.: Prentice Hall.

Francis, Diane

1986 *Controlling Interest. Who Owns Canada?* Toronto: Macmillan of Canada.

Franzoi, Stephen L., Jennifer J. Kessenich, and Patricia A. Sugrue

1989 "Gender differences in the experience of body awareness: an experiential sampling study." *Sex Roles* 21: 499–515.

Freud, Sigmund

1935 *A General Introduction to Psychoanalysis*. Garden City, NY: Doubleday.

Frideres, James

1988 *Native Peoples in Canada: Contemporary Conflicts*. (3rd ed.) Scarborough, Ont.: Prentice Hall.

Fried, M.

1973 *The World of the Urban Working Class*. Cambridge: Harvard University Press.

Frieze, I.H., J.E. Parsons, P.B. Johnson, D.N. Rubble, and G.I. Zellman

1978 *Women and Sex Roles*. New York: W.W. Norton.

Fukuyama, Francis

1989 "The end of history?" *The National Interest* 16: 3–18.

Gabor, Thomas

1990 "Crime displacement and situational prevention: toward the development of some principles." *Canadian Journal of Criminology* 32: 41–73.

Gabor, T. and E. Gottheil

1984 "Offender characteristics and spatial mobility: an empirical study and some policy implications." *Canadian Journal of Criminology* 26: 267–81.

Gamson, W.A.

1992 "The social psychology of collective action." Pp. 53-76 in A.D. Morris and C.M. Mueller (eds.), *Frontiers in Social Movement Theory*. New Haven: Yale University Press.

Gans, Herbert

1970 "Urbanism and suburbanism as ways of life: a re-evaluation of definitions." Pp. 84–100 in J.J. Palen and K.H. Fleming (eds.), *Urban America*. New York: Holt, Rinehart and Winston.

Gardner, Howard

1991 *The Unschooled Mind: How Children Think and How Schools Should Teach*. New York: Basic Books.

Garfield, Chad

1990 "The social and economic origins of contemporary families." Pp. 23–40 in M. Baker (ed.), *Families: Changing Trends in Canada*. (2nd ed.) Toronto: McGraw-Hill Ryerson.

Geipel, John

1969 *The Europeans*. New York: Pegasus.

Gerber, Linda

1984 "Community characteristics and out-migration from Canadian Indian reserves: path analyses." *Canadian Review of Sociology and Anthropology* 21: 145–65.

Gero, Joan

1991 "Genderlithics: women's role in stone tool production." Pp. 163–193 in Joan M. Gero and Margaret W. Conkey (eds.), *Engendering Archaeology: Women and Prehistory*. Cambridge, MA: Blackwell.

Gerth, Hans H. and C. Wright Mills

1946 *From Max Weber: Essays in Sociology*. New York: Oxford University Press.

Ghalam, Nancy

1993 "Women in the workplace." *Canadian Social Trends* 28: 2–6.

Giddens, Anthony

1973 *The Class Structure of the Advanced Societies*. London: Hutchinson and Co.

1981 *A Contemporary Critique of Historical Materialism, Volume 1: Power, Property, and the State*. London: Macmillan.

Giffen, P.J., S. Endicott, and S. Lambert

1991 *Panic and Indifference-The Politics of Canada's Drug Laws*. Ottawa: Canadian Centre on Substance Abuse.

Gilligan, Carol

1982 *In a Different Voice*. Cambridge, MA: Harvard University Press.

Glass, R.

1982 "Some fear abuses in premenstrual tension decisions." *Philadelphia Inquirer*, January 24: 8C.

Gliksman, L. and B. Rush

1986 "Alcohol availability, alcohol consumption and alcohol related damage, II: the role of demographic factors." *Journal of Studies on Alcohol* 47: 11–18.

Glock, Charles and Rodney Stark

1967 *Religion and Society in Tension*. Berkeley, CA: University of California Press.

Goffman, Erving

1974 *Frame Analysis: An Essay on the Organization of Experience*. New York: Harper.

Goldscheider, Frances Kobrin and Linda Waite

1986 "Sex differences in the entry into marriage." *American Journal of Sociology* 92: 91–109.

Goldstein, Jay

1985 "The prestige dimension of ethnic stratification." Pp. 181–98 in R. Bienvenue and J. Goldstein (eds.), *Ethnicity and Ethnic Relations in Canada*. (2nd ed.) Toronto: Butterworths.

Goode, William J.

1977 "World revolution and family patterns." Pp. 47–58 in A.S. Skolnick and J.H. Skolnick (eds.), *Family in Transition*. Boston: Little, Brown.

Gordon, Margaret T.

1985 "The urban condition: 'plates' beneath city surfaces and a new research agenda." *Urban Affairs Quarterly* 21: 25–36.

Gordon, Milton

1964 *Assimilation in American Life: The Role of Race, Religion, and National Origin*. New York: Oxford University Press.

Gorman, Christine

1992 "Sizing up the sexes." *Time* 139(3): 36–43.

Gotlib, Ian H. and William R. Avison

1993 "Children at risk for psychopathology." Pp. 271–319 in Charles G. Costello (ed.), *Basic Issues in Psychopathology*. New York: Guilford Press.

Gottfredson, M. and T. Hirschi

1990 *A General Theory of Crime*. Stanford, CA: Stanford University Press.

Gough, E. Kathleen

1959 "The Nayars and the definition of marriage." *Journal of the Royal Anthropological Institute* 89: Part 1.

Gould, Stephen Jay

1981 *The Mismeasure of Man*. New York: W.W. Norton.

Gouldner, Alvin W.

1979 *The Future of Intellectuals and the Rise of the New Class*. New York: Seabury.

Gove, Walter

1990 "The effect of marriage on the well-being of adults: a theoretical analysis." *Journal of Marriage and the Family* 11: 4–35.

Government of Canada

1971 "Statement by the Prime Minister (Response to the Report of the Royal Commission on Bilingualism and Biculturalism, Book 4, House of Commons)." Ottawa: Press Release, October 8, 1971.

Goyder, John C. and James E. Curtis

1977 "Occupational mobility in Canada over four generations." *Canadian Review of Sociology and Anthropology* 14: 303–19.

Grabb, Edward G.

1988 "Occupation, education, and feelings of powerlessness." Chapter 39 in J. Curtis, E. Grabb, N. Guppy, and S. Gilbert (eds.), *Social Inequality in Canada: Patterns, Problems, Policies*. Scarborough, Ont.: Prentice Hall.

1993a "Conceptual issues in the study of social inequality." Chapter 1 in J. Curtis, E. Grabb, and N. Guppy (eds.), *Social Inequality in Canada: Patterns, Problems, Policies*. (2nd ed.) Scarborough, Ont.: Prentice Hall.

1993b "Who owns Canada?" Chapter 2 in J. Curtis, E. Grabb, and N. Guppy (eds.), *Social Inequality in Canada: Patterns, Problems, Policies*. (2nd ed.) Scarborough, Ont.: Prentice Hall.

1997 *Theories of Social Inequality: Classical and Contemporary Perspectives*. (3rd ed.) Toronto: Harcourt Brace.

Grabb, Edward G. and James E. Curtis

1992 "Voluntary association activity in English Canada, French Canada, and the United States: a multivariate analysis." *Canadian Journal of Sociology* 17: 371–388.

Grabb, Edward G. and S.L. Waugh

1987 "Family background, socioeconomic attainment, and the ranking of self-actualization values." *Sociological Focus* 20: 215–26.

'Grande São Paulo registra queda em homicídios.'

1996 *Folha de São Paulo* December 10.

Granovetter, Mark

1978 "Threshold models of collective behavior." *American Journal of Sociology* 83: 1420–43.

Grayson, J. Paul, D. Alan Pomfret, and S.N. Gilbert

1993 "Expectations and Experiences of Female Science Students: The First Few Months." Paper presented at the Canadian Institutional Researchers and Planners Conference, Vancouver, B.C.

Greer, Germaine

1992 *The Change: Women, Aging, and the Menopause*. New York: Alfred A. Knopf.

Grenier, Gilles

1987 "Earnings by language group in Quebec in 1980 and emigration from Quebec between 1976 and 1981." *Canadian Journal of Economics* 20: 774–91.

Grindstaff, Carl F.

1990 "Long-term consequences of adolescent marriage and fertility." Pp. 137–54 in *Report on the Demographic Situation in Canada 1988*, Statistics Canada, Catalogue No. 91-209. Ottawa: Minister of Supply and Services Canada.

Grindstaff, Carl F., T.R. Balakrishnan, and Paul S. Maxim

1989 "Life course alternatives: factors associated with differential timing patterns in fertility among women recently completing childbearing, Canada, 1981." *Canadian Journal of Sociology* 14: 443–60.

Groneman, Carol

1995 "Nymphomania: the historical construction of female sexuality." Pp. 219-249 in Jennifer Terry and Jacqueline Urla (eds), *Deviant Bodies*. Bloomington, IN: Indiana University Press.

Guindon, Hubert

1964 "Social unrest, social class and Quebec's bureaucratic revolution." *Queen's Quarterly* 71: 150–62.

1977 "Class, nationalism and ethnic tension." Pp. 18–28 in Christopher Beattie and Stewart Crysdale (eds.), *Sociology Canada: Readings*. Toronto: Butterworths.

Gunderson, Morley

1982 "The male-female earnings gap in Ontario: a summary." Toronto: Research Branch, Ontario Ministry of Labour.

Guppy, Neil and A. Bruce Arai

1993 "Who benefits from higher education? Differences by sex, social class, and ethnic background." Chapter 16 in J. Curtis, E. Grabb, and N. Guppy (eds.), Social Inequality in Canada: Patterns, Problems, Policies. (2nd ed.) Scarborough, Ont.: Prentice Hall.

Guppy, Neil, James Curtis, and Edward Grabb

1993 "Aging, human rights, and economic opportunities." Chapter 28 in J. Curtis, E. Grabb, and N. Guppy (eds.), *Social Inequality in Canada: Patterns, Problems, Policies*. (2nd ed.) Scarborough, Ont.: Prentice Hall.

Guppy, Neil, S. Freeman, and S. Buchan

1988 "Economic background and political representation." Chapter 33 in J. Curtis, E. Grabb, N. Guppy, and S. Gilbert (eds.), *Social Inequality in Canada: Patterns, Problems, Policies*. Scarborough, Ont.: Prentice Hall.

Gusfield, J.

1986 [1963] *Symbolic Crusade*. Urbana, IL: University of Illinois Press.

Hacker, Andrew

1992 *Two Nations, Black and White, Separate, Hostile, Unequal*. New York: Ballantine Books.

Hackler, J. and K. Don

1990 "Estimating system biases: crime indices that permit comparisons across provinces." *Canadian Journal of Criminology* 32: 243–64.

Hagan, John

1988 *Structural Criminology*. Cambridge: Polity.

1991 *The Disreputable Pleasures: Crime and Deviance in Canada*. (3rd ed.) Toronto: McGraw-Hill Ryerson.

1992 "The poverty of classless criminology: the American Society of Criminology 1991 Presidential Address." *Criminology* 30: 1–19.

Hagan, J., R. Gillis, and J. Chan

1980 "Explaining official delinquency: a spatial study of class, conflict and control." In Robert Silverman and James Teevan (eds.), *Crime in Canadian Society*. (2nd ed.) Toronto: Butterworths.

Hagan, J. and F. Kay

1990 "Gender and delinquency in white collar families: a power-control perspective." *Crime and Delinquency* 36: 391–407.

Hamel, Pierre

1991 *Action collective et démocratie locale: les mouvements urbains montréalais*. Montreal: Les presses de l'Université de Montréal.

1995 "Mouvements urbains et modernité: l'exemple montréalais." *Recherches sociographiques* 36: 279-305.

Hamilton, Roberta

1978 *The Liberation of Women: A Study of Patriarchy and Capitalism*. London: George Allen and Unwin.

Handleby, J.B., L. Keating, and C.L. Hooper

1990 "A follow-up of Ontario training school boys." Paper presented at Ontario Psychological Association meeting, Feb. 16.

Harman, Lesley D.

1986 "The well-preserved woman, or 'How old do you think I am?'" *Human Affairs* 10: 19–31.

1989 *When a Hostel Becomes a Home: Experiences of Women*. Toronto: Garamond Press.

1992 "The feminization of poverty: an old problem with a new name." *Canadian Woman Studies* 13 (Summer): 6–9.

Harmatz, M.G. and M.A. Novak

1983 *Human Sexuality*. New York: Harper and Row.

Harrell, W. Andrew

1985 "Husband's involvement in housework: the effects of relative earnings power and masculine orientation." University of Alberta: Edmonton Area Series Report No. 39.

Harris, Chauncy D. and Edward L. Ullman

1945 "The nature of cities." *Annals of the American Academy of Political and Social Science* 242: 7–17.

Harris, Marvin

1985 *Good to Eat: Riddles of Food and Culture*. New York: Simon and Schuster.

Harrison, Trevor and Gordon Laxer (eds.)

1995 *The Trojan Horse: Alberta and the Future of Canada*. Montreal: Black Rose Books Montreal, 1995.

Hartnagel, Timothy

1996 "Correlates of criminal behavior." Pp. 95–138 in Rick Linden (ed.), *Criminology: A Canadian Perspective*. (3rd ed.) Toronto: Holt, Rinehart and Winston.

Hartnagel, T. and J. Tanner

1986 "Class, schooling and delinquency." Pp. 157–68 in R. Silverman and J. Teevan (eds.), *Crime in Canadian Society*. (3rd ed.) Toronto: Butterworths.

Harvey, Pierre

1969 "Pourquoi le Québec et les Canadiens français occupent-ils une place inférieure sur le plan économique?" Pp. 113–27 in R. Durocher and P.A. Linteau (eds.), *Le "Retard" du Québec*. Quebec: Editions Boréal Express.

Hasselback, P., K. Lee, Y. Mao, R. Nichol, and D. Wigle

1991 "The relationship of suicide rates to sociodemographic factors in Canadian census divisions." *Canadian Journal of Psychiatry* 36: 655–59.

Hawley, A.

1950 *Human Ecology: A Theory of Community Structure*. New York: Ronald.

Head, Wilson

1981 *Adaptation of Immigrants: Perceptions of Ethnic and Racial Discrimination*. Toronto: York University.

Heimer, Karen and Ross Matsueda

1994 "Role-taking, role commitment, and delinquency." *American Sociological Review* 59: 365–90.

Heinz, Walter

1991 "Youth and labour markets: promises of comparative research on transition processes." Pp. 196–203 in David Ashton and Graham Lowe (eds.), *Making Their Way: Education, Training and the Labour Market in Canada and Britain*. Toronto: University of Toronto Press.

Helmes-Hayes, Richard

1994 "Canadian sociology's first textbook: C.A. Dawson and W.E. Getty's *An Introduction to Sociology* (1929)." *Canadian Journal of Sociology* 19: 461–97.

Helmes-Hayes, R. and D. Wilcox-Magill

1993 "A neglected classic: Leonard Marsh's *Canadians In and Out of Work*." *Canadian Review of Sociology and Anthropology* 30: 83–109.

Henripin, J.

1972 *Trends and Factors of Fertility in Canada*. Ottawa: Statistics Canada.

Henripin, Jacques and Evelyne Lapierre-Adamcyk

1986 *Essai d'Evaluation du Cout de l'Enfant*. Report submitted to the *Bureau de la Statistique du Québec*.

Henry, Frances and Effie Ginsberg

1985 *Who Gets the Work? A Test of Racial Discrimination in Employment*. Toronto: Urban Alliance on Race Relations and Social Planning Council of Metropolitan Toronto.

1993 "Racial discrimination in employment." Chapter 24 in J. Curtis, E. Grabb, and N. Guppy (eds.), *Social Inequality in Canada: Patterns, Problems, Policies*. (2nd ed.) Scarborough, Ont.: Prentice Hall.

Henshel, Richard L.

1990 *Thinking about Social Problems*. Toronto: Harcourt Brace Jovanovich.

Herman, Harry

1978 *Men in White Aprons: Macedonian Restaurant Owners in Toronto*. Toronto: Peter Martin.

Herold, Edward S.

1984 *Sexual Behaviour of Canadian Young People*. Markham: Fitzhenry and Whiteside.

Hesse-Biber, Sharlene

1989 "Eating patterns and disorders in a college population: are college women's eating problems a new phenomenon?" *Sex Roles* 20: 71–89.

Heyns, Barbara

1986 "Educational effects: issues in conceptualization and measurement." Pp. 305–40 in John G. Richardson (ed.), *Handbook of Theory and Research for the Sociology of Education*. New York: Greenwood Press.

Hiller, Harry H.

1979 "The Canadian sociology movement: analysis and assessment." *Canadian Journal of Sociology* 4: 125–50.

1982 *Society and Change: S.D. Clark and the Development of Canadian Sociology*. Toronto: University of Toronto Press.

Hirschi, T.

1969 *Causes of Delinquency*. Berkeley: University of California Press.

Hobart, Charles W.

1988 "Relationships in remarried families." *Canadian Journal of Sociology* 13: 261–82.

1993 "Sexual behaviour." Pp. 52–72 in G.N. Ramu, *Marriage and Family in Canada Today*. (2nd ed.) Scarborough, Ont.: Prentice Hall.

Hofley, John M.

1992 "Canadianization: a journey completed?" In Wm. K. Carroll et al. (eds.), *Fragile Truths: 25 Years of Sociology and Anthropology in Canada*. Ottawa: Carleton University Press.

Holland, Dorothy C. and Margaret A. Eisenhart

1990 *Educated in Romance: Women, Achievement, and College Culture*. Chicago: The University of Chicago Press.

Hou, Feng and T.R. Balakrishnan

1996 "The integration of visible minorities in contemporary Canadian society." *Canadian Journal of Sociology* 21: 307-326.

Hoult, T.F., L.F. Henze, and J.W. Hudson

1978 *Courtship and Marriage in America*. Boston: Little, Brown.

House, James, Karl Landis, and Debra Umberson

1988 "Social relationships and health." *Science* 241: 540–545.

Houston, Susan E. and Alison Prentice

1988 *Schooling and Scholars in Nineteenth-Century Ontario.* Toronto: University of Toronto Press.

Hoyt, Homer

1939 *The Structure and Growth of Urban Areas.* Washington, DC: Federal Housing Authority.

Huang, C. and J. Anderson

1991 "Anomie and deviancy: reassessing racial and social status differences." Paper presented at the Annual Meeting of the American Sociological Association, Cincinnati, OH.

Hughes, Everett C.

1943 *French Canada in Transition*. Chicago: University of Chicago Press.

Human Resources Committee, National Advisory Board on Science and Technology

1993 *Winning with Women in Trades Technology, Science, and Engineering*. Ottawa: Government of Canada.

Hunter, Alfred A.

1993 "The changing distribution of income." Chapter 7 in J. Curtis, E. Grabb, and N. Guppy (eds.), *Social Inequality in Canada: Patterns, Problems, Policies*. (2nd ed.) Scarborough, Ont: Prentice Hall.

Hurn, Christopher J.

1985 [1978] *The Limits and Possibilities of Schooling: An Introduction to the Sociology of Education*. Boston: Allyn and Bacon.

1993 *The Limits and Possibilities of Schooling: An Introduction to the Sociology of Education.* (3rd ed.) Boston: Allyn and Bacon.

Hutter, Mark

1988 *The Changing Family: Comparative Perspectives.* (2nd ed.) New York: Wiley.

Huyssen, Andreas

1986 *After the Great Divide: Modernism, Mass Culture, Postmodernism*. Bloomington: Indiana University Press.

Indian and Northern Affairs Canada

1988 *Basic Departmental Data*. Ottawa: Minister of Supply and Services Canada.

Innis, Harold

1956 *Essays in Canadian Economic History*. Toronto: University of Toronto Press.

Isajiw, Wsevolod

1990 "Ethnic-identity retention." Pp. 34–91 in Raymond Breton, Wsevolod Isajiw, Warren Kalbach, and Jeffrey Reitz (eds.), *Ethnic Identity and Equality*. Toronto: University of Toronto Press.

Isajiw, W., A. Sev'er, and L. Driedger

1993 "Ethnic identity and social mobility: a test of the drawback model." *Canadian Journal of Sociology* 18: 177–96.

Ishwaran, K.

1977 *Family, Kinship and Community: A Study of Dutch Canadians*. Toronto: McGraw-Hill Ryerson.

Jain, Harish, Simaon Taggar, and Morley Gunderson

1997 "The Status of Employment Equity in Canada: An Assessment." Paper presented at the 49th Annual Conference of the Industrial Relations Research Association, January 4-6, 1997.

Jencks, C.

1994 *The Homeless*. Cambridge: Harvard University Press.

Johnson, Holly and Peter Chisholm

1989 "Family homicide." *Canadian Social Trends* 14: 17–18.

Juteau, Danielle and Louis Maheu

1989 "Sociology and sociologists in francophone Quebec: science and politics." *The Canadian Review of Sociology and Anthropology* 26: 363–93.

Kalbach, Warren E.

1978 "Growth and distribution of Canada's ethnic populations, 1871–1971." Pp. 82–104 in Leo Driedger (ed.), *The Canadian Ethnic Mosaic: A Quest for Identity*. Toronto: McClelland and Stewart.

1990 "Ethnic residential segregation and its significance for the individual in an urban setting." Pp. 92–134 in Raymond Breton, Wsevolod Isajiw, Warren Kalbach, and Jeffrey Reitz (eds.), *Ethnic Identity and Equality*. Toronto: University of Toronto Press.

Kalbach, Warren E. and Wayne McVey

1971 *The Demographic Bases of Canadian Society.* Toronto: McGraw-Hill Ryerson.

1979 *The Demographic Bases of Canadian Society*. (2nd ed.) Toronto: McGraw-Hill Ryerson.

Kalmijn, Matthijs

1991 "Status homogamy in the United States." *American Journal of Sociology* 97: 496–523.

Kaplan, H. and H. Fukurai

1992 "Negative social sanctions, self-rejection and drug use." *Youth and Society* 23: 275–98.

Kaplan, Marcie

1983 "A woman's view of DSM-III." *American Psychologist* 38: 786–92.

Karabel, Jerome and A.H. Halsey (eds.)

1977 *Power and Ideology in Education*. New York: Oxford University Press.

Kates, N. and E. Krett

1988 "Socio-economic factors and mental health problems: can census-tract data predict referral patterns?" *Canadian Journal of Community Mental Health* 7: 89–98.

Katz, Jack

1988 *Seductions of Crime: Moral and Sensual Attractions of Doing Evil*. New York: Basic Books.

Kaufman, Michael (ed.)

1993 *Cracking the Armor: Power, Pain and the Lives of Men*. Toronto: Viking.

Kennedy, L. and S. Baron

1993 "Routine activities and a subculture of violence: a study of violence on the street." *Journal of Research in Crime and Delinquency* 30: 88–112.

Kennedy, L.W. and D.R. Forde

1990 "Routine activities and crime: an analysis of victimization in Canada." *Criminology* 28: 101–15.

Kennedy, L., R. Silverman, and D. Forde

1991 "Homicide in urban Canada: testing the impact of economic inequality and social disorganization." *Canadian Journal of Sociology* 16: 397–410.

Kent, Stephen

1990 "Deviance labelling and normative strategies in the Canadian 'new religions/countercult' debate." *Canadian Journal of Sociology* 15: 393–416.

1993 "New religious movements." Pp. 83–106 in W.E. Hewitt (ed.), *The Sociology of Religion: A Canadian Focus*. Toronto: Harcourt Brace.

Koenig, D.

1991 *Do Police Cause Crime? Police Activity, Police Strength, and Crime Rates*. Ottawa: Canadian Police College.

Kohlberg, Lawrence

1984 *Essays in Moral Development: The Psychology of Moral Development*. New York: Harper and Row.

Kohn, Melvin, A. Naoi, C. Schoenbach, C. Schooler, and K. Slomczynski

1990 "Position in the class structure and psychological functioning in the United States, Japan and Poland." *American Journal of Sociology* 95: 964–1008.

Kopinak, Kathryn M.

1985 "Women in Canadian municipal politics: two steps forward, one step back." *Canadian Review of Sociology and Anthropology* 22: 394–410.

1987 "Gender differences in political ideology in Canada." *Canadian Review of Sociology and Anthropology* 24: 23–38.

1996 "Effects of NAFTA on Mexican and Canadian industrial workers." Paper presented at the NAFTA Conference, Indiana Center on Global Change and World Peace, November 1996.

Krahn, Harvey and L.W. Kennedy

1985 "Producing personal safety: the effects of crime rates, police force size and fear of crime." *Criminology* 23: 697–710.

Krahn, Harvey and Graham Lowe

1991 "Transitions to work: findings from a longitudinal study of high-school and university graduates in three Canadian cities." Pp. 130–170 in David Ashton and Graham Lowe (eds.), *Making Their Way: Education, Training and the Labour Market in Canada and Britain*. Toronto: University of Toronto Press.

1993 *Work, Industry, and Canadian Society*. (2nd ed.) Toronto: Nelson.

Krauter, Joseph and Morris Davis

1978 *Minority Canadians: Ethnic Groups*. Toronto: Methuen.

Krupat, E. and P. Kubzansky

1987 "Designing to deter crime." *Psychology Today* 21: 58–61.

Kubat, Daniel and David Thornton

1974 *A Statistical Profile of Canadian Society*. Toronto: McGraw-Hill Ryerson.

Lachapelle, Rejean and Jacques Henripin

1982 *The Demolinguistic Situation in Canada*. Montreal: The Institute for Research on Public Policy.

Langford, Tom and J. Rick Ponting

1992 "Canadians' responses to aboriginal issues: the roles of prejudice, perceived group conflict, and economic conservatism." *Canadian Review of Sociology and Anthropology* 29: 140–166.

Lapidus, Ira M.

1986 "Cities and societies: a comparative study of the emergence of urban civilization in Mesopotamia and Greece." *Journal of Urban History* 12: 257–82.

La Prairie, Carol

1990 "The role of sentencing in the over-representation of aboriginal people in correctional institutions." *Canadian Journal of Criminology* 32: 429–40.

Lautard, Hugh and Neil Guppy

1990 "The vertical mosaic revisited: occupational differentials among Canadian ethnic groups." Pp. 189–208 in Peter Li (ed.), *Race and Ethnic Relations in Canada*. Toronto: Oxford University Press.

Law, B. (ed.)

1992 *Corpus Almanac and Canadian Sourcebook*. Toronto: Southam.

Laws, Sophie, Valerie Hey, and Andrea Eagan

1985 *Seeing Red: The Politics of Pre-menstrual Tension*. London: Hutchinson.

Laxer, Gordon

1989 *Open for Business: The Roots of Foreign Ownership in Canada*. Toronto: Oxford University Press.

Leacock, Eleanor

1983 "Interpreting the origins of gender inequality: conceptual and historical problems." *Dialectical Anthropology* 7: 263–284.

LeBlanc, M., P. McDuff, et al.

1991 "Social and psychological consequences, at 10 years old, of an earlier onset of self-reported delinquency." *Psychiatry* 54: 133–47.

LeBlanc, M., E. Vallieres, and P. McDuff

1993 "The prediction of males' adolescent and adult offending from school experience." *Canadian Journal of Criminology* 35: 459–78.

LeBon, Gustave

1960 [1895] *The Crowd*. New York: Viking Press.

Leck, J.D. and D.M. Saunders

1996 "Achieving diversity in the workplace: Canada's Employment Equity Act and members of visible minorities," *International Journal of Public Administration* 19: 299–322.

Lee, John Allan

1975 "The romantic heresy." *Canadian Review of Sociology and Anthropology* 12: 514–28.

LeMasters, E.E. and J. DeFrain

1989 *Parents in Modern America*. (5th ed.) Belmont, CA: Wadsworth.

Lemert, Edwin

1951 *Social Pathology*. New York: McGraw-Hill.

Lengermann, Patricia M. and Jill Niebrugge-Brantley

1990 "Feminist sociological theory: the near-future prospects." In George Ritzer (ed.), *Frontiers of Sociological Theory: The New Synthesis*. New York: Columbia University Press.

Lenneberg, Eric

1967 *Biological Foundations of Language*. New York: John Wiley.

Lenski, Gerhard E.

1966 *Power and Privilege*. New York: McGraw-Hill.

Lenton, Rhonda L.

1992 "Home versus career: attitudes towards women's work among Canadian women and men." *Canadian Journal of Sociology* 17: 89–98.

Leroux, T. and M. Petrunik

1990 "The construction of elder abuse as a social problem: a Canadian perspective." *International Journal of Health Services* 20: 651–63.

Letkemann, Peter

1973 *Crime as Work*. Englewood Cliffs, NJ: Prentice Hall.

Levitt, Kari

1970 *Silent Surrender: The Multinational Corporation in Canada*. Toronto: Macmillan.

Lewis, David

1993 "Canada's Native peoples and the churches." Pp. 235–252 in W.E. Hewitt (ed.), *The Sociology of Religion: A Canadian Focus*. Toronto: Harcourt Brace.

Lewis, Oscar

1961 *The Children of Sanchez: Autobiography of a Mexican Family*. New York: Random House.

Li, Peter

1988 *Ethnic Inequality in a Class Society*. Toronto: Wall and Thompson.

1992 "Race and gender as bases of class fractions and their effects on earnings." *Canadian Review of Sociology and Anthropology* 29: 488–510.

Link, Bruce

1991 "The stigma of mental illness." Paper read at the Annual Meeting of the Society for the Study of Social Problems.

Link, Bruce and Francis Cullen

1990 "The labeling theory of mental disorder: a review of the evidence." *Research in Community and Mental Health* 6: 75–105.

Linton, Ralph

1936 *The Study of Man*. New York: Appleton-Century Crofts.

Lipset, Seymour Martin

1985 *Consensus and Conflict*. Oxford: Transaction.

1990 *Continental Divide*. New York: Routledge.

Lo, Celia

1995 "Gender differences in collegiate alcohol use." *Journal of Drug Issues* 25: 817–36.

The Los Angeles Times

1992 "Slum jewel—a Canadian triumph." November 28: A1, A17, A18.

Lowe, Graham S.

1993 "Jobs and the labor market." Chapter 11 in J. Curtis, E. Grabb, and N. Guppy (eds.), *Social Inequality in Canada: Patterns, Problems, Policies*. (2nd ed.) Scarborough, Ont.: Prentice Hall.

Lowe, Graham S. and Harvey J. Krahn (eds.)

1984 *Working Canadians*. Toronto: Methuen.

Lowe, Graham S. and Herbert C. Northcott

1986 *Under Pressure: A Study of Job Stress*. Toronto: Garamond Press.

Lower, J.A.

1973 *Canada: An Outline History*. Toronto: McGraw-Hill Ryerson.

Lowman, John

1989 "The geography of social control: clarifying some themes." Pp. 228–59 in D.J. Evans and D.T. Herbert (eds.), *The Geography of Crime*. London: Routledge.

1992 "Street prostitution." In Vincent Sacco (ed.), *Deviance-Conformity and Control in Canadian Society*. (2nd ed.) Scarborough Ont.: Prentice Hall.

Luke, T.W.

1989 *Screens of Power: Ideology, Domination, and Resistance in Informational Society*. Urbana: University of Illinois Press.

Lundberg, Olle

1991 "Causal explanations for class inequality in health: an empirical analysis." *Social Science and Medicine* 32: 385–93.

Lupri, Eugen, Elaine Grandin, and Merlin Brinkerhoff

1994 "Socioeconomic status and male violence in the Canadian home: a reexamination." *Canadian Journal of Sociology* 19: 47–73.

Lupri, Eugen and James Frideres

1981 "The quality of marriage and the passage of time: marital satisfaction over the family life cycle." *Canadian Journal of Sociology* 6(3): 283–306.

Lupri, Eugen and Donald L. Mills

1987 "The household division of labour in young dual-earner couples: the case of Canada." *International Review of Sociology* 2: 33–54.

Lupri, Eugen and Gladys Symons

1982 "The emerging symmetrical family: fact or fiction?" *International Journal of Comparative Sociology* 23: 166–89.

Luxton, Meg

1990 "Two hands for the clock: changing patterns in the gendered division of labour in the home." In M. Luxton, H. Rosenberg, and S. Arat-Koc (eds.), *Through the Kitchen Window: The Politics of Home and Family*. (2nd ed.) Toronto: Garamond.

Lynch, J.

1979 *The Broken Heart: The Medical Consequences of Loneliness*. New York: Basic Books.

Maccoby, Eleanor and Carol Jacklin

1974 *The Psychology of Sex Differences*. Stanford, CA: Stanford University Press.

Mackie, Marlene

1987 *Constructing Women and Men: Gender Socialization*. Toronto: Holt, Rinehart and Winston.

1991 *Gender Relations in Canada*. Toronto: Butterworths.

MacKinnon, Catharine A.

1989 *Toward a Feminist Theory of the State*. Cambridge, MA: Harvard University Press.

Madoo-Lengermann, P. and J. Niebrugge

1996 "Contemporary feminist theory." Pp. 436–86 in George Ritzer (ed.) *Contemporary Sociological Theory*. (4th ed.) New York: McGraw-Hill.

Malinowski, Bronislaw

1927 *Sex and Repression in Savage Society*. New York: Harcourt, Brace.

1929 [1920] *The Sexual Life of Savages in Northwestern Melanesia*. New York: Harcourt, Brace.

1954 [1925] *Magic, Science and Religion*. New York: Doubleday.

Marchak, M. Patricia

1983 *Green Gold: The Forest Industry in British Columbia*. Vancouver: University of British Columbia Press.

1990 "Sociology, ecology, and a global economy." *Cahiers de Recherche-sociologique* 14: 97–109.

Marchand, Philip

1989 *Marshall McLuhan: The Medium and the Messenger, A Biography*. Toronto: Random House.

Marcil-Gratton, Nicole

1988 *Les Modes de Vie Nouveaux des Adultes et Leur Impact sur les Enfants au Canada*. Health and Welfare Canada: Report for Review of Demography.

Marcuse, Herbert

1964 *One-Dimensional Man: Studies in the Ideology of Advanced Industrial Society*. Boston: Beacon.

Marsh, Leonard

1943 *Report on Social Security for Canada*. Ottawa: King's Printer. Reprinted, University of Toronto Press, 1975.

Marshall, Katherine

1990a "Women in professional occupations: progress in the 1980s." Pp. 109–12 in Craig McKie and Keith Thompson (eds.), *Canadian Social Trends*. Toronto: Thompson Educational Publishing.

1990b "Household chores." *Canadian Social Trends* 16: 18–19.

Martin, Wilfred B.W. and Allan J. Macdonell

1982 [1978] *Canadian Education: A Sociological Analysis*. (2nd and 1st eds.) Scarborough, Ont.: Prentice Hall.

Marx, Karl

1932 [1864] *Economic and Philosophic Manuscripts of 1844*. Edited by Dirk J. Struik. New York: International Publishers.

1964 [1843] *Selected Writings in Sociology and Social Philosophy*. Edited by T.B. Bottomore and M. Rubel. Baltimore, MD: Penguin.

Marx, Karl and F. Engels

1964 *On Religion*. New York: Schocken Books.

Maslow, A.H.

1954 *Motivation and Personality*. New York: Harper.

Mason, David

1988 "Introduction, controversies and continuities in race and ethnic relations theory." Pp. 1–19 in John Rex and David Mason (eds.), *Theories of Race and Ethnic Relations*. Cambridge: Cambridge University Press.

Matza, David

1990 *Delinquency and Drift*. New Brunswick, NJ: Transaction.

Maxim, Paul S.

1993 "Ethno-religious diversity and local option in Ontario, 1906–14." Paper presented at the International Congress on the Social History of Alcohol, London, Ontario.

McAdam, Doug, J.D. McCarthy, and M.N. Zald (eds.)

1996a *Comparative Perspectives on Social Movements: Political Opportunities, Mobilizing Structures, and Cultural Framings*. New York: Cambridge University Press.

McAdam, Doug, J.D. McCarthy, and M.N. Zald

1996b "Introduction: opportunities, mobilizing structures, and framing processes - toward a synthetic, comparative perspective on social movements." Pp. 1-40 in Doug McAdam, J.D. McCarthy, and M.N. Zald (eds.), *Comparative Perspectives on Social Movements: Political Opportunities, Mobilizing Structures, and Cultural Framings*. New York: Cambridge University Press.

McCarthy, B. and J. Hagan

1987 "Gender, delinquency and the Great Depression: a test of power-control theory." *Canadian Review of Sociology and Anthropology* 24: 153–77.

McClelland, David

1961 *The Achieving Society*. New York: Free Press.

McDonald, Kevin and Ross D. Parke

1986 "Parent-child physical play: the effects of sex and age on children and parents." *Sex Roles* 15: 367–78.

McDonald, Ryan

1991 "Canada's off-reserve Aboriginal population." *Canadian Social Trends* 23: 2–7.

McGahan, P.

1995 *Urban Sociology in Canada*. (3rd ed.) Toronto: Harcourt Brace.

McKie, Craig

1990 "Lifestyle risks: smoking and drinking in Canada." Pp. 86–92 in Craig McKie and Keith Thompson (eds.), *Canadian Social Trends*. Toronto: Thompson Educational Publishing.

McLuhan, Marshall

1962 *The Gutenberg Galaxy: The Making of Typographic Man*. Toronto: University of Toronto Press.

1964 *Understanding Media: The Extensions of Man*. New York: McGraw Hill.

McMillan, S.

1987 "Forty years of social housing in Toronto." *Canadian Social Trends* 7: 24–30.

McPherson, Barry

1990 *Aging as a Social Process*. (2nd ed.) Toronto: Butterworths.

McQuillan, Kevin

1992 "Falling behind: the income of lone-mother families, 1970–1985." *Canadian Review of Sociology and Anthropology* 29: 511–523.

McRoberts, Kenneth

1988 *Quebec: Social Change and Political Crisis*. (3rd ed.) Toronto: McClelland and Stewart.

McVey, W. and W. Kalbach

1995 *Canadian Population*. Toronto: Nelson.

Mead, George H.

1934 *Mind, Self and Society*. Edited by Charles Morris. Chicago: University of Chicago Press.

Mead, Margaret

1935 *Sex and Temperament in Three Primitive Societies*. New York: Morrow.

1971 *The Mountain Arapesh III*. Garden City, NY: Natural History Press.

Mendel-Meadow, C. and S. Diamond

1991 "Content, method, and epistemology of gender in sociolegal studies." *Law and Society Review* 25: 221–38.

Merton, Robert K.

1957 *Social Theory and Social Structure*. New York: Free Press.

Michels, Robert

1958 [1915] *Political Parties*. Glencoe, IL: The Free Press.

Miedzian, Myriam

1991 *Boys Will Be Boys: Breaking the Link Between Masculinity and Violence*. New York: Basic Books.

Miliband, Ralph

1977 *Marxism and Politics*. London: Oxford University Press.

1985 "The new revisionism in Britain." *New Left Review* 150: 5–28.

Mills, C. Wright

1956 *The Power Elite*. Oxford: Oxford University Press.

Milner, Henry and Sheilagh Hodgins Milner

1973 *The Decolonization of Quebec*. Toronto: McClelland and Stewart.

Miner, Horace

1963 [1939] *The Parish of St. Denis*. Chicago: University of Chicago Press.

Mirowsky, J. and C. Ross

1995 "Sex differences in distress: real or artifact?" *American Sociological Review* 60: 449–68.

Moghaddam, Fathali and Donald Taylor

1987 "The meaning of multiculturalism for visible minority immigrant women." *Canadian Journal of Behavioural Science* 19: 121–36.

Moghaddam, Fathali, Donald Taylor, and Richard Lalonde

1987 "Individualistic and collective integration strategies among Iranians in Canada." *International Journal of Psychology* 22: 301–13.

Moore, Maureen

1987 "Women parenting alone." *Canadian Social Trends* 7: 31–36.

1989a "Female lone parenting over the life course." *Canadian Journal of Sociology* 14: 335–52.

1989b "Dual-earner families: the new norm." *Canadian Social Trends* 12: 24–26.

1990 "Women parenting alone." Pp. 121–27 in Craig McKie and Keith Thompson (eds.), *Canadian Social Trends*. Toronto: Thompson Educational Publishing.

Morgan, Gareth

1986 *Images of Organizations*. Newbury Park, CA: Sage.

Morgan, Michael

1982 "Television and adolescents' sex role stereotypes: a longitudinal study." *Journal of Personality and Social Psychology* 43: 947–55.

Morris, Raymond

1991 "The literary conventions of sociological writing in Quebec and English Canada." *Society* 15: 10–15.

Mosca, Gaetano

1939 *The Ruling Class*. New York: H.D. Kahn.

Mowbray, C., S. Herman, and K. Hazel

1992 "Gender and serious mental illness: a feminist perspective." *Psychology of Women Quarterly* 16: 107–26.

Muller, J.

1990 "Co-ordinating the re-organization of ruling relations: management's use of human resource development for the New Brunswick community colleges." In J. Mueller (ed.), *Political Economy of Community Colleges: Training Workers for Capital*. Toronto: Garamond Press.

Murdie, Robert A.

1969 *Factorial Ecology of Metropolitain Toronto, 1951–1961*. Chicago: Dept. of Geography, University of Chicago, Research Paper No. 116.

Murdock, George P.

1957 "World ethnographic sample." *American Anthropologist* 59: 664–87.

1960 *Social Structure*. New York: Macmillan.

Nader, George A.

1975 *Cities of Canada*. Toronto: Macmillan of Canada.

National Council of Welfare

1990 *Women and Poverty Revisited*. Ottawa: Ministry of Supply and Services.

1993 "Poverty in Canada." Chapter 9 in J. Curtis, E. Grabb, and N. Guppy (eds.), *Social Inequality in Canada: Patterns, Problems, Policies*. (2nd ed.) Scarborough, Ont.: Prentice Hall.

Nault, Francois and Alain Belanger

1996 *The Decline in Marriage in Canada, 1981 to 1991*. Ottawa: Statistics Canada. Catalogue No. 84-536-XPB.

Navarro, Vincente

1982 "The labor process and health: an historical materialist interpretation." *International Journal of Health Services* 12: 5–29.

Neallani, Shelina

1992 "Women of colour in the legal profession: facing the familiar barriers of race and sex." *Canadian Journal of Women and the Law* 5: 148–165.

Needleman, Lionel

1986 "Canadian fertility trends in perspective." *Journal of Biosocial Science* 18: 43–56.

Neuman, W. Lawrence

1997 *Social Research Methods.* (3rd ed.) Boston: Allyn and Bacon.

Newman, Peter C.

1981 *The Acquisitors*. Toronto: McClelland and Stewart-Bantam.

Newman, S.C. and R.C. Bland

1987 "Canadian trends in mortality from mental disorders, 1965–83." *Acta Psychiatrica Scandinavica* 76: 1–7.

Nicks, Trudy

1985 "Mary Anne's dilemma: the ethnohistory of an ambivalent identity." *Canadian Ethnic Studies* 17: 103–14.

Nock, D.A.

1983 "Education and the correspondence principle." Pp. 345–71 in J. Paul Grayson (ed.), *Introduction to Sociology: An Alternative Approach*. Toronto: Gage.

1987 "Cult, sect, and church in Canada: a re-examination of Stark and Bainbridge." *Canadian Review of Sociology and Anthropology* 24: 514–25.

1993 "The organization of religious life in Canada." Pp. 41–63 in W.E. Hewitt (ed.), *The Sociology of Religion: A Canadian Focus*. Toronto: Harcourt Brace.

Noh, S., W. Zheng, and W. Avison

1994 "Social support and quality of life: sociocultural similarity and effective social support among Korean immigrants." *Advances in Medical Sociology* 5: 115–37.

O'Connor, Julia

1989 "Welfare expenditure and policy organization in Canada in comparative perspective." *Canadian Review of Sociology and Anthropology* 26: 127–50.

1993 "Ownership, class, and public policy." Chapter 6 in J. Curtis, E. Grabb, and N. Guppy (eds.), *Social Inequality in Canada: Patterns, Problems, Policies*. (2nd ed.) Scarborough, Ont.: Prentice Hall.

Ogmundson, R. and J. McLaughlin

1992 "Trends in the ethnic origins of Canadian elites: the decline of the BRITS?" *Canadian Review of Sociology and Anthropology* 29: 227–242.

Olsen, Dennis

1980 *The State Elite*. Toronto: McClelland and Stewart.

Ortega, S. and J. Corzine

1990 "Socioeconomic status and mental disorders." *Research in Community and Mental Health* 6: 149–92.

Osberg, Lars and Pierre Fortin, (eds.)

1996 *Unnecessary Debts*. Toronto: James Lorimer and Company.

Pahl, Robert E.

1969 "Urban social theory and research." *Environment and Planning* 1: 143–48.

1989 "Is the emperor naked? Some questions on the adequacy of sociological theory in urban and regional research." *International Journal of Urban and Regional Research* 13: 709–20.

Palantzas, T.

1991 "A search for 'autonomy' at Canada's first sociology department." *Society/Société* 15: 10–18.

Pallas, A.M., D. Entwisle, K. Alexander, and M. Stluka

1994 "Ability–group effects: instructional, social, or institutional." *Sociology of Education* 67: 27–46.

Pareto, Vilfredo

1935 *The Mind and Society*. Translated by Arthur Livingston. New York: Dover.

Park, Robert E.

1950 *Race and Culture*. New York: Free Press.

1952 *Human Communities*. New York: Free Press.

Park, Robert E. and E.W. Burgess

1967 *The City*. Chicago: University of Chicago Press.

Parkin, Frank

1979 *Marxism and Class Theory: A Bourgeois Critique*. London: Tavistock.

Parlee, M.B.

1982 "New findings: menstrual cycles and behavior." *Ms.* (September): 126–28.

Parliament, Jo-Anne

1990 "Increased life expectancy, 1921–1981." Pp. 64–65 in Craig McKie and Keith Thompson (eds.), *Canadian Social Trends*. Toronto: Thompson Educational Publishing.

Parsons, Talcott

1937 *The Structure of Social Action*. New York: The Free Press.

1951 *The Social System*. Glencoe, IL: The Free Press.

1953 "A revised analytical approach to the theory of social stratification." Pp. 92–128 in Reinhard Bendix and S.M. Lipset (eds.), *Class, Status and Power*. Glencoe, IL: The Free Press.

1968 "The distribution of power in American society." In G. William Domhoff and Hoyt B. Ballard (eds.), *C. Wright Mills and the Power Elite*. Boston: Beacon Press.

Parsons, Talcott and Robert F. Bales

1955 *Family, Socialization and Interaction Process*. New York: Free Press.

Patai, Daphne

1994 "U.S. academics and Third-World women: Is ethical research possible?" In *Feminist Nightmares, Women at Odds*. New York: New York University Press.

Patterson, Jeffrey

1991a "Things that matter to urban dwellers." *Institute of Urban Studies Newsletter* (University of Winnipeg) 37(Dec.): 1–4.

1991b "Introducing sustainable cities." *Institute of Urban Studies Newsletter Supplement* (University of Winnipeg) 1(Dec.): 1–6.

1992 "A quarter century of Canada's metropolitan fringe development." *Institute of Urban Studies Newsletter Supplement* (University of Winnipeg) 4(Autumn): 1–6.

Pelgrum, W.J., I.A.M. Janssen Reinen, and T. Plomp (eds.)

1993 *Schools, Teachers, Students and Computers: a Cross-National Perspective*. Enschede, IEA.

Péron, Ives and Jacques Légaré

1988 *L'Histoire Matrimoniale et Parentale des Générations Atteignant le Seuil de la Vieillesse d'Ici l'An 2000*. Ottawa: Health and Welfare Canada, Report for Review of Demography.

Petrunik, M. and C. Shearing

1988 "'The 'I,' the 'me,' and the 'it': moving beyond Meadian conception of self." *Canadian Journal of Sociology* 13: 435–448.

Piaget, Jean

1977 [1965] *The Moral Judgment of the Child*. New York: Free Press.

Pichardo, N.A.

1988 "Resource mobilization: an analysis of conflicting theoretical variations." *Sociological Quarterly* 29: 97–110.

Picot, Garnet and Ted Wannell

1993 "Who suffers permanent job loss?" Chapter 13 in J. Curtis, E. Grabb, and N. Guppy (eds.), *Social Inequality in Canada: Patterns, Problems, Policies*. (2nd ed.) Scarborough, Ont.: Prentice Hall.

Pike, Robert M.

1988 "Recommendations on access to post-secondary education." Chapter 16 in J. Curtis, E. Grabb, N. Guppy, and S. Gilbert (eds.), *Social Inequality in Canada: Patterns, Problems, Policies*. (1st ed.) Scarborough, Ont.: Prentice Hall.

1993 "Problems around educational opportunity." Chapter 15 in J. Curtis, E. Grabb, and N. Guppy (eds.), *Social Inequality in Canada: Patterns, Problems, Policies*. (2nd ed.) Scarborough, Ont.: Prentice Hall.

Pinard, Maurice

1968 "Mass society and political movements: a new formulation." *American Journal of Sociology* 73: 682–90.

Pineo, Peter

1986 "The social standing of ethnic and racial groupings." Pp. 256–72 in L. Driedger (ed.), *Ethnic Canada: Identities and Inequalities*. Toronto: Copp Clark Pitman.

1988 "Socioeconomic status and the concentric zonal structure of Canadian cities." *Canadian Review of Sociology and Anthropology* 25: 421–38.

Pineo, Peter and John Porter

1985 "Ethnic origin and occupational attainment." Pp. 357–92 in Monica Boyd et al. (eds.), *Ascription and Achievement*. Ottawa: Carleton University Press.

Pirie, M.

1988 "Women and the illness role: rethinking feminist theory." *Canadian Review of Sociology and Anthropology* 25: 628–48.

Platiel, Rudy

1993 "Inuit to sign deal for 'our land'." *The Globe and Mail*, May 25: 1.

Plomin, Robert

1989 "Environment and genes: determinants of behavior." *American Psychologist* 44: 105–11.

PMSP—Prefeitura do Município de São Paulo

1992 *Dossiê São Paulo*. São Paulo: PMSP-Sempla.

Polakowski, Michael

1994 "Linking self- and social control with deviance: illuminating the structure underlying a general theory of crime and its relation to deviant activity." *Journal of Quantitative Criminology* 10: 41–78.

Pomfret, Alan and Sid Gilbert

1991 "'Did they jump, or were they pushed?': gendered perceptions and preferences affecting attrition among science and engineering students." Paper presented at Women in Engineering. Fredericton, NB.

Ponting, J. Rick (ed.)

1986 *Arduous Journey. Canadian Indians and Decolonization.* Toronto: McClelland and Stewart.

Poplin, Denis E.

1979 *Communities*. New York: Macmillan.

Porter, John

1965 *The Vertical Mosaic: An Analysis of Social Class and Power in Canada*. Toronto: University of Toronto Press.

1980 "Canada: dilemmas and contradictions of a multiethnic society." Pp. 325–36 in Jay Goldstein and Rita Bienvenue (eds.), *Ethnicity and Ethnic Relations in Canada*. Toronto: Butterworths.

Posgate, Dale and Kenneth McRoberts

1976 *Quebec: Social Change and Political Crisis*. Toronto: McClelland and Stewart.

Prentice, Alison et al.

1988 *Canadian Women: A History*. Toronto: Harcourt Brace Jovanovich.

Propper, Alice

1984 "The invisible reality: patterns and power in family violence." Pp. 104–28 in M. Baker (ed.), *The Family: Changing Trends in Canada*. Toronto: McGraw-Hill Ryerson.

Ram, Bali

1990 *New Trends in the Family*. Statistics Canada, Catalogue No. 91-535. Ottawa: Minister of Supply and Services Canada.

Ramu, G.N.

1984 "Family background and perceived marital happiness: a comparison of voluntarily childless couples and parents." *Canadian Journal of Sociology* 9: 47–68.

Ratner, A. and C. McKie

1990 "The ecology of crime and its implications for prevention: an Ontario study." *Canadian Journal of Criminology* 32: 155–71.

Raudenbush, Stephen W. and Anthony S. Byrk

1988 "Methodological advances in analyzing the effects of schools and classrooms on student learning." Pp. 423–475 in Ernst Z. Rothkopf (ed.), *Review of Research in Education*. Washington: American Educational Research Association.

Ray, Carol Axtell and Roslyn Arlin Mickelson

1993 "Restructuring students for restructured work: the economy, school reform, and non-college-bound youths." *Sociology of Education* 66: 1–20.

Reitsma-Street, Marge

1993 "Canadian youth court charges and dispositions for females before and after implementation of the *Young Offenders Act*." *Canadian Journal of Criminology* 35: 437–58.

Reitz, Jeffrey

1980a "Language and ethnic community survival." Pp. 111–29 in Jay Goldstein and Rita Bienvenue (eds.), *Ethnicity and Ethnic Relations in Canada*. Toronto: Butterworths.

1990 "Ethnic concentrations in labor markets and their implications for ethnic inequality." Pp. 135–195 in Raymond Breton, Wsevolod Isajiw, Warren Kalbach, and Jeffrey Reitz (eds.), *Ethnic Identity and Equality*. Toronto: University of Toronto Press.

1993 "Racial conflict in Canada and Britain." Chapter 25 in J. Curtis, E. Grabb, and N. Guppy (eds.), *Social Inequality in Canada: Patterns, Problems, Policies*. (2nd ed.) Scarborough, Ont.: Prentice Hall.

Reitz, Jeffrey and Raymond Breton

1994 *The Illusion of Difference: Realities of Ethnicity in Canada and the United States*, Toronto: C.D. Howe Institute.

Renaud, Marc, Suzanne Doré, and Deena White

1989 "Sociology and social policy: from a love-hate relationship with the state to cynicism and pragmatism." *Canadian Review of Sociology and Anthropology* 26: 426–56.

Renzetti, Claire M. and Daniel J. Curran

1992 *Women, Men and Society: The Sociology of Gender*. (2nd ed.) Boston: Allyn and Bacon.

Resnick, Philip

1990 *Letters to a Québécois Friend*. Montreal and Kingston: McGill-Queen's Press.

Rhodes, A. and P. Goering

1994 "Gender differences in the use of outpatient mental health services." *Journal of Mental Health Administration* 21: 338–46.

Rice, Patricia C.

1981 "Prehistoric Venuses: symbols of motherhood or womanhood?" *Journal of Anthropological Research* 37: 402–414.

Richer, Stephen

1988 "Equality to benefit from schooling: the issue of educational opportunity." Pp. 262–86 in Dennis Forcese and Stephen Richer (eds.), *Social Issues: Sociological Views of Canada*. (2nd ed.) Scarborough, Ont.: Prentice Hall.

Richer, Stephen and Pierre Laporte

1971 "Culture, cognition, and English-French competition." Pp. 141–50 in Jean L. Elliott (ed.), *Minority Canadians II: Immigrant Groups*. Scarborough, Ont.: Prentice Hall.

Rindfuss, Ronald R. and Audrey VandenHeuvel

1990 "Cohabitation: precursor to marriage or an alternative to being single." *Population and Development Review* 16: 703–26.

Rinehart, James W.

1996 *The Tyranny of Work*. (3rd ed.) Toronto: Harcourt Brace.

Rioux, Marcel

1971 *Quebec in Question*. Toronto: James, Lewis and Samuel.

1978a "Bill 101: a positive anglophone point of view." *Canadian Review of Sociology and Anthropology* 15: 142–44.

1978b *Quebec in Question*. Toronto: James Lorimer.

Robbins, Tom

1988 *Cults, Converts, and Charisma*. London: Sage.

Roberts, Julian and Thomas Gabor

1990 "Lombrosian wine in a new bottle: research on crime and race." *Canadian Journal of Criminology* 32: 291–314.

Robinson, Patricia

1986 "Women's work interruptions and the family." Paper presented at meetings of the Federation of Canadian Demographers, Ottawa, November.

Rocher, G.

1977 "The future of sociology in Canada." In Christopher Beattie and Stewart Crysdale (eds.), *Sociology Canada: Readings*. Toronto: Butterworths.

1992 "The two solitudes between Canadian sociologists". In Wm. K. Carroll et al. (eds.), *Fragile Truths: 25 Years of Sociology and Anthropology in Canada*. Ottawa: Carleton University Press.

1996 "Préface." In Marc Brière (ed.), *Le goût du Québec: l'après référendum 1995*. La Salle: Hurtubise.

Rohde-Dascher, C. and S. Price

1992 "Do we need a feminist psychoanalysis?" *Psychoanalysis and Contemporary Thought* 15: 241–59.

Rondinelli, D.

1988 "Increasing the access of the poor to urban services." Pp. 19–57 in D. Rondinelli and G. Cheema (eds.), *Urban Services and Developing Countries*. London: Macmillan.

Roscoe, Paul

1996 "Incest." Pp. 631-34 in D. Levinson and M. Ember (eds), *The Encyclopedia of Cultural Anthropology*. Volume 2. New York: Henry Holt.

Rosenau, P.M.

1992 *Post-modernism and the Social Sciences: Insights, Inroads, and Intrusions*. Princeton: Princeton University Press.

Rosenberg, Harriet

1990 "The home is the workplace". In M. Luxton, H. Rosenberg, and S. Arat-Koc (eds.), *Through the Kitchen Window: The Politics of Home and Family*. (2nd ed.) Toronto: Garamond.

Rosenberg, M. Michael and Jack Jedwab

1992 "Institutional completeness, ethnic organizational style and the role of the state: the Jewish, Italian, and Greek communities of Montreal." *Canadian Review of Sociology and Anthropology* 29: 266–287.

Rosenfield, Sarah

1982 "Sex roles and societal reactions to mental illness: the labeling of 'deviant' deviance." *Journal of Health and Social Behavior* 23: 18–24.

Rosser, S.V.

1990 *Female-Friendly Science: Applying Women's Studies Methods and Theories to Attract Students*. New York: Pergamon.

Rossi, A. and P. Rossi

1990 *Of Human Bonding: Parent-Child Relations Across the Life Course*. New York: A. de Gruyter.

Rossi, Alice S.

1985 *Gender and the Life Course*. New York: Aldine de Gruyter.

Rothman, Robert A.

1993 *Inequality and Stratification: Class, Color, and Gender*. (2nd ed.) Englewood Cliffs, NJ: Prentice Hall.

Rowe, Geoff

1989 "Union dissolution in a changing social context." Pp. 141–64 in J. Légaré et al. (eds.), *The Family in Crisis: A Population Crisis*. Ottawa: The Royal Society of Canada.

Royal Commission on Bilingualism and Biculturalism

1967 *Report. Book I: The Official Languages*. Ottawa: Queen's Printer.

1969 *Report. Book IV: The Cultural Contribution of the Other Ethnic Groups*. Ottawa: Information Canada.

Rudé, George

1964 *The Crowd in History: A Study of Popular Disturbances in France and England, 1730–1848*. New York: Wiley.

Ruth, Sheila

1990 *Issues in Feminism*. (2nd ed.) Toronto: Mayfield.

Rutter, Michael

1985 "Family and school influences on behavioral development." *Journal of Child Psychology and Psychiatry* 26: 349–68.

Sacco, Vincent

1988 "Public definitions of crime problems and functionalist processes: a reassessment." *Canadian Review of Sociology and Anthropology* 25: 84–97.

1992 *Deviance—Conformity and Control in Canadian Society*. (2nd ed.) Scarborough, Ont.: Prentice Hall.

Sacco, V. and H. Johnson

1990 *Patterns of Criminal Victimization in Canada*. Ottawa: Minister of Supply and Services.

Sacco, V., H. Johnson, and R. Arnold

1993 "Urbanism and criminal victimization." *Canadian Journal of Sociology* 18: 431–51.

Salutin, Rick

1993 "Men and feminism." *This Magazine* 26: 12–18.

Sampson, R. and J. Laub

1990 "Crime and deviance over the life course: the salience of adult social bonds." *American Sociological Review* 55: 609–27.

Sampson, R. and J. Wooldredge

1987 "Linking the micro- and macro-level dimensions of lifestyle-routine activity and opportunity models of predatory victimization." *Journal of Quantitative Criminology* 3: 371–93.

Satzewich, Victor and Peter Li

1987 "Immigrant labour in Canada: the cost and benefit of ethnic origin on the job market." *Canadian Journal of Sociology* 12: 229–41.

Scanzoni, Letha and John Scanzoni

1988 *Men, Women and Change: A Sociology of Marriage and Family*. (3rd ed.) New York: McGraw-Hill.

Scheff, Thomas

1984 [1966] *Being Mentally Ill: A Sociological Theory*. Chicago: Aldine.

Schissel, Bernard

1992 "The influence of economic factors and social control policy on crime rate changes in Canada, 1962–1988." *Canadian Journal of Sociology* 17: 405–28.

Schur, Edwin

1971 *Labeling Deviant Behavior*. New York: Harper and Row.

1984 *Labeling Women Deviant*. New York: Random House.

Scott, Alan

1990 *Ideology and the New Social Movements*. London: Unwin Hyman.

Sellin, T.

1938 *Culture Conflict and Crime*. New York: Social Science Research Council.

Semple, R. Keith

1988 "Urban dominance, foreign ownership, and corporate concentration." Pp. 343–56 in J. Curtis et al. (eds.), *Social Inequality in Canada: Patterns, Problems, Policies*. Scarborough, Ont.: Prentice Hall.

Sharp, R.L.

1952 "Steel axes for stone age Australians." *Human Organization* 11: 17–22.

Shaw, C. and H. McKay

1942 *Juvenile Delinquency in Urban Areas*. Chicago: University of Chicago Press.

Shea, Catherine

1990 "Changes in women's occupations." *Canadian Social Trends* 18: 21–23.

Sheehan, M. Nancy, J. Donald Wilson, and David C. Jones (eds.)

1986 *Schools in the West: Essays in Canadian Educational History*. Calgary: Detselig.

Sheldon, William

1949 *Varieties of Delinquent Youth: An Introduction to Constitutional Psychiatry*. New York: Harper and Row.

Sherman, Lawrence, P. Gartin, and M. Buerger

1989 "Hot spots of predatory crime: routine activities and the criminology of place." *Criminology* 27: 27–55.

Shore, Marlene

1987 *The Science of Social Redemption: McGill, the Chicago School, and the Origins of Social Research in Canada*. Toronto: University of Toronto Press.

Shorter, Edward

1977 *The Making of the Modern Family*. New York: Basic Books.

Siggner, Andrew

1986 "The socio-demographic conditions of registered Indians." Pp. 57–83 in J.R. Ponting (ed.), *Arduous Journey, Canadian Indians and Decolonization*. Toronto: McClelland and Stewart.

Silverman, Robert

1992 "Street crime." Pp. 236–77 in Vincent Sacco (ed.), *Deviance—Conformity and Control in Canadian Society*. (2nd ed.) Scarborough, Ont.: Prentice Hall.

Silverman, Robert, James Teevan, and Vincent Sacco (eds.)

1995 *Crime in Canadian Society*. (5th ed.) Toronto: Harcourt Brace.

Simpson, Sally

1991 "Caste, class, and violent crime: explaining differences in female offending." *Criminology* 29: 115–35.

Skogan, W.

1990 *Disorder and Decline*. NY: Free Press.

Skolnick, Arlene S.

1987 *The Intimate Environment*. Boston: Little, Brown.

1991 *Embattled Paradise: The American Family in an Age of Uncertainty*. New York: Basic Books.

Slife, Brent D. and Joseph F. Rychlak

1982 "Role of affective assessment in modeling aggressive behavior." *Journal of Personality and Social Psychology* 43: 861–68.

Smelser, Neil J.

1962 *Theory of Collective Behavior*. New York: Free Press.

1991 *Social Paralysis and Social Change: British Working-Class Education in the Nineteenth Century*. Berkeley, CA: University of California Press.

Smith, Adam

1977 [1776] *The Wealth of Nations*. Chicago: University of Chicago Press.

Smith, Dorothy

1989 "Feminist reflections on political economy." *Studies in Political Economy* 30: 37–60.

Smith, Michael D.

1990a "Sociodemographic risk factors in wife abuse: results from a survey of Toronto women." *Canadian Journal of Sociology* 15: 39–58.

1990b "Patriarchal ideology and wife beating: a test of a feminist hypothesis." *Violence and Victims* 5: 257–73.

Smith, S.

1989 "Social relations, neighbourhood structure, and the fear of crime in Britain." Pp. 193–227 in D.J. Evans and D.T. Herbert (eds.), *The Geography of Crime*. London: Routledge.

Snider, Laureen

1991 "Critical criminology in Canada: past, present and future." In Robert Silverman, James Teevan, and Vincent Sacco (eds.), *Crime in Canadian Society*. (4th ed.) Toronto: Butterworths.

1992 "Commercial crime." Pp. 313–62 in Vincent Sacco (ed.), *Deviance: Conformity and Control in Canadian Society*. (2nd ed.) Scarborough, Ont.: Prentice Hall.

Sniderman, P., D. Northrup, J. Fletcher, P. Russell, and P. Tetlock

1993 "Psychological and cultural foundations of prejudice: the case of anti-Semitism in Quebec." *Canadian Review of Sociology and Anthropology* 30: 242–70.

Snow, D.A. and R.D. Benford

1988 "Ideology, frame resonance, and participant mobilization." Pp. 197-217 in Bert Klandermans, Hanspeter Kriesi, and Sidney Tarrow (eds.), *From Structure to Action: Social Movement Participation Across Cultures*. Greenwich: JAI.

1992 "Master frames and cycles of protest." Pp. 133-155 in A.D. Morris and C.M. Mueller (eds.), *Frontiers in Social Movement Theory*. New Haven: Yale University Press.

Snow, D.A., E.B. Rochford, Jr., S.K. Worden, and R.D. Benford

1986 "Frame alignment processes, micromobilization, and movement participation." *American Sociological Review* 51: 464-81.

Snyderman, M. and S. Rothman

1987 "Survey of expert opinion on intelligence and aptitude testing." *American Psychologist* 42: 137–44.

Solomon, R. and T. Madison

1986 "The evolution of non-medical drug use in Canada." In Robert Silverman and James Teevan (eds.), *Crime in Canadian Society*. (3rd ed.) Toronto: Butterworths.

Sparks, Allister

1995 *Tomorrow Is Another Country: The Inside Story of South Africa's Road to Change*. Chicago: University of Chicago Press.

Sperling, Susan

1991 "Baboons with briefcases vs. langurs in lipstick." Pp. 204–234 in Micaela di Leonardo (ed.), *Gender at the Crossroads of Knowledge*. Berkeley, CA: University of California Press.

Spitzer, S.

1975 "Toward a Marxian theory of deviance." *Social Problems* 22: 638–51.

Stanbridge, K. A. and Samuel Clark

1997 "Varieties of new social movements: universalistic versus particularistic." Unpublished manuscript.

Stanton, Elizabeth C.

1895 *The Woman's Bible*. New York: European Publishing.

Stark, Rodney and William Sims Bainbridge

1985 *The Future of Religion: Secularization, Revival, and Cult Formation*. Berkeley, CA: University of California Press.

Stebbins, Robert

1988 *Deviance: Tolerable Differences*, Toronto: McGraw-Hill Ryerson.

Steffensmeier, D. and C. Streifel

1991 "Age, gender, and crime across three historical periods: 1935, 1960, and 1985." *Social Forces* 69: 869–94.

Stevenson, David Lee and David P. Baker

1992 "Shadow education and allocation in formal schooling: transitions to university in Japan." *American Journal of Sociology* 97: 1639–1657.

Stone, Leroy O.

1988 *Family and Friendship Ties among Canada's Seniors*. Statistics Canada, Catalogue No. 89-508. Ottawa: Minister of Supply and Services Canada.

Stone, Leroy and Susan Fletcher

1977 *Migration in Canada*. Profile Studies. Ottawa: Information Canada.

Stonequist, Everett

1963 "The marginal man: a study in personality and culture conflict." Pp. 327–45 in E.W. Burgess and Donald Bogue (eds.), *Contributions to Urban Sociology*. Chicago: University of Chicago Press.

Stout, Cam

1991 "Common law: a growing alternative." *Canadian Social Trends* 23: 18–20.

Strasburger, Victor C.

1995 *Adolescents and the Media: Medical and Pscyhological Impact*. Thousand Oaks, CA: Sage.

Streitmatter, J.L.

1988 "Ethnicity as a mediating variable of early adolescent identity development." *Journal of Adolescence* 11: 335–46.

Strong, Bryan, Christine DeVault, Murray Suid, and Rebecca Reynolds

1983 *The Marriage and Family Experience*. St.Paul, MN: West Pub. Co.

Stubbs, Michael

1983 *Language, Schools, and Classrooms*. (2nd ed.) London: Methuen.

Sudnow, David

1967 *Passing On: The Social Organization of Dying*. Englewood Cliffs, NJ: Prentice Hall.

Sulloway, Frank

1996 *Born to Rebel*. New York: Pantheon Books.

Sumner, William G.

1940 *Folkways*. Boston: Ginn.

Sutherland, Edwin

1939 *Principles of Criminology*. (3rd ed.) Philadelphia: Lippincott.

Swan, Neil and John Serjak

1993 "Analysing regional disparities." Chapter 30 in J. Curtis, E. Grabb, and N. Guppy (eds.), *Social Inequality in Canada: Patterns, Problems, Policies*. (2nd ed.) Scarborough, Ont.: Prentice Hall.

Swanson, Guy

1960 *Birth of the Gods*. Ann Arbor, MI: University of Michigan Press.

Swatos, William H.

1981 "Church-sect and cult: bringing mysticism back in." *Sociological Analysis* 42: 17–26.

Sykes, G. and D. Matza

1957 "Techniques of neutralization: a theory of delinquency." *American Sociological Review* 22: 664–70.

Symons, Thomas H.B.

1976 *To Know Ourselves, the Report of the Commission on Canadian Studies*. Volumes 1 and 2. Ottawa: Association of Universities and Colleges of Canada.

Szelenyi, Ivan and Bill Martin

1988 "The three waves of new class theories." *Theory and Society* 17: 645–67.

Tancred-Sheriff, Peta (ed.)

1988 *Feminist Research: Prospect and Retrospect*. Kingston and Montreal: McGill-Queen's Press.

Tannenbaum, Frank

1938 *Crime and the Community*. Boston: Ginn.

Tanner, Julian

1992 "Youthful deviance." Pp. 203–35 in Vincent Sacco (ed.), *Deviance: Conformity and Control in Canadian Society*. (2nd ed.) Scarborough, Ont.: Prentice Hall.

Tanner, J. and H. Krahn

1991 "Part-time work and deviance among high school seniors." *Canadian Journal of Sociology* 16: 281–302.

Taylor, F.W.

1911 *Scientific Management*. New York: Harper.

Temple, M. et al.

1991 "A meta-analysis of change in marital and employment status as predictors of alcohol use on a typical occasion." *British Journal of Addiction* 86: 1269–81.

Tepperman, Lorne

1977 *Crime Control*. Toronto: McGraw-Hill Ryerson.

Thomas, W.I.

1923 *The Unadjusted Girl*. Boston: Little, Brown.

Thompson, E.P.

1971 "The moral economy of the English crowd in the eighteenth century." *Past and Present* 50: 76–136.

Thompson, J.H. and Allen Seager

1985 *Canada, 1922–1939: Decades of Discord*. Toronto: McClelland and Stewart.

Thorne, Barrie

1990 "Children and gender: construction of difference." Pp. 100–113 in Deborah Rhode (ed.), *Theoretical Perspectives on Sexual Difference*. New Haven, CT: Yale University Press.

Tilly, Charles

1978 *From Mobilization to Revolution*. Reading, MA: Addison-Wesley.

Tilly, Charles, Louise Tilly, and Richard Tilly

1975 *The Rebellious Century, 1830–1930*. Cambridge, MA: Harvard University Press.

Tittle, C.

1989 "Urbanness and unconventional behavior." *Criminology* 27: 273–306.

1995 *Control Balance: Toward a General Theory of Deviance*. Boulder, CO: Westview Press.

Tocqueville, Alexis de

1955 [1856] *The Old Regime and the French Revolution*. New York: Doubleday.

Touraine, Alain

1971 *The Post-Industrial Society: Tomorrow's Social History: Classes, Conflicts and Culture in the Programmed Society*. Translated by L.F.X. Mayhew. New York: Random House 1971.

Townsend, Joan B.

1990 "The Goddess: fact, fallacy and revitalization movement." Pp. 179–203 in Larry W. Hurtado (ed.), *Goddesses in Religions and Modern Debate*. Atlanta, GA: Scholars Press.

Trible, Phyllis

1979 "Eve and Adam: Genesis 203 reread." In Carol Christ and Judith Plaskow (eds.), *Womanspirit Rising*. San Francisco: Harper and Row.

Trigg, Linda J. and Daniel Perlman

1983 "Extramarital sex: the standards of Canadians." Pp. 263–76 in K. Ishwaran (ed.), *The Canadian Family*. Toronto: Gage.

Troeltsch, Ernst

1931 *The Social Teachings of the Christian Churches*. Vol. 2, translated by Olive Wyon. New York: Macmillan.

Trovato, Frank

1987 "A macrosociological analysis of Native Indian fertility in Canada, 1961, 1971, and 1981." *Social Forces* 66: 463–85.

1991 "Sex, marital status, and suicide in Canada: 1951–1981." *Sociological Perspectives* 34: 427–45.

Trovato, Frank and N. M. Lalu

1995 "The narrowing sex differential in mortality in Canada since 1971." *Canadian Studies in Population* 22: 145-167.

Turner, Ralph and L.M. Killian

1957 *Collective Behavior*. Englewood Cliffs, NJ: Prentice Hall.

Tylor, Edward

1964 [1871] *Primitive Culture: Researches into the Development of Mythology, Philosophy, Religion, Language, Art and Custom*. London: J. Murray.

Ueda, Yoko

1990 "The learning corporation: Japanese experience in occupational training." Pp. 197–211 in Jacob Mueller (ed.), *Canada's Changing Community Colleges*. Toronto: Garamond Press.

Urla, Jacqueline and Alan C. Swedlund

1996 "The anthropometry of Barbie: unsettling ideas of the feminine body in popular culture." Pp. 277-313 in Jennifer Terry and Jacqueline Urla (eds), *Deviant Bodies*. Bloomington: Indiana University Press.

Ursel, Jane

1986 "The state and the maintenance of patriarchy: a case study of family, labour and welfare legislation in Canada." Pp. 150–91 in J. Dickinson and B. Russell (eds.), *Family, Economy and State*. Toronto: Garamond Press.

Van den Berghe, Pierre

1967 *Race and Racism: A Comparative Perspective*. New York: Wiley.

van Poppel, F. and L. Day

1996 "A test of Durkheim's theory of suicide." *American Sociological Review* 61: 500–507.

Veevers, J.E.

1980 *Childless by Choice*. Toronto: Butterworths.

Visano, Livy

1987 *This Idle Trade*. Concord, Ont.: VitaSana.

Waddell, Eric

1986 "State, language and society: the vicissitudes of French in Quebec and Canada." Pp. 67–110 in Alan Cairns and Cynthia Williams (eds.), *The Politics of Gender, Ethnicity, and Language in Canada*. Toronto: University of Toronto Press.

Waite, Linda J. and Lee A. Lillard

1991 "Children and marital disruption." *American Journal of Sociology* 96: 930–953.

Waller, Willard

1937 "The rating and dating complex." *American Sociological Review* 2: 727–34.

Walmsley, Ann

1992 "Trading places." *The Globe and Mail Report on Business Magazine*, March: 17–27.

Walsh, A. and R. Gordon

1995 *Biosociology: An Emerging Paradigm*. Westport, CT: Praeger.

Wanner, Richard A.

1993 "Patterns and trends in occupational mobility." Chapter 12 in J. Curtis, E. Grabb, and N. Guppy (eds.), *Social Inequality in Canada: Patterns, Problems, Policies*. (2nd ed.) Scarborough, Ont.: Prentice Hall.

Ward, Martha

1996 *A World Full of Women*. Boston: Allyn and Bacon.

Warren, R., D. Taylor, M. Powers, and J. Hyman

1989 "Acceptance of the mental illness label by psychotic patients: effects on functioning." *American Journal of Orthopsychiatry* 59: 398–409.

Weber, Max

1946 *From Max Weber: Essays in Sociology*. New York: Oxford University Press.

1946a [1922] "Religious rejections of the world and their directions." Pp. 323–62 in Hans H. Gerth and C. Wright Mills (eds.), *From Max Weber*. New York: Oxford University Press.

1946b [1922] "The sociology of charismatic authority." Pp. 245–52 in Hans H. Gerth and C. Wright Mills (eds.), *From Max Weber*. New York: Oxford University Press.

1954 *Max Weber on Law in Economy and Society*. Cambridge, MA: Harvard University Press.

1958 [1904–5] *The Protestant Ethic and the Spirit of Capitalism*. New York: Charles Scribner and Sons.

1964 [1947] *The Theory of Social and Economic Organization*. New York: The Free Press.

1964 *Sociology of Religion*. Boston: Beacon Press.

1978 [1958] *From Max Weber: Essays in Sociology*. Translated by H. H. Gerth and C. Wright Mills. New York: Oxford University Press.

Weimann, Gabriel

1987 "New religions: from fear to faith." *Canadian Journal of Sociology* 12: 216–28.

Weitzman, N., B. Birns, and R. Friend

1985 "Traditional and nontraditional mothers' communication with their daughters and sons." *Child Development* 56: 894–96.

Wellman, Barry and Scott Wortley

1990 "Different strokes for different folks: community ties and social support." *American Journal of Sociology* 96: 558–588.

Wells, Gordon

1986 *The Meaning Makers: Children Learning Language and Using Language to Learn*. Portsmouth, NH: Heinemann.

Wells, L. Edward and Joseph H. Rankin

1991 "Families and delinquency: A meta-analysis of the impact of broken homes." *Social Problems* 38: 71–93.

White, Pamela

1990 *1986 Census of Canada: Ethnic Diversity in Canada*. Ottawa: Minister of Supply and Services Canada.

Whorf, Benjamin Lee

1956 *Language, Thought and Reality*. New York: John Wiley.

Wiegman, O., M. Kuttschreuter, and B. Baarda

1992 "A longitudinal study of the effects of television viewing on aggressive and prosocial behaviours." *British Journal of Social Psychology* 31: 147-164.

Wien, Fred

1993 "Regional inequality: explanations and policy issues." Chapter 31 in J. Curtis, E. Grabb, and N. Guppy (eds.), *Social Inequality in Canada: Patterns, Problems, Policies*. (2nd ed.) Scarborough, Ont.: Prentice Hall.

Wilkins, Leslie T.

1964 *Social Deviance: Social Policy, Action, and Research*. London: Tavistock.

Wilkins, Russell, Owen Adams, and Anna Brancker

1989 "Changes in mortality by income in urban Canada from 1971 to 1986." *Health Reports* 1(2) Statistics Canada, 820-003: 137–74. Ottawa: Minister of Supply and Services Canada.

Williams, D., D. Takeuchi, and R. Adair

1992 "Marital status and psychiatric disorders among blacks and whites." *Journal of Health and Social Behavior* 33: 140–57.

Wilson, J. and R. Herrnstein

1985 *Crime and Human Nature*. New York: Simon and Schuster.

Wilson, Susannah J.

1991 *Women, Families, and Work*. (3rd ed.) Toronto: McGraw-Hill Ryerson.

Wilson, William J.

1987 *The Truly Disadvantaged: the Inner City, the Underclass and Public Policy*. Chicago, IL: University of Chicago Press.

Wilson, J. and G. Kelling

1982 "Broken windows." *Atlantic Monthly*, March, 29–38.

Wilson, Paul, Robyn Lincoln, and Duncan Chappell

1986 "Physician fraud and abuse in Canada: a preliminary examination." *Canadian Journal of Criminology* 28: 129–46.

Wirth, Louis

1938 "Urbanism as a way of life." *American Journal of Sociology* 44: 1–24.

Wolf, Naomi

1990 *The Beauty Myth*. London: Chatto and Windus.

Wolff, Lee

1991 "Drug crimes." *Canadian Social Trends* 20: 26–9.

Wood, Wendy, Frank Y. Wong, and Gregory Chachere

1991 "Effects of media violence on viewers' aggression in unconstrained social interaction." *Psychological Bulletin* 109: 371–83.

Wordes, M. and T. Bynum

1995 "Policing juveniles: is there bias against youths of color?" Pp. 47–65 in K. Leonard et al. (eds.), *Minorities in Juvenile Justice*. Thousand Oaks, CA: Sage.

Wotherspoon, Terry (ed.)

1991 *Hitting the Books: The Political Economy of Retrenchment*. Toronto: Garamond.

Wotherspoon, Terry and Vic Satzewich

1993 *First Nations. Race, Class, and Gender Relations*. Scarborough: Nelson Canada.

Yi, Sun-Kyung

1991 "Crime statistics based on race promote hatred, board told." *The Globe and Mail*, Aug. 23.

Young, J. and R. Matthews

1992 *Rethinking Criminology: The Realist Debate*. London: Sage.

Subject Index

Accounts of behaviour 31
Achieved characteristic 138
Acheived status 169
Acculturation 228
Acute diseases 424
Adopted children 114
Aggression 86
  myth of male 147
  television and 95
  and testosterone 114
Age, *see also* Life expectancy
  and alcoholism 123
  and collective action 396
  compostition in Canada 438
  and crime 122
  at life course events 256
  migration 434
  and new religions 292
  poverty and 123
  social stratification 193–194
Age specific birth rate 428
Age specific death rate 423
Aging
  elder abuse 107
  and family 245
  and gender 156
  and menopause 156
  and mental illness 123
  and retirement 193
  and suicide 3
  and women 194
Alcoholism
  and deviance 103
  factors in 119
  and income 112
  labeling 130
  and masculinity 119
  and Native peoples 219
  rates of 106, 116
  and unemployment 112
Alienation of workers 364
  four types 364–365
  Marxism and 362
  and industrial sociology 365
Altruistic suicide 4
Anomie theory 116–119
  criticism of 119–121
Anomic suicide 4
Acribed status 168, 179, 186, 187, 206
Arunta 277–278
Assimilationism 226–229231
Authority 331–333, 362
Axiomatic logic 23

Behaviour
  cognitive theory 89
  conformity 116
  imitation 82
  modelling 85
  nature vs. nurture 76
  participant observation of 30–31
  rates of 4, 5
  rule governed 85
  symbolic interactionism 85
  vicarious punishment 86
  vicarious reinforcement 85
Bilateral disent 241
Bill 101 222–224
Binary opposition 78
Biological determinism 144
  functionalist view 146
  history of 145
  myths of 144–148
Biological reproduction 143, 144, 154,
Biological theory of deviance 112–114
Blacks
  segregation 229
  two-category view 229–230
Bloc Québécois 224, 346
Bourgeoisie 172
  in Marxism 336
British Canadians 220–224
British North America (BNA) Act 221, 346
Bureaucracy 358–362
  dysfunctions of 362
  and environment 363
  ideal type 361
  Marxist view 363
  six principles of 362
  in socialism 176
  types of authority 362
  universal class 341–342
  Weber's analysis 175

Canadian Constitution 224, 347–349
Capital accumulation theory 306–307
Capitalism
  alienation of workers 363
  change from 181–183
  control of workers 363
  and crime 106, 119
  and deviance 103–134
  and patriarchy 142
  and Protestantism 11
  and wife abuse 124
Chain migration 202, 225
Charisma 281–284
Charismatic authority 333
Charlottetown Agreement 345–348
Charter of Rights and Freedoms 345–348
Charter of French Language *see* Bill 101
Child abuse
  and deviance 107
  family change 267
  variables in 264
Childbearing
  age at 256, 429
  childlessness 263
  in marriage 261–263
  unmarried women 429
  women in labour force 248
Childrearing
  day care centres 94
  and division of labour 154, 248, 249
  and divorce 264–265
  and marriage 236–264
  self-esteem 91
  single parents 97–99

socialization 73, 74, 77, 75, 82,
Children
adopted 77
and aggression 86
child labour 344
confluence model 78
divorce 98, 264
family change 256, 267, 268
orphanhood 256
parental death 98
personality development 87
and poverty 268, 344
single-parent families 97
and television 95–96
Chronic diseases 424
Church 285
Circular reaction 383
Circulation of elites 335
Cities
and crime 116, 460
gentrification 448
housing in 459
human ecology view 449–452, 460
immigration to 225
inner 448
origin and growth 444–445
social choice view 452–454
social power view 454–459
urban renewal 457
urbanization 443–462
Civil religion 294–295
Civil society 341
Class 169, 170
collective action 397
education 316, 318–323
for itself 172
functionalist view 176–177
hierarchies 178–179
in itself 172
Marxist view 170–174
polarization 181
political participation 348–349
Weber's analysis 174–176
Collective action 387
in Canada 389
criticism of 389
defense of 389
Native peoples 387–388
Collective behaviour
criticism of 385
emergent norm theory 384
game theory 384
riots 386
Smelser's theory 383–384
social contagion 383
Collective conscience 104, 360
Colonialism 215
and capitalism 229
descrimination 211–215
and Native peoples 211–215
Common law union 241
and family change 268
Family Law Reform Act 260
fertility 430
increase in 248, 253
and single parenthood 260, 262
Comparative analysis 36
Concentric zone theory 450–451
Communism 174
Communist Manifesto 174
Conflict theory 8–9,
culture 63–65
deviance 105–106,
of gender relations 141–142
of marital power 259
of religion 286–288
and socialist feminism 143
view of anomie theory 116–117
view of functionalism 125
Conformity 104, 123, 126
Consanguine family 242–244
Constitution Act 345, 347
Consumer religion 294–296
Content analysis 31
Contraception 429, 432
Contraculture 118
Control variables 30
Cooperative Commonwealth Federation 290, 400, 401
Correlations 35
Correspondance principle 307
Craze 382
Crime
and age 122
anomie theory of 116–119
biological theories 112–114
in city 116, 460–461
and defensible space 461
human ecology theory 116
and poverty 117
psychological theories112–114
rates 108, 109
symbolic interactionist view 126
white collar 121, 125, 126,
Critical school 105
Cross sectional research 34, 35
Crowd
collective effervescence 275
emergent norm theory 384
game theory 384
social contagion 383
Crude birth rate 427
Crude death rate 423
Cult 285, 286, 289
Cult of man 289
Cultural
integration 57, 58
learning 83–87
markets theory 308
transmission 75
universals 55–57
values
Canadian 228
and language 148
learned 85
and television 95
variations 52–55
Culture, *see also* Subculture
androcentrism 61
conflict theory 63–65
cultural materialtist theory 65–67
dependancy theory 340
feminist theory 67–69
functionalist theory 62–63
islands 225
and television 95

Dating 251–253
Day care centres
conflict theory 126
liberal feminist view 143
and single mothers 158
and socialization 94
Deductive logic 23, 33

Defensible space 461
Demographic transition 415–419
Demography *see* Population
fertility 426–433
migration 433–437
mortality 421–426
Denominations 285, 291
Dependency theory 340
Deviance
amplifying process 127
anomie theory 116–117
biological theory 112, 113, 114
conflict theory 105, 106
definitions of 103
dramatization of evil 127
functionalist view of 104–105
human ecology theory 115
labeling 127
primary 128
psychological theory 112, 113, 114
social choice theory 452–456
rates of 108–109
reaction to 107
relativist view 107
secondary 128
social control theory 121, 122, 123
structural conflict theory 124–126
symbolic interactionist theory 116, 126
two stage hypothesis 107
Discrimination
age 193
explanations of 213–214
French Canadians 189
institutionalized 211
Native peoples 190
race/ethnicity 187–188
segregation 212–213
systemic 211
visible minorities 187
women 193
Disenchantment of the world 289, 361
Division of labour
functionalist view 177
gendered 154–156
housework 154
Marxist conflict view 141
wifework 154
Divorce
age at 266
and children 265
and cities 116
Divorce Act 267
Family Law Reform Act 260
grounds for 267
length of marriage 266
and socialization 98
statistics 266
and women 266
Double ghetto 155
Drug abuse
anomie theory 116
Native peoples 117
youth 117
Dysfunctions 8

Eating disorders 153
Ecclesia 285, 287
Economic power 168
cities 191
elite 189
and fertility 429
inequality 173, 180, 181
occupation 183, 184
regional cleavage 397–398
women 193
Ectomorphs 113
Education
apprenticeships 324
in Canada 302
capital accumulation theory 306–307
cultural markets theory 307–309
enrollment 302–303
expansion 301–310
functional theory 304–306
inequality 311, 312, 313, 323
process model 309–310
reform movement 311
social construction approach 310
social mobility 186–187
and women 158
Ego 87, 114
Egoistic suicide 4
Elaborated code 320
Elective affinity 281
Elitism 334–336, 348–350
Emergent norm theory 384
Endogamy 207, 241, 277, 294
Equalitarian authority 241
Environmentalism 339–341
Ethnic community
chain migration 202, 225
cultural values 206
formation202–205
institutions 203, 204
network 206
Ethnic group
assimilations 226–229
characteristics 205–207
discrimination 211–215
identity 208
regional cleavage 397–398
Ethnic mosaic, *see* Vertical mosaic
Ethnic relations
assimilation 226–229
in Canada 226
discrimination 211–215
institutions 203–204
nationalism 231
pluralism 230–232
segregation 212
two-category perspective 229–230
Ethnicity
ascribed status 168–169
assimilation 226–229
and collective action 389
and fertility 432
and mortality 426
as social organization 206–207
and socioeconomic status 187–188
statification 187
as subculture 207–208
Ethnocentrism 59
Ethnomethodology 369
Eurocentrism 59–60
Exogamny 241
Experimental group 28
Expressive dimension 139,
Extended family 241
External validity 29

Fad 382
Familism 249, 263
Family

and aging 256
functionalist view of change 245–247
gender stratification 192
incest taboo 244, 245, 277
and language 79
looking-glass self 90
Oedipal conflict 88
parental death 98
patriarchy 124
single parent 97
social control theory 122
as a social institution 154
socialization 74–76, 78
Fatalistic suicide 4
Federalism 345–347
Femininity 148–150
Feminism
and gender 11
liberal 143
maternal 143
methodology 57, 58
radical 143
religion 287
socialist 143
Feminization of poverty 157–158, 259, 261
Feral children 73
Fertility
in Canada 263
determinants of 426–427
differentials 430–431
and family planning 432
marital 262
measures of 427–428
models of 426–427
in Quebec 263
Folkways 47
Formal organization 358
Cooley's view 361
development of 358–359
division of labour 359
Durkheim's view 359–360
human relations school 366–367
moral order 360
scientific management 365–366
social contract 360
structuralist view 367
symbolic interactionist view 368–369
theoretical prepectives 359–370
work in 363–365
Free Trade Agreement 343
union view 375
French Canadians
Bill 101 222–224
Bloc Québécois 221
fertility 263
French fact 221
income 189
Meech Lake Accord 224
prejudice 189
pluralism 230–232
Quiet Revolution 222
as a race 220–221
relations with British Canada 220
seigneurial system 220
social mobility 189
social stratification 189
French Revolution 5–6
Functional theory of education 301
Functionalism 7–8
and anomie theory 116
and assimilationism 226
and biological determinism 146
and change in family 245–247
conflict theory view 64
consensus 176–177
and culture 62–63
and deviance 104–105
and education 186, 304–305
and gender relations 139, 140
male sexual jealousy 63
and Marxism 141
social control theory 123
view of conflict theorists 106

Game theory 384
Gender 138
aggression 95
aging 156, 157
blenders 140
confusion 140
and collective action 397
deviance 158, 159
division of labour 154–156
income/education 323
Marxist view 141
nature vs. nurture 144–148
norms 138
socialization 73, 74, 77
stereotyping 95
srtatification 192
Gender inclusive language 149
Gender inequality
androcentrism 61
anomie theory 116
in Canada 193
cultural universal 55–57
and deviance 111, 158, 159
division of labour 154–156
and education 314–316
feminist view 142–144
functionalist view 139–140
idoeology 137, 138
infanticide 103
language and 148–150
Marxist view 141–142
and premarital sex 251
poverty 157
self-esteem 91
Gender relations
body and sexuality 152–154
and dating 251
deviance 158–159
feminist view 142–144
functionalist view 139–140
Marxist conflict view 141–142
symbolic interactionist view 140–141
Gender roles
Canadian 159
childrearing 154
and dating 251
in family 247–250, 267–269
mother 49
father 57
functionalist view 139–140
maternal feminism 143
nature vs. nurture 144–146
socialization 137–138
spouse roles 247
symbolic interactionist view 140–141
Gendered division of labour, *see* Division of labour
Gendered identity 137–138, 150–152
Gendered order
feminization of poverty 157–158

heterosexual assumption 141
language 148–150
nature vs. nurture 144–146
pervasiveness 159
socialization 150
Generalized other 92
Geopolitics 332–333
Globalization 343, 345
Government 333
Group marriage 240–242

Hegelian political theory 340–342
civil society 341
ideal state 341
liberal democracy 340–341
universal class 341
Heterosexual assumption 141, 158
Heterogamy 241
Homelessness 157, 158
Homosexuality
as deviance 104, 158, 159
discouraged 244
gay rights movement 144
gender relations 138, 141
gender socialization 151
and hyopthalamus size 153
rule breakers 107
social stigma 243
techniques of neutralization 126
and the United Church 290
Horizontal mobility 169
Human ecology 115
Chicago school 227
concentric zone theory 450–451
multiple nuclei theory 452
natural areas 449
sector theory 451
urbanization 444

I and me 92
Id 87, 114
Ideal state 341
Ideology 287
Ideology of gender inequality 137, 138
Immigration
to Canada 224–226
chain migration 202, 225
culture islands 225
education 226, 323
ethnic identity 204, 206
fertility 431
Immigration Act 222
and international migration 435
Italian 202–205
to Quebec 220
race 211
refugee status 225
religion 291
return to homeland 226
sponsored 203
statistics 223
Income
by age
distribution of 180
and edcuation 185, 323
family statistics 192
fertility 430
French Canadians 189
Native peoples 190
by occuptation 183
race/ethnicity 188
regional inequality 191
women 193
Individualism
and action 178
assimilation 226–227
Canada vs. US 55
and crime 54
and functionalism 178
and government 54
and religion 54, 291
Industrial Revolution 5–6
education 246
and Marxism 170
motherhood 246
population growth 413–415
religion 279
Infant mortality rate 423
Informal organizations 358
Inner worldly asceticism 280
Innovation 117
Institution 49
ethnic 203–204
functionalist view 177
Institutional completedness 204
Institutionalized discrimination 211
Institutionalized power 167
Instrumental dimension 139
Instrumental exchange 240
Intergenerational mobility 169
Intrageneraltional mobility 169
Inuit
colonialism 215
deviance rates 112
Indian Act 211, 216
infanticide 103
land claim settlements 216
language 82
marginality 218
poverty 218
Tapirisat 230
Iron Law of Oligarchy 176, 335

Japanese management styles 371–376
cultural resistance 372
quality circle 372–373
union response 374
Juvenile delinquence
adult crime 127
alcoholism 123
anomie 119
bias in justice 110, 111
broken homes 121, 127
gang theory 118
gender 125
labelling 127
opportunity 119
part time work 123
power 119
race/ethnicity 113
school 123
unemployment 119, 125

Kin
aging 244
in consanguine family 243
group 243
in nuclear family 243
social control 244

Labelling theory
bias 127, 129, 130
discretion 129, 130
race/ethnicity 209

social hierarchy 209
symbolic interactionist theory 127–131
Labour force
fertility 431–432
and gender inequality 248
segregation 248
women 248–249
Language
acquisition of 81
in the Charter of Rights and Freedoms 346
coded 320
ethnic groups 209–210
French 221
functions 80
gendered 148, 149
linguistic
empiricism 81
nativism 81
relativism 82
sexism 149
universalism 82
mother tongues in Canada 223
role taking 91
socialization 79
Learning 83–87
Legitimation 362
Liberal democracy 333, 341–342, 348
Liberal feminism 143
Life expectancy
marriage 243, 257
mortality differentials 424–426
social class 426
statistcs 156
stratification 193
Longitudinal research 35, 36
Looking glass self 90

Marginality 208
Marital structures 241, 264
Marriage 240
age at 255
breakdown 264–266
childbearing 261–263
childrearing 263–264
commitment 240
and deviance 122
duration 257
empty nest stage 256
exchange 240
female social mobility 192
fertility 261
gay 244, 267
inheritance 185, 245
life expectancy 256
love 254
maintenance 240
mate selection 254
mating gradient 255
and mental illness 122
number of partners 240
power 259
premarital sex 251
remarriage 259, 266, 267
reproduction 244–245
status 241
structures 241, 259
suicide 122
widowhood 257
Marxism, *see also* Conflict theory
alienation of workers 364
bureaucracy 363
and collective action 392–393
dialectical approach 37
education 310
elite switching 336
functionalism 141
gender relations 141–142
ideology 286
political theory 336–337
means of production 171
praxis 37
religion 286
research methods 37
social class 170–171
social control 287
socialist feminism 143
state control theory 337
stratification 172–174
structuralist 337
symbolic interactionism 37
Weber's criticism of 174–176
Masculinity
appearance 152
childrearing 154, 155
and deviance 119
gay rights movement 144
gender blending 140, 142
mens' movements 144
in patriarchal society 143
physical fitness 154
profeminist movement 144
violence 158
Material culture 49
Maternal feminism 143
Mating gradient 255
Matriarchy 219, 241
Matrilineal descent 241
Matrilocal residence 241
Mechanical solidarity 246, 360
Meech Lake Accord 224, 407
Mental illness
aging 118, 123
biological theories 114
cities 115
deviance 112–118
friends 123
homelessness 157
homosexuality 107, 109
labelling 111
marriage 121
men 111
poverty 118
rates of 111
single parent families 97–98
social class 118
treatment bias 111, 112
women 111
Mesomorphs 113
Middle class 179
education 186
expanding 184
French Canada 189
income levels 180
language 320
life expectancy 193
society 175
in state elite 189, 195
white-collar occupations 183
Migration 433
cities 434–435
and deviance 116
internal 433–434

international 435–437
motives 433
social organization 433
Minority group 209–211
Model 32, 37
Monogamy 240, 241
Moral autonomy
development 89
ecconomy 386
entrepreneurs 105
order 360
Morality of constraint 89
Morality of cooperation 89
Mores 47
Mortality
causes of 423–424
differentials 424–426
measures of 422–423
Multiculturalism 187, 346

Nationalism 230
Native peoples
alcoholism 219
assimilation 402–403
birth rate 402, 432
colonialism 215
and crime 117, 118
culture 218, 219
education 219
employment equity 227
erosion of power 190
ethnogenesis 209
factionism 406
identity 190
income 219
Indian Act 216
land claims 190, 216, 217
language 208
matriarchy 219
Meech Lake Accord 407
Métis 216
migration 224–225
movement 406
Native Council of Canada 230
Oka crisis 190
pluralism 230
population 216
prejudice 213
reserve system 207, 229
residential schools 208
segregation 212
socioeconomic status 190
sovereignty 219
stratification 190
suicide 219
two-category perpective 229
unemployment 217, 218
verticle mosaic 190
visble minority 209
women 219
Naturalization of history 145
Nature vs. nurture 144–146
Negotiated order theory 368
Neoconservatism 343–345
deficit reduction 344–345
free trade 343
reduction incorporate taxes 345
zero inflation 344
Neolocal residence 241
New Democratic Party 290, 348, 349
New Keynesians 344
New industrial sociology 370–371
New religious movement 291–293
Non industrial society 245–246
Non-marriage statistics 258
Norms
bodies 153
boundaries 207
consensus 176
cults 289
cultural 54
deviance 103, 104
division of labour 154
ethnic groups 207
fertility 427
gender 138
gender roles 250
marriage 240
sexual 63
socialization 73–75, 94–96
social reproduction of 152
television 151
North American Free Trade Agreement 331, 343
Nuclear family 242–243
Objectification of women 143, 153, 155
Occupation
blue collar 183, 184
education 186, 308, 323–324
French Canadian 221
immigrant specialization 205
income by 183
migration 434
shifts in 182
social mobility 185
specialization 205
stratification 185
variety 184
white collar 183, 184
Operational definition 24
Organization 357–370
Other worldly mysticism 280

Panic 381
Participant observation 31, 32, 33, 36
Parti Québécois 189, 407
Party 175
Patriarchy 241
crime 124
deviance 124
family change 267
feminist view 144
feminization of poverty 157
gender blending 140, 142
homless women 157
marital power 259
Marxist conflict view 141–142
masculinity 144, 146
origins 141
pro feminist movement 144
wife abuse 124
Patrilineal descent 241
Partilocal residence 241
Personality development
cognitive perspective 89
Freud's stages 87–88
genetic influences 78
nature vs. nurture 76–77
psychosocial theory 88–89
role taking 91
socialization 73–75
twins 77
Pluralism 105

Canada 230, 346, 348
ethnic mosaic 231
functionist view 177
immigration 232
power 177–178
Pluralistic society 177
ethnic groups 205
French fact 221
hierarchical 202
race 209
Political economy 339–340
Politics 331–351
Polyandry 240, 241
Polygamy 241
Polygyny 240, 241
Population
demographic transition 415–419
growth in Canada 420–421, 422
Malthusian theory 419–420
natural increase 422
projected 439
pyramid 437–438
sex/age composition 437
world growth 413–414
Positivism 21
Post test 29
Poverty
aging 123
crime 112, 118
deviance 112, 118, 119
education 323
ethnic/racial segregation 213
family change 268
homelessness 157
mental illness 118
Native peoples 219
wife abuse 127
women in 157
Power
abuse of 176
cities 191
conflict theory 125
deviance 125
economic 168
elite 335
group 308
ideological 168
institutionalized 168
marital 259
Marxism 37
Native peoples 192
political 168, 194
race/ethnicity 187
sacred 275–276
social mobility 184
structured 176
Weber's view 175
women 191–192
Praxis 37, 125
Predestination 281
Prejudice 213
Pre test 29
Primary group 361
Profane 278
Progressive Conservative Party 348–349
Primary deviance 128
Primary sources 37
Private realm 139
Prodestant ethic 283
Protestantism 288
Proletariet 172, 173, 174, 175, 176
Property 171, 172, 173, 174, 175
Protestantism 3, 11, 12
Psychology
cognitive view 89
psychodynamic view 87
Public realm 139

Quebec 13, 15, 16
Quebec, *see also* French Canadians
Americanization 346
birth rate 221, 431
culture 221
distinct society 16
education 405
as ethnic minority 16
fertility rate 264
French English relations 222
immigration to 220
labour code 405
la survivance 404–406
language 405–406
Marxist view 16
Meech Lake Accord 407
nationalism 346, 405–406
pluralistic values 346
population 346
religion 289
separatisim 405–407
social services 406
sociology in 12–16
sovereignty association 345
War Measures Act 332
Welfare Reform Law 342

Race
ascribed status 168
crime 127
ethnic groups as 206
income
inequality
minorities
mortality differential 426
Native peoples 190
relations
assimilation 226–228
in Canada 215–226
conflict 231
cycle 228
discrimination 187–189, 192, 193
ethnic cleansing 231
French and English in Canada 220–224
labelling 209
nationalism 231
pluralism 230–232
segregations 211
two-category perspective 229–230
socioeconomic status 187
stratification 187–188
terminology 210
visible minorities 187
Racism 209–210
Radical feminism 143
Rationalization 361
Rational legal authority 333, 361
Reaction to deviance 128, 129, 130.
Rebellion 117
Reconstituted family 241, 264
Reform Party 348, 401, 402
Relative deprivation 386–387
Reliability 24

Religion
- Arunta 276–278
- in Canada 289–291
- causes 275
- civil 293
- consumer 294
- cultural materialist view 66
- cultural variation 53
- emotions 289
- feminist view 287
- functionalist view 275–279
- functions of 278–279
- growth in 291
- Marxist view 286–288
- Mother Teresa 64
- new definitions 293–296
- new movements 291–293
- parish of St. Denis 278–279
- retreatism 117
- sacred 275
- salvation 280
- secularization 288–289
- and society 276
- suicide 123
- symbolic interactionist view 279–286
- totemism 276–277
- and well-being 274

Replication 34

Research methods
- analysis 29, 33
- comparative analysis 36
- content analysis 31
- cross-cultural 38
- experiment 28, 29
- generalizability 34–35
- Hawthorne effect 29
- historical analysis 36
- measurement 22, 24, 32
- methods of observation 22, 25
- participant observation 31
- qualitative 22
- quantitative 21
- questionnaires 28
- statistics 125, 126
- survey 23
- triangulation 36
- validity 24, 29

Research paper 38–40

Resocialization 78

Resources theory of urban development 454–459

Retreatism 117

Revolution
- Marxist 170
- potential for 170–171
- program for 172
- proletariat 172

Ritualism 117

Role conflict 48

Roles
- and biological determinism 144
- and culture 47–48
- and division of labour 154
- education 312
- language 148–150
- nature vs. nurture 146
- parental death 98
- religion 276
- resocialization 78

Routinization of charisma 281–282

Rule breakers 107, 109, 110, 115

Rural–urban inequities
- collective action 397
- fertility differential 431
- migration 434–435
- regional cleavage 397–398
- rural renaissance 447–449
- shift 447

Sampling 26
- accidental 27
- cluster 27
- cost of 27, 29, 31, 32, 38
- in cross cultural research 338
- in experimental research 28, 29
- frame 27
- in Marxist research 37
- non-random quota 33
- in participant observation 31
- quota 27
- random 26
- random digit dialing 28
- representatives 26
- secondary deviance 128

Secondary analysis 38

Secondary group 361

Secondary sources 37

Sect 284
- Marxist view 287, 288
- new religious movement 291

Sector theory 451

Secularization 288–291
- in Canada 289–291
- Christian response 290
- limits to 290
- response to 289

Segregation 211
- human ecology view 450
- Native peoples 219
- and socioeconomic status 219
- and poverty 219

Selective incentives 390

Sex 138
- ascriptive trait 138, 168
- bargainning for 252
- bias in education 315
- blocked 254
- -change operation 141
- codes 242
- dating 251
- extramarital 242
- gender 138
- mortality differential 424–426
- premarital 251
- ratio 424
- roles 52

Sexual
- assult 159
- deviance 106, 107
- harrassment 155

Sexuality 141, 142, 152–154

Significant others 92

Single parent family 241
- benefits 262
- challenges 262
- common law unions 253, 260, 261
- divorced parents 264, 265
- education 262
- family change 264
- feminization of poverty 157, 261
- fertility differential 432
- housing 459
- income 262
- men 260

mental illness 97–98
never–married parents 262
separated parents 262
standard of living 264
statistics 262
widowed parent 260
women in 260
Social
breakdown approach 385
category 209–210
choice theories 452–454
class 170
and crime 112
deviance 125
Hegelian theory 340–342
homogamy 254, 255
inequality in education 319–320
Marxist conflict view 141–142
mental illness 118
mortality differential 426
new class 342
oppression of women 142
socialist feminist view 143
cleavage
ethnic 397
regional 397–398
contagion 383
contract 360
control
citizen participation 460–461
crime 460–461
criticism of 123
deviance 103
discrimination 211–215
education 306
gatekeepers 457
religion 287
segregation 211
subordination of minorities 210–211
theory of deviance 121
and language 81
Social credit party 290, 400
Social
death 369
differentiation 8
facts 3
groups
behaviour 47
consensus 176
constraint of individual 12
culture of 48–49
experience of 10
formal organizations 358
inequality 178
kinship 277
membership 3
power of 278
religion 276–277
inequality 178
institutions
education 302–323
families 239–269
religion 273–275
mobility 169
assmilation 226–228
education 186
ethnic identity 208
ethnicity 205
French Canadians 224
marriage 192
occupation 169, 184
vertical intergenerational 169
movement 382
in Canada
collective action 387–393
collective behaviour 381, 383–385
ethnic cleavage 397
regional cleavage 397–398
relative deprivation 386–387
social breakdown 385
theoretical approaches 381–396
order
community size and social choice theory 453–454
organization
age composition 434
boundaries 207
consensus 176
and ethnic groups 206
fertility 430
formal 358
hierarchy 206
immigrants 224
migration 433
mortality 424
norms 206
population growth 413–415
sex compostition 437
socialization 206
spatial separation 206
relationships
mortality differentials 424
reproduction 138, 151, 151
stratification
age 193
analysis 167
in Canada 179–194
class 169
closed vs. open 168, 169
combining theories 177–179
conflict theory view 63–65
as distributive process 167
and education 186
gender 192
institutionalized power 167
Marxist view 170–174
Native peoples 190
and political power 194
and power 167194–197
racial/ethnic 187
regional inequalitites 190
social mobility 169
and status 168
and stratum 168
structural functionalism 170, 176–177
theories of 170–177
Weber's view 174–176
Socialism
Marxist view 170
postmodernist view 337–339
Weber's view 174
Socialist feminism 143
Socialization
behaviour 84
biological determinism 144
childrearing 73, 75
children raised with animals 74
cognitive view 89
confluence model 78
cultural 73
to deviance 126, 127
divorce 98

and ethnic groups 206
ethnic identity 208
family 73–75, 244
feral children 73
gender 144, 149, 151, 154, 250
implications of 137, 138
isolation 74
juvenile delinquency 73
and language 79
and life cycle 77
males 137
and marriage 244
for marriage 250
modeling 93
nature vs. nurture 76–77
parental death 98
primary 93
process 73–75
psychodynamic view 87
and psychology 87–92
purpose of
research 36
results of 73
separation 98
single parents 97
symbolic interactionist view 90
television 94–96
and toys 151

Society 3
bureaucracy 11
composition of 3
conflict in 12
constraint of individuals 12
development 5–7
Durkheim's view 3–5
equilibrium 8
and French Revolution 5–6
inadequate socialization 99
Industrial Revolution 5–6
Marx's view 6–7
pro-fertility 428

Socioeconomic hierarchies 179–194

Socioeconomic status 188

Sociology
careers in 17
concerns of 3, 5, 6
conflict theory 8–9
ethnocentrism 59
eurocentrism 59–60
feminist model 11–12
French Revolution 5–6
functionalism 7–8
history of 5–7, 13–16
Industrial Revolution 5–6
as a Liberal discipline 9
modern origins 5
new industrial 370
and other social sciences 4
urban 443

Spurious relationships 35

Staples theory 339–340

State 332
in bureaucracy 358
composition of 195
control 334–342
dependency 340
economic elite 194
elite 194
Hegel's view 340–342
ideal 341
laws 194
legitimacy of 332
Marxist 336–337
political power 195
pluralist 334
postmodern 337–339

Status 168
consistency 168
education 308, 323–324
functionalism 175
groups 168
hierarchy 168
honour 175
inconsistency 168
marriage 250
mobility 169
set 168

Stereotypes 213
gender 150
Native peoples 190
and television 95

Stratum 168
in capitalism 178
income distribution 180–181
occupations 182
Weber's view 175

Structural assimilation 227

Structuralism
anomie theory of deviance 116–118
criticism of human relations school 367
criticism of scientific management theory 367
social control theory 121–123
view of formal organizations 367

Subculture 48
counterculture 292
ethnic 207–208
regional 230

Suicide
aging 121
deviance 103
Durkhiem's study of 3–5
men 121
social causes of 3
suttee 104
types of 4
women 121

Superego 87, 114

Symbolic interactionism 9–11
behaviour 90
definition of the situation 92
and deviance 116, 126–131
differential association 126
escape 280
ethnomethodology 369
and formal organizations 369
and gender relations 140–141
inner worldly ascetism 280
labelling 127
looking glass self 90
and organizations 368
other worldly ascetism 280
prostitution 10
Protestant ethic thesis 281–284
religion 279–286
role-taking 91
routinization of charisma 281–282
salvation 280
suicide 4
types of religious organizations 284–286
use in research 11

Systematic discrimination 211

Techniques of neutralization 126
Theory 23, 25, 31, 37
Traditional authority 333, 362
Triangulation 36
Two-category perspective 229–230

Unemployment
- alcoholism 112
- crime 110
- education 186
- juvenile delinquency 126
- mental illness 111
- Native peoples 219
- prison 127
- wife abuse 127
- youth 111–112
- zero inflation 344

Unions 374
Universal class 341
Upper class 172, 179–197
Urban development
- human ecology theory 449–452
- social choice theory 452–454
- social power theory 454–459

Urbanization 443
- Canadian urban settlements 445–447
- citizen participation 457
- crime 459–462
- in the developing world 461
- general patterns of 446
- history of cities 444–445
- housing 459–460
- rural renaissance 447–448
- rural-urban shift 447
- suburbanization 447–448
- theories of 449–459

Urban legends 49–51
Urban renewal 457–458
Urban social issues 459–462

Values 45
- Canadian vs. American 54–55
- consensus 176
- cultural 52
- deviance 104
- education 306
- French 221
- physical environment 453
- religious 286
- secularization 287
- social choice 452
- social reproduction 137, 138
- subgroup 452
- television 95
- urban life styles theory 451
- use of surveys in research on 55

Variable 23, 24, 29, 30
Vertical mobility 169
- assimilationism 226
- in Canada 179
- occupation184
- pluralism 230

Vertical mosaic
- Canadian culture 230
- Canadian values 230
- ethnic groups 202, 203
- inequality 203, 226
- multiculturalism 231
- Native peoples 190
- pluralism 230
- social stratification 179

Violence
- against women 158
- child abuse 264
- crime 112
- domestic 111
- homelessness 157
- testosterone 119

Visible minorities 188, 210, 226

Wealth
- distribution of 180
- education 186
- political power 194

Welfare state 342–344
Women
- aging 106, 156
- alcoholism 121
- anomie theory 116
- Charter of Rights and Freedoms 349
- collective action 390
- crime 120
- cultural integration 58
- deviance 158
- domestic violence 127
- eating disorders 153
- education 186
- entry into the labour force 192
- family change 264–265
- fertility rates 426–433
- gender stratification 192
- housework 154
- income 183
- marriage 192
- mental illness 118
- Native 219
- pay equity 350
- politics 349–350
- poverty 157, 193, 259, 268
- power 192
- premarital sex 251
- retreatism 117
- ritualism 117
- single mothers 192, 260, 261
- socioeconomic rank 192
- violence 158
- violence 127
- in science 25
- in sociology 11
- wifework 154
- widowhood 256

Women's movement
- change in family 268
- consciousness-raising 138
- social change 159, 160

Work
- alienation of workers 364
- control of workers 364–365
- Japanese management styles 371–375
- Marxist views 363–365
- new industrial sociology 370

Working class
- blue collar occupations 183
- class voting 348
- education 186, 316, 318, 320–323
- income levels 183
- language 320
- Marxist theory 336–337
- new working class 183
- passivity 181
- in state elite 195
- underclass 179

Writing research papers 38–40

Name Index

Abella, Judge 349
Aberhart, William 400
Adair, R 122
Adam, B.A. 395
Adams, O.B. 248, 266
Adamson, Nancy 382, 391, 398
Agnew, Robert 118
Agócs, Carol 188, 189, 202, 205, 213, 229
Akerlind, I. 123
Akyeampong, E.K. 186
Alder, Christine 119, 121
Alexander, K.L. 321
Allahar, Anton A. 193
Allen, Robert C. 353
Amagoalik, John 217
Amato, Paul R. 98
Ambert, Anne-Marie 265, 271
Anderson, J. 117
Anisef, Paul 186, 187, 328
Arai, A. Bruce 186, 189, 316
Archibald, W. Peter 189
Aries, Philippe 271
Armour, Lisa K. 372
Armstrong, Hugh 192
Armstrong, Pat 192
Arnold, R. 115
Avison, William R. 98, 123
Axelrod, Paul 186, 328

Badets, Jane 225
Baer, Douglas 9, 54, 55, 197
Bainbridge, William Sims 295
Baker, David P. 317, 324
Bala, Nicholas 133
Balakrishnan, T.R. 188, 213, 263, 266, 431, 450
Bales, Robert F. 139
Bandura, Albert 83, 85, 86, 87, 96, 101
Baron, S. 130
Barr, Rebecca 323
Bart, Pauline 40
Barth, Fredrik 206
Beaujot, Roderic P. 22, 216, 222, 267, 420, 427, 441
Becker, Howard S. 105
Behiels, Michael 346
Beisner, M. 114
Béland, Francois 16
Belaney, Archie 208, 209
Belanger, Alain 257, 267
Belenky, M. 315
Bell, Daniel 341
Bellah, Robert 293, 294
Bellamy, Raymond 335
Benford, R.D. 390
Berger, Peter 294
Berk, Richard A. 129, 324
Berman, Dr. Edgar 149
Berns, Roberta M. 101
Bernstein, Basil 320, 321
Bertrand (Parti Québécois) 406
Beveridge, William 13
Bibby, Reginald 289, 290, 291, 292, 293, 294, 295, 296, 299
Bidwell, Charles E. 319, 322
Bielby, William 212
Bienvenue, Rita 190
Bird, T. 459
Birns, B. 151
Bishop, Patricia 349
Black, Naomi 410
Blais, Andre 16
Bland, Roger 110, 111, 114, 123, 125
Bleier, Ruth 61
Bloch, Herbert 119
Blumenfeld 318
Blumer, Herbert 383, 384
Blumstock, Robert 294
Bongaarts, John 427
Bourassa, Henri 404, 405, 406
Bourne, L. 448
Bourne, Paula 410
Boutilier, Marie 249
Bowles, Samuel 307
Boyd, Monica 188, 189, 202, 205, 212
Bozinoff, Lorne 49
Brabant, S. 5
Brandt, Gail 410
Brannigan, Augustine 106
Braverman, Harry 183, 306
Brehm, Sharon S. 244
Breton, Raymond 16, 188, 204, 207, 211, 212, 215, 222, 231
Brickey, Steven 105
Brinkerhoff, Merlin 124, 259
Briskin, Linda 382, 391, 398
Brooks, N. 110
Broude, Gwen 53
Brown, M. 125
Brown, Steven 54
Brownfield, D. 121
Bruke, M.A. 460
Brunvand, Jan Harold 49
Brym, Robert J. 348
Bryner, John 323
Buchan, S. 349
Bumpass, Larry L. 264
Burawoy, Michael 339
Burch, Thomas K. 253, 256
Burgess, E.W. 449, 450, 451, 452
Burr, Catherine 229
Bush, George 331, 337
Bynum, T. 111
Byrk, Anthony S. 322, 323
Byrne, C. 114

Caldwell, G. 346, 418
Caldwell, John C. 243
Calvin 281
Calzavara, Liviana 156, 192
Campani, Giaovanna 203
Campbell, Douglas F. 12
Campbell, K.E. 453
Campbell, Kim 349
Canel, Eduardo 393, 395
Capeling-Alakija, Sharon 160
Capone, Al 331
Caroll, W.K. 410
Carroll, William K. 18, 170, 181
Cassin, A.M. 369

Cato 249
Chalk, Frank 211
Chan, J. 111
Chappel, Duncan 120, 126
Chawla, Raj K. 180, 260
Che-Alfred, J. 459
Cherlin, Andrew J. 262
Chisholm, Peter 118
Chodorow, Nancy 88
Chomsky, Noam 334
Chou, S 116
Chretien, Jean 81, 331, 341, 343, 346
Christ, Carol 287
Christiansen-Ruffman, Linda 18
Christie, Nils 125
Christofides, L.N. 212
Chui, Tina 196, 197
Clark, Peter 47
Clark, S.D. 282, 283
Clark, Samuel D. 13, 14, 15, 395
Clarke, Juanne 5, 196
Clement, Wallace 170, 189, 191, 193, 194, 336
Clinard, Marshall 126
Cloward, Richard 120, 121
Cockerham, William C. 114
Cohen, Albert 118, 126
Coleman W.D. 405, 406
Collins, Randall 306, 307, 308, 333
Comack, Elizabeth 105
Combes-Orme, T. 130
Comte, Auguste 6, 360
Condry, J. 147
Condry, S. 147
Connidis, Ingrid 245, 259
Connor, Steven 394
Conway, John F. 268, 271, 353
Cook, M. 22
Cooley, Charles H. 90, 91, 361
Copp, Terry 307
Corrado, Raymond 133
Corwin, Ronald G. 368
Corzine, J. 118
Coser, Lewis 104
Côté, James E. 193
Creese, G. 323
Crompton, Susan 260
Crosby, Faye J. 154
Cullen, Francis 112
Cuneo, Michael W. 288
Curran, Daniel J. 140, 146, 148
Currie, Raymond 18
Curtis, Bruce 6, 197, 316, 328
Curtis, James 54, 168, 185, 199

Dabbs, James 113
Dagg, Anne Innis 317
Dahrendorf, Ralf 178
Daly, Mary 287
Darwin, Charles 13, 64, 75
Das Gupta, Tania 212, 235
Davis, Anthony 47
Davis, Arthur K. 191
Davis, Kingsley 7, 73, 176, 444, 445
Davis, Morris 210
Dawson, Charles 225, 227
Dawson, D. 116
Day, L. 3
de Tocqueville, Alexis 387
Decima 215
DeFrain, J. 263
Dekeseredy, Walter S. 124
DeMello, Margo 395
Derber, Charles 150
Derrida, Jacques 337
Desai, Sonalde 260
Devor, Holly 140, 141, 142, 159
Di Leonardo, Micaela 58
Diamond, S. 124
Dickens, Charles 170
Dickson, Lovat 208
Dionne, Claude 262
Dobasch, R.E. 124
Dobasch, R.P. 124
Dohrenwend, B. 118
Don, K. 111, 116
Doob A. 110
Downing, Christine 104
Dreeben, Robert 323
Driedger, Leo 205, 211, 453, 464
Dryden, Ken 86
Duleep, Harriet 212
Dumas, Jean 13, 16, 266
duPays, Jean 407
Duplessis, Maurice 405, 406
Durkheim, Emile 3, 4, 7, 11, 12, 21, 37, 38, 43, 104, 107, 113, 115, 116, 123, 131, 226, 246, 273, 274, 275, 276, 277, 278, 279, 275, 279, 293, 299, 358,.359, 361, 385, 393
Dyck, Ronald 116, 123

Eagan, Andrea 148
Eccles, Jacquelynne S. 318
Edgerton, Robert B. 103, 104, 110
Edsall, T.B. 180
Edwards, Richard 370, 371
Ehrlich, Anne H. 414, 441
Ehrlich, Paul R. 414, 441
Eichar, Douglas 196
Eichler, Margrit 11, 23, 67, 263
Eisenhart, Margaret A. 318
Eliany, Marc 114, 116, 118, 119, 123
Elliott, Jean Leonard 213, 231
Endicott, S. 105
Engels, Friedrich 142, 174, 287
English, Christine 149
Erikson, Erik H., 87, 88, 101, 104
Esping-Anderson, Gosta 342
Ethington, Corrina A. 317
Evans, John 127

Falardeau, Jean-Charles 13
Fallding, Harold 293
Fausto-Sterling, Anne 147, 164, 317
Feeley, M. 121
Felson, Marcus 460
Finkel, Alvin 390, 40
Fiorenza, Elisabeth Schussler 287
Fischer, C. 453
Fisher, Helen 254
Fleras, Augie 213, 231
Florida, Richard 375
Foote, David K. 439, 441
Forcese, Dennis 191, 196, 334
Forde, D. 116, 119, 460
Form, William H. 196
Foucault 338
Fournier, D 346
Fox, Bonnie 193, 195
Frances, Henry 235
Francis, Diane 170, 181, 189, 191, 193
Frankel, Linda 40
Franklin, Rosalind 145

Franzoi, Stephen L. 153
Freeman S 349
Freud, Sigmund 87, 88
Frideres, James S. 190, 235, 256
Fried, M. 457
Friedkin, Noah E. 319, 322
Friend, R. 151
Frieze I.H. 148
Frye, Northrop 14
Fukurai, H. 129
Fukuyama, Francis 340, 341
Fustel de Coulanges, Numa Denis 464

Gabor, Thomas 107, 113, 116, 130
Gamson, W.A. 393, 395
Gandhi 104
Gans, Herbert 453
Gardner, Howard 322
Garfield, Chad 249
Gaskell, Jane 328
Geipel, John 209
General Motors 373
Geran, Leslie 260
Gerber, Linda 218
Gero, Joan 61
Gerth, Hans H. 362
Ghalam, Nancy 260
Giddens, Anthony 168, 170, 172, 173, 175, 179
Giffen, P.J. 105
Gilbert, S.N. 315, 318
Gillespie, Michael W. 348
Gilligan, Carol 317
Gillis, R. 111
Gintis, Herbert 307
Ginzberg, Effie 187, 212
Glass, R. 149
Gliksman, L 118, 120
Glock, Charles 275
Goering, P. 111
Goffman, Erving 389
Goldenberg, Sheldon 106
Goldscheider, Frances Kobrin 248
Goldstein, Jay 190
Goltz, J. Walter 271
Goode, William J. 245
Gordon, Milton 228
Gordon, R. 114
Gorman, Christine 148
Gotlieb, Ian H. 98
Gottfredson, Michael 121, 133
Gottheil, E. 116
Gough, Kathleen 242
Gould, Stephen Jay 210
Gouldner, Calvin W. 342
Gove, Walter 122
Goyder, John C. 185
Grabb, Edward 54, 55, 168, 178, 179, 181, 194, 196, 197, 199
Gramsci 392
Grandin, Elaine 124
Granovetter, Mark 384
Grant, B. 116
Grayson, J. Paul 315, 318
Greene, Sarah 53
Greer, Germaine 152
Grenier, Gilles 224
Gretzky, Wayne 81
Grey Owl 208, 209
Grey, Deborah 402
Grindstaff, Carl F. 248, 261, 263, 266, 430, 432, 441
Groneman, Carol 69
Groulx, Abbe 405
Groulx, Lionel 405
Group of Seven 81
Guindon, Hubert 222, 405
Gunderson, Morley 192
Guppy, Neil 186, 189, 193, 194, 197, 199, 205, 316, 349
Gusfield, J. 107

Hacker, Andrew 213, 215
Hackler, J. 111, 116
Hagen, John 109, 111, 117, 121, 124, 125, 127
Hall, Glenn 86
Hall, Richard 379
Halsey, A.H. 320
Hamel, Pierre 390, 393, 394
Hamilton, Roberta 247, 249
Handleby, J.B. 129
Harman, Lesley D. 152, 157
Harmatz, M.G. 147
Harrell, W. Andrew 260
Harris, Chauncy D. 452
Harris, Marvin 66, 67, 71
Harris, Mike 340
Harrison, Deborah 18
Harrison, Trevor 340, 342
Hartnagel, Timothy 112, 121, 123
Harvey, Pierre 189
Hasselback, P 116, 122, 123
Hawley, A. 460
Hazel, K. 111
Head, Wilson 211
Hegel 341
Heidegger 338
Heimer, Karen 126
Heinz, Walter 324
Helmes-Hayes, Richard 13
Henripin, Jacques 224, 262
Henry, Frances 187, 212
Henshel, Richard L. 112
Herman, Harry 205
Herman, S. 111
Hernstein, R. 120
Herold, Edward 251
Hesse-Biber, Sharlene 153
Hewitt, Foster 86
Hewitt, W.E. 299
Hey, Valerie 148
Heyns, Barbara 318
Hill, Donald 295
Hiller, Harry H. 12, 13, 15, 16
Himmelfarb, A. 127
Hirschi, Travis 121, 123, 133
Hobart, Charles W. 47, 251, 264, 271
Hobbes, 360
Hoecker-Drysdale, Susan 18
Hofley, John M. 16
Holland, Dorothy C. 318
Hornquist, J. 123
Hou, Feng 188
Hoult, T.F. 249
Houston, Susan E. 307
Howe, Gordie 86
Hoyt, Homer 451
Huang, C. 117
Hudson's Bay Company 220
Hughes, Everett 13
Humphrey, Hubert 149
Hunter, Alfred A. 180
Hurn, Christopher J. 309

Hutter, Mark 259
Huyssen, Andreas 394

Iaconno, W. 114
Innis, Harold 13, 14, 15, 339, 340
Isajiw, Wsevolod 205, 207, 208
Ishwaran, K. 205

Jacklin, Carol 146, 147, 317
Jarvis, George K. 450
Jedwab, Jack 204
Jencks, C. 459
Jesus 104
Johnson (Parti Québécois) 406
Johnson, P.B. 148
Johnson,Holly 115, 118, 130
Johnston, William 54, 55
Jonassohn, Kurt 211
Jones, Deborah Perkins 317
Jorgensen, Christine 141
Juteau, Danielle 16

Kalback, Warren E. 213, 225, 437, 448
Kalmijn, Matthijs 254
Kaplan, H. 129
Kaplan, Marcie 105
Karabel, Jerome 320
Kates, N. 110, 116, 118
Katz, Jack 126
Kaufman, Michael 158, 164
Kay, Barry 54
Kay, F. 125
Keith, Bruce 98
Kelling, G. 460
Kennedy, L.W. 116, 119, 130, 460
Kenney, Martin 375
Kent, Stephen 106, 291, 292
Kessenich, Jennifer J. 153
Keynes, John Maynard 344
Killian, L.M. 384
Klein, Ralph 340
Klymquiw, Julian 86
Koenig, D. 110
Kohlberg, Lawrence 62, 89
Kohn, Melvin 196
Kopinak, Kathryn M 343, 351
Krahn, Harvey 123, 125, 184, 194, 323, 324, 371, 379, 460
Krauter, Joseph 210
Krett, E. 110, 116, 118
Krosenbrink-Gelissen, Lilianne 235
Krotov, Pavel 339
Krupat, E. 461
Kubzansky, P. 461

Lachepelle, Rejean 224
Lalonde, Richard 231
Lalu, N.M. 425
Lambert, Ronald 54
Lambert, S. 9, 105
Langford, Tom 190
Lapidus, Ira M. 444
Lapierre-Adamcyk, Evelyne 262
Laporte, Pierre 189
LaPrairie, Carol 120
Larson, Lyle J. 271
Laub, J. 122, 126
Lautard, Hugh 205
Law, B. 459
Laws, Sophie 148
Laxer, Gordon 340, 342
Leacock, Eleanor 60
LeBlanc, Marc 121, 123, 129, 133
LeBon, Gustave 275, 383
Lee, Barrett A. 453
Lee, John Allan 254
Legare, Jacques 257, 258
LeMasters, E.E. 263
Lemert, Edwin 127, 128
Lengermann, Patricia M. 317
Lenin 363
Lenneberg, E. 82, 83
Lenski, Gerhard E. 167, 168, 178
Lenton, Rhonda L. 250, 348
LePlay, Frederic 12
Leroux, T. 107
Lesage, Jean 405, 406
Letkemann, Peter 129
Lévesque, Rene 347
Lewis, Oscar 75
Li, Peter 188, 193, 205, 209, 212, 231
Light, Beth 410
Lightstone, J. 294
Lillard, Lee A. 264
Lincoln, Robyn 120, 126
Linden, Rick 133
Link, Bruce 112
Linton, Ralph 254
Lipset, Seymour Martin 54, 55, 71, 119, 342
Livingston, D.W. 328
Locke 360
Lockheed Missile and Space Company 372
Lofland, John 42
Lofland, Lyn 42
Lowe, Graham S. 183, 184, 199, 323, 324, 365, 371, 379
Lower, J.A. 220
Lowman, John 9, 457
Luke, T.W. 393, 394
Lundberg, Olle 118
Lupri, Eugen 124, 248, 250, 256, 259
Luxton, Meg 155, 252
Lynford, John 386

Maccoby, Eleanor 146, 147, 317
Macdonell, Allan J. 187
Mackenzie King, William Lyon 346
Mackie, Marlene 23, 25, 140, 141, 192, 193
MacKinnon, Catherine A. 142, 143
MacLean, Brian 134
Madan, Ashok 253
Madison, T. 105
Madoo-Lengerman, P. 11
Maheu, Louis 16
Mahovlich, Frank 86
Malinowski, Bronislaw 242, 293
Malthus, Thomas 419, 420
Mandella, Nelson 212
Manning, Preston 401
Marchak, Patricia M. 339, 340
Marchand, Philip 15
Marcil-Gratton, Nicole 264
Marcuse, Herbert 394
Marsh, Leonard 13
Marshall, Katherine 155, 260
Martin, Wilfred B.W. 187, 342
Marx, Karl 6, 9, 11, 12, 63, 124, 125, 141, 142, 169, 170, 171, 172, 173, 174, 176, 178, 226, 273, 275, 285, 287, 306, 308, 337, 341, 363, 364, 365, 370, 392, 393
Maslow, A.H. 87
Mason, David 209

Matsueda, Ross 126
Mattel Corporation 51, 52
Matthews, R. 125
Matza, D. 126
Maxim, Paul S. 107
Mayo 366
McAdam, Doug 393
McAlpine, Donna D. 91
McCarthy, B. 121
McClelland, David 169
McClung, Nellie 143
McDonald, Ryan 151, 218
McDuff, P. 123
McGahan, P. 445, 446, 464
McKay, H. 115, 460
McKenzie, Roderick 12
McKie, Craig 112, 117, 119, 120, 157
McLaren, Arlene 328
McLaughlin, J. 189, 197
McLuhan, Marshall 13, 14, 15
McMillan, S. 459
McPhail, Margaret 382, 391, 398
McPherson, Barry 193
McQuillan, Kevin 261
McRoberts, Kenneth 189, 405, 410
McVey, W. 437, 448
Mead, George Herbert 90, 368
Mead, Margaret, 52, 53, 71, 245
Mendel-Meadow, C. 124
Merton, Robert K. 116, 117, 118, 119, 120, 210
Mezoff, Richard 211
Michels, Robert 176, 334, 335, 347, 348, 364
Mickelson, Roslyn Arlin 324
Miedzian, Myriam 154, 158, 159
Milliband, Ralph 337, 348
Mills, Donald L. 250
Mills, Wright C. 335, 362
Milner, Henry 189
Milner, Sheilagh Hodgins 189
Miner, Horace 278, 279
Mirowsky, J. 111
Mitchinson, Wendy 410
Moghaddam, Fathali 209, 211, 231
Mooney, L. 5
Moore, Maureen 158, 260, 261
Moore, Wilbert E. 176
Morgan, Michael 96, 372
Morris, Raymond 16
Mosca, Gaetano 334, 335, 347
Mother Teresa 64
Mowbray, C. 111
Mulroney, Brian 331, 342, 343, 349
Murdie, Robert A. 452
Murdock, George P. 241, 242
Murphy, Emily 143

Nagnur, D.N. 248, 266
Nault, Francois 257, 267
Navarro, Vincente 365
Navratilova, Martina 141
Neallani, Shelina 212
Neeldeman, Lionel 263
Neuman, W. Lawrence 37, 39, 42
Newman, Stephen 110, 111, 114, 116, 123, 191
Nicks, Trudy 208
Niebrugge-Brantley, Jill 11, 317
Niederhoffer, A. 119
Nietzche 338
Nock, David 42, 284, 317
Noh, S. 123
Northcott, Herbert C. 365
Novak, M.A. 147

O'Connor, Julia 180, 181, 343
Ogmundson, R 189, 197
Okihiro, Norm 187
Olsen, Dennis 195
Onlin, L. 120, 121
Orn, Helene 110, 111, 123
Ornstein, Michael 195
Ortega, S. 118

Pahl, Robert E. 457, 458
Palantzas, T. 13
Pallas, A.M. 322
Palmer, Bud 86
Pareto, Vilfredo 334, 335, 3347, 348
Park, Robert 12, 443, 449
Parke, Ross D. 151
Parlee, M.B. 149
Parliament, Jo-Anne 156, 157
Parsons J.E. 148
Parsons, Talcott 139, 169, 176, 334
Patai, Daphne 60
Patterson, Jeffery 448
Perlman, Daniel 242
Peron, Ives 257, 258
Petrunik, M. 107, 127
Piaget, Jean 61, 89
Pichardo, N.A. 391
Pickering, R. 116
Picot, Garnet 186
Pierre-Aggamaway, Marlene 219
Pike, Robert M 186, 187
Pinard, Maurice 395
Pineo, Peter 189, 190, 450, 452
Pirie, M 105
Plaskow, Judith 287
Platiel, Rudy 216
Plomin, Robert 77
Polakowski, Michael 114
Pomfret, D. Alan 315, 318
Ponting, J. Rick 190
Porter, John 13, 170, 179, 186, 187, 189, 194, 195, 202, 227, 335, 336
Posgate, Dale 405
Prentice, Alison 307, 382, 391, 402, 410
Price, S. 105, 107
Propper, Alice 264
Purich, Donald 235

Queresma, Isabel 74

Ram, Bali 258, 260, 261
Ramu, G.N. 263
Rankin, Joseph H. 98, 121
Raskind, Richard 141
Ratner, A. 112, 117, 119, 120
Raudenbush, Stephen W. 322, 323
Ray, Carol Axtell 324
Reagan, Ronald 331, 337
Rebick, Judy 332
Reitsma-Street, Marge 121
Reitz, Jeffrey 187, 205, 208, 212, 215
Renaud, Marc 16
Renzetti, Claire M. 140, 146, 148
Resnick, Philip 346
Rhodes, A. 111
Rice, Patricia C. 59
Richards, Renee 141
Richer, Stephen 189, 319, 320

Riel, Louis 81, 216
Rindfuss, Ronald R. 253
Rinehart, James W. 183, 184, 196, 365, 367, 371, 372, 379
Rioux, Marcel 222, 332
Ritzer, George 18
Robbins, Tom 292
Roberts, Julian 113
Robinson, Patricia 248
Rocher, G. 12, 16, 407
Rohde-Dascher, C. 105, 107
Roscoe, Paul 56
Rosenberg, Harriet 154
Rosenberg, Michael, M 204
Rosenbluth, Giedon 353
Roseneau, P.M. 394
Rosenfield, S. 111
Ross, C. 111
Rosser, Sue V. 25, 315
Rossi, Alice S. 245, 259
Rossi, P. 245
Rothman, S. 77
Rothman, Robert A. 168
Rousseau 360
Rowe, Geoff 266
Rubble, D.N. 148
Rude, George 385
Rush, B. 118, 120
Ruth, Sheila 158, 164
Rutter, Michael 98
Rychlak, Joseph F 96

Sacco, Vincent 103, 106, 110, 115, 130, 134
Sadker, David 145
Sadker, Myra 145
Saint Paul 249
Salutin, Rick 144
Sampson, R. 122, 126, 460
Sanchez, Jesus 75
Sanders, Seth 212
Satzewich, Victor 190, 205
Sauvé, Paul 405
Sawchuk, Terry 86
Scanzoni, John 240, 259
Scanzoni, Letha, 240, 259
Scheff, Thomas 111, 129
Schissel, Bernard 117, 119, 125, 129
Schur, Edwin 127, 154
Schwarzenegger, Arnold 158
Scott, Alan 393, 395
Scott, W. Richard 379
Seager, Allen 390, 400
Sellin, T. 113
Selvanathan, K.E. 256
Semple, R. Keith 191
Sen, Amartya 160, 161
Serjak, John 191
Sev'er, A. 205
Sharp, R.L. 57
Shaw, C. 115, 460
Shearing, C. 127
Sheehan, M. Nancy 307
Sheldon, William 112
Sherman, Lawrence 461
Shore, Marlene 12, 13
Shorter, Edward 254
Sidnow, David 369
Sifton, Clifford 225
Siggner, Andrew 190
Silverman, Robert 110, 114, 115, 116, 119, 121, 134
Simpson, Sally 125
Skogan, W. 461
Skolnick, Arlene S. 244, 249, 250
Slife, Brent D. 96
Smaller, Harry 328
Smelser, Neil J. 310, 383, 384
Smith, Adam 365
Smith, Dorothy 349
Smith, Michael D. 124
Smith, Sandie 149, 457
Snider, Laureen 120, 125
Sniderman, P. 213
Snow, D.A. 390
Snyderman M. 77
Solomon, R. 105
Somerset, Felicity 229
Sparks, Allister 212
Sperling, Susan 68
Stanbridge, K.A. 395
Stark, Rodney 275, 295
Stebbins, Robert 107, 112, 114, 123
Steffensmeier, D. 118
Stevenson, David Lee 324
Stevenson, Harold W. 328
Stigler, James W. 328
Stoffman, Daniel 439, 441
Stone, Leroy 258
Stonequist, Everett 208
Strasburger, Victor C. .95, 101
Streifel, C. 118
Streitmatter, J.L. 208
Strong, Bryan 267
Stubbs, Michael 321
Sugrue, Patricia A. 153
Sulloway, Frank 74
Sumner, William G., 47
Sutherland, Edwin 126, 127
Swan, Neil 191
Swanson, Guy 52
Swedlund, Alan C. 51, 52
Swidinsky, R. 212
Sykes, G. 126
Symons, Gladys 248
Symons, Thomas H.B.16

Takeuchi, D. 122
Talon, Jean 220
Tancred-Sherrif, Peta 25
Tannenbaum, Frank 127
Tanner, Julian 118, 123, 125
Tardivel, Jules Paul 405
Tator, Carol 235
Taylor, F.W. 365
Taylor, Donald 209, 211, 231
Teevan, James 110, 115, 134
Temple, M 118, 122
Tepperman, Lorne 119
Thatcher, Margaret 337
Thomas, W.I. 10, 90, 91, 127, 210
Thompson, Dr. Eugene 295, 385, 386
Thompson, J.H. 390, 400
Thompson, K. 121
Thompson, Patricia J 317
Thorne, Barry 53, 69
Tilly, Charles 387, 410
Tilly, Louise 387
Tilly, Richard 387
Tite, R. 11
Tittle, C. 131, 454
Touraine, Alain 393, 394
Townsend, Joan B., 59
Toyota 373, 375
Trible, Phyllis 287

Trigg, Linda J 242
Troeltsch, Ernst 284, 285
Trotsky 363
Trovato, Frank 218, 425, 441
Trudeau, Pierre 231, 332, 333, 346, 347, 401
Turcotte, Andre 49
Turner, Ralph 384
Tylor, Edward 43

Ueda, Yoko 324
Ullman, Edward C. 452
Urla, Jacqueline 51, 52
Ursel, Jane 247

Vallieres, E. 123
van Poppel, F. 3
VandenHeuvel, Audrey 253
Veevers, J.E. 263
Visano, Livy 10

Waddell, Eric 224
Waite, Linda J. 248, 260, 264
Waller, Willard 251
Walmsley, Ann 373, 375
Walsh, A. 114
Wannell, Ted 186
Wanner, Richard A. 185
Ward, Martha C. 53, 71
Warner, B. 125
Warren, R. 130
Waters, Stanley 402
Waugh, S.L. 1966
Weber, Max 11, 21, 22, 37, 38, 105, 169, 170, 174, 175, 176, 206, 226, 273, 275, 279, 280, 281, 282, 284, 285, 289, 291, 299, 308, 332, 333, 348, 358, 361, 362, 363, 364, 365, 368, 370, 393
Weitzman, N. 151
Wellman, Barry 453
Wells, Gordon 321
Wells, L. Edward 98, 121
White, Pamela 203
Whorf, Benjamin Lee, 83
Wiegman, O. 94
Wien, Fred 191
Wilcox-Magill, D. 13
Wilkins, Leslie T. 127
Wilkins, Russell 426
Williams, D. 122
Wilson, J. 120, 126, 460
Wilson, Paul 120
Wilson, Susannah J. 192, 199
Wilson, William J. 215
Wirth, Louis 452, 453
Wolf, Naomi 153, 154, 155
Wolfe, Lee M. 10, 317
Wood, Wendy 96
Wooldredge, J. 460
Wordes, M. 111
Wortley, Scott 453
Wotherspoon, Terry 187, 190

Yeager, P 126
Yi, Sun-Kyung 113
Young, J 125

Zajonc, Robert B. 78
Zellman, G.I. 148
Zheng, W. 123

Photo Credits

CHAPTER 1
Page 2, Bob Carroll; page 6, National Archives of Canada, #C46356; page 8, Marco Shark; page 10, Jeanette Andrews-Bertheau; page 14, National Archives of Canada, #C17341

CHAPTER 2
Page 20, Dick Hemingway; page 26, Metropolitan Toronto Convention and Visitors Association; page 27, Bob Carroll; page 32, Marco Shark; page 34, Prentice Hall Canada Archives; page 35, UPI/Bettman

CHAPTER 3
Page 44, Dick Hemingway; page 48, Metropolitan Toronto Convention and Visitors Association; page 50, Bob Carroll; page 56, National Archives of Canada; page 60, Corbis-Bettmann; page 65, Canadian Museum of Civilization/#1876; page 68, Canadian Forces Photography

CHAPTER 4
Page 72, Dick Hemingway; page 75, John McNeill; page 76, Government of Canada, Tourist Branch; page 80, Dick Hemingway; page 84, Dick Hemingway; page 90, Dick Hemingway; page 95, Bob Carroll

CHAPTER 5
Page 102, Fanzio/Toronto Sun; page 105, John McNeill; page 110, UPI/Bettmann; page 111, Dick Hemingway; page 117, Dick Hemingway; page 122, Reekie/Toronto Sun; page 127, Kathleen Bellesiles

CHAPTER 6
Page 136, Dick Hemingway; page 139, Al Harvey/The Slide Farm; page 146, Dick Hemingway; page 151, Dick Hemingway; page 153, Retna/Pono Presse; page 155, Al Harvey/The Slide Farm; page 158, Dick Hemingway;

CHAPTER 7
Page 166, Michael Gibson; page 169, John McNeill; page 171, National Archives of Canada/PA42949; page 177, Rosenfeld/Tony Stone Images; page 185, Prentice Hall Canada Archives; page 193, Dick Hemingway; page 195, Office of the Lieutenant Governor of Ontario

CHAPTER 8
Page 200, John McNeill; page 204, Bob Carroll; page 208, NCC/CCN; page 212, Reuters/Bettmann; page 218, David Smiley; page 224, Peter Jones/Reuters/Archive Photos; page 227, Al Harvey/The Slide Farm; page 231, courtesy Alka Venugopal

CHAPTER 9
Page 238, Al Harvey/The Slide Farm; page 243, courtesy of Stanley and Janet Morais; page 248, Alice Walter; page 255, Prentice Hall Canada Archives; page 257, Metropolitan Toronto Convention and Visitors Association; page 261, Chip Henderson/Tony Stone Images

CHAPTER 10
Page 272, Dick Hemingway; page 276, Canapress; page 280, Jeanette Bertheau; page 285, British Tourist Authority; page 291, Prentice Hall Canada Archives; page 296, Dick Hemingway

CHAPTER 11
Page 300, Al Harvey/The Slide Farm; page 305, Prentice Hall Canada Archives; page 309, Dick Hemingway; page 311, Metropolitan Toronto Convention and Visitors Association; page 314, Dick Hemingway; page 316, Al Harvey/The Slide Farm; page 321, Dick Hemingway

CHAPTER 12
Page 330, Dick Hemingway; page 332, Director General of Public Affairs; page 336, Jean-Marc Carisse, Office of the Prime Minister; page 339, Greenpeace; page 347, Shaun Best/Reuters/Archive Photos

CHAPTER 13
Page 356, Prentice Hall Canada Archives; page 359, V. Last/Geographical Visual Aids; page 361, Northern Telecom; page 365, William Chan; page 368, Dick Hemingway; page 371, courtesy of Chrysler Canada Ltd.; page 373, Matsushita Electric of Canada Ltd.

CHAPTER 14
Page 380, Temagami Wilderness Society; page 382, Prentice Hall Canada Archives; page 388, Glowacki/Winnipeg Free Press/Canapress; page 391, Jim Young/Canapress; page 399, Manitoba Archives; page 404, National Archives of Canada/C-27360; page 407, Canapress Photo Service

CHAPTER 15
Page 412, Al Harvey/The Slide Farm; page 416, Archives of Ontario/A)532, Acc. 4437-2; page 420, Canapress; page 423, John McNeill; page 425, Health & Welfare Canada; page 429, Al Harvey/The Slide Farm; page 436, NCC/CCN

CHAPTER 16
Page 442, Metropolitan Toronto Convention and Visitors Association; page 448, Prentice Hall Canada Archives; page 449, Dick Hemingway; page 454, Prentice Hall Canada Archives; page 458, City of Toronto Archives (Heath32-259)